1997

MORAL DEVELOPMENT

A Compendium

Series Editor
BILL PUKA
Rensselaer Institute

A GARLAND SERIES

Series Contents

VOLUME

7

REACHING OUT

Caring, Altruism, and Prosocial Behavior

Edited with introductions by
BILL PUKA

GARLAND PUBLISHING, Inc.
New York & London
1994

Library of Congress Cataloging-in-Publication Data

Moral development : a compendium / edited with introductions by Bill
Puka.
    p.   cm.
    Includes bibliographical references.
    Contents: v. 1. Defining perspectives in moral development — v.
2. Fundamental research in moral development — v. 3. Kohlberg's
original study of moral development — v. 4. The great justice
debate — v. 5. New research in moral development — v. 6. Caring
voices and women's moral frames — v. 7. Reaching out.
    ISBN 0–8153–1554–6 (v. 7 : alk. paper).
    1. Moral development.   I. Puka, Bill.
BF723.M54M66 1994
155.2'5—dc20   94–462
                                          CIP

Printed on acid-free, 250-year-life paper
Manufactured in the United States of America

CONTENTS

SERIES INTRODUCTION

Moral development is an interdisciplinary field that researches moral common sense and interpersonal know-how. It investigates how children evolve a sense of right and wrong, good and bad, and how adults hone their abilities to handle ethical issues in daily life. This includes resolving value conflicts, fermenting trusting, cooperative, and tolerant relationships, and setting ethical goals. It focuses most on how we think about these ethical issues (using our cognitive competences) and how we act as a result.

These seven volumes are designed to function as a standard, comprehensive sourcebook. They focus on central concerns and controversies in moral development, such as the relation between moral socialization and development, moral judgment and action, and the effects of culture, class, or gender on moral orientation. They also focus on central research programs in the field, such as the enduring Kohlberg research on moral stages, Gilligan research on ethical caring and women's development, and related prosocial research on altruism.

The studies contained here were compiled from the "wish lists" of researchers and educators in the field. These are the publications cited as most important (and, often, least available) for effective teaching and research training and for conveying the field to others. Unfortunately, the most crucial studies and essays in moral development are widely scattered across hard-to-find (sometimes out-of-print) volumes. Compiling them for a course is difficult and costly. This compendium eases these problems by gathering needed sources in one place, for a single charge. Regrettably, rising reprint fees frustrated plans to include *all* needed resources here, halving the original contents of these volumes and requiring torturous excising decisions. Even so, compared to other collections, this series approaches a true "handbook" of moral development, providing key sources on central issues rather than "further essays" on specialized topics.

A major aim of this series is to represent moral development accurately to related fields. Controversies in moral development have sparked lively interest in the disciplines of philosophy, education, sociology and anthropology, literary criticism, political science, gender and cultural studies, critical legal studies, criminology and corrections, and peace studies. Unfortunately, members of these fields were often introduced to moral development through the highly theoretical musings of Lawrence Kohlberg, Carol Gilligan, or Jean Piaget—or by highly theoretical commentaries on them. Jumping into the fray over gender or culture bias in stage theory, theorists in the humanities show virtually no familiarity with the empirical research that gave rise to it. Indeed, many commentators seem unaware that these controversies arise in a distinct research field and are context-dependent.

This compendium displays moral development as a social science, generating research findings in cognitive developmental, and social psychology. (Students are invited to recognize and approach the field as such.) Theory is heavily involved in this research—helping define the fundamental notions of "moral" and "development," for example. But even when philosophically or ethically cast, it remains psychological or social scientific theory. It utilizes but does not engage in moral philosophy per se. Otherwise, it is not moral development theory, but meta-theory. (Several extensively criticized Kohlberg articles on justice are meta-theory.) The confusion of these types and levels of theory has been a source of pervasive confusion in the field. The mistaken assessment of psychological theory by moral-philosophical standards has generated extremely damaging and misguided controversy in moral development. Other types of theory (moral, social, interpretive, anthropological) should be directed at moral development science, focusing on empirical research methods and their empirical interpretation. It should be theory of data, that is, not meta-theoretical reflection on the "amateur" philosophizing and hermeneutics interpolations of psychological researchers. (Likewise, social scientific research should not focus on the empirical generalizations of philosophers when trying to probe social reality or seek guidance in doing so from this theoretical discipline.) The bulk of entries in this compendium present the proper, empirically raw material for such "outside" theoretical enterprise.

To researchers, theorists, and students in related fields, this series extends an invitation to share our interest in the fascinating phenomena of moral development, and to share our findings thus far. Your help is welcomed also in refining our treacherously qualitative research methods and theories. In my dual disciplines of psychology and philosophy, I have found no more inspiring area of study. Alongside its somewhat dispassionate research orientation, this field carries on the ancient "cause" of its pre-scientific past. This is to show that human nature is naturally good—that the human psyche spontaneously unfolds in good will, cleaving toward fair-mindedness, compassion, and cooperative concern.

The first volume, *Defining Perspectives*, presents the major approaches to moral development and socialization in the words of chief proponents: Kohlberg, Bandura, Aronfreed, Mischel, Eysenck, and Perry. (Piaget is discussed in detail.) This first volume is required reading for those needing to orient to this field or regain orientation. It is crucial for clarifying the relations and differences between moral development and socialization that define research.

The second volume, *Fundamental Research*, compiles the classic research studies on moral levels and stages of development. These studies expose the crucial relation of role-taking and social perspective to moral judgment and of moral judgment to action. They also divine the important role of moral self-identity (viewing oneself as morally interested) in moral motivation.

The third volume contains *Kohlberg's Original Study*, his massive doctoral research project. The study, which has never before been published, sets the parameters for moral development research, theory, and controversy. (Major critical alternatives to Kohlberg's approach share far more in common with it than they diverge.) Here the reader sees "how it all started," glimpsing the sweep of Kohlberg's aspiration: to uncover the chief adaptation of humankind, the evolving systems of reasoning and meaning-making that, even in children, guide effective choice and action. Most major Kohlberg critiques fault features of this original study, especially in the all-male, all-white, all-American cast of his research sample. (Why look here for traits that characterize all humans in all cultures through all time?) It is worth checking these criticisms against the text, in context, as depictions of unpublished work often blur into hearsay. It is also worth viewing this study through the massive reanalysis of its data (Colby, Kohlberg, et al.) and the full mass of Kohlberg research that shaped stage theory. Both are liberally sampled in Volume Five.

The Great Justice Debate, the fourth volume, gathers the broad range of criticisms leveled at moral stage theory. It takes up the range of "bias charges" in developmental research—bias by gender, social class, culture, political ideology, and partisan intellectual persuasion. Chief among these reputed biases is the equation of moral competence and development with justice and rights. Here key features of compassion and benevolence seem overlooked or underrated. Here a seemingly male standard of ethical preference downplays women's sensibilities and skills. Responses to these charges appear here as well.

Volume Five, *New Research*, focuses on cross-cultural re-search in moral development. Studies in India, Turkey, Israel, Korea, Poland, and China are included. While interesting in itself, such research also supports the generalizability of moral stages, challenged above. Indeed, Volume Five attempts to reconceive or re-start the central research program of moral development from the inception of its matured research methods and statistically well-validated findings. From this point research is more data-based than theory-driven. It can address criticism with hard evidence. Regarding controversy in moral development, Volumes Four and Five go together as challenge and retort.

Volume Six, *Caring Voices*, is devoted to the popular "different voice" hypothesis. This hypothesis posits a distinct ethical orienta-tion of caring relationship, naturally preferred by women, that complements justice. Compiled here is the main record of Gilligan's (and colleagues') research, including recent experiments with "narrative" research method. The significant critical literature on care is well-represented as well, with responses. While Gilligan's empirical research program is more formative than Kohlberg's, her interpretive observations have influenced several fields, espe-cially in feminist studies. Few research sources have more common-sense significance and "consciousness-raising" potential. The stu-dent reader may find Gilligan's approach the most personally relevant and useful in moral development.

Reaching Out, the final volume, extends moral development concerns to "prosocial" research on altruism. Altruistic helping behavior bears close relation to caring and to certain ideals of liberal justice. This volume emphasizes the role of emotions in helping (and not helping), focusing on empathic distress, forgive-ness, and guilt. It also looks at early friendship and family influ-ences. Moral emotions are related to ethical virtues here, which are considered alongside the "vices" of apathy and learned help-lessness. Leading researchers are included such as Hoffman, Eisenberg, Batson, and Staub.

INTRODUCTION

This volume presents research on altruism, empathy, and other moral emotions, and prosocial behavior in general. Increasing the quality of moral thinking matters most where it yields desirable actions (often it does not, however, and, at lower levels of development, thank goodness). At higher levels, sophisticated moral reasoning can weave brilliantly self-deceptive rationalizations, ideal for hypocrisy. It not only weaves paths around responsibilities, but helps us feel justified in avoiding them. (Research cited on unresponsive bystanders to crime bears testimony.) Here bringing action in line with judgment is no help. Thus, it makes sense to research moral development from the action/output standpoint itself, asking what causes better behavior. Here it makes sense also to investigate the most powerful motivators of action, emotional needs and feelings.

This volume surveys important research on altruistic behavior and the roots of altruism within family relations and children's friendships. Among these roots are the altruistic emotions of sympathy, empathy, and forgiveness, which must compete against aggression and depression (also researched here) for nourishment. Guilt fuels both tendencies, sometimes promoting, sometimes inhibiting altruism. Together, altruistic emotions and actions produce virtues of unselfishness. The structure and substance of altruistic virtues, and their role in education, are discussed in this volume as well by Spieker, Steutel.

Unselfishness seems prerequisite to all ethical action, whether obligatory, righteous, just, or more expansively generous. And, to many, it seems the ultimate ethical ideal—to sacrifice one's interest, perhaps one's life, for a friend or stranger. Clearly ethical caring involves helping behavior and do-gooding for others, typical of altruistic behavior. So does ideal or "liberal" (Stage 6) justice for Kohlberg. Unlike justice, however, caring requires the expression of certain emotions and emotional skills. Compassion and empathy are the most obvious, but there are many other "natural responses," involving emotion, prerequisite to caring responsiveness and consensus-seeking. Thus research on moral emotion and its relation to helping is key to care and, most likely, to revealing general moral competence. This is virtue approached empirically.

As might be expected, many research programs in this area seek accommodation between competing ethical themes such as care and justice, and potentially rival foci, such as moral reasoning and emotion. Hoffman's approach, sampled here, is most prominent among them. Shweder and I discuss ethical pluralism in our essays—the aspiration to integrate conflicting moral perspectives—still, there is an abiding tension between research in prosocial behavior and moral development. And readers should be aware of confusion. As moral action validates moral cognition, so moral cognition qualifies action for moral assessment. Moral action is part intention; it is behavior done for the right reasons or sprung from appropriate sensibilities and feelings. Altruism motivated by guilt, depression, or a host of other causes is nothing special—nothing of positive moral relevance. But some researchers in altruism do not seem to notice. The more sociobiologically inclined, not sampled here, note the altruism of animals (most notably bees) and then morally praise it. This sort of confusion shows the need for moral philosophy in moral development, recognized by Piaget and Kohlberg. Other altruism researchers do not care about the relation of intentions and behavior, typically defining altruism amorally. ("Altruism" is sometimes defined amorally in common speech, referring simply to behavior that benefits others, perhaps disadvantaging oneself.) The reader should distinguish when prosocial research is morally cast and has relevance to moral development, and when it is not, meriting separate assessment.

Developmental Psychology
1991, Vol. 27, No. 5, 849–857

Prosocial Development in Adolescence: A Longitudinal Study

Nancy Eisenberg, Paul A. Miller, Rita Shell, Sandra McNalley, and Cindy Shea
Arizona State University

Change in prosocial moral reasoning over an 11-year period, gender differences in prosocial reasoning in adolescence, and the interrelations of moral reasoning, prosocial behavior, and empathy-related emotional responses were examined with longitudinal data and data from adolescents interviewed for the first time. Hedonistic reasoning declined in use until adolescence and then increased somewhat (primarily for boys). Needs-oriented reasoning, direct reciprocity reasoning, and approval and stereotypic reasoning increased until midchildhood or early adolescence and then declined. Several modes of higher level reasoning emerged in late childhood or adolescence. Girls' overall reasoning was higher than boys'. Consistent with expectations, there was some evidence of high level prosocial reasoning being associated with prosocial behavior and empathy and of a relation between sympathy or empathy and prosocial behavior.

The roles of cognition and affect in morality have been a topic of discussion for centuries (e.g., Hume, 1777/1966; Kant, 1797/1964). In recent years, psychologists such as Kohlberg (1981) have argued that cognition is the foundation of morality, whereas others such as Batson (1990) or Hoffman (1987) have emphasized the role of sympathy and empathy in moral behavior, particularly in altruism. In recent research and writings, the role of each has been acknowledged (e.g., Hoffman, 1987; Underwood & Moore, 1982).

The cognitive process most closely linked with morality, including prosocial behavior, is moral reasoning. Cognitive developmentalists have argued that developmental advances in the sociocognitive skill of perspective taking underlie age-related changes in moral reasoning and that the quality of individuals' thinking about moral issues affects the maturity of their moral functioning. In support of this view, higher level moral reasoning or self-attributions have been associated with frequency of prosocial behavior and with higher quality (e.g., more altruistic) behavior (Bar-Tal, 1982; Eisenberg, 1986; Underwood & Moore, 1982).

Although most researchers studying moral judgment have focused on reasoning about moral dilemmas in which rules, laws, authorities' dictates, and formal obligations are central (Kohlberg, 1981; Rest, 1983), some investigators have studied issues related to positive morality (e.g., Damon, 1977; Eisenberg, 1986; Gilligan & Attanucci, 1988). One type of reasoning that investigators have explored is prosocial moral reasoning, that is, reasoning about moral dilemmas in which one person's needs or desires conflict with those of another (or others) in a

context in which the role of prohibitions, authorities' dictates, and formal obligations is minimal.

In cross-sectional research on the prosocial moral reasoning of children and adolescents in industrialized cultures, age-related changes in prosocial moral judgment have been delineated. These changes are, in general, consistent with Kohlberg's (1969, 1981) view that the capability for complex perspective taking and for understanding abstract concepts is associated with advances in moral reasoning. However, levels of prosocial moral reasoning are not viewed as hierarchical, integrated structures (with the result that individuals' reasoning is primarily at one stage) or as being invariant in sequence and universal (Eisenberg, 1986). Specifically, young children tend to use primarily hedonistic or needs-oriented (primitive empathic) reasoning. In elementary school, children's reasoning begins to reflect concern with approval and enhancing interpersonal relationships as well as the desire to behave in stereotypically good ways, although such reasoning also appears to decrease in use from the elementary to high school years. Contrary to initial expectations, direct reciprocity reasoning, which reflects an orientation to self-gain, has been found to increase in the elementary school years, perhaps because of the cognitive sophistication involved in thinking about reciprocity over time. In late elementary school and beyond, children begin to express reasoning reflecting abstract principles, internalized affective reactions (e.g., guilt or positive affect about the consequences of one's behavior for others or living up to internalized principles), and self-reflective sympathy and perspective taking. Nonetheless, even in adolescence people frequently verbalize less mature modes of reasoning, although hedonistic reasoning decreases with age (Eisenberg-Berg, 1979a; see Eisenberg, 1986).

In the limited longitudinal research on prosocial reasoning, change in moral reasoning has been examined from age 4–5 years to 11–12 years (Eisenberg, Lennon, & Roth, 1983; Eisenberg et al., 1987). A longitudinal study of prosocial moral reasoning was initiated because intraindividual change can be examined only with longitudinal data and because longitudinal procedures overcome the confound between developmental

This research was supported by National Science Foundation Grant BNS8807784 and National Institute of Child Health and Development Career Development Award K04 HD00717 to Nancy Eisenberg. We thank the mothers and students in our longitudinal samples and the principals, students, and teachers at Connolly Junior High School and Tempe High School for their participation.

Paul Miller is now at Arizona State University, West Campus.

Correspondence concerning this article should be addressed to Nancy Eisenberg, Psychology, Arizona State University, Tempe, Arizona 85287.

change and cohort inherent in cross-sectional research. In this research, we have for the most part replicated the aforementioned findings in the cross-sectional research for preschool and elementary school children. However, consistent with Gilligan's (Gilligan & Attanucci, 1988) argument that females use more care-oriented reasoning than do males, we found that the initial increase in self-reflective other-oriented modes of reasoning in late elementary school was primarily for girls. Because no longitudinal study has included participants older than age 12, the declines in some modes of reasoning (e.g., stereotypic, approval oriented) noted during adolescence in cross-sectional research have not been replicated with a longitudinal design; nor has the developmental course of direct reciprocity reasoning (primitive other-oriented reasoning, which increases during elementary school) or needs-oriented reasoning (which has been found to increase into the midelementary school years and then to level off in usage) been adequately delineated. Furthermore, some of the higher level modes of reasoning that seem to emerge in adolescence have not been examined longitudinally, even though sociocognitive changes during this age period are substantial (Colby, Kohlberg, Gibbs, & Lieberman, 1983; Hoffman, 1987; Selman, 1980).

Thus, the primary purpose of this study was to examine change in prosocial moral reasoning during early and midadolescence (i.e., at ages 13–14 and 15–16). The subjects in this study have been followed since age 4–5 years for 11 years. Because of the changes in early and midadolescence in logical reasoning, perspective-taking skills (Selman, 1980), and Kohlbergian moral reasoning (Colby et al., 1983), it seemed reasonable to expect the development of more abstract and morally sophisticated modes of reasoning during this period of development. Moreover, changes in the complexity of the child's social environment as he or she moves into adolescence might be expected to stimulate perspective taking and, consequently, moral reasoning (see Kohlberg, 1981). In addition, given the debate over the possible existence of a gender difference in moral reasoning in adolescence and adulthood (Gilligan & Attanucci, 1988; Walker, 1984), we were also interested in determining whether the sex difference in the emergence of other-oriented modes of reasoning found at age 11–12 persisted into adolescence.

The second purpose of this study was to examine the relations among prosocial moral reasoning, prosocial behavior, and empathy-related emotional reactions in adolescence. Few investigators have examined prosocial reasoning or empathy in adolescence, and even studies of adolescents' prosocial behavior are relatively few in number (Eisenberg, 1990). Indeed, the prosocial side of morality in adolescence has been neglected by researchers.

Theorists such as Kohlberg (1981) and Rest (1983) have argued that moral reasoning influences individuals' moral decisions and behavior. Consistent with this view, moral reasoning, including prosocial moral judgment, does seem to be correlated with the performance of prosocial behaviors, although the empirical associations generally are modest (Eisenberg, 1986; Underwood & Moore, 1982). Specifically, elementary school children's prosocial behavior generally has been positively related to needs-oriented reasoning and negatively related to hedonistic reasoning (Eisenberg, 1986; Eisenberg et al., 1987). In one of the only studies on this topic involving adolescents, Eisenberg-Berg (1979b) found that the level of moral judgment was positively correlated with helping behavior, but only for males. In this study, we sought to further examine the relation of prosocial moral reasoning to prosocial behavior in early and midadolescence. Investigators have hypothesized that the relation between reasoning and behavior increases with age because higher level reasoning is associated with the "progressive stripping away of bases for justifying behavior that are extrinsic to principle" (Rholes & Bailey, 1983, p. 104), resulting in a stronger motive to maintain consistency between attitudes and behaviors at higher stages of development. Thus, we hypothesized that helping behavior in adolescence would be positively correlated with other-oriented modes of reasoning, as well as with overall level of reasoning, and negatively related to hedonistic reasoning.

The relation of empathy to prosocial moral reasoning has been studied very infrequently, although some modes of moral reasoning explicitly reflect cognitive role taking, empathy, and sympathy. Indeed, investigators have suggested that sympathy (concern for others based on the apprehension of another's state) and empathy (an emotional reaction elicited by and congruent with another's state) stimulate the development of internalized moral principles reflecting concern for others' welfare (Hoffman, 1987) and prime the use of preexisting moral cognitions reflecting concern for others (Eisenberg, 1986).

The very limited empirical data are consistent with the argument that there is an association between empathy and prosocial moral reasoning. In the last two follow-ups of our longitudinal research, we found that scores on Bryant's (1982) empathy scale were positively related to needs-oriented and higher level moral reasoning and negatively related to hedonistic reasoning. However, the associations generally were stronger at age 9–10 years than at age 11–12 years. Thus, it was unclear whether the association would continue into adolescence, although level of prosocial reasoning was associated with global empathy in one study of high school students (Eisenberg-Berg & Mussen, 1978).

In addition, in previous research on the relation of prosocial reasoning to vicarious emotional responding, only the association of empathy to moral reasoning has been examined. However, researchers have found that it is important to differentiate among various emotionally based reactions that often stem from empathy, including sympathy and personal distress (i.e., a self-oriented aversive response to another's state; Batson, 1987). Sympathy, which is viewed as stemming from perspective taking (e.g., Batson, 1987; Hoffman, 1987) and as leading to other-oriented, altruistic motivations (Batson, 1987), has been positively related to altruistic behavior (e.g., Batson, 1987, 1990). In contrast, personal distress appears to be associated with egoistic motives and behavior (Batson, 1987; Eisenberg & Fabes, 1991), particularly with the motive to alleviate one's own negative emotional state. Thus, at the most recent follow-up, we examined the relations of sympathy and personal distress, as well as perspective taking, to prosocial moral reasoning.

The positive relation between empathy and prosocial behavior has been documented more frequently than has the relation between empathy and moral reasoning (see Barnett, 1987; Eisenberg & Miller, 1987). Indeed, empathy and sympathy are viewed by many theorists as important motivators of altruism

(Batson, 1990; Hoffman, 1987; Staub, 1978). Consistent with this view and with the finding of weaker relations in childhood than during adulthood (Eisenberg & Miller, 1987), in our longitudinal research empathy was associated with prosocial behavior at age 11–12 years but not 10–11 years. In other studies, there does seem to be some positive relation between empathy and prosocial behavior in adolescence (Eisenberg & Miller, 1987; Underwood & Moore, 1982); however, the research on this association in adolescence is quite limited, and no one, to our knowledge, has published research concerning the relations of sympathy and personal distress to adolescents' prosocial behavior. Thus, another goal of this study was to examine the aforementioned relations at two ages during adolescence.

Finally, in any study in which moral development is assessed with self-report data one must be concerned with the possibility that responses are contaminated by self-presentational concerns. Thus, in this study we examined the relation of social desirability to our other moral indexes.

In summary, the purposes of this study were to examine change in prosocial moral reasoning in adolescence and the interrelations among moral reasoning, prosocial behavior, and empathy-related responses at that stage of life. To do so, we conducted two longitudinal follow-ups of children studied since the age of 4–5 years, one at age 13–14 years and one at age 15–16 years, and also tested additional students at each age.

Method

Subjects

Three groups of middle-class children participated in this study. The primarily longitudinal cohort (C1) consisted of 16 girls and 16 boys (all White except 2) who had been interviewed five times previously, at ages 4–5, $5\frac{1}{2}$–$6\frac{1}{2}$, 7–8, 9–10, and 11–12 (at 108, 90, 72, 48, and 24 months before the first assessment in this study); the seven testing sessions henceforth are referred to as T1 through T7. The mean ages of the children at T6 and T7 were 163 months (range = 154–171 months; approximately 13–14 years of age) and 187 months (approximately 15–16 years of age). No children have been lost since T3 (in 8 years); 1 was lost in the past 9.5 years and 5 have been lost over the 11-year period (3 boys and 2 girls; the original sample was 37 children).

The second sample (C2) consisted of 39 eighth graders from a middle-class, predominantly White neighborhood (20 girls and 19 boys; mean age = 164 months, range = 154–176 months). These children attended a school in the suburban city in which the longitudinal subjects lived at the beginning of the study. They were interviewed for the first and only time at T6. A similar group (C3) of 34 tenth graders (17 of each sex) was interviewed for the first and only time at T7 (mean age = 189 months, range = 180–199 months).

Instruments

Children's prosocial moral reasoning was assessed with the same four moral reasoning stories used in prior follow-ups (see Eisenberg et al., 1983, 1987), although a few words were changed to make the stories sound less childlike (e.g., "birthday party" was changed to "birthday celebration"). However, an additional story previously used with school-aged children and adolescents in another study (concerning going into the hospital to donate a rare type of blood at a cost to the self; Eisenberg-Berg, 1979a) was also used in these two follow-up sessions. This story was added because the costs of helping in some of the other stories appeared to be rather low for adolescents (e.g., missing a birth-

day celebration), whereas the costs of helping in the giving-blood story would likely be substantial for adolescents (losing time at work and school).

As at T4 and T5, subjects at T6 in C1 and C2 were also administered Bryant's (1982) 22-item Empathy scale (αs = .78 and .69) and Crandall's 47-item Social desirability (SD) Scale for children (αs = .92 and .87, respectively; Crandall, Crandall, & Katkovsky, 1965). To assess social desirability at T7, children in C1 and C3 completed 25 items from the Marlowe-Crowne Social Desirability Scale (αs = .86 and .74, respectively; Crowne & Marlowe, 1964), which appeared to be more age-appropriate for adolescents than the Crandall et al. index. To assess capabilities related to empathy, students in C1 and C3 at T7 were also administered three subscales of Davis's Interpersonal Reactivity Scale: Sympathy (α = .83), Perspective Taking (.73), and Personal Distress (.74). In addition, at both T6 and T7, children filled out a 23-item adapted version of Rushton, Chrisjohn, and Fekken's (1981) self-report Altruism scale (αs = .86 and .90 at T6 and T7, respectively). Children indicated on a 5-point scale (ranging from *never* to *very often*) how frequently they engaged in 23 behaviors such as giving money to charity or volunteer work. Finally, children at T6 and T7 were given an opportunity to assist the experimenter by filling out some additional questionnaires and returning them in a stamped, addressed envelope.

Mothers of children in C1 also filled out the modified Rushton et al. Altruism scale; however, they filled it out in regard to their child rather than themselves. Because they were given the additional option of "don't know," alphas could not be computed for these scales (due to the fact that items with this response were considered missing, resulting in few mothers with all items completed).

For all of the aforementioned questionnaires, scores for the various items were summed (after reversing their direction, if necessary). For mothers' reports of children's prosocial behavior, this sum was divided by the number of items the mothers answered. Two indexes of helping behavior were computed: whether the students returned the questionnaires and whether all parts of the questionnaires were completed.

Procedures

C1. Interviews for C1 took place in the home or at the university. In either case, mother and child were interviewed in different rooms, the mother by a woman (at T6) and the child by a man (at T6) or a woman (at T7) who had not been involved in any previous follow-ups. For the children, the prosocial dilemmas were presented first in random order; they were read to the children while the children read along (responses were taped). Children repeated dilemmas to check for comprehension, and a standard sequence of questioning was followed (Eisenberg et al., 1983). The moral reasoning task was always administered first because it was considered most important and we did not want to influence the children's responses by having it follow other procedures.

Subsequent to the moral interview, the children completed the measures of empathy, social desirability, and self-reported prosocial behavior (presented in random order). The students were told that their responses were confidential. Next, after the children were paid for their participation ($5 at T6 and $10 at T7), the experimenter told the students that he or she would appreciate their filling out a few more forms at home, but that they need not do so if they did not want to. If the student agreed to take the questionnaires (all did), they were given the forms and a stamped envelope.

C2 and C3. C2 and C3 students were individually administered the procedures at their schools. Their mothers were not present. Tapes for moral interviews of 4 C2 students were lost due to mechanical difficulties.

Scoring

Prosocial reasoning stories. Scoring of prosocial reasoning was done in two ways. First, the children's judgments were coded into the categories of reasoning outlined by Eisenberg et al. (1983, 1987; Eisenberg-Berg, 1979a). Those used by children with any frequency were as follows:

Hedonistic reasoning—(a) *hedonistic gain to the self* (orientation to gain for oneself), (b) *direct reciprocity* (orientation to personal gain because of direct reciprocity or lack of reciprocity from the recipient of an act), and (c) *affectional relationship* (orientation to the individual's identification or relationship with another or liking for the other);

Pragmatic (orientation to practical concerns that are unrelated to selfish considerations);

Needs-oriented (orientation to the physical, material, or psychological needs of the other person; e.g., "He needs blood," or "He's sad");

Stereotypes of a good or bad person (orientation to stereotyped images of a good or bad person);

Approval and interpersonal orientation (orientation to others' approval and acceptance in deciding what is the correct behavior);

Self-reflective empathic orientation—(a) sympathetic orientation (expression of sympathetic concern and caring for others), (b) role taking (the individual explicitly takes the perspective of the other or has the story protagonist do so), (c) internalized positive affect related to consequences (orientation to internal positive affect as a result of a particular course of action because of the consequences of one's act for the other person), and (d) internalized negative affect related to consequences (the same as [c] but for negative affect);

Internalized affect because of loss of self-respect and not living up to one's value—(a) positive (orientation to feeling good, often about oneself, as a consequence of living up to internalized values), (b) negative (concern with feeling bad as a consequence of not living up to internalized values);

Internalized law, norm, and value orientation (orientation to an internalized responsibility, duty, or need to uphold the laws and accepted norms or values);

Other abstract or internalized types of reasoning—(a) *generalized reciprocity* (orientation to indirect reciprocity in a society, that is, exchange that is not one-to-one but eventually benefits all or a larger group), (b) *concern with the condition of society* (orientation to improving the society or community as a whole), (c) *concern with individual rights and justice* (orientation to protecting individual rights and preventing injustices that violate another's rights), and (d) *equality of people* (orientation to the principle of the equal value of all people).

Children were assigned scores indicating the frequency with which they used each of the various types of reasoning when discussing both the pros and cons of helping the needy other in the story dilemma (1 = no use of category; 2 = vague, questionable use; 3 = clear use of a mode of reasoning; and 4 = a major type of reasoning used). Next, the scores for each category were summed across the stories. At each time period, two coders scored either half or all the data; interrater reliabilities for T1, T2, T3, T4, and T5 have been presented in previous articles (Eisenberg et al., 1983, 1987; Eisenberg-Berg & Roth, 1980). For all time periods, the primary coder was the same person, whereas five persons have served as reliability coders over the 7 time periods. To prevent bias in scoring, the coders were blind to the identity of the children. The primary coder was also blind to any information regarding the subjects' scores on other measures (e.g., prosocial behavior and empathy); this was usually the case for the reliability coder. Interrater reliabilities (Pearson product–moment correlations) computed for each reasoning category at T6 and T7 (using data for all subjects at T6 and for half the subjects at T7) ranged from .81 (for positive affect–self at T6) to 1.00, with most being above .85. (These reliabilities are for four stories; those for five stories were very similar.)

As was just noted, the primary coder for the moral reasoning protocols was the same person who scored the data at all previous follow-ups. This procedure was used to prevent differences across different coders at different times being interpreted as age-related changes in

reasoning. To determine if there was any change in the primary coder's scoring over the years (and to prevent the primary coder from knowing the age of subjects being coded), five protocols from each of the previous follow-ups were mixed together with the various protocols from T6 and T7 and were rescored by the primary coder to determine if there was any change in her scoring over the years (the coder was blind to which protocol was from which follow-up). Scoring of the data from earlier sessions was highly similar to the original scores for the same data (agreement on codings within one point was 75% or higher on all categories; correlations were .89 and higher).

The categories of reasoning are viewed as representing components of developmental levels of prosocial moral reasoning; these levels were derived from the results of cross-sectional research (Eisenberg-Berg, 1979a; see Eisenberg, 1986). Briefly, the levels are as follows: Level 1, hedonistic, self-focused orientation; Level 2, needs of others orientation; Level 3, approval and interpersonal orientation and stereotyped orientation; Level 4, self-reflective, empathic orientation; and Level 5, strongly internalized orientation. On the basis of these levels, a score representing level of moral judgment was computed for each child. The level score was constructed in a manner similar to that used to score Kohlbergian reasoning; that is, subjects were assigned composite scores by weighing the proportion of the child's reasoning at each level (see Eisenberg et al., 1983, for more detail). Because it is debatable whether Level 5 is more moral than Level 4 and because Levels 4 and 5 were weighted equally in previous follow-ups, they were weighted equally in the analyses presented in this article (although the data changed little if Level 5 was weighted higher).

Results

Age Changes in Moral Judgment

To examine age changes in moral reasoning for C1 over the 11 years, multivariate analyses of variance (MANOVAs) and univariate trend analyses of variance (ANOVAs) were computed with one within-subjects factor (time; adjusted for unequal time gaps when appropriate) and one between-subjects factor (sex). On the basis of prior research and theoretical formulations in which types of reasoning involving more complex perspective taking and abstract concepts are expected to increase with age (Eisenberg, 1986; Kohlberg, 1981), we expected the self-reflective and internalized–abstract modes of reasoning to increase with age into adolescence. In contrast, direct reciprocity, approval, and stereotypic modes of reasoning, which increased in childhood, were expected to decrease in usage in adolescence, whereas levels of needs-oriented and hedonistic reasoning were not expected to change much in adolescence (although the latter modes of reasoning do exhibit dramatic change in childhood).

Different MANOVAs had to be computed for groups of reasoning that emerged at different ages because of the linear dependencies in the data that occur if a particular mode of reasoning is not used at more than one time period (and because quadratic trends could occur if a type of reasoning was not used much in childhood and then emerged in adolescence). Only categories of reasoning used with some frequency during at least one time period were included in the analyses. Because types of reasoning that were used infrequently tended to be positively skewed, a logarithmic transformation was performed on the data (although the means presented in Table 1 and in the text are nontransformed means). Linear, quadratic, and cubic trends were examined when possible because from early child-

Table 1
Moral Reasoning Categories: Means for Cohort 1

Reasoning category	1	2	3	4	5	6	7
Hedonistic	12.12	8.66	6.31	5.88	4.69	4.75	5.28
Direct reciprocity	4.00	4.09	4.09	4.31	5.38	5.91	4.88
Affectional relationship	4.03	4.38	4.00	4.25	4.19	4.09	4.53
Pragmatic	4.12	4.47	4.28	5.03	5.25	5.81	6.28
Needs-oriented	8.53	11.59	13.62	13.12	13.59	12.25	12.00
Stereotypic	4.50	4.31	4.68	5.12	5.62	6.72	6.47
Approval–interpersonal	4.00	4.06	4.22	4.44	4.88	5.34	4.97
Sympathetic	4.00	4.03	4.00	4.19	4.38	4.06	4.19
Role taking	4.00	4.00	4.06	4.59	4.62	5.12	5.81
Positive affect–simple or related to consequences	4.00	4.00	4.09	4.56	4.78	5.09	5.53
Negative affect–simple or related to consequences	4.00	4.00	4.00	4.16	4.28	4.22	4.44
Positive affect regarding self-respect	4.00	4.00	4.09	4.03	4.00	4.19	4.28
Negative affect regarding self-respect	4.00	4.00	4.00	4.06	4.00	4.09	4.06
Internalized law, norm, or value orientation	4.00	4.00	4.03	4.00	4.00	4.16	4.47
Generalized reciprocity	4.00	4.00	4.00	4.00	4.00	4.03	4.38
Condition of society	4.00	4.00	4.00	4.00	4.00	4.03	4.16
Individual rights	4.00	4.00	4.00	4.00	4.12	4.16	4.03
Equality of individuals	4.00	4.00	4.00	4.00	4.03	4.00	4.25

Note. Means are based on the nontransformed data.

hood to adolescence some categories of reasoning were expected to show both increases and decreases in usage, sometimes with a period of relative stability in use (which could result in a cubic trend analysis, for example, when a period of little use of a type of reasoning was followed by an increase in use during midchildhood and then a decline in its use in adolescence). In the first analysis, the categories of reasoning were those that had been used with some frequency (by at least one sex) at six or more time periods (i.e., hedonistic, needs-oriented, pragmatic, direct reciprocity, approval-oriented, and stereotypic; see Eisenberg et al., 1987). Scores were computed from the four stories used at all seven follow-ups. The multivariate Fs for the linear, quadratic, and cubic effects of time were highly significant, Fs(7, 24) = 40.86, 9.60, and 4.58, ps < .001, .001, and .002, respectively. For hedonistic reasoning, the univariate Fs for the linear and quadratic trends were highly significant, Fs(1, 30) = 116.72 and 53.58, ps < .001, respectively. Hedonistic reasoning decreased sharply with age until 11–12 years and then increased slightly in adolescence (see Table 1). Interestingly, perusal of the means indicated that the scores in hedonistic reasoning for girls changed little in adolescence (Ms = 4.56, 4.56, and 4.62 for T5, T6, and T7, respectively), whereas such reasoning clearly increased during adolescence for boys (Ms = 4.81, 4.94, and 5.28 for T5, T6, and T7, respectively). For needs-oriented reasoning, there was a highly significant quadratic trend and weaker (but highly significant) linear and cubic trends, Fs(1, 30) = 47.04, 11.89, and 10.02, ps < .001, .002, and .004, respectively; needs-oriented reasoning increased with age until 7–8 years, was relatively stable from 7–8 to 11–12 years (with a small decrease at age 9–10 followed by a small increase at age 11–12, and declined somewhat through early to midadolescence; see Table 1). According to a highly significant linear trend and

weaker quadratic and cubic trends, Fs(1, 30) = 49.02, 4.13, and 20.93, ps < .001, .051, and .001, respectively, direct reciprocity reasoning was used with little frequency until age 9–10, increased in use until early adolescence (13–14 years), and then started to decline. Similarly, stereotypic and approval-oriented judgments exhibited strong linear trends, Fs(1, 30) = 42.24 and 25.20, ps < .001, respectively, and weaker cubic trends, Fs(1, 30) = 4.52 and 4.29, ps < .042 and .047, respectively; these types of reasoning were used infrequently until mid to late elementary school, increased in use until age 13–14, and then decreased slightly in use in midadolescence. Finally, pragmatic reasoning increased in a linear fashion with age, F(1, 30) = 34.20, p < .001, whereas affectional relationship reasoning fluctuated in amount of use in elementary school (but was never used much) and then increased somewhat at T7, cubic F(1, 30) = 8.73, p < .006.

A second 2 (sex) × 5 (time) trend analysis was computed for those higher level categories of reasoning used with any frequency at T3 or T4 (sympathetic, role taking, internalized positive affect about consequences, internalized negative affect about consequences, internalized positive affect about values, internalized negative affect about values, and internalized law, norm, or value orientation reasoning). The multivariate F for the linear effect of time was significant, F(7, 24) = 5.28, p < .001. Role taking, positive affect/consequences, and internalized norm, rule, and law reasoning increased in usage with age, Fs(1, 30) = 13.37, 31.77, and 6.46, ps < .001, .001, and .016, respectively.

Although the multivariate Fs for sex and for Sex × Time (ps < .12 and .92, respectively) were not significant, it is important to look at the univariate Fs because of the gender differences in trends noted in some of these types of reasoning at T5. None of the Sex × Time interactions were significant, although across all time periods, girls used more role-taking and positive affect/values reasoning than did boys, $F_s(1, 30) = 4.41$ and 4.21, $ps < .044$ and $.049$, respectively.

In a third 2 (sex) × 3 (time) analysis, we examined age changes in the use of categories of reasoning that emerged only in adolescence (generalized reciprocity, concern with society, rights and justice, and equality of people reasoning). These categories of reasoning were used quite infrequently (see Table 1); nonetheless, the multivariate F for time was marginally significant, $F(7, 24) = 2.40$, $p < .075$, and there was a linear increase with age in generalized reciprocity reasoning, $F(1, 30) = 4.97$, $p < .033$.

In a summary analysis, we examined change in C1 students' moral reasoning composite scores from the follow-up preceding the two reported in this article, that is, T5 to T6 and T7. According to a 2 (sex) × 3 (time) trend analysis, there were main effects of both sex and the linear trend, $F(1, 30) = 12.00$ and 11.29, $ps < .002$, respectively. Girls scored higher than boys on the composite scores, and scores increased with age ($Ms = 227$, 241, and 254 for T5, T6, and T7, respectively).[1]

It is also of interest to examine intraindividual patterns of change. However, given that children frequently used a variety of types of moral reasoning (reflecting different levels of moral judgment) and higher levels of reasoning were weighted more heavily, a composite score at a given level did not necessarily indicate the predominance of a given mode of reasoning. For example, a score of 200 was obtained when subjects verbalized all needs-oriented reasoning or when they used half hedonistic reasoning and half stereotypic reasoning.

Nonetheless, we examined whether individuals' composite scores dropped considerably at any point in development (in comparison to any prior point). A drop of 50 points is roughly equivalent to a change of half a stage (because all hedonistic reasoning equals a score of 100, all needs-oriented reasoning equals a score of 200, etc). Nine children exhibited a drop of 50 points or more (3 dropped about 100 points) at one point in their development. Thus, although reasoning generally increased in sophistication with age, there were sizable declines in some children's reasoning at various points in their development.

According to additional analyses using the five (instead of four) moral reasoning stories at T6 and T7 (with the scores multiplied by .8 to adjust for the number of stories), the findings were generally the same or stronger. Moreover, the age trends in the children's reasoning did not seem to be the result of repeated testing. If they were, one would not expect the reasoning for C1 to be similar to that of children of the same age interviewed for the first time at T6 or T7 (C2 or C3). However, at T6, the only difference in reasoning between C1 and C2 was that C1 used more direct reciprocity reasoning, $t(65) = -2.32$, $p < .032$. At T7, the only differences were that C1 used more affectional relationship and role-taking reasoning, $t(64) = -2.25$ and -2.11, $ps < .028$ and $.039$, respectively, whereas C3 used more rights/justice reasoning, $t(64) = 2.28$, $p < .026$. Affectional relationship and rights/justice reasoning were used infrequently in both groups, and there were clear age trends for these types of reasoning. Thus, it seems unlikely that the repeated testing significantly affected the results of the analyses.[2]

Consistency of Indexes From T6 to T7

Most of the measures for C1 were fairly consistent from T6 to T7. The Bryant empathy scale from T6 ($M = 33.28$) was positively related to Davis' measures of sympathy ($M = 27.39$) and perspective taking at T7 ($M = 23.74$), but not to personal distress ($M = 18.38$), $rs(30) = .48$ and $.45$, $ps < .006$ and $.01$, respectively.[3] Social desirability, although measured with different scales at the two time periods ($Ms = 60.63$ and 34.35 at T6 and T7, respectively), was also consistent over time, $r(30) = .37$, $p < .037$, as were the children's ($Ms = 62.28$ and 71.75 at T6 and T7, respectively) and mothers' reports ($Ms = 2.71$ and 3.00 at T6 and T7, respectively) of prosocial behavior (on the modified Rushton et al., 1981, scale), $rs(30)$ and $(29) = .59$ and $.51$, $ps < .001$ and $.003$, respectively. Similarly, whether subjects helped was positively correlated from T6 to T7 (percentage of subjects helping at T6 and T7 were 46% and 53%, respectively), $r(30) = .41$, as was the composite index of helping, $r(30) = .37$, $p < .038$ (see next section); whether subjects completed all questions was nonsignificantly positively related ($r = .23$; 33% and 48% of subjects at T6 and T7, respectively, completed all parts). The only correlations that dropped substantially when sex was partialed out were those between the Bryant scale at T6 and the Sympathy and Perspective-Taking scales at T7; nonetheless, these correlations were still marginally significant, partial $rs(29) = .32$ and $.34$, $ps < .083$ and $.059$, for sympathy and perspective taking, respectively.

Interrelations of Prosocial Indexes

The two indexes of helping—whether subjects returned the questionnaires and whether all parts were completed (those

---

[1] For the entire sample of longitudinal and cross-sectional subjects, there was not a significant sex difference in the moral reasoning composite scores at T6 (although girls were somewhat higher), whereas at T7 girls scored higher than boys on the composite scores composed of both four and five stories, $ps < .008$ and $.006$. For the entire sample at T7, girls scored higher than boys on stereotypic and positive affect/self-reasoning, $ps < .047$ and $.024$, respectively, whereas boys scored higher on hedonistic reasoning, $p < .03$ (ps are for five stories; those for four stories are similar).

[2] On the basis of a small replication sample of 10 children interviewed six times between 4–5 and 13–14 years of age (a younger sample than C1; four girls, six boys; M age = 139 months at T5 and 163 months at T6), hedonistic reasoning decreased with age, $F(1, 8) = 20.40$, $p < .024$, whereas needs-oriented and approval-oriented reasoning increased with age, $F(1, 8) = 8.11$ and 16.42, $ps < .022$ and $.004$, respectively. Stereotypic reasoning increased with age until 13–14 years, and then dropped in use at age 15–16; linear and quadratic trends were $F(1, 8)$ 12.76 and 10.24, $p < .007$ and $.013$, respectively. Finally, according to Linear and Sex × Time quadratic trends for direct reciprocity reasoning, $F(1, 8) = 7.16$ and 10.24, $ps < .028$ and $.015$, respectively; direct reciprocity reasoning increased steadily with age for boys but increased for girls until age 13–14 ($M = 5.00$) and dropped off in use at age 15–16 ($M = 4.00$).

[3] Nineteen C1 subjects also returned the Davis perspective-taking, sympathy, and personal distress scales as part of the helping task at T6. For them, sympathy, perspective-taking, and personal distress were highly correlated from T6 to T7, $rs(17) = .72$, $.48$, and $.63$, $ps < .001$, $.039$, and $.004$, respectively.

who did not return anything were coded as not completing the questionnaires—were highly intercorrelated at both T6 and T7 (using C1 and either C2 or C3), $rs(69)$ and $(64) = .58$ and $.91$, $ps < .001$, respectively. Thus, the two indexes of helping were standardized and combined at both T6 and T7; these composite scores were then used in subsequent analyses.

At T6, the composite index of helping was significantly related to mothers' reports of children's prosocial behavior, $r(29) = .51$, $p < .003$, but not with children's reports on the modified Rushton self-report scale. Mothers' and children's reports of prosocial behavior were significantly, positively related, but only for boys, $r(13) = .53$, $p < .041$. At T7, the composite index of helping was not significantly correlated with either mothers' or children's reports of helpfulness; nor were mothers' and children's reports of prosocial behavior significantly related.

Relation of Sex to Prosocial Behavior, Empathy and Related Constructs, and Social Desirability

T tests were performed to determine whether there were sex differences in scores for the indexes of prosocial behavior, empathy, and social desirability at either T6 or T7. In these and all subsequent analyses, data from C2 and C3, as well as C1, were used when possible. At T6, girls scored higher than boys on the empathy scale and the composite index of helping, $ts(69) = 6.89$ and 2.17, $ps < .001$ and $.037$, respectively. At T7, girls also scored higher on the empathy-related scales, that is, on sympathy, perspective taking, and personal distress, $ts(64) = 5.11$, 2.27, and 2.52, $ps < .001$, $.027$, and $.014$, respectively, as well as on students' and mothers' reports of prosocial behavior, $t(64) = 2.56$ and $t(30) = 2.38$, $ps < .013$ and $.024$, respectively. This pattern of findings is, of course, consistent with sex role stereotypes.

Relation of Social Desirability to Moral Judgment, Moral Behavior, and Empathy

In these and subsequent analyses involving moral judgment, results for the composite scores based on all five stories are reported because composite scores based on more stories are generally assumed to be more reliable (Rushton, Brainerd, & Pressley, 1983) and the new story was considered to be more age-appropriate than some of the other four stories. However, the findings based on these composite scores generally were very similar to those based on data from the four stories.

At T6 and T7, the Social Desirability scale was not significantly related to the moral judgment composite scores. In addition, social desirability was not significantly correlated with any moral reasoning category used with some frequency at T6 (i.e., those categories in the first 2 MANOVAs conducted for C1 in the *Age Changes in Moral Judgment* section; only these categories of reasoning were used in any correlational analyses). At T7, the Social Desirability scale was negatively related to sympathy reasoning, $r(64) = -.29$, $p < .017$.

Children's social desirability was unrelated to helping at either T6 or T7, although their self-reported prosocial behavior was positively related to social desirability at T7, $r(64) = .37$, $p <$

$.002$. In addition, social desirability was significantly, positively related to most of the various indexes of empathy-related reactions. At T6, the Empathy scale was positively correlated with social desirability, $r(69) = .29$, $p < .015$, although this relation was due solely to the correlation for boys, $r(33) = .42$, $p < .012$; $r(34) = -.01$ for girls). At T7, social desirability was positively related to the Sympathy and Perspective-Taking scales, $rs(64) = .38$ and $.51$, $ps < .002$ and $.001$, respectively, and these correlations were substantial for both sexes. Because of the aforementioned relations between social desirability or sex and some of our measures (particularly empathy-related indexes and the modified Rushton helping scale), partial correlations controlling for social desirability and sex were computed in addition to zero-order correlations in subsequent analyses. In addition, we note when the pattern of findings was markedly different for boys and girls.

Relation of Moral Reasoning to Prosocial Behavior

At T6, the helping composite index was not significantly related to the moral reasoning composite scores. However, consistent with findings in prior follow-ups, helping was negatively related to hedonistic reasoning, $r(67) = -.28$, $p < .023$; partial $r(63) = -.25$, $p < .048$, controlling for sex and social desirability. Children's self-reported prosocial behavior was unrelated to moral reasoning; mothers' reports of children's prosocial behavior were positively related to children's pragmatic moral reasoning, $r(29) = .45$, $p < .001$; partial $r(27) = .52$, $p < .004$.

At T7, the helping behavior was positively related to higher scores on the moral reasoning composite score, $r(64) = .30$, $p < .015$; partial $r(62) = .25$, $p < .049$. Mothers' and children's reports of the children's prosocial behavior were not significantly related to the moral judgment composite score, although children's reports of prosocial tendencies were negatively related to hedonistic reasoning, $r(64) = -.38$, $p > .002$; partial $r(62) = -.30$, $p < .017$, particularly for boys, $r(31) = -.45$, $p < .009$; $r(31) = -.11$ for girls).

Relations of Moral Reasoning to Empathy and Related Constructs

At T6, the Bryant empathy index was not significantly related to the moral judgment composite scores, although it was negatively related to hedonistic moral reasoning, $r(65) = -.43$, $p < .001$; partial $r(63) = -.41$, $p < .001$, controlling sex and social desirability. At T7 there were more relations between empathy-related indexes and moral judgment, although the relations were nearly always due to the boys' data. Scores for perspective taking were positively related to the composite judgment scores, $r(64) = .28$, $p < .022$; partial $r(62) = .27$. The correlation between perspective taking and the composite reasoning score was due primarily to the data for boys, $r(30) = .44$, $p < .01$. In addition, sympathy and perspective taking were negatively related to hedonistic reasoning, $rs(64) = -.40$ and $-.35$, $ps < .001$ and $.004$, respectively, whereas sympathy was positively related to needs-oriented reasoning, $r(64) = .32$, $p < .008$, and these correlations remained significant when sex and social desirability were partialed, partial $rs(62) = -.29$, $-.28$, and $.35$, $ps <$

.019, .027, and .005, respectively. Again, however, these relations were due to the boys' data: $rs(31) = -.46, -.43,$ and .44, $ps < .008, .012,$ and $.011$, respectively, and partialing social desirability had virtually no effect on these correlations ($rs = -.06, -.17,$ and .17 for girls). Moreover, when sex and social desirability were partialed, scores on perspective taking tended to be positively correlated with sympathetic moral reasoning, partial $r(62) = .28, p < .027$; partial $r(30) = .49, p < .004,$ for boys; $r = .08$ for girls. None of the relations for personal distress were significant when social desirability was partialed from the correlations.

Relation of Prosocial Behavior to Empathy and Related Constructs

At T6, helping was positively correlated with Bryant empathy scores, $r(71) = .33, p < .006,$ although this correlation dropped somewhat when the effects of sex and social desirability were partialed, partial $r(67) = .22, p < .068.$ Similarly, children's self-reported prosocial behavior was positively related to Bryant empathy scores, $r(69) = .27, p < .023$; partial $r(67) = .24, p < .043.$ At T7, the empathy-related indexes were unrelated to helping behavior. However, children's reported prosocial behaviors (but not maternal reports) were positively related to both sympathy and perspective taking, $rs(64) = .52$ and .57, $ps < .001,$ respectively; partial $rs(62) = .34$ and .43, $ps > .006$ and .001.

Discussion

Several important findings were obtained in this study. First, we clarified the pattern of some modes of prosocial moral reasoning that previously were unclear. For example, we obtained the first longitudinal data indicating that approval and stereotypic prosocial moral reasoning start to decline in use in mid-adolescence. With this finding, we can reconcile the potentially discrepant findings that such reasoning increases in the elementary school years (Eisenberg et al., 1987) but that it has been found to decrease in use in a cross-sectional study of elementary and high school students (Eisenberg-Berg, 1979a). Moreover, the pattern obtained in this study for approval and stereotypic reasoning is consistent with that for Kohlbergian moral reasoning (Colby et al., 1983). However, given the relatively weak cubic trends obtained for approval and stereotypic reasoning (due to either periods of no change or minor fluctuations, followed by an increase and then a drop in usage), it is important to examine the further development of these modes of reasoning in late adolescence.

In addition, the developmental course of direct reciprocity reasoning has been clarified somewhat. Direct reciprocity reasoning, which is scored as a low level of prosocial moral judgment, increased significantly with age in elementary school and then decreased in use in adolescence. The initial increase with age in this mode of reasoning may be because it involves cognitive concepts of exchange and coordination between people and consequently is more sophisticated cognitively than merely a focus on what the self desires (e.g., hedonistic reasoning). Thus, direct reciprocity reasoning seems to be a relatively so-

phisticated mode of self-oriented reasoning, but one that decreases in use in mid-adolescence.

Moreover, in these follow-ups, we were able to observe the emergence of some of the higher level modes of reasoning (e.g., internalized norm, rule, and law reasoning and generalized reciprocity) during adolescence. An additional finding of interest was that although role taking and sympathetic reasoning emerged earlier for girls than for boys (i.e., at age 11–12; Eisenberg et al., 1987), the developmental curves for these modes of reasoning were very similar in adolescence. Girls did use somewhat higher levels of reasoning overall; however, there was little evidence of girls using more of the other-oriented modes of reasoning after age 11–12. Thus, it appears that girls used other-oriented, self-reflective modes of reasoning earlier than did boys, but boys caught up in their use of these modes of reasoning within 2 years.

The fact that girls exhibited a higher level of reasoning overall was probably due in part to the modest increase in boys' hedonistic reasoning in adolescence (which had decreased in use until adolescence), as well as to the tendency for girls to use somewhat more of some higher level modes of reasoning. Consistent with our data, Ford, Wentzel, Wood, Stevens, and Siesfeld (1989) found that high school boys made fewer socially responsible choices on a questionnaire index than did girls and their choices were more a function of self-interested emotions. As Ford et al. concluded, perhaps issues concerning responsibility for others are more problematic for adolescent boys than girls.

Another important finding is that we obtained some evidence of relations between moral reasoning and adolescents' prosocial behavior. At T6, helping was negatively related to hedonistic reasoning; at T7, helping was positively related to overall level of moral reasoning. Thus, as at younger ages, children's level of prosocial moral judgment seemed to be reflected in actual behavior (although the direction of causality is unclear). These relations are impressive given that the index of helping was fairly weak (i.e., did not involve much cost to the helper).

Adolescents' moral reasoning also was related to their empathy (at T6) and sympathy and perspective taking (at T7), although the relations at T7 held primarily for boys. The reason for the sex difference in the patterns of relations at T7 is unclear; global empathy was positively related to level of moral reasoning for both sexes in a previous study conducted with adolescents (Eisenberg-Berg & Mussen, 1978). The lack of a relation for girls' sympathy at T7 could be due to the restricted range of their responses (mean for sympathy was 30.30 out of a range of 7–35; for boys, $M = 24.48$); recall that girls scored higher on both sympathy and perspective taking. However, a ceiling effect was not evident for perspective-taking scores (means for girls and boys were 25.15 and 22.33) and the standard deviations for boys' and girls' sympathy and perspective taking were not markedly different. Although social desirability was significantly, positively related to both boys' and girls' sympathy ($rs = .38$ and .47, $ps < .029$ and .005, respectively) and perspective taking ($rs = .41$ and .60, $ps < .017$ and .001, respectively), these relations were somewhat stronger for girls—a finding that suggests that the indexes of sympathy and perspective taking were slightly more valid for boys. Whatever the reason, the data for T6 and for boys at T7 are consistent with the view that other-oriented concerns and perspective-taking tendencies

8

are intimately involved in moral reasoning (Eisenberg, 1986; Hoffman, 1987).

The findings in regard to the relations between empathy-related responses and prosocial behavior were mixed, albeit all findings were in the predicted direction. Empathy-related reactions were significantly, positively related to helping behavior only at T6. At T7, children's reports of sympathy and perspective taking were positively related to their reported helping behavior; however, the validity of the students' self-reported prosocial behavior is questionable because of the relation of these indexes to social desirability and the lack of their relation to actual helping behavior. Given the relations of indexes of empathy-related reactions with social desirability, it would be useful in the future to replicate the positive relations between adolescents' prosocial actions and empathy-related responses by means of non-self-report indexes. Moreover, given the relatively small number of subjects in this study, replication of these findings with larger samples would be useful.

In summary, in this study we obtained longitudinal data confirming, for the most part, the predicted pattern of development for prosocial moral reasoning in adolescence. In addition, prosocial moral reasoning, prosocial behavior, and empathy/sympathy and perspective taking were interrelated in theoretically meaningful ways, although sex differences in the relations of sympathy and perspective taking to moral reasoning merit further attention.

References

Bar-Tal, D. (1982). Sequential development of helping behavior: A cognitive-learning approach. *Developmental Review, 2,* 101–124.

Barnett, M. A. (1987). Empathy and related responses in children. In N. Eisenberg & J. Strayer (Eds.), *Empathy and its development* (pp. 146–162). Cambridge, England: Cambridge University Press.

Batson, C. D. (1987). Prosocial motivation: Is it ever truly altruistic? In L. Berkowitz (Ed.), *Advances in experimental social psychology* (Vol. 20, pp. 65–122). New York: Academic Press.

Batson, C. D. (1990). How social an animal? The human capacity for caring. *American Psychologist, 45,* 336–346.

Bryant, B. K. (1982). An index of empathy for children and adolescents. *Child Development, 53,* 413–425.

Colby, A., Kohlberg, L., Gibbs, J., & Lieberman, M. (1983). A longitudinal study of moral judgment. *Monographs of the Society for Research in Child Development, 48*(1–2, Serial No. 200).

Crandall, V. C., Crandall, V. J., & Katkovsky, W. (1965). A child's social desirability questionnaire. *Journal of Consulting Psychology, 29,* 27–36.

Crowne, D. P., & Marlowe, D. (1964). *The approval motive.* New York: Wiley.

Damon, W. (1977). *The social world of the child.* San Francisco: Jossey-Bass.

Eisenberg, N. (1986). *Altruistic emotion, cognition and behavior.* Hillsdale, NJ: Erlbaum.

Eisenberg, N. (1990). Prosocial development in early and mid adolescence. In R. Montemayor, G. R. Adams, & T. P. Gullotta (Eds.), *From childhood to adolescence: A transitional period? Advances in adolescence* (Vol. 2, pp. 240–269). Newbury Park, CA: Sage.

Eisenberg, N., & Fabes, R. A. (1991). Prosocial behavior and empathy: A multimethod, developmental perspective. In P. Clark (Ed.), *Re-view of personality and social psychology.* (pp. 34–61). Newbury Park, CA: Sage.

Eisenberg, N., Lennon, R., & Roth, K. (1983). Prosocial development: A longitudinal study. *Developmental Psychology, 19,* 846–855.

Eisenberg, N., & Miller, P. A. (1987). The relation of empathy to prosocial and related behavior. *Psychological Bulletin, 101,* 91–119.

Eisenberg, N., Shell, R., Pasternack, J., Lennon, R., Beller, R., & Mathy, R. M. (1987). Prosocial development in middle childhood: A longitudinal study. *Developmental Psychology, 23,* 712–718.

Eisenberg-Berg, N. (1979a). Development of children's prosocial moral judgment. *Developmental Psychology, 15,* 128–137.

Eisenberg-Berg, N. (1979b). The relationship of prosocial moral reasoning to altruism, political liberalism, and intelligence. *Developmental Psychology, 15,* 87–89.

Eisenberg-Berg, N., & Mussen, P. (1978). Empathy and moral development in adolescence. *Developmental Psychology, 14,* 185–186.

Eisenberg-Berg, N., & Roth, K. (1980). The development of children's prosocial moral judgment: A longitudinal follow-up. *Developmental Psychology, 16,* 375–376.

Ford, M. E., Wentzel, K. R., Wood, D., Stevens, E., & Siesfeld, G. A. (1989). Processes associated with integrative social competence: Emotional and contextual influences on adolescent social responsibility. *Journal of Adolescent Research, 4,* 405–425.

Gilligan, C., & Attanucci, J. (1988). Two moral orientations: Gender differences and similarities. *Merrill-Palmer Quarterly, 34,* 223–238.

Hoffman, M. L. (1987). The contribution of empathy to justice and moral judgment. In N. Eisenberg & J. Strayer (Eds.), *Empathy and its development* (pp. 47–80). Cambridge, England: Cambridge University Press.

Hume, D. (1966). *Enquiries concerning the human understanding and concerning the principles of morals* (2nd ed.). Oxford, England: Clarendon Press. (Original work published 1777)

Kant, I. (1964). *The doctrine of virtue.* New York: Harper & Row. (Original work published 1797)

Kohlberg, L. (1969). Stage and sequence: The cognitive-developmental approach to socialization. In D. A. Goslin (Ed.), *Handbook of socialization theory and research* (pp. 325–480). Chicago: Rand McNally.

Kohlberg, L. (1981). *The philosophy of moral development: Moral stages and the idea of justice.* San Francisco: Harper & Row.

Rest, J. R. (1983). Morality. In P. Mussen (Ed.), *Handbook of child psychology: Vol. 3. Cognitive development* (pp. 556–629). New York: Wiley.

Rholes, W. S., & Bailey, S. (1983). The effects of level of moral reasoning in consistency between moral attitudes and related behaviors. *Social Cognition, 2,* 32–48.

Rushton, J. P., Brainerd, C. J., & Pressley, M. (1983). Behavioral development and construct validity: The principle of aggregation. *Psychological Bulletin, 94,* 18–38.

Rushton, J. P., Chrisjohn, R. D., & Fekken, G. C. (1981). The altruistic personality and the self-report altruism scale. *Personality and Individual Differences, 2,* 1–11.

Selman, R. L. (1980). *The growth of interpersonal understanding.* San Diego, CA: Academic Press.

Staub, E. (1978). *Positive social behavior and morality: Social and personal influences* (Vol. 1). New York: Academic Press.

Underwood, B., & Moore, B. (1982). Perspective-taking and altruism. *Psychological Bulletin, 91,* 143–173.

Walker, L. (1984). Sex differences in the development of moral reasoning: A critical review. *Child Development, 55,* 677–691.

Received September 13, 1990
Revision received March 28, 1991
Accepted April 11, 1991 ∎

9

5 A conception of the determinants and development of altruism and aggression: motives, the self, and the environment

Ervin Staub

The time has come to develop theories and conduct research that jointly consider the most basic, central elements of moral conduct: aggression and altruism. How are such behaviors determined? What influences contribute to their occurrence? How do personal characteristics develop that make their occurrence more or less likely? A simple theory that focuses on one or two elements will necessarily be inadequate. What might be the central elements of a comprehensive theory of the development and determinants of aggression and altruism?

A major purpose of this chapter is to consider socialization and childhood experiences that contribute to the development of aggressive and altruistic behaviors. It is not possible, however, to consider their development meaningfully without understanding how such behaviors are determined. What psychological processes promote and inhibit aggression and altruism? What personal characteristics are likely to give rise to these psychological processes and to influence whether they gain expression in behavior? A reasonable strategy is to specify these characteristics and then to proceed to consider their sources in children's socialization and experience (Atkinson, 1981; Staub, 1979).

In order to understand the determinants of altruism and aggression, we have to consider three classes of influences: (1) environmental conditions that instigate or activate such behavior (e.g., someone's distress or an insult or attack), (2) personal characteristics that affect how people respond to external activators, and can also result in internal activation or initiation of altruism or aggression (e.g., empathic capacity, values, the self-concept), and (3) psychological states (e.g., empathy, anger) that are the result of activation and are the direct determinants of ways of dealing with it. Although altruism or aggression is frequently the result of environmental forces or external instigation, personal characteristics and psychological states can lead to self-instigation. Others in need can always be found. Reasons for victimization and violence can always be created.

Environmental instigation of altruism and aggression

Aggressive and prosocial behavior will be broadly defined. Prosocial behavior is behavior intended to benefit other people. However, the reason for benefiting them may be to gain reciprocal benefits, or approval – that is, some kind of self-gain. Altruism is behavior intended to help other people for no other purpose but to improve their welfare, to benefit them. Obviously, good feeling for having done so may follow, as may the reduction of empathic distress or the arousal of positive empathic feelings, but the motive or reason for action is not self-related. Aggression, in the truest sense, is behavior meant to harm others. It is important to recognize, however, that much of aggressive behavior is in the service of other goals, for example physical or psychological self-defense, while the actor accepts or even takes for granted that the object of aggression will be harmed. Such behaviors will be called aggressive, although the different motivational sources are important to recognize. Also, the motivational sources of aggression are often likely to be mixed – hostility, the desire to harm, added to the desire to defend the self.

The primary instigator of altruism is the need of others. The need may result from a condition of deficiency – someone is physically hurt or injured or a life is in danger; a person is in psychological distress or is sad or grieving; someone is hungry or cold; individuals or groups are deprived or unjustly treated or are suffering relative to some standard of reasonable welfare or some standard of comparison applicable to all human beings or to the specific class of individuals in question. The instigating power of need may arise out of our hereditary makeup, as geneticists and recently sociobiologists (Wilson, 1975) and psychologists have argued (see Hoffman, 1981, for an extensive discussion of biological origins of altruism), and it may arise out of social values and socialization that transmits those values to the young. There is likely to be an overall genetic inclination, in my judgement (Staub, 1978b), but it is socialization and individual experience that determine the extent to which specific individuals or members of specific cultures will respond to others' needs as activating conditions for prosocial or altruistic action. In addition to need that results from deficiency in someone's welfare, there can be need for help to pursue a positive goal that will enhance someone's welfare above and beyond a standard. A person's own state of well-being, comparison between the self and the other person, the relationship to the other, and other factors influence the perception of, and response to, the need of others (Staub, 1978b).

A genetic potential for aggression is also likely. Sociobiologists, particularly Wilson (1978), argue that an examination of the probabilities of aggressive behavior under certain environmental conditions, over time and across cultures, suggests that aggressive behavior is part of the human genetic makeup. In response to threat to survival or reproduction, the probability of aggression – not of any specific type, but some aggressive behavior out of the whole range of possible aggressive actions – will increase. However, the malleability of human beings is great. Culture and individual personality that evolves through socialization and experience will strongly affect, increase, or decrease the likelihood of aggression and altruism.

Consistent with the ideas of sociobiologists, psychologists found that certain conditions make aggressive behavior more likely. The primary instigators of aggression seem more varied and complex than those of altruism, but all involve loss, danger, or threat to the self. Frustration (i.e. interference with goal-directed behavior), increases the likelihood of aggression. However, many reactions other than aggression can follow frustration. Even more than frustration, physical attack such as electric shocks and psychological attack on the self (insult, humiliation) or threat to the self make aggressive reactions probable (see Baron, 1977; Averill, 1982). In sum, threat to existence, to the self-concept, and to fulfillment of goals all appear to increase the probability of aggressive responses. These conditions at times directly and physically, at other times potentially or symbolically, threaten a person's existence. Even when threat to survival is not immediate, aggressive responses can be genuinely self-protective in that attack or threat can predict later attacks. Lack of self-defense or retaliation makes continued and often more intense aggressive acts directed at the self more probable. The instigating conditions noted here can give rise to a number of motivations – anger, hostility, and the desire to harm another ("hostile" aggression); self-defense; and the defense of the self-concept. Instrumental aggression (aggression in the service of personal gain) need not be in response to instigation. Nonetheless, under difficult life circumstances, when the fulfillment of goals is difficult, instrumental aggression may increase the real or imagined probability of goal attainment.

An analysis of historical events suggests that the conditions that are likely to give rise to aggression on an individual level also increase the probabilities of violence within or between societies. Economic problems, chaos, and political disorganization within a society, increase the likelihood of violence and of scapegoating and persecution of subgroups in the society (Staub, 1982, 1984a, 1985b).

Value orientations, altruism, and aggression

Certain value orientations that children acquire during the course of so-cialization and experience can both contribute to positive behavior and inhibit the likelihood of aggression. The stages of Kohlberg's (1969) moral reasoning can be seen, for example, as describing different value orien-tations. Different investigations have described and assessed different moral value orientations that characterize people, such as humanistic versus con-ventional (Hoffman, 1970) or rule-centered versus person-oriented (Gil-ligan, 1982). These have different probable (and as some research shows, actual) consequences on behavior.

In a number of studies with adult participants, my associates and I found that persons characterized by a moral value orientation, which I called prosocial orientation, are more likely to respond helpfully to someone's need. We used a variety of tests to assess prosocial orientation (Staub, 1974, 1978a, 1978b, 1980). These tests, in our view, tap three interrelated domains: (1) a positive view or positive evaluation of human beings; (2) concern about and valuing of other people's welfare; and (3) a feeling of personal responsibility for others' welfare. When several weeks after the assessment of their prosocial orientation individuals were faced with an-other person's need, those with a stronger prosocial orientation responded more helpfully to either the physical (Staub, Erkut, and Jaquette, as de-scribed in Staub, 1974; and Erkut, Jacquette, & Staub, 1981), or the psy-chological distress of another (Feinberg, 1977; Grodman, 1979; Staub, 1978a, 1978b, 1980).

Value orientations are characterized by desired ends they specify and associated "cognitive networks." Different value orientations are expected to give rise to different actions. For example, an orientation to maintaining the social order, sometimes described as a duty or obligation orientation – in essence a conventional orientation that focuses on maintaining rules and conventions – (Durkheim, 1961; Hoffman, 1970; Staub, 1978b, 1980) might frequently lead to prosocial behavior. However, when a person in need is seen as having been at fault, particularly as having brought about his or her need by contravening societal norms or conventions, this person may be seen as deserving his or her suffering (Lerner, 1980; Rubin & Peplau, 1973, 1975). Individuals characterized by a concern with rules and feelings of duty or obligation to them may be more likely to make the judgment that victims deserve their suffering and be less helpful under such conditions.

The extent to which the relationship between personal characteristics such as value orientations and either prosocial or aggressive behavior has

14

been explored is limited. Our research on the relationship between a pro-social value orientation and prosocial behavior was briefly noted. As yet the relationship between prosocial orientation and aggression has not been explored. A strong prosocial orientation is assumed to make it less likely that motives for aggression arise, and more likely that behavior that harms other people is inhibited. Limited evidence does exist that value related personal characteristics are associated with less aggression (Baron, 1977; Kohlberg, 1969). Most research that has explored such relationships was not guided by a conception of behavior as the result of varied influences, both environmental and personal. Instead, usually a correlation between some individual characteristic and a specific behavior was investigated. Since any behavior is multidetermined, and individual characteristics and circumstances will usually join in affecting behavior, a conception of how different influences join is essential to come to understand and be able to predict the occurrence of altruistic and aggressive behaviors. Such a conception, described in more detail elsewhere (Staub, 1978a, 1978b, 1980, 1984a, 1984b) is briefly presented below. How different moral orientations and other relevant individual characteristics develop will then be considered.

Instigation, value orientations, and personal goals: a theory of social behavior

A motivational disposition, for example a strong prosocial orientation, obviously does not guarantee that such a motive will become active and gain out over other motives. Faced with another person's need, people may aim to benefit them or may choose another, self-related, end or purpose, or may continue with an already ongoing pursuit of a goal. Similarly, conditions that are instigators for aggression might give rise to aggression, or to non-aggressive self-defense, or to no outward response, or to flight. A person may also continue to work toward a blocked goal in nonaggressive ways or choose and proceed to pursue a different goal. Self-instigation also occurs, so that altruism or aggression is not merely a response to environmental conditions. *In order to understand how altruism or aggression comes about, we must consider both how people select the aims of their behavior from a multiplicity of aims, and what determines whether they actually pursue aims they selected.*

I have proposed a theory of social behavior, with the primary purpose of accounting for how prosocial behavior comes about (Staub, 1978a, 1978b, 1980, 1984b). Recently I began to extend this concept to embody aggressive behavior, as a beginning toward a comprehensive theory of moral conduct (Staub, 1984a).

15

The theory assumes that the characteristics of persons and their circumstances jointly affect the selection of aims. During the course of their development, people develop varied motives. In recognition of the fact that much of human behavior is purposive in character, the focus is placed on motivation to reach desired ends or to avoid aversive ones. Such motivation is conceptualized in the theory as goals (Lewin, 1938, 1948) or as personal goals, or as goal orientations. Personal goals embody desired preferences or end states. In most cases the person has developed an associated cognitive network consisting of beliefs, thoughts, elaborations, and meanings in relation to the valued outcomes. Goals are potentials that become active under certain conditions. As potentials, goals can be arranged in hierarchies according to the value or importance of each goal to a person. Environmental (as well as internal) conditions can have activating potentials for goals for one, two, or more goals. Activating potentials vary in their intensity. The activation of a goal is a function of its importance to the person, which is at least partly relative, a function of its position in the hierarchy of goals, and the intensity of the activating potential for that goal. It is possible for more than one goal to be activated; the result is goal conflict, with the actual motivation a function of the way in which the conflict is resolved. One focus of this model is how the aims of benefiting or harming others is selected from the multiplicity of a person's potential aims; another is a specification of conditions that promote or influence the expression of aims in goal-directed behavior.

Value orientations can be seen as embodying personal goals in moral domains and as incorporating both the desire for outcomes and ways of thinking – cognitive networks – in relation to the welfare of other people and to "right" or "wrong" conduct. A prosocial value orientation can be seen as embodying the personal goal of benefiting and not harming others. Research findings (Staub, 1974, 1978b) show that the stronger their prosocial orientation, the more people respond with positive behavior to activating conditions (physical or psychological distress), supporting the theoretical model. Given the nature of this value orientation, with its focus on personal responsibility for others' welfare, it can also be expected to inhibit aggression under some activating conditions.

This approach provides useful ways of explaining a variety of research findings. Consider one example. Darley and Batson (1973) asked seminary students to give a public lecture. Some, but not others, were told that they were late to the lecture; each student *then* proceeded to the building where the lecture was to be given. Those who believed they were late were more likely to pass by – practically step over – a person lying in their path than were the seminary students who were not in a hurry. Giving a public lecture probably served an important goal for these students, as it was an activity they would later engage in as part of their profession. Being late presumably intensified the focus of attention on their goal. Since the goal was in a highly active state, they were less open to the activating potential of their environment for another goal. Research findings of other psychologists (e.g., Schwartz et al., 1969; Gergen et al., 1972; and London, 1970) were discussed from the perspective of this theory in other publications (Staub, 1978a, 1978b, 1980).

Although the focus here is on prosocial value orientation as the motivational source of unselfish behavior that aims to benefit other people (or inhibits harming them), two additional motivational sources should be noted. Prosocial orientation is person centered, its focus others' welfare. However, some people, both children and adults (Karylowski, 1984; Hoffman, 1970; Gilligan, 1982; Staub, 1979) are characterized by a rule-centered moral orientation with a focus on adherence to rules or principles of conduct. The aims that arise from these two different moral orientations will be different – concern with the welfare of persons versus obligation to rules or principles.[1] In general, the precise nature of internalized rules or norms or motives (Schwartz & Howard, 1984) will affect motivation and action.

These two types of moral value orientations can have different effects on behavior, and are brought about by different socialization and experience of children. For example, Hoffman (1970) found that parental withdrawal of love was an important source of conventional moral orientation in seventh-grade boys, whereas induction was a source of humanistic orientation; these two value orientations are comparable to the prosocial and rule-centered orientations discussed here.

Empathy is the third important motivational source of altruism and potential inhibitor of causing harm to people (Staub, 1971). Empathy is currently receiving substantial theoretical and research attention (e.g., Hoffman, 1975; Batson et al, 1981; Eisenberg & Lennon, 1983). Briefly, what are the sources of empathy and the characteristics of persons that enhance their empathic potential, what is the likelihood that they will respond empathically to others, and finally what is the relationship of empathy to this model?

Possibly, one source of empathy is a primitive emotional responsiveness in the child to others' distress, which Hoffman (1975a) called primitive empathy. Another source is the cognitive elaboration of the sense of other people as separate, differentiated individuals, which Hoffman (1975a) described. This is a value-free characteristic, a cognitive knowledge and awareness. For a person to respond empathically to other people it is probably also necessary to develop a positive evaluation of other people. As Hoffman (1976) also noted, the primitive "empathy" appears to be a connection with and responsiveness to others that is not necessarily empathic; for example, the experience of the infant can be fear, rather than shared distress (Staub, 1979). Given the malleability of human beings this responsiveness can evolve not only in positive, but also in negative ways (fear and avoidance).

We can expect it to evolve as a source of empathic responsiveness only if, in addition to an elaboration of the sense of others, a positive valuing of others develops. This positive valuing is one component of prosocial orientation. Whereas empathy and prosocial orientation are not identical, the latter is a likely source of empathic response, particularly if it is accompanied by an elaborate cognitive sense of others or an in depth capacity for role taking.

Although Hoffman does not assume that a positive evaluation of human beings is a precondition for more forms of empathy, he proposes that children in the course of development discover "both that others react as persons in their own right, and that their responses are often very similar to his own. The realization that his feelings resemble those experienced independently by others in similar situations must inevitably contribute to a sense of 'oneness' which preserves and may even enhance the child's developing motivation to alleviate others' distress" (Hoffman, 1976, p. 136).

A sense of oneness with other human beings is important for identification, a basis for empathy. Experiencing a sense of oneness will depend on positive evaluation of other people; without that, the similarity of others' distress to one's own may not be noticed or acknowledged. However, a feeling of identification and a positive evaluation may have bidirectional influences on each other. Although the two are not regarded here as identical, they probably evolve under similar conditions of socialization and experience, such as warmth and inductive reasoning by parents (Hoffman, 1976; Staub, 1979). They will not evolve under conditions of hostility and rejection by parents.

Finally, a related source of empathy is the self concept, which affects the self–other bond. Empathy is, in part, an extension of the self to other people. It is not surprising, therefore, that people respond more empathically to similar others, even if the similarity is limited in nature (Krebs, 1975; Stotland, 1969). Victims of mistreatment of whole groups of people are usually defined as dissimilar, an outgroup, as "them" rather than "us" (Hornstein, 1976; Staub, 1982, 1984a). A poor self-concept makes it more difficult to extend the boundaries of the self in benevolent ways.

The preceding discussion suggests that empathy arises out of a multiplicity of sources: an emotional connectedness that evolved from primitive empathy and that may require a positive self-concept, a well-developed sense of other people, and the positive valuation of human beings. The empathic response has an emergent quality. It arises as a unitary response from these varied characteristics of persons, usually in response to environmental events. The quality of empathic response, whether it is an emotion similar to that of another person or includes a sympathetic responsiveness, needs to be further defined and investigated (Staub and Feinberg, 1980).

Hoffman (1982) proposed that sympathy is developmentally more advanced than empathy and a qualitatively different feeling. Staub and Feinberg (1980) found that empathy (which they called "parallel empathy") and sympathetic responsiveness (which they called "reactive empathy") have different behavioral correlates. Girls who showed reactive empathy on a test engaged in somewhat more positive behavior and were the recipients of substantially more positive behavior from peers. (There were no reactive empathy responses among the third- and fourth-grade boys in the study.)

One consequence of empathy can be the desire to benefit another, which diminishes one's empathic distress or gives rise to empathic enjoyment of another's increased well-being. Empathy differs from the desire to benefit another that arises from prosocial orientation in that the former does not include a feeling of responsibility for others' welfare. This difference may make prosocial orientation a more reliable source of positive behavior than empathic capacity. It is the lack of this feeling of responsibility, and the more specifically affective nature of the response, that might account for escape from empathy arousing situations, which can be one mode of reducing empathic distress (Piliavan, Dividio, Goertner, & Clark, 1981). However, escape is less likely when the affective response is sympathetic or reactive.

A conscious valuing of other people's well-being and a desire for benefiting them may not be prerequisites for empathy. Most likely, though, these characterize persons with a well-developed capacity for empathy, especially "reactive" empathy.

The emergent quality of empathic emotion gives it immediacy. However, in selecting an aim for behavior, empathy is still in competition with other motives, which give rise to the desire for one or another outcome. That is, in the current perspective empathy is a source of motivation that must be viewed in conjunction with other motivational sources such as value orientations and personal goals, for its relative influence to be understood.

Motivation alone does not determine behavior. The nature of the self-concept is also important, particularly for altruism and aggression. (This will be discussed in the next section.) Moreover, a variety of supporting characteristics are essential for motivation to be expressed in action, and sometimes for motivation to become active.

For example, competencies are important in determining whether altruistic motivation will gain expression in behavior. Frequently without seeing the possibility of reaching a desired outcome, of fulfilling a goal, the goal may not become active (Benesh and Weiner, 1982). Three types of competencies are important: a general belief in one's ability to influence events and successfully pursue goals; the capacity to generate plans of action or the knowledge of action on specific occasions; and specific competence to act in required ways, (such as the ability to swim in order to save a drowning person) (Staub, 1978a, 1978b, 1980). Other supporting characteristics sometimes include the ability to make fast decisions, if the opportunity for action might come to pass (Denner, 1968) and a role-taking capacity to perceive others' needs when those needs are not obvious. Such characteristics are seen, however, as being in the service of motivation. Without a motivational source, they will not give rise to altruistic behavior.

The self-concept and self-other connections

A substantial body of research findings shows that positive experience, such as success, luck or kindness by other people, increases subsequent helpfulness and generosity. Although negative experiences often decrease helpfulness or generosity, sometimes they do not and can even increase positive behavior (for reviews, see Rosenhan, Salovey, Karylowski, & Hargis, 1981; Staub, 1978b). This variation following negative experiences seems partly a function of the type of negative experience. For example, shared misfortune can increase a sense of communality with other people and enhance positive behavior. In some cases, after failure people might engage in positive behavior in an attempt to repair others' assessment of them, or even their self-assessment, diminished by the failure (Isen, Horn, & Rosenhan, 1973).

Why do positive and negative experiences have these effects? They can affect temporary levels of self-esteem and attention to self versus others. First, negative experiences, or even the expectation of stress or of evaluation by other people, can lead to self-preoccupation (Berkowitz, 1970). The result is diminished attention to other people and their needs. In an important study, Reykowski and Yarymovitz (1977) found that children with low self-esteem showed substantial increase in their perception of the need of another child once their self-esteem improved as a result of a series of success experiences. Second, negative experiences can result in motivation to enhance or protect the self and thereby diminish concern for other people's needs. Positive experiences can free people of self-concern, which is often present to some degree in social relationships. As a result, the ability to attend to other people's needs increases and the motivation to help others can come to the fore, becoming active and gaining expression. I am implying that the effects of positive and negative experiences, particularly of success and failure, will depend on a person's self-esteem (see also Karylowski, 1976). Moreover, differences in self-esteem will be related to altruistic behavior. However, according to the conception presented here, the influence on prosocial behavior of a person's self-concept and self-esteem, and how it is modified by current experience, will also depend on the strength of their prosocial orientation or other altruistic motivation.

Since positive and negative behaviors are expressions of the connection between the self and others, it is not surprising that how people feel about or experience themselves would affect the way they feel about others, as well as their willingness to extend themselves for others. It is interesting, in this context, that some research findings with children suggest that an extremely positive self-concept is less related to positive behavior (Reykowski & Yarymovitz, 1976) and to positive peer relations (Loban, 1953, Reese, 1961; see Staub, 1979, p. 236) than a positive but more moderate self-concept. Children with a very positive self-concept may feel sufficient unto themselves and less concerned with their connection to other children. They may have less of a sense of connectedness to others. However, the relationship between self-esteem and positive behavior would be modified by the degree of prosocial motivation that children developed and the relative importance of their prosocial versus other motives.

There are also indications that a weak sense of self, a low self-esteem, contributes to aggression. It makes it more likely that the behavior of others is perceived as threatening, as dangerous, if not physically, then at least to one's self-esteem. Certain kinds of danger, or threats to self will be more acutely experienced, or even imagined, by people who have low self-esteem or a vulnerable self-concept. The need or desire to protect the self will more easily arise and dominate other motives. The clinical literature suggests that young aggressive delinquents tend to perceive others' behavior as threatening, and they respond with what might be called pre-retaliation (Staub, 1971; Slavson, 1965). The study of violent criminals also shows that a frequent source of violence is sensitivity to insult or threat by other people. In a careful study of prison inmates who committed crimes

of violence, with other trained inmates or former inmates acting as interviewers, Toch (1969) found that a large percentage (25%) of these violent
individuals reacted to mild or imagined insults. These insults gave rise to
motivation to defend their reputation or self-image. As Toch (1969) writes,
"he invariably responds with violence to defend himself against the belit-
tlement" (p. 148). Another group of violent individuals, also characterized
by feelings of worthlessness, would seek violent encounters to convince
others that they are fearless (Toch, 1969). When the defense or enhancement of the self become important goals – either as persistent individual
characteristics or aroused on specific occasions – in some individuals these
motivations are fulfilled by aggression.

Self-awareness, or knowledge of oneself, and acceptance of the varied
aspects of the self so that they become part of the self-concept can also be
of great importance in affecting altruism and aggression. Freud, Jung, and
Rogers all theorized, on the basis of their clinical experience, about the
negative consequences of individuals not being aware of certain impulses
or emotions within themselves or of not accepting them and failing to
incorporate them into their conscious self-concept. The denial of feelings
of anger or of sexual impulses can lead to the projection of such characteristics into other people. But when such characteristics are seen as wrong,
as unacceptable – which is the reason for their denial or repression – a
desire to punish them in other people can arise. That is, lack of self-
awareness and of self-acceptance and the lack of self-fulfillment that results
can be a source of hostility toward others. The existing research on the
authoritarian personality (Adorno, Frenkel-Brunswik, Levinson, & Sanford, 1950; Cherry & Bryne, 1977; Sanford, 1973) – some with better and
others with less adequate methodology – indicates that authoritarian individuals are characterized by such tendencies of denial and projection and
by the desire to punish other people who presumably have these unacceptable characteristics. Such individuals also show a tendency toward
obedience and submission to authority and a disregard for those without
power. The combination of these characteristics provides a potential for
their becoming tools of malevolent authority in perpetrating violence against
others (Staub, 1982, 1985b).

Developmental psychologists have not been much concerned with the
acceptance of aspects of the self. As an incidental finding, Hoffman (1970),
described children characterized by a conventional moral orientation as
having also learned to inhibit anger as well as sexual and other impulses
in themselves. Self-awareness and the acceptance of varied aspects of oneself have basic importance for many aspects of functioning, including ways
of relating to other people. This received substantial attention from psy-

chologists who developed theories based on clinical experience. Research exploring the origins and consequences of differences in self-awareness and self-acceptance are greatly needed.

Summary of determinants of altruism and aggression

The conception presented here identifies important influences on altruistic and aggressive behaviors. Moral value orientations and empathic potential, the sources of a person's altruistic motivation, probably diminish hostility or its expression in behavior (Staub, 1971). Their influence is also a function of their position in a hierarchy of motives. The self-concept, self-esteem, self-awareness, and self-acceptance all affect connectedness to other people. Jointly with moral value orientation and empathy, they affect openness to others' needs as opposed to a focus on the self, as well as sensitivity to instigators of aggression such as frustration or threat. Competence, role taking and other supporting characteristics affect the engagement of motivational potentials, and the expression of motives in action. To understand the development of altruism and aggression, we must understand the sources of these personal characteristics in socialization and experience.

A question of profound discussion and controversy in personality and social psychology has been the extent of consistency in behavior across different (but related) circumstances (Mischel, 1968; Mischel and Peake, 1982; Epstein, 1979). The model presented here suggests that moderate to fairly high consistency can be expected in general, and in prosocial and aggressive behaviors in particular, when a relevant goal or motive is important to a person (high in the person's hierarchy of goals) and when this person possesses positive self-esteem and supporting characteristics that lead to the expression of the goal in behavior. Still, very high consistency would not be expected because (1) the environment will at least occasionally offer a strong potential to satisfy another goal important to the person, which then gains dominance; or (2) an already active goal will interfere with the activation of the goal. The seminary students who ignored a person lying in their path in their hurry to get to their assignment provide an example of the latter.

Motivational sources in human nature

A number of basic motivational systems seem to be present at birth, or to develop as humans mature, if minimal supporting conditions exist. They are the sources of a variety of personal goals. Some are importantly involved in the development of altruistic and aggressive behaviors. How these motivational potentials unfold, however, is a function of socialization and experience.

These motivational systems or potentials include primary needs and sex. They include intrinsic motivation, an interest in stimulation and in novelty, and in the ability to manipulate and work with objects. With favorable experience, out of this, can grow a sense of agency, a belief in one's ability to influence events. As a conception of the self and the world begins to develop, it guides the way the individual makes sense of the world, of himself or herself, and of the relationship between the two (Epstein, 1973, 1980). There appears to be a strong motivation to protect and maintain one's existing self-concept, and to protect and enhance self-esteem. The relevance of this system to prosocial behavior and aggression was noted earlier.

Motivational sources of specific relevance

Certain stimuli appear to have biological meaning, such as contact comfort and crying by another infant. There is evidence that infants, on their first day of life, cry in response to crying by another infant, although not in response to the same-intensity noise (Simner, 1971; Sagi and Hoffman, 1976). This may provide support for a notion of genetically based connectedness to other human beings, a genetically based sociotropic orientation. The observation of infants and young children also indicates a tendency to respond to certain experiences with rage or anger. With increasing age, undirected forms of anger decline while anger directed at other children increases (Goodenough, 1931). How the potential for anger and for aggression that it sometimes gives rise to develops depends on socialization and experience.

Attachment, an early affectional tie to specific others, is another motivational potential present at birth. It has long been believed that the first important relationship of infants to parents represents a prototype of later relationships. Recent research findings provide support (see Sroufe, 1979).

The human infant, like the infant of many species of animals, has the capacity to form strong attachments to members of its species. Recent research findings show that the quality of attachment of infant to parents – usually the mother – varies, and that the quality of this attachment is associated with later social behaviors of the child in interactions with peers. Children who form secure attachments to their caretakers, in contrast to anxious or ambivalent attachments (Ainsworth, 1979), later manifest more effective or positive peer relations (Sroufe, 1979). In one study, secure attachment was associated with more effective peer relations when combined with early experience with peers (Lieberman, 1976). In part, the reason for these differences in social relations to peers is probably motivational. Children who experience conditions leading to secure attachment and who develop such attachment may feel safer and less anxious. They may experience less need to protect themselves. They may also experience greater positivity of feelings towards other people and would, therefore, be more motivated to approach and interact with peers. From earlier research on institutionalized infants who, because of lack of a consistent caretaker in their environment and of social stimulation and responsiveness to their needs, had no opportunity to develop attachment to an adult, we know that such children later have serious problems in their personal relationships (Thompson and Grusec, 1970).

A secure attachment, which is associated with responsiveness by caretakers to the child's needs, bodily contact, mutual gazing, as well as other types of contact (Shaffer, 1979), is likely to be an important starting point for the development of altruism and might lessen the probability of aggression. It provides a basis for positive feelings for and positive evaluation of other human beings, the most basic component of prosocial orientation. It is probably also a component of empathic responsiveness. The positive contact to a caretaker probably contributes to the beginnings of a positive self concept. The nature of continuing socialization and experience of the child is crucial, of course, to expand this rudiment of positive relatedness to other human beings, and to the self.

At the time that attachments to primary caretakers develop, stranger anxiety also appears, a fear and/or avoidance of unfamiliar individuals. This may be a rudimentary appearance of a very basic human tendency, to divide people into ingroups and outgroups, into "us" and "them" (Staub, 1982; Tajfel, 1982). In turn, we are more likely to help those we identify as "us" (Hornstein, 1976). Consistent with this is the substantially greater altruism toward mothers than toward lesser known adults in the first years of children's life (Zahn-Waxler and Radke-Yarrow, 1982). The evolving perceived similarity and identification with "us" is a source of empathy and presumably leads to the application of values that promote altruism (Krebs, 1975; Stotland, 1969).

Obviously, it is socialization and experience that shape the course of development of the early rudimentary differentiation. More varied early experience, for example, exposure to and familiarity with more people, is associated with less stranger anxiety (Shaffer, 1979). The quality of attachment also affects stranger anxiety, less stranger anxiety accompanying secure attachment. At a later age the family or tribe, identifying outsiders as dangerous, or as enemies, will further promote differentiation, while creating new boundaries along which enemies are made. The culture, including its most basic aspects, such as language can embody such differentiation. For example, among the Mundurucu, the word for non-Mundurucu also means enemy (Wilson, 1978).

Differentiation between "us" and "them" is so basic an aspect of human thinking that it is worth considering its bases in the human genetic makeup. The differentiation of the known and familiar from the unknown and unfamiliar, of which stranger anxiety is an important example, and the categorization of classes of objects by which the human mind works, may be such bases. Usually people defined as outsiders, as "them," are also devalued (Piaget and Weil, 1951). They can become the object of prejudice, hostility, and violence, even to the point of extermination. When people are so identified they come to be excluded from the application of moral value orientations (Staub, 1982, 1984a, 1984b). This seems a general principle, suggesting that extending the boundaries of "us" in the course of socialization may increase helpfulness and diminish aggression. Secure attachment, varied social experience, and socialization (and culture), which identify other human beings as similar and which positively evaluate them, would best contribute to the rudiments of prosocial orientation and empathic responsiveness applied to a broad range of people.

We are reminded of the multiple influences on aggression and altruism by the substantial degree of ingroup violence in contemporary America, such as child abuse, abuse of spouses, and the large proportion of murders occurring among intimates. It is consistent with the previous theorizing that identifying some people as part of one's ingroup will not alone determine altruism or aggression toward them. Differentiation between "us" and "them" affects the arousal and application of altruistic and aggressive motivations and their expression. However, these motivations depend primarily on the personal characteristics identified earlier.

Socialization practices and their consequences

A great deal of laboratory and socialization research shows that prosocial behavior is influenced by a combination of (1) parental warmth and nurturance, (2) *induction*, pointing out to children the consequences of their behavior on other people, and (3) firm control by parents, so that children actually behave in accordance with important values and rules (Staub, 1979, 1981).[2] These practices expand the original attachment that children develop toward important caretakers. The experience of warmth can contribute to the development of positive assumptions about human beings as well as trust in their benevolence. Induction, particularly if it is accompanied by control, can lead children to become aware of and take others' needs seriously and to feel responsible for others' welfare. By enhancing awareness of others' needs, induction can contribute to empathy.

From a theoretical perspective, warmth, nurturance, induction, control, and actual participation in positive behavior implied by control can be expected to contribute to positive assumptions about human beings and concern about, and a feeling of personal responsibility for, their welfare. These are elements of the prosocial value orientation. However, research on how socialization practices contribute to personal characteristics in general, and value orientations in particular, is quite sparse. Much of the research has been laboratory analogue research. Such research can demonstrate immediate cognitive or affective consequences of experimental treatments, which possibly mediate behavioral consequences, as for example research by Grusec and associates (Chapter 8, this volume). Having identified such cognitive and affective consequences, we can extrapolate and hypothesize that the repeated application of such "treatments" or practices by parents will lead to the acquisition of the mediating cognitive-affective tendencies, which thus become personal characteristics of children.

The limited research that has explored the relationship of parental socialization practices to children's characteristics has sometimes focused on the relationship of those practices to children's behavior (Baumrind, 1975). At other times, children's value orientations were explored, with a primary focus on the extent to which children demonstrated internalization of values. Many of the actual values assessed were proscriptive in nature, prohibiting misconduct (Hoffman and Saltzstein, 1967). However, the limited research findings that are available do show a relationship between specific parental socialization practices discussed above and the acquisition of concern about the welfare of other humans (Hoffman and Saltzstein, 1967; Hoffman, 1970, 1975b). For example, Hoffman's (1970) humanistic-flexible children, who demonstrate a value orientation similar to prosocial orientation in that it embodies concern for others' welfare, have parents who demonstrate warmth and inductive reasoning as important aspects of child rearing.

What is needed, however, is research in which the correlates of the enduring use by parents or socializing agents of the *whole pattern* of practices are identified. The more parents and socializers in other settings, such as schools, particularly in the early school years (Staub, 1981), use such a pattern, the more we can expect prosocial orientation, empathic responsiveness, and behavioral tendencies for increased altruism and less aggression in children. Practices that are expected to contribute to a rule-centered moral orientation can also be identified. For example, the focus of parents' reasoning with the child would be not the consequences of the child's behavior (and human behavior in general) on others' welfare, but the importance of adherence to rules. Very early in life, parents more or less characterized by such patterns may be selected for study, with continued assessment of the evolution of the pattern. Alternatively, parents may be willing to undergo, in the context of a study, early training in "optimum" socialization practices for the development of an altruistic behavioral disposition.

While reasonable parental control is important, it is also important that parents respond to the child's own reasoning and be willing to consider the child's point of view (Baumrind, 1975). Autocratic control has negative effects. In general, the mode of control employed by parents can be crucial. There is evidence of an association between overly power-assertive control, with a substantial amount of physical punishment, and aggressive behavior displayed by children (Aronfreed, 1968; Bandura and Walters, 1959). Such controlling practices break the connection of love and trust in other people, generate anger, and create concern in the child about his or her well-being, safety, and goodness. Thus both prosocial orientation and the self-concept may be affected. There is some evidence that the combination of power-assertive control and autocratic parenting contributes to the development of authoritarian personalities (Cherry & Byrne, 1977).

Another consequence of the mode of parental control has been shown in a study by Hoffman (1970). In assessing children's moral orientations and parental childrearing practices, Hoffman found love withdrawal to be associated with a conventional rule-oriented morality. This gained expression in concern about rules in contrast to the welfare of individuals. A characteristic of conventional children was an inhibition of expression of impulses. There are hidden elements in most parental socialization practices; a primary one is the content of what is rewarded or punished, what is promoted or inhibited. Love withdrawal may result in pervasive concern by the child about being loved and accepted as he or she is. As a result, children become cautious and therefore inhibited. Or love withdrawal may be an expression of parental sensitivity that leads to prohibiting specific behaviors, particularly expressions of anger. Certainly the effects of love withdrawal will depend on its severity, generality, and the total pattern of parental practices, including the type of behaviors which parents punish by love withdrawal. However, the possibility that extensive use of love withdrawal leads to a focus on adherence to rules and social convention, and perhaps interferes with self acceptance and self awareness, is important.

Children learn from the specific types of behaviors that are encouraged or discouraged, rewarded or punished. The example of parents and others is another mode, a highly influential one, through which specific behaviors, standards of conduct, and value placed on human welfare are learned. The influence of such examples will depend on the total context, on socialization practices, and on other experiences.

Modeling clearly affects prosocial behavior (Grusec, 1981; Eisenberg, 1982; Staub, 1979). The evidence also suggests (Barron, 1977; Eron, 1982; Maccoby, 1980; Theiss, 1983) that the more exposure children had to aggression in the course of growing up – in the form of physical punishment or violence directed at them by parents, or exposure to violence in their own families, or these combined with television aggression – the more they later demonstrate aggressive behavior. Aggression directed at them can lead children to develop hostility, mistrust, and generally negative feelings and perceptions of other people. Antagonism between boys and their fathers has itself been found to be related to the boys' aggressiveness (Bandura and Walters, 1959). Frequent and varied exposure to violence can lead to viewing aggression as a basic and acceptable mode of conflict resolution and as a basic plan or strategy toward interpersonal relationships. Competence, both in the sense of plans and strategies for the use of aggression, and for specific skills in enacting aggression, will be available.

Apart from their specific child-rearing practices, parents vary in their emphasis on prescriptive versus proscriptive orientation to morally relevant behaviors (McKinney, 1971; Olejnik and McKinney, 1973). Some parents tend to prohibit undesirable behaviors while others focus their efforts more on promoting desirable, including prosocial, behaviors in their children. Obviously, love withdrawal is a proscriptive practice, while induction can be either proscriptive or prescriptive. There is evidence that children whose parents are more prescriptively oriented are more generous (Olejnik and McKinney, 1973). The differences in personality that result from such variation are unexplored. A focus on prohibition may result in concern about doing wrong, hence reducing harmdoing but also reducing the initiative frequently required for benefiting other people. A focus on prohibition may also promote self concern, thereby diminishing attention to others' needs. Probably a balance is desirable with parents *proscribing* certain forms of aggressive behavior (without prohibiting the underlying emotions, while teaching children to constructively deal with these emotions) and of *prescribing* positive conduct.

The socialization practices that apparently contribute to a prosocial orientation and positive behavior in children are similar to those that contribute to the development of positive self-esteem, at least among boys. Coopersmith (1967) found in his research with 10- to 11-year-old boys that parents who are genuinely concerned with the welfare of their children

29

and who use reasoning with their children, set high standards for them, and enforce these standards, had children who developed high self-esteem. It seems that the development of a positive self-esteem and of prosocial value orientation, two personal characteristics that in my view are crucial influences on both altruistic and aggressive behavior, are the result of overlapping socialization practices. These practices share an interest in and desire to promote the child's welfare, reasoning with the child, and effective control. Clearly, the antecedents of the two in parental socialization can be highly supportive of each other. Caring about the child's welfare can be expressed through nurturance and in other ways; reasoning can apply to personal relations, as in induction, and to other aspects of the child's life.

It is possible to postulate a pattern of practices that might be antecedents of all the personal characteristics that were identified as important in promoting altruism and diminishing aggression. For example, to those already mentioned we could add fostering self-reliance in children, so that they can experience and meet challenges, and experience success and reinforcement by other people for their achievements. This is an elaboration of the high standards set by parents of high self-esteem children. It would contribute to a positive self-esteem but would also promote a particular aspect of a positive self-concept, a belief in one's ability to influence events. Both by promoting such a belief and by helping develop other aspects of competence, it would enhance the likelihood that motives of any kind are expressed in action, including that of benefiting other people. At the same time, the characteristics resulting from all these practices would diminish the likelihood of aggression, for reasons discussed earlier.

It is essential that we also begin to study the sources or origins of parental socialization practices, which may be regarded as methods, in parental values and goals that underlie these methods. The goals of parents regarding the kind of child they want to raise, the everyday behavior of the child they want to promote or inhibit, as well as their own behavior or the kind of persons they themselves want to be, particularly in relation to their children, are all important (Staub, 1985a).

Natural socialization: learning by doing

Just as the ancient philosophers had proposed (see Peters, 1970), moral behavior is learned through action, through engagement in moral conduct. A prosocial behavioral tendency develops, in part, through participation in prosocial behavior. In fact, learning by doing is a hidden aspect of most socialization. The extent to which the child is or is not guided to do or to act will determine whether the child does or does not learn certain behavioral orientations. It would be unusual to have a prosocial person who, in the course of growing up, had heard a great deal about how desirable it is to benefit others but rarely engaged in helpful, charitable, or generous conduct. The same is true of achievement or other forms of conduct. It is also difficult to imagine that a person who as a child and adolescent was freely allowed to engage in aggressive behavior and has been successful in aggressing against others would not continue to behave aggressively. The development of valuing certain outcomes, an important characteristic of personal goals, as well as the learning of competencies to execute one's goals, crucially depend on actual participation in goal-directed behavior.[3]

There is substantial evidence that prior participation in prosocial behavior increases adults' subsequent positive actions (Harris, 1972; for a review of research on the foot-in-the-door phenomenon that is also an example, see DeJong, 1979; Staub, 1978) as well as children's (Staub, 1979). In the realm of aggression, there is less clear evidence, partly because clear evidence is more difficult to come by. Children allowed a substantial amount of aggressive behavior who would later exhibit aggressiveness would constitute such evidence. However, a substantial amount of aggression can be taken as an already learned aggressive behavioral tendency that then continues to demonstrate itself. Another kind of evidence might be the inhibition of aggressive behavior associated with less aggression at a later time. However, limited aggression by children can be the result of direct and forceful control, which would increase the likelihood of aggression in different settings or at later times. The combination of discouragement of aggressive behavior by reasonably enforced rules, and helping children to learn and allowing them to exercise effective self-assertion, combined with socialization practices and experience that contribute to a prosocial behavioral tendency, may be most effective in diminishing the potential for aggression.

Participation in prosocial action, particularly when it is not the result of forceful demands by adults, and when it is accompanied by induction and/or the experience of having benefited others, will have important psychological consequences (Staub, 1979). First, it will affect the evaluation of the importance of both such action and the welfare of its intended (or actual) beneficiaries, thereby promoting prosocial orientation. Second, it will result in self-attribution and the perception of oneself as a helpful person (DeJong, 1979; Grusec, 1981; Staub, 1979). Nonparticipation in aggression, when it is not the result of forceful prohibition by adults, may also result in increased concern with others' welfare and in self attribution. Induction that is offered concurrently (Staub, 1975, 1979) or prior experience that results in a network of cognitions that enter into self-guidance and the inductive interpretation of events would contribute to these changes. In other words, existing characteristics, participation, and how its meaning and effects are interpreted evolve and mutually influence each other.

Existing personality as a source of later development

The already existing personal characteristics and behavioral tendencies of children become an important source of their later development. Children shape their environment and others' response to them, which in turn affect their own further development. Through their behavioral expression, rudiments of empathic responsiveness, prosocial or rule-enforced orientation, self-esteem, and other characteristics themselves become influences on children's further development.

In one of our studies, we observed the relationship between children's behaviors and the behaviors directed toward them by their peers during the course of natural interactions in open classrooms (Staub and Feinberg, 1980). This study showed strong reciprocity in boys' aggressive behaviors. Boys who initiated aggression were also the recipients of aggressive behavior from others. Among both boys and girls, there was fairly substantial reciprocity in positive behaviors. Girls who were empathic on a test that we developed, who responded to pictures with sympathetic concern and sympathetic distress to others' fate, were the recipients of many positive behaviors from their peers. Presumably, girls who showed this kind of empathy, which we called *reactive empathy* in contrast to the *parallel* emotional reactions to others' feelings that some boys and girls demonstrated (what is usually seen as the empathic emotion) were sensitive to their peers' desires and needs. Children's aggressive behaviors, their positive behaviors, and their sensitivity to others presumably shape and form their environments and their experience. Their experiences in interactions with peers will, however, affect their feelings about themselves, their feelings about other people, and the types of strategies for interaction that they develop, master, and habitually use.

Concluding remarks

A major purpose of this chapter is to present a *conception* of how prosocial behavior comes about, as well as the relationship between influences promoting altruism and inhibiting aggression. This conception is then used to consider the development of the tendency to behave prosocially (and not behave aggressively). Certain personal characteristics are described as a basis of selecting, usually in interaction with environmental influences, the benefit of other people rather than other outcomes as one's aim and as contributing to people acting on this aim. On the basis of this view and supporting research, the development of these personal characteristics should become a focus of research on the socialization of altruistic (and aggressive) behavior. Relevant personal characteristics include broad value orientations (and the consideration of their importance relative to other values and goals), the self-concept and self-esteem, and competencies. This view implies that the development of prosocial and aggressive tendencies must be seen in the context of the development of the totality of the child's personality and social behavior.

The discussion has focused more on the development of altruistic and prosocial behavior and on how characteristics that promote altruism will inhibit aggression than on the sources and origins of aggression. Although social psychologists have paid much attention to aggressive behavior, and recently developmental psychologists have concerned themselves with the determinants and origins of altruism and prosocial behavior (Eisenberg, 1982; Grusec, 1981; Staub, 1979, 1981; Staub et al. 1984; Radke-Yarrow et al., 1984), research on the development of aggressive behavioral tendencies has been less extensive. However, some of the discussion did suggest origins of the motivation for aggression and of characteristics that contribute to its behavioral expression. The development of negative perception of people, devaluing people in general or specific groups, a negative self-concept, and plans, strategies, and skills for aggressive interactions are central elements.

There is substantial support for the "personal goal theory" account (Staub, 1978b, 1980, 1985) of how social behavior in general and altruistic behavior in particular are determined. There is also good evidence, in this writer's view, that the influences that were presented as contributing to the tendency for altruistic-prosocial behaviors actually do so. There is little evidence, however, that these influences contribute to the development of the motivations for altruistic behavior that were identified as central – prosocial orientation, or a rule-centered value orientation, and empathy – and to a positive self-concept and other supporting characteristics. Research needs to focus on collecting such evidence.

In concluding I will note some unfortunate limitations in theory and research. First, theories of the development of altruism or prosocial behavior, with some exceptions (Hoffman, 1975a), are limited or lacking. The same is true of theories of the development of aggression. In the concept presented here a theory of the determinants of altruistic-positive behavior and/or aggression is an important starting point for a theory of their development. Second, the focus of much research on development is on limited forms of altruism and aggression. We do not know whether this research is of much relevance to the development of characteristics that give rise to heroic acts by individuals, to tremendous sacrifices endured and danger accepted for the sake of saving the lives of persecuted people (London, 1970), to continued self-sacrifice of any kind to benefit other people, or even to the capacity for genuine kindness in everyday relationships. The conception presented here assumes that there are core characteristics relevant to a broad range of altruistic acts. However, special motivation and special personal characteristics are required for special forms of beneficial acts, which must be identified by an analysis of the nature of the need, the behavior required, and other properties (Smithson, Amato, & Pearce, 1983). Heroic acts require competence and a strong "action tendency" (Staub, 1974); rescuing the lives of persecuted people requires courage and perhaps an enjoyment of adventure (London, 1970); helping the poor and needy requires a view of them as deserving, rather than a belief that they are the cause of their own misfortune (Rubin and Peplau, 1973, Weiner, 1980). We also need to differentiate types of aggression and the developmental course of different types. We need research that informs us about the antecedents of people participating in a life of violence, or in torture, or genocide and other mistreatment of groups of people. To understand the latter, we must study the characteristics not only of individuals but of cultures and of social organizations as well (Staub, 1982, 1984a, 1985b).

Considering such examples of human altruism and violence, we must question and carefully analyze the extent of continuity and discontinuity, or degree of isomorphism, in the influences on and developmental origins of such behaviors among animals and humans. The recognition of the extent to which human altruism and aggression are guided by ideas and ideals is essential: we defend our self-concept when no danger to survival is present, act according to our self-concept in performing altruistic acts, or follow ideologies that offer the hope of a better life, while identifying some people as interfering with the better future that the ideology promises. While ideologies, systems of beliefs, can offer hope, meaning, a sense of significance, they have also been the origins of mass murder and genocide – as in Nazi Germany, or recently in Cambodia. Psychologists have been inattentive to such truly large-scale violence. Such symbolically based violence appears uniquely human. However, it is threatening, frustrating, and chaotic life conditions that give rise to ideologies of mass murder. Comparable environmental conditions may lead to aggression among animals.

How human beings come to deal with difficult life conditions, when these give rise to violence, and how cooperative efforts to deal with them can be promoted are important questions (Staub, 1982, 1985a, 1985b). How human beings create and come to embrace ideologies that justify the mistreatment of other people and how such mistreatment serves personal goals on both the individual and cultural-societal level must be one of our concerns.

Acknowledgement

The preparation of this chapter was facilitated and some of the research referred to was supported by NIMH grant MH23886.

Notes

1. Rule-centered moral orientations can vary in important ways that cannot be fully discussed here. They may vary in the *level* at which rules are of concern, either specific standards and norms, the conventions of the social group (Hoffman, 1970), or higher principles such as the social contract, justice, or mercy. The rules or principles may focus on obligation to persons, although frequently the implicit or explicit focus is obligation to the social group.

2. This discussion focuses on generalizations that can be drawn from past research and does not examine the intricacies of research findings that have been reviewed and analyzed by a number of workers (Eisenberg, 1982; Staub, 1979, 1981; Staub, Bar-Tal, Reykowski, & Karylowski, 1984; Yarrow, Zahn-Waxler, & Chapman, 1984). For example, both socialization research in which parental practices and child characteristics and behavior are examined and laboratory analogue research exploring influences on children's helping behavior found a *positive* relationship between parental warmth and positive behavior by children. By contrast, laboratory studies of generosity (children sharing rewards they just acquired) found no such relationship. According to one view (Staub, 1979) this is because children want to maximize their gains in a situation wherein the adult had no opportunity to transmit his or her values to the child in an effective manner. The generalizations presented here are likely to apply, however, when these practices are jointly used, in the usual contexts of the child's life (Staub, 1979).

3. Certain exceptions might exist. At least in the realm of religion, important conversion experiences have been described. St. Francis and St. Augustine are described as young men who lived a life of debauchery followed by conversion and lives of sainthood. It is probable, however, that the childhood of these important religious figures did include important influences, including some forms of learning by doing, which formed the basis of their later conversion. Religious influences were common in their days. It may also be the case that such conversion experiences, which result in the adoption of whole ideologies, may be different in nature from the gradual development of value orientations and behavioral tendencies.

References

Adorno, T. W., Frenkel-Brunswik, E., Levinson, D. J., & Sanford, R. N. (1950). *The authoritarian personality*. New York: Norton.

Ainsworth, M. D. S. (1979). Infant–mother attachment. *American Psychologist, 34*, 932–937.

Aronfreed, J. (1968). *Conduct and conscience*. New York: Academic Press.

Atkinson, W. (1981). Studying personality in the context of an advanced motivational psychology. *American Psychologist, 36*, 117–129.

Averill, J. R. (1982). *Anger and aggression. An essay on emotion*. New York: Springer-Verlag.

Bandura, A., & Walters, R. H. (1959). *Adolescent aggression: A study of the influence of child training practices and family interrelationship*. New York: Ronald.

Baron, R. A. (1977). *Human aggression*. New York: Plenum.

Batson, C. D., Duncan, B., Ackerman, P., Buckley, T., & Birch, K. (1981). Is empathic emotion a source of altruistic motivation? *Journal of Personality and Social Psychology, 40*, 290–302.

Baumrind, D. (1975). *Early socialization and the discipline controversy*. Morristown, NJ: General Learning Press.

Benesh, M., & Weiner, B. (1982). On emotion and motivation: From the notebooks of Fritz Heider. *American Psychologist, 37*, 887–895.

Berkowitz, L. (1970). Reactance and the unwillingness to help others. *Psychological Bulletin, 79*, 310–317.

Cherry, F., & Byrne, D. (1977). Authoritarianism. In T. Blass (Ed.), *Personality variables in social behavior* (pp. 109–135). Hillsdale, NJ: Erlbaum.

Coopersmith, S. (1967). *Antecedents of self-esteem*. San Francisco: Fremont.

Darley, J., & Batson, C. (1973). From Jerusalem to Jericho: A study of situational and dispositional variables in helping behavior. *Journal of Personality and Social Psychology, 27*, 100–108.

DeJong, W. (1979). An examination of the self perception mediation of the foot in the door effect. *Journal of Personality and Social Psychology, 37*, 2221–2239.

Denner, B. (1968). Did a crime occur? Should I inform anyone? A study of deception. *Journal for Personality, 36*, 454–466.

Durkheim, E. (1961). *Moral education*. New York: Free Press.

Eisenberg, N. (1982). *The development of prosocial behavior*. New York: Academic Press.

Eisenberg, N., & Lennon, R. (1983). Sex differences in empathy and related capacities. *Psychological Bulletin, 94*, 100–132.

Epstein, S. (1973). The self-concept revisited. Or a theory of a theory. *American Psychologist, 28*, 404–416.

Epstein, S. (1979). The stability of behavior: I. On predicting most of the people much of the time. *Journal of Personality & Social Psychology, 37*, 1097–1126.

Epstein, S. (1980). The self-concept: A review and the proposal of an integrated theory of personality. In E. Staub (Ed.), *Personality: Basic aspects and current research* (pp. 81–133). Englewood Cliffs, NJ: Prentice-Hall.

Erkut, S., Jaquette, D., & Staub, E. (1981). Moral judgment–situation interaction as a basis for predicting social behavior. *Journal of Personality, 49*, 1–44.

Eron, L. D. (1982). Parent–child interaction, television violence, and aggression of children. *American Psychologist, 37*, 197–211.

Feinberg, H. K. (1977). *Anatomy of a helping situation: Some personality and situational determinants of helping in a conflict situation involving another's psychological distress*. Unpublished doctoral dissertation, University of Massachusetts, Amherst.

Gergen, K. J., Gergen, M. M., & Meter, K. (1972). Individual orientations to prosocial behavior. *Journal of Social Issues, 8*, 105–130.

Gilligan, C. (1982). *In a different voice. Psychological theory and women's development*. Cambridge: Harvard University Press.

Goodenough, F. L. (1931). *Anger in young children.* Minneapolis: University of Minnesota Press.

Grodman, S. M. (1979). *The role of personality and situational variables in responding to and helping an individual in psychological distress.* Unpublished doctoral dissertation, University of Massachusetts, Amherst.

Grusec, J. (1981). Socialization processes and the development of altruism. In J. P. Rushton & R.M. Sorrentino (Eds.), *Altruism and helping behavior* (pp. 65-91). Hillsdale, NJ: Erlbaum.

Harris, M. B. (1972). The effects of performing one altruistic act on the likelihood of performing another. *Journal of Social Psychology, 88*, 65-73.

Hoffman, M. L. (1970). Conscience, personality and socialization technique, *Human Development, 13*, 90-126.

Hoffman, M. L. (1975a). Developmental synthesis of affect and cognition and its implications for altruistic motivation. *Developmental Psychology, 11*, 607-622.

Hoffman, M. L. (1975b). Altruistic behavior and the parent–child relationship. *Journal of Personality and Social Psychology, 31*, 937-943.

Hoffman, M. L. (1976). Empathy, role-taking, guilt, and development of altruistic motives. In T. Lickona (Ed.), *Moral development and behavior: Theory research and social issues* (pp. 124-144). New York: Holt, Rinehart and Winston.

Hoffman, M. L. (1981). Is altruism part of human nature? *Journal of Personality and Social Psychology, 40*, 121-137.

Hoffman, M. L. (1982). Development of prosocial motivation: Empathy and guilt. In Eisenberg, N. (Ed.), *The development of prosocial behavior* (pp. 218-231). New York: Academic Press.

Hoffman, M. L., & Saltzstein, H. D. (1967). Parent discipline and the child's moral development. *Journal of Personality & Social Psychology, 5*, 45-57.

Hornstein, H.A. (1976). *Cruelty and kindness: A new look at aggression and altruism.* Englewood Cliffs, NJ: Prentice-Hall.

Isen, A. M., Horn, N., & Rosenhan, D. L. (1973). Effects of success and failure on children's generosity. *Journal of Personality and Social Psychology, 27*, 239-248.

Karylowski, J. (1976). Self esteem, similarity, liking and helping. *Personality and Social Psychology Bulletin, 2*, 71-74.

Karylowski, J. (1984). Focus of attention and altruism: endocentric and exocentric sources of altruistic behavior. In Staub, E., Bar-Tal, D., Karylowski, J., & Reykowski, J. (Eds.) *The development and maintenance of prosocial behavior. International perspectives* (pp. 139-155). New York: Plenum.

Kohlberg, L. (1969). Stage and sequence: The cognitive-developmental approach to socialization. In D. Goslin (Ed.), *Handbook of socialization theory and research* (pp. 347-480). Chicago: Rand McNally.

Krebs, D. L. (1975). Empathy and altruism. *Journal of Personality and Social Psychology, 32*, 1134-1146.

Lerner, M. J. (1960). *The belief in a just world: A fundamental delusion.* New York: Plenum.

Lewin, K. (1938). *The conceptual representation and measurement of psychological forces.* Durham, NC: Duke University Press.

Lewin, K. (1948). *Resolving social conflicts.* New York: Harper.

Lieberman, A. F. (1976). *The social competence of preschool children: Its relation to quality of attachment and to amount of exposure to peers in different preschool settings.* Unpublished doctoral dissertation, John Hopkins University.

Loban, W. (1953). A study of social sensitivity (sympathy) among adolescents. *Journal of Educational Psychology, 44*, 102-112.

London, P. (1970). The rescuers: Motivational hypotheses about Christians who saved Jews from the Nazis. In J. Macaulay & L. Berkowitz (Eds.), *Altruism and helping behavior* (pp. 241–251). New York: Academic Press.

Macoby, E. E. (1980). *Social development.* New York: Harcourt Brace Jovanovich.

McKinney, J. P. (1971). The development of values: Prescriptive or proscriptive? *Human Development, 14,* 71–80.

Mischel, W. (1968). *Personality and assessment.* New York: Wiley.

Mischel, W., & Peake, P. K. (1982). Beyond deja-vu in the search for cross-situational consistency. *Psychological Review, 89,* 730–755.

Olejnik, A. B., & McKinney, J. P. (1973). Parental value orientation and generosity in children. *Developmental Psychology, 8,* 311.

Peters, R. S. (1970). Concrete principles and the rational passions. In J. M. Gustafson, R. S. Peters, L. Kohlberg, B. Bettelheim, & K. Keniston, (Eds.), *Moral education: five lectures* (pp. 29–57). Cambridge: Harvard University Press.

Piaget, J., & Weil, A. (1951). The development in children of the idea of the homeland and of relations with other countries. *International Social Science Bulletin, 3,* 570.

Piliavin, J. A., Dividio, J. F., Goertner, S. L., & Clark, R. D. (1981). *Emergency intervention.* New York: Academic Press.

Radke-Yarrow, M. R., Zahn-Waxler, C., & Chapman, M. (1984). Children's prosocial dispositions and behavior. In P. H. Mussen (Ed.), *Carmichael's manual of child psychology* (4th ed.) (Vol. IV, pp. 469–545). New York: Wiley.

Reese, H. (1961). Relationships between self-acceptance and sociometric choices. *Journal of Abnormal and Social Psychology, 62,* 472–474.

Reykowski, J., & Yarymovitz, M. (1976). *Elicitation of the prosocial orientation.* Unpublished manuscript. Warsaw, Poland: University of Warsaw.

Rosenhan, D. L., Salovey, P., Karylowski, J., & Hargis, K. (1981). Emotion and altruism. In J. P. Rushton & R. M. Sorrentino (Eds.), *Altruism and helping behavior* (pp. 233–251) Hillsdale, NJ: Erlbaum.

Rubin, Z., & Peplau, L. A. (1973). Belief in a just world and reactions to another's lot: A study of participants in the national draft lottery. *Journal of Social Issues, 29,* 73–93.

Rubin, Z., & Peplau, L. A. (1975). Who believes in a just world? *Journal of Social Issues, 31,* 65–89.

Sagi, A., & Hoffman, J. L. (1976). Empathic distress in the newborn. *Developmental Psychology, 12,* 175–176.

Sanford, R. N. (1973). Authoritarian personality in contemporary perspective. In Knutson, J. N. (Ed.), *Handbook of political psychology* (pp. 139–171). San Francisco: Jossey-Bass.

Schwartz, S. H., Feldman, K. A., Brown, M. E., & Heingarter, A. (1969). Some personality correlates of conduct in two situations of moral conflict. *Journal of Personality, 37,* 41–57.

Schwartz, S. H., & Howard, J. (1984). Internalized values as motivators of altruism. In Staub, E., Bar-Tal, D., Karylowski, J., & Reykowski, J. (Eds.), *The development and maintenance of prosocial behavior. International perspectives* (pp. 229–257). New York: Plenum.

Shaffer, D. R. (1979). *Social and personality development.* Monterey, CA: Brooks-Cole.

Simner, M. L. (1971). Newborn's response to the cry of another infant. *Developmental Psychology, 5,* 136–150.

Slavson, S. R. (1965). *Reclaiming the delinquent.* New York: Free Press.

Smithson, M., Amato, P. R., & Pearce, P. (1983). *Dimensions of helping behavior.* New York: Pergamon.

Sroufe, L. A. (1979). The coherence of individual development: Early care, attachment, and subsequent developmental issues. *American Psychologist, 34,* 834–841.

Staub, E. (1971). The learning and unlearning of aggression: The role of anxiety, empathy, efficacy and prosocial values. In J. Singer (Ed.), *The control of aggression and violence: Cognitive and physiological factors* (pp. 94–125). New York: Academic Press.

Staub, E. (1974). Helping a distressed person: Social, personality, and stimulus determinants. In L. Berkowitz (Ed.), *Advances in experimental social psychology* (Vol. 7, pp. 113–136). New York: Academic Press.

Staub, E. (1975). To rear a prosocial child: Reasoning, learning by doing, and learning by teaching others. In D. DePalma and J. Folley (Eds.), *Moral development: Current theory and research* (pp. 113–137). Hillsdale, NJ: Erlbaum.

Staub, E. (1978a). Predicting prosocial behavior: A model for specifying the nature of personality-situation interaction. In L. Pervin & M. Lewis (Eds.), *Internal and external determinants of behavior* (pp. 87–111). New York: Plenum.

Staub, E. (1978b). *Positive social behavior and morality: Vol. 1. Social and personal influences.* New York: Academic Press.

Staub, E. (1979). *Positive social behavior and morality: Vol. 2. Socialization and development.* New York: Academic Press.

Staub, E. (1980). Social and prosocial behavior: Personal and situational influences and their interactions. In E. Staub (Ed.), *Personality: Basic aspects and current research* (pp. 236–295). Englewood Cliffs, NJ: Prentice-Hall.

Staub, E. (1981). Promoting positive behavior in schools, in other educational settings, and in the home. In J. P. Rushton & R.M. Sorrentino (Eds.), *Altruism and helping behavior* (pp. 109–137). Hillsdale, NJ: Erlbaum.

Staub, E. (1982, June). Social evil: *The psychology of perpetrators and bystanders.* Presented at the meetings of the International Association of Political Psychology, Washington, DC.

Staub, E. (1984a). Steps toward a comprehensive theory of moral conduct: Goal orientation, social behavior, kindness and cruelty. In J. Gewirtz and W. Kurtines (Eds.), *Morality and moral development* (pp. 241–261). New York: Wiley-Interscience.

Staub, E. (1984b). Notes toward an interactionist–motivational theory of the determinants and development of prosocial behavior. In E. Staub, D. Bar-Tal, J. Karylowski, & J. Reykowski (Eds.), *The development and maintenance of prosocial behavior: International perspectives* (pp. 29–51). New York: Plenum.

Staub, E. (1985a). *Social behavior and moral conduct: A personal goal theory account of altruism and aggression.* Unpublished manuscript, Amherst: University of Massachusetts.

Staub, E. (1985b). The psychology of perpetrators and bystanders. *Political Psychology, 6,* 61–86.

Staub, E., Bar-Tal, D., Karylowski, J., & Reykowski, J. (Eds.), *The development and maintenance of prosocial behavior. International perspectives.* New York: Plenum.

Staub, E., & Feinberg, H. (1980). *Regularities in peer interaction, empathy, and sensitivity to others.* Presented at the symposium on the development of prosocial behavior and cognitions at the American Psychological Association Meeting, Montreal.

Stotland, E. (1969). Exploratory studies of empathy. In L. Berkowitz (Ed.), *Advances in experimental social psychology* (Vol. 4, pp. 271–313). New York: Academic Press.

Tajfel, H. (1982). Intergroup relations. In M. R. Rosenzweig and L. W. Porter (Eds.), *Annual review of psychology* (pp. 1–41). Palo Alto: Annual Reviews.

Theiss, A. (1983). *Violence. A problem for and of society.* Unpublished manuscript, Amherst: University of Massachusetts.

Thompson, W. R., & Grusec, J. (1970). Studies of early experience. In P. H. Mussen (Ed.), *Carmichael's manual of child psychology* (3rd ed.) (Vol. 2, pp. 567–657). New York: Wiley.

Toch, H. (1969). *Violent men.* Chicago: Aldine.

Weiner, B. (1980). A cognitive (attribution)–emotion–action model of motivated behavior: An analysis of judgments of help giving. *Journal of Personality and Social Psychology, 37*, 186–200.

Wilson, E. O. (1975). *Sociobiology: The new synthesis.* Cambridge, MA: Belknap Press (Harvard University Press).

Wilson, E. O. (1978). *On human nature.* Cambridge, MA: Harvard University Press.

Yarymovitz, M. (1977). Modification of self-worth and increment of prosocial sensitivity. *Polish Psychological Bulletin, 8*, 45–53.

Zahn-Waxler, C., & Radke-Yarrow, M. (1982). The development of altruism: Alternative research strategies. In Eisenberg, N. (Ed.), *The development of prosocial behavior.* New York: Academic Press.

JOURNAL OF EXPERIMENTAL SOCIAL PSYCHOLOGY 8, 438–445 (1972)

Social Influence and Diffusion of Responsibility in an Emergency[1]

Leonard Bickman
Smith College

Latané and Darley have proposed a model of the intervention
process which stresses the series of decisions a bystander makes
before intervention will occur. The present research examined two
of the more important decisions concerning the definition of the
situation as an emergency and the responsibility for acting. Ninety
female undergraduates overheard one of three different interpretations of an emergency from a confederate who was or was not able
to help. The more the confederate indicated that an emergency
was taking place the quicker the subjects helped ($p < .001$).
Subjects also responded faster when the confederate was not able
to help ($p < .025$). It was concluded that the results strongly
support the decision-making model of bystander intervention.

Latané and Darley (1970b) have proposed a theoretical model of the
determinants of bystander intervention in an emergency. Based on the
results of their research and on evidence drawn from real life situations,
their model examines the series of decisions an individual makes before
intervention will occur. The purpose of the present research is to examine two aspects of their theory.

Latané and Darley's (1970b) first stage in their model is concerned
with the bystander noticing that some event has occurred. Once a person
has attended to some event, he enters the second stage where he must
decide whether or not the event is an emergency. In most emergencies the
bystander confronts an ambiguous situation which he must define if he is
to intervene. Latané and Darley point out that at this defining stage
in their model many factors determine the bystander's choice of interpretation. However, they stress the role of the behavior of other bystanders
as an important influence on the interpretation an individual gives to a
situation.

The interpretation of the situation that other bystanders are making
may be ascertained by discussing the situation with them or by merely

[1] Requests for reprints should be sent to the author, Department of Psychology,
Clark Science Center, Smith College, Northampton, Massachusetts 01060.

42

observing what they do. If other witnesses appear to regard some event as not being serious and therefore not requiring intervention, then this apparent consensus would lead a single bystander to draw the conclusion that no emergency exists, thus inhibiting him from helping. Latané and Darley describe this as a state of "pluralistic ignorance." Until someone acts, each witness observes only other nonreacting individuals and is probably influenced not to intervene himself. This social-influence process will determine the interpretation of the situation and consequently the probability of intervention by a bystander.

Latané and Darley (1970a,b) interpreted the findings of their research to support the hypothesis that social influence affects bystander intervention. However, they point out that explanations other than social influence could account for their findings. In situations in which a subject observed passive others, the presence of these individuals could have affected the subject's helping behavior by reducing his fear, increasing his embarrassment, or increasing the diffusion of responsibility. While taken together much of the research indicates a social-influence effect, no single experiment has effectively demonstrated this effect. Moreover, no evidence has been presented that indicates that others' behavior affect the subject's interpretation of the situation. In Latané and Darley's theory, the interpretation of the situation mediates the social-influence effect. None of the previous research has attempted to explicitly and directly manipulate the interpretation others give to an emergency. The present research tests the hypothesis that a bystander's communication of a greater or lesser emergency will affect the subject's own definition of the situation and subsequently his helping behavior.

According to the Latané and Darley model, once an individual has noticed and interpreted an event he still has to decide what he will do about it. Noticing and defining an event as an emergency does not necessarily mean that an individual will assume responsibility for intervening. One of the factors that Darley and Latané (1968) have explored is the effect of the number of other bystanders on intervention. They have found that the more bystanders perceived to be present the less likely it is for the subject to help. They explained this result using the concept of diffusion of responsibility. When several bystanders are present the pressure to intervene is shared by all bystanders. However, when the subject realizes that he is the only one aware of the emergency the responsibility for acting focuses on him.

Previously reported research (Bickman, 1971) has shown that the diffusion of responsibility is dependent upon the subject's perception of the ability of another bystander to help. If this bystander is seen as not being able to help then the subject's response time was no different than when the subject was alone. This research investigated the effect of the ability of this other bystander to help under conditions where there was no communication from this bystander to the subject. The present research examines the interaction of the other bystander's ability to intervene and the interpretation he gives to the emergency. By defining the incident in a particular way does the bystander also affect the operation of the diffusion of responsibility?

Latané and Darley (1970b) include other situational variables in their model. Such factors as deciding the mode of intervention and the implementation of intervention are considered. In addition, they consider modifications of their model which include factors other than the overly rational decisions the subject makes before intervention will occur. However, the key aspects of their theory are defining the situation and degree of personal responsibility. The present research directly tests the social influence hypothesis as mediated by another bystander's interpretations, and examines the operation of diffusion of responsibility.

METHOD

Subjects and Design

The subjects were 90 Brooklyn College female undergraduates, who were either freshmen or sophomores, between the ages of 17 and 20. The subjects were all enrolled in introductory psychology courses. Participation in the experiment was voluntary and the subjects were not paid. Subjects were randomly assigned to the experimental conditions with the limitation that there be 15 subjects in each of the six conditions.

The three principal individuals involved in this experiment were the naive subject, a confederate who provided the interpretation of the situation, and whose ability to help was manipulated (called the bystander) and a confederate who acted as if she might have been hurt (called the victim). A 3 × 2 factorial design was used employing three levels of interpretation (No Emergency, Possible Emergency, Certain Emergency) provided by the bystander and two levels of the bystander's ability to help (Able, Not Able).

Procedure

The subject was met and escorted down a corridor. In the middle of the corridor, the experimenter stopped in front of an office door which had a sign on it saying "Mr. Bickman, ESP Project." The experimenter then told the subject that he had to get something from his office. The experimenter entered his office and remained there for about 30 sec. He then took the subject across the hall to the experimental cubicle. The purpose of this maneuver was to ensure that the subject knew the location of the experimenter's office.

Once in the experimental cubicle the subject was told that she was participating in an ESP experiment. It was explained to her that there were two other subjects in separate cubicles taking part in the experiment and to avoid any criticism of collusion between the subjects on the ESP experiment she would not meet any of the others until after the experimental session was completed. Actually, tape recordings simulated the presence of the other subjects.

The experimenter then gave detailed instructions on how to take part in the experiment. The subject had to be able to understand and operate a fairly complex panel. The purpose of the elaborate control panel and the detailed instructions was to help convince the subject that she was taking part in an ESP experiment and that the voices she would hear later in the experiment were those of other subjects.

After the details of the procedure were explained to the subject, the ability of the bystander to help was manipulated by the procedure used by Bickman (1971). Subjects in the Able Condition were told that the victim and the bystander were located in cubicles nearby. In the Not Able condition subjects were informed that the victim was located nearby but the bystander was in another building. In this condition it was intended that the subject perceive that the bystander was unable to help because she was located about a thousand feet away in another building. Since the experiment supposedly dealt with the effects of distance on ESP, it was expected that it would not be viewed as unusual that one of the other subjects was located in another building.

After delivering the instructions, the experimenter left the subject's cubicle and crossed the hall to his office. However, before leaving the cubicle the experimenter stressed that he did not have an intercom in his office because he did not want to influence the ESP guessing. Thus, the subject was aware that she and the bystander were the only persons who could know about the emergency.

The Emergency

The pseudo-ESP experiment progressed smoothly until it was the subject's turn to send the ESP symbols. After the subject had "sent" two symbols (4 min after the start of the ESP experiment), the subject heard a guess from the recorded voice; then the subject heard the voice say: "Wait a minute, I think something is falling off the bookcase. I'd better fix it." This was followed by sounds of the victim getting off her chair. She then cried out, "It's falling on me!" followed by a scream and a loud crash. Nothing more was heard from the victim. At this point the experimental manipulation of the bystander's interpretation of the situation was introduced on the tape.

No Emergency Interpretation

In this condition, after the crash, the bystander (subject 2), stated in a matter of fact, unemotional tone: "Hey what happened? Subject 1 (the victim) something must've fallen on the intercom... Hey subject 3 (the subject)...what do we do now? Oh yeah, you can't answer. Well I guess she'll tell the guy it's not working. We'd better wait for him to tell us what to do next. O.K.?" In this condition the bystander defined the common experience in a way which weakened the idea that the victim was in trouble.

Possible Emergency Interpretation

Following the crash, the bystander stated in a puzzled voice: "What happened? Hey subject 1, are you O.K.? Why don't you answer? It sounds like the whole bookcase fell ... Hey subject 3 what do you think? ... Oh yeah, you can't answer ... I hope it's nothing serious, I hope she's O.K." The bystander, with this interpretation, defined the incident as one in which the victim might have gotten hurt.

Certain Emergency Interpretation

Following the crash the bystander stated in a very emotional and concerned voice: "What happened, Hey subject 1 please answer me. Are you O.K.? Are you alright?... She's not answering - something must have fallen on her - she's hurt... Hey subject 3... she must have gotten hurt."

Because of the automatic operation of the microphones the subject was no longer able to communicate with the other "subjects." Thirty seconds after the bystander finished her interpretation all the lights on the ESP panel went off.

The experimenter waited in his office until either the subject informed him of the incident or until 6 min after the crash of the bookcase at which point he entered the subject's cubicle. In all cases the experimenter acted as if he did not know about the disruption. If the subject did not help, the experimenter, as he entered the cubicle, behaved as if it was just the end of the ESP experiment and asked the subject how she did on the ESP test. At this point subjects invariably informed the experimenter about the disruption. The experimenter then asked the subject to explain what she thought happened. After a few other questions the subject was informed of the true nature of the experiment and assured that no one was hurt. All subjects were given a structured postexperimental interview to determine the effectiveness of the experimental manipulations.

The dependent variable was the time it took the subjects to leave the cubicle to report the emergency. This time was measured from the end of the bystander's interpretation to the point at which the subject went for help. In order for a response to count as a helping response, the subject had to inform the experimenter about the emergency by either knocking at his office door or calling out to him for help. Subjects who did not leave the cubicle were given a time score of 6 min.

RESULTS

Efficacy of Experimental Manipulations

Three subjects were excluded from the data analysis because they reported to the experimenter with a great deal of certainty that they thought the emergency was staged. An additional six subjects were excluded from the data analysis because they left the cubicle before they heard at least 85% of the bystander's communication. This criteria was decided upon before the experiment was conducted. All excluded subjects were replaced by others.

The effectiveness of the manipulation of the interpretation of the emergency was evaluated in two ways. In a pilot study three groups of 30 female undergraduates each listened to and evaluated one of the three tapes in order to determine if the interpretations did convey different probabilities that an emergency was taking place. The findings of the pilot study provided very strong support for the effectiveness of the taped statements of the bystander.

Subjects in the actual experiment were asked for their reactions to the emergency. Before they were told that the incident was staged the subjects were asked "Did the other subject (bystander) say anything?" "What did she say?—what did she think?" The subjects' verbatim responses were coded into whether she thought the bystander said the victim was hurt, not hurt or not sure if she was hurt. The subjects' perceptions of what the bystander said strongly coincided with what she actually said [$\chi^2(4) = 97.8$, $p < .001$].

If the bystander's interpretation of the emergency affects helping behavior by influencing the subject's own interpretation of the situation then it would be expected that subjects in the three interpretation conditions would differ in whether they thought the victim got hurt. The first question subjects were asked (before they were told that the emergency was part of the experiment) was "what happened?" From the answer to this question it was determined that 93% of the subjects in the Certain Emergency, 73% in the Possible Emergency, and 54% of the subjects in the No Emergency condition thought that the victim had been hurt [$\chi^2(2) = 10.58$, $p < .01$]. Although all the subjects heard the same incident the way in which the bystander interpreted the emergency influenced the subjects' perceptions of the incident.

The diffusion of responsibility was manipulated by varying the ability of the bystander to intervene. To determine if this manipulation was successful, subjects were asked if they thought the other subject (bystander) could help. Only one subject in the Able condition reported that she thought the bystander could not help. In the Not Able condition 78% of the subjects correctly perceived that the bystander could not help. There is a significant relationship between the perceived ability of the bystander to help and the experimental instructions [$\chi^2(1) = 50.4$, $p < .001$]. However, 10 of the 45 subjects in the Not Able condition (three in the No and Possible Emergency and four in the Certain Emergency condition) reported that the bystander was able to help. These subjects were confused as to the location of the victim and the bystander; they thought the victim was located in another building and the bystander near them. These subjects were included in the data analysis as a more conservative test of the diffusion of responsibility hypothesis.

Effect of Interpretation and Diffusion on Helping Behavior

Table 1 shows the mean speed score (multiplied by 100) for each of the experimental conditions. The speed score was obtained by taking the reciprocal of each subject's time score. This transformation served to decrease the differences between the longer time scores, thus deemphasizing the effect of the arbitrary 6-min time limit. A high speed score represents a fast response. Inspection of the table shows that the more the bystander's interpretation indicated that an emergency was taking

TABLE 1
EFFECT OF INTERPRETATION AND ABILITY ON SPEED OF HELPING[a]

Ability	Interpretation		
	No emergency	Possible emergency	Certain emergency
Able	2.72	3.69	8.28
Not able	2.00	9.80	14.97

[a] Speed scores are reciprocal time scores multiplied by 100.

place, the faster the subjects responded. Subjects also responded faster in the Not Able condition where they perceived that the bystander could not help, than in the Able condition. A two-way analysis of variance indicates that the interpretation [$F(2,84) = 10.72$, $p < .001$] and ability [$F(1,84) = 5.87$, $p < .025$] manipulations significantly affected the speed with which subjects helped. There was no significant interaction effect between the bystander's ability to help and her interpretation of the incident.

DISCUSSION

Social Influence

The results of the present research strongly support the social influence aspect of the Latané and Darley (1970b) model of helping behavior. Subjects' definition of the emergency and their helping behavior was influenced by the interpretation of the situation given by a confederate.

In the present research the subject could not observe the confederate's behavior. The confederate essentially supplied only an interpretation of the situation. Thus, the social influence effect, in the present experiment, is mediated by the interpretation. This can be related to research conducted on models and helping behavior, in that models often provide a definition of the situation (Krebs, 1970). However, unlike most experiments on modeling, this effect was obtained not by observing the model's behavior and assuming that it affected the subject's interpretation, but by just presenting the interpretation.

Diffusion of Responsibility

Previous research (Bickman, 1971) has shown that diffusion of responsibility does not occur when another bystander is perceived as not being able to help. The present research extends this relationship to conditions in which the other bystander communicated with the subject. Other methods of varying bystander ability should be attempted. For example, Ross (1971) recently manipulated ability by using adults and children (ages 4 and 6) as confederates. Ross assumed that children would not serve to diffuse responsibility. Although more subjects helped when children were present than when adults were present, helping behavior was still more frequent when the subject was alone.

In the Latané and Darley model of bystander intervention the subject first interprets the situation and then a decision is made whether to take personal responsibility. It is at this latter point that diffusion of responsibility operates. If diffusion operates in this manner then it should affect helping behavior without affecting the interpretation given to the situation by the subject. In order to determine if this assumption was correct subjects were asked, before being told the true nature of the experiment, what they thought happened. Sixty percent of the subjects in the Able condition thought the victim got hurt compared to 71% in the Not Able condition [$x^2(1) = .004$, NS]. It appears that when diffusion occurs, an individual recognizes and continues to believe that help is needed and should be given but also believes that this help will be given by other bystanders. Therefore, he himself does not have to help.

REFERENCES

BICKMAN, L. The effect of another bystander's ability to help on bystander intervention in an emergency. *Journal of Experimental Social Psychology*, 1971, **7**, 367–379.

DARLEY, J. M., & LATANÉ, B. Bystander intervention in emergencies: Diffusion of responsibility. *Journal of Personality and Social Psychology*, 1968, **8**, 377–383.

KREBS, D. L. Altruism—An examination of the concept and a review of the literature. *Psychological Bulletin*, 1970, **73**, 258–302.

LATANÉ, B., & DARLEY, J. M. Social determinants of bystander intervention in emergencies. *In* J. Macauley & L. Berkowitz (Eds.). *Altruism and helping behavior.* New York: Academic Press, 1970. (a)

LATANÉ, B., & DARLEY, J. M. *The unresponsive bystander: why doesn't he help?* New York: Appleton-Century-Crofts, 1970. (b)

ROSS, A. S. Effect of increased responsibility on bystander intervention: The presence of children. *Journal of Personality and Social Psychology*, 1971, **19**, 306–310.

(Received February 15, 1972)

JOURNAL OF EXPERIMENTAL SOCIAL PSYCHOLOGY 7, 313–318 (1971)

Sex Differences in Bystander Reactions to Physical Assault[1]

GERALD L. BOROFSKY, GARY E. STOLLAK, AND LAWRENCE A. MESSÉ

Michigan State University

In a "psychodrama" situation, a "spontaneous" fight occurred between two male and/or female accomplices. As predicted, significantly more male Ss attempted to interfere with the fight than did female Ss. Contrary to prediction, however, none of six male Ss interfered when a male was "injuring" a female. A number of possible explanations for this latter finding were presented, among them the speculation that males obtained vicarious sexual and/or hostile gratification from seeing a male "hurt" a female.

Among the many dimensions of social role that could affect bystander reactions to persons in trouble, the most obvious is sex role differences. The degree to which sex roles are a determinant of responses in situations where intervention behavior is relevant has not been studied extensively. Piliavin, Rodin, and Piliavin (1969) found that, in groups of men and women, significantly more males than females helped a male accomplice who feigned collapse from illness or drunkenness. Further, several studies (e.g., Berkowitz, Klanderman, & Harris, 1964; Bryan & Test, 1967; Buss & Brock, 1963) have produced findings that are indirectly relevant to sex differences in bystander intervention. However, none of the studies has examined a situation in which physical assault occurred.

The present research was designed to examine the propensity of a bystander to interfere when confronted with a situation in which one person was beating up another. The relevant variable was the sex of the participants. Based upon the results of the studies cited above and the popular conception in Western culture that males should and do assume the role of "protector," it was predicted that (a) more males than females would intervene in the fight, and (b) males would interfere most often when a female was being hurt, especially when her "aggressor" was a male.

[1] This article is an elaboration of a paper presented at the 1969 Midwestern Psychological Association Convention, Chicago, Illinois. The authors wish to thank Andrew Barclay and Arthur A. Seagull, for their comments on an earlier draft of this paper. This research was supported, in part, by USAF Office of Scientific Research Grant (F44620-69-C-0114).

51

METHOD

Subjects and design. Twenty-one male and 21 female undergraduate students enrolled in introductory psychology classes served as Ss. They were given extra credit for participating in what they were told was a study of psychodrama. A $2 \times 2 \times 2$ factorial design was used, with sex of S, sex of "aggressor," and sex of "victim" as the independent variables. The design yielded four "fight" conditions: (a) one male beating up another male; (b) one female beating up another female; (c) a male beating up a female; and (d) a female beating up a male.

Procedure. There were always six people (in addition to the E) present during an experimental session. This group was composed as follows: (a) the *actual* S; (b) one female and two male undergraduate confederates who pretended to be Ss;[2] and (c) two actors, drama students at Michigan State University, who also pretended to be Ss and who engaged in what appeared to be a spontaneous fight sequence.[3] In each condition every actor played every appropriate role at least once. Thus, e.g., in the female "aggressor"–male "victim" condition, each actress played the role of "aggressor" once and each actor served as the "victim" once. All accomplices, both confederates and actors, always acted as if they were strangers to each other.

In all four fight conditions, the E selected two confederates (non-actors) to act out in front of the rest of the group—who were seated in chairs along one side of the room—what was supposed to be the first in a series of psychodrama exercises. After 4- or 5-min, the E stopped the "Ss"—whose exercise always consisted of a pattern of prearranged behaviors—and made some positive comments regarding the quality of the performance. He then suggested some improvements to be used by future pairs in their exercises.

The first pair then sat down and the E selected the two actors to be the participants in the second exercise. The situation to be acted out, a family argument, was explained and then the E mentioned that he had to leave the room for a short time to get some forms that he had left in his office. He told the Ss to start their exercise in his absence since he would be right back. The actors then engaged in a prearranged sequence of behaviors, a slowly developing argument that after a few minutes exploded into a physical fight.

The argument developed slowly from the initial disagreement inherent in the specifications of the exercise. The intensity of the argument gradually increased until one of the actors, apparently losing his temper, slapped the other actor across the face. The person who was slapped then responded, "Look, this is only acting. This is just supposed to be an experiment (3-sec pause). You can't get away with hitting me like that." At this point the actors began to fight in a violent and convincing manner. The actor who was slapped was always the "aggressor" and he more or less beat up the other person. The fight continued until the S made an attempt to stop it or until the E returned to the room, 45 sec after the fight began.

Every effort was made before the experiment began to make the fights equivalent

[2] The authors wish to express their thanks to the following people who served as confederates and coders: Frank Benison, Sandy Bierowicz, Leon Brenner, Janet Keinath, Maria Levy, Marlene Martin, Pat Southwell, Dennis Staulauskas, and Frank Winn.

[3] The authors also wish to express their thanks to the *dramatis personae*: Thomas Clark, Karen Grossman, Michael Oberfield, Vicki Sanchez, Bernie Tato, and Debbie Tomlinson.

in intensity across all conditions. Two judges, who independently viewed from behind one-way mirrors at least one S in each experimental condition, both perceived no systematic differences in the intensity of the fights. Further, their is direct evidence that the "aggressor" did not "pull his punches" in the one condition in which such behavior was the most likely, the fight in which a male beat up a female. Towards the end of the experiment, one of the actresses had to be taken to the student health center because she suffered some cracked ribs from being flung across the floor by her male aggressor.

After the E returned to the room, he always debriefed the S in detail and pledged him to secrecy.

Index of interference. A group of raters was trained to decide if the behavior of an S during the fight constituted interference. They were trained to rate behavior as interference if (a) the S approached the actors and attempted (in any manner) to stop the fight, or (b) the S spoke directly to the actors, telling or asking them to stop fighting. All other behaviors, such as moving restlessly in the chair, turning away from the fight, talking to oneself or the confederates, etc., were rated as noninterference. At least two raters independently viewed each S from behind one-way mirrors. Percentage of agreement on whether or not the S interferred with the fight was 98 overall, and it did not differ systematically across conditions.

RESULTS

Table 1 presents the number of Ss in each condition who interfered with the fight. The upper number in each cell is the frequency of Ss who interfered, the lower number, in parentheses, is the total frequency of Ss who served in that condition. Table 1 indicates that, as predicted, more male Ss interfered with the fight than did female Ss. A chi-square test (corrected for continuity) revealed that this difference in the frequency of interference as a function of sex was statistically significant ($\chi^2 = 5.75$, $p < .05$).

On the other hand, contrary to prediction, Table 1 indicates that

TABLE 1

DISTRIBUTION OF INTERFERING Ss CLASSIFIED BY SEX OF "VICTIM," SEX OF "AGGRESSOR," AND SEX OF SUBJECT

Sex of aggressor	Sex of victim	Sex of subject	
		Male	Female
Male	Male	4	0
		(5)[a]	(5)
	Female	0	1
		(6)	(4)
Female	Male	2	0
		(3)	(7)
	Female	4	1
		(7)	(5)

[a] The number in parentheses is the total frequency of subjects in that condition.

males did not interfere more when the "victim" in the fight was female; in fact, they tended to interfere less. This is most evident in the male "aggression"–female "victim" condition in which none of the six male Ss interfered. This number is significantly different from the frequency of interference by male Ss in the male "aggressor"–male "victim" condition ($p < .04$, two-tailed Fisher test) and marginally different from the number of males who interfered in the female "aggressor"-female "victim" condition ($p < .10$, two-tailed Fisher test). Thus, the behavior of male Ss did not support the popular conception of the male as protector of women.

DISCUSSION

The results indicate that, when undergraduates are confronted with a situation in which a person is being injured by direct physical assault, they react differently as a function of their sex, and, for males, as a function of the sex of the people fighting. Female Ss tended not to interfere at all, while males interfered about half of the time. These findings are congruent with the results of past studies (e.g., Piliavin, et al., 1969) which indicated that male bystanders were more likely to help persons in distress.

There is some evidence (Darley & Latané, 1968) which indicates that, under some circumstances, males and females do not differ with respect to intervention behavior. However, as these authors point out, there is a difference between *direct* intervention—where the bystander must be willing, if necessary, to become a participant in the situation, perhaps with some danger to himself—and *reportial* intervention—where the bystander merely reports to a third party that something is amiss. In the present research, the most obvious mode of interference was direct intervention. In the Darley and Latané (1968) study, intervention took the form of reporting to the E that another S was having an epileptic seizure. Thus, taken together, the results of the two studies support the hypothesis of Darley and Latané (1968) that males will interfere more when the situation demands direct intervention, but there will be no difference as a function of sex when reportial intervention is an adequate response.

It is possible, however, that females would interfere more frequently in situations like that of the present research if there were no males present. It could be that females did not respond in the present research because they expected the male Ss in the room to interfere; if they had been in an all female group, they might have intervened with the same frequency as would males in an all male group. The fact remains, though, that females did not interfere directly in the mixed-sex groups of the present research nor did they ask a male S to do so. Further, the sexual composition of the groups in the present study was probably an accurate representation of most real-life situations in which it is likely that both males and females would witness an unfortunate event.

Why didn't the male Ss interfere when a man was injuring a woman? There is the possibilty that the uniqueness of the situation inhibited their responses. However, for most men, the sight of two women fighting should be just as unique as the sight of a man fighting with a woman, and yet males tended to interfere more in the former condition. Perhaps, males failed to interfere because they were deriving some kind of vicarious sexual and/or hostile gratification from seeing a man injure a woman.

While appealing, an explanation that assumes such complex motivations on the part of Ss must be treated as highly speculative, especially since it was derived from data that were contrary to what was predicted. Moreover, there are other explanations that are also plausible. For example, it is certainly possible that the "Gestalt" of a fight between a male "aggressor" and a female "victim" is very different from one between two males. It could be that a fight between two males was entirely plausible, while the sight of a man beating up a woman was too ridiculous to merit a response. The result that two of three males interfered in the even more "ridiculous" situation in which a woman beat up a man argues against this explanation. However, it is probably true that the fights did appear somewhat different to Ss in spite of the fact that every effort was made to equate them across conditions and to make them as realistic as possible.

It is apparent that a more definitive answer to the question of why males did not interfere when a man beat up a woman must await further research. Another problem for future research is the question of whether or not there are conditions in which the frequency of direct intervention by females would be as great as it seems to be for males. Research on these and similar issues should be fruitful since, as the present study indicates, sex roles, and probably social roles in general, are an important dimension of bystander intervention behavior.

REFERENCES

BERKOWITZ, L., KLENDERMAN, S., & HARRIS, R. Effects of experimenter awareness and sex of subject on reactions to dependency relationships. Sociometry, 1964, 27, 327–329.

BRYAN, J., & TEST, M. Models and helping: naturalistic studies in aiding behavior. Journal of Personality and Social Psychology, 1967, 6, 400–407.

BUSS, A., & BROCK, T. Repression and guilt in relation to aggression. Journal of Abnormal and Social Psychology, 1963, 66, 345–350.

DARLEY, J., & LATANÉ, B. Bystander intervention to emergencies; diffusion of responsibility. *Journal of Personality and Social Psychology*, 1968, **8**, 377–383.

PILIAVIN, I. M., RODIN, J., & PILIAVIN, J. A. Good Samaritanism: An underground phenomenon? *Journal of Personality and Social Psychology*, 1969, **13**, 289–299.

(Received November 11, 1969)

Distress and Empathy: Two Qualitatively Distinct Vicarious Emotions with Different Motivational Consequences

C. Daniel Batson, Jim Fultz, and Patricia A. Schoenrade
University of Kansas

ABSTRACT   The construct of empathy may be located conceptually at several different points in the network of interpersonal cognition and emotion. We discuss one specific form of emotional empathy—other-focused feelings evoked by perceiving another person in need. First, evidence is reviewed suggesting that there are at least two distinct types of congruent emotional responses to perceiving another in need: feelings of personal distress (e.g., alarmed, upset, worried, disturbed, distressed, troubled, etc.) and feelings of empathy (e.g., sympathetic, moved, compassionate, tender, warm, softhearted, etc.). Next, evidence is reviewed suggesting that these two emotional responses have different motivational consequences. Personal distress seems to evoke egoistic motivation to reduce one's own aversive arousal, as a traditional Hullian tension-reduction model would propose. Empathy does not. The motivation evoked by empathy may instead be altruistic, for the ultimate goal seems to be reduction of the other's need, not reduction of one's own aversive arousal. Overall, the recent empirical evidence appears to support the more differentiated view of emotion and motivation proposed long ago by McDougall, not the unitary view proposed by Hull and his followers.

Psychologists are noted for using terms loosely, but in our use of empathy we have outdone ourselves. It is not possible to review here all the dif-

Preparation of this paper was supported in part by University of Kansas General Research Fund Grant #3375-XO-0038, C. Daniel Batson, Principal Investigator, and by NSF Grant #BNS-8507110, C. Daniel Batson, Principal Investigator. Jim Fultz is now an NIMH Postdoctoral Fellow in the Department of Psychology, Arizona State University. Requests for reprints should be addressed to C. Daniel Batson, Department of Psychology, University of Kansas, Lawrence, KS 66045.

Journal of Personality 55:1, March 1987. Copyright © 1987 by Duke University Press. CCC 0022-3506/87/$1.50

(1851/1875), who first coined the term altruism, did not deny the existence of self-serving motives, even for helping. Comte labeled the impulse to seek self-benefit and self-gratification egoism. But Comte also believed that some social behavior was an expression of an unselfish desire to "live for others" (1851, p. 556). He called this second type of prosocial motivation altruism. Building upon Comte's distinction, we may say that prosocial motivation is *egoistic* when the ultimate goal is to increase one's own welfare; it is *altruistic* when the ultimate goal is to increase another's welfare.

At times, the personal gain derived from helping is obvious—as when one receives material rewards or public praise, or escapes public censure. But even when one helps in the absence of obvious external rewards, one may still benefit. One can self-reward, congratulating oneself for being kind and caring, or one can avoid self-censure, escaping guilt and shame (Bandura, 1977; Cialdini & Kenrick, 1976). In such cases the pat on the back may come from oneself rather than from someone else, but it is a reward nonetheless. Alternatively, seeing someone in distress may cause one distress, and a person may act to relieve the other's distress as an instrumental means to reach the ultimate goal of relieving his or her own distress.

Even heroes and martyrs can benefit from their acts of apparent selflessness. Consider the soldier who saves his or her comrades by diving on a grenade or the person who dies after relinquishing his or her place in a rescue craft. These persons may have acted to escape anticipated guilt and shame for letting others die. They may have acted to gain rewards—the admiration and praise of those left behind or the benefits expected in a life to come. Or they simply may have misjudged the consequences of their actions.

Insofar as the helper's goal in each of these situations is some form of self-benefit, the motivation to help is egoistic. Even though the helper acts to relieve another's distress, the other's benefit is not the ultimate goal: It is only instrumental in allowing the helper to relieve his or her own distress, gain social or self-rewards, or avoid feeling guilty. If, on the other hand, the helper acts to relieve another's distress as an ultimate goal, then the motivation is altruistic. By relieving the other's distress the helper may relieve his or her own distress, receive social or self-rewards, and avoid feeling guilty. Yet, if these outcomes are not ultimate goals but only consequences of the action, then the motivation is altruistic (see Batson & Coke, 1981, and Batson, in press, for more extensive discussions of the definitions of egoism and altruism).

Other's distress   → Vicarious   → Motivation to   → Behavior
                     emotional   reduce one's   (possibly
                     arousal   own arousal   helping) to
                     ("empathic   achieve
                     pain" or   reduction of own
                     "empathic   arousal
                     distress")

Figure 1
Outline of Traditional Tension-Reduction View of Vicarious Emotion and
Associated Motivation

Two Views of the Empathy-Prosocial Motivation Link

The Traditional View. Our two-part thesis is then that the emotional reactions of distress and empathy are distinct, and distress leads to egoistic
motivation and empathy leads to altruistic motivation. This thesis contradicts the traditional view of the role of emotion in motivating behavior.
The traditional view assumes that all motivation evoked by emotional
arousal is directed toward reducing that arousal. This view of the emotion-motivation link emerged from the combined impact of (*a*) studies
of infrahuman motivation, (*b*) studies of emotion-employing physiological measures, (*c*) homeostatic principles, and (*d*) Cannon's (1927) critique of the James-Lange theory of emotion. This view is perhaps most
clearly expressed in the drive-reduction model of Hull (1943, 1952).
When applied to the motivation to help evoked by arousal of empathic
emotion, this tension-reduction view may be outlined as in Figure 1.

According to the traditional view, the vicarious emotional reactions
that we have labeled personal distress and empathy are not qualitatively
distinct, at least not in any psychologically significant way. Instead, these
emotions combine to produce an overall level of physiological arousal.
This arousal is experienced as aversive, and it leads to motivation directed toward the goal of reducing the aversive arousal. One, but not the
only, behavioral means of reaching this goal is to help, because eliminating the other's distress eliminates the stimulus causing one's own
aversive arousal. In this traditional view, the motivation to help evoked
by empathy is fundamentally egoistic. The ultimate goal is to reduce
one's own aversive empathic arousal; reducing the distress of the person
in need is simply one means of reaching this ultimate goal.

Perhaps the best known exponents of this traditional tension-reduction view of the vicarious emotion-prosocial motivation link are Piliavin and Piliavin (1973; see also J. Piliavin, Dovidio, Gaertner, & Clark, 1981) and Hoffman—at least in his recent writings (1981a, 1981b, 1982).[1] The Piliavins speak of an aversive vicarious emotion of "empathic pain" while Hoffman speaks of "empathic distress." Both assume that the empathically aroused individual helps in order to reduce this vicarious emotion. As might be expected, both also minimize the difference between egoistic and altruistic motivation for helping. Two statements by Hoffman summarize the traditional view succinctly: "Empathy may be uniquely well suited for bridging the gap between egoism and altruism, since it has the property of transforming another person's misfortune into one's own feeling of distress" (Hoffman, 1981a, p. 133). "Empathic distress is unpleasant and helping the victim is usually the best way to get rid of the source" (Hoffman, 1981b, p. 52).

The Archaic View. This traditional tension-reduction view is not the only view of the emotion-motivation link. There is another, older, less parsimonious view. Largely derived from armchair reflection on an assortment of examples of real and imagined human and animal behavior— and largely ignored for the past half-century—this older view is perhaps most clearly expressed in the writings of William McDougall (1908). We shall call it the archaic view. In this view it is assumed that there are qualitative distinctions between different emotions. Moreover, it is assumed that different emotions evoke different goals and, hence, different types of motivation. Emotions do not all just tumble together into one seething cauldron of tension or arousal, producing a generalized drive state and directing all behavior toward the single goal of tension reduction. Instead, the emotions and their associated motives are qualitatively distinct.

McDougall believed that the different emotions and associated motives defined different instincts. But one need not adopt McDougall's in-

---

1. In some of his earlier writings, Hoffman (1975, 1976) made a distinction between empathic distress and sympathetic distress that parallels our distinction between personal distress and empathy. But in his recent writings, Hoffman (1981a, 1981b) tends to minimize this distinction, using the term empathic distress "generically" to refer to both empathic and sympathetic distress, and ignoring any motivational difference.

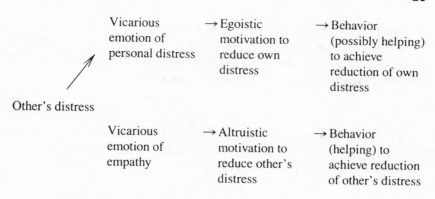

Figure 2
Outline of Archaic View of Vicarious Emotion and Associated Motivation

stinct theory in order to adopt his view that there are qualitatively distinct emotions with different motivational consequences.

When applied to motivation to help evoked by emotional reactions to another's distress, this archaic view makes a clear distinction between the nature of the motivation to help associated with personal distress and the nature of the motivation associated with empathy. The motivation associated with distress is claimed to be egoistic, whereas the motivation associated with empathy is claimed to be altruistic. The archaic view may be outlined as in Figure 2.

McDougall (1908) himself applied his differentiated view of the emotion-motivation link to prosocial motivation resulting from emotional reactions to the suffering of others. He suggested that there were two distinct vicarious emotions—sympathetic pain and the tender emotion. These two vicarious emotions are essentially the same as those described by our terms personal distress and empathy, respectively. Moreover, he suggested that sympathetic pain leads to egoistic motivation and the tender emotion leads to altruistic motivation, and that the gap between these two types of motivation cannot be bridged. McDougall's argument is nicely summarized in his delightfully fanciful interpretation of the parable of the Good Samaritan:

No doubt the spectacle of the poor man who fell among thieves was just as distressing to the priest and the Levite, who passed by on the other side, as to the good Samaritan who tenderly cared for him. They may well have been exquisitely sensitive souls, who would have fainted away if they had been compelled to gaze upon his wounds. The great difference between them and the Samaritan was that in him the tender emotion and its impulse were evoked, and that this impulse overcame, or prevented, the aversion naturally induced by the painful and, perhaps, disgusting spectacle (1908, p. 65).

The two-part thesis that we stated earlier is reminiscent of Mc-Dougall's archaic view of the vicarious emotion-prosocial motivation link. But we are not suggesting that McDougall's armchair reflections should be uncritically accepted. Before such a view is taken seriously, empirical evidence in its support is needed.

Part 1: Evidence that Distress and Empathy Are Distinct Vicarious Emotions

Concerning the first part of our thesis—that personal distress and empathy are qualitatively distinct vicarious emotions—two types of evidence seem relevant. First, we have factor-analyzed individuals' self-reported emotional responses to witnessing another's distress to see if adjectives reflecting personal distress and adjectives reflecting empathy load on two different factors. We have done this in a series of studies, now six in number (Batson, Cowles, & Coke, 1979; Batson et al., 1983; Coke, 1980; Coke et al., 1978; Fultz, 1982; Toi & Batson, 1982). Subjects in each study were asked to report on a 7-point scale (1 = not at all; 7 = extremely) how strongly they were feeling each emotion described in a list of emotion-related adjectives. The list included eight adjectives assumed to reflect the vicarious emotion of personal distress (alarmed, grieved, upset, worried, disturbed, perturbed, distressed, and troubled) and six adjectives assumed to reflect empathy (sympathetic, moved, compassionate, tender, warm, and softhearted). If distress and empathy are qualitatively distinct emotions, then subjects' ratings of the adjectives in these two sets should load on separate components in a principal components analysis. Alternatively, if these emotions combine to form a single vicarious emotion of "empathic distress," then responses to all 14 adjectives should load on a single component. To provide a clear comparison of these alternatives, an orthogonal rotation was used, thereby ensuring that the different components were entirely unrelated.

Before turning to the results from the component analyses, it should be noted that the correlations between responses to the eight distress adjectives (averaged) and the six empathy adjectives (averaged) were positive in each of the six studies (the r's ranged from .44 to .75; all

$ps = .01$). These correlations may seem to suggest that adjectives of both types reflect a single dimension of emotional response. Although the correlations are certainly consistent with this possibility, they do not provide clear support for it. There are at least three other reasons to expect subjects' reports of these emotions to be positively correlated. First, because both distress and empathy are emotions, they should be similarly affected by individual differences in general emotionality and in readiness to report emotions. Second, because both distress and empathy are evoked by perceiving a person in need, individual differences in perceptions of the magnitude of the need should have similar effects on both. Third, in each of the six studies in this series, emotions were measured by self-reports on unidirectional adjective rating scales, with adjectives reflecting distress and empathy intermixed. Using this form of measurement, response-sets could easily produce a positive correlation between reports of the two emotions.

Principal components analysis can control for these potential confounds in the correlations, because a components analysis using orthogonal rotation reflects systematic, independent patterns within and across individuals' responses. Accordingly, varimax-rotated principal components analyses were performed in each of the six studies on subjects' responses to the 14 emotion adjectives. Results in each study revealed that a two-component solution was more appropriate than a one-component solution. The two-component solution included all components with eigenvalues above 1.0, and only eigenvalues above 1.0, in five of the six studies, and all eigenvalues above 1.3 in the sixth (Batson, Cowles, & Coke, 1979). The variance accounted for by the two-component solution ranged from 65 percent to 73 percent across the six studies. Furthermore, whereas a two-component solution included all components accounting for at least 10 percent of the total variance in all six studies, a one-component solution failed to meet this criterion in any study. Component loadings for each of the 14 emotion adjectives in the two-component solution are reported in Table 1.

As is apparent from Table 1, the loadings reveal a component structure that is highly consistent across studies. In each, the eight distress adjectives tend to load on one component and the six empathy adjectives tend to load on a second, orthogonal component. The first component, which we have called the distress component, received high loadings ($> .60$) from "alarmed," "upset," "disturbed," and "distressed" in all six studies, from "worried" and "perturbed" in five of the six, and from

Table 1
Varimax-Rotated Principal-Components Factor Structure of Self-Reported Emotional Responses to Witnessing Another in Need (Six Studies)

Study[a]	1		2		3		4		5		6	
	D	E	D	E	D	E	D	E	D	E	D	E
Distress adjectives												
Alarmed	.75*	.01	.72*	.49	.63*	.15	.72*	.34	.77*	.11	.80*	.19
Grieved	.51	.49	.65*	.48	.55	.58	.70*	.33	.68*	.42	.72*	.30
Upset	.84*	.39	.82*	.32	.74*	.38	.80*	.38	.87*	.17	.89*	.28
Worried	.40	.60*	.87*	.18	.67*	.35	.72*	.34	.78*	.18	.81*	.39
Disturbed	.83*	.35	.82*	.38	.76*	.20	.76*	.38	.89*	.18	.90*	.24
Perturbed	.84*	.17	.59	-.11	.76*	-.18	.69*	-.13	.82*	-.02	.68*	.11
Distressed	.62*	.56	.65*	.48	.81*	.32	.67*	.48	.87*	.25	.86*	.28
Troubled	.88*	.23	.58	.54	.80*	.22	.75*	.33	.59	.39	.87*	.32
Empathy adjectives												
Sympathetic	—	—	.58	.53	.23	.74*	.29	.69*	.04	.84*	.20	.82*
Moved	.31	.75*	.37	.78*	.41	.78*	.42	.74*	.31	.67*	.40	.72*
Compassionate	.25	.80*	.09	.82*	.40	.73*	.24	.80*	.14	.86*	.17	.90*
Tender	—	—	.66*	.32	.18	.86*	.28	.78*	.31	.78*	.36	.74*
Warm	.05	.82*	.23	.71*	-.03	.80*	.19	.80*	.20	.68*	.15	.66*
Softhearted	.12	.85*	.14	.73*	.11	.80*	.17	.86*	.05	.83*	.29	.86*

*Denotes loading above .60.

Note. Tabled values are factor loadings. D = Distress component (Component 1); E = Empathy component (Component 2).

a. Studies are as follows:

1. Coke et al. (1978, Experiment 2) N = 33; females only; 2. Batson et al. (1979) N = 30; females only; 3. Coke (1980) N = 63; females only;
4. Toi & Batson (1982) N = 78; females only; 5. Fultz (1982) N = 61; 35 females, 26 males; 6. Batson et al. (1983) N = 88; 49 females, 39 males. —From Batson (in press). Table reproduced courtesy of Academic Press.

64

"grieved" and "troubled" in four of the six studies. The second component, which we have called the empathy component, received high loadings (> .60) from "moved," "compassionate," "warm," and "softhearted" in all six studies and from "sympathetic" and "tender" in four of five studies. (These last two adjectives were not used by Coke et al., 1978.)

The consistency of the component structure across the six studies suggests that the two-component solution is robust, because these studies employed a variety of need situations. In the first study in this series (Coke et al., 1978, Experiment 2), the need was not especially great, and it was relatively remote in time and place: A graduate student in the School of Education needed subjects for her Master's research. In the next three studies, the victim's need was great, but it was still relatively remote in time and place: Subjects learned that the victim was struggling to deal with the consequences of a tragic automobile accident. She had horrible scars on her face (Batson et al., 1979), on her legs (Coke, 1980), or was confronted with having to give up her career aspirations (Toi & Batson, 1982). In each of these first four studies, subjects learned of the victim's need by listening to an audiotape of a (bogus) radio announcement. In the remaining two studies, the victim's need was great and was highly proximate in time and place: Subjects watched over closed-circuit television (actually a videotape) while the victim, thought to be in a nearby room, reacted with increasing discomfort to a series of electric shocks.

The consistency of the component structure across need situations not withstanding, the particular configurations of emotions experienced as distress and empathy, as well as the relationship between these configurations, may well vary across different need situations. As revealed in Table 2, "grieved" and "worried" were sometimes more closely associated with the empathy than the distress factor, and in one study, both "sympathetic" and "tender" were more closely associated with the distress than the empathy factor. Moreover, in some need situations—for example, when an innocent child or pet is suffering—it seems likely that distress and empathy will be closely intertwined. In other need situations—for example, when a peer is suffering—distress and empathy may both be present but more clearly differentiated. Presumably, one can more easily imagine the peer's plight befalling oneself, and thus one oscillates between focusing on the other's need and focusing on one's own need if in the same situation. Focusing on the other's need should pro-

Batson et al.

Table 2

Proportions of Low and High Empathy Subjects who Offered Help
when Escape was Easy or Difficult (Seven Studies)

Study[a]	1	2	3	4	5	6	7
Low empathy							
Easy escape	$.38_x$	$.00_x$	$.18_x$	$.33_x$	$.39_x$	$.40_x$	$.25_x$
	(16)	(15)	(11)	(12)	(23)	(10)	(8)
Difficult escape	—	—	$.64_y$	$.75_y$	$.81_y$	$.89_y$	$.89_y$
			(11)	(12)	(21)	(9)	(9)
High empathy							
Easy escape	$.94_y$	$.60_y$	$.91_y$	$.83_y$	$.71_y$	$.70_y$	$.86_y$
	(17)	(15)	(11)	(12)	(17)	(10)	(7)
Difficult escape	—	—	$.82_y$	$.58_{xy}$	$.75_y$	$.63_{xy}$	$.63_{xy}$
			(11)	(12)	(20)	(8)	(8)

Note. Numbers in parentheses are the number of subjects in each cell. Cell means within a given study (column) that do not share a common subscript differ significantly, $p <$ .05.

a. Studies are as follows:

1. Coke et al. (1978, Experiment 2). Empathy condition determined by median split on empathic concern index. (A false-feedback manipulation of emotion produced parallel effects on helping in this study.)

2. Batson et al. (1979). Empathy condition determined by median split on empathy component (orthogonal rotation).

3. Batson et al. (1981, Experiment 1). Empathy condition determined by similarity manipulation.

4. Batson et al. (1981, Experiment 2). Empathy condition determined by drug mis-attribution manipulation.

5. Toi & Batson (1982). Empathy condition determined by median split on index of predominant emotional response (empathy index minus distress index). (A perspective-taking manipulation of empathy produced parallel effects on helping in this study.)

6. Batson et al. (1983, Experiment 1). Empathy condition determined by median split on index of predominant emotional response (empathy index minus distress index).

7. Batson et al. (1983, Experiment 2). Empathy condition determined by median split on index of predominant emotional response (empathy index minus distress index).

—From Batson (in press). Table reproduced courtesy of Academic Press.

duce both distress and empathy; focusing on one's own imagined need should produce only distress.

The robustness of the two-factor structure is further supported by the findings of other researchers at another institution. Using principal axes factor analyses rather than principal components, Archer, Diaz-Loving,

Gollwitzer, Davis, and Foushee (1981) and Davis (1983) have reported similar factor structures, with distress adjectives loading on one factor and empathy adjectives loading on a second factor.[2]

This robust two-factor structure seems inconsistent with the traditional view that distress and empathy are components of a single vicarious emotion; however, it is entirely consistent with the archaic view that these vicarious emotions are qualitatively distinct. Still, the factor analytic evidence cannot be considered conclusive because some other discriminating feature of the two sets of adjectives—for example, differences in social desirability or positivity between distress and empathy adjectives—might be producing the two factors. Corroborating evidence using a different research strategy is needed.

Another strategy for examining whether the two emotions are qualitatively distinct is to look for evidence of the motivational differences claimed to result from the two emotions. If, as asserted by the second part of our two-part thesis, the two emotions evoke recognizably different types of motivation, then they must be distinct, as asserted by the first part of our thesis. Ultimately, evidence from research using this second strategy is the more crucial. For even if we were to find evidence that the emotions were experienced as distinct, but we found that both distress and empathy led to motivation directed toward the ultimate goal of reducing one's own emotional arousal, then the distinction would not support the two-path archaic model. Although such a finding would suggest the need for a slight modification of the traditional view in order to account for the qualitative difference between these two vicarious emotions, it would support the heart of the traditional view—that the moti-

2. Shelton and Rogers (1981) reported a study in which both distress and empathy adjectives loaded on a single factor. But that study differed from the studies discussed in this section in two important respects: First, the victims in the Shelton and Rogers study were an endangered species (whales) rather than humans. Second, subjects in all conditions of the studies discussed in this section received the same information about the victim's needs. However, subjects in different conditions of the Shelton and Rogers study were given different information about the victims. One-half of the subjects saw a gory film clip in which whales were hunted, killed, and processed for market. The remaining subjects saw neutral scenes describing whales' natural habitats and behavior. The differences in information across conditions in the Shelton and Rogers study could easily account for subjects' distress and empathy responses loading on a single factor. Half of the subjects had little reason to experience either emotion; the other half had reason to experience both emotions (R. W. Rogers, personal communication, February, 1986).

vation to help associated with both distress and empathy is directed toward the ultimate goal of reducing the helper's own aversive emotional state. Is there, then, any evidence for the second part of our two-part thesis, that is, that distress leads to egoistic and empathy to altruistic motivation to help?

Part 2: Evidence that Distress Leads to Egoistic Motivation to Help and Empathy Leads to Altruistic Motivation to Help

To answer this question, we needed a research strategy that enabled us to determine whether empathy led to altruistic motivation, as suggested by the archaic view, or to egoistic motivation to reduce one's own empathic arousal, as suggested by the traditional view. Batson et al. (1981) proposed that it is possible empirically to separate these two alternative views of the nature of the motivation evoked by empathy by varying the ease of escape without helping. If the motivation evoked by empathy is directed toward the egoistic goal of reducing one's own vicarious empathic emotion, then either helping or escaping can enable one to reach this goal. So if it is moderately costly to help, then helping should be likely when escape is difficult but not when escape is easy. If, on the other hand, the motivation evoked by empathy is directed toward the altruistic goal of reducing the other's need, then helping can enable one to reach this goal, but escaping cannot. Thus, helping should be as likely when escape is easy as when it is difficult.

The kind of escape at issue here is psychological escape. A potential helper needs to get away from the *awareness* of the victim's suffering— not merely to get away from the suffering physically. But the old adage "out of sight, out of mind" suggests that these two kinds of escape are likely to be closely linked. Physical escape from exposure to the victim's distress may often permit psychological escape as well.

To date, there have been seven studies that provide evidence concerning the effect of empathy on likelihood of helping when escape is easy. The results of these studies are summarized in Table 2.

In the first two studies in Table 2, ease of escape was not manipulated; the need situation was always presented so that escape was easy. In the first study (Coke et al., 1978, Experiment 2), subjects learned of a graduate student's need for research participants indirectly by listening to a (bogus) taped radio broadcast. Subjects were then given a written appeal for help from the graduate student. All that was necessary to escape continued exposure to the need situation was to lay the appeal aside and forget it. Yet higher levels of self-reported empathy were associated with higher rates of helping (see Column 1 of Table 2). This pattern was what would be expected if increased empathy led to altruistic motivation.

Results of the second study in Table 2 (Batson et al., 1979) provided additional evidence that greater self-reported empathy leads to higher rates of helping when escape is easy, whereas greater personal distress does not lead to increased helping when escape is easy. The procedure of this study was quite similar to that of the previous one, but a different need situation was employed. In this study, the taped radio broadcast presented the consequences of a rather gory automobile accident. Unlike the situation used in the first study, this situation produced moderately high levels of self-reported distress as well as empathy. Escape without helping was made easy by the same technique used by Coke et al. (1978). Greater self-reported empathy was again associated with increased helping, but greater self-reported personal distress was not.

In these first two studies, it was simply assumed that escape was sufficiently easy that egoistic motivation would not lead to increased helping, whereas altruistic motivation would. A far stronger test of whether empathy leads to altruistic motivation is provided by a design in which both the level of vicarious emotion and the ease of escape are varied. The last five studies in Table 2 employed such a design. In each, ease of escape was manipulated by leading some participants to believe that if they did not help they would never again see the person in need; other participants were led to believe that if they did not help they would continue to see the suffering victim.

If empathy evokes altruistic motivation, what pattern of helping would be expected across the four cells of this empathy (low vs. high) by escape (easy vs. difficult) 2×2 design? Presumably, if empathy is kept low, then distress will be the predominant vicarious emotion produced by witnessing the other's suffering. This distress should produce egoistic motivation to reduce one's own aversive arousal. As a result, when empathy is low, if escape is made easier, then there should be less helping (assuming helping involves some cost). But when empathy is high, it should be the predominant vicarious emotion, evoking altruistic motivation. This should mean that when empathy is high, if escape is made easier, then there should be no reduction in helping. Across the four cells of the 2×2 design, then, we would expect a one versus three pattern of helping. That is, the rate of helping should be relatively low in the low empathy-easy escape cell and high in the other three.

But if, as predicted by the traditional view of the vicarious emotion-prosocial motivation link, empathy evokes egoistic motivation to reduce one's own empathic arousal, then we would expect an escape manipulation to have the same effect on helping among high empathy subjects as among low. That is, this view leads to the prediction of a main effect for escape—higher helping in the difficult escape condition than in the easy escape condition for *both* low and high empathy subjects. There might also be a main effect for empathy, with high empathy leading to more helping than low empathy because the higher level of vicarious emotion in the high empathy condition should lead to stronger motivation to reduce that emotion. Thus, if empathy evokes egoistic tension-reduction motivation, we would expect to observe a definite main effect for ease of escape and a possible main effect for empathy; if, however, empathy evokes altruistic motivation, we would expect the one versus three pattern described above.

Five published studies have examined the nature of the motivation to help associated with empathy using an Empathy × Escape design. In these studies low and high empathy conditions have been created by four different techniques: (*a*) subjects' self-reports of their vicarious emotion (using essentially the same measurement instrument employed in the factor analyses described earlier—Batson et al., 1983, Studies 1 and 2), (*b*) a perspective-taking instruction manipulation (Toi & Batson, 1982), (*c*) a similarity manipulation (Batson et al., 1981, Experiment 1), and (*d*) an emotion-specific misattribution manipulation (Batson et al., 1981, Experiment 2). Ease of escape has been manipulated in two ways: (*a*) Subjects believed that they either would or would not continue to watch another introductory psychology student take electric shocks (Batson et al., 1981, Experiments 1 and 2; Batson et al., 1983, Studies 1 and 2), or (*b*) subjects believed that they either would or would not see the needy person the next week in their introductory psychology class (Toi & Batson, 1982). Finally, two different need situations have been used—the victim's need for relief from painful shocks (Batson et al., 1981; Batson et al., 1983) and need for assistance in going over class notes (Toi & Batson, 1982).

Results of each of these five studies (the last five in Table 2) clearly conform to the one versus three pattern predicted if personal distress leads to egoistic motivation and empathy leads to altruistic motivation. In each study, the planned comparison testing this pattern accounted for all reliable between-cell variance. Moreover, pairwise comparisons of

cells in each study revealed that, as predicted, the low empathy-easy escape cell differed significantly, $p < .05$, from the low empathy-difficult
escape cell, but the high empathy-easy escape and high empathy-difficult escape cells did not differ. These results do not support the traditional tension-reduction view that empathy evokes egoistic motivation to
reduce aversive arousal; rather, they support the archaic view that distress evokes egoistic and empathy evokes altruistic motivation to help.

The consistency of the one versus three pattern across the last five
studies summarized in Table 2 suggests that the pattern is fairly robust,
because, as already noted, the studies differed in the need situations employed and the techniques used to vary level of empathy and ease of escape. Across these different need situations and techniques for varying
the levels of empathy and ease of escape, helping responses consistently
conformed to the one versus three pattern that would be predicted if distress leads to egoistic and empathy leads to altruistic motivation to help.

New Egoistic Alternatives to the Traditional and Archaic Views

The suggestion that empathy evokes altruistic motivation to help has not,
however, gone unchallenged. Archer et al. (1981), Cialdini (1984), Dovidio (1984), and Meindl and Lerner (1983) have each proposed alternative explanations for all or part of the evidence (summarized in Table 2)
that supports the second half of the two-part archaic thesis. In essence,
the alternative explanations suggest that, although empathy may not
evoke motivation to reduce one's empathic distress as has been assumed
by the traditional tension-reduction view, the motivation to help associated with empathy may still be egoistic. The empathically aroused individual may help in order to avoid anticipated punishments (such as shame
or guilt) or to gain anticipated rewards (such as enhanced self-esteem)
that arise specifically when a person is feeling empathy.

Several studies have recently been conducted to explore these alternative explanations for the results summarized in Table 2. Fultz, Batson,
Fortenbach, McCarthy, and Varney (1986) provided evidence that empathically aroused individuals help more even when no other person—
not even the person in need—will know if they do not help. This finding
seems to rule out the possibility that the empathy-helping relationship is
mediated by a desire to avoid socially administered punishments for not
helping, such as social censure or negative evaluation. Batson, Bolen,
Cross, and Neuringer-Benefiel (1986), using partial correlations, pro-

vided evidence that part of the motivation to help associated with self-reported empathic emotion might be directed toward avoiding self-censure or guilt, but only part. Interestingly, it was the part of self-reported situational empathy that was associated with a self-report measure of the disposition to show empathic concern for people in need (Davis, 1983) that appeared to be directed toward avoiding self-censure. The part of situational empathy not associated with this measure of dispositional empathy was correlated with the pattern of helping across an ease of escape manipulation that would be expected if the underlying motivation was altruistic.

These recent studies provide at least partial answers to the questions raised by the suggestion that empathy increases helping because it evokes special concern about anticipated social or self-punishments for not helping. Additional research is needed to explore the role of anticipated social and self-rewards in the empathy-helping relationship. The evidence thus far does not suggest that the new egoistic explanations can provide adequate alternatives to the archaic view, but the evidence is still incomplete.

CONCLUSION

Taken together, the factor analyses of self-reported emotional response and the effects of distress and empathy on helping when escape is easy contradict the traditional tension-reduction view of the relationship between vicarious emotion and prosocial motivation. Instead, they provide strong support for the first part of our two-part archaic thesis, that distress and empathy are distinct vicarious emotions. They also provide considerable support for the second part of the archaic thesis, that distress leads to egoistic motivation and empathy leads to altruistic motivation. Still, additional research is needed before we can be confident that this second part of the archaic thesis is correct.

Although our review has focused specifically on the vicarious emotion-prosocial motivation link, we believe that the evidence we have reviewed may have more general implications for an understanding of the nature of emotion and the relationship between emotion and motivation. For if there are important qualitative distinctions between the vicarious emotions of distress and empathy and between their associated prosocial motivations, then may there not be similar important qualitative distinctions among other emotions as well? Perhaps there is less plasticity and more uniqueness among emotions than is implied by Schachter's (1964) popular formulation of emotion as undifferentiated physiological arousal paired with a cognitive label. In retrospect, psychologists may have been led into a limited view of emotion by the relative emphases on (*a*) the association between cognition and emotion, and (*b*) emotion as a dependent variable, to the relative exclusion of (*c*) the association between emotion and motivation, and (*d*) emotion as a mediating variable. To assess potentially important qualitative distinctions among emotions, we may need to change our research perspective. It may be necessary, as suggested by Abelson (1983) and Roseman (1984), to look at emotions in the context of goal-directed behavior rather than simply as the end point of an inference process about one's current internal states.

REFERENCES

Abelson, R. P. (1983). What ever became of consistency theory? *Personality and Social Psychology Bulletin, 9*, 37–54.

Archer, R. L., Diaz-Loving, R., Gollwitzer, P. M., Davis, M. H., & Foushee, H. C. (1981). The role of dispositional empathy and social evaluation in the empathic mediation of helping. *Journal of Personality and Social Psychology, 40*, 786–796.

Bandura, A. (1977). *Social Learning Theory.* Englewood Cliffs, NJ: Prentice-Hall.

Batson, C. D. (in press). Prosocial motivation: Is it ever truly altruistic? In L. Berkowitz (Ed.), *Advances in experimental social psychology* (Vol. 21). New York: Academic Press.

Batson, C. D., Bolen, M. H., Cross, J. A., & Neuringer-Benefiel, H. (1986). Where is the altruism in the altruistic personality? *Journal of Personality and Social Psychology, 50*, 212–220.

Batson, C. D., & Coke, J. S. (1981). Empathy: A source of altruistic motivation for helping? In J. P. Rushton & R. M. Sorrentino (Eds.), *Altruism and helping behavior* (pp. 167–187). Hillsdale, NJ: Erlbaum.

Batson, C. D., & Coke, J. S. (1983). Empathic motivations of helping behavior. In J. T. Cacciopo & R. E. Petty (Eds.), *Social psychophysiology: A sourcebook* (pp. 417–433). New York: Guilford.

Batson, C. D., Cowles, C., & Coke, J. S. (1979). *Empathic mediation of the response to a lady in distress: Egoistic or altruistic?* Unpublished manuscript, University of Kansas.

Batson, C. D., Darley, J. M., & Coke, J. S. (1978). Altruism and human kindness: Internal and external determinants of helping behavior. In L. Pervin & M. Lewis (Eds.), *Perspectives in interactional psychology* (pp. 111–140). New York: Plenum.

Batson, C. D., Duncan, B. D., Ackerman, P., Buckley, T., & Birch, K. (1981). Is empathic emotion a source of altruistic motivation? *Journal of Personality and Social Psychology, 40*, 290–302.

Batson, C. D., O'Quin, K., Fultz, J., Vanderplas, M., & Isen, A. (1983). Self-reported distress and empathy and egoistic versus altruistic motivation for helping. *Journal of Personality and Social Psychology, 45*, 706–718.

Borke, H. (1971). Interpersonal perception of young children: Egocentrism or empathy? *Developmental Psychology, 5,* 263–269.

Cannon, W. B. (1927). The James-Lange theory of emotion: A critical examination and an alternative theory. *American Journal of Psychology, 39,* 106–124.

Cialdini, R. B. (1984, August). *Altruism, or the elimination of negative affect?* Paper presented at the annual convention of the America Psychological Association, Toronto.

Cialdini, R. B., & Kendrick, D. T. (1976). Altruism as hedonism: A social development perspective on the relationship of negative mood state and helping. *Journal of Personality and Social Psychology, 34,* 907–914.

Coke, J. S. (1980). Empathic mediation of helping: Egoistic or altruistic? (Doctoral dissertation, University of Kansas, 1979). *Dissertation Abstracts International, 41B* (01), 405. (University Microfilms No. 8014371)

Coke, J. S., Batson, C. D., & McDavis, K. (1978). Empathic mediation of helping: A two-stage model. *Journal of Personality and Social Psychology, 36,* 752–766.

Comte, I. A. (1875). *System of positive polity* (Vol. 1). London: Longmans, Green, & Co. (Original work published 1851)

Davis, M. H. (1983). The effects of dispositional empathy on emotional reactions and helping: A multidimensional approach. *Journal of Personality, 51,* 167–184.

Dovidio, J. F. (1984). Helping behavior and altruism: An empirical and conceptual overview. In L. Berkowitz (Ed.), *Advances in experimental social psychology* (Vol. 17, pp. 362–427). New York: Academic.

Dymond, R. (1949). A scale for measurement of empathic ability. *Journal of Consulting Psychology, 13,* 127–133.

Fultz, J. N. (1982). *Influence of potential for self-reward on egoistically and altruistically motivated helping.* Unpublished Master's thesis, University of Kansas.

Fultz, J., Batson, C. D., Fortenbach, V. A., McCarthy, P. M., & Varney, L. L. (1986). Social evaluation and the empathy-altruism hypothesis. *Journal of Personality and Social Psychology, 50,* 761–769.

Heider, F. (1958). *The psychology of interpersonal relations.* New York: Wiley.

Hoffman, M. L. (1975). Developmental synthesis of affect and cognition and its implications for altruistic motivation. *Developmental Psychology, 11,* 607–622.

Hoffman, M. L. (1976). Empathy, role-taking, guilt, and development of altruistic motives. In T. Lickona (Ed.), *Moral development and behavior: Theory, research, and social issues* (pp. 124–143). New York: Holt, Rinehart, & Winston.

Hoffman, M. L. (1981a). Is altruism part of human nature? *Journal of Personality and Social Psychology, 40,* 121–137.

Hoffman, M. L. (1981b). The development of empathy. In J. P. Rushton & R. M. Sorrentino (Eds.), *Altruism and helping behavior: Social, personality, and developmental perspectives* (pp. 41–63). Hillsdale, NJ: Erlbaum.

Hoffman, M. L. (1982). Development of prosocial motivation: Empathy and guilt. In N. Eisenberg (Ed.), *The development of prosocial behavior* (pp. 281–311). New York: Academic Press.

Hogan, R. (1969). Development of an empathy scale. *Journal of Consulting and Clinical Psychology, 33,* 307–316.

Hull, C. L. (1943). *Principles of behavior.* Englewood Cliffs, NJ: Prentice–Hall.

Hull, C. L. (1952). *A behavior system*. New Haven, CT: Yale University Press.

Hume, D. (1896). *A treatise of human nature*. Oxford: Oxford University Press. (Original work published 1740)

Krebs, D. L. (1975). Empathy and altruism. *Journal of Personality and Social Psychology*, **32**, 1134–1146.

Krebs, D., & Russell, C. (1981). Role-taking and altruism: When you put yourself in the shoes of another will they take you to their owner's aid? In J. P. Rushton and R. M. Sorrentino (Eds.), *Altruism and helping behavior* (pp. 137–165). Hillsdale, NJ: Erlbaum.

McDougall, W. (1908). *Introduction to social psychology*. London: Methuen.

Mehrabian, A., & Epstein, N. (1972). A measure of emotional empathy. *Journal of Personality*, **40**, 525–543.

Meindl, J. R., & Lerner, M. J. (1983). The heroic motive: Some experimental demonstrations. *Journal of Experimental Social Psychology* **19**, 1–20.

Piliavin, J. A., Dovidio, J. F., Gaertner, S. L., & Clark, R. D., III (1981). *Emergency intervention*. New York: Academic Press.

Piliavin, J. A., & Piliavin, I. M. (1973). *The Good Samaritan: Why does he help?* Unpublished manuscript, University of Wisconsin.

Roseman, I. J. (1984). Cognitive determinants of emotion: A structural theory. In P. Shaver (Ed.), *Review of personality and social psychology. Vol. 5: Emotions, relationships, and health* (pp. 11–36). Beverly Hills, CA: Sage.

Schachter, S. (1964). The interaction of cognitive and physiological determinants of emotional state. In L. Berkowitz (Ed.), *Advances in experimental social psychology* (Vol. 1, pp. 49–81). New York: Academic Press.

Shelton, M. L., & Rogers, R. W. (1981). Fear-arousing and empathy-arousing appeals to help: The pathos of persuasion. *Journal of Applied Social Psychology*, **11**, 363–378.

Smith, A. (1759). *The theory of moral sentiments*. London: A. Miller.

Stotland, E. (1969). Exploratory studies of empathy. In L. Berkowitz (Ed.), *Advances in experimental social psychology* (Vol. 4, pp. 271–314). New York: Academic Press.

Toi, M., & Batson, C. D. (1982). More evidence that empathy is a source of altruistic motivation. *Journal of Personality and Social Psychology*, **43**, 281–292.

Underwood, B., & Moore, B. (1982). Perspective-taking and altruism. *Psychological Bulletin*, **91**, 143–173.

Wispé, L. G. (1968). Sympathy and empathy. In D. L. Sills (Ed.), *International encyclopedia of the social sciences* (Vol. 15, pp. 441–447). New York: Free Press.

Wispé, L. G. (1986). The distinction between sympathy and empathy: To call forth a concept, a word is needed. *Journal of Personality and Social Psychology*, **50**, 314–321.

Manuscript received January 6, 1986; revised September 10, 1986.

INTERPERSONAL RELATIONS AND GROUP PROCESSES

Five Studies Testing Two New Egoistic Alternatives to the Empathy–Altruism Hypothesis

C. Daniel Batson, Janine L. Dyck, J. Randall Brandt, Judy G. Batson, Anne L. Powell,
M. Rosalie McMaster, and Cari Griffitt
University of Kansas

The empathy–altruism hypothesis claims that prosocial motivation associated with feeling empathy for a person in need is directed toward the ultimate goal of benefiting that person, not toward some subtle form of self-benefit. We explored two new egoistic alternatives to this hypothesis. The empathy-specific reward hypothesis proposes that the prosocial motivation associated with empathy is directed toward the goal of obtaining social or self-rewards (i.e., praise, honor, and pride). The empathy-specific punishment hypothesis proposes that this motivation is directed toward the goal of avoiding social or self-punishments (i.e., censure, guilt, and shame). Study 1 provided an initial test of the empathy-specific reward hypothesis. Studies 2 through 4 used three procedures to test the empathy-specific punishment hypothesis. In Study 5, a Stroop procedure was used to assess the role of reward-relevant, punishment-relevant, and victim-relevant cognitions in mediating the empathy–helping relationship. Results of these five studies did not support either the empathy-specific reward or the empathy-specific punishment hypothesis. Instead, results of each supported the empathy–altruism hypothesis. Evidence that empathic emotion evokes altruistic motivation continues to mount.

Feeling empathy—defined as an other-oriented emotional response congruent with the perceived welfare of another person—can evoke motivation to help that person (Coke, Batson, & McDavis, 1978; Eisenberg & Miller, 1987; Krebs, 1975). Several researchers have suggested that this motivation is, at least in part, altruistic; they claim that empathy evokes motivation directed toward the ultimate goal of benefiting the person for whom empathy is felt, not toward some subtle form of self-benefit (see Batson, 1987; Batson, Duncan, Ackerman, Buckley, & Birch, 1981; Hóffman, 1976; Krebs, 1975). If valid, this empathy–altruism hypothesis seems very important. It contradicts the general assumption in psychology that all motivation, including all prosocial motivation, is ultimately egoistic (Wallach & Wallach, 1983).

Initial support for the empathy–altruism hypothesis comes from a series of studies using Empathy × Ease of Escape designs. Researchers have consistently found that when empathy is low, helping drops dramatically if escape is easy. When empathy is high, however, helping remains high even if the empathically aroused individuals can easily reduce their arousal by escaping exposure to the suffering victim (Batson et al., 1981; Batson, O'Quin, Fultz, Vanderplas, & Isen, 1983; Fultz, Batson, Fortenbach, McCarthy, & Varney, 1986; Toi & Batson, 1982). This pattern of results seems to rule out the most popular egoistic explanation of the empathy–helping relationship: that the empathically aroused individual helps in order to reduce his or her own aversive empathic arousal (Hoffman, 1981; Piliavin & Piliavin, 1973).

NEW EGOISTIC ALTERNATIVES TO THE EMPATHY–ALTRUISM HYPOTHESIS

Even if the motivation to help associated with empathy is not directed toward the goal of aversive-arousal reduction, it may still be egoistic. Archer, Diaz-Loving, Gollwitzer, Davis, and Foushee (1981), Batson (1987), Cialdini et al. (1987), Dovidio (1984), and Thompson, Cowan, and Rosenhan (1980) have each proposed possible new egoistic explanations for all or part of the evidence presented in support of the empathy–altruism hypothesis. In essence, these new egoistic explanations suggest that apart from any general rewards and punishments associated with helping, there are *empathy-specific* rewards or punish-

This research was supported by National Science Foundation Grant BNS-8507110 awarded to C. Daniel Batson.

We wish to thank Margaret Schadler and David Thissen for assistance with the Stroop equipment used in Study 5 and Marcy Sheridan, Randy Rash, and Mickey Waxman for assistance in preparing the Stroop materials. Thanks to Jack Brehm, Brian Cohen, William Graziano, Patricia Schoenrade, Abraham Tesser, Joy Weeks, and Robert Wicklund for helpful comments on part or all of this article.

Correspondence concerning this article should be addressed to C. Daniel Batson, University of Kansas, Lawrence, Kansas 66045.

Editor's note: This article was submitted as three separate manuscripts. Each received positive reviews. They were combined at the editor's suggestion prior to a final decision about publication.

ments. Feeling empathy changes the anticipated reward or punishment structure of the situation, making helping more beneficial to the self and so increasing the egoistic motivation to help.

Empathy-Specific Reward Hypothesis

According to one new egoistic explanation, people learn through prior reinforcement either that (a) special rewards in the form of praise, honor, and pride are attendant on helping when feeling empathy (Batson, 1987; Thompson et al., 1980; see also Meindl & Lerner, 1983) or (b) empathy creates a special need for these rewards of helping (Cialdini et al., 1987). When people feel empathy, they think of these social and self-rewards and are egoistically motivated to obtain them.

This empathy-specific reward hypothesis can easily account for the results of the studies cited earlier that provide support for the empathy–altruism hypothesis, because all of those studies involved manipulation of ease of escape. Empathy-specific rewards should accrue only when one helps, so the empathy-specific reward hypothesis predicts that a chance to escape will not reduce helping by empathically aroused individuals. No reduction in helping under easy escape is precisely what has been found.

Empathy-Specific Punishment Hypothesis

According to a second new egoistic explanation, feeling empathy may lead to increased helping because of anticipated empathy-specific punishments for failing to help (Archer et al., 1981; Batson, 1987; Dovidio, 1984). Presumably, people learn through prior reinforcement that a special obligation to help—and special guilt and shame for not helping—are attendant on feeling empathy. When people feel empathy, they think of these social and self-punishments and are egoistically motivated to avoid them.

This empathy-specific punishment hypothesis also can account for the results of the studies that seem to support the empathy–altruism hypothesis. The empathy-specific punishment hypothesis predicts reduced helping by empathically aroused individuals when it is easy to escape the anticipated punishments for failing to help. However, escape from the victim's suffering, which was the form of escape made easy in the studies supporting the empathy–altruism hypothesis, might not have allowed escape from the anticipated guilt and shame for doing so. Even in the easy-escape condition of those studies, empathically aroused individuals might have found it difficult to escape these anticipated punishments.

We report five studies designed to test these two new egoistic alternatives to the empathy–altruism reward hypothesis. Study 1 provided an initial test of the empathy-specific reward hypothesis. Studies 2, 3, and 4 used three procedures to test the empathy-specific punishment hypothesis. In Study 5 we used a different procedure to test both new egoistic alternatives, as well as the empathy–altruism hypothesis.

TESTING THE EMPATHY-SPECIFIC REWARD HYPOTHESIS: EFFECTS ON MOOD OF NOT BEING ALLOWED TO HELP

Social and self-rewards associated with helping produce enhanced mood (Yinon & Landau, 1987) as long as the helping

act has a low cost and is clearly beneficial to the person in need (Weyant, 1978). This fact suggests that one way to test the relative merits of the empathy–altruism and the empathy-specific reward hypotheses is to compare (a) the mood of individuals who believe that the need of a person for whom they feel empathy has been relieved as a result of their own action with (b) the mood of individuals who believe that the person's need has been relieved, but not as a result of their own action. Because the mood-enhancing rewards for helping should be available only to the helper, the empathy-specific reward hypothesis predicts that individuals feeling a high degree of empathy will be in a more positive mood when they have been the agent of the victim's relief than when they have not. Moreover, to the extent that empathy-specific reward is the only motivational process operating, the mood of high-empathy individuals deprived of the opportunity to help should be unaffected by whether the victim's need is relieved by other means. Neither relief of the need nor lack of relief per se is relevant to the egoistic goal of obtaining mood-enhancing rewards for helping.

In contrast, the empathy–altruism hypothesis predicts that individuals feeling a high degree of empathy will be in as positive a mood when the victim's need is relieved by other means as when by their own action. Moreover, the empathy–altruism hypothesis predicts that when empathically aroused individuals are deprived of the opportunity to help, they should be in a more positive mood when the victim's need is relieved by other means than when it is not relieved. Relief, by whatever means, brings attainment of the altruistic goal of increasing the victim's welfare. This goal attainment should increase positive mood.

Manipulation and Measurement of Empathy

In the studies providing evidence for the empathy–altruism hypothesis, empathy sometimes has been experimentally manipulated (Batson et al., 1981, Experiments 1 and 2), sometimes allowed to occur naturally and then measured through self-reports (Batson et al., 1983, Studies 1 and 2; Batson, Bolen, Cross, & Neuringer-Benefiel, 1986; Fultz et al., 1986, Study 1), and sometimes both manipulated and measured (Coke et al., 1978, Experiment 2; Fultz et al., 1986, Study 2; Toi & Batson, 1982). Exactly the same pattern of helping, the pattern predicted by the empathy–altruism hypothesis, has been found when empathy is manipulated and when it is measured, suggesting the interchangeability of these two techniques for operationalizing empathy as an independent variable.

In most cases, of course, experimental manipulation of an independent variable is preferable to measurement because manipulation permits clearer causal inference. In our case, however, measurement of empathy actually seemed preferable to manipulation. Our goal was to determine whether the empathy-specific reward hypothesis merited further consideration, so we wished to give this hypothesis the best possible chance to display its power. Because this hypothesis was based on a socialization model that implied individual differences and awareness of one's empathic state, the predicted self-reward effects seemed most likely to appear among subjects who reported themselves to be feeling empathy.

If high-empathy subjects report a more positive mood when

they are the agent of the victim's relief than when they are not, as the empathy-specific reward hypothesis predicts, then additional research would be required to ensure that feeling empathy, and not some correlate of feeling empathy, causes the effect. If, however, these subjects fail to report a more positive mood when they are the agent of the victim's relief, this finding would count against the empathy-specific reward hypothesis as clearly as failure to find this predicted effect in an experimental design in which empathy is manipulated. As Campbell and Stanley (1963) pointed out long ago, failure to find predicted effects in a correlational design counts against a causal hypothesis as clearly as failure to find these effects in an experimental design. Given both this equal power to detect lack of support for the hypothesis and our desire to optimize chances of finding empathy-specific reward effects if they exist, it seemed best in this case to operationalize empathy through measurement, not manipulation.

Study 1: Empathy and Not Being Allowed to Help

Design and Predictions

To test the predictions of the empathy-specific reward hypothesis, we created a situation in which all subjects were (a) confronted with a person in need and (b) informed that they could perform a task that would, at little or no cost to them, relieve the victim's need. (Low-cost helping was necessary because research by Weyant, 1978, and Yinon & Landau, 1987, suggested that the mood-enhancing effects are limited to low-cost, clearly beneficial help.) Subjects then completed a measure of self-reported empathic emotional reaction to the victim, followed by an initial measure of mood. Later, half of the subjects learned that by chance they would not be performing the helping task after all. Moreover, both among subjects allowed to perform the task and those not allowed, half learned that the victim was still in need, and half learned that by chance the victim was no longer in need. Finally, subjects completed a second measure of mood. A median split on the measure of self-reported empathy was combined with the two experimental manipulations to produce a 2 (low vs. high empathy) × 2 (no prior relief of victim's need vs. prior relief) × 2 (perform the helping task vs. not perform) factorial quasi-experimental design.[1]

The major dependent measure was change in self-reported mood after subjects were or were not allowed to help the victim. The empathy-specific reward hypothesis predicted a 1 versus 3 pattern of mood change among high-empathy subjects: In the no-prior-relief/perform cell, mood should not change or should become more positive, whereas in each of the other three cells—in which subjects had in different ways been deprived of the anticipated opportunity to obtain the empathy-specific rewards for helping—mood should become more negative. The empathy–altruism hypothesis also predicted a 1 versus 3 pattern of mood change among high-empathy subjects, but a different one: In the no-prior-relief/not-perform cell, mood should become more negative, whereas in each of the other three cells—in which in one way or another the victim's need had been relieved—mood should not change or should become more positive.

Method

Subjects

Eighty students (40 men, 40 women) in an introductory psychology course at the University of Kansas served as subjects, partially fulfilling a course requirement. Within sex, a randomized-block procedure was used to assign 20 subjects (10 men, 10 women) to each of the four cells of the 2 (no prior relief of victim's need vs. prior relief) × 2 (perform the helping task vs. not perform) experimental design.[2]

Procedure

Subjects were run individually. A written introduction described the study as concerning "how a variety of task characteristics and outcome consequences affect people's task performance and attitudes." Four task characteristics were being examined: (a) for whom one's performance has consequences—self only, another person only, or both; (b) the kind of outcome consequences—positive, negative, or neutral; (c) stability of the task situation—stable or unstable in opportunity to perform the task, outcome consequences, or both; and (d) complexity of the task situation—simple (varying only in whether the consequences for self are positive, negative, or neutral) or complex (varying in type of consequences, for whom, and stability).

Ostensibly, 2 same-sex subjects were participating in the study. One would be randomly assigned to the simple task situation and the other to some variant of the complex task situation. The 2 subjects were not to meet face-to-face during the study, but the one assigned to the complex task situation was to receive an audio communication from the one assigned to the simple task situation.

The outcome consequences—positive, negative, and neutral—were then described. Positive consequences involved either receiving a raffle ticket or avoiding an electric shock for each correct response. Negative consequences involved receiving a "mild but uncomfortable" electric shock for each incorrect response. Neutral consequences involved simply being informed whether each response was correct or incorrect.

Finally, the introduction explained that unstable task situations could vary either in opportunity to perform the task or in outcome consequences. Variance in opportunity to perform was illustrated by second-string players on sports teams and understudies in the theater, "people who must keep their skills honed and be ready to take over when necessary but who may never get a chance to perform." Variance in outcome consequences was illustrated by the change from positive to negative consequences that occurs when an underdog sports team becomes the favorite. The former may have nothing to lose, whereas the latter has much to lose.

Condition 9: benefiting the other person; unstable task situation. Once they had read this information, all subjects learned that they had (ostensibly randomly) been assigned to Condition 9, a complex task situation in which they were to perform a task with positive consequences

---

[1] In the prior-relief condition, the task could no longer benefit the victim, so it may seem inappropriate to label it a helping task. We have retained this label for two reasons. First, the task was originally presented to subjects as one on which their performance could help the victim. Second, we wish to emphasize that the task was the same in both the no-prior-relief and the prior-relief conditions and that only the consequences of the task were different.

[2] Ten additional students (6 men, 4 women) were excluded from the sample and replaced because of suspicion. The suspicion rate did not differ reliably across experimental conditions, $\chi^2(3, N = 90) = 6.08$, $p > .10$. Moreover, analyses the same as those reported here but including the 10 suspicious individuals produced the same, albeit somewhat weaker, pattern of reliable results.

for another person under unstable conditions. A sheet provided more detailed information about this condition:

> Your performance will have no consequences for yourself; it will have positive consequences for the other research participant. . . . That person has been initially assigned to the negative consequences condition of the simple task situation, which means that he or she will receive an electric shock after every error he or she makes (most people make about 9–10 errors in the simple task situation). But you can help that person avoid the negative consequences. For every correct response you make on your task, the person in the simple task situation will be given neutral consequences—just information—instead of shocks after one of his or her errors. If you make enough correct responses, he or she will receive no shocks at all.

Because the task situation was unstable, there was a 1 in 3 chance that either the opportunity to perform the task or the outcome consequences or both would change just before time to perform the task.

This sheet also explained that before performing their task subjects would complete a practice task "like the one you will be asked to perform" and would then "get to know" the person assigned to the simple task situation by listening as he or she talked to them briefly over an audio intercom. Finally, it was explained that the other person was not aware of the subject's opportunity to help him (her) avoid the shocks.

Learning of the other person's need. After performing the practice task and receiving positive feedback (to allay fears about not being able to succeed at the helping task), subjects were left alone to listen to the other subject—Brian for men, Janet for women—talk over the intercom. What they heard was actually a prerecorded tape. Explaining that he (she) was supposed to talk about "what's on my mind right now," Brian (Janet) hesitated and said:

> Well . . . , I guess if I'm really honest, I'd have to say I'm thinking about this shock thing. I mean, when I came in here I didn't really expect anything quite like this. . . . When I found out I'd get shocked for every mistake I make on my task, I wasn't crazy about the idea, but I thought, it's probably no big deal. Well . . . , they gave me a couple of sample shocks so that I'd know what to expect. . . . Wow! (nervous laugh) I don't want to sound like a wimp or anything, but I was surprised. Those shocks kinda hurt! I mean, they weren't terrible and I guess I'll go through with it, but I'm not looking forward to making mistakes on my task. And I guess from what they say I'll probably make some. . . . Oh well, I'm sure it won't be that bad.

Empathic reaction to learning of the other's need. After listening, subjects completed an emotional response questionnaire, which was designed to assess their empathic feelings toward Brian (Janet). This questionnaire listed 24 adjectives describing different emotional states. Subjects were to indicate on 7-point scales (1 = *not at all*, 7 = *extremely*) how they were feeling. Included in the list were 6 adjectives that had been previously found through factor analysis (in six studies; see Batson, 1987, for a review) to reflect feelings of empathy: *sympathetic, moved, compassionate, tender, warm,* and *softhearted.*

Measure of mood prior to experimental manipulations. Once subjects completed the emotional response questionnaire, they were given the first mood measure. This measure consisted of fifteen 9-point bipolar scales; subjects were to indicate their present feelings by circling the number on each scale "that best represents how you are feeling *right now.*" Seven of the scales were used to provide a measure of the evaluative tone of subjects' mood: bad mood–good mood, sad–happy, depressed–elated, dissatisfied–satisfied, gloomy–cheerful, displeased–pleased, and sorrowful–joyful. The first 4 items in this list had been used by Rosenhan, Salovey, and Hargis (1981); the last 3 were added on the basis of face validity. The other eight scales were related to either the tension (e.g., nervous–calm, tense–relaxed) or potency (e.g., lethargic–energetic, passive–active) dimensions of mood; they served as filler

items. (Factor analysis of our subjects' responses revealed that the seven evaluative scales defined a mood dimension orthogonal to the tension and potency dimensions.)

Experimental manipulation of prior relief of need and of opportunity to perform. While subjects completed this first mood measure, the experimenter went to "consult the random number table to see whether there are any changes in either your opportunity to perform the task or your outcome consequences." The experimenter, who was blind to subjects' empathy scores throughout the procedure, had up to this point also been blind to the experimental condition. The experimenter now checked the subject's condition, selected a prepared sheet describing the task characteristics for that condition, returned, and asked the subject to read the sheet carefully.

Prior relief of the victim's need was manipulated by what subjects read on the sheet about Brian's (Janet's) consequences. Subjects in the no-prior-relief condition read that there was no change in the consequences: "The person in the simple task situation remains in the negative consequences condition. He or she will receive an electric shock after every error." Subjects in the prior-relief condition read that Brian's (Janet's) consequences had changed: "The person in the simple task situation has been reassigned to the neutral consequences condition. He or she will receive no shocks but will simply be informed whether a response is correct or incorrect."

Performance of the helping task was manipulated by what subjects read about their own performance. Subjects in the perform condition read that there was no change: "You will be performing your task." Subjects in the not-perform condition read, "You will not be performing the task."

The two manipulations were varied factorially, producing a 2 (no prior relief of victim's need vs. prior relief) × 2 (perform the helping task vs. not perform) experimental design. Subjects in the no-prior-relief/perform condition were the only ones who could still help the victim. For subjects in the no-prior-relief/not-perform condition, Brian (Janet) would still receive shocks for errors, but they could no longer do anything to prevent it. For subjects in the two prior-relief conditions, Brian's (Janet's) need had been relieved without their action.

Measure of mood after the experimental manipulations. Subjects who were still to perform the task did so. The task involved working for 120 s from left to right, line by line through a sheet filled with numbers, circling as many combinations of 13 and 47 as possible. The task was designed so that subjects could get the 9 to 10 combinations necessary to eliminate all of Brian's (Janet's) shocks. (Mean number of combinations circled was 11.38, SD = 1.67.) After the task, subjects in the perform condition completed a second mood measure that was identical to the first. Subjects in the not-perform condition completed this second mood measure immediately after reading the information about the change(s) in their task characteristics. As before, instructions on the mood measure emphasized that subjects were to circle the number on each bipolar scale "that best represents how you are feeling *right now.*"

Debriefing. Subjects were carefully debriefed, thanked for their participation, and excused.

Results and Discussion

Effect on Mood of Not Being Allowed to Help

To control for the individual differences typically found on mood measures, we assessed change of mood from the point at which all subjects believed that they would have a chance to help to the point at which some had and some had not been allowed to help. First, ratings on the seven evaluative-tone mood scales that subjects completed prior to the introduction of the experimental manipulations were averaged to form an index of mood at the point that all subjects believed that they would have a chance to help (Cronbach's alpha = .90). In all conditions, the average mood at this point was moderately positive, overall $M = 6.01$ on the 9-point scale ($1 = bad\ mood$, $9 = good\ mood$), with no reliable differences among the four experimental conditions (all Fs < 1.0).

Next, ratings on the same seven scales after the introduction of the experimental manipulations were averaged to form an index of mood after subjects either had or had not been allowed to help (Cronbach's alpha = .94). At this point too, the average mood was moderately positive ($M = 6.35$), although across the four experimental conditions there was a significant Prior Relief × Perform interaction, $F(1, 76) = 4.25$, $p < .05$, suggesting that the experimental manipulations had affected subjects' moods (both main effect Fs < 1.20). The mean response on this postmanipulation mood index for subjects in each of the four experimental conditions is reported in Table 1.

Empathic Response to the Other Person's Need

To determine whether the mood effects of the experimental manipulations reflected in Table 1 were those predicted by either the empathy-specific reward or the empathy–altruism hypothesis, we had to take into account the level of empathy reported in response to Brian's (Janet's) need. Therefore, we constructed an empathy index by averaging each subject's ratings of the six adjectives on the emotional response questionnaire that have been found in previous research to reflect empathy: *sympathetic, moved, compassionate, tender, warm,* and *soft-hearted* (Cronbach's alpha = .83). Scores on this empathy index were moderately high ($M = 3.81$) and variable ($SD = 1.27$) on the 7-point response scale ($1 = not\ at\ all$, $7 = extremely$). We then performed a median split on the empathy index ($Mdn = 3.90$). This split produced the 2 (low vs. high empathy) × 2 (no prior relief vs. prior relief) × 2 (perform helping task vs. not perform) design needed to test the predictions of the empathy-specific reward and the empathy–altruism hypotheses.

Mood Change for Low- and High-Empathy Subjects Who Were and Were Not Allowed to Help

To assess mood change in the 2 × 2 × 2 design, we created a mood change score by subtracting each subject's premanipulation mood score from his or her postmanipulation mood score.[3] The mean mood change for subjects in each cell of this design

Table 1
Mean Ratings on the Mood Index (After Introduction of the Experimental Manipulations) by Subjects Who Were or Were Not Allowed to Help: Study 1

Status of other's need	Perform helping task	Not perform helping task
No prior relief	6.56$_{a,b}$	5.84$_a$
Prior relief	6.29$_{a,b}$	6.73$_b$

Note. $N = 20$ in each cell. Only subjects in the no-prior-relief/perform cell could actually help. Ratings on the seven-item mood index were on a 9-point scale ($1 = bad\ mood$, $9 = good\ mood$). Cell means not sharing a common subscript differ, $p < .05$, by a t test.

Table 2
Mean Mood Change for Low- and High-Empathy Subjects Who Were or Were Not Allowed to Help: Study 1

	Low empathy		High empathy	
Other's need	Perform helping task	Not perform helping task	Perform helping task	Not perform helping task
No prior relief				
M	.13	.10	.50	−.30
n	12	11	8	9
Prior relief				
M	.27	.43	.31	1.36
n	10	10	10	10

Note. Positive mood-change scores indicate more positive mood after introduction of the experimental manipulations; negative scores indicate less positive mood after introduction of the experimental manipulations.

is reported in Table 2. The empathy-specific reward and the empathy–altruism hypotheses each had predicted a distinct 1 versus 3 pattern of mood change among high-empathy subjects. To test these predictions we conducted planned comparisons.

The empathy-specific reward hypothesis predicted that mood change among high-empathy subjects would be more positive in the one cell in which they were able to gain the empathy-specific rewards for helping, the no-prior-relief/perform cell, than in the other three cells. A planned comparison contrasting the mood change in this cell with the change in the other three high-empathy cells did not support this prediction, $F(1, 72) < 1.0$. Pairwise comparisons revealed that, as predicted, the mood change was more positive in the no-prior-relief/perform cell than in the no-prior-relief/not-perform cell, $t(72) = 1.70$, $p < .05$, one-tailed. Contrary to the predictions of the empathy-specific reward hypothesis, however, there was no reliable evidence of a more positive mood change in the no-prior-relief/

---

[3] As may be expected, analysis of subjects' premanipulation mood scores in the 2 × 2 × 2 design revealed a significant main effect for empathy, $F(1, 72) = 4.60$, $p < .04$; high-empathy subjects were in a worse mood ($M = 5.69$) than low-empathy subjects ($M = 6.28$). This main effect accounted for all reliable between-cell variance, residual $F(6, 72) = 0.37$.

Included among the 24 adjectives on the emotional response questionnaire were 6 that had previously been found to reflect feelings of personal distress caused by witnessing another person suffer: *upset, worried, disturbed, perturbed, distressed,* and *troubled* (see Batson, 1987). It was clear from discussions with subjects during debriefing that most interpreted these distress adjectives differently than had subjects in previous studies involving more immediate, higher impact need situations (for example, watching another person apparently receive, and react with obvious discomfort to, a series of electric shocks; Batson, Duncan, Ackerman, Buckley, & Birch, 1981; Batson, O'Quin, Fultz, Vanderplas, & Isen, 1983). Rather than reporting the degree to which they were distressed *by* witnessing the victim's potential suffering, most subjects in this study reported the degree to which they were distressed *for* the victim, a response that we would consider empathic. The issue of when the distress adjectives reflect a self-directed and when they reflect an other-directed response needs to be explored in future research.

perform cell than in either the prior-relief/perform cell, $t(72) = 0.15$, or the prior-relief/not-perform cell, $t(72) = -1.82$.

The empathy–altruism hypothesis predicted that mood change among high-empathy subjects would be more positive in the three cells in which Brian's (Janet's) need was relieved than in the one cell in which it was not (no prior relief/not perform). A planned comparison contrasting the mood change in this cell with the change in the other three high-empathy cells provided clear support for this prediction, $F(1, 72) = 7.09$, $p < .02$. Moreover, this effect appeared to be empathy specific; the same comparison among low-empathy subjects was not statistically significant, $F(1, 72) = 0.20$. Indeed, the 1 versus 3 comparison among high-empathy subjects predicted by the empathy-altruism hypothesis accounted for all reliable between-cell variance in mood change in the entire $2 \times 2 \times 2$ design, residual $F(6, 72) = 1.17$, ns, even though the 1 versus 3 pattern was only marginally stronger among high-empathy subjects than among low-empathy subjects, $F(1, 72) = 2.45$, $.10 < p < .15$. Pairwise comparisons revealed that the predicted differences among the high-empathy subjects were reliable between the no-prior-relief/not-perform cell and both the no-prior-relief/perform cell, $t(72) = 1.70$, $p < .05$, one-tailed, and the prior-relief/not-perform cell, $t(72) = 3.52$, $p < .001$, one-tailed. (The particularly high mood-change score in the prior-relief/not-perform cell probably reflected a combination of motives: pleasure that the victim's need was relieved and pleasure at relief from any lingering performance apprehension.) The difference between the no-prior-relief/not-perform cell and the prior-relief/perform cell was in the predicted direction but was not reliable, $t(72) = 1.31$.[4]

Task Performance

Further evidence that low- and high-empathy subjects differed in their goals is provided by the differences in task performance in the perform condition. Performance was assessed by the number of combinations that subjects correctly circled during the 2 min they worked on the final task. Mean performance scores for subjects in each cell are reported in Table 3. As can be seen, high-empathy subjects circled more combinations when Brian's (Janet's) welfare still depended on their performance ($M = 12.38$) than when it did not ($M = 10.20$), $t(36) = 3.37$, $p < .001$. In contrast, low-empathy subjects circled more combinations when the victim's welfare did not depend on their performance ($M = 12.40$) than when it did ($M = 10.83$), $t(36) = 2.43$, $p < .02$. An analysis of variance (ANOVA) revealed that although neither main effect was significant, both $Fs(1, 36) < 1.0$, the Empathy $\times$ Prior-Relief interaction was highly significant, $F(1, 36) = 16.78$, $p < .001$. This pattern of results suggests that high-empathy subjects were more motivated to do well on the task when Brian's (Janet's) welfare depended on their performance, whereas for low-empathy subjects the opposite was true. The higher performance of the low-empathy subjects in the prior-relief condition, although not predicted by either of the hypotheses tested, seemed readily interpretable as a product of (a) these subjects being more self-focused and (b) prior-relief information leading them to focus more on personal performance standards (Wicklund, 1975).

Table 3
Mean Number of Combinations Circled on the Task (Perform Condition Only): Study 1

Other's need	Low empathy	High empathy
No prior relief		
M	10.83	12.38
SD	1.27	1.51
n	12	8
Prior relief		
M	12.40	10.20
SD	0.97	1.87
n	10	10

Implications of Study 1

The empathy-specific reward hypothesis predicted that high-empathy subjects would feel better if they were the cause of relief of the victim's need than if they were not: Only if they were the cause would they be in line for the mood-enhancing rewards attendant on helping. Contrary to this prediction, subjects' self-reported mood provided no evidence that high-empathy subjects felt better when the victim's need was relieved by their own action than when it was relieved by other means. Thus, our data did not support the empathy-specific reward hypothesis.

Instead, both the mood change data and the performance data were entirely consistent with the claim of the empathy-altruism hypothesis that high-empathy subjects were directed toward the goal of having the victim's need reduced. If they could obtain this goal by their own action, these subjects worked relatively hard to do so and felt relatively good about the result. Even if they were not the cause, they felt relatively good if the victim's need was relieved.

Self-Presentation

Although our data patterned very much as predicted by the empathy–altruism hypothesis, it would be erroneous for us to conclude that they prove the validity of this hypothesis. Self-presentation (Jones & Pittman, 1982) provides a possible alternative explanation for at least some of our results consistent with the empathy–altruism hypothesis. Especially when subjects were informed that they would not be performing the helping task, their subsequent mood reports might have been affected by what they thought was the appropriate response. Subjects informed that the victim would still receive shocks might have thought they should report feeling bad; subjects informed that the victim would not receive shocks might have

---

[4] There was a sex difference on the empathy index; women reported more empathy for Janet ($M = 4.24$) than men reported for Brian ($M = 3.32$), $F(1, 72) = 11.55$, $p < .001$. Such a sex difference has often been found for self-report measures of empathy, but not for physiological measures, suggesting that the sexes differ more in the appropriateness of reporting empathic feelings than in the experience of them (Eisenberg & Miller, 1987). In this study, supplemental analyses revealed that the sex difference could not account for the observed pattern of mood change. The same pattern of significant results was found when the median split on empathy was performed separately within sex.

thought they should report feeling good. That this difference was reliable only among high-empathy subjects may be due to high-empathy subjects having a greater concern for positive self-presentation than low-empathy subjects. After all, to report that one feels a high degree of empathy for someone in need, as the high-empathy subjects had done, could itself be a product of a concern for positive self-presentation.

If self-presentation is to account for all of the support we found for the empathy–altruism hypothesis, then it must be a pervasive form of self-presentation. It must have affected not only subjects' self-reports of their mood but also their task performance. Still, the possibility that our results consistent with the empathy–altruism hypothesis were a product of self-presentation cannot be ruled out entirely.

Could self-presentation also account for our failure to find the pattern of results predicted by the empathy-specific reward hypothesis? We think not. As noted earlier, it seems possible that the mood change reported by subjects who were not to perform the task could be a product of self-presentation. However, the empathy-specific reward hypothesis also predicted a difference in mood between the no-prior-relief and the prior-relief conditions for subjects who were to perform the task. It seems implausible that the lack of difference in mood change between these two conditions was a product of self-presentation. In each of these conditions the victim's need had been relieved, so any concern to present oneself as feeling good because of this should have been the same in the two conditions. In the no-prior-relief condition, however, the relief had been caused by the subject's help; in the prior-relief condition it had not. To the degree that high-empathy subjects feel better only as a result of themselves having helped the person for whom they feel empathy, as the empathy-specific reward hypothesis claims, then we would expect our high-empathy subjects to report significantly more positive mood change in the no-prior-relief/perform cell than in the prior-relief/perform cell. They did not, $t(72) = 0.15$.

Thus, the lack of support for the empathy-specific reward hypothesis does not appear to be attributable to self-presentation. If, as intended, our strategy of measuring naturally occurring empathy provided maximal opportunity for any self-reward effects associated with empathy to appear, then our results seem to suggest that the motivation to help evoked by empathy is not directed toward obtaining special rewards available to the empathically aroused helper.

A Second Version of the Empathy-Specific Reward Hypothesis: Negative-State Relief

There is another version of the empathy-specific reward hypothesis, recently proposed by Cialdini et al. (1987). Rather than suggesting that special mood-enhancing rewards are associated with empathically induced helping, Cialdini et al. suggested that because feeling empathy for a person in need is a negative affective state, it produces an increased need for some mood-enhancing experience, including (but not limited to) the self-rewards following helping. In this version of the empathy-specific reward hypothesis, it is not the self-rewards that are empathy specific but the need for these rewards.

Study 1 was not designed to test the Cialdini et al. (1987) negative-state relief version of the empathy-specific reward hypothesis, and, frankly, we do not know whether our results contradict negative-state relief predictions. As far as we know, the negative-state relief literature has never addressed the question of whether, once a negative state is induced, removal of the inducing conditions is sufficient to relieve the negative state. Clearly, termination of these conditions has not been assumed to be necessary: Money, praise, or other forms of self-reward that do not remove the negative-state-inducing conditions have been assumed to work (Cialdini et al., 1987). Whether termination of the inducing conditions is sufficient is unclear.

If we assume that termination of the inducing conditions is sufficient to relieve a negative state, then the negative-state relief perspective predicts the same pattern of mood change in Study 1 as the empathy–altruism hypothesis, the pattern we observed. Therefore, a different research paradigm will be needed to provide a clear test of the relative merits of the negative-state relief version of the empathy-specific reward hypothesis and the empathy–altruism hypothesis.

TESTING THE EMPATHY-SPECIFIC PUNISHMENT HYPOTHESIS: PROVIDING JUSTIFICATION FOR NOT HELPING

The empathy-specific punishment hypothesis claims that people have learned through prior reinforcement that a special obligation to help—and special guilt and shame for failure to help—are attendant on feeling empathy. As a result, when people feel empathy they are faced with impending empathy-specific social or self-censure that is above and beyond any general punishment associated with not helping, and they are egoistically motivated to avoid these empathy-specific punishments.

Socially Administered Empathy-Specific Punishments

One version of the empathy-specific punishment hypothesis, proposed by Archer et al. (1981; see also Archer, 1984), assumes that empathy-specific punishments are socially administered. According to this version, empathy leads to increased helping only when the empathic individual anticipates negative social evaluation for failing to act in a manner consistent with his or her reported feelings of concern. To test this suggestion, Fultz et al. (1986) both manipulated and measured empathy for a person in need; they then assessed the rate of helping this person under conditions of high and low social evaluation. In the high social-evaluation condition, both the experimenter and the person in need would know if the research participant decided not to help; in the low social-evaluation condition, no one but the participant would know, not the experimenter, not even the person in need. Fultz et al. (1986) found that anticipated low social evaluation did not produce less helping than high social evaluation for either low- or high-empathy subjects. Knowing that there was no cause to worry about socially mediated punishments for a failure to help did not diminish the empathy–helping relationship.

Self-Administered Empathy-Specific Punishments

The Fultz et al. (1986) results clearly count against a version of the empathy-specific punishment hypothesis that assumes that the relevant punishments are socially administered. It does not, however, rule out the possibility that high-empathy individuals are motivated to help to avoid self-administered punishments and negative self-evaluation (Dovidio, 1984; Hoffman, 1976; Schwartz & Howard, 1981). To do this, one must manipulate expectations of self-punishment for not helping.

How is one to manipulate expectations of self-punishment? If these expectations have been internalized to the degree that they are automatic and invariant across all situations, then manipulation seems impossible. Yet, we suspect that few people, if any, have internalized procedures for self-punishment to such a degree. Even those who reflexively slap themselves with guilt and self-recrimination whenever they do wrong are likely to be sensitive to situational cues in determining when they have done wrong (see Milgram, 1963, 1974). Also, given the discomfort produced by guilt and self-recrimination, we suspect that most people will not reflexively self-punish but will, if possible, overlook their failures to do good. They will dole out self-punishments only in situations in which such failures are salient and inescapable.

If it is true that self-punishment will be avoided when possible, then expectation of such punishment after a failure to help may be effectively manipulated simply by varying ease of physical escape (i.e., the expectation of continued visual exposure to the suffering victim). Individuals who expect continued exposure should find their failure to help inescapable, so they should anticipate self-punishment. Those who expect no continued exposure should be able to put their failure out of sight and, following the old adage, out of mind, allowing self-punishment to be avoided. Batson et al. (1986) found that varying the ease of physical escape did indeed seem to have this effect on anticipated self-punishment.

If physical escape reduces anticipated self-punishment for not helping, then the studies that have used an ease of physical escape manipulation to test the empathy–altruism hypothesis against an aversive-arousal reduction explanation (Batson et al., 1981; Batson et al., 1983; Toi & Batson, 1982) may also provide a test of the empathy-specific punishment hypothesis. To the degree that these studies do provide a test, they do not offer support. These studies have consistently shown that individuals feeling high empathy for a person in need do not help less when physical escape is easy than when it is difficult.

Providing Justification for Not Helping

Although suggestive, the previous research using an ease of physical escape manipulation was not explicitly designed to test the empathy-specific punishment hypothesis. We sought to provide a more explicit test by reducing the expectation of self-punishment in a different way. If, as proposed earlier, there is leeway in interpreting a given failure to help as wrong and hence deserving of self-punishment, then the expectation of self-punishment may be reduced by providing some individuals with information that would justify not helping. We did not believe that this information could be provided directly by, for example, telling individuals not to feel guilty about not helping, because calling direct attention to the failure in this way may have the reverse effect; it may highlight the associated punishments. Instead, we wished to supply justifying information in a more subtle, indirect way. We were able to think of three ways this could be done: justifying not helping through others' inaction, justifying not helping through attributional ambiguity, and justifying not helping because qualifying to help is difficult.

Justification for Not Helping Through the Inaction of Others

One way to justify not helping, suggested by the study of social influence and social norms (Moscovici, 1985; Sherif, 1936), was to provide individuals confronted with a request for help with information about how their peers had responded to this request. If most peers had decided to help, then the belief that they too ought to help should be strengthened, leading them to anticipate more self-censure if they did not. Assuming that avoidance of this censure is their goal, helping should increase. If, however, most peers had decided not to help, then the belief that they too ought to help should be weakened, leading them to anticipate less self-censure if they did not. Assuming that avoidance of this censure is their goal, helping should decrease. Not to be confused with diffusion of responsibility, which occurs when one knows there are other potential helpers but not whether anyone else has helped (Darley & Latané, 1968), learning that others had decided not to help should produce exclusion from responsibility. It should reduce the sense that one ought to help in the situation.

Justification for Not Helping Through Attributional Ambiguity

A second way to justify not helping, suggested by the attributional-ambiguity technique developed by Snyder, Kleck, Strenta, and Mentzer (1979), was to confront individuals with a choice between one activity that would benefit the self and another that would help a person in need. For some potential helpers, helping-irrelevant attributes of the two activities could then be highlighted, as well as information that these helping-irrelevant attributes justified choosing the activity benefiting the self. This information should make these individuals less likely to anticipate self-punishment were they to choose this activity; they could justify their choice as being due to the helping-irrelevant attributes. If avoidance of punishment is their goal, helping should decrease. Snyder et al. (1979) had found a similar attributional-ambiguity technique effective in allowing individuals to justify an act that they may otherwise consider morally wrong: avoiding a handicapped person.

Justification for Not Helping Because Qualifying to Help is Difficult

A third way to justify not helping was to make qualifying to help difficult. Imagine a person who feels sorry for someone needing a bone-marrow transplant. Imagine further that, as the empathy-specific punishment hypothesis predicts, this person anticipates feeling guilty about not volunteering to undergo the rather painful marrow-donation operation that would help the needy individual. This person should be relieved, and content, to learn of a blood-type mismatch that disqualifies him or her as a possible donor. Even if no other source of help is available, he or she cannot be blamed for not helping.

What if, as the empathy–altruism hypothesis predicts, this person is concerned not about avoiding guilt but about reducing the needy individual's suffering? Learning about the blood-type mismatch should not cause relief and contentment. If no other source of help is available, the altruistically motivated individual should be upset over not being eligible.

In this example, qualifying to help is entirely out of the potential helper's control; blood types either match or they do not. Now imagine a slightly different situation in which, rather than potential helpers simply learning that they are or are not eligible, they must perform a task requiring effort in order to qualify to help. In such a situation, how hard the potential helper tries on the qualifying task should give us a behavioral measure of whether he or she is motivated to reduce the needy individual's suffering (which requires qualifying) or to avoid self-punishment (which does not). This should be true, however, only if failure to qualify can be justified. Failure should be justifiable if the performance standard on the qualifying task is so difficult that most people fail.

Having no basis for choosing between these three ways of providing justification for not helping, we conducted three studies, one using each technique. We reasoned that if the three studies produced consistent results, providing conceptual replication, then our confidence in the results of each would be increased. To add generality, we used different need situations and helping responses in the three studies. We also used different techniques for operationalizing empathy. In Study 2, we manipulated empathic feelings for the person in need; in Studies 3 and 4, we measured these feelings through self-reports.

Study 2: Justification for Not Helping Through the Inaction of Previous Potential Helpers

To test the empathy-specific punishment hypothesis by providing justification for a failure to help through the inaction of previous potential helpers, we needed a research paradigm in which (a) the empathy–helping relationship was known to occur and (b) previous helping (or lack of helping) by others would not eliminate the victim's need for help from the subject. The paradigm developed by Coke et al. (1978, Experiment 1) seemed to meet these requirements. In this paradigm, subjects learn of a young woman's need by listening to a (bogus) pilot radio newscast and are given an unexpected chance to help her. Empathy is manipulated by instructing subjects to take a particular perspective while listening to the newscast (Stotland, 1969).

To manipulate justification for not helping, we modified the pledge form used by Coke et al. (1978) to include spaces for the responses of 8 individuals. Seven spaces were already filled, ostensibly by previous subjects. In the low-justification condition, 5 of the 7 previous subjects had volunteered to help. In the high-justification condition, only 2 of the 7 had volunteered. To ensure that we had reproduced the empathy–helping relationship, we also included two replication cells, one low empathy and one high, in which the pledge form had space only for the subject's response. Individuals in these cells received no information about the helping of previous subjects.

Predictions

In the replication cells, both the empathy-specific punishment hypothesis and the empathy–altruism hypothesis predicted more overall helping in the high-empathy condition than in the low, because both assumed that increased empathy leads to increased helping. These two hypotheses differed, however, in their predictions for the effects of the justification manipulation on helping. The empathy-specific punishment hypothesis predicted less helping in the high-justification condition than in the low for subjects in both empathy conditions. In the low-empathy condition, subjects should be motivated to avoid general shame and guilt associated with a failure to help; in the high-empathy condition, subjects should be even more highly motivated to avoid shame and guilt because of the added empathy-specific punishments. In both conditions, it should be easier to avoid shame and guilt without having to help in the high-justification condition than in the low.

The empathy–altruism hypothesis predicted less helping in the high-justification condition than in the low for subjects in the low-empathy condition, but it predicted little or no effect of the justification manipulation in the high-empathy condition. It predicted that subjects in the high-empathy condition would be, at least partly, motivated to reduce the need of the person for whom empathy was felt; reduction in anticipated general and empathy-specific self-punishment provided by the justification information would not be relevant to reaching this goal. Across the four cells of the 2 (low vs. high empathy) × 2 (low vs. high justification) design, then, the pattern of results most consistent with the empathy–altruism hypothesis would be a 1 versus 3 pattern; the rate of helping in the low-empathy/high-justification cell should be lower than the rate in the other three cells.

Method

Subjects

For Study 2, 120 students (60 men, 60 women) in an introductory psychology course at the University of Kansas served as subjects, partially fulfilling a course requirement. By use of a randomized-block procedure, 20 subjects (10 men, 10 women) were assigned to each cell of the 2 (low vs. high empathy) × 2 (low vs. high justification for not helping) factorial design. In addition, 20 subjects (10 men, 10 women) were assigned to both the low- and high-empathy replication cells.[5]

Procedure

Ostensibly as part of an ongoing project for pilot testing new programs for the local university radio station, subjects listened to two pilot tapes, one for "Bulletin Board," a program announcing campus activities, and one for "News From the Personal Side," a program attempting to go beyond the facts of local news events "to report how these events affect the lives of the individuals involved." Subjects were asked to adopt

---

[5] Twelve additional students (8 men, 4 women) were excluded from the sample and replaced because of suspicion. Degree of suspicion did not differ reliably across the six conditions, $F(5, 126) = 1.43$, $p > .20$, and analyses the same as those reported here but including suspicious individuals produced the same, albeit somewhat weaker, pattern of reliable results.

a particular listening perspective for each broadcast, and reactions were measured by questionnaires. The specific procedure was similar to that used by Coke et al. (1978, Experiment 1), except for insertion of the justification manipulation and omission of their misattribution manipulation. Therefore, we present in detail only the experimental manipulations and dependent measures.

Manipulation of empathy. Before listening to the "News From the Personal Side" tape, which presented a young woman in need, subjects were given one of two listening perspectives. Subjects in the low-empathy condition were instructed to do the following:

Try to *focus on the technical aspects of the broadcast.* Try to concentrate on those techniques and devices that are used to make the broadcast have an impact on the listener.

Subjects in the high-empathy condition were instructed to do the following:

Try to *imagine how the person who is being interviewed feels* about what has happened and how the events have affected her life. Try to feel the full impact of what this person has been through and how she feels as a result.

Subjects were led to believe that all previous research participants had been given the same listening-perspective instructions they received. This ensured that, when interpreting the justification information, subjects would perceive the other research participants to be responding to the same helping situation as they were. The experimenter was blind to which listening-perspective instructions subjects received.

Listening to the "News From the Personal Side" *tape.* On the "News From the Personal Side" tape, a male announcer interviewed Katie Banks, a senior at the university. Katie's parents and a sister had recently been killed in an automobile crash. Her parents did not have life insurance, and Katie was desperately struggling to support her surviving younger brother and sister while she finished her last year of college. If she did not finish, she would have to put the children up for adoption.

After the tape, the experimenter returned and prepared to administer a reaction questionnaire, only to find that an apparent mimeograph malfunction had left a blank streak across the page, rendering several questions illegible. While the experimenter went to get another copy, the subject was directed to read two letters that the professor in charge of the study had asked be given to participants.

Katie's request for help. The first letter was from the professor. He thanked subjects for participating in the research and explained that it had occurred to him that some participants may want to help Katie, so he had encouraged her to write a letter telling what they could do if they wished. The second letter was from Katie; she presented subjects with a range of possible ways to help: sitting with her younger brother and sister while she attended her night classes, fixing things around the house, providing transportation, helping with telephone calls, and stuffing envelopes for a fundraising project.

Manipulation of justification for not helping. Enclosed with the two letters was a response form on which subjects were to indicate whether they wished to help Katie. In both justification conditions, this form had spaces for the responses of 8 subjects; the first 7 were already filled with the handwritten names of same-sex individuals (actually fictitious). In the low-justification condition, 5 of the 7 previous subjects had volunteered to help Katie: 3 subjects volunteered 1 to 2 hr, 1 subject 3 to 5 hr, and 1 subject 6 to 8 hr. In the high-justification condition, only 2 of the 7 had helped: 1 subject volunteered 1 to 2 hr, the other 3 to 5 hr. (Subjects in the justification conditions filled in the last blank on the form so that they could be assured that the form with their name on it would not be seen by other subjects. This avoided concern over praise or censure from friends or acquaintances who could learn of their response.) In the replication condition, the form provided exactly the same response options as in the justification conditions but was designed for only one person's response; subjects were not provided with information about the action of their peers.

To ensure that subjects did not feel that they were Katie's last chance for help, the experimenter made it clear that theirs was not the only response form and that Katie's request would be presented to other research participants. The experimenter was blind to which version of the response form subjects received.

Dependent measure: volunteering to help Katie. Each version of the response form asked subjects to provide their name, to indicate whether they wished to help Katie and, if so, to check the number of hours they wished to volunteer: 1 to 2, 3 to 5, 6 to 8, or 9 to 10 hr. The amount of time, if any, that subjects volunteered to help Katie was the dependent measure of helping.

Ancillary measures. After subjects filled out the response form, the experimenter returned, collected the form, and gave them a legible copy of the reaction questionnaire. In addition to asking subjects how interesting, informative, and worthwhile they felt the broadcast was, this questionnaire included an item concerning Katie's need (i.e., "How great is the need of the person who was interviewed?") and two items designed to check the effectiveness of the empathy manipulation (i.e., "While listening to this broadcast, to what extent did you concentrate on the technical aspects of the broadcast?" "To what extent did you concentrate on the feelings of the person being interviewed?").

The experimenter also gave subjects a help-opportunity questionnaire. The experimenter explained that although this questionnaire was not part of the pilot-testing study, the professor in charge wished to learn how research participants felt about being given the chance to help Katie. Included on this questionnaire was an item designed to check the effect of the justification manipulation on perceived obligation to help Katie: "Do you believe that KU students ought to help Katie?"

Debriefing. Subjects were left alone to complete these questionnaires; then they were carefully debriefed, thanked for their participation, and excused.

Results and Discussion

Perception of Katie's Need

On the reaction questionnaire, subjects indicated the magnitude of Katie's need ($1 = $ *very little,* $9 = $ *very great*). Subjects in all six conditions perceived her need to be great (cell Ms ranged from 7.65 to 8.45; overall $M = 8.17$), with no reliable differences for either main effect or for the interaction. Apparently, the perspective-taking instructions used to manipulate empathy did not prevent subjects in the low-empathy condition from perceiving Katie to be in considerable need. Moreover, as intended, subjects perceived her need to be as great when 5 of 7 previous subjects had helped ($M = 8.38$) as when only 2 of 7 had helped ($M = 8.05$) or when there was no information about the helping of previous subjects ($M = 8.08$).

Effectiveness of the Empathy Manipulation

Subjects also indicated on the reaction questionnaire the extent to which they concentrated on (a) the technical aspects of the broadcast and (b) the feelings of the person being interviewed ($1 = $ *not at all,* $9 = $ *very much* for each question). Across all six conditions, subjects in the low-empathy condition reported more concentration on the technical aspects ($M = 6.70$) than did subjects in the high-empathy condition ($M = 4.55$), $F(1, 114) = 30.71$, $p < .001$. In addition, subjects in the low-empathy condition reported less concentration on feelings

($M = 6.63$) than did subjects in the high-empathy condition ($M = 7.95$), $F(1, 114) = 19.31$, $p < .001$. For neither measure was there a significant main effect for the justification manipulation or interaction, all $Fs(2, 114) < 1.80$. We concluded that the empathy manipulation was successful.[6]

Effectiveness of the Justification for Not Helping Manipulation

After about one third of the subjects were run, we began asking subjects during debriefing (before the true purpose of the research was revealed) for the total number of previous subjects whose names appeared on the response form and the number who volunteered to help Katie. These reports were available for 54 of the 80 subjects in the two justification conditions. Creating a proportion for each subject by dividing the reported number of previous subjects volunteering by the total and then averaging these proportions, we found that subjects in the low-justification condition recalled previous subjects helping more often ($M = .72$) than did subjects in the high-justification condition ($M = .33$), $F(1, 50) = 231.53$, $p < .0001$. These mean proportions closely approximated the proportions that subjects in the two conditions had actually been given: .71 (5 of 7) in the low-justification condition and .29 (2 of 7) in the high. Neither the empathy main effect nor the interaction was significant, $Fs(1, 50) < 1.60$. Thus, even though subjects in the justification conditions were not instructed to attend to the information about the helping of others, it seemed clear that they did.

The manipulation-check question on the help-opportunity questionnaire provided evidence that this information had the intended effect on perceptions of the obligation to help Katie. When asked whether they believed students ought to help Katie ($1 = not at all$, $9 = very much$), subjects in the low-justification condition felt more strongly that they should ($M = 7.45$) than did subjects in the high-justification condition ($M = 6.55$), $F(1, 76) = 4.47$, $p < .04$. Neither the empathy main effect, $F(1, 76) = 1.38$, nor the interaction, $F(1, 76) < 1.0$, were significant. In the replication condition, perceived obligation was intermediate in both the low-empathy condition ($M = 6.75$) and the high ($M = 6.95$), with no reliable difference between these conditions, $t(114) = 0.34$.

Effect of Justification for Not Helping on Helping in the Low- and High-Empathy Conditions

Helping responses were coded in two ways. First, the proportion of subjects who volunteered any amount of time served as a dichotomous measure of helping ($0 = no help$, $1 = help$); second, scores on the 5-point scale of number of hours volunteered ($0 = 0$ hr, $1 = 1$ to 2 hr, $2 = 3$ to 5 hr, $3 = 6$ to 8 hr, and $4 = 9$ to 10 hr) served as a continuous measure.

Roughly paralleling the results reported by Coke et al. (1978), who had found that 19 of 44 subjects (.43) volunteered to help Katie, we found that 61 of our 120 subjects (.51) volunteered some time. Given that almost half of our subjects did not help, scores on the continuous measure were badly skewed. Therefore, we adopted the dichotomous measure as our major index of helping, but as a check we also analyzed the scaled measure. The proportion of subjects volunteering to help Katie in each

Table 4
Proportion of Subjects in Each Justification Condition Who Helped in Low- and High-Empathy Conditions: Study 2

Justification condition	Low empathy		High empathy	
	%	M	%	M
Replication condition (no justification information)	.35	.45	.70	1.20
Low justification for not helping	.55	.85	.70	.95
High justification for not helping	.15	.20	.60	.80

Note. $N = 20$ (10 men, 10 women) per cell. Means are for the scaled measure of helping (0 = no helping, 1 = 1 to 2 hr, 2 = 3 to 5 hr, 3 = 6 to 8 hr, and 4 = 9 to 10 hr).

of the six cells is presented in Table 4; the means on the scaled measure are also shown.

Table 4 reveals that we successfully replicated the empathy-helping relationship in the replication cells, in which subjects were provided no information about the helping response of others. As predicted by both the empathy-specific punishment and the empathy–altruism hypotheses, the proportion of subjects helping was lower in the low-empathy condition (.35) than in the high (.70), $z = 2.26$, $p < .02$ (normal-approximation analysis of arc sine transformed proportions; see Langer & Abelson, 1972; Winer, 1971).

Effects of the justification manipulation on the proportion of subjects helping in each cell of the 2 (low vs. high empathy) × 2 (low vs. high justification for not helping) design appear in the last two rows of Table 4. As can be seen, the pattern of helping across the four cells of the 2 × 2 design is consistent with predictions from the empathy–altruism hypothesis: lower helping in the low-empathy/high-justification cell than in the other three. A planned comparison testing this 1 versus 3 pattern was highly significant, $\chi^2(1, N = 80) = 15.39$, $p < .001$, and accounted for all reliable between-cell variance, residual $\chi^2(2, N = 80) = 1.35$. Pairwise comparisons revealed that the rate of helping in the low-empathy/high-justification cell was significantly lower than in each of the other three cells, all $zs > 2.75$, $ps < .005$, and there were no reliable differences among the other three (all $zs < 1.0$).

Analysis of the scaled measure of helping produced exactly the same pattern of significant effects, although the pattern was a little weaker than for the dichotomous measure, presumably

---

[6] There was a significant effect of sex on reported concentration on Katie's feelings; women reported more concentration on her feelings ($M = 7.60$) than did men ($M = 6.98$), $F(1, 108) = 4.31$, $p < .04$. However, there were no interactions of sex with the experimental manipulations, all $Fs(1, 108) < 1.70$. The main effect for sex suggested that women either were more inclined than men to imagine the feelings of our female victim or were more inclined to present themselves as having imagined her feelings. In either case, given the absence of interactions, this main effect did not call into question the effectiveness of the listening-perspective instructions in focusing both men and women subjects' attention either away from or toward Katie's feelings about her plight.

due to the skew. For the scaled measure, the planned comparison testing the 1 versus 3 pattern predicted by the empathy–altruism hypothesis was highly significant, $F(1, 76) = 11.04$, $p < .001$, and accounted for all reliable between-cell variance, residual $F(2, 76) < 1.0$. Mean helping in the low-empathy/high-justification cell was significantly lower than in each of the other three cells, all $ts(76) > 2.40$, $ps < .02$, and there were no reliable differences among the other three, all $ts(76) < 1.0$.

These analyses indicated that subjects' helping responses conformed closely to the pattern predicted by the empathy–altruism hypothesis. There was no evidence of the significant effect of justification manipulation in the high-empathy condition that had been predicted by the empathy-specific punishment hypothesis.

Finally, some empirical evidence for the validity of our manipulation-check question concerning perceived obligation was provided by the correlation between responses to this question and helping. Across the entire design, subjects who reported feeling more strongly that students ought to help Katie were indeed somewhat more likely to help, $r_{pbis}(118) = .23$, $p < .02$, and to help more, $r(118) = .26$, $p < .01$. There were no reliable between-cell differences in these correlations, although they tended to be highest in the high-empathy/low-justification cell (both $rs = .32$) and lowest in the low-empathy/high-justification cell ($rs = .04$ and .14 for the dichotomous and scaled helping measures, respectively).

Study 3: Justification for Not Helping Through Attributional Ambiguity

Study 3 provided a generalized replication of the same Empathy × Justification design used in Study 2. In Study 3, however, the need situation, helping response, and both independent variables—empathy and justification for not helping—were operationalized differently. The person in need was a same-sex peer who had been (ostensibly) randomly assigned to receive a moderately uncomfortable electric shock for each error he or she made on a task. Subjects were to perform a different task; they would have a choice of two options and would not be punished for errors. Instead, for each correct response on Option A, they would receive one ticket for a raffle with a prize worth $30; for each correct response on Option B, they would reduce by one the shocks the peer was to receive. Spending time working on Option B rather than on Option A constituted helping. An attempt to manipulate empathy by varying similarity to the person in need proved ineffective; our similarity information had no reliable effect on either subjects' reports of empathy or their helping. Therefore, we relied on subjects' self-reports of empathy to define low- and high-empathy groups. As pointed out earlier, this measurement technique has proved as effective as experimental manipulation in operationalizing empathy as an independent variable and in producing the empathy–helping relationship.

Justification for not helping was manipulated by varying information about helping-irrelevant attributes of the two task options. In the low-justification condition both options involved either numbers or letters, and no information was given about other people's preferences. In the high-justification condition, the two options differed in that one involved numbers and the

other letters. Subjects in this condition were told that most people prefer to work with the numbers (letters), whichever appeared on the nonhelpful Option A. (Pairing of the numbers and letters with the two options was counterbalanced.)

We reasoned that individuals who were given two different task options and were told that most people prefer one over the other would be provided with attributional ambiguity for their choice of that option (Snyder et al., 1979). They could attribute choosing to work on the nonhelpful option to the type of task (numbers or letters) rather than to selfishness, reducing anticipated self-punishment. Individuals for whom both options involved either numbers or letters could not justify choosing to work on Option A in this way.

Predictions

Predictions for Study 3 were essentially the same as for Study 2. The empathy-specific punishment hypothesis predicted less helping in the high-justification condition than in the low for both low- and high-empathy subjects. The empathy–altruism hypothesis predicted less helping in the high-justification condition than in the low for low-empathy subjects but little or no effect of the justification manipulation among high-empathy subjects. Across the four cells of the 2 (low vs. high empathy) × 2 (low vs. high justification) design, then, the pattern of results most consistent with the empathy–altruism hypothesis would be the same 1 versus 3 pattern as in Study 2; the rate of helping in the low-empathy/high-justification cell should be lower than the rate in the other three cells.

Method

Subjects

For Study 3, 88 students (48 men, 40 women) in an introductory psychology course at the University of Kansas served as subjects, partially fulfilling a course requirement. Within sex, a randomized-block procedure was used to assign subjects to the two justification conditions, 43 (23 men, 20 women) to the low-justification condition and 45 (25 men, 20 women) to the high. (A blocking error caused the unequal number of men in the cells.)[7]

Procedure

Because the procedure was very similar to the one used in Study 1, we discuss in detail only the new features. As before, subjects were told that the study concerned "how a variety of task characteristics and outcome consequences affect people's task performance and attitudes." This time, however, the task characteristics being examined were (a) whether one has a choice of tasks on which to work; (b) for whom one's performance has consequences—for self only, for another person only, or both; (c) the kind of outcome consequences—positive, negative, or neutral; and (d) complexity of the task situation—simple (varying only in whether the consequences for self are positive, negative, or neutral) or complex (varying on choice, type of consequences, and for whom).

---

[7] Thirteen additional students (5 men, 8 women) were excluded from the sample and replaced because of suspicion. The suspicion rate did not differ reliably between the justification conditions, $\chi^2(1, N = 101) = 0.11$, and analyses the same as those reported here but including suspicious individuals produced the same pattern of significant effects.

Positive consequences were tickets in a raffle for a $30 gift certificate; negative consequences were mild but uncomfortable electric shocks; and neutral consequences were just information.

Condition 9: choice of tasks, one benefiting self and one benefiting another person. All subjects were informed that they had (ostensibly randomly) been assigned to Condition 9, a complex task situation in which they would have a choice between two task options, both with positive consequences. They could divide their time between the two options in any way they chose: Option A would have positive consequences for them, and Option B would have positive consequences for the person assigned to the simple task situation. A sheet provided more detailed information about Condition 9:

> Since you have been assigned to the positive consequences condition, you will be given a raffle ticket for every point you receive on Option A. Depending on the condition initially assigned to the person in the simple task situation—negative or positive—he or she will be given fewer shocks or more raffle tickets for each point you receive on Option B.

The sheet also informed subjects that before performing their task they would get to know something about the person assigned to the simple task situation (Brian for men, Janet for women) by listening as he (she) talked to them briefly over an audio intercom.

Once subjects read this sheet, the experimenter told them that Brian (Janet) had been initially assigned to the negative consequences condition; he (she) would receive an electric shock for each error on his (her) task. Each point the subject received on Option B would eliminate one of those shocks. Brian (Janet) was not aware of the subject's opportunity to help him (her) avoid the shocks.

Empathic reaction to learning of the other person's need. After being given this information, subjects were left alone to listen to Brian (Janet) over the intercom. As before, what they heard was actually a prerecorded tape on which Brian (Janet) confessed to having concern about the shocks and a desire to get as few as possible.

Subjects next completed an emotional response questionnaire designed to assess their empathic feelings toward Brian (Janet). This questionnaire listed 24 adjectives describing different emotional states. Subjects were to indicate on 7-point scales (1 = *not at all*, 7 = *extremely*) how they were feeling. Included in the list were 5 adjectives that had been found in previous research (Batson, 1987) to reflect feelings of empathy: *sympathetic, moved, compassionate, tender,* and *softhearted.* (*Warm* was inadvertently omitted from the questionnaire in this study.)

The combination-circling task. When subjects finished this questionnaire, the experimenter returned with the two task options. Each option consisted of a page filled with lines of randomly ordered numbers or letters. The task was to work from left to right, line by line, circling all combinations of 13 and 47 (or AB and JX) on the page. All numbers (letters) that were not part of one of these combinations were to be drawn through with a horizontal line. Each combination correctly circled was worth 1 point. Subjects would have 120 s to work on the task; they could divide this time between the two options in any way they chose.

Manipulation of justification for not helping. For subjects in the low-justification condition, both Option A and Option B involved circling either exactly the same combinations of numbers or exactly the same combinations of letters; the only difference between the two options was the order of lines on the page, which was varied to prevent copying. When showing the options to subjects in this condition, the experimenter simply said, "You can work on whichever option you wish."

For subjects in the high-justification condition, one option involved circling combinations of numbers, the other circling combinations of letters. Pairing of the numbers and letters with the two options was counterbalanced. When showing the options to subjects in this condition, if Option A involved numbers the experimenter said, "Some people seem to prefer working on numbers and some seem to prefer letters, although

most people seem to prefer numbers. You can, however, work on whichever option you wish." If Option A involved letters, the words *numbers* and *letters* were reversed. The experimenter was blind to the subject's justification condition until just prior to presenting the options.

Dependent measure: choosing to reduce Brian's (Janet's) shocks by working on Option B. The experimenter then started the timer and left subjects alone for 120 s to perform the task. The dependent measure of helping was the ratio of the number of correct combinations subjects circled on Option B divided by the total number they circled.

Debriefing. After subjects completed the task, they were carefully debriefed. They were also informed that a raffle for a $30 gift certificate would actually be held and that they would receive 10 tickets regardless of their task performance. Following debriefing, subjects were thanked for their participation and excused. Once all 88 subjects had been run, the raffle was held and the gift certificate awarded to the winner.

Results and Discussion

Empathic Response to Brian's (Janet's) Need

To provide an index of empathic reaction to Brian's (Janet's) need, responses to the five adjectives on the emotional response questionnaire that had been found in previous research to reflect empathy were averaged to form an index of empathic emotion (Cronbach's alpha = .87). Scores on this empathy index did not differ across justification conditions, $t(84) < 1.0$ (overall $M = 3.88$). We then performed a median split to identify low- and high-empathy subjects ($Mdn = 4.01$). Crossing this low- versus high-empathy classification with the justification manipulation produced the Empathy × Justification design needed to test the empathy-specific punishment and empathy-altruism hypotheses.[8]

Effect of Justification for Not Helping on the Helping of Low- and High-Empathy Subjects

The measure of helping was the ratio of number of combinations correctly circled on Option B—the option that would reduce the number of shocks Brian (Janet) would receive—divided by total number of combinations correctly circled on both options. This ratio could range in value from 0 if all of the combinations circled were on Option A, the option that would earn tickets for the $30 raffle, to 1.0 if all of the combinations circled were on Option B. The mean helping response on this ratio scale for subjects in each cell of Study 3 is presented in Table 5.

As can be seen, the pattern of helping across the four cells of the 2 × 2 design was highly consistent with the predictions of the empathy-altruism hypothesis: lower helping in the low-empathy/high-justification cell than in the other three. A planned comparison testing this 1 versus 3 pattern was highly significant,

---

[8] As in Study 1, we found a significant sex difference on the empathy index; women reported more empathy for Janet ($M = 4.36$) than men reported for Brian ($M = 3.47$), $F(1, 84) = 9.17$, $p < .003$. This sex difference could not, however, account for the observed pattern of helping; the same pattern of significant results was found when the median split on empathy was performed separately within sex.

We did not attempt to create an index of personal distress in this study because, as in Study 1, our distress adjectives seemed to measure an other-oriented, empathic response in this research paradigm.

Table 5

Mean Helping in Each Justification Condition by Subjects Reporting Low and High Empathy: Study 3

Justification condition	Self-reported empathy	
	Low	High
Low justification for not helping		
M	.65	.61
n	21	22
High justification for not helping		
M	.28	.50
n	23	22

Note. Helping was measured by the ratio of combinations circled on Option B (which reduced shocks to the victim) divided by the total number of combinations circled on both options.

$F(1, 84) = 12.69$, $p < .001$, and accounted for all reliable between-cell variance, residual $F(2, 84) < 1.0$. Pairwise comparisons revealed that the rate of helping in the low-empathy/high-justification cell was significantly lower than in each of the other three cells, all $ts(84) > 2.10$, $ps < .04$, and there were no reliable differences among the other three, all $ts(84) < 1.35$. There were no reliable sex effects on helping.

The results of Study 3 provided a clear conceptual replication of the results of Study 2. There was no evidence of the significant effect of the justification manipulation on the helping of high-empathy subjects predicted by the empathy-specific punishment hypothesis. Instead, subjects' helping responses conformed closely to the pattern predicted by the empathy–altruism hypothesis. In Study 4, we again tested the empathy-specific punishment hypothesis using a third technique to provide justification for not helping: We varied the difficulty of the performance standard on a task that subjects performed in order to qualify to help.

Study 4: Justification for Not Helping Because Qualifying to Help is Difficult

If subjects motivated to avoid self-punishment are told that the performance standard to qualify to help is easy enough that most people meet it, they should not feel that they can gracefully justify failing to qualify. Therefore, to avoid self-recrimination, they should try to do well on the qualifying task. If they are told, however, that the performance standard is so difficult that most people do not meet it, they can easily justify failing to qualify. Knowing this, they should not have to help. Instead, they should either (a) decline to offer help because of the low objective probability of their being qualified or (b) offer to help but not try very hard on the qualifying task, thus ensuring that they do not qualify. Bluntly put, they should take a dive.

If, on the other hand, individuals altruistically motivated to reduce the suffering of the person in need are confronted with this situation, they should not take a dive. They should offer help regardless of the difficulty of the qualifying standard. They should also try harder at the qualifying task when the standard is difficult than when it is easy. This is because only by offering

to help and qualifying can they reach their altruistic goal of reducing the other person's suffering.

To test the relative merits of the empathy-specific punishment and the empathy–altruism hypotheses using this logic, we needed a research paradigm in which (a) helping is personally costly, (b) the empathy–helping relationship is known to occur, and (c) it is plausible to introduce a qualifying task for helping. The shock paradigm developed by Batson et al. (1981; see also Batson et al., 1983, 1986) seemed to meet these requirements.

Introducing a Qualifying Task Into the Shock Paradigm

In this paradigm, female subjects watched over closed-circuit TV (actually a videotape) as a young woman, Elaine, appeared to receive electric shocks while performing a digit recall task. Elaine's reactions made it clear that she was finding the shocks highly uncomfortable. After Elaine completed only two of her scheduled 10 digit recall trials, subjects were unexpectedly given a chance to relieve her distress by taking the remaining eight trials, and the shocks, in her stead.

We introduced a qualifying task into this shock paradigm by explaining that we were interested in studying auditory numeric facility, measured by the digit recall task, of only those individuals who displayed a certain level of visual numeric facility, which was measured by a digit scan recognition task. Thus, even if subjects were willing to help Elaine by taking her place, they would be allowed to do so only if they met a certain performance standard on the digit scan recognition task.

Operationalizing Empathy Through Self-Reported Predominant Emotional Response

As in Study 1, we operationalized empathy as an independent variable through measurement rather than manipulation. Batson et al. (1983) pointed out that when assessing self-reported empathy in a high-impact, proximate situation such as watching a peer receive shocks, it is important to differentiate empathic feelings from feelings of personal distress. Both personal distress and empathy are possible emotional reactions to witnessing another person suffer, and they often occur together. Feelings of personal distress are more self-oriented; they are the upset and discomfort one feels as a result of witnessing another person's suffering. Feelings of empathy, on the other hand, are more other-oriented; they are the sympathy and compassion one feels for the suffering person. There are both theoretical and empirical grounds for believing that these two emotional reactions to witnessing another person suffer have different motivational consequences: Whereas the motivation to help associated with feeling empathy may be altruistic, the motivation to help associated with personal distress seems clearly egoistic (see Batson, 1987, for a discussion of the distinction between personal distress and empathy and a review of the evidence).

In order to assess the nature of the motivation to help associated with self-reported empathy in a situation in which both distress and empathy are felt, Batson et al. (1983) recommended the use of an index of predominant emotional response, created by subtracting each subject's score on an index of personal distress from his or her score on an index of empathy. This index of predominant emotional response should reflect the relative strength of competing motives associated with distress and empathy. If, for example, an individual experiencing a high degree of empathy were experiencing an even higher degree of personal distress, motivation associated with the latter emotion should dominate.

Following the recommendation of Batson et al. (1983), we operationalized empathy as an independent variable by performing a median split on subjects' scores on an index of predominant emotional response. This split produced two groups, one experiencing a relative predominance of personal distress and the other a relative predominance of empathy.

Ease of Escape

One final aspect of the shock paradigm needed to be considered. In previous studies using this paradigm, ease of physical escape from Elaine's suffering had been manipulated. This was done by leading some subjects to believe that even if they chose not to help, they would not watch Elaine take the remaining shocks (easy escape); other subjects believed that if they chose not to help, they would watch Elaine's remaining eight trials (difficult escape). Because we wished to examine the effects of difficulty of the performance standard both on whether subjects would offer to help and, if they offered, on their performance on the qualifying task, we decided that it was best to lead all subjects to believe that if they chose not to help, they would watch Elaine's remaining eight trials. In previous studies, this difficult-escape information had produced a high rate of helping among subjects reporting a predominance of distress, as well as among those reporting a predominance of empathy.

Predictions

The empathy-specific punishment hypothesis predicted that the difficulty of the qualifying standard would have much the same effect on the behavior of subjects feeling a relative predominance of distress and those feeling a relative predominance of empathy because the motivation to help of subjects in both groups would be egoistic: Either the rate of helping or performance on the qualifying task, or both, should be lower when the qualifying standard was difficult than when it was easy. The empathy-altruism hypothesis made the same prediction for subjects feeling a relative predominance of distress. It predicted, however, that the rate of helping of subjects feeling a relative predominance of empathy should be high regardless of the difficulty of the qualifying standard and that, if anything, the performance of these subjects on the qualifying task should be higher when the qualifying standard was difficult than when it was easy. Only by both volunteering to help and qualifying could they reach the altruistic goal of relieving Elaine's suffering.

Method

Subjects

In Study 4, 60 female students in an introductory psychology course at the University of Kansas served as subjects, partially fulfilling a course requirement. By use of a randomized-block procedure, 25 subjects were assigned to an easy qualifying-standard condition and 35 to a difficult qualifying-standard condition. More subjects were assigned to the difficult-standard condition because we anticipated a lower rate of helping in that condition (at least among subjects reporting a relative predominance of distress), and we wished to ensure that even in this condition we had enough subjects offering help that we could meaningfully analyze performance on the qualifying task. Nine additional students (5 in the easy- and 4 in the difficult-standard condition) were excluded from the design and replaced because they expressed suspicion that the confederate was not actually receiving shocks.

Procedure

Subjects were run individually. Because the experimental procedure was much the same as that used by Batson et al. (1986), we describe in detail only the new features.

Initial administration of the digit scan recognition task. When subjects arrived, they were first asked to complete a digit scan recognition task, ostensibly while waiting for the other scheduled participant, Elaine (actually fictitious). Subjects were told that the purpose of the digit scan task would become clear later. The task was the same as in Study 1; it involved working for 120 s from left to right, line by line down a page filled with randomly ordered digits, circling all occurrences of the combinations 13 and 47. Unknown to subjects, this was exactly the same task they would later be asked to perform in order to qualify to help Elaine. This initial administration served to familiarize them with the task and provided a context for introducing the qualifying-standard manipulation.

Manipulation of qualifying-standard difficulty. After performing the task, subjects read an introduction that described the study as being concerned with the effects of aversive conditions on task performance and impression projection. Subjects learned that one participant would serve as a worker, performing a numeric recall task while receiving mild electric shocks at random. The other participant would serve as the observer, watching over closed-circuit TV while the worker performed the recall task. The observer's job was to form and report a general impression of the worker.

The introduction also explained that the numeric recall task performed by the worker involved only one aspect of numeric facility: auditory recall of number sequences. Because it was necessary that anyone serving as the worker have numeric facility, everyone first completed the digit scan task, which was a visual measure of numeric facility. The introduction explained that, "Only individuals who display numeric facility by performing at a certain standard on the digit scan task will be able to be the worker on the numeric recall task."

The experimental manipulation of qualifying-standard difficulty was introduced in the last paragraph of the introduction. In the easy qualifying-standard condition, subjects read the following: "A moderately stringent standard has been adopted for performance on the digit scan task. On the average, about 7 of 10 college students meet the standard." In the difficult qualifying-standard condition, subjects read the following: "An extremely difficult standard has been adopted for performance on the digit scan task. On the average, only 1 of 5 college students meet the standard, so do not be surprised or disturbed if you do not." In both conditions subjects were informed that "numeric facility is not generally associated with intelligence or mathematical ability. It is simply a capacity that some people display and some do not." The experimenter did not know which version of the introduction a subject received and so remained blind to the subject's experimental condition.

Observer role. Once subjects had read the introduction and agreed to participate in the study, they were all (ostensibly randomly) assigned to the observer role; Elaine was assigned to the worker role. Noting that Elaine had met the standard on the digit scan task, the experimenter commented, "Since you'll be the observer, we don't need your digit scan task; I didn't even score it," and tossed it in the wastebasket.

Self-reported emotional response to Elaine's distress. Subjects were then left alone to observe Elaine over closed-circuit TV as she performed 10 digit recall trials while receiving the shocks. By the end of the second trial, the shocks seemed to be hurting Elaine so much that Marsha, the assistant administering the shocks, interrupted the procedure and asked whether Elaine was all right. Elaine hesitantly said yes, then asked for a glass of water before going on. Marsha agreed and left to get the water.

During this break, the experimenter spoke to subjects over an audio intercom, explaining that because there was going to be a short delay, they should complete the first impression questionnaire. This questionnaire, called the emotional response questionnaire, consisted of a list of 28 adjectives describing emotions. Subjects were asked to indicate on 7-point scales (1 = *not at all,* 7 = *extremely*) how much they were experiencing each emotion as a result of observing the worker. The list of emotions included adjectives that have been found in past research (Batson, 1987; Batson et al., 1983; Coke et al., 1978; Toi & Batson, 1982) to reflect the two distinct vicarious emotions: personal distress and empathy.

After about 90 s, Marsha returned and asked Elaine whether she had ever before been bothered by electric shock. Elaine then confessed to having had a traumatic experience with shock as a child. (This information was provided in order to ensure that subjects would consider Elaine's extreme reaction to the shocks atypical and would not expect to find the shocks as unpleasant if they chose to take her place.) Hearing this, Marsha suggested that the experiment be stopped, but Elaine expressed a firm desire to continue: "I started; I want to finish. I'll go on. . . . I know your experiment is important, and I want to do it." At this point, Marsha had an idea: The observer was also an introductory psychology student; maybe she would be willing to help Elaine out by taking her place as the worker. Elaine, with a mixture of reluctance and relief, agreed to allow the observer to be asked. The tape ended with Marsha turning off the video equipment to go check with the experimenter about this possibility.

Helping opportunity. About 20 s later, the experimenter's voice, sounding somewhat agitated, came over the intercom and outlined the subject's options: either to remain as the observer, watching Elaine's remaining eight trials, or to help Elaine out by taking her place "doing the recall task and receiving the shocks." The experimenter then added the following:

Oh, I almost forgot. Even if you volunteer to take Elaine's place, you'll be able to do so only if you meet the qualifying standard on the digit scan task—you know, the number-circling task on which, on the average, [*easy qualifying-standard condition:* 7 of 10 college students qualify] [*difficult qualifying-standard condition:* only 1 of 5 college students qualify]. Oh, I guess I messed up your earlier try at that, so I'll need you to do that task again to see if you qualify.

Finally, the experimenter emphasized, "whichever you want to do is fine." This communication was prerecorded, one tape for each qualifying-standard condition. At this point in the procedure, the experimenter simply selected the appropriate tape and played it over the intercom.

Helping response. The subject was left alone for about 30 s after the tape ended, giving her time to decide. The experimenter then entered the observation room and asked for the subject's decision, which was the measure of helping.

Performing the qualifying task. If the subject decided to help Elaine, the experimenter placed a new copy of the digit scan task, identical to the one completed earlier, in front of the subject and left her alone for 120 s to work on it. After completing this task, subjects were asked to fill out a second impression questionnaire and then a digit scan task questionnaire while the experimenter went to score their digit scan task.

If the subject decided not to help, she did not perform the qualifying task or complete the digit scan task questionnaire. She simply com-

pleted the second impression questionnaire while the experimenter went to tell Marsha what had been decided.

Ancillary measures. The second impression questionnaire assessed subjects' perceptions of the worker, including how uncomfortable the shocks were for her. This assessment provided a measure of the perceived severity of Elaine's need. The first item on the digit scan task questionnaire provided a check on the effectiveness of the performance standard manipulation; it asked subjects how difficult it would be to meet the qualifying standard.

Debriefing. After subjects completed these questionnaires, the experimenter returned and informed them that it had been decided that the session would not continue; neither Elaine nor they would do any more recall trials or receive any more shocks. The experimenter then expressed a desire to talk with subjects for a few minutes, getting their reactions to the study. All subjects readily agreed. After discussing their reactions, subjects were carefully debriefed, thanked for their participation, and excused.

Results and Discussion

Effectiveness of the Qualifying-Standard Manipulation

The manipulation-check item on the digit scan task questionnaire suggested that the qualifying-standard manipulation was successful. An ANOVA indicated that the only reliable effect on responses to the question "How difficult do you think it will be for you to meet the performance standard on the digit scan task?" (1 = *not at all difficult,* 9 = *extremely difficult*) was a main effect for the qualifying-standard manipulation, $F(1, 32) = 5.36, p < .03$. Subjects in the difficult qualifying-standard condition rated meeting the standard as being more difficult ($M = 6.25$) than did subjects in the easy qualifying-standard condition ($M = 4.90$).

Perceptions of Elaine's Need

Subjects in both experimental conditions perceived Elaine to be in considerable need. The overall mean response to the question of how uncomfortable the shocks were for the worker, rated on a 7-point scale (1 = *not at all,* 7 = *extremely*), was 6.50. Mean response did not differ reliably across conditions, $t(58) < 1.0$.

Index of Predominant Emotional Response: Personal Distress Versus Empathy

Each subject's responses to eight adjectives on the emotional response questionnaire found in past research to reflect feelings of personal distress (*alarmed, grieved, troubled, distressed, upset, disturbed, worried,* and *perturbed*) were averaged in order to form an index of self-reported personal distress at watching Elaine suffer (Cronbach's alpha = .94); responses to the six adjectives previously found to reflect feelings of empathy (*sympathetic, moved, compassionate, warm, softhearted,* and *tender*) were averaged to form an index of self-reported empathy (Cronbach's alpha = .89). As in previous studies, observing Elaine evoked relatively high levels of both distress and empathy; the mean on the 7-point response scale was 5.34 for the distress index and 4.58 for the empathy index. For neither index was there a reliable effect for the qualifying-standard manipulation, both $ts(58) < 1.10$.[9]

Following the same procedure as Batson et al. (1983), we created an index of predominant emotional response by subtracting each subject's score on the distress index from her score on the empathy index. We then performed a median split on this index of predominant emotional response ($Mdn = -.20$), dividing our subjects into those who felt a relative predominance of distress and those who felt a relative predominance of empathy. This median split, combined with the experimental manipulation, produced the 2 (easy vs. difficult qualifying standard) × 2 (predominant distress vs. empathy) design needed to test the predictions of the empathy-specific punishment and the empathy-altruism hypotheses.

Rate of Helping in Each Condition of the 2 × 2 Design

Of the 60 subjects, 36 offered to help Elaine by taking the shocks in her stead. The proportion of subjects who offered help in each cell of the 2 × 2 design is presented in Table 6. As in Studies 2 and 3, the pattern of helping across the four cells was highly consistent with the predictions of the empathy-altruism hypothesis: less helping in the difficult standard/distress cell (.28) than in the other three cells (.65 or higher). A planned comparison testing this 1 versus 3 pattern was highly significant, $\chi^2(1, N = 60) = 10.47, p < .001$, and accounted for all reliable between-cell variance; residual $\chi^2(2, N = 60) = 1.84$ (analyses using normal approximation based on arc sine transformation; see Study 2). Pairwise comparisons revealed that the proportion of subjects offering help in the difficult standard/distress cell was significantly lower than in each of the other three cells, all $zs > 2.04$, $ps < .025$, and there were no reliable differences among the other three (all $zs < 1.35$).

Performance on the Qualifying Task

We then examined performance on the qualifying task by those subjects who agreed to help. Across the four cells of the 2 × 2 design, the empathy-specific punishment hypothesis predicted a main effect for difficulty of the qualifying standard; performance should be worse when the standard was difficult. In contrast, the empathy-altruism hypothesis predicted that performance by prospective helpers reporting a predominance of empathy would be the same or better when the standard was

Table 6
Proportion of Subjects Who Helped Elaine in Each Cell of 2 × 2 Design: Study 4

| Qualifying standard | Predominant emotional response | |
	Distress	Empathy
Easy		
%	.73	.86
n	11	14
Difficult		
%	.28	.65
n	18	17

Table 7
Performance on Qualifying Task by Subjects Offering Help in Each Cell of 2 × 2 Design: Study 4

| Qualifying standard | Predominant emotional response | |
	Distress	Empathy
Easy		
M	$11.30_{b,c}$	$9.90_{a,b}$
n	10	10
Difficult		
M	8.25_a	13.00_c
n	8	8

Note. Performance was measured by the number of combinations correctly circled. Cell means not sharing a common subscript differ, $p < .05$, by a t test.

difficult. Rather than predicting a main effect for difficulty of the qualifying standard, the empathy-altruism hypothesis predicted a Difficulty of Standard × Predominant Emotional Response interaction.

Measuring performance. The number of combinations correctly circled on the second digit scan task served as our performance measure. Because only the 36 subjects who offered to help performed the qualifying task, we created a new median split on the index of predominant emotion for these 36 helpers ($Mdn = .00$), providing a balanced 2 (easy vs. difficult standard) × 2 (predominant distress vs. empathy) design. (To ensure that this new split did not introduce some artifact, we also examined performance using the old split. The pattern of means was the same reported here, as was the pattern of significant effects.)

Performance on the digit scan task. The mean number of combinations circled correctly by subjects in each cell of the 2 × 2 design are presented in Table 7. An ANOVA revealed a marginally significant main effect for predominant emotional response, $F(1, 32) = 3.02, p < .10$; subjects reporting a predominance of empathy circled more combinations ($M = 11.28$) than did subjects reporting a predominance of personal distress ($M = 9.94$). This main effect was, however, qualified by a highly significant Difficulty of Standard × Predominant Emotional Response interaction, $F(1, 32) = 10.17, p < .003$. There was no evidence of the main effect for the qualifying-standard manipulation predicted by the empathy-specific punishment hypothesis, $F(1, 32) < 1.0$.

Pairwise comparisons indicated that the interaction was the same as that predicted by the empathy-altruism hypothesis. Subjects reporting a predominance of distress circled significantly fewer combinations when the qualifying standard was difficult ($M = 8.25$) than when it was easy ($M = 11.30$), $t(32) = 2.24$, $p < .02$, one-tailed. Subjects reporting a predominance

---

[9] A varimax-rotated principal-components analysis of all 14 of these emotional response adjectives produced a two-component solution similar to the solutions found in previous studies (see Batson, 1987); all 8 distress adjectives loaded above .65 on one component, and all 6 empathy adjectives loaded above .65 on the other orthogonal component.

of empathy circled significantly more combinations when the qualifying standard was difficult ($M = 13.00$) than when it was easy ($M = 9.90$), $t(32) = 2.27$, $p < .02$, one-tailed. The performance difference in the difficult qualifying-standard condition between subjects reporting a predominance of distress and those reporting a predominance of empathy was highly reliable, $t(32) = 3.30$, $p < .001$, one-tailed.

Implications of Studies 2 Through 4

Providing justification for not helping—whether by the inaction of others (Study 2), by introducing attributional ambiguity (Study 3), or by making it difficult to qualify to help (Study 4)—had a dramatic effect on the helping of low-empathy subjects; it had little effect on the helping of high-empathy subjects. This pattern of results, which was highly consistent across studies, suggested that although the helping of low-empathy subjects was motivated at least partly by a desire to avoid the self-punishment associated with a failure to do the right thing, the helping of high-empathy subjects was not. The relatively high rate of helping by high-empathy subjects, even when justification for not helping was high, was precisely what we would expect if, as claimed by the empathy–altruism hypothesis, feeling empathy for the person in need evoked altruistic motivation to have that person's need reduced. It was not what we would expect if, as claimed by the empathy-specific punishment hypothesis, feeling empathy evoked increased egoistic motivation to avoid anticipated self-punishment.

Did Our Justification Manipulations Really Reduce Empathy-Specific Punishment?

Even though the results of these three studies certainly seem to count against the empathy-specific punishment hypothesis, they do not entirely rule it out. Our manipulations of justification for not helping were indirect, so we cannot be absolutely certain that they reduced anticipated empathy-specific self-punishment. The finding that our justification manipulations had a significant effect on helping of low-empathy subjects, coupled with the finding by Fultz et al. (1986) of no reduction even in a low-empathy condition for a powerful manipulation of anticipated social punishment, suggests that our manipulations did reduce anticipated self-punishment for a failure to help. But to press the point, perhaps the information that we provided to justify not helping was only effective in reducing general and not empathy-specific self-punishments. Perhaps anticipation of the latter is so well internalized that it is impervious to information about the inactivity of other potential helpers, the helping-irrelevant attributes of the helping task, or the difficulty of qualifying. If this were true, could the empathy-specific punishment hypothesis not still account for the observed pattern of results: substantially reduced helping in the high-justification condition for low- but not for high-empathy subjects?

Indeed it could, but the relevant evidence suggests that our justification manipulations were not ineffective in reducing anticipated empathy-specific punishment. Recall that on the perception of obligation measure in Study 2 there was evidence that learning most peers had not helped reduced the perception of obligation to help Katie as much in the high-empathy condi-

tion as in the low. If high-empathy subjects are impervious to justification information, there should have been no change in their perception of obligation. Recall also that the perception of obligation by subjects in the replication cells of Study 2, who were provided with no information about the helping of others, was essentially the same in the high-empathy condition as in the low, and in neither replication condition did perceived obligation differ reliably from the perception in the high-justification condition. On our obligation measure, then, there was no evidence of the increased sense of obligation associated with feeling empathy claimed by the empathy-specific punishment hypothesis.

But to persist, perhaps our obligation measure was flawed. Perhaps high-empathy subjects in the replication condition perceived a change in their own personal obligation to help Katie that was not picked up by our measure, which (to be less reactive) had asked whether "students" ought to help. Perhaps the effect of the justification manipulation on perceived obligation in the high-empathy condition reflected a change in perception of what other students ought to do, but not what the empathically aroused subject felt he or she ought to do. This may be true, but recall that responses on the perception of obligation measure were positively correlated with subjects' own helping, suggesting that it reflected implications for their own behavior.

Could the Lack of Difference Among High-Empathy Subjects Be Due to a Ceiling Effect?

Another possibility is that the lack of difference in helping between the high- and low-justification conditions for high-empathy subjects was caused by a ceiling effect. Recall that the obligation measure indicated that the information about other helpers in Study 2 might have increased perceived obligation to help in the low-justification condition at least as much as it decreased the perceived obligation to help in the high-justification condition. This might have been because, as suggested in the replication condition, the perceived obligation to help was not especially high even in the absence of justifying information. Whatever the reason, the increase in obligation raises the possibility that in Study 2 a ceiling effect might have prevented us from observing an increase in helping among high-empathy/low-justification subjects. The proportion of helping in the high-empathy/replication cell was .70. Even though this proportion is not close to the absolute ceiling of 1.00, perhaps it is close to a functional ceiling. Perhaps helping in the high-empathy/low-justification cell would have been significantly higher than in the high-empathy/high-justification cell had this functional ceiling not prevented it from rising. A similar argument can be made concerning helping in Study 4.

A close look at our data renders this ceiling-effect explanation implausible. In Study 2 we found exactly the same pattern of significant effects on the scaled measure of helping (on which the mean in the high-empathy/replication cell was 1.20 on a 0 to 4 scale) as we found for the dichotomous measure based on proportions. In Study 3, we again found the same pattern of significant effects on a scaled measure, and in that study, unlike Study 2, there was no information provided in the low-justification condition to increase the obligation to help. Given the same pattern of helping across measures and across studies, it is not likely that the absence of an effect of our justification manipulations on the helping of high-empathy subjects was caused by a ceiling effect.

Instead, we believe that the results of these three studies seriously challenge the anticipated self-punishment version of the empathy-specific punishment hypothesis. Still, in a final attempt to find evidence for this hypothesis, and for the empathy-specific reward hypothesis, we examined the goal-relevant cognitions associated with empathy-induced helping.

GOAL-RELEVANT COGNITIONS ASSOCIATED WITH EMPATHY-INDUCED HELPING

The empathy-specific reward, empathy-specific punishment, and empathy–altruism hypotheses each postulate a different motive underlying the helping associated with feeling empathy. These different motives have different goals: seeking rewards, avoiding punishments, and relieving the victim's need, respectively. Because each hypothesis assumes that the empathically aroused individual, when considering whether to help, has in mind one of these goals, each assumes that cognitions relevant to that goal should be especially salient. Determining whether reward-relevant, punishment-relevant, or victim-relevant cognitions are associated with empathy-induced helping should provide some evidence as to the goal of empathically aroused helpers. A Stroop task seemed to be one means of determining the salient goal-relevant cognitions.

Assessing Goal-Relevant Cognitions Using a Stroop Task

A Stroop task (Stroop, 1938) involves having subjects name as quickly as possible the color of the ink in which a word or other visual stimulus appears. As Geller and Shaver (1976, p. 101) observed: "In general, it appears that latency of color naming for a particular word will increase whenever a subject has been thinking about something related to that word" (see also Schadler & Thissen, 1981; Warren, 1974). This Stroop procedure seemed capable of providing a measure of the nature of the motivation underlying the empathy–helping relationship, one that was relatively nonreactive and did not rely on subjects' conscious awareness of or willingness to report their goals.

Predictions

If the increased helping associated with empathic emotion is motivated by the desire to reach a given goal, then this helping should be positively correlated with the latency to name the color of words relevant to that goal. This observation leads to three distinct predictions: (a) If the motivation to help associated with feeling empathy is directed toward the egoistic goal of obtaining social and self-rewards, as the empathy-specific reward hypothesis claims, then the increased helping associated with empathic emotion should be positively correlated with color-naming latency for reward-relevant words. (b) If the motivation to help associated with feeling empathy is directed toward the egoistic goal of avoiding social and self-punishments, as the empathy-specific punishment hypothesis claims, then the

increased helping associated with empathic emotion should be positively correlated with color-naming latency for punishment-relevant words. (c) If the motivation to help associated with feeling empathy is directed toward the altruistic goal of reducing the victim's suffering, as the empathy–altruism hypothesis claims, then the increased helping associated with empathic emotion should be positively correlated with color-naming latency for victim-relevant words. Although distinct, these three predictions are not mutually exclusive; correlations may be found supporting any or all.

If we could assume a one-to-one correspondence between either manipulated or measured empathic emotion and increased reward-seeking, punishment-avoiding, or altruistic motivation, then we could predict a direct association between increased empathy and increased color-naming latency for words of one or more of the three types. It seemed likely, however, that situational factors would make it impossible for some empathically aroused individuals to help. This could inhibit their motivation and the salience of related goal-relevant cognitions (see Brehm, Wright, Solomon, Silka, & Greenberg, 1983). Therefore, it seemed best to direct our attention to the more precise relationship predicted by the three hypotheses: the relationship between increased helping associated with feeling empathy and increased color-naming latency for words of one or more of the three types. If empathically induced helping is directed toward gaining rewards, avoiding punishments, or reducing the victim's suffering, then the color-naming latency for words relevant to one or more of these goals should mediate the relationship between feeling empathy and helping (Baron & Kenny, 1986).

A Preliminary Attempt to Test the Predictions

C. D. Batson, J. Orendain, D. Shetrompf, and M. L. Templeton made a preliminary attempt to test these predictions. They conducted a pilot study in which 23 female undergraduates read about Sandy, a lonely, disadvantaged 12-year-old girl seeking a surrogate grandparent to be an adult friend and guide. After reading about Sandy, subjects were informed that they would soon be given a chance to volunteer time to write letters to prospective "grandparents" on her behalf. First, however, ostensibly as a baseline control for a measure of cognitive reactions to the information about Sandy, subjects were asked to name as quickly as possible the color (red, blue, green, or brown) in which each word in a series appeared. Some of the words were reward relevant (*good, merit, honor,* and *praise*); some were punishment relevant (*duty, guilt, shame,* and *should*); some were victim relevant (*hope, child, needy,* and *friend*); and some were neutral (*left, rapid, large,* and *breath*). Using a millisecond timer and voice-operated relay, it was possible to assess color-naming latencies for the different types of words by repeated measures within subjects (see Schadler & Thissen, 1981; Warren, 1974) rather than by the more gross between-group comparisons used by Stroop (1938) and Geller and Shaver (1976). After completing this Stroop task, helping was measured by the amount of time, if any, subjects volunteered to spend writing letters for Sandy.

In an attempt to manipulate empathy, written instructions directed some subjects to focus on technical aspects of the information about Sandy (low empathy) and others to imagine how she felt (high empathy), but this manipulation proved unsuccessful. The amount of help offered did not differ reliably between the low- and high-empathy conditions, $t(21) < 1.0$, and in debriefing, subjects assigned to the low-empathy condition consistently reported that they had been unable to keep from imagining how Sandy felt. Because it appeared that all subjects either were placed or placed themselves in a high-empathy condition, correlations between the amount of helping and color-naming latencies were computed for all 23 subjects combined.

These correlations revealed a significant positive relationship between amount of help volunteered and color-naming latency for the victim-relevant words (averaged and adjusted for individual differences in reaction time by subtracting the average latency to the neutral words), $r(21) = .53$, $p < .004$, one-tailed. Correlations between amount of helping and adjusted average latencies for the reward-relevant and punishment-relevant words were $-.06$ and $-.10$, respectively.

These correlations patterned as predicted by the empathy–altruism hypothesis, but not as predicted by either the empathy-specific reward or the empathy-specific punishment hypothesis. However, because in this pilot study the empathy manipulation failed and all subjects were assumed to be experiencing a high degree of empathy, results were not conclusive.

Study 5: Empathy, Helping, and a Stroop Task

Because the results were not conclusive, we conducted a new study, using a need situation and empathy manipulation known to produce the customary empathy–helping relationship. The need situation and empathy manipulation we used were the same as the ones used in Study 2 (see also Coke et al., 1978), in which subjects adopted a particular perspective while listening to a (bogus) radio broadcast that informed them of the need of another undergraduate, Katie Banks.

Method

Subjects

Forty-eight female introductory psychology students at the University of Kansas served as subjects, partially fulfilling a course requirement. By use of a randomized-block procedure, 24 subjects were assigned to each of the two empathy conditions (low and high), and within these conditions, two female experimenters each ran 3 subjects with each of four Stroop slide sets (used to counterbalance words with colors and order of presentation). Type of word (reward relevant, punishment relevant, victim relevant, and neutral) was a repeated measures factor.[10]

Materials and Equipment

We used 16 stimulus words in the Stroop procedure, 4 of each type. Reward-relevant words were *nice, proud, honor,* and *praise;* punishment-relevant words were *duty, guilt, shame,* and *oblige;* victim-relevant words were *loss, needy, adopt,* and *tragic;* and neutral words were *pair, clean, extra,* and *smooth.* Across type, words were matched for length (one 4-letter word, two 5-letter words, and one 6-letter word) and approximate frequency of appearance in American English (Kučera & Francis, 1967).

To assess the appropriateness of the words selected to represent each type, five independent judges first listened to the tape presenting Katie Banks's need, then classified the 16 words into the 4 types. Reward-relevant words were correctly classified 80% of the time, punishment-

relevant words 100% of the time, victim-relevant words 100% of the time, and neutral words 85% of the time. These results suggested that the words were adequate representatives of the types.

Sixty-four Stroop slides were prepared, 1 of each of the 16 stimulus words in each of four colors (red, blue, green, and brown) against a black field. These slides were then arranged into four slide sets. Each word appeared in each slide set, but in a different color. Moreover, within each slide set, a word of each type and a word in each color appeared in the first 4 words presented, also in the next 4, and so on, with no repetition of specific word–color pairing or order across slide sets.

In each slide set, the 16 stimulus words were preceded by five buffer slides. The first 4 presented a row of Xs in one of the four colors; the fifth presented a neutral word, added because pretesting had revealed an atypically long latency on the first word following the Xs. Opaque slides were alternated with the slides of Xs and words to provide a dark screen during the 5-s intertrial interval.

The slides were shown on a square 28-cm rear-projection screen placed approximately 80 cm in front of subjects; letters of the projected words were approximately 1 cm high and 0.5 cm wide. When each slide was shown, a light-sensitive phototransistor attached to the projector lens started a digital millisecond timer. The timer was stopped by the electrical impulse from a Grayson-Stadler E7300A-1 voice-operated relay, which was activated by input from a throat microphone as subjects named the color in which the Xs or word was printed.

Procedure

The procedure was similar to that used by Coke et al. (1978), except for the inclusion of the Stroop task and an emotional response questionnaire to measure self-reported empathy and the omission of their misattribution manipulation. Therefore, we describe in detail only these new aspects. The Stroop task was presented to subjects in a written introduction as a reaction time measure of the effect of the pilot radio broadcasts on thoughts, and the emotional response questionnaire was presented as a measure of the effect of the broadcasts on feelings.

The reaction time (Stroop) task. After the introduction, subjects read a written description of the reaction time measure. This measure involved looking at a series of words after each broadcast; some of the words would be relevant to possible thoughts after hearing the broadcast, others would not. Different words would appear in different colors. For each word, participants assigned to the "test group" would say as quickly as possible whether it was relevant to their thoughts; participants assigned to the "control group" would say as quickly as possible the color in which the word was printed. The written description explained, "Responses of people in the control group will provide a baseline needed to interpret the responses of the people in the test group. Therefore, it is important that you do your best no matter to which group you have been assigned."

Once subjects read this information, the experimenter consulted a chart and informed each subject that she had (ostensibly randomly) been assigned to the control group, so her task would be to name the color (red, blue, green, or brown) in which each word appeared. (Inclusion of the test group in the cover story made it plausible not only that the reaction time measure be taken but also that some of the words be relevant to thoughts evoked by the broadcast.) To acquaint subjects with the reaction time task, the experimenter next showed them slides, each of a row of Xs in one of the four colors, and had subjects practice the color-naming procedure until they felt comfortable with it.

---

[10] Seven additional students were excluded from the sample and replaced, 1 in each empathy condition because of suspicion, 3 in the low-empathy condition because they reported being unable to maintain their assigned listening perspective, and 1 in each empathy condition because of failure to give a clear response to the request for help.

Manipulation of empathy. Before listening to the "News From the Personal Side" broadcast, which presented Katie Banks's need, subjects were instructed to adopt one of two listening perspectives. The perspective instructions were identical to those used Study 2 to create low- and high-empathy conditions, as was the broadcast about Katie's need. The experimenter remained blind to which listening-perspective instructions the subjects received.

Empathic reaction to learning of Katie's need. At the conclusion of the tape, subjects completed the emotional response questionnaire, which listed 24 adjectives describing different emotional states. Subjects were asked to indicate on 7-point scales ($1 = not at all, 7 = extremely$) how much they had experienced each emotion while listening to the tape. Included in the list were the same six adjectives used in Studies 1 and 4 to measure empathy.

The experimenter then returned and prepared to administer the reaction time measure, only to discover that she had failed to bring the second slide carousel. While she went to get the carousel, the experimenter left the subject two letters to read, explaining that these two letters, which the professor in charge of the study had asked be given to participants, could be read now to save time.

Katie's request for help. The first letter, from the professor, introduced the opportunity to help Katie. The second letter, from Katie, enumerated various ways students could help her if they wished. Subjects were encouraged to think about the possibility of helping for a few minutes before deciding. To that end, no response form was provided at this point; it was to be provided later.

Measurement of color-naming latencies for reward-, punishment-, and victim-relevant words, and of desire to help Katie. Once subjects had read both letters, the experimenter returned and administered one of the four counterbalanced Stroop slide sets. The experimenter then gave subjects (a) a brief response form on which to indicate how many hours, if any, they wished to volunteer to help Katie; (b) an envelope in which to seal the response form to assure their anonymity; and (c) a reaction questionnaire. The experimenter left subjects alone, directing them first to complete the response form (or leave it blank, as they wished), seal it in the envelope, and then complete the questionnaire. The questionnaire asked how interesting, informative, and worthwhile subjects thought the broadcast was. It also contained a question assessing perceptions of Katie's need: "How great is the need of the person who was interviewed?" ($1 = very little, 9 = very great$).

Debriefing. Finally, subjects were carefully debriefed, thanked for their participation, and excused.

Results and Discussion

Perceptions of Katie's Need

In both empathy conditions, subjects reported on the reaction questionnaire that Katie's need was very great (overall $M = 8.65$ on the 9-point scale), with no reliable differences between conditions, $t(46) < 1.0$. Apparently, the perspective-taking instructions used to manipulate empathy did not prevent subjects in the low-empathy condition from perceiving Katie to be in considerable need.

Effectiveness of the Empathy Manipulation

To assess the effectiveness of the empathy manipulation in inducing empathic feelings for Katie, we compared scores for subjects in the low- and high-empathy conditions on an index of self-reported empathy. This index was created by averaging responses to the six adjectives on the emotional response questionnaire found in previous research to reflect feelings of empathy: *sympathetic, moved, compassionate, tender, warm,* and *softhearted* (Cronbach's alpha $= .89$). As expected, scores on the 7-point empathy index ($1 = not at all, 7 = extremely$) were lower for subjects in the low-empathy condition ($M = 4.54$) than in the high ($M = 5.38$), $t(46) = 2.10, p < .03$, one-tailed, indicating that the empathy manipulation successfully induced the intended differences in empathic emotional response to Katie's plight. Still, it should be noted that the level of reported empathy was fairly high even in the low-empathy condition.[11]

Empathy-Induced Desire to Help Katie

To adjust for a severe positive skew in the number of hours volunteered, subjects' desire to help Katie was coded using the same scale used by Coke et al. (1978): $0 =$ no help volunteered, $1 = 1$ hr, $2 = 2$ to 3 hr, $3 = 4$ to 5 hr, $4 =$ more than 5 hr. This scale was much less skewed. Consistent with previous research demonstrating a positive relationship between empathy and helping (Coke et al., 1978; Krebs, 1975; Toi & Batson, 1982), our subjects volunteered more help in the high-empathy condition ($M = 1.50$) than in the low ($M = 0.50$), $t(46) = 2.94, p < .005$.[12] Moreover, as expected, scores on the empathy index were positively correlated with the amount of help volunteered, both overall, $r(46) = .46, p < .001$, and in the low- and high-empathy conditions, $rs(22) = .58$ and $.30, ps = .001$ and $.07$, respectively.

These results suggested that we had successfully replicated the empathy–helping relationship. Having done this, we turned to the Stroop measure to assess the nature of the goal-relevant cognitions associated with this empathy-induced helping.

Assessing Goal-Relevant Cognitions

To obtain three color-naming latency scores for each subject—one for reward-relevant, one for punishment-relevant, and one for victim-relevant words—we first averaged each subject's color-naming latencies for the four words of each type: reward relevant (M [in milliseconds] $= 692.54, SD = 173.61$), punishment relevant ($M = 709.57, SD = 161.34$), victim relevant ($M = 685.08, SD = 176.66$), and neutral ($M = 691.57, SD = 190.70$). The counterbalancing within and across slide sets ensured that for each subject all four averages included one response to each of the four colors (red, blue, green, and brown) and that each word–color pairing was equally represented in each empathy condition. To adjust for the individual differences in response latencies that typically occur with reaction time

---

[11] Included on the emotional response questionnaire were eight adjectives that had been found in previous studies to reflect feelings of personal distress caused by witnessing another person suffer: *alarmed, grieved, upset, worried, disturbed, perturbed, distressed,* and *troubled.* As in Studies 1 and 3, subjects in this broadcast paradigm seemed to interpret and respond to the distress adjectives more in terms of an other-oriented feeling of distress for Katie than a feeling of being personally distressed by her need.

[12] Similarly, a dichotomous measure ($0 =$ no help, $1 =$ help) revealed that more subjects helped in the high-empathy condition (.63; 15 of 24) than in the low (.29; 7 of 24), $z = 2.36, p < .01$, one-tailed (normal-approximation analysis based on arc sine transformations; see Langer & Abelson, 1972; Winer, 1971).

Table 8

Mean Adjusted Average Color-Naming Latency for Victim-Relevant Words by Low- and High-Empathy Subjects Who Did and Did Not Help: Study 5

	Empathy condition	
Helping response	Low	High
No help		
M	−24.66	−44.22
n	17	9
Help		
M	−29.11	47.32
n	7	15

measures, we subtracted each subject's average latency to the neutral words from her average latency to the reward-, punishment-, and victim-relevant words.

These adjusted averages served as our measures of color-naming latency for the three types of words. These measures were, in turn, our index of the degree to which a person was thinking about three possible goals for helping: obtaining rewards, avoiding punishments, or reducing the victim's need. Each of the three hypotheses we were testing claimed that the empathy-helping relationship is a function of motivation directed toward one of these goals, and each predicted that the increased helping evoked by empathy would be positively associated with the color-naming latency for words related to that goal.

Goal-Relevant Cognitions Associated With Empathy-Induced Helping

The empathy manipulation had no reliable main effect on any of the three adjusted average latency measures, all $Fs(1, 46) < 2.25$, $ps > .15$. Consistent with the more precise prediction of the empathy–altruism hypothesis, however, the means in Table 8 reveal that latency for the victim-relevant words for helpers in the high-empathy condition was higher than latency for these words for nonhelpers in the high-empathy condition and for both helpers and nonhelpers in the low-empathy condition.

To test this predicted pattern, we conducted a planned comparison in this 2 (low vs. high empathy) × 2 (no help vs. help) design, contrasting the mean latency of the high-empathy helpers with the mean latency in the other three cells. This 1 versus 3 planned comparison was significant, $F(1, 44) = 4.34$, $p < .05$, and accounted for all reliable between-cell variance, residual $F(2, 44) < 1.0$. Parallel analyses of latencies for the reward- and punishment-relevant words did not reveal this pattern, both planned comparison $Fs(1, 44) < 1.10$.

There was also a positive correlation between self-reported empathy and latency to name the victim-relevant words, both overall, $r(46) = .28$, $p < .03$, and in the high-empathy condition, $r(22) = .38$, $p < .04$. There were no reliable correlations between self-reported empathy and latency to name the reward-relevant words. There was a reliable positive correlation between self-reported empathy and latency to name the punishment-relevant words overall, $r(46) = .24$, $p < .05$, but this correlation was not reliable in the high-empathy condition.

Turning from the empathy–latency relationships to the latency–helping relationships predicted by the three hypotheses, betas for the three latency measures when regressing helping on these measures, overall and separately for subjects in the low- and high-empathy conditions, are presented in Table 9. As can be seen, the only positive association in the high-empathy condition was the correlation between helping and color-naming latency for the victim-relevant words, which had been predicted by the empathy–altruism hypothesis ($\beta = .62$, $p < .01$). The finding that in the low-empathy condition, in which empathic feelings had not been explicitly aroused, there was not a positive correlation between helping and latency for the victim-relevant words suggested that the positive correlation for victim-relevant words in the high-empathy condition was not due to some general characteristic of these words or their association with helping. The relationship seemed to be empathy specific.

Victim-Relevant Cognitions as Mediators of the Empathy–Helping Relationship

Given the positive association between self-reported empathy and helping and between self-reported empathy and latency for the victim-relevant words, it was possible to examine the degree to which victim-relevant cognitions mediated the relationship between subjects' self-reported empathy and helping. (Because the empathy manipulation did not have a significant overall effect on latency for the victim-relevant cognitions, it was not appropriate to test the role of victim-relevant cognitions in mediating the relationship between the empathy manipulation and helping; see Baron & Kenny, 1986.) Figure 1 provides path coefficients (betas) for the regression equation specified by Baron and Kenny to test mediation. Coefficients are presented for two equations, one for subjects in the low- and one for subjects in the high-empathy condition.

The significant positive path coefficient for the victim-relevant words in the high-empathy condition indicates that victim-relevant cognitions did indeed serve as a mediator of the relationship between self-reported empathy and helping in this condition ($\beta = .51$, $p < .03$). Indeed, in this condition the indirect (mediated) effect was substantial; it accounted for 63% of the total effect of self-reported empathy on helping (Pedhazur, 1982). In the low-empathy condition, however, there was no evidence of an indirect (mediated) effect of self-reported empathy on helping. Instead, there was a strong relationship that was un-

Table 9

Betas From Regressing Amount of Help Offered on Adjusted Average Color-Naming Latency for Reward-, Punishment-, and Victim-Relevant Words: Study 5

		Empathy condition	
Type of word	Overall[a]	Low[b]	High[b]
Reward relevant	−.20	−.15	−.30
Punishment relevant	−.20	−.29	−.30
Victim relevant	.48*	−.06	.62*

[a] $N = 48$. [b] $n = 24$.
* $p < .01$, one-tailed.

LOW-EMPATHY CONDITION   HIGH-EMPATHY CONDITION

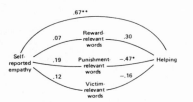
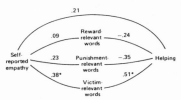

Figure 1. Path coefficients (betas) from regression analyses to test the mediation of the empathy–helping relationship by goal-relevant cognitions in Study 5. (*$p < .05$. **$p < .001$, one-tailed.)

mediated by any of the latency measures ($\beta = .67, p < .001$) and some evidence of negative mediation by punishment-relevant cognitions ($\beta = -.47$).

Implications of Study 5

Once again, we found no support for either the empathy-specific reward or the empathy-specific punishment hypothesis; there was no evidence of a positive correlation between empathy-induced helping and color-naming latency for either the reward- or punishment-relevant words. Instead, analyses revealed that the increased helping associated with empathy was positively correlated with and mediated by latency to name the color of victim-relevant words. These results provided further support for the empathy–altruism hypothesis, which claims that the goal of empathy-induced helping is to reduce the victim's need. Indeed, given that correlations and tests for mediation are weakened by any error in measurement (Baron & Kenny, 1986)—both our self-report measure of empathy and our color-naming latency measure of salient cognitions almost certainly involved error—the support we found for the empathy–altruism hypothesis seemed striking.

Recall, too, that a positive correlation between amount of helping and color-naming latency for victim-relevant words had also been found in a preliminary study, the interpretation of which was clouded by failure of the empathy manipulation. This failure notwithstanding, the agreement between our results and the results of the preliminary study increased our confidence in the evidence for the empathy–altruism hypothesis found in each study.

At the same time, our analyses also revealed that not all of the observed empathy–helping relationship was mediated by victim-relevant cognitions. Although we have no way of knowing with certainty what accounted for the relatively high levels of self-reported empathy and the relationship between self-reported empathy and helping in the low-empathy condition, previous research (see Batson et al., 1986; Eisenberg & Miller, 1987) revealed that self-presentation concerns (Jones & Pittman, 1982) often account for some, but not all, of women's reported empathy, presumably because the female sex role script (Abelson, 1981; Eagly & Crowley, 1986) says that women should care about others' suffering. Such self-presentation concerns could easily have produced some of the reported empathy in Study 5. At the same time, previous research (Coke et al.,

1978; Stotland, 1969) also indicates that such concerns are not likely to account for the difference in reported empathy between the low- and high-empathy conditions. Moreover, Batson et al. (1986) found evidence that only the part of subjects' self-reported empathy that did not reflect self-presentation concerns was associated with motivation to help that appeared altruistic.

Using these previous findings to help us interpret our results, subjects more concerned with presenting themselves as being caring and sympathetic might have also been more likely, when presented with Katie's appeal for help, to comply with her request. In each condition, then, self-presentation might have been at least one source of that part of the empathy–helping relationship that was not mediated by any of our latency measures.

Could Our Results Be an Artifact of Priming?

It may appear that the observed positive correlation between latency for the victim-relevant words and empathy-induced helping could be an artifact of a simple priming effect. After all, the victim-relevant words were by design closely associated with what subjects heard and read about Katie's need. Would not the mere exposure to this material make these words more salient, increasing the color-naming latency? Although such priming certainly might have occurred, there was no evidence that it did. Recall that mean latency for the victim-relevant words was actually slightly lower than mean latency for words of the other three types.

Could priming have occurred specifically in the high-empathy condition, in which the perspective-taking instructions explicitly directed subjects to focus on Katie's feelings? Again, although it might have, there was no evidence that it did. Mean latency for the victim-relevant words was slightly lower in the high-empathy condition ($M = 664.01$) than in the low ($M = 706.16$), $t(46) < 1.0$. A similar lack of effect of the empathy manipulation on mean latency was found for the reward-relevant, punishment-relevant, and neutral words.

Even if there had been priming of the victim-relevant words, either overall or in the high-empathy condition, it is not clear how this priming could account for the observed pattern of correlations predicted by the empathy–altruism hypothesis. Presumably, priming would occur for all subjects (or at least for all subjects in the high-empathy condition). The empathy–altruism hypothesis, however, predicted that the color-naming latency for the victim-relevant words would not increase for all subjects, even all subjects in the high-empathy condition. It predicted an increase specifically for those subjects whose increased empathic feelings led them to help. It was this specific, complex pattern of correlations that we observed. These correlations suggested that victim-relevant cognitions were associated not simply with learning of or focusing on Katie's need but with the link between the empathic emotion evoked by this information and subsequent helping behavior.

Strengths and Weaknesses of the Stroop Procedure

As a research strategy to test the empathy–altruism hypothesis and various egoistic alternatives, the Stroop procedure has both strengths and weaknesses. One strength is that it permitted us to extend research on the empathy–helping relationship into the cognitive domain, testing different motivational hypotheses by exploring possible goal-relevant thoughts associated with empathic emotion. As far as we know, this had not previously been done. Another strength is that the predicted correlations between empathy, helping, and color-naming latencies were subtle and not likely to be produced by experimental demand (Orne, 1962) or self-presentation (Jones & Pittman, 1982). The major weakness of the Stroop procedure is that its validity rests on two plausible but not fully tested assumptions: (a) Color-naming latencies reflect salience of current cognitions and (b) the specific words we used adequately represent the appropriate reward-, punishment-, and victim-relevant cognitions.

Some justification for the first assumption lies in the consistent finding in previous research of increased color-naming latencies specifically for words associated with salient cognitions (Geller & Shaver, 1976; Stroop, 1938; Warren, 1974). Some justification for the second assumption lies in the face validity of the words used and in the finding that they were correctly classified with a high degree accuracy by independent judges. Moreover, there is evidence that color-naming latency for each of the three word sets used is capable of being associated with helping. In Study 5, color-naming latency for both the punishment- and victim-relevant words was, at times, correlated with helping, although the correlation for the punishment-relevant words was the opposite of that predicted by the empathy-specific punishment hypothesis. In a subsequent study by Batson and Dyck (1988) using the same need situation, latency for the reward-relevant words was positively correlated with the helping of subjects scoring relatively high on an intrinsic, end orientation to religion (Allport & Ross, 1967; Batson & Ventis, 1982).

GENERAL CONCLUSIONS

When the results of all five studies are considered, a remarkably consistent pattern emerges. Using different need situations, techniques for operationalizing empathy, and dependent measures, our results consistently conformed to the pattern predicted by the empathy–altruism hypothesis. In no study did the results show a pattern predicted by either the empathy-specific reward or the empathy-specific punishment hypothesis.

Four of the studies were designed to test the empathy-specific punishment hypothesis. Studies 2 through 4 used different techniques to provide justification for not helping, and Study 5 assessed the salience of punishment-relevant cognitions for empathically aroused helpers. We failed to find support for the empathy-specific punishment hypothesis in any study. When these results are considered in conjunction with the results of studies of the empathy–helping relationship using an ease of physical escape manipulation (Batson et al., 1981, 1983; Toi & Batson, 1982) and studies eliminating the possibility of social punishment (Fultz et al., 1986), the claim that the motivation to help evoked by empathy is directed toward the egoistic goal of avoiding empathy-specific punishments seems very doubtful. As with a claim for the existence of unicorns, we cannot categorically say that it is wrong, but we have looked hard in a number of likely places to find supporting evidence and have found none.

Two studies were designed to test the empathy-specific reward hypothesis. Study 1 measured mood after relief of a victim's need was or was not the result of one's own helpful act; Study 5 assessed the salience of reward-relevant cognitions for empathically aroused helpers. We found no support for the empathy-specific reward hypothesis in either study. Thus, the claim that the motivation to help evoked by empathy is directed toward the egoistic goal of gaining empathy-specific rewards also seems doubtful.

As we noted when discussing the results of Study 1, however, there is a second version of the empathy-specific reward hypothesis that was not clearly addressed in that study, nor was it clearly addressed in Study 5. Cialdini et al. (1987; see also Schaller & Cialdini, in press) claimed that it is not the rewards but the need for the rewards that is empathy specific: Feeling empathy for a person who is suffering involves a state of temporary sadness or depression, which can be relieved by any mood-enchancing experience, including obtaining the social and self-rewards that accompany helping. Cialdini et al. (1987) provided some evidence consistent with this view, but recent research reported by Dovidio, Allen, and Schroeder (1987) and Schroeder, Dovidio, Sibicky, Matthews, and Allen (in press) seems to challenge the Cialdini et al. claim. Still, at this point the possibility that a negative-state relief version of the empathy-specific reward hypothesis can account for the empathy–helping relationship cannot be entirely ruled out.

Moreover, the empathy-specific reward and empathy-specific punishment hypotheses are not the only new egoistic explanations proposed to account for the empathy–helping relationship. Piliavin, Dovidio, Gaertner, and Clark (1981) offered an empathy-cost explanation. They claimed that the empathically aroused individual is motivated to avoid not present but anticipated future aversive empathic arousal produced by the knowledge that the person in need is continuing to suffer. As far as we know, this empathy-cost explanation has yet to be tested directly.

Clearly, before the empathy–altruism hypothesis is accepted, more evidence is needed. At the same time, the consistency and diversity of evidence for the claim that empathic emotion evokes altruistic motivation is becoming hard to ignore. Plausible egoistic explanations of the evidence are increasingly difficult to find. The empathy–altruism hypothesis certainly seems to be the most parsimonious explanation for the results of the five studies reported here. More and more, it appears that the motivation to help evoked by feeling empathy is at least partly altruistic. If it is, then psychologists will have to make some fundamental changes in their conceptions of human motivation and, indeed, of human nature.

References

Abelson, R. P. (1981). Psychological status of the script concept. *American Psychologist, 36,* 715–729.

Allport, G. W., & Ross, J. M. (1967). Personal religious orientation and prejudice. *Journal of Personality and Social Psychology, 5,* 432–443.

Archer, R. L. (1984). The farmer and the cowman should be friends: An attempt at reconciliation with Batson, Coke, and Pych. *Journal of Personality and Social Psychology, 46,* 709–711.

Archer, R. L., Diaz-Loving, R., Gollwitzer, P. M., Davis, M. H., & Foushee, H. C. (1981). The role of dispositional empathy and social evaluation in the empathic mediation of helping. *Journal of Personality and Social Psychology, 40,* 786–796.

Baron, R. M., & Kenny, D. A. (1986). The moderator–mediator variable distinction in social psychological research: Conceptual, strategic, and statistical considerations. *Journal of Personality and Social Psychology, 51,* 1173–1182.

Batson, C. D. (1987). Prosocial motivation: Is it ever truly altruistic? In L. Berkowitz (Ed.), *Advances in experimental social psychology* (Vol. 20, pp. 65–122). New York: Academic Press.

Batson, C. D., Bolen, M. H., Cross, J. A., & Neuringer-Benefiel, H. (1986). Where is the altruism in the altruistic personality? *Journal of Personality and Social Psychology, 50,* 212–220.

Batson, C. D., Duncan, B., Ackerman, P., Buckley, T., & Birch, K. (1981). Is empathic emotion a source of altruistic motivation? *Journal of Personality and Social Psychology, 40,* 290–302.

Batson, C. D., & Dyck, J. L. (1988). *Goal-relevant cognitions associated with the religion–helping relationship.* Unpublished manuscript, University of Kansas.

Batson, C. D., O'Quin, K., Fultz, J., Vanderplas, M., & Isen, A. (1983). Self-reported distress and empathy and egoistic versus altruistic motivation for helping. *Journal of Personality and Social Psychology, 45,* 706–718.

Batson, C. D., & Ventis, W. L. (1982). *The religious experience: A social-psychological perspective.* New York: Oxford University Press.

Brehm, J. W., Wright, R. A., Solomon, S., Silka, L., & Greenberg, J. (1983). Perceived difficulty, energization, and the magnitude of goal valence. *Journal of Experimental Social Psychology, 19,* 21–48.

Campbell, D. T., & Stanley, J. C. (1963). *Experimental and quasi-experimental designs for research.* Chicago: Rand McNally.

Cialdini, R. B., Schaller, M., Houlihan, D., Arps, K., Fultz, J., & Beaman, A. L. (1987). Empathy-based helping: Is it selflessly or selfishly motivated? *Journal of Personality and Social Psychology, 52,* 749–758.

Coke, J. S., Batson, C. D., & McDavis, K. (1978). Empathic mediation of helping: A two-stage model. *Journal of Personality and Social Psychology, 36,* 752–766.

Darley, J. M., & Latané, B. (1968). Bystander intervention in emergencies: Diffusion of responsibility. *Journal of Personality and Social Psychology, 8,* 377–383.

Dovidio, J. F. (1984). Helping behavior and altruism: An empirical and conceptual overview. In L. Berkowitz (Ed.), *Advances in experimental social psychology* (Vol. 17, pp. 361–427). New York: Academic Press.

Dovidio, J. F., Allen, J., & Schroeder, D. A. (1987, May). *The specificity of empathy-induced helping: Evidence for altruistic motivation.* Paper presented at the annual meeting of the Eastern Psychological Association, New York.

Eagly, A. H., & Crowley, M. (1986). Gender and helping behavior: A meta-analytic review of the social-psychological literature. *Psychological Bulletin, 100,* 283–308.

Eisenberg, N., & Miller, P. (1987). Empathy and prosocial behavior. *Psychological Bulletin, 101,* 91–119.

Fultz, J., Batson, C. D., Fortenbach, V. A., McCarthy, P. M., & Varney, L. L. (1986). Social evaluation and the empathy–altruism hypothesis. *Journal of Personality and Social Psychology, 50,* 761–769.

Geller, V., & Shaver, P. (1976). Cognitive consequences of self-awareness. *Journal of Experimental Social Psychology, 12,* 99–108.

Hoffman, M. L. (1976). Empathy, role-taking, guilt, and development of altruistic motives. In T. Lickona (Ed.), *Moral development and behavior: Theory, research, and social issues* (pp. 124–143). New York: Holt, Rinehart & Winston.

Hoffman, M. L. (1981). The development of empathy. In J. P. Rushton & R. M. Sorrentino (Eds.), *Altruism and helping behavior: Social, personality, and developmental perspectives* (pp. 41–63). Hillsdale, NJ: Erlbaum.

Jones, E. E., & Pittman, T. S. (1982). Toward a general theory of strategic self-presentation. In J. Suls (Ed.), *Psychological perspectives on the self* (pp. 231–262). Hillsdale, NJ: Erlbaum.

Krebs, D. L. (1975). Empathy and altruism. *Journal of Personality and Social Psychology, 32,* 1134–1146.

Kučera, H., & Francis, N. W. (1967). *Computational analysis of present-day American English.* Providence, RI: Brown University Press.

Langer, E. J., & Abelson, R. P. (1972). The semantics of asking a favor: How to succeed in getting help without really dying. *Journal of Personality and Social Psychology, 24,* 26–32.

Meindl, J. R., & Lerner, M. J. (1983). The heroic motive: Some experimental demonstrations. *Journal of Experimental Social Psychology, 19,* 1–20.

Milgram, S. (1963). Behavioral study of obedience. *Journal of Abnormal and Social Psychology, 67,* 371–378.

Milgram, S. (1974). *Obedience to authority: An experimental view.* New York: Harper & Row.

Moscovici, S. (1985). Social influence and conformity. In G. Lindzey & E. Aronson (Eds.), *Handbook of social psychology: Vol. 2. Special fields and applications* (3rd ed., pp. 347–412). New York: Random House.

Orne, M. (1962). On the social psychology of the psychological experiment: With particular reference to demand characteristics and their implications. *American Psychologist, 17,* 776–783.

Pedhazur, E. J. (1982). *Multiple regression in behavioral research: Explanation and prediction* (2nd ed.). New York: Holt, Rinehart & Winston.

Piliavin, J. A., Dovidio, J. F., Gaertner, S. L., & Clark, R. D., III. (1981). *Emergency intervention.* New York: Academic Press.

Piliavin, J. A., & Piliavin, I. M. (1973). *The Good Samaritan: Why does he help?* Unpublished manuscript, University of Wisconsin—Madison.

Rosenhan, D. L., Salovey, P., & Hargis, K. (1981). The joys of helping: Focus of attention mediates the impact of positive affect on altruism. *Journal of Personality and Social Psychology, 40,* 899–905.

Schadler, M., & Thissen, D. M. (1981). The development of automatic word recognition and reading skill. *Memory & Cognition, 9,* 132–141.

Schaller, M., & Cialdini, R. B. (in press). The economics of empathic helping: Support for a mood management motive. *Journal of Experimental Social Psychology.*

Schroeder, D. A., Dovidio, J. F., Sibicky, M. E., Matthews, L. L. , & Allen, J. L. (in press). Empathy and helping behavior: Egoism or altruism. *Journal of Experimental Social Psychology.*

Schwartz, S. H., & Howard, J. (1981). A normative decision-making model of altruism. In J. P. Rushton & R. M. Sorrentino (Eds.), *Altruism and helping behavior* (pp. 189–211). Hillsdale, NJ: Erlbaum.

Sherif, M. (1936). *The psychology of norms.* New York: Harper.

Snyder, M. L., Kleck, R. E., Strenta, A., & Mentzer, S. J. (1979). Avoidance of the handicapped: An attributional ambiguity analysis. *Journal of Personality and Social Psychology, 37,* 2297–2306.

Stotland, E. (1969). Exploratory studies of empathy. In L. Berkowitz (Ed.), *Advances in experimental social psychology* (Vol. 4, pp. 271–313). New York: Academic Press.

Stroop, J. R. (1938). Factors affecting speed in serial verbal reactions. *Psychological Monographs, 50,* 38–48.

Thompson, W. C., Cowan, C. L., & Rosenhan, D. L. (1980). Focus of attention mediates the impact of negative affect on altruism. *Journal of Personality and Social Psychology, 38,* 291–300.

Toi, M., & Batson, C. D. (1982). More evidence that empathy is a source of altruistic motivation. *Journal of Personality and Social Psychology, 43,* 281–292.

Wallach, M. A., & Wallach, L. (1983). *Psychology's sanction for selfishness: The error of egoism in theory and therapy.* San Francisco: Freeman.

Warren, R. E. (1974). Association, directionality, and stimulus encoding. *Journal of Experimental Psychology, 102,* 151–158.

Weyant, J. M. (1978). Effect of mood states, costs, and benefits on helping. *Journal of Personality and Social Psychology, 36,* 1169–1176.

Wicklund, R. A. (1975). Objective self awareness. In L. Berkowitz (Ed.), *Advances in experimental social psychology* (Vol. 8, pp. 233–275). New York: Academic Press.

Winer, B. J. (1971). *Statistical principles in experimental design* (2nd ed.) New York: McGraw-Hill.

Yinon, Y., & Landau, M. O. (1987). On the reinforcing value of helping behavior in a positive mood. *Motivation & Emotion. 11,* 83–93.

Received October 15, 1986
Revision received February 16, 1988
Accepted February 17, 1988 ■

Comment
The Psychological Definitions of Morality
Augusto Blasi

The paper by Richard Shweder is a part of a larger and very ambitious project. His intention is not only to criticize Kohlberg's and Turiel's accounts of moral development but also to offer a constructive alternative description and explanation of moral development. Although Shweder qualifies his conclusions as preliminary, he suggests that his findings support the following claims: (1) Kohlberg is incorrect in postulating a universal sequence, in which the understanding of conventionality always precedes the understanding of morality; (2) Turiel is incorrect in postulating that the differentiation between conventionality and morality is universally present from a very early age; (3) the understanding of morality is universally present in children and adults, but the understanding of conventionality is a specialization of the former and only occurs in certain cultures; (4) moral understanding is not contructed by each individual but is "tacitly communicated" to the members of each culture through their participation in certain cultural practices.

These claims are more radical than they may appear initially. By rejecting the assumption of constructivism, Shweder places himself outside the currently popular cognitive-developmental understanding of moral de-

103

velopment and seems to subscribe to a form of cultural determinism. In particular, his notion of cultural influence through "tacit communication," although ill-defined, is intriguing and worthy of reflection.

It is impossible to deal with each of Shweder's claims in such a short paper. Instead, I will limit myself to a central issue, namely, the ways in which morality, moral understanding, and moral behavior have been defined by psychologists. The relevance for Shweder's conclusions is obvious. If what Shweder means by morality is not what Kohlberg or Turiel mean by the same term, then his data may not be relevant to their accounts. But the issue of meanings goes beyond Shweder's, Kohlberg's, and Turiel's work and deserves to be considered in broad terms.

To simplify (and perhaps oversimplify) the history of psychological research in this field, one can say that morality was first defined as a list of specific behaviors, ranging from helping others to resisting the temptation to cheat. These behaviors were not understood by psychologists and social scientists in general as sharing any intrinsic characteristics; instead, their moral relevance was thought to exclusively depend on culturally relative classifications and labels.

The important shift occurred when it was acknowledged that morality does not consist of any specific behaviors but of a special perspective of the agent, a certain kind of understanding that the agent has of actions and situations. The "assumption of phenomenalism," as Kohlberg (Kohlberg, Levine, and Hewer 1983) calls it, was the starting point of cognitive developmentalism and remains one of its central characteristics. The reason why this definition is important and in my opinion should not be abandoned is that it made psychological research on morality (and not simply on moral reasoning) congruent with the meanings embedded in ordinary language. In fact, the level of ordinary language, or common understanding, not only creates shared social meanings, but allows interactions among people to be genuinely social.

Despite Kohlberg's contribution, two important questions still remain to be answered: first, which perspective is characteristic of morality and defines it; and second, which level of abstraction is most appropriate in studying people's moral understanding? The cognitive-developmental approach, particularly under Kohlberg's influence, relies for answers on philosophical theory or, at least, on the most common philosophical views. It takes justice to be the central characteristic of morality and one's understanding of justice as defining the moral perspective. Concerning the second question, the solution was to follow a formalistic approach to morality. Moral understanding would then consist of the most basic conceptual structure that determines the criteria used to justify one's moral actions.

It is useful to emphasize that these solutions are choices among several possible alternatives. These choices, moreover, do not necesarily depend on the meanings of ordinary language. In other words, it is possible to settle on a more concrete, more content-oriented, level of moral understanding. Moreover, one could have emphasized, together with or as alternatives to justice, other moral issues, such as kindness or obligations to oneself.

Another important observation concerns the influence of philosophy on psychology. As I noted elsewhere (Blasi 1986), even though this influence has been positive, there may be negative side effects when psychologists choose for their study of morality definitions that derive from specific philosophical theories. The reason is that philosophy is concerned with establishing a coherent and rational foundation for morality; namely, with determining what morality should be. Psychology, instead, is (or should be) interested in describing what morality in fact is, the way it is actually experienced by people, and in providing an account in terms of psychological processes, both rational and nonrational.

As a result of these different perspectives, philosophical theory may disregard, or eliminate as irrelevant to morality, behaviors and feelings that are relevant to the psychologist's questions. For instance, some philosophers (e.g., Habermas 1971; Hamm and Daniels 1979), starting from a theoretical conception of what morality should be, distinguish between moral issues and "good life" issues. In contrast with morality, good life issues would be relativistic, nonobligatory and mostly personal rather than interpersonal in content. They would include not only the pursuit of one's interests and the fulfillment of one's personality, but also loyalty to cultural customs and traditions and religious obligations.

If a psychologist were to follow the same guideline, he or she might disregard large samples of practices that in fact are viewed by many people as falling in the same category as moral obligations. The psychological theory of morality that would be based on this unnecessarily restricted sample of behaviors would consequently be much too narrow.

While it may generally be problematic to rely on philosophy to define what is to be studied as morality, the risks are even more serious in cross-cultural research. The reason is that those moral institutions on which the researcher relies, as well as Western moral philosophy that builds on them, may be inadequate to represent morality as it is understood in other cultures. One cannot rely on the similarities and differences among the practices, because morality cannot be defined without taking into account those subjective perspectives by which these practices are understood. And, in attempting to take these subjective perspectives into account, one cannot rely either on the simple use of terms such as "should," "right," "good," and "obligation," because it is precisely the meanings of these terms that are in question.

A possible approach to cross-cultural moral research would be to select a large number of culturally meaningful "practices" (in Shweder's sense of the term) and, for each, to gather rich networks of meanings (attitudes, reasons). This can be done at the level of the culture as a whole (e.g., through fairy tales, popular books, and newspaper accounts) as well as with groups of individuals of various ages and social backgrounds. Even then a working definition will be needed to differentiate moral from non-moral perspectives. The starting definition should be descriptive (i.e., involving a low level of theoretical reconstruction), emphasize psychological processes, and rely on as few philosophical assumptions as possible beyond the level of common understanding.

Elsewhere (Blasi 1986) I suggested a set of three criteria for morality. For the purpose of psychological research, a behavior or a practice is considered moral if it is intentional, a response to some sense of obligation, and if the obligation is a response to an ideal, even if vaguely understood. This definition may very well offer an adequate starting point, a middle ground between a behavioristic approach to practices and language on the one hand and a prematurely narrow philosophical view on the other. One may be able to determine, from the beginning, which practices are understood to be moral in different cultures. By relying on the network of meanings that are attached to each practice, one may be able to construct different categories of moral understanding and to establish, eventually, theoretical relations among these categories.

We can now return to Shweder's study and consider his claims in the light of these very general considerations. Shweder began his project with the decision to use as concrete material large samples of practices, not two or three dilemmas as Kohlberg and his associates used. These practices form a very heterogeneous group; while some seem to be good candidates for eliciting a universal moral response, others seem to be important only within certain cultures, and others, at least from the perspective of Western intuition and philosophy, seem to be irrelevant to morality. This last group includes hygienic and eating practices and prescriptions concerning dependence or independence, sex roles, and ethnic identity.

Shweder's selection of practices runs counter to the definition of morality as justice commonly accepted within cognitive developmentalism. But Shweder was probably correct in following his anthropological intuition rather than philosophical definitions. As I suggested earlier, his strategy seems to offer the only possible starting point, if one wants to find out to what extent moral understanding is universal, or whether justice is indeed the universal structural core of moral knowledge.

Unfortunately, this investigation, at least as presented in this paper, cannot keep its promise. In fact, Shweder relies on people's use of simple terms, such as "wrong," "best," and "okay," to indicate the presence of a moral judgment and does not seem to inquire how these and other terms are specifically understood by children and adults of different cultures.

He has asked eight questions concerning the necessity and the violation of each practice; each question contained key terms, whose meaning is ambiguous and open to different interpretations. Some of these are: "violation," "offense," "sin," "wrong," "serious," "best," and "okay." Childrens' and adults' answers were of two types. The first consisted in the choice of one of four alternatives concerning the degree of "seriousness" of violating a practice. On this basis, Shweder could find out how the practices are ranked by each subject in terms of their importance. He could then compare the rankings and determine the degree of similarity among children and adults of the same culture, as well as among the children and adults of different cultures.

The answers to the other seven questions consisted essentially of yes or no. Three of these questions are particularly important for Shweder: (1) Would it be best if everyone in the world followed practice X?; (2) In country Z people do practice X all the time. Would country Z be a better place if they stopped doing that?; and (3) What if most people in country Z wanted to change practice X? Would it be okay to change it? Shweder constructed the three most central categories of his analysis on the basis of the answers to these three questions. According to his classification, a practice is understood as establishing a universal moral obligation if one answers yes to the first question and not to the other two. The obligation is understood to be moral but context-dependent if one answers no to all three questions. Finally, the obligation is understood to be nonmoral but simply based on convention and consensus if one answers no to the first two questions and yes to the last. Shweder believes that these three categories represent "the more formal and structural aspects of normative judgments" (p. 35), and they allow him to address Kohlberg's and Turiel's views concerning the relations between conventionality and morality.

I believe, instead, that Shweder's findings are largely irrelevant to, and leave untouched, Kohlberg's and Turiel's claims. I will focus my discussion on Kohlberg's case. There are two reasons for my judgment. One is that Shweder tends to misinterpret Kohlberg's claims in important ways and ends up criticizing his own construction rather than the claims themselves. The second reason is that Kohlberg and Shweder define morality so differently in their respective empirical operations that it is impossible to see how their data can be relevant to each other.

Concerning the first point, Shweder misinterprets three central ideas of Kohlberg's scheme. First, he confuses the type of objectivity and universality characteristic of Kohlberg's postconventional level with his own concept of natural law. In Shweder's vocabulary, the idea of natural law seems to refer to a recognition that morality is based on the objective nature of things and actions. According to Kohlberg (Kohlberg, Levine, and Hewer 1983), instead, the postconventional understanding of universality seems to be based on the recognition that only a certain kind of ideal consensus establishes the ultimate moral rationality. Because of this confusion, Shweder interprets children's objectivistic approach to morality as indicating an understanding of natural law and concludes, then, that children are postconventional in Kohlberg's sense.

Second, Shweder appears to think that the conventionality of Kohlberg's level two (stages three and four) includes both the idea of conformity to rules and authority and the idea that the value of social rules is based on consensus. However, in Kohlberg's description, this level is social and authoritarian in perspective, but neither relativistic nor consensual, as Shweder seems to think. From Kohlberg's viewpoint, the moral value of consensus is understood much better at the postconventional than at the conventional level.

Finally, Shweder interprets Kohlberg's theory as claiming that genuine morality develops from the understanding of conventionality, namely, from a nonmoral position. But, again, Kohlberg's view is quite different. For him, moral development is always a matter of progressively clarifying those criteria that are specifically moral and differentiating them from those that are not. Thus, he believes that during level two there is a global understanding in which conventional and moral criteria are fused together and in which conventional criteria are given moral value. Level three, based on the understanding that moral criteria cannot be reduced to conventional criteria, would develop out of a genuinely moral, though partially undifferentiated, understanding.

However, even if Shweder had correctly represented Kohlberg's ideas, his data would not be adequate to test or criticize them. To use the currently accepted terminology, Shweder's data concern the *content* of people's thinking, whereas Kohlberg tries to capture the basic *structures* of moral understanding. More precisely, Kohlberg's stages are based on the reasons that people give to justify certain practices. Starting from these reasons, more basic criteria are isolated and the logic from which these criteria are derived is finally reconstructed. This information is missing in, and irretrievable from, Shweder's data, even from those categories that, in his view, reflect more formal aspects. For example, when a person says that a certain practice should be followed by everybody, in every culture, regardless of people's consensus, we still don't know why she or he thinks that this should be the case.

Faced with Shweder's finding that children's answers are more similar to the answers given by the adults of the same culture, Kohlberg would reply that similarity in content may hide more fundamental differences, while differences in content are compatible with similarity in structural criteria. In fact, Kohlberg (1969) has already pointed out that from an early age, children are familiar with and accept those attitudes and concrete judgments that are typical of their culture, but he has taken this fact to indicate the inadequacy of content responses to reveal structural moral development.

Of course, these considerations do not invalidate Shweder's findings. When they are considered alone and not in relation to Kohlberg's or Turiel's theories, Shweder's data are interesting and raise questions about the actual meaning and the limits of moral universals at the level of structural analysis. Shweder may say that the type of structural account that Kohlberg and others offer is only partial and ultimately not very useful to an understanding of how and why people do what they actually do. He may have a point, even if it does not seem useful to argue about the relative usefulness of approaches as different as Kohlberg's, Turiel's, and Shweder's. The real issue is one of integration; namely, of understanding how concrete moral judgments and abstract moral structures go together both at the level of individual consciousness and in functionally affecting behavior. This question of integration, it is fair to say, has not been solved; indeed, it is rarely asked.

However—and this brings us back to the main theme of my commentary—this work of integration presupposes that concrete judgments, as well as abstract criteria, are genuinely moral; that is, that they are understood to be moral by the individual who formulates them. Most of my doubts with regard to Shweder's research concern this point. It is of secondary importance that he did not intend to gather structurally relevant material. However, one frequently wonders whether the responses that Shweder accepts as having moral meaning are indeed understood as moral by his informants. When a person (American or Indian, child or adult) agrees that it would be best if everyone in the world followed a certain practice and that the world would not be a better place if other societies stopped the same practice, can Shweder be sure that this person understands and uses "best" and "better" in a moral sense?

In the methodological tradition that characterizes cognitive developmentalism, it is acknowledged that people's response only ambiguously reflect their conceptual competence. Therefore, an effort is made to facilitate the interpretive analysis and to clarify the subjects' real understanding by resorting to probes, alternative hypothetical situations, and countersuggestions. However, Shweder avoided this methodology and did so consciously. In his view and in the opinions of many others, this strategy unnecessarily relies on linguistic skills that many people do not possess and leads investigators to underestimate the actual level of conceptual competence. One may sympathize with Shweder's concern; however, the problem of inferring real meanings from the use of simple words still remains.

This inference is, of course, more problematic in the cases of children. And yet, it is this type of evidence that Shweder uses to conclude that even young children commonly approach cultural practices with the belief that they establish universal moral obligations and, thus, with a genuine moral understanding. My doubts are not simply based on the ambiguity of "better" and "best." We know from Piaget's (1932) studies that very young children do indeed attach some kind of strict necessity to social rules and generalize this necessity to everybody. However, Piaget had also pointed out that, in this case, necessity is not equivalent to moral obligation but reflects a confusion between physical laws and social rules, while generalization is not equivalent to moral universality but indicates children's basic inability to differentiate other people's perspectives from their own. Unless this type of ambiguity is resolved, it is very difficult to determine the precise way in which Shweder's findings are relevant to a theory of moral development.

References

Blasi, A. 1986 Psychologische oder philosophische Definition der Moral. Schädliche Einflüsse der Philosophie auf die Moralpsychologie (How should psychologists define morality? Or, the negative side-effects of philosophy's influence on psychology). In W. Edelstein and G. Nunner-Winkler, eds., *Zur Bestimmung der Moral*. Frankfurt am Main: Suhrkamp.

Habermas, J. 1971. *Knowledge and Human Interests*. Boston: Beacon Press.

Hamm, C. M., and L. B. Daniels, 1979. Moral Education in Relation to Values Education. In D. B. Cochrane, C. M. Hamm, and A. C. Kazepides, eds., *The Domain of Moral Education*. New York: Paulist Press.

Kohlberg, L. 1969. Stage and Sequence: The Cognitive-Development Approach to Socialization. In D. A. Goslin, ed., *Handbook of Socialization Theory and Research*. Chicago: Rand McNally.

Kohlberg, L., C. Levine, and A. Hewer, 1983. *Moral Stages: A Current Formulation and a Response to Critics*. Basel: Karger.

Piaget, J. 1932. *The Moral Judgment of the Child*. New York: Free Press.

Positive Mood and Helping Behavior: A Test of Six Hypotheses

Michael Carlson, Ventura Charlin, and Norman Miller
University of Southern California

Past research has shown rather consistently that positive mood states lead to increased helpfulness. In an expanded analysis of the published literature, we examined six distinct views about this relation: the focus of attention, objective self-awareness, separate process, social outlook, mood maintenance, and concomitance hypotheses. For each of 61 positive affect conditions in which it was possible to generate an effect-size estimate corresponding to the relative degree of helpfulness exhibited by positive mood subjects (compared with neutral affect subjects), judges assessed the contextual levels of variables relevant to each of the six hypotheses by reading the Method section of each article. Higher-order partial correlation coefficients were then calculated to isolate the independent contribution of each of the theoretically relevant variables to the variation among the 61 effect sizes. The results support the focus of attention, separate process, social outlook, and mood maintenance hypotheses, and partially support the objective self-awareness and concomitance hypotheses.

A substantial body of research shows that, with relatively few exceptions, a good mood promotes helpfulness. Some of the types of positive mood experiences that do so include succeeding on an experimental task (e.g., Isen, 1970; Weyant, 1978), unexpectedly finding a dime in the return slot of a public phone (Cunningham, Steinberg, & Grev, 1980; Isen & Levin, 1972), listening to soothing music (Fried & Berkowitz, 1979), being on the winning team when participating in a football game (Berg, 1978), being given a free packet of stationery (Isen, Clark, & Schwartz, 1976), imagining oneself to be enjoying a marvelous vacation in Hawaii (Rosenhan, Salovey, & Hargis, 1981), and being labeled a charitable person (Kraut, 1973). At least six hypotheses attempt to account for various aspects of these effects. Prior to introducing them, the notion of priming, which is directly relevant to several of them, is briefly reviewed.

Priming

A good mood causes people to perceive things in a more positive light (Bower, 1981; Carson & Adams, 1980; Clark & Teasdale, 1985; Forgas, Bower, & Krantz, 1984; Isen, Shalker, Clark,

& Karp, 1978; Teasdale & Fogarty, 1979). Presumably, people store material in memory in part on the basis of its affective tone. Consequently, a good mood state is hypothesized to function as a cue that temporarily increases the likelihood that positive cognitions will be generated in response to a subsequent stimulus. This process, called *priming*, can set a self-perpetuating cognitive loop of positive thoughts and associations into motion. Consequently, individuals who feel positive will tend to evaluate a given prosocial opportunity more favorably than will others, and therefore will more readily offer assistance (Clark & Isen, 1982; Isen et al., 1978). The finding that a good mood increases the affective positivity of cognitions linked to a potential helping situation (Clark & Waddell, 1983) is very much in harmony with this notion. This priming effect, however, is not assumed to be invariant. In particular, unambiguously unpleasant stimuli are hypothesized to be relatively immune to any positive perceptual biasing that results from a good mood (Clark & Isen, 1982).

To an extent, the general notion of priming is pertinent to each of the hypotheses discussed in the following section. In addition, it is important to note that the six hypotheses are not mutually exclusive, but tend to be partially overlapping and, in certain cases, complexly interrelated.

The Six Hypotheses

Focus of Attention

Rosenhan and his colleagues have proposed that attentional focus mediates the relation between good mood and helpfulness (Rosenhan, Karylowski, Salovey, & Hargis, 1981; Rosenhan, Salovey, et al., 1981). In this view, positive events promote benevolence only when they are directed toward oneself. Pleasant

The Haynes Foundation, by providing Fellowship support to Michael Carlson for the 1986–87 academic year, greatly facilitated this research and its preparation for publication.

We thank Alice Isen and Len Berkowitz for helpful comments on an early draft of this article. In addition, we thank Norbert Kerr and three anonymous reviewers for their very constructive criticism of a subsequent draft.

Correspondence concerning this article should be addressed to Norman Miller, Department of Psychology, University of Southern California, Los Angeles, California 90089-1061.

Journal of Personality and Social Psychology, 1988, Vol. 55, No. 2, 211–229
Copyright 1988 by the American Psychological Association, Inc. 0022-3514/88/$00.75

mood states that result from focusing on another person's good fortune fail to heighten helpfulness and may even reduce it below normal levels.

Rosenhan, Salovey, and Hargis (1981) confirmed these expectations in an experiment that manipulated attentional focus toward oneself or toward another among subjects in whom a positive mood had been induced. Individuals made to feel good by intensely imagining themselves experiencing a wonderful Hawaiian vacation subsequently helped more than did neutral mood controls; however, when good mood was induced by instructing subjects to imagine instead that their best friend was enjoying this pleasant vacation, the level of helpfulness dropped below that exhibited by the affectively neutral controls. Rosenhan, Salovey, and Hargis speculated that a type of social comparison accounts for these results. Being the primary recipient of good fortune elicits a general feeling of advantage relative to others, along with a concomitant desire to restore a general sense of equity by donating time and resources to the service of others. If instead another person's good fortune is salient, one feels disadvantaged and thus dispenses resources less freely to others. In addition to equity restoration, attentional focus effects may reflect the operation of priming processes. When a person is the recipient of unwarranted good fortune, it may generate positive thoughts that in turn promote helpfulness (Isen et al., 1978). In contrast, when it is another's good fortune that is salient, negative cognitions related to jealousy or other selfish concerns may neutralize or reverse positive priming effects.

Thus, although the focus of attention hypothesis fundamentally describes a key boundary condition for the facilitative effects of positive mood on helping (i.e., that the primary recipient of the positive event is oneself), underlying explanatory processes, such as social comparison or priming, may nonetheless be associated with it.

Objective Self-Awareness

The theory of objective self-awareness (Duval & Wicklund, 1972; Wicklund, 1975) furnishes a further explanation for the finding that a positive event tends to augment helpfulness if, but only if, it is directed primarily at oneself. Objective self-awareness is defined as a state in which one focuses on oneself as an object of attention. It may occur when one is either the cause or the recipient of a positive event. In a pair of experiments reported by Berkowitz (1987), objective self-awareness was induced, following a manipulation of positive affect, by having subjects either view themselves in a mirror or write a self-referencing essay. As predicted, among elated individuals self-awareness was associated with increased effort in scoring data sheets on behalf of the experimenter. There are two primary ways in which objective self-awareness might augment positive mood-based helpfulness. The first is based on the finding that those made self-aware tend to conform to salient behavioral ideals to a greater degree than do others, presumably in an effort to avoid any negative affect that results from perceptions of falling short of such ideals (e.g., Duval & Wicklund, 1972; Gibbons & Wicklund, 1982; Vallacher & Solodky, 1979). Research has consistently found that a negative mood state that is accompa-

nied by objective self-awareness augments helpfulness if a salient plea for aid is present, or if prosocial values are otherwise psychologically prominent (e.g., Carlson & Miller, 1987; Gibbons & Wicklund, 1982; Rogers, Miller, Mayer, & Duval, 1982). Thus, to the extent that a positive mood state engenders objective self-awareness, increased helpfulness may result if a person seeks to avoid an intraself discrepancy that would result from failing to fulfill one's responsibility to help. In line with this, Berkowitz (1987) has suggested that, in the context of a pleasant mood, a self-aware person may adhere more strongly to social responsibility ideals in an effort to maintain a positive self-conception.

A second reason why self-awareness might augment helpfulness in the context of positive affect is that it may intensify many of the self-relevant pleasant feelings and cognitions that accompany a good mood and that generally promote helpfulness (Berkowitz, 1987). For example, self-focus may enhance one's good mood (Scheier & Carver, 1977) and thereby further facilitate priming processes or feelings of social attraction.

As previously noted, in some instances a self-directed positive event may increase objective self-awareness, for example, as when one has received bogus feedback to the effect that one is intelligent (Strenta & DeJong, 1981) or vividly imagines oneself engaging in pleasant activities (Rosenhan, Salovey, et al., 1981). Nonetheless, an individual may be the primary recipient of good fortune, yet fail to become objectively self-aware. For example, after unexpectedly being given a free box of candy, a person's attention may primarily center on the generous individual who provided the treat, or perhaps on the candy itself.[1] Although studies involving negative affective states have shown that viewing oneself as the cause of a negative event increases objective self-awareness, which in turn promotes helpfulness provided that a salient prosocial behavioral standard is present (e.g., Rogers et al., 1982), nevertheless, perceptions of oneself as the recipient of a negative event do not invariably generate objective self-awareness and its motivational dynamic (e.g., Thompson, Cowan, & Rosenhan, 1980). In the case of positive mood and helping, it is likewise possible that the act of focusing on oneself as the primary cause of the mood-elevating event (e.g., after succeeding on an experimental task) is generally necessary in order to elicit objective self-awareness and its motivational effects on helpfulness. To date, however, we know of no empirical evidence that addresses this question.

Separate Processes

Subjects made to feel guilty typically show increased helpfulness (e.g., Carlsmith & Gross, 1969; Carlson & Miller, 1987; McMillen & Austin, 1971; J. W. Regan, 1971; Regan, Williams, & Sparling, 1972). After reviewing such evidence, as well as a body of research that points to the presence of neurologically distinct punishment and reward centers in animals, Cunning-

---

[1] Thus, while the focus of attention hypothesis stresses the importance of perceptions concerning the fact that one has been the recipient of a positive event, the objective self-awareness hypothesis instead emphasizes the role of directly focusing on oneself as the object of attention.

ham et al. (1980) advanced the notion that separate, mutually inhibitory, motivational processes underlie the respective increases in helpfulness that result from positive and negative mood. In the first of two field experiments, Cunningham et al. found that subjects who experienced either a positive event (finding a dime in the coin return slot of a public phone) or a guilt-producing event (ostensibly breaking someone's camera) helped more than did neutral mood controls. However, individuals who were subjected to both the positive event and the guilt induction helped nonsignificantly less than did affectively neutral persons. Presumably, this result reflects a cancellation of effects when positive and negative motivational systems are concurrently activated. In the second study, the authors reasoned that, to the extent that distinct motivational systems are involved, positive and negative mood states should produce a differential responsiveness to requests for aid that emphasize, respectively, either positive or negative aspects of helping. In support of this prediction, a good mood state was found to be associated with increased donations made to a children's fund if, but only if, a positive request for aid was given (subjects were exposed to a poster portraying a smiling child, along with a caption stating "Help keep the children smiling"). Guilty subjects, however, donated more only when exposed to a negatively toned plea that emphasized obligation (the poster in this case pictured a frowning child, with the words "You owe it to the children").

In addition to positing the presence of a mutually inhibitory effect of sequential events that separately induce good mood and guilt, the separate process hypothesis also implies that a single event that simultaneously engenders both good mood and guilt will produce less helpfulness than will either good mood or guilt alone (Cunningham et al., 1980). Thus, a positive mood state that contains guilt as one of its elements should fail to produce the typical increase in prosocial responding that occurs as a result of positive affect. This idea counters the suggestion (e.g., Forbes & TeVault, 1975) that some manipulations of positive mood, such as finding a dime in the coin return slot of a pay phone, have produced increased helpfulness as a consequence of making subjects feel guilty.

Note that other than stating that the mediating events differ, the separate process hypothesis does not explain why positive and negative moods augment helpfulness. In this sense, it is not at odds with other explanatory attempts, but merely postulates a boundary condition (i.e., the absence of negative affect) for the facilitative effects of positive mood on helpfulness.

Social Outlook

The fourth interpretation to be considered, the social outlook hypothesis, rests on the notion that certain positive events directly alter the favorableness of an individual's perception of the social community (Holloway, Tucker, & Hornstein, 1977; Hornstein, LaKind, Frankel, & Manne, 1975). It argues that irrespective of any mood changes, a given pleasant event may heighten a person's readiness to respond prosocially toward a stranger if one of its side effects is that it temporarily promotes a positive perception of human nature or the general social community when considered as a cooperative collective. In an experimental test of this idea, Holloway et al. (1977) exposed

subjects to a radio broadcast featuring good news that was either social (e.g., hearing about a stranger who risked his life in successfully rescuing a family from a burning home) or nonsocial (e.g., hearing how a freak wind saved a family from a forest fire) in nature. Compared with no-broadcast control subjects, only those who listened to good news stories that emphasized a positive side of human nature exhibited increased cooperation when making subsequent nonzero-sum game choices. Furthermore, positive mood was ruled out as a potential mediator of the results because a manipulation check showed that the good news broadcasts failed to elevate mood. Thus, the social outlook hypothesis suggests that helpfulness that appears to result from positive mood may sometimes be caused instead by cognitions that emphasize human kindness and cooperation. In addition, a pleasant event that originates in the context of a social interaction (e.g., meeting a wonderful new friend) would generally be expected to promote a more favorable social outlook than one that is impersonal in nature (e.g., finding a nugget while panning for gold when alone), in that in the former case the cognitions surrounding the good mood are more socially relevant. Therefore, we believe that the social outlook hypothesis can be extended to suggest that prosocial interactions should promote greater helpfulness than equally positive nonsocial events.

The underlying process responsible for the social outlook effect has not been clearly elaborated. It may entail the priming of cognitions pertinent to positively toned social interaction. These might include cognitions concerning a sense of community or trust, but also those related to attraction, empathy, and cooperation. In addition, a positive social outlook may make salient help-dictating norms such as those for reciprocity and social responsibility, and thus overlap with the segment of the objective self-awareness model that emphasizes adherence to prosocial ideals.

Mood Maintenance

Given that a pleasant mood has commenced, it can best be maintained in the face of a subsequent social event if a response is made that fosters further positive feelings. In line with this notion, the mood maintenance hypothesis posits that happy individuals help more in part because doing so enables them to prolong their good mood state (Clark & Isen, 1982; Isen et al., 1978; Isen & Simmonds, 1978). Several studies show that those who feel good exhibit increased helpfulness when the helping task is inherently pleasant, but tend to help less than others when the act of helping is distasteful (Forest, Clark, Mills, & Isen, 1979; Harada, 1983; Isen & Levin, 1972; Isen & Simmonds, 1978). Such results argue for the operation of a mood maintenance motive among elated individuals, in that enjoyable prosocial tasks prolong a positive affective state, whereas unpleasant ones disrupt it.

In principle, a motive to maintain a positive mood will promote helping to a greater extent when positive priming processes are also present. The reason for this is that according to the mood maintenance hypothesis, a good mood is hypothesized to augment helpfulness to a greater degree when the helping task is viewed in a favorable manner. To the extent that priming processes increase the likelihood of favorably perceiving the prosocial opportunity, fulfilling the helping task will therefore be seen as better able to prolong one's good mood state. Likewise, if a motive to maintain one's prior good mood is activated, then the positive perceptual biases that result from priming processes will be more readily acted on.

We think, however, that these relations will be qualified by other considerations. If a desire to prolong one's prior good mood state is in fact operative, then an extremely satisfying positive experience (e.g., winning an Olympic gold medal) might be expected to generally produce less subsequent helpfulness than a more moderate one (e.g., enjoying a sunset). Presumably, when one is savoring an especially gratifying experience, directing subsequent attention to a neutral or moderately pleasant activity (such as helping another person) may represent an undesirable trade-off with respect to the hedonic quality of one's affective state. On the other hand, when a person's positive feelings only slightly exceed affective neutrality, the strength of a mood maintenance motive should be minimal, in that in such cases one's positive mood state is more likely to be unnoticeable or to lack any salience, and therefore will not produce any attempts to prolong it. Thus, given that good mood is present, intermediate levels of elation should generally lead to more helpfulness than either very high or very low levels.[2] It should be stressed that this expectation is neither directly implied by the mood maintenance formulation nor has it previously been specifically mentioned in the literature. It assumes that perceivers gauge the net impact that a prosocial activity might have on their mood by averaging their perceived existing level of positive affect with the corresponding level expected to result from a subsequent contemplated helping activity. In contrast, an additive model would suggest that any positive activity, no matter how slight, will be engaged in more readily when a person is feeling good. On theoretical grounds, we feel that the averaging model is more likely to be correct. For example, evidence supporting the unidirectional nature of human attention (e.g., Anderson, 1980) implies that directing one's efforts to help another will detract from one's ability to consciously focus upon a prior, extremely elating experience. Thus, cognitions surrounding a subsequent helping task are expected primarily to replace, and not additively coexist with, positive affect generating thoughts that stem from the prior positive event.

Concomitance

Cialdini and his associates have proposed a concomitance hypothesis to account for the increased helpfulness that typically follows a happy mood state (Cialdini, Kenrick, & Baumann, 1982; Manucia, Baumann, & Cialdini, 1984). According to this perspective, positive affect per se does not directly augment helpfulness. Instead, increased benevolence is a psychological by-product of other effects of a good mood (such as an increased liking for others, priming processes, or a feeling of emotional advantage that should be shared equitably with others).

The proponents of the concomitance model explicitly deny the operation of a mood maintenance motive in accounting for the greater helpfulness exhibited by elated individuals. The outcome of an experiment conducted by Manucia et al. (1984) is offered as support for this rejection. In this study, half of the positive mood subjects were led to believe that their temporary mood state was unalterable, whereas the other half received no such information. The results showed that although subjects in the two positive mood conditions exhibited more helpfulness than neutral mood control subjects, they nonetheless failed to differ from each other. Because the operation of any desire to prolong good mood presumably was irrelevant for subjects who believed that their mood was temporarily unchangeable, Manucia et al. concluded that mood maintenance does not contribute to the helpfulness exhibited by happy individuals. These negative results are in apparent harmony with the outcome of a study by Weyant (1978), in which the reward-cost matrix associated with a given helping opportunity was not found to affect the level of compliance exhibited by elated subjects.

Despite the results of Manucia et al. (1984) and Weyant (1978), available evidence does not rule out mood maintenance. As noted in the preceding discussion of the mood maintenance hypothesis, a series of studies that manipulated the pleasantness of a helping opportunity consistently supported its predictions by showing that a good mood augments helpfulness when the prosocial task is pleasant, but decreases it when the task is effortful or unpleasant (Forest et al., 1979; Harada, 1983; Isen & Levin, 1972, Study I; Isen & Simmonds, 1978).[3] Manucia et al., in attempting to account for the results of the Forest et al. and Isen and Simmonds studies within the framework of the concomitance model, suggested that the manipulation of the helping task's pleasantness in these latter studies (reading either positive or negative mood statements) altered patterns of helpfulness by creating mood changes after the helping task had commenced. In other words, the mood cards themselves and not any prior willingness to help were responsible for the increased number of positive, as well as the decreased number of negative, cards that were read by the elated subjects. Although plausible, such an explanation seems to admit that happy individuals, relative to those feeling neutral, are more likely to sustain ongoing help only if doing so is consistent with the perpetuation of the prior good mood state. Despite the fact that affectively neutral subjects were expected to experience mood changes in either a positive or negative direction after reading the mood-inducing statements, those who had experienced a prior good mood nonetheless read more of the positive statements, as well as fewer of the negative statements, than did those who initially felt neutral. Thus, a motive to maintain or enhance one's good mood apparently does operate to sustain ongoing helping behavior. With respect to the possible role of

---

[2] A questionnaire study conducted by Harris (1977) supports the idea that the fulfillment of most types of brief, interpersonal helping acts is perceived as moderately positively reinforcing.

[3] A study conducted by Shaffer and Graziano (1983) likewise found this expected interaction between mood and task pleasantness when the dependent measure was the duration for which help was actually given. However, positive mood subjects were not more likely than others to volunteer help in the first place. Consequently, this study does not unequivocably support the mood maintenance formulation. The negative results for help volunteered, however, may artifactually be due to a ceiling effect: 33 out of 36 total subjects in the experiment agreed to help.

mood maintenance in affecting future, nonongoing helping acts, however, prior studies show mixed results. In some cases, elated subjects have shown increased sensitivity to the hedonic consequences of a contemplated helping task (Harada, 1983; Isen & Levin, 1972, Study I), whereas in other instances they have not (Shaffer & Graziano, 1983; Weyant, 1978). Further research is needed to clarify the possible role of mood maintenance in such situations.

It should be noted that, other than denying the role of mood maintenance, the concomitance hypothesis does not add any new explanatory concepts. It merely provides a common label for the set of helpfulness-enhancing considerations that are not based on mood management. Thus, explanations based on processes related to attentional focus, priming, altered social outlook, and objective self-awareness can be viewed as separate instances of concomitant factors.

Theoretically Based Correlation Analysis

These six hypotheses suggest that the relation between positive affect and prosocial behavior may be affected by a large number of variables that pertain to either a positive mood state or a helping request (e.g., the degree of positive affect present, objective self-awareness, guilt, pleasantness of the helping task, etc.). Consequently, it may be difficult to arrive at a general explanation by conducting a single experiment or a small set of experiments. For example, although in a given study good mood may fail to interact with task pleasantness in affecting helpfulness (as, for example, in Weyant, 1978), it is nonetheless quite conceivable that such a negative result is due to some particular and perhaps unknown contextual feature of the experiment (e.g., some aspect of the particular helping task that is called for) and merely represents a special exception that contradicts a generally valid phenomenon.

A research strategy that relates the effect-size estimates of meta-analytic procedures to specialized measurements of theoretically relevant mediating and moderating variables represents a potentially fruitful means of overcoming this problem. Drawing from the fairly sizable positive mood-helping literature, we have implemented such a strategy in the present study by (a) obtaining a sample of research instances in which the helpfulness of positive mood subjects is compared with that of neutral mood controls; (b) measuring for each case within the sample the levels of theoretically relevant mediating and moderator variables that accompany the subject characteristics, the positive mood induction, or the request for help; (c) calculating for each case a standardized estimate of experimental effect that reflects the relative degree of helpfulness exhibited by the positive affect experimental group; and (d) observing the extent to which the proposed mediating variables correlate with the effect sizes in the expected direction, given that the effects of the set of measured extraneous moderator and mediating variables are statistically controlled. If a given variable associated with some positive mood induction is in fact at least partially responsible for the increase in helpfulness found among elated individuals, then within the sampled set of cases, the magnitude of experimental effect should be larger for those instances in which high contextual levels of the variable in question are present. By si-

multaneously controlling for the effects of a large number of potential confounding variables via the use of partial correlation analysis, it is possible in principle to isolate the unique effects of helpfulness that result from a given theoretical variable. Thus, the proposed analytic technique greatly reduces the complexity that would otherwise be present in attempting to assess which variables among an intercorrelated set are in fact responsible for differences in helpfulness that arise from positive mood.

Moreover, the calculation of experimental effect sizes, by enabling the detection of differing degrees of positive mood-based increases in helpfulness (as opposed to simply tabulating whether positive mood increased helpfulness, as is routinely done in individual studies, as well as in qualitative reviews), greatly increases the precision that is available in testing proposed hypotheses of the effect. In testing a given predictor variable by obtaining its higher-order partial correlation coefficient with experimental effect size, one is in actuality performing a simple correlation between the unique variance associated with the predictor variable (i.e., that part of its variability that is not due to its covariation with the set of variables whose effects are controlled) and the residualized effect-size estimates (i.e., the difference between the actual effect size and the value that would be predicted on the basis of the particular combination of control variable values). Therefore, a given variable will significantly correlate with effect sizes to the extent that it uniquely predicts any systematic departures of effect sizes from those that would otherwise be expected. This implies that the proposed analytic strategy is viable even if, as Cialdini et al. (1982) have argued, the consistent tendency within the literature for positive mood to increase helpfulness ordinarily precludes or makes it difficult to pinpoint underlying causal mechanisms.

Finally, testing of theoretically relevant explanatory variables across an entire literature permits a broader range of generalization than would be possible after conducting a single study or a small series of studies, in that the conclusions that emerge reflect principles that hold over a wider array of combinations of subjects, settings, positive mood manipulations, and helping requests than have been studied in any single experiment. At the same time, however, we recognize that a negative result for a given variable does not imply that it is always unrelated to helpfulness. Instead, a certain set of boundary conditions that are underrepresented in the research literature may be necessary in order for it to affect helpfulness. Thus, the proposed correlational strategy is intended to complement but not invalidate the results obtained from any individual experiments.

Table 1 lists the primary predictions pertaining to the six hypotheses about the relation between good mood and helpfulness.

Method

Literature Search

The following procedure produced the sample of studies used to assess the impact of a given positive mood state on helpfulness. First, a search was made of *Psychological Abstracts* (January 1974 through December 1985), as well as recent volumes of several key social psychological journals (*Journal of Personality and Social Psychology, Personality*

Table 1
Between-Study Helping Predictions for the Six Hypotheses

Focus of attention

1. The degree to which oneself, as opposed to another, is the perceived primary recipient of the pleasant event correlates positively with effect size.

Objective self-awareness

1. Positive moods that produce high levels of objective self-awareness are associated with larger effect sizes, given that a salient helping request or prosocial values are present.
2. The extent of objective self-awareness correlates positively with effect size when the effects of concomitant variables, such as positive social outlook and self as the target of the positive event, are operative.

Separate processes

1. The degree to which a positive mood engenders feelings of guilt correlates negatively with effect size.

Social outlook

1. The extent to which a positive mood fosters positive perceptions of the social community correlates positively with effect size.
2. Positive experiences that are based on interacting with another person (as opposed to being impersonal) are associated with larger effect-size estimates.[a]

Mood maintenance

1. Intermediate levels of positive affect lead to larger effect sizes than do either very low or very high levels of positive affect.[a]
2. The overall degree of helping-task pleasantness correlates positively with effect size.

Concomitance

1. The overall degree of helping-task pleasantness fails to correlate positively with effect size.
2. At least some factors other than mood maintenance that accompany a positive mood state correlate positively with effect size.

[a] The prediction is not made by proponents of the hypothesis, but rather is based on our own theoretical extrapolation.

---

and *Social Psychology Bulletin, Journal of Experimental Social Psychology,* and *Social Psychology Quarterly,* 1982–1985), to locate empirical articles that examined a positive mood state's effect on helpfulness. For each potential qualifying case, the Reference section was checked for possible citations of other relevant studies. This backwards search process was repeated until no new citations appeared, ensuring that the search for qualifying studies was reasonably exhaustive.

Inclusionary Criteria for Studies

To qualify for inclusion, a given study had to (a) be published in a journal;[4] (b) compare the level of helpfulness exhibited by a group of positive-mood subjects with the corresponding level exhibited by a neutral mood control group;[5] and (c) provide sufficient statistical information to enable the calculation of an effect-size estimate of the relative amount of helpfulness exhibited by the positive mood group (Glass, McGaw, & Smith, 1981).

Experimental groups that were exposed to negative mood-inducing

events were excluded from the analysis (e.g., the subjects in Weyant & Clark, 1977, whose fingers were soiled with lead graphite while recovering a dime from the return slot of a public phone), as were cases in which the control subjects were exposed to an event or set of events that typically might be expected to produce either positive or negative affect (e.g., the instances contained in Rosenhan, Underwood, & Moore, 1974, and Barden, Garber, Duncan, & Masters, 1981, in which children were allowed to indulge themselves with candy prior to the measurement of helpfulness).

An additional requirement was that the measurement of helpfulness took place within 30 min of the positive mood induction. This restriction was imposed in order to avoid including cases for which the effects of positive mood had worn away prior to the presentation of the helping opportunity (Isen et al., 1976, for example, found that increases in helpfulness that resulted from receiving a free gift dissipated within approximately 20 min). Because the focus of our analysis concerns the effects of positive affect on helpfulness that is directed toward others generally (as opposed to helpfulness that is directed toward a specific individual in a possible attempt to reciprocate a favor), instances in which the ultimate benefactor of the subjects' help was the same individual who was personally responsible for causing the prior good mood state were also omitted. Finally, studies were excluded if helpfulness was assessed by having subjects engage in a game or task that was a required part of an ongoing laboratory experiment (e.g., Berkowitz & Connor, 1966; Berkowitz & Daniels, 1964; and Simmons & Lerner, 1968, in which the dependent measure consisted of the amount of effort subjects exerted on a task in order to benefit another subject, or Greenglass, 1969, in which helpfulness was operationalized by requiring subjects to rate the level of task motivation exhibited by a peer). Such cases were eliminated because (a) the helping opportunity was psychologically connected to the laboratory setting, and was therefore not incidental with respect to the induction of positive affect; (b) the helping opportunity may not have been overtly defined as such by the subjects, as it was partially masked by virtue of its embeddedness within an ostensible laboratory task; and (c) the experimental effect-size estimates arising from such cases may not be comparable with those in other studies, in that all subjects were forced to engage in a helping-relevant task without being able to decline altogether.

A total of 34 separate studies (listed in Appendix A) met the criteria for inclusion. This set featured a wide variety of positive mood-inducing events, including, for example, instances that involved succeeding on an experimental task (e.g., Weyant, 1978), finding money (e.g., Isen & Levin, 1972; Weyant & Clark, 1977), viewing a series of pleasant slides (Donnerstein, Donnerstein, & Munger, 1975), listening to soothing music (Fried & Berkowitz, 1979), receiving a prosocial label (Strenta & DeJong, 1981), being exposed to pleasant weather (Cunningham, 1979), receiving positive self-feedback (e.g., Kazdin & Bryan, 1971), and experiencing empathic joy (Rosenhan, Salovey, et al., 1981). In addition, a diverse array of helping tasks, such as donating to charity (e.g., Cunningham et al., 1980), mailing a lost letter (e.g., Levin & Isen, 1975), volunteering free time for experimental participation (e.g., Donnerstein et al., 1975), agreeing to solicit for Little League baseball or for

---

[4] Because our intent was to correlate, with effect size, variables that were generally not intentionally manipulated, the absence of unpublished articles in our sample does not pose a significant problem (i.e., as the decision to publish an article is relatively independent of the outcome for variables that were controlled or otherwise not ostensibly being researched).

[5] This second criterion was applied independently by two judges (Michael Carlson and Ventura Charlin) on an initial set of potentially qualifying cases, with the result being a 97% agreement rate as to which studies should be included.

the American Cancer Society (Weyant, 1978), opting to make a phone call on behalf of a stranger (Isen et al., 1976), agreeing to donate blood (Kazdin & Bryan, 1971), or helping to pick up dropped packages (Blevins & Murphy, 1974), were represented.

Criteria for Inclusion as Distinct Cases Within Studies

Many of the articles contained more than one positive mood versus control group comparison. Separate positive mood inductions within a study were treated as distinct observations if and only if they differed on one or more of the theoretical variables (Variables 5–14) presented in Table 2. (The definition and measurement of these variables is discussed in a subsequent section.) For example, positive affect groups were collapsed if they differed only on the basis of subjects' sex. Groups distinguished on the basis of minor age differences were also collapsed. When more than one neutral mood control group was compared with a positive affect group, the relevant control groups were combined to produce a single observation. Together, the 34 articles yielded a total sample size of 61 distinct positive mood versus neutral mood comparisons on the basis of the preceding criteria.

Definition and Measurement of Moderator Variables

Sixteen variables were initially measured in order to ultimately create the final set of theoretical and control variables used in the analysis. Table 2 lists the variables and, in addition, includes for each the definition, possible range of scale values, method of measurement, and reliability where appropriate. For each of the subjectively rated variables (see following discussion), a representative example of a case judged to be near the high end of the scale is also provided in Table 2. The 16 variables may be grouped into three major categories: (a) subject and design characteristics (Variables 1–4); (b) features associated with the positive affect induction (Variables 5–10); and (c) variables related to the helping opportunity (Variables 11–16). The measurement of the subject and design variables (i.e., age of subjects, sex of subjects, sex of helpee, and year of study) was very straightforward in that, with the exception of subject age in some field studies, information concerning the proper values was explicitly provided.

With the exception of Variables 1–4, 12, 15, and 16, each of the study characteristics listed in Table 2 was measured by having two judges independently make ratings based on reading the Method sections of the sampled studies. To achieve this, the following procedure was undertaken. First, the two raters briefly went over the definition of each of the variables in question and, in addition, for each variable, discussed how (and on what basis) they would rate each of a set of standard manipulation examples. (The examples did not correspond to any of the manipulations used in the actual studies. For instance, one such example consisted of the positive mood state that would result from the humorous observation of a clown slipping into a puddle of mud.) Prior to the calculation of any effect-size estimates, for each of the qualifying cases the entire Method section was photocopied and detached from the other portions of the article. One complete set of cut-out Method sections was provided for each of the two judges, who then independently read through the entire set of Method sections and underlined the portion describing the positive mood induction, as well as that describing the helping opportunity. During this first reading, values on the variables age of subjects, sex of subjects, and time delay were recorded by each rater. Following this, each of the remaining variables was assessed by each of the two judges independently, one variable at a time, with a separate randomly ordered sequence of the variables assigned to each rater. In addition, for each variable, a separate random sequence of the studies was assigned for each judge. The judges made their ratings by imagining themselves to be the actual subjects who were exposed to

the positive mood induction (or helping situation) in question. When making a given rating, each judge was careful to attend to the nature of the particular subject population being studied, and referred to a sheet containing the definition of the construct in question along with the possible scale values (see Table 2 for the ranges of scale values and their corresponding anchors for each of the rated variables). The average reliability coefficient among the subjectively rated variables was .83.[6]

For the variables age of subjects and time delay, the mean of the two judges' estimates was used to arrive at the final value for each case. For the remaining nondichotomous variables that are presented in Table 2, the value for each observation was obtained by summing the two judges' ratings. Finally, for the dichotomous variables (i.e., sex of subject and salience of the helping request), the mean scale value was used.

According to the version of the objective self-awareness position that highlights the importance of intraself discrepancy reduction, self-focus promotes helpfulness to the extent that the request for help or the presence of prosocial values is salient. A single variable, termed *objective self-awareness* (OSA) + *request salience*, was created in order to capture the nature of this interaction. For each case in which either (a) a salient helping request was present, or (b) the value on either the variable responsibility to help or the variable salience of prosocial values was greater than or equal to the 75th percentile (i.e., relative to the entire set of cases), the value of OSA + request salience was made equal to the score on objective self-awareness if self-awareness was judged to be elevated. However, when neither of these two conditions was satisfied, the score on OSA + request salience was set equal to 10.0, which is the score that corresponds to no change from baseline in objective self-awareness.

We interpreted the mood maintenance hypothesis as suggesting that positive affect that is either very mild or very intense should enhance helpfulness to a lesser extent than should middling levels of good mood. To create a variable that reflected the presence of either high or low levels of positive affect, the absolute value of each observation's distance from a positive affect value of 6.5 (31 cases were above this value and 30 cases were below it) was obtained. This variable was named *high/low positive affect*.

---

[6] Michael Carlson and Ventura Charlin served as the two raters. The possibility of experimenter bias was minimal due to the following considerations. First, the Method sections that were rated had been detached from the remaining portions of the articles; thus, the results of the studies were not ascertainable. Second, Ventura Charlin was unaware of any of the hypotheses or specific studies at the time she performed her ratings, and Michael Carlson was aware only of the hypothesis test results of a small handful of the studies. (Note that, in the absence of specific effect-size information, the knowledge that a given study produced a significant effect is of little consequence because of the general robustness of the positive mood–helping relation.) Finally, given the complex nature of the data analytic strategy (i.e., 11th-order partial correlation analysis), in order to exhibit bias the judges would have had to estimate how the unique variability of each predictor variable correlated with the residual transformed effect-size estimates after statistically adjusting for the effects of 11 other variables, which seems highly implausible.

Several additional variables other than those reported on were also measured (i.e., whether the positive mood induction involved the presentation of a tangible object to the subject, whether the study was of a lab or field nature, the extent to which the positive mood induction involved a helping act being performed for the subject, the degree to which the positive event would make subjects feel competent generally, and whether the helping act involved interaction with another person). Each of these variables had a low level of reliability, was not relevant theoretically, or possessed a severely restricted range. Thus, they are not considered further.

Table 2
Definitions, Range of Scale Values, Measurement Procedures, and Reliability Estimates for Each of the Potential Moderator Variables

Variable	Definition	Example of observation with high value	Potential range of scale values	Measurement procedure	Reliability
1. Age of subjects	Mean age of subjects	—	0–100 years	Mean of two judges' estimates	.98[*]
2. Sex of subjects	Sex of the experimental subjects	—	1 = 80% or more males; 2 = less than 80% males and less than 80% females, or unspecified; 3 = 80% or more females	Recorded by two judges	1.0[b]
3. Sex of helpee	Sex of the ultimate benefactor of help	—	1 = Male(s); 2 = Both male(s) and female(s), or unspecified; 3 = Female(s)	Recorded by Michael Carlson	—
4. Year of study	Year the study was published	—	1950–1985	Recorded by Michael Carlson	—
5. Positive affect	The extent to which the positive mood induction would be expected to increase the subjects' level of positive affect	Subjects received computerized feedback stating that they were very intelligent (Strenta & DeJong, 1981).	1 to 7 (1 = *The positive mood induction does not differ from affective neutrality; 7 = The positive mood induction would make subjects feel extremely good)*	Sum of two judges' ratings	.92[*]
6. Objective self-awareness	The extent to which the positive mood induction would be expected to alter subjects' self-awareness	Subjects received evaluative feedback stating that they were creative and had a high level of aesthetic ability (Kazdin & Bryan, 1971).	1 to 9 (1 = *The positive mood induction would tend to make subjects extremely subjectively self-aware; 5 = The positive mood induction would not tend to alter subjects' levels of self-awareness; 9 = The positive mood induction would tend to make subjects extremely objectively self-aware)*	Sum of two judges' ratings	.86[*]
7. Target of the positive event	The extent to which the subject, as opposed to someone else, was the primary beneficiary of the positive event	Subjects were unexpectedly given a free gift (Isen, Shalker, Clark, & Karp, 1978).	1 to 5 (1 = *The primary beneficiary of the positive event is another person; 5 = The primary beneficiary of the positive event is oneself)*	Sum of two judges' ratings	.91[*]
8. Guilt/inequity arousal	The extent to which the positive mood induction promotes feelings of guilt or inequity	During the experiment, subjects received a personal favor from another subject; the situational context prevented them from fulfilling any perceived obligation to reciprocate (D. T. Regan, 1971).	1 to 7 (1 = *The positive mood induction produces no guilt or inequity arousal whatsoever; 7 = The positive mood induction produces an extreme amount of guilt or inequity arousal)*	Sum of two judges' ratings	.91[*]
9. Human nature	The extent to which the positive mood induction would lead subjects to view human nature and human interaction as being kind and pleasant (as opposed to being selfish, "every-man-for-himself," etc.)	Subjects found a dropped envelope containing a wallet, along with an attached note indicating that the sender obtained pleasure from being "able to help somebody in the small things that make life nicer" (Hornstein, Fisch, & Holmes, 1968).	1 to 11 (1 = *The positive mood induction would lead subjects to view human nature/interaction as being selfish and unpleasant to a great degree; 6 = The positive mood induction would not affect subjects' view of human nature/ interaction one way or the other; 11 = The positive mood induction would lead subjects to view human nature/interaction as unselfish and pleasant to a ...*	Sum of two judges' ratings	.63[*]

Table 2 (Continued)

Variable	Definition	Example of observation with high value	Potential range of scale values	Measurement procedure	Reliability
10. Sociality of the positive event	The extent to which the positive mood directly resulted from interaction with another person or persons	Subjects were given cookies while studying in the library (Isen & Levin, 1972).	1 to 5 (1 = The positive mood in no way depended on interaction with another person or persons; 5 = The positive mood completely depended on interaction with another person or persons)	Sum of two judges' ratings	.67*
11. Pleasantness of the helping task	The extent to which performing the helping task is associated with high rewards and low costs	Subjects were asked by a female experimenter to read a set of statements described as cheerful and happiness-inducing (Forest, Clark, Mills, & Isen, 1979).	1 to 7 (1 = Performing the helping task is extremely unrewarding and costly; 7 = Performing the helping task is extremely rewarding and uncostly)	Sum of two judges' ratings	.82*
12. Salience of the helping request	Whether the helping request is a direct, face-to-face plea (or involves an intentional experimental manipulation of high salience)	—	1 = No, 2 = Yes	Recorded by two judges	1.0^b
13. Salience of prosocial values	The extent to which the possibility or call for help involves cues or content that stimulate normative or value-related pressures for helping	Subjects were exposed to a plea asking them to volunteer to collect funds for the American Cancer Society (Weyant, 1978).	1 to 7 (1 = The possibility or call for help does not feature cues that stimulate normative or value-related pressures to help; 7 = To an extreme degree, the possibility or call for help stimulates normative or value-related pressures to help)	Sum of two judges' ratings	.84*
14. Responsibility to help	The extent to which subjects would feel the helping act itself is legitimate or urgent to perform	Subjects found a lost set of keys with tags bearing the name and address of a private individual owner; the helping act consisted of whether subjects returned the keys (Forbes & TeVault, 1975).	1-5 (1 = Not at all legitimate or urgent; 5 = Extremely legitimate or urgent)	Sum of two judges' ratings	.88*
15. Time delay	The amount of time that elapsed between the positive affect induction and the presentation of the request for help	—	1–30 min	Mean of two judges' estimates	.85*
16. Sustained helpfulness	Whether the dependent measure entailed sustained effort on an ongoing helping task	—	1 = No, 2 = Yes	Recorded by Michael Carlson	—

* Spearman–Brown reliability coefficient for the sum/mean of the two judges' ratings.
b Proportion of agreement between the two judges.

Table 3

*Possible Range, Observed Range, Median, Mean, and
Standard Deviation for Each of the Continuous
Moderator Variables and Effect Size*

Variable	Possible range	Observed range	Mdn	M	SD
Age of subjects	0–100	8–36	18	21.8	7.6
Positive affect	2–14	4–14	7	7.4	2.8
Low/high positive affect	.5–7.5	.5–7.5	1.5	2.3	1.8
Objective self-awareness	2–18	3–17	10	10.9	4.2
OSA + request salience	10–18	10–17	10	11.9	2.4
Target of the positive event	2–10	2–10	10	8.9	2.4
Guilt/inequity arousal	2–14	2–10	2	3.1	1.8
Human nature	2–22	11–22	13	13.9	2.0
Sociality of the positive event	2–10	2–10	4	4.4	2.5
Social outlook	−7–7	−2.1–3.2	−.2	0.0	1.5
Pleasantness of the helping task	2–14	2–13	6	6.2	2.2
Salience of prosocial values	2–14	3–13	8	7.7	2.6
Responsibility to help	2–10	2–10	5	5.3	1.9
Time delay	0–30	.5–20	3	4.3	3.5
Effect size	−∞–∞	−1.32–2.78	.50	.54	.80

Note. OSA = Objective self-awareness.

The social outlook hypothesis implies that the variables human nature and sociality of the positive event should each correlate positively with helpfulness. However, because these two variables share a good deal of conceptual overlap, and because the measure of each had a relatively low degree of reliability (below .7 in both cases), a composite variable, termed *social outlook,* was created in order to provide a more powerful statistical test of the social outlook hypothesis. To arrive at this summary variable, the individual z-scores for human nature and for sociality of the positive event were added together for each observation.

Table 3 presents for each of the continuous variables listed in Table 2 and for the aforementioned additional variables and effect size, the possible and the observed range of scores, the median, the mean, and the standard deviation for the 61 observations. Evidence concerning the validity of the variables measured by judges' ratings is discussed in Appendix B. The intercorrelations among the 12 variables that entered the final results shown in Table 4 are presented in Appendix C.

Effect-Size Calculation

For cases in which a helpfulness mean and standard deviation were reported for both the experimental and control group, effect-size estimates were generated by subtracting the control group mean from the experimental group mean and dividing by the pooled estimate of standard deviation, as advocated by Hunter, Schmidt, and Jackson (1982). Because many of the sample sizes were quite small, this pooled estimate, used in place of the control group standard deviation, is preferable in that it minimizes sampling error. The formulas found in Glass et al.

(1981) were used to calculate effect-size estimates on the basis of F, t, or r statistics. For dichotomous measures of helpfulness, probit transformation procedures (Glass et al., 1981) were used. If more than one effect-size calculation was possible for a given positive mood versus neutral mood comparison, the mean of the available effect-size estimates was used. Likewise, when multiple positive affect groups or multiple control groups were collapsed to form a single observation, effect size was estimated by obtaining the mean effect size of the possible comparisons.

Because small samples tend to produce spuriously large effect-size estimates, all effect-size estimates were corrected for sample-size bias in accordance with the table provided by Hedges that is reproduced in Glass et al. (1981, p. 113).

For many of the predictor variables, as well as for effect size, the distribution of scores was noticeably positively skewed. (The predictor variables in question, which in each case possessed a skewness coefficient larger than .5, were pleasantness of the helping task, high/low positive affect, social outlook, OSA + request salience, guilt, and time delay.) For these variables, a logarithmic transformation was applied to each score in order to better approximate the assumption of normality. Because the variables social outlook and effect size included negative values, an appropriate constant was added to the scores prior to log-transforming them (5.0 and 4.0 for the two variables, respectively). The variable self as target of the positive event was negatively skewed; consequently, the scores were raised to the power of 1.5 in order to achieve a greater degree of normality.

Statistical Analysis

The major method of data analysis consisted of testing the extent to which each of the theoretically relevant variables correlated with helpfulness effect-size estimates in the expected fashion, given that the effects of measured extraneous variables were statistically controlled. Higher-order partial correlation coefficients were generated to achieve this purpose.

Results and Discussion

The mean of the 61 effect-size estimates, .54, significantly exceeded zero, $t(60) = 5.27$, $p < .0001$. The fairly sizable standard deviation of .8 suggests that the effects of positive mood on helpfulness are substantially moderated by other variables.

The first two columns of Table 4 present, respectively, the zero-order correlation and the higher-order partial correlation between each of the primary 12 potential mediating and moderator variables and the log-transformed effect-size estimates. In computing the higher-order correlation coefficient for each variable, the effects of each of the other 11 variables were removed. The results of partial correlation analysis suggest that subject age, helping task pleasantness, social outlook, and self as target are all positively associated with, whereas guilt, high/low positive affect, and sustained helpfulness are negatively associated with, increases in the relative amount of helpfulness exhibited by individuals who are experiencing a positive mood.[7] As a set, the 12 predictors account for nearly one third of the variability

---

[7] Performing a partial correlation analysis by using untransformed values for each variable, including effect size, does not alter the hypothesis test result for any of the 12 predictors.

Table 4

Correlations of Theoretical and Control Variables With Helpfulness

Variable	Zero-order correlation coefficient (59 df)	Higher-order partial r[a] (48 df)	Jackknifed higher-order partial r[a] (33 df)
Pleasantness of the helping task[b]	.21	.34**	.29**
High/low positive affect[b]	.02	−.38**	−.40**
Social outlook[b]	−.02	.31**	.40*
OSA + request salience[b]	−.03	−.03	−.11
Self as target of positive event[b]	.35**	.49***	.50**
Guilt[b]	.08	−.44***	−.46**
Age of subjects	.22	.33****	.39****
Year of study	−.12	−.20	−.19
Sex of subjects	.09	−.09	−.14
Sex of helping target	.05	−.10	−.02
Time delay[b]	−.02	−.09	−.06
Sustained helpfulness	−.39****	−.37****	−.49

Note. OSA = Objective self-awareness.
[a] After removing effects of all other variables.
[b] The correlations are based on the transformed version of the variable in question (see discussion in the Effect-Size Calculation section).
* $p < .05$, one-tailed. ** $p < .015$, one-tailed. *** $p < .001$, one-tailed. **** $p < .05$, two-tailed.

among the transformed effect-size estimates (adjusted R^2 = .33), $F(12, 48) = 3.46$, $p = .0001$.[8]

Three of the variables for which the partial correlation analysis yielded theoretically predicted effects (high/low positive affect, social outlook, and guilt) had a zero-order correlation with effect size that was nonsignificantly opposite in sign to the theoretical prediction. This outcome highlights the critical importance of controlling for confounding variables in order to avoid a misleading assessment of the manner in which a given facet of a positive mood uniquely affects helpfulness.

Because, in some instances, more than one positive mood condition within a given study was sampled, the partial correlation coefficients were additionally assessed by applying Tukey's jackknife technique. This procedure, which takes into account the interdependencies that are common in meta-analytic data (Glass et al., 1981), was used in order to ensure that the obtained results were not artifactually based on statistical dependencies (the mean number of effect sizes sampled per article was equal to 1.8). Column 3 of Table 4 presents the jackknifed higher-order partial correlation coefficients; inspection of this column reveals that applying the jackknife procedure does not substantially alter the results for any of the variables.

With the exception of subject age and sustained helpfulness, none of the control variables were significantly associated with the relative helpfulness of positive mood subjects. Although the correlation between the transformed effect-size estimates and subject age was positive, the sample contained only six cases in which subjects were younger than college age. The limited number of observations that used children as subjects makes it

difficult to assess the effect of positive mood on their helpfulness in comparison with that of adults. If the variable age of subjects is dichotomized into the categories children (mean age 10 years or younger) and adults (mean age 18 years or older), a weak positive partial correlation with the transformed effect-size estimates emerges (after statistically removing the effects of the other variables listed in Table 4, with the exception of subject age, this correlation is equal to .05, $p > .5$).

Closer inspection of the data reveals that the significant correlation between subject age and transformed effect-size estimates is due primarily to the increased potency of good mood in promoting helpfulness among older adults relative to younger adults. If age is dichotomized at 30 years, a significant effect results such that those who are 30 and older tend to exhibit larger helpfulness effect-size estimates than younger individuals (after removing the set of variables listed in Table 4—except subject age—the partial correlation of this dichotomous variable with effect size is equal to .32, $p < .025$). The finding of greater mood-based helpfulness for older, as opposed to younger, adults is consistent with the predictions of several of the hypotheses. For example, older individuals may potentially have more fully elaborated mood-maintenance strategies as well as better developed interconnective networks among positive items in memory (Clark & Isen, 1982), which could facilitate the priming of material relevant to an enhanced social outlook. Interpretational caution should be exercised, however, because it was not possible to adequately assess the more critical age distinction, namely, differences between children and adults. Moreover, these comparisons are confounded with cohort effects, as the older adults generally were members of an earlier generation.

The relative increase in helpfulness due to positive mood was reduced when the dependent measure featured sustained task effort (partial $r = -.37$, $p < .05$). In accounting for this result, it is likely that some combination of both the passage of time and sustained mental absorption with a task causes the prior mood state and its psychological by-products to progressively wear away, thereby reducing the advantage in helpfulness as a result of elation that is present in the case of mere volunteering.[9] In addition, it is possible that forcing oneself to focus on a given helping task is generally less rewarding than allowing one's prior good mood to continue uninterrupted. Sustained help may therefore be terminated when a person senses that his or her pleasant affect is slipping away, which fails to happen in the case of mere agreement to help.

---

[8] An examination of the tolerance values of the predictors, as well as of the proportion of variance for each variable's estimate shared with principal components having high condition indexes (SAS User's Guide: Statistics, 1985), suggested that multicollinearity was not a problem with the present set of predictors.

[9] Note that the variable time delay, defined as the amount of elapsed time between the positive event and the presentation of the helping request, does not control for the passage of time occurring after a helping task has commenced. Although it correlated with effect size in the proper direction, time delay was not statistically significant. This nonsignificant outcome seems largely due to restricted range: For nearly every observation, the amount of elapsed time prior to the helping request was estimated to be less than 10 min.

Focus of Attention

The present results support the focus of attention hypothesis. Even after statistically adjusting for the effects of objective self-awareness, positive events that were experienced for the self, as opposed to being empathically based, were associated with higher degrees of relative helpfulness (partial $r = .49$, $p < .001$). As Rosenhan, Salovey, et al. (1981) note, this result is opposite to that which occurs in the case of negative affect. Among subjects who have been made to feel bad, higher levels of helpfulness are exhibited when the negative event is directed toward another person as opposed to oneself.

In attempting to tie these findings together, Rosenhan and his colleagues (1981) have posited that individuals respond to positive or negative mood in such a way as to restore a sense of relative social equity. Those who are the recipients of a fortuitous event, as well as those who witness unmerited harm that occurs to another person, may feel unduly advantaged in some sense relative to others. Increased helpfulness may serve to lessen such feelings. However, if a positive event is targeted at a person other than oneself, or if one is the victim of a negative circumstance, then one will experience a feeling of relative disadvantage that would only be exacerbated if one chose to offer aid to a further party.

This line of reasoning suggests that, among individuals who have experienced a positive mood, perceptions of the degree to which one had earned or had deserved the mood-elevating event should be negatively associated with the extent to which a good mood increases helping. If a person believes that he or she has earned a pleasant outcome (e.g., as might occur after being given cash payment for having worked hard), then a feeling of undue advantage, and hence increased helpfulness, should largely be absent. However, when one experiences a pleasant event that is perceived as lucky or otherwise unmerited, one should experience a feeling of emotional advantage and consequently exhibit increased benevolence.

To test this prediction, an additional variable, termed *deservedness of the positive event,* was measured. This variable was defined as the extent to which the typical subject would feel that he or she had earned or deserved the positive event that produced the good mood in question.[10] Contrary to expectations, neither the zero-order correlation ($-.01$) nor the higher-order partial correlation ($-.09$) between deservedness of the positive event and the transformed effect-size estimates significantly departed from zero. In addition to this nonsignificant outcome, the large negative correlation between the transformed guilt scores and effect-size estimates (partial $r = -.44$, $p < .001$) likewise argues against the notion that considerations pertaining to a general sense of equity restoration significantly mediate the effects of good mood on benevolence. Because those who feel guilty might generally be expected to feel unfairly advantaged relative to others (e.g., after receiving an expensive gift), they should be expected to help more than others, yet the present results reveal an opposite pattern.

As noted in the beginning of this article, a further possible explanation for the effect of focus of attention centers on the potential difference between the content of cognitions that surround positive events directed toward another as opposed to oneself. As Rosenhan, Salovey, et al. (1981) note, emotions such as jealousy may result when an individual reflects on the good fortune of another person. Such feelings may impede the normal operation of cognitive consequences that follow good mood and that generally promote helpfulness, such as priming or social outlook effects. We feel that such an account represents the most promising explanation for the attentional focus effect.

Objective Self-Awareness

As previously noted, there are two conceptually distinct processes whereby objective self-awareness might increase helpfulness in the context of positive mood. First, self-aware individuals may behave prosocially in an effort to avoid any negative affect that would result from failing to fulfill a perceived helping obligation; second, objective self-awareness may augment helpfulness by enhancing the impact of those psychological by-products of a good mood that promote prosocial responding. Our results are consistent only with the latter of these two possibilities, and are discussed in the following sections.

OSA and intraself discrepancy reduction. The results contained in Table 4 contradict the idea that an interaction between objective self-awareness and prosocial behavioral standards mediates the relation between positive affect and helpfulness. When positive mood inductions produced high levels of objective self-awareness and were coordinated with a salient request for help or with salient prosocial values, the transformed effect-size estimates were nonsignificantly lower than for opposing cases (e.g., the higher-order partial r for OSA + request salience in Column 2 of Table 4 is equal to $-.03$).

To assess the notion that perceptions of having personally caused the mood-elevating positive event are necessary in order to produce objective self-awareness and its associated motivational dynamic, the effect of an additional variable, termed *cause of the positive event,* was assessed. This variable was defined as the extent to which the typical subject would perceive that he or she had caused the mood-elevating event in question.[11] When its effect was examined, either singly or in combination with a salient helping request or the presence of salient prosocial values, it uniformly failed to systematically influence the relative degree of helpfulness exhibited by elated subjects.

In attempting to account for this negative result, it should be noted that theoretical complications arise when one invokes the aspect of objective self-awareness theory that posits intraself discrepancy reduction as an explanation of behavioral phenomena surrounding positive affect. In particular, among self-aware individuals the dynamic that underlies their increased adherence to behavioral standards is generally conceived to be negative in character. Adherence to behavioral standards presumably serves the function of avoiding the discomfort that would otherwise arise from perceiving a discrepancy between one's ac-

---

[10] The Spearman–Brown reliability estimate of this variable was equal to .79. Thanks are due to Sharon Gross and Gaye Davidson-Podgorny for providing these ratings.

[11] The Spearman–Brown reliability estimate of this variable was equal to .92. The ratings were made by Michael Carlson and Ventura Charlin.

tual self and one's ideals (Duval & Wicklund, 1972). It is therefore possible that the presence of positive affect is capable of disrupting this discrepancy-reduction process by either (a) reducing the aversiveness of any failure to conform to a given behavioral standard; or (b) decreasing the psychological salience of prosocial norms that obligate one to help others by inclining one instead to focus on one's current good fortune (in that doing so is more reinforcing).

OSA and the enhancement of concomitant factors. To the extent that objective self-awareness enhances helpfulness by amplifying the prosocially relevant feelings and perceptions that arise from a good mood, it is inappropriate to remove statistically the effects of such concomitant factors when assessing whether objective self-awareness generally augments helpfulness. On an a priori basis, the variables social outlook and self as target of the positive event were singled out as being likely to reflect the operation of such relevant concomitant factors.[12] If only the remaining variables listed in Table 4 are partialed out (except, of course, OSA + request salience), then the variable objective self-awareness correlates positively with the transformed effect-size estimates, partial $r(50) = .37$, $p < .01$, one-tailed. This positive outcome for objective self-awareness is in agreement with the findings of Berkowitz (1987) in that, provided that one does not statistically remove the effects of key cognitive mediators, objective self-awareness is associated with the increased helpfulness produced by positive affect. Because in the present study objective self-awareness fails to correlate with effect size after additionally removing the effects of social outlook and self as target of the positive event, partial $r(48) = .00$, we conclude that self-awareness augments helping only to the extent that it bolsters the experience of (or the inclination to act on) the prosocially relevant concomitant factors that accompany a positive mood.

In addition to reflecting a possible tendency for objective self-awareness to amplify the experience of concomitant factors, however, the significant correlation reported in the preceding paragraph may merely be due to confounding, in that after statistically removing the effects of all other variables in Table 4, the higher-order correlations between OSA and both social outlook and self as target of the positive event are significantly positive (partial $rs = .58$ and $.74$, respectively). Thus, events that produce high levels of self-awareness also tend to induce perceptions of oneself as the target of a positive event as well as an enhanced social outlook. Further research is needed to better understand whether self-awareness interacts to augment these concomitant factors, or instead is merely confounded with them.

Separate Processes

Among subjects made to feel positive, higher levels of guilt are associated with decreased relative helpfulness. This result is consistent with Cunningham et al.'s (1980) notion that the prosocial behavior that occurs in response to positive affect will be attenuated to the extent that a competing motivational process is simultaneously activated. The tendency for other-directed positive events to be associated with lower effect-size estimates within the sample (i.e., the variable self as target of the

positive event is positively correlated with relative helpfulness) is also consistent with the separate-process formulation. As noted earlier, this attentional focus effect may result from disruptive cognitions or emotions (e.g., jealousy) that are elicited when one perceives that another person and not oneself is the recipient of a fortuitous event.

Social Outlook

Our results are also consistent with the social outlook hypothesis in that the composite variable social outlook is positively associated with increases in helpfulness among those who experience positive affect (partial $r = .31$, $p < .015$, one-tailed). This variable was obtained by adding together the z-scores of the variables degree of sociality of the positive event and enhancement of perceptions of human nature (see Table 2 for a definition of these variables). When examined separately, each of these underlying variables correlates in a positive fashion with the transformed effect-size estimates after statistically removing the set of variables listed in Table 4 (with the exception of social outlook), partial $r(48) = .26$, $p = .035$, one-tailed, for degree of sociality of the positive event, and partial $r(48) = .25$, $p = .037$, one-tailed, for enhancement of perceptions of human nature.

Mood Maintenance and Concomitance

The facilitative effects of positive affect on helpfulness were stronger when (a) the helping task was relatively pleasant to perform; and (b) a middling level (as opposed to either higher or lower levels) of positive affect was induced (see Column 2 of Table 4). These results are consistent with the predictions of the mood maintenance hypothesis, and are discussed in the following paragraphs.

Pleasantness of the helping task. The positive correlation between the pleasantness of the helping task and the degree to which positive mood promotes helpfulness, partial $r(48) = .34$, $p < .015$, one-tailed, supports the notion of mood maintenance in that, as noted previously, the performance of a pleasant helping task relative to an unpleasant one better enables an individual to perpetuate his or her prior good mood state.

To further explore the generality of the effects of task pleasantness on helpfulness among elated individuals, the effect-size estimates were divided into two classes: (a) those based on helping acts that were either actually performed or were expected to be performed immediately (i.e., present helping situations); and (b) those featuring a helping task that ostensibly would not be commenced until at least 1 or more hr had elapsed (i.e., future helping situations). With respect to present helping situations, the correlation between task pleasantness and the transformed

---

[12] Given the presence of mood-enhanced perceptions of the favorability of social interaction (i.e., an elevated social outlook), self-awareness would be expected to produce a juxtaposition of oneself with this disposition and thereby intensify the propensity to act prosocially. When oneself is the target of a positive event, concomitant factors, such as the priming of positive material in memory (e.g., Isen, Shalker, Clark, & Karp, 1978), have been shown to follow.

helpfulness effect-size estimates, after partialing out the significant variables listed in Table 4, is equal to .34 (36 df, $p < .02$, one-tailed). In addition, task pleasantness increases the relative helpfulness of elated individuals in the case of agreement to engage in future prosocial activity, partial $r(13) = .58$, $p < .015$, one-tailed.[13] Although the difference between the two correlations is not significant, this is not surprising in that the test lacks power. In any case, however, the obtained effect for delayed help is troublesome for the concomitance model. As noted in the beginning of this article, the concomitance theorists posit that prior findings ostensibly favoring the operation of a mood maintenance motive were based instead on mood alteration arising during the performance of the helping task itself (Manucia et al., 1984). The present result, however, suggests that elated individuals are more sensitive than those in a neutral mood to the hedonic consequences of helping opportunities that are merely agreed to, but not expected to be immediately performed. The obtained effect for unperformed delayed helping tasks cannot be attributed to the effect of performing the task, and therefore seems to be particularly supportive of the mood maintenance hypothesis.

Several explanations can account for the interaction between mood and task pleasantness in affecting agreement to engage in future helping tasks. First, it is likely that the mere act of agreeing to engage in a pleasant helping task functions as a self-reinforcer that helps maintain one's prior good mood state. A second explanation is that elated individuals exhibit a heightened concern for obtaining positive reinforcement, and that this concern extends into future situations in which one's present mood state will have worn off. The emphasis here is not on a specific motivation to maintain one's current positive mood state, but rather on a more general increase in the salience of positive reinforcers and positive reinforcement. Finally, the strong effect found for future prosocial action may be a consequence of an actor's own cognitive analysis of factors that bear on mood maintenance. Whereas the good mood that exists at the moment will persist for a while without additional buttressing, as more time elapses one's current pleasant state will dissipate, and the need for actions that will maintain or restore it will become more pressing. Such thought points to the fact that mood-elevating actions performed in the more distant future are more relevant to and will have greater net positive impact on promoting a good mood than the immediate performance of that act.

Our conclusion that a mood-management motive regulates the relation between positive affect and agreement to engage in future helping tasks is in apparent conflict with the results of studies by both Manucia et al. (1984) and Weyant (1978). As described in the beginning of this article, in both of these studies positive affect increased the amount of volunteered help, yet the extent of such increases was not strongly influenced by factors that on the surface might be relevant to mood management (i.e., having the capacity to alter one's mood in Manucia et al., or the rewards and costs of helping in Weyant's study). We speculate that these negative findings resulted from the use of helping opportunities that stimulated feelings of obligation, which in turn reduced the salience of positive reinforcement considerations. In Manucia et al.'s study, the helping act involved collecting in-

formation for a nonprofit blood organization by calling potential donors, whereas in Weyant's study, the low cost–high benefit (i.e., the most reinforcing) helping task consisted of soliciting for the American Cancer Society. In both cases, subjects were confronted with a direct plea to assist in a worthwhile, potentially life-saving cause.[14] Cunningham et al.'s (1980) finding that the motivation to seek rewards ordinarily elicited by a positive mood is largely inoperative when the helping request stimulates feelings of obligation strongly suggests that specifically reward-based motives were minimized in these two studies. In this context, it is noteworthy that none of the experiments directly supporting mood maintenance (Forest et al., 1979; Harada, 1983; Isen & Levin, 1972; Isen & Simmonds, 1978) featured a helping request that potentially fostered feelings of obligation to a socially worthy cause. Therefore, drawing from the separate process hypothesis, we tentatively suggest that a boundary condition for the operation of mood maintenance is the absence of strong feelings of prosocial obligation.

Degree of mood elevation. Middling degrees of positive affect produce greater levels of relative helpfulness than other more mild or intense levels of elation, for high or low positive affect, partial $r(48) = -.38$, $p < .015$, one-tailed.[15] Such a result is consistent with the mood maintenance hypothesis because the motive to manage one's mood via prosocial responding should operate maximally when a person's positive feelings exceed affective neutrality to a significant enough extent to render the cognitive and motivational by-products of a good mood (i.e., priming and mood-management concerns) effective, but fail to invoke such extreme feelings of elation that fulfilling or agreeing to fulfill a typical, moderately positive helping request will represent a diminution in one's degree of experienced positive affect. A consideration of the variety of inductions that were considered low (e.g., exposure to classical music; Fried & Berkowitz, 1979), moderate (e.g., intensively imagining oneself on a wonderful Hawaiian vacation; Rosenhan, Salovey, et al., 1981), or high (e.g., receiving computerized feedback stating that one is highly intelligent; Strenta & DeJong, 1981) in their capacity to elevate mood reveals a range that intuitively seems sufficient to produce the curvilinear relation. For example, a

---

[13] In computing the correlations for present and for future helping situations, the log-transformed effect-size estimates were used (although very similar results are obtained if the effect-size estimates are left untransformed). To preserve degrees of freedom, only the statistically significant variables in Column 2 of Table 4 were partialed out (this strategy was followed throughout the study whenever dichotomous subsets of the data were analyzed separately). In the case of future help, when all variables contained in Table 4 are partialed out, a significant correlation is still present between task pleasantness and relative helpfulness on the part of positive mood subjects, partial $r(8) = .67$, $p < .02$, one-tailed. In the case of present help, the corresponding partial r value is .37 ($df = 31$, $p < .02$, one-tailed).

[14] The values on the variables responsibility to help and salience of prosocial values were noticeably above average for the two helping tasks in question.

[15] In generating the variable high or low positive affect, the absolute value of the difference from 6.5 was used. If instead middling values other than 6.5 were used (e.g., the adjacent values 6.0 and 7.0), the significant negative correlation with relative helpfulness was still obtained.

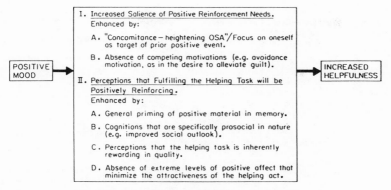

I. Increased Salience of Positive Reinforcement Needs.
Enhanced by:

A. "Concomitance – heightening OSA"/Focus on oneself
as target of prior positive event.

B. Absence of competing motivations (e.g. avoidance
motivation, as in the desire to alleviate guilt).

II. Perceptions that Fulfilling the Helping Task will be
Positively Reinforcing.
Enhanced by:

A. General priming of positive material in memory.

B. Cognitions that are specifically prosocial in nature
(e.g. improved social outlook).

C. Perceptions that the helping task is inherently
rewarding in quality.

D. Absence of extreme levels of positive affect that
minimize the attractiveness of the helping act.

POSITIVE MOOD → INCREASED HELPFULNESS

Figure 1. General sequence of events hypothesized to produce increased helpfulness in response to positive affect.

person who finds out from a highly credible source, perhaps for the first time, that he or she is highly intelligent, might well be expected to momentarily savor such a thought to the exclusion of bothering to help others.

To further explore the nonlinear relation between the degree of positive affect and subsequent helpfulness, the observations were divided into two groups: (a) those that were at or above the sample median with respect to the rated level of positive affect; and (b) those that were below the median in terms of positive affect. Then, separately within each set of cases, a higher-order partial correlation coefficient was calculated between the variable degree of positive affect and the transformed effect-size estimates. As expected, greater levels of positive affect were associated with reduced levels of relative helpfulness given that the rated degree of positive affect was high, that is, at or above the median, partial $r(23) = -.45$, $p < .012$, one-tailed. When levels of positive affect were rated below the sample median, a weak, nonsignificant positive correlation between the degree of positive affect and relative helpfulness on the part of elated subjects emerged, partial $r(22) = .03$, $p > .5$. The difference between these two correlations is statistically significant ($z = 1.70$, $p < .05$, one-tailed) and is in the direction specified by the mood maintenance hypothesis.[16]

The cumulative pattern of results concerning the effects of both task pleasantness and high levels of positive affect is counter to the concomitance theorists' notion that a desire to prolong or enhance good mood fails to affect helpfulness among elated individuals. Although we believe that under certain circumstances a mood management motive is inoperative (as in Manucia et al., 1984), we nonetheless conclude that it often does in fact partially mediate the effect of a positive mood on helpfulness. On the other hand, the results contained in Table 4 do support the notion that concomitant factors (i.e., those other than the motive to maintain a pleasant mood state, such as an enhanced social outlook) contribute to the increased helpfulness of happy individuals.

Positive Mood and Helping: An Overview

The various outcomes of our analysis can be subsumed under a common principle of heightened sensitivity among elated individuals to concerns about positive reinforcement. Specifically, we posit that a good mood will increase a person's helpfulness to the extent that the mood-elevating experience itself or other situational features increase either (a) the salience of concerns related to obtaining positive reinforcement for oneself; or (b) perceptions of the reward value of responding prosocially. Figure 1 outlines this scheme and incorporates the major pattern of obtained results. The overall framework is nicely consistent with Cunningham et al.'s (1980) assertion that happy individuals possess a salient motivational orientation of seeking positive reinforcement. Self-focus, in the form of objective self-awareness or a more general perception of oneself as the recipient of an immediately prior good fortune, may serve to augment such a motivational orientation in that the salience of oneself is enhanced within the context of a pleasant atmosphere. Our findings additionally emphasize the importance of mood-altered cognitions that dovetail with the posited motivational bias. The cognitive consequences of a positive mood may be either general (e.g., global priming effects) or help-specific (e.g., enhanced social outlook), and influence helpfulness by altering the perceived capacity of a given prosocial opportunity to provide self-reinforcement. In addition, perceptions of the inherent reward

[16] If the observations are instead divided into those above the median versus those at or below the median in terms of positive affect, a similar, although slightly weaker, pattern of results emerges. Given that positive affect was rated above the median, the partial correlation between the degree of positive affect and the transformed effect-size estimates is equal to $-.32$ (16 *df*, $p < .10$, one-tailed). For the set of observations at or below the median, this correlation is equal to $.20$ (29 *df*, $p = .14$, one-tailed). The difference between these two correlations remains significant ($z = 1.68$, $p < .05$, one-tailed).

value of the helping task, as well as one's current degree of elation, influence whether or not one views engaging in the prosocial act as likely to maximize one's outcomes.

Situational features that are incongruent with the proposed emphasis on positive reinforcement (e.g., a guilt-based motive to avoid negative affect that would result from failing to help, or cognitions such as jealousy that may disrupt the priming of positive material) detract from the overall sequence and therefore are generally expected to lessen positive mood-based helpfulness. This also holds true for negative perceptions of the contemplated helping task. When one or more of these disruptive considerations is strongly operative, the increases in prosociality that are based on perceptions of oneself as the recipient of a positive event, priming of positive material, objective self-awareness, or an enhanced social outlook may be eliminated. Thus, a central prerequisite for the positive mood-helping link is the absence of such incongruent factors.

References

Anderson, J. R. (1980). *Cognitive psychology and its implications*. San Francisco, CA: Freeman.

Barden, R. C., Garber, J., Duncan, S. W., & Masters, J. C. (1981). Cumulative effects of induced affective states in children: Accentuation, inoculation, and remediation. *Journal of Personality and Social Psychology, 40,* 750–760.

Berg, B. (1978). Helping behavior on the gridiron: It helps if you're winning. *Psychological Reports, 42,* 531–534.

Berkowitz, L. (1987). Mood, self-awareness, and willingness to help. *Journal of Personality and Social Psychology, 52,* 721–729.

Berkowitz, L., & Connor, W. (1966). Success, failure, and social responsibility. *Journal of Personality and Social Psychology, 4,* 664–669.

Berkowitz, L., & Daniels, L. (1964). Affecting the salience of the social responsibility norm: Effects of past help on the response to dependency relationships. *Journal of Abnormal and Social Psychology, 68,* 275–281.

Blevins, G., & Murphy, T. (1974). Feeling good and helping: Further phonebooth findings. *Psychological Reports, 34,* 326.

Bower, G. H. (1981). Mood and memory. *American Psychologist, 36,* 129–148.

Carlsmith, J., & Gross, A. (1969). Some effects of guilt on compliance. *Journal of Personality and Social Psychology, 11,* 232–239.

Carlson, M., & Miller, N. (1987). An explanation of the relation between negative mood and helping. *Psychological Bulletin, 102,* 91–108.

Carson, T. P., & Adams, H. E. (1980). Activity valence as a function of mood change. *Journal of Abnormal Psychology, 89,* 368–377.

Cialdini, R. B., Darby, B. L., & Vincent, J. E. (1973). Transgression and altruism: A case for hedonism. *Journal of Experimental Social Psychology, 9,* 502–516.

Cialdini, R. B., & Kenrick, D. (1976). Altruism as hedonism: A social development perspective on the relationship of negative mood state and helping. *Journal of Personality and Social Psychology, 34,* 907–914.

Cialdini, R. B., Kenrick, D. T., & Baumann, D. J. (1982). Effects of mood on prosocial behavior in children and adults. In N. Eisenberg-Berg (Ed.), *The development of prosocial behavior* (pp. 339–359). New York: Academic Press.

Clark, D. M., & Teasdale, J. D. (1985). Constraints on the effects of mood on memory. *Journal of Personality and Social Psychology, 48,* 1595–1608.

Clark, M. S., & Isen, A. M. (1982). Toward understanding the relationship between feeling states and social behavior. In A. Hastorf & A. M. Isen (Eds.), *Cognitive social psychology.* New York: Elsevier.

Clark, M. S., & Waddell, B. A. (1983). Effects of moods on thoughts about helping, attraction, and information acquisition. *Social Psychology Quarterly, 46,* 31–35.

Cunningham, M. R. (1979). Weather, mood, and helping behavior: The sunshine Samaritan. *Journal of Personality and Social Psychology, 37,* 1947–1956.

Cunningham, M. R., Steinberg, J., & Grev, R. (1980). Wanting to and having to help: Separate motivations for positive mood and guilt-induced helping. *Journal of Personality and Social Psychology, 38,* 181–192.

Donnerstein, E., Donnerstein, M., & Munger, G. (1975). Helping behavior as a function of pictorially induced moods. *Journal of Social Psychology, 97,* 221–225.

Duval, S., & Wicklund, R. A. (1972). *A theory of objective self-awareness.* New York: Academic Press.

Forbes, G. B., & TeVault, R. K. (1975). The facilitation of anonymous helpfulness by a fortuitous pleasant event. *Journal of Social Psychology, 97,* 299–300.

Forest, P., Clark. M., Mills, J., & Isen, A. M. (1979). Helping as a function of feeling state and nature of the helping behavior. *Motivation and Emotion, 3,* 161–169.

Forgas, J. P., Bower, G. H., & Krantz, S. E. (1984). The influence of mood on perceptions of social interactions. *Journal of Experimental Social Psychology, 20,* 497–513.

Fried, R., & Berkowitz, L. (1979). Music hath charms . . . and can influence helpfulness. *Journal of Applied Social Psychology, 9,* 199–208.

Gibbons, F. X., & Wicklund, R. A. (1982). Self-focused attention and helping behavior. *Journal of Personality and Social Psychology, 43,* 462–474.

Glass, G. V., McGaw, B., & Smith, M. L. (1981). *Meta-analysis in social research.* Beverly Hills, CA: Sage.

Greenglass, E. R. (1969). Effects of prior help and hindrance on willingness to help another: Reciprocity or social responsibility. *Journal of Personality and Social Psychology, 11,* 224–231.

Harada, J. (1983). The effects of positive and negative experiences on helping behavior. *Japanese Psychological Research, 25,* 47–51.

Harris, M. B. (1977). Effects of altruism on mood. *Journal of Social Psychology, 102,* 197–208.

Holloway, S., Tucker, L., & Hornstein, H. A. (1977). The effects of social and nonsocial information on interpersonal behavior of males: The news makes news. *Journal of Personality and Social Psychology, 35,* 514–522.

Hornstein, H. A., Fisch, E., & Holmes, M. (1968). Influence of a model's feeling about his behavior and his relevance as a comparison other on observers' helping behavior. *Journal of Personality and Social Psychology, 10,* 222–226.

Hornstein, H. A., LaKind, E., Frankel, G., & Manne, S. (1975). Effects of knowledge about remote social events on prosocial behavior, social conception, and mood. *Journal of Personality and Social Psychology, 32,* 1038–1046.

Hunter, J. E., Schmidt, F. L., & Jackson, G. B. (1982). *Meta-analysis: Cumulating research findings across studies.* Beverly Hills, CA: Sage.

Isen, A. M. (1970). Success, failure, attention, and reaction to others. *Journal of Personality and Social Psychology, 15,* 294–301.

Isen, A. M., Clark, M., & Schwartz, M. F. (1976). Duration of the effect of good mood on helping: "Footprints on the sands of time." *Journal of Personality and Social Psychology, 34,* 385–393.

Isen, A. M., & Levin, P. F. (1972). Effect of feeling good on helping: Cookies and kindness. *Journal of Personality and Social Psychology, 21,* 384–388.

Isen, A. M., Shalker, T. E., Clark, M., & Karp, L. (1978). Affect, accessibility of material in memory, and behavior: A cognitive loop? *Journal of Personality and Social Psychology, 36*, 1–12.

Isen, A. M., & Simmonds, S. F. (1978). The effect of feeling good on a helping task that is incompatible with good mood. *Social Psychology, 41*, 346–349.

Kazdin, A. E., & Bryan, J. H. (1971). Competence and volunteering. *Journal of Experimental Social Psychology, 7*, 87–97.

Kraut, R. E. (1973). Effects of social labeling on giving to charity. *Journal of Experimental Social Psychology, 9*, 551–562.

Levin, P. F., & Isen, A. M. (1975). Further studies on the effect of feeling good on helping. *Sociometry, 38*, 141–147.

Manucia, G. K., Baumann, D. J., & Cialdini, R. B. (1984). Mood influences on helping: Direct effects or side effects? *Journal of Personality and Social Psychology, 46*, 357–364.

McMillen, D. L., & Austin, J. B. (1971). Effect of positive feedback on compliance following transgression. *Psychonomic Science, 24*, 59–60.

Regan, D., Williams, M., & Sparling, S. (1972). Voluntary expiation of guilt: A field experiment. *Journal of Personality and Social Psychology, 24*, 42–45.

Regan, D. T. (1971). Effects of a favor and liking on compliance. *Journal of Experimental Social Psychology, 7*, 627–639.

Regan, J. W. (1971). Guilt, perceived injustice, and altruistic behavior. *Journal of Personality and Social Psychology, 18*, 124–132.

Rogers, M., Miller, N., Mayer, F. S., & Duval, S. (1982). Personal responsibility and salience of the request for help: Determinants of the relation between negative affect and helping behavior. *Journal of Personality and Social Psychology, 43*, 956–970.

Rosenhan, D. L., Karylowski, J., Salovey, P., & Hargis, K. (1981). Emotion and altruism. In J. P. Rushton & R. M. Sorrentino (Eds.), *Altruism and helping behavior* (pp. 233–248). Hillsdale, NJ: Erlbaum.

Rosenhan, D. L., Salovey, P., & Hargis, K. (1981). The joys of helping:

Focus of attention mediates the impact of positive affect on altruism. *Journal of Personality and Social Psychology, 40*, 899–905.

Rosenhan, D. L., Underwood, B., & Moore, B. (1974). Affect moderates self-gratification and altruism. *Journal of Personality and Social Psychology, 30*, 546–552.

SAS user's guide: Statistics, version five edition. (1985). Cary, NC: SAS Institute.

Scheier, M. F., & Carver, C. S. (1977). Self-focused attention and the experience of emotion: Attraction, repulsion, elation, and depression. *Journal of Personality and Social Psychology, 35*, 625–636.

Shaffer, D. R., & Graziano, W. G. (1983). Effects of positive and negative moods on helping tasks having pleasant or unpleasant consequences. *Motivation and Emotion, 7*, 269–278.

Simmons, C. H., & Lerner, M. J. (1968). Altruism as a search for justice. *Journal of Personality and Social Psychology, 9*, 216–225.

Strenta, A., & DeJong, W. (1981). The effect of a prosocial label on helping behavior. *Social Psychology Quarterly, 44*, 142–147.

Teasdale, J. D., & Fogarty, S. J. (1979). Differential effects of induced mood on retrieval of pleasant and unpleasant events from episodic memory. *Journal of Abnormal Psychology, 88*, 248–257.

Thompson, W., Cowan, C., & Rosenhan, D. (1980). Focus of attention mediates the impact of negative affect on altruism. *Journal of Personality and Social Psychology, 38*, 291–300.

Vallacher, R. R., & Solodky, M. (1979). Objective self-awareness, standards of evaluation, and moral behavior. *Journal of Experimental Social Psychology, 15*, 254–262.

Weyant, J. M. (1978). Effects of mood states, costs, and benefits on helping. *Journal of Personality and Social Psychology, 36*, 1169–1176.

Weyant, J., & Clark, R. D. (1977). Dimes and helping: The other side of the coin. *Personality and Social Psychology Bulletin, 3*, 107–110.

Wicklund, R. A. (1975). Objective self-awareness. In L. Berkowitz (Ed.), *Advances in experimental social psychology* (Vol. 8, pp. 233–275). New York: Academic Press.

Appendix A

The 34 Qualifying Articles

Aderman, D., & Berkowitz, L. (1970). Observational set, empathy, and helping. *Journal of Personality and Social Psychology, 14,* 141–148.

Barnett, M. A., King, L. M., & Howard, J. A. (1979). Inducing affect about self or other: Effects on generosity in children. *Developmental Psychology, 15,* 164–167.

Batson, C. D., Coke, J. S., Chard, F., Smith, D., & Taliaferro, A. (1979). Generality of the "glow of good will": Effects of mood on helping and information acquisition. *Social Psychology Quarterly, 42,* 176–179.

Benson, P. L. (1979). Social feedback, self-esteem state, and prosocial behavior. *Representative Research in Social Psychology, 9,* 43–56.

Blevins, G., & Murphy, T. (1974). Feeling good and helping: Further phonebooth findings. *Psychological Reports, 34,* 326.

Cunningham, M. R. (1979). Weather, mood, and helping behavior: The sunshine Samaritan. *Journal of Personality and Social Psychology, 37,* 1947–1956.

Cunningham, M. R., Steinberg, J., & Grev, R. (1980). Wanting to and having to help: Separate motivations for positive mood and guilt-induced helping. *Journal of Personality and Social Psychology, 38,* 181–192.

Donnerstein, E., Donnerstein, M., & Munger, G. (1975). Helping behavior as a function of pictorially induced moods. *Journal of Social Psychology, 97,* 221–225.

Forbes, G. B., & TeVault, R. K. (1975). The facilitation of anonymous helpfulness by a fortuitous pleasant event. *Journal of Social Psychology, 97,* 299–300.

Forest, P., Clark, M., Mills, J., & Isen, A. M. (1979). Helping as a function of feeling state and nature of the helping behavior. *Motivation and Emotion, 3,* 161–169.

Fried, R., & Berkowitz, L. (1979). Music hath charms . . . and can influence helpfulness. *Journal of Applied Social Psychology, 9,* 199–208.

Harris, M. B., & Siebal, C. E. (1975). Affect, aggression, and altruism. *Developmental Psychology, 11,* 623–627.

Hornstein, H. A., Fisch, E., & Holmes, M. (1968). Influence of a model's feeling about his behavior and his relevance as a comparison other on observers' helping behavior. *Journal of Personality and Social Psychology, 10,* 222–226.

Isen, A. M. (1970). Success, failure, attention, and reaction to others. *Journal of Personality and Social Psychology, 15,* 294–301.

Isen, A. M., Clark, M., & Schwartz, M. F. (1976). Duration of the effect of good mood on helping: "Footprints on the sands of time." *Journal of Personality and Social Psychology, 34,* 385–393.

Isen, A. M., Horn, N., & Rosenhan, D. L. (1973). Effects of success and failure on children's generosity. *Journal of Personality and Social Psychology, 27,* 239–247.

Isen, A. M., & Levin, P. F. (1972). Effect of feeling good on helping: Cookies and kindness. *Journal of Personality and Social Psychology, 21,* 384–388.

Isen, A. M., Shalker, T. E., Clark, M., & Karp, L. (1978). Affect, accessibility of material in memory, and behavior: A cognitive loop? *Journal of Personality and Social Psychology, 36,* 1–12.

Isen, A. M., & Simmonds, S. F. (1978). The effect of feeling good on a helping task that is incompatible with good mood. *Social Psychology, 41,* 346–349.

Kazdin, A. E., & Bryan, J. H. (1971). Competence and volunteering. *Journal of Experimental Social Psychology, 7,* 87–97.

Kidd, R. F., & Berkowitz, L. (1976). Effect of dissonance arousal on helpfulness. *Journal of Personality and Social Psychology, 33,* 613–622.

Kidd, R. F., & Marshall, L. (1982). Self-reflection, mood, and helpful behavior. *Journal of Research in Personality, 16,* 319–334.

Levin, P. F., & Isen, A. M. (1975). Further studies on the effect of feeling good on helping. *Sociometry, 38,* 141–147.

Manucia, G. K., Baumann, D. J., & Cialdini, R. B. (1984). Mood influences on helping: Direct effects or side effects? *Journal of Personality and Social Psychology, 46,* 357–364.

McMillen, D. L., Sanders, D. Y., & Solomon, G. S. (1977). Self-esteem, attentiveness, and helping behavior. *Personality and Social Psychology Bulletin, 3,* 257–261.

Moore, B. S., Underwood, B., & Rosenhan, D. L. (1973). Affect and altruism. *Developmental Psychology, 8,* 99–104.

Regan, D. T. (1971). Effects of a favor and liking on compliance. *Journal of Experimental Social Psychology, 7,* 627–639.

Rosenhan, D. L., Salovey, P., & Hargis, K. (1981). The joys of helping: Focus of attention mediates the impact of positive affect on altruism. *Journal of Personality and Social Psychology, 40,* 899–905.

Sahoo, F. M., & Misra, S. (1983). Effects of success and failure on helping behavior. *Journal of Psychological Researches, 27,* 70–74.

Schellenberg, J. A., & Blevins, G. A. (1973). Feeling good and helping: How quickly does the smile of dame fortune fade? *Psychological Reports, 33,* 72–74.

Shaffer, D. R., & Graziano, W. G. (1983). Effects of positive and negative moods on helping tasks having pleasant or unpleasant consequences. *Motivation and Emotion, 7,* 269–278.

Strenta, A., & DeJong, W. (1981). The effect of a prosocial label on helping behavior. *Social Psychology Quarterly, 44,* 142–147.

Weyant, J. M. (1978). Effects of mood states, costs, and benefits on helping. *Journal of Personality and Social Psychology, 36,* 1169–1176.

Weyant, J., & Clark, R. D. (1977). Dimes and helping: The other side of the coin. *Personality and Social Psychology Bulletin, 3,* 107–110.

Appendix B

Validity of the Rated Predictor Variables

Determinations on some of the predictor variables (e.g., subject age, subject sex, year of study, sex of the helping target, and salience of the helping request) were made on the basis of information directly provided in the reports; consequently, their validity should not pose potential problems. Other variables (e.g., helping task pleasantness, guilt, objective self-awareness, positive affect) were measured by having judges, after reading relevant information provided in each Method section, make continuously scaled ratings of the dimension in question. The available evidence is supportive of the essential validity of these ratings, and is reviewed below.

As an inspection of Table 4 reveals, the rated predictor variables associated with the different models tend to correlate with transformed effect-size estimates in theoretically anticipated ways. This general result is consistent with the notion that the ratings are valid indicators of the underlying theoretical constructs in question.

A number of sampled cases ($N = 13$) included a dependent measure (in addition to helping) that assessed the presence of positive affect differences between the experimental group and the neutral mood subjects. For such instances, it is possible to generate an effect-size estimate that corresponds to the standardized direction and extent of mood positivity in the experimental group relative to the control group. To the degree that the judges' ratings of positive affect in the present study are valid, a positive correlation should be present between the judges' summed ratings and the mood positivity effect-size estimates. This is

what precisely occurs, $r(11) = .69$, $p < .005$, one-tailed; if corrected for measurement unreliability in the positive affect ratings, this correlation increases to .72. Within this sample of 13 cases, the positive affect effect-size estimates were on the average .39 units larger for each increase of one standard deviation in the sum of the judges' ratings. Thus, despite the use of different measures of mood among the sampled cases, it is evident that the judges' ratings of mood among the sampled cases, it is positive affect that results from exposing subjects to a given treatment condition.

Finally, the validity of the measurement scheme is supported by the results of a previous study in which the same procedure was applied in assessing the relation between negative mood and helping (Carlson & Miller, 1987). For example, variables that were either identical to (e.g., guilt, objective self-awareness) or similar to those rated in the present study were found to correlate with relative helpfulness on the part of the negative mood subjects in theoretically predicted ways, the exclusive exception to this pattern being the uniformly negative result for the variables pertaining to Cialdini's negative state relief model (Cialdini, Darby, & Vincent, 1973; Cialdini & Kenrick, 1976), all of which consistently failed to correlate with helpfulness in the manner predicted. Further, in line with the results for the variable positive affect, significant positive correlations were found between judges' ratings of various dimensions (e.g., sadness) and effect-size estimates that were based on dependent measures of the constructs in question.

Appendix C

Zero-Order Intercorrelations Among the 12 Predictor Variables

Variables	1	2	3	4	5	6	7	8	9	10	11	12
1. Pleasantness of the helping task[a]	—											
2. High/low positive affect[a]	-.130	—										
3. Social outlook[a]	-.275	.056	—									
4. OSA + request salience[a]	-.296	.453	.203	—								
5. Self as target of positive event[a]	-.091	.309	-.192	.198	—							
6. Guilt[a]	.059	-.478	.222	-.443	.274	—						
7. Age of subjects	.295	-.168	-.187	-.571	.091	.470	—					
8. Year of study	.201	.026	-.312	.085	-.017	-.276	-.026	—				
9. Sex of subjects	.225	.141	-.337	.084	.194	-.258	.110	.332	—			
10. Sex of helping target	-.219	.357	.111	.284	.374	-.132	-.161	.198	.260	—		
11. Time delay[a]	-.117	.054	.066	.054	.036	-.047	.111	-.219	.055	.020	—	
12. Sustained helpfulness	.142	-.176	-.131	-.074	-.320	-.112	-.014	.070	-.032	-.314	.144	—

Note. OSA = Objective self-awareness.
[a] The correlations are based on the transformed version of the variable.

Received September 5, 1987
Revision received March 14, 1988
Accepted March 15, 1988 ∎

The Role of Sympathy and Altruistic Personality Traits in Helping: A Reexamination

Nancy Eisenberg, Paul A. Miller, Mark Schaller,
Richard A. Fabes, Jim Fultz, Rita Shell,
and Cindy L. Shea

Arizona State University

ABSTRACT The purposes of this study were (*a*) to examine the role of social evaluative concerns in the self-report of sympathy and in the relation of sympathy to helping; and (*b*) to determine the role of "altruistic personality" traits and situationally induced vicarious emotional responses in the intention to help. Dispositional and situational self-reports of sympathy and other vicarious emotional reactions were obtained for persons who also were given the opportunity to assist a needy other. Moreover, dispositional measures of concern with social evaluation and an altruistic orientation were obtained, and a bogus pipeline manipulation was instituted for half the study participants. Both dispositional and situational self-reported sympathy were positively related to helping, as were other personality indices viewed as reflecting altruistic characteristics. The relations for the dispositional indices of sympathy were not due solely to social evaluative concerns or to other egoistic concerns. The effects on intended helping of dispositional sympathy, perspective taking, and the tendency to ascribe responsibility for others to the self appeared to be both direct and mediated by

This research was supported by grants from the National Science Foundation (BNS-8509223) and the National Institute of Child Health and Development (1 KO4 HD00717-01) to the first author, as well as by fellowships from the National Institute of Mental Health to Paul Miller (1 F32 MH0926301-01) and Jim Fultz (1 F32 MH09181-01). The authors gratefully acknowledge the contributions of the following persons: Denise Bustamante, Stacey Fowler, Michele Paxton, Kelly Rhodes, and Michele Wilson. Special appreciation is due to George Knight for his statistical consultation. Requests for reprints should be addressed to Nancy Eisenberg, Department of Psychology, Arizona State University, Tempe, AZ 85287.

Journal of Personality 57:1, March 1989. Copyright © 1989 by Duke University Press. CCC 0022-3506/89/$1.50

situational sympathetic responding. Finally, situational sadness did not mediate the effects of sympathetic responsiveness.

Researchers frequently have claimed that sympathy is positively related to prosocial behavior (Batson, 1987; Hoffman, 1982).[1] In relevant research, sympathy most often refers to an actual affective reaction to information or cues concerning another in a specific situation (henceforth labeled situational sympathy). However, people also may vary in the general trait or disposition to react sympathetically. People who are predisposed to respond sympathetically should be relatively likely to process others' needs and to respond sympathetically in sympathy-evoking contexts (Eisenberg & Miller, 1987; Staub, 1986). Thus, both types of sympathy might be expected to relate positively to altruistic behavior and to an altruistic disposition (Batson, 1987; Eisenberg, 1986).

In fact, there does seem to be an empirical association between prosocial behavior and both situational and dispositional indices of sympathy or empathy (Eisenberg & Miller, 1987). For example, in an initial series of studies, Batson and his colleagues (Batson, Duncan, Ackerman, Buckley, & Birch, 1981; Batson, O'Quin, Fultz, Vanderplas, & Isen, 1983; Toi & Batson, 1982) have examined the relation between situational sympathy and helping. In this work, Batson has differentiated between empathy (sympathy in our terminology) and personal distress, that is, an aversive self-oriented response (such as alarm, distress, or worry) that is associated with the egoistic motive of diminishing one's own distress. In general, Batson and his colleagues have found that situational sympathy, assessed by means of various manipulations or self-reports, is positively related to helping, regardless of whether or not the individual might easily escape from the distress-inducing stimulus (e.g., the victim). In contrast, feelings of personal distress tend to be associated with low levels of helping if individuals can easily escape from the aversive situation. However, if people experiencing personal distress

1. Sympathy is defined as an affective reaction stemming from the apprehension of another's emotional state or condition, which is characterized by other-oriented feelings of concern (Eisenberg & Strayer, 1987; Wispé, 1986). It should be differentiated from empathy, which we (Eisenberg & Strayer, 1987) define as a vicarious affective response based on the apprehension of another's state or condition. Empathy is neither other-oriented nor self-oriented, but frequently may be transformed (due to cognitive processing) into either sympathy or a self-oriented affective response (i.e., personal distress).

cannot easily escape from the aversive situation, helping is relatively high, presumably because it is used as a means to reduce one's own personal distress (by eliminating the aversive situation).

Investigators usually have suggested that the relation between indices of sympathy and prosocial responding exists because situational and dispositional sympathy result in the altruistic motive to alleviate another's need or distress (Batson, 1987; Eisenberg, 1986; Staub, 1986). Specifically, situational sympathy is viewed as inducing other-oriented concern, which results in the desire to alleviate the other's distress, whereas the effects of a sympathetic disposition are both mediated by situational sympathy and due to the altruistic values and orientation inherent in such a disposition. However, some researchers also have asserted that indices of sympathy (both dispositional and situational) frequently may be related to prosocial behavior for egoistic reasons (Archer, Diaz-Loving, Gollwitzer, Davis, & Foushee, 1981; Batson, Bolen, Cross, & Neuringer-Benefiel, 1986; Cialdini et al., 1987). Such reasons include concerns with others' evaluations and avoidance of negative self-evaluations or other aversive affective states. Indeed, some researchers have even challenged the notion that there is an altruistic personality (Batson et al., 1986; Cialdini et al., 1987). These issues, as well as the role of situational versus trait sympathy in prosocial responding, are discussed below.

The Role of Social Evaluative Processes

Archer and his colleagues (Archer et al., 1981) have suggested that individuals' concern with social evaluation, by either the experimenter or the professor conducting the study, may mediate the association between their sympathy and helping in many studies, and that high sympathizers may be especially motivated to behave in a socially desirable manner. In two separate studies, Fultz, Batson, Fortenbach, McCarthy, and Varney (1986) tested Archer's assertions by (a) reducing the visibility of cues related to social evaluation and (b) manipulating the possibility for social evaluation. They obtained no evidence that social evaluative concerns caused the relation between sympathy and helping. This conclusion is dependent, however, upon a null interaction between level of sympathy and level of potential for negative social evaluation. In addition, some participants might have helped in order to obtain a positive social evaluation (rather than avoid social disapproval) because the situation was one in which the recipient of help would eventually know who offered to assist. Moreover, subjects' written self-reports of emotional responses to the needy other, in these and other studies, might have been affected by the desire to respond in socially desirable ways. In fact, Davis (1983) found that dispositional indices of sympathy, personal distress, and fantasy empathy (i.e., the tendency to transpose oneself imaginatively into the feelings of fictitious characters) were positively related to one or more indices of sensitivity to others' evaluations (perspective taking, however, was negatively related). Finally, it is possible that the positive relation between dispositional indices of sympathy/empathy and prosocial behavior found in the empirical literature is due, in part, to the fact that it is socially desirable (especially for females; Block, 1983; Eisenberg & Lennon, 1983) both to express concern and to behave as a nurturer. Consequently, we hypothesized that social evaluative concerns (as assessed with dispositional indices and the bogus pipeline [BPL] procedure; Jones & Sigall, 1971) would affect report of emotion in a gender-role stereotypic manner (that is, females would be especially likely to attempt to appear emotionally responsive because such responsivity is defined as feminine; Shields, 1987), and that social evaluative concerns would account for some, but not all, of the relation between sympathy (dispositional and situational) and helping.

The Role of Guilt and Sympathy: Is There an Altruistic Personality?

At present, support for the assertion that there is an altruistic personality is modest. There is some evidence of cross-situational consistency in prosocial behavior, but it is not strong (Krebs & Miller, 1985; Mussen & Eisenberg-Berg, 1977; Rushton, 1980). Indeed, it has been suggested that one might be able to construct a better measure of an altruistic disposition than the existing pencil and paper indices of prosocial behavior by computing a composite prosocial index of various dispositional indices of prosocial traits such as sympathy and social responsibility (Krebs & Miller, 1985). Moreover, some researchers have questioned whether those who score high on indices of an altruistic disposition help others because of concern for others or the desire to avoid guilt. Thus, there is a need to examine further the role of dispositional and situational sympathy in prosocial behavior, as well as other potentially important aspects of a prosocial orientation (e.g., dispositions related to perspective taking, social responsibility, and the tendency to ascribe responsibility for others to the self).

Batson et al. (1986) are among those who have recently examined the notion of Rushton (1980), Staub (1986), and others that there is an altruistic personality. They found that questionnaire indices of an altruistic personality were positively correlated with helping in a situation in which it was difficult to escape contact with the needy other but not in a situation in which it was easy to escape contact. Based on this finding, they argued that the people who were high on these indices did not help for altruistic reasons (or they would have assisted when escape was easy); they assisted merely to avoid aversive self-censure. In addition, they suggested that their indices of an altruistic personality actually reflected the egoistic desire to avoid guilt or shame.

In contrast, Batson et al.'s (1986) self-report index of situational sympathy was significantly related to helping in the easy escape but not in the difficult escape condition when the aforementioned personality variables were partialled from the correlation with helping. On the basis of these findings, they argued that their self-report measure of situational sympathy reflected altruistic concern in the easy escape condition because the correlation between situational sympathy and helping was still significant when the effects of the tendency to experience guilt or shame (i.e., the personality indices) were removed.

Another implication of Batson et al.'s (1986) findings is that altruistic personality characteristics (including the trait of sympathy) do not play a role in the relation of situational sympathy to helping, especially in situations in which helping is likely to be altruistically motivated (i.e., in easy escape situations). However, the degree to which situationally induced reactions versus personality attributes influence subsequent prosocial behavior would be expected to vary as a function of characteristics of the given situation (because situational and personal factors can be expected to interact; Gergen, Gergen, & Meter, 1972; Romer, Gruder, & Lizzadro, 1986). In "strong" situations, "those that provide salient cues to guide behavior and have a fairly high degree of structure" (Snyder & Ickes, 1985, p. 904), the cause of behaviors typically should be situational. In contrast, in psychologically weak situations, dispositional factors seem to have a relatively strong impact on behavior (Snyder & Ickes, 1985). In addition, one might expect strong situations containing evocative emotional cues to elicit more intense situational reactions than weak situations.

In the Batson et al. (1986) study, the context was more emotionally arousing (the nearby needy other was being electrically shocked) than in most other studies of sympathy. The strong cues concerning the other's immediate need, as well as her physical proximity to the subject and the intensity of her distress, may have elicited strong situational sympathy. In fact, participants' ratings of the other's need were quite high, more so than in some other studies (e.g., Fultz et al., 1986). These emotion-inducing characteristics of the situation may have heightened the role of situational sympathy in helping and diluted the influence of dispositional sympathy/altruism. If the situation were not so highly evocative or salient, dispositional variables would be expected to be better predictors of behavior than situational reactions. In such weak situations, motivation to help is likely to stem from internalized values and needs and the predisposition to take the cognitive role of another as well as from situational sympathy.

In the present study, we examined helping in a situation in which the other's need was somewhat less immediate and dramatic than in the Batson et al. (1986) study. Therefore, in addition to our earlier hypotheses concerning social evaluation, we hypothesized as follows: (a) that dispositional indices of altruism would be positively related to helping in the present study, as in much of the literature (Eisenberg & Miller, 1987; Krebs & Miller, 1985) but not Batson et al.; (b) that the relation of situational sympathy to helping would be affected by individual differences in altruistic and sympathetic tendencies; and (c) that indices of an altruistic personality would be linked to helping in part as a function of their effect on situational sympathy. Specifically, we expected indices of a sympathetic, altruistic personality orientation to relate to prosocial intentions both directly (due to the values and other-orientation associated with having an altruistic orientation; Eisenberg, 1986; Hoffman, 1987) and indirectly, as mediated by the situational sympathy experienced in the given context. To test these assumptions, models including both direct and indirect (mediated) effects of a given variable (e.g., dispositional sympathy) on the intention to assist were compared with models including only direct effects or only indirect effects. Although the intent to assist is not identical to actual helping behavior, intentions do tend to be related to actual behavior (Pomazal & Jaccard, 1976; see also Ajzen & Fishbein, 1977) and generally relate to other variables in a manner similar to that for indices of actual helping (see Batson's [1987] various studies). Therefore, intention to help was considered to be a relevant indicator of prosocial responding.

Sadness as a Mediator of Sympathy

Cialdini et al. (1987) have suggested that sadness may frequently mediate the relation between situational sympathy and helping, and that people who report responding sympathetically assist primarily to relieve their own personal sadness. This notion also was examined with mediational analyses.

METHOD

Subjects

Seventy-eight undergraduate students (37 females, 41 males) participated in the experiment for partial class credit. Four additional subjects (two of each sex; one BPL, three control) were dropped because they expressed strong suspicions about the experiment.

Procedures

Approximately equal numbers of males and females were randomly assigned to the two experimental conditions: the BPL and the control group. The objective of the BPL condition was to induce individuals to report their affective reactions and attitudes honestly (Jones & Sigall, 1971). This is a procedure in which participants are persuaded that their "true" attitudes and feelings can be assessed reliably by means of physiological indices (Quigley-Fernandez & Tedeschi, 1978). All participants were tested in circumstances comparable to Batson's easy escape condition because differences in the relations of sympathy and personal distress to helping are clearest (both empirically and conceptually) in this condition (Batson, 1987).

Questionnaire Session: Measuring the Personality Variables

One to two weeks prior to the experimental session, participants completed a battery of personality measures including the Ascription of Responsibility Scale (Schwartz, 1968; $\alpha = .74$); the Social Responsibility Scale (Berkowitz & Lutterman, 1968; $\alpha = .60$); the Marlowe-Crowne Social Desirability Scale (Crowne & Marlowe, 1964; $\alpha = .78$); the Fear of Negative Evaluation Scale (Leary, 1983; $\alpha = .85$); Snyder's (1986) Self-Monitoring Scale ($\alpha = .70$); and Mehrabian and Epstein's (1972) measure of emotional empathy ($\alpha = .83$). Demographic data were also obtained. Order of the measures was counterbalanced. It is important to note that the Social Desirability and Self-Monitoring questionnaires assess the desire to elicit others' positive reactions as well as to avoid negative social reactions.

Participants appearing for the session were informed that the materials for the actual experiment were not yet prepared and that another experimenter was conducting a study and needed subjects to complete several questionnaires. Subjects also were told they would receive an extra research credit if they agreed to participate in both studies. Those who agreed to participate (virtually all) completed the questionnaires and were then scheduled for the second (experimental) session approximately a week later. The second part of the experiment took place in a different part of the building and was conducted by different experimenters. The sessions were arranged in this way to reduce the likelihood that participants would perceive a relation between the two sessions.

Experimental Session: The Opportunity to Assist Needy Others

This study was introduced as a project being conducted for a local TV station interested in obtaining individuals' emotional and physiological reactions to the content of actual, but unaired, news broadcasts (adopted from Toi & Batson, 1982).

BPL condition. For persons in the BPL condition, the experimenter handed the subject a clipboard with several forms, the top one of which was a brief "attitude survey" about the content of TV shows. A piece of carbon paper, placed several pages down, transferred the subject's responses to a matching form without the subject's awareness. After completing the survey, the subject removed it from the clipboard and kept it from the experimenter's view. Then the experimenter explained that a new technique for measuring the intensity of individuals' attitudes and emotional reactions had recently been developed. Offering to show the equipment to the subject, the experimenter picked up the clipboard (containing the concealed carbon copy of the subject's responses) and took the subject to the equipment room. There the "ECG technician" briefly described the recording equipment and reemphasized its capacity to accurately monitor individuals' internal reactions. The experimenter then took the subject back to the experimental room, leaving the clipboard behind. Next the experimenter placed two electrodes on the subject and indicated that it was necessary to calibrate the ECG measuring equipment. In order to get accurate "readings," the experimenter asked the subject to complete the attitude survey form again using the original survey to copy their responses onto the second form of the survey. (This procedure avoided the possibility that subjects' might record an answer different from their original response.) Before seeing the subject's response, the experimenter asked the technician for a "reading" from the machine. According to a prearranged plan, the technician reported a reading that was off by one number from the subject's response. The technician then adjusted the equipment. This procedure was repeated until on the third item the technician reported a value that matched the subject's response. Noting that the machine was operating properly, the experimenter asked the subject to complete the remaining items and to try to "fool" the machine by putting down answers that were clearly different from their "true" responses on the original survey form. The technician's readings exactly matched all the subject's original "real" answers (see Quigley-Fernandez & Tedeschi, 1978).

Control condition.   The same procedure was followed (without the calibration process) for the control group except there was no attempt to induce subjects to believe their true responses could be ascertained by the equipment. They were merely told that the experimenter wanted to measure their physiological responses to the tapes.

Empathy questionnaire.   All subjects were then asked to complete the Davis Interpersonal Reactivity Index (IRI; Davis, 1983), which contains four 7-item subscales (EC, sympathetic concern; PT, perspective taking; FE, fantasy empathy; PD, personal distress; α's = .82, .80, .73, and .69, respectively). Participants were told the questionnaire information was to be used in later analyses of their responses to the upcoming TV programs. The experimenter indicated that to avoid influencing the individual's responses, he or she would leave the room. The subject was asked to tap a small bell when finished to call the experimenter back.

Presentation of the films.   Next the experimenter introduced the first TV program. Subjects were told, " . . . We have quite a number of different tapes so that only one participant will watch each tape, and who watches which tape is determined by a random procedure." The experimenter started the videotape, asked the subject to tap the bell when the film ended, and then left the room. The primary purpose of this film was to promote the notion that no two persons would view the same programs. The context of this film (a newscast on local events) was very bland and (according to many subjects) rather boring.

139

After the film, the experimenter returned with a reaction questionnaire and an evaluation form to be used in rating the TV program. The subjects responded to 12 adjectives (on a 7-point scale, 1 = not at all; 7 = extremely), indicating their current emotional state. Order of the adjectives was counterbalanced across participants. Based upon previous research, these adjectives reflected individuals' personal distress, sympathetic concern, and sad reactions to another's need (Fultz, Schaller, & Cialdini, 1988). Subjects next rated (on 7-point scales) how interesting and evocative the broadcast was. The experimenter again left the room to avoid "biasing" the subject's responses.

The experimenter returned when the bell was rung and introduced the second film as another randomly assigned tape, this time from a series called "News From the Personal Side." The tapes were described as short programs about real events that happened to people in the local community. As before, subjects were asked to watch the film carefully because they would be the only person seeing that particular program. All subjects actually viewed the same film in which a woman (Mrs. Fulton) seated in a local hospital room with her "injured" children, described to a reporter a serious car accident, the injuries it caused her two children, and the adjustment problems they were having as a result. She explicitly noted her children's fears of getting behind in school and failing and her problem as a single parent finding enough time to be with them at the hospital.

Helping response. The experimenter returned at the sound of the bell and "discovered" that one part of the evaluation form was misplaced; he/she asked the subject to start rating the 12 adjectives and went to search for another form. About a minute after the subject completed the form, the experimenter returned (slightly out of breath), placed the evaluation form on the clipboard, and then said:

> I also have this [envelope] to give you. I don't know what is in it, but the professor in charge of this research said to give it to the student scheduled to watch tape #24, so I guess that's you. So why don't you read this note first, and then work on the evaluation form and ring the bell when you are through.

In the envelope were two letters. One letter was from the professor in charge of the research. She said that she had encouraged the mother to write a letter requesting assistance from the subject who rated her film. In the second letter, the mother said that it had been difficult for her to write the letter, but because of mounting difficulties in handling problems related to the accident, she agreed to ask for some assistance with certain household tasks (e.g., shopping, yard work) so she could spend more time tutoring and supporting her children. As in Batson's easy escape condition, individuals were led to believe they would have no contact with the Fulton family if they refused to help, and that the experimenter would be unaware of their decision. Enclosed with the letters was a small slip of paper indicating the number of hours that could be donated to helping her around the house, in 3-hour increments from 1 to 3 to more than 18 hours (i.e., there were seven possible levels of helping). As indicated in the professor's cover letter, the subject then placed the (possibly unsigned) slip in an envelope and sealed it. Finally, subjects filled out the program evaluation, which included a question regarding the degree to which the persons interviewed in the film needed help.

Debriefing. The experimenter returned and indicated that the session was nearly over. Prior to debriefing, the experimenter asked the participant for reactions to the films and probed for information that would suggest awareness of the experimental manipulation.

RESULTS

Perceptions of the Fultons's Need

Ratings of the Fultons's need averaged 5.16 (on a 7-point scale), which is somewhat lower than in some other studies (e.g., Batson et al., 1983, 1986). These ratings did not vary by condition, but they were positively related to several personality indices: the Mehrabian and Epstein, partial $r(69) = .27$, $p < .021$; FE, partial $r(72) = .29$, $p < .014$; PT, partial $r(72) = .27$, $p < .018$; EC, partial $r(72) = .20$, $p < .09$; and social responsibility, partial $r(73) = .20$, $p < .08$ (sex was partialled in all correlations). Thus, people who scored high on measures of dispositional sympathy and altruistic characteristics were especially likely to view the Fultons's need as substantial.

Situational Sympathy, Distress, and Sadness

To measure situational sympathetic concern, four adjectives from the emotional response questionnaire administered after the second film were averaged: sympathetic, touched, soft-hearted, and compassionate ($\alpha = .89$). Similar composite scores were computed for personal distress (distressed, disturbed, troubled, uneasy; $\alpha = .89$) and sadness (low-spirited, heavy-hearted, sad, feeling low; $\alpha = .88$).[2] Mean values

2. A three-factor, varimax-rotated principal components analysis of all 12 adjec-

for the sympathy, distress, and sadness composites (on a 1 to 7 scale) were 4.11 (SD = 1.50), 3.04 (SD = 1.39), and 3.21 (SD = 1.42). These values are somewhat lower than those obtained by Batson et al. (1986), suggesting that our film was less emotion-provoking than theirs.[3]

The Role of Social Evaluative Concerns

The role of social evaluative concerns both in self-report of emotional reactivity (dispositional and situational indices) and in the relation of sympathy and other self-reported reactions to helping was examined in two ways. First, we determined whether these variables and relations differed under BPL versus control conditions. If people generally consciously attempt to present themselves in socially desirable ways, they should be more likely to act in a manner consistent with their gender role (females more emotionally reactive and concerned than males) under control as opposed to BPL conditions. Moreover, if more honest reports of sympathy were obtained with BPL procedures, one would expect the relation between reported sympathy and helping to be somewhat stronger in the BPL than the control condition (although this may not be so if social evaluative concerns affect both reports of sympathy and offers to assist in the control condition). Second, we assessed the role of social evaluation in emotional responding and helping by examining the relations of the three personality indices designed to tap social evaluation concerns (i.e., the Self-Monitoring, Social Desirability, and Fear of Negative Evaluation Scales) to self-reported affective reactions and helping behavior.

Self-report of emotion: BPL.   The effects of the BPL procedure on participants' reports of emotional response were examined with two 2 × 2 (Sex × Condition: BPL vs. Control) multivariate analyses of variance (MANOVAs): (*a*) one in which the dependent variables were the four subscales of the

---

tives produced a factor solution quite similar to that found by Batson (1987) in previous research. The three factors reflected the items in our three composite indices, with the exception that *uneasy* loaded higher on the sadness than distress factor. However, given that this item had an interitem correlation of .64 with the other items on the distress scale, its removal increased the α negligibly, and its face meaning is not sadness, we left it in the distress composite. According to auxiliary analyses, removal of this item did not affect the pattern of results.
3. Note, however, that the overlap in adjectives in the two studies was only partial.

Davis Dispositional Empathy/Sympathy Scale, and (*b*) one for the three situational self-report emotional composites (sympathy, personal distress, sadness). For the four Davis subscales, the multivariate Fs were significant for the main effect of sex and the Sex × Condition interaction, Fs $(4, 69) = 5.57$ and 2.74, $ps < .001$ and $.035$, respectively. The univariate Fs for sex were significant for all four subscales, Fs $(1, 72) = 20.16, 5.10, 4.58$, and 9.86, $ps < .001, .027, .036$, and $.002$, respectively, for EC, PT, FE, and PD. Consistent with gender-role expectations and prior research (Lennon & Eisenberg, 1987), women scored higher on all scales.

The univariate Condition × Sex interaction was significant only for FE, $F(1, 72) = 4.28, p < .042$. Males and females differed little in FE in the BPL condition ($Ms = 23.45$ and 23.53 for males and females, respectively), but females ($M = 25.84$) scored significantly higher than males ($M = 21.42$) when they did not think the experimenter could detect their true responses (i.e., in the control group), $F(1, 37) = 8.30, p < .007$.

Similar analyses were performed for the three situational emotional composites. According to the 2×2 (Sex × Condition) MANOVA, only the effect of sex was marginally significant, $F(3, 72) = 2.52, p < .065$. Females reported more sympathy and sadness ($M = 4.57$ and 3.54) than did males ($M = 3.70$ and 2.91), Fs$(1, 74) = 7.54$ and 4.13, $ps < .008$ and $.046$, respectively.

Self-report of emotion: Questionnaires. The self-report indices of emotion were correlated with the three scales related to social evaluative concerns. EC, PT, and situational sympathy were all positively related to social desirability; EC, PD, and situational sympathy, distress, and sadness were at least marginally, positively related to fear of negative evaluations; and PT and FE were related to low self-monitoring (see Table 1). There were no marked or significant gender differences in this pattern of findings. In summary, it appears that self-report of sympathetic and other emotional reactions was affected to some degree by social evaluative concerns as indexed by the self-report questionnaires (see Table 2 for the interrelations of the indices).

The relation of reported affect to helping: BPL. The role of social evaluative concerns (as assessed by the BPL) in the relation of reported affective response (dispositional and situational) to helping first was examined with a series of 2×2 (Sex × Condition) unique sums of squares analyses of variance (ANOVAs), one for each of the four Davis subscales and for each of the three situational emotional indices. In each of these analyses, one Davis subscale or one situational index was treated as a continuous independent variable (using a regression procedure) along with sex and condition; amount of helping was the dependent variable in all analyses (SPSS, 1983). By means of these analyses, we sought to determine whether the relation

Table 1
Relation of Affective Self-Report Indices to Personality Indices: Pearson Correlations

Personality indices		Davis scales				Situational report		
		EC	PT	FE	PD	Sympathy	Distress	Sadness
Self-Monitoring	Total	-.12***	-.22***	-.11	-.26***	.03	.11	.08
	Females	-.07	-.06	-.17	-.35**	-.01	.02	.08
	Males	-.06	-.31*	.01	-.13	.17	.26	.15
Fear of Negative Evaluation	Total	.30***	-.03	.17	.32***	.36***	.29**	.21*
	Females	.26	-.05	.15	.32*	.32*	.27	.06
	Males	.15	-.16	.08	.18	.29*	.24	.27*
Social Desirability	Total	.39***	.50***	.04	-.02	.24**	.11	.14
	Females	.50***	.67***	.05	-.15	.23	.05	.08
	Males	.20	.31*	-.01	-.05	.14	.08	.10
Ascription of Responsibility	Total	.49***	.32***	.18	.33***	.30***	.07	.12
	Females	.23	.32*	-.03	.20	.27	.03	.05
	Males	.40**	.14	.09	.21	.08	-.04	.01
Social Responsibility	Total	.27**	.11	.30***	.07	.27**	.15	.19
	Females	.14	.13	.39**	.05	.11	-.03	.07
	Males	.24	.02	.16	.03	.32**	.20	.20
Mehrabian & Epstein Empathy Scale	Total	.65***	.19	.44***	.53***	.47***	.21*	.36**
	Females	.56**	.34*	.25	.36**	.42**	.00	.22
	Males	.52***	-.09	.47**	.45**	.38*	.22	.36**

Table 1
Continued

Personality indices		Davis scales				Situational report		
		EC	PT	FE	PD	Sympathy	Distress	Sadness
Sympathy	Total	.55***	.31***	.27***	.21*	—	.64***	.70***
	Females	.55***	.35**	.11	.12	—	.45***	.53***
	Males	.45***	.16	.34**	.14	—	.81***	.85***
Distress	Total	.26**	.13	.26**	.17	.64***	—	.81***
	Females	.17	.12	.19	.07	.45***	—	.81***
	Males	.26	.08	.26*	.17	.81***	—	.72***
Sadness	Total	.34***	.13	.21*	.23**	.70***	.81***	—
	Females	.21	.14	.05	.12	.53***	.72***	—
	Males	.34**	.03	.28*	.22	.85***	.87***	—
EC	Total	—	.54***	.39***	.47***			
	Females	—	.65***	.13	.34**			
	Males	—	.36**	.49***	.42***			
PT	Total	.54***	—	.23***	.05			
	Females	.65***	—	.06	.06			
	Males	.36**	—	.28*	-.12			
FE	Total	.39***	.23**	—	.24***			
	Females	.13	.06	—	.07			
	Males	.49***	.28*	—	.27*			
PD	Total	.47***	.05	.24**	—			
	Females	.34**	.06	.07	—			
	Males	.42***	-.12	.27*	—			

Note. EC = sympathetic concern; PT = perspective taking; FE = fantasy empathy; PD = personal distress.

*p < .10
**p < .05
***p < .01.

145

Table 2
Interrelations of Indices of Social Evaluative and Altruistic Personality Indices

Personality Indices	Self-Monitoring	Fear of Negative Evaluation	Social Desirability	Ascription of Responsibility	Social Responsibility
Self-Monitoring					
Total		.10	−.28**	−.31***	.10
Females		.01	−.16	−.26	.04
Males		.31*	−.36	−.31	.23
Fear of Negative Evaluation					
Total			−.20*	.05	.16
Females			−.27	−.01	.06
Males			−.26	−.17	.16
Social Desirability					
Total				.49***	.06
Females				.35**	−.15
Males				.53***	.07
Ascription of Responsibility					
Total					.06
Females					−.18
Males					−.02

*p < .10
**p < .05
***p < .01.

146

between self-reported indices of vicarious response and helping differed in the BPL and control conditions, and whether any higher-order interactions were significant. In these and other analyses, only data for amount of helping are reported. In most cases, the findings for the dichotomous index of helping versus not helping were similar to those for the continuous variable for amount of helping, but slightly weaker. Because the helping data were very skewed (55% of participants did not assist at all), a square root transformation was performed on the continuous measure of helping.

For the ANOVA including EC as a predictor, only the main effect for EC was significant, $F(1, 68) = 8.82, p < .004$. EC was positively related to helping, $r(74) = .33, p < .003$. Similarly, for the ANOVA including PT, only the main effect for PT was significant, $F(1, 68) = 4.99, p < .03$. PT was positively related to helping, $r(74) = .28, p < .013$. There were no significant interactions for EC or PT; nor were there any significant effects for the analyses involving PD and FE. The results of these analyses are consistent with the view that the positive relation of PT and EC to helping was not a function of social evaluative concerns as gauged by the BPL procedure (means for helping [untransformed] in the control and BPL conditions were 1.42 and 1.54, respectively).

Similar analyses were computed for the three situational indices of emotional response. For the three 2×2 (Sex $\times$ Condition) ANOVAs in which an index of emotional response was treated as a continuous independent variable, there were no significant effects for distress or sadness. However, for the analysis involving the sympathy index, there was a main effect of sympathy, $F(1, 70) = 4.77, p < .032$. Sympathy was positively related to helping, $r(76) = .27, p < .016$.

The relation of reported affect to helping: Questionnaires. Next, we examined whether the relations between helping and Davis subscale scores and the self-report adjectives were altered when the effects of concern with social evaluation, as indexed by the three personality scales, were partialled (along with sex) from the correlations. The results of the partial correlations suggest that the relations of EC and PT to helping were not weakened greatly by partialling the effects of scores on the three personality questionnaires, partial $rs(63) = .26$ and $.24$, $ps = .04$ and $.053$, for EC and PT. Thus, social evaluative concerns did not seem to account for most of the variance in the relation between EC or PT and helping. However, the correlation between situational empathy and helping was reduced somewhat when social evaluative concerns were partialled, partial $r(63) = .18, p < .16$. Partialling these same indices did not alter the relations between helping and the sadness and distress indices.

In an additional set of nine regressions, we examined whether the three indices of social evaluative concern moderated (Baron & Kenny, 1986) the relation between helping and EC, PT, and situational sympathy. EC was moderated by fear of negative evaluation (i.e., the Fear of Negative Evaluation × EC interaction increased prediction of helping significantly), multiple $r = .41$, r^2 change $= .05$, $F(1, 71)$ for the r^2 change $= 4.05$, $p < .05$. Similarly, the relation of situational sympathy to helping was moderated by social desirability, multiple $r = .36$, r^2 change $= .06$, $F(1, 67)$ for the r^2 change $= 4.78$, $p < .032$. The relation of EC to helping intent was higher among persons high in fear of negative evaluation than among those low on fear of evaluation. Similarly, the correlation of situational sympathy with helping was stronger among those who scored high on social desirability than among those who scored low. Thus, it appears that the relations of EC and situational sympathy (but not PT) to helping were higher among those high in social evaluative concerns, although the correlation of EC to helping held even when the effects of social evaluative concerns were removed.

Relation of Indices of Altruistic Personality to Helping

As discussed previously, Batson et al. (1986) argued that if there is such a thing as an altruistic (rather than guilt-avoiding) personality, measures of altruistic dimensions of personality such as the tendency to ascribe responsibility for others' welfare to the self, to feel sympathy, and to have internalized the norm of social responsibility should be positively correlated with helping when escape from the guilt- or shame-inducing situation is easy. In our experimental situation, which included features that should have made escape quite easy, the altruistic personality variables ascription of responsibility, social responsibility, perspective taking, and empathy/sympathy (as assessed by both the Mehrabian and Epstein Scale and the EC Scale) were positively related to helping for one sex or the other (see Table 3).[4]

Contribution of Altruistic Personality Measures to the Relation Between Situational Sympathy and Helping

Altruistic personality variables accounted for much of the variance in the association between situational sympathy and helping. Sympathy was un-

---

4. Batson et al. (1986) found that birth order was significantly related to ascription of responsibility and helping. We found no significant relations between birth order and any variable (including helping) with the exception that latter borns were marginally significantly higher on scores of situational sympathy, partial $r(75) = .19$, $p < .095$ (partialling out sex).

Table 3
Relation of Personality and Situational Variables to Helping [a]

Personality measure	Both sexes	Women	Men
Social Responsibility	.22*	− .02	.36**
	(.24)**	(.02)	(.35)**
Ascription of Responsibility	.31***	.46***	.12
	(.28)**	(.40)**	(.09)
Mehrabian & Epstein Empathy	.29**	.43**	.16
Scale	(.31)***	(.38)**	(.23)
Social Desirability	.17	.14	.17
	(.14)	(.08)	(.13)
Self-Monitoring	− .07	.01	− .13
	(− .04)	(.01)	(− .05)
Fear of Negative Evaluation	.19*	.37**	− .04
	(.16)	(.31)*	(− .05)
Interpersonal Reactivity (Davis Scale)			
Sympathetic concern	.33***	.36**	.29*
	(.31)***	(.20)	(.37)**
Perspective taking	.28**	.18	.34**
	(.21)*	(.09)	(.28)*
Fantasy empathy	.15	.17	.10
	(.17)	(.16)	(.13)
Personal distress	.04	− .11	.11
	(.02)	(− .20)	(.15)
Situation Indices			
Sympathy	.27**	.29*	.22
	(.21)*	(.14)	(.09)
Personal distress	.14	.21	.06
	(.13)	(.14)	(.09)
Sadness	.16	.15	.13
	(.18)	(.14)	(.17)

a. Data for the dichotomous variables of helping/not helping are in parentheses.
*$p < .10$, two-tailed test
**$p < .05$, two-tailed test
***$p < .01$, two-tailed test.

related to helping after partialling the effects of SR, AR, and EC ($rs = .08$ or less for combined sample and for men; $rs = .18$ or less for women). This was not surprising given that situational sympathy was positively related to EC (see Table 1). In contrast, there were still significant correlations between helping and both EC and ascription of responsibility after controlling

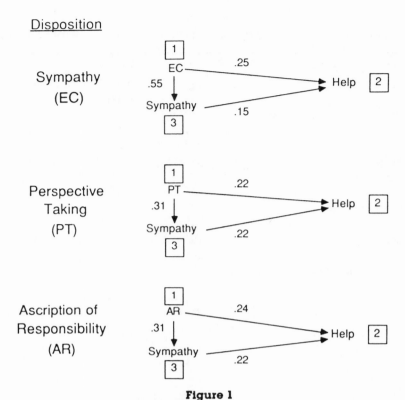

Figure 1
Models of the Relations of Dispositional Indices and Situational Sympathy
to Intent to Help

Note. $N = 76$. Path coefficients are for an unstandardized solution.

for sex and situational sympathy, partial $r(72) = .24, p < .041$ and partial $r(67) = .27, p < .027$, respectively.

To examine further the relations of EC, PT, and ascription of responsibility to helping, we compared several plausible path models using the procedures outlined by Pedhazur (1982). The full (just-identified) models are presented in Figure 1; they contain both direct and mediated paths from the dispositional index to helping. This full model was compared with two alternatives: (a) the model when the path from the dispositional index to helping (from 1 to 2) was set to 0 (a model with no direct effect of the dispositional measure), and (b) the model when the path from the dispositional index to situational sympathy (1 to 3) was set to 0 (a model with direct effects for both the dispositional and situational indices and no mediate effect). For EC, the full model accounted for the data better than either the solely mediated or solely direct effects models, $W(1) = 4.06$ and 21.36, $ps < .05$ and $.001$ (chi-square distribution; a significant difference indicates that there is a significant difference between the variance accounted for by the just-identified and alternative model). The same pattern held for both PT, $W = 3.83$ and 4.86, $p < .055$ and $.05$, and ascription of responsibility, $W = 4.61$ and 5.23, $ps < .05$. Thus, the effects of EC, PT, and ascription of responsibility on helping intentions were both direct and partially mediated through sympathetic responding in the experimental context.[5] Total variance in helping accounted for in the three models was 13%, 13%, and 14%, respectively, for EC, PT, and ascription of responsibility.

Sadness, Distress, or Sympathy: Which Mediates Helping?

The mediational role of sadness in the relation of dispositional sympathy to helping was also examined with simple regression procedures (Loehlin, 1987). Although situational sympathy was correlated with both sadness and helping (Table 1), sadness was not significantly related to helping, $r = .17$, *ns*. Thus, sadness could not be a mediator of the effect of situational sympathy on helping. Moreover, sympathy was still a predictor of helping when sadness was entered prior to sympathy in a regression analysis, multiple $R = .28$, R^2 change $= .048$, $F(1, 74)$ for change in $R^2 = 3.76$, $p < .056$ (whereas the reverse was not true, R^2 change $= .002$), a finding which reinforces the conclusion that sadness did not mediate the effect of sympathy on helping. According to similar analyses, report of situational personal distress also did not mediate the relation between situational sympathy and helping.

DISCUSSION

Our findings are consistent with the view that altruistic, other-oriented personality dispositions enhance prosocial behavior in some contexts. Social evaluative concerns were significantly related to (or moderated) some indices of sympathy or empathy (PT), but did not account for most of the variance between these dispositional indices and helping. Moreover, the BPL procedures had a significant effect only for dispositional fantasy empathy, which was unrelated to helping. Nonetheless, the fact

---

5. The pattern of findings for the relation of the Mehrabian and Epstein Empathy Scale to helping was quite similar. One also could argue that the dispositional characteristics mediate the effect of situational sympathy on helping. However, it seems unlikely that a stable disposition measured 1 to 2 weeks prior to a given emotional response mediated or caused the effect of that emotional reaction.

that adults do seem to respond in gender-stereotypic ways to the fantasy empathy subscale is informative because there are a number of items of this sort on several frequently used scales of empathy for which there are large gender differences in scores (Eisenberg & Lennon, 1983).

It is interesting that self-reports on the other subscales of the Davis Scale were related to one or more of the three dispositional (i.e., questionnaire) indices reflecting social evaluative concerns, but were not affected by the BPL. This pattern of findings suggests that people who tend to be concerned about others' negative evaluations and adjust their behavior accordingly either really are more sympathetic or believe they are more sympathetic. Perhaps such individuals actually learn to attend to (and perhaps respond to) others' emotional cues because of their desire to be evaluated favorably and to avoid censure. This could result in more sympathetic responsiveness (and a more sympathetic self-image) among people who are sensitive to others' evaluations. Alternatively, subjects who were sensitive to others' evaluations may have been deceiving themselves—believing that they were more altruistic than they really were (see Paulhus, 1986). This kind of self-deception should not be detected by the BPL procedure but may be assessed by the social evaluative personality indices (because individuals evaluate themselves in socially desirable domains when filling out these indices). Of course, it is also possible that the BPL procedure was not maximally effective, although few subjects expressed suspicions about the procedure.

In contrast to the findings for dispositional indices, social evaluation concerns, as assessed by the questionnaire indices, did account for about half the variance between helping and situational sympathy. Moreover, as was found by Cialdini et al. (1987), the relation of helping to situational sympathy was moderated, to some degree, by social evaluative concerns. Thus, it seems that the relation between helping and situational sympathy is significantly affected by social evaluative concerns, although situational sympathy also shared variance with indices of an altruistic personality even when social evaluation concerns (and sex) were partialled (e.g., partial r between EC and sympathy $= .38, p <$ .002).

In our experimental setting, indices of dispositional sympathy, perspective taking, and altruistic norms tended to be positively related to helping. These findings differ from those of Batson et al. (1986) and suggest that altruistic and sympathetic traits (i.e., an altruistic personality) may motivate helping. Perhaps the reason for the difference in findings is due to differences between the studies in the sympathy-evoking circumstances. It is possible that people with altruistic personality characteristics are more likely than other persons to generate both altruistic, other-oriented motivations and guilt-related motives for helping. In situations in which the other's need is quite apparent and dramatic (as in Batson et al.'s situation involving electric shock), these people may be especially prone to the experience or anticipation of guilt (because they will violate their altruistic principles if they do not help). They also may be more likely than other people to experience sympathetic concern in less dramatic (and perhaps less guilt-inducing) situations. If Hoffman (1982) is correct that guilt and sympathy are positively related developmentally and within persons, it is reasonable to expect sympathetic persons to be relatively vulnerable to feelings of guilt. These individuals may internalize norms related to helping and others' needs to a greater degree than other persons, and reference to these norms may elicit sympathy in some situations and guilt in others. Alternatively, persons who score high on indices of an altruistic personality may experience sympathy in situations that evoke moderate levels of vicarious responding and experience personal distress when overaroused (see Hoffman, 1982), which could account for Batson et al.'s findings.

Unlike Batson et al. (1986), we found that dispositional indices of an altruistic personality accounted for much of the variance in the correlation between situational sympathy and helping. Situational sympathy appeared to serve as a mediator of part of the effects of EC, PT, and ascription of responsibility on helping intentions. Moreover, there appeared to be direct effects of EC, PT, and ascription of responsibility on helping (independent of the effects of situational sympathy). The difference in findings between our and Batson et al.'s studies was likely due to a difference in the degree to which the two situations evoked situational sympathy. If a situation is emotionally evocative, one would expect emotional responses in that situation to predict behavior more than dispositional indices of sympathy and altruism. However, in less emotionally evocative situations, characteristic ways of responding may be an important determinant of both the individual's emotional reaction and his or her behavior (Snyder & Ickes, 1985). Those with altruistic personality characteristics may be particularly likely to have previously internalized norms and values related to helping and the importance of others' needs; these values could be activated by situational cues even if the individual were not highly emotionally involved and might facilitate sympathetic responding. Our findings, in combination with those of Batson and others (see Snyder & Ickes, 1985), suggest that the relative role of enduring traits versus situationally induced reactions in behavioral intention varies depending on the "pull" for a given response in a particular situation and the "push" for responses reflecting relevant enduring values or norms accessible to the individual.

Despite the aforementioned relations between helping and the indices of traits and situational responding, the models including PT, EC, and ascription of responsibility (along with situational sympathy) do not account for most of the variance in helping. This is probably due to a variety of factors, including weaknesses in the measures and the potential role of other person variables (e.g., sociability; Stanhope, Bell, & Parker-Cohen, 1987) in prosocial behavior. Moreover, practical considerations such as hours of employment and access to a car no doubt influenced the decisions of many study participants.

Although there were relatively few gender differences in the relations of personality variables to helping, it is interesting to note that social responsibility was strongly related to helping for males but not females, whereas ascription of responsibility, fear of negative evaluation, and Mehrabian and Epstein empathy scores were significantly related to helping for females but not males. This pattern of results is not especially consistent with the notion that women often assist due to norms related to needs of others and social concerns whereas men often assist because of norms regarding chivalry (which would tend to result in a focus on one's own duty rather than the other's needs; see Eagly & Crowley, 1986). However, none of the correlations differed significantly across the two sexes (although the differences for social responsibility and fear of negative evaluation were significant at $p < .10$). Moreover, the pattern of findings may be due in part to the fact that men scored higher on ascription of responsibility than did women ($p < .001$) whereas women tended to score higher on social responsibility, empathy, and fear of negative evaluation ($ps < .062, .001,$ and $.02$; the variances did not differ much).

Cialdini et al. (1987) have suggested that sadness mediates the relation between sympathy and helping. We obtained no support for this assumption. It is possible, however, that differences in the emotion-eliciting stimuli used in our and their research (e.g., Cialdini et al. used a situation similar to Batson's shock paradigm in one study) account in part for this discrepancy in findings. However, the level of sadness reported by our subjects was not much lower than that found by Cialdini et al. (1987); thus, it is not clear why we failed to substantiate their claim.

In summary, our findings support the view that there is indeed an altruistic personality, and that the effects of an altruistic disposition on the intention to assist a needy other are partially mediated through individuals' sympathetic reactions to needy others in the given context. Interesting issues that merit further consideration include (*a*) the role of the situation (particularly its emotional evocativeness) in determining the degree to which dispositional factors affect helping (especially real helping behavior), and (*b*) the precise mechanisms by which a prosocial orientation is related to helping independent of situational sympathetic responding.

REFERENCES

Ajzen, I., & Fishbein, M. (1977). Attitude-behavior relations: A theoretical analysis and review of empirical research. *Psychological Bulletin*, **84**, 888–918.

Archer, R. L., Diaz-Loving, R., Gollwitzer, P. M., Davis, M. H., & Foushee, H. C. (1981). The role of dispositional empathy and social evaluation in the empathic mediation of helping. *Journal of Personality and Social Psychology*, **40**, 786–796.

Baron, R. M., & Kenny, D. A. (1986). The moderator-mediator variable distinction in social psychological research: Conceptual, strategic, and statistical considerations. *Journal of Personality and Social Psychology*, **51**, 1173–1182.

Batson, C. D. (1987). Prosocial motivation: Is it ever truly altruistic? In L. Berkowitz (Ed.), *Advances in experimental social psychology* (Vol. 20, pp. 65–122). New York: Academic Press.

Batson, C. D., Bolen, M. H., Cross, J. A., & Neuringer-Benefiel, H. E. (1986). Where is the altruism in the altruistic personality? *Journal of Personality and Social Psychology*, **50**, 212–220.

Batson, C. D., Duncan, B. D., Ackerman, P., Buckley, T., & Birch, K. (1981). Is empathic emotion a source of altruistic motivation? *Journal of Personality and Social Psychology*, **40**, 290–302.

Batson, C. D., O'Quin, K., Fultz, J., Vanderplas, M., & Isen, A. M. (1983). Influence of self-reported distress and empathy on egoistic versus altruistic motivation to help. *Journal of Personality and Social Psychology*, **45**, 706–718.

Berkowitz, L., & Lutterman, K. G. (1968). The traditional socially responsible personality. *Public Opinion Quarterly*, **32**, 169–185.

Block, J. H. (1983). Differential premises arising from differential socialization of the sexes: Some conjectures. *Child Development*, **54**, 1335–1354.

Cialdini, R. B., Schaller, M., Houlihan, D., Arps, K., Fultz, J., & Beaman, A. L. (1987). Empathy-based helping: Is it selflessly or selfishly motivated? *Journal of Personality and Social Psychology*, **52**, 729–758.

Crowne, D. P., & Marlowe, D. (1964). *The approval motive*. New York: Wiley.

Davis, M. H. (1983). Measuring individual differences in empathy: Evidence for a multi-dimensional approach. *Journal of Personality and Social Psychology*, **44**, 113–126.

Eagly, A. H., & Crowley, M. (1986). Gender and helping behavior: A meta-analytic review of the social psychological literature. *Psychological Bulletin*, **100**, 282–308.

Eisenberg, N. (1986). *Altruistic emotion, cognition and behavior*. Hillsdale, NJ: Lawrence Erlbaum.

Eisenberg, N., & Lennon, R. (1983). Sex differences in empathy and related capacities. *Psychological Bulletin*, **94**, 100–131.

Eisenberg, N., & Miller, P. (1987). The relation of empathy to prosocial and related behaviors. *Psychological Bulletin*, **101**, 91–119.

Eisenberg, N., & Strayer, J. (1987). Introduction. In N. Eisenberg & J. Strayer (Eds.), *Empathy and its development* (pp. 3–13). Cambridge: Cambridge University Press.

Fultz, J., Batson, C. D., Fortenbach, V. A., McCarthy, P. M., & Varney, L. L. (1986). Social evaluation and the empathy-altruism hypothesis. *Journal of Personality and Social Psychology*, **50**, 761–769.

Fultz, J., Schaller, M., & Cialdini, R. B. (1988). Empathy, sadness, and distress: Three related but distinct vicarious affective responses to another's suffering. *Personality and Social Psychology Bulletin*, **14**, 312–325.

Gergen, K. J., Gergen, M. M., & Meter, K. (1972). Individual orientations to prosocial behavior. *Journal of Social Issues*, **8**, 105–130.

Hoffman, M. L. (1982). Development of prosocial motivation: Empathy and guilt. In N. Eisenberg (Ed.), *The development of prosocial behavior* (pp. 218–231). New York: Academic Press.

Hoffman, M. L. (1987). The contribution of empathy to justice and moral judgment. In N. Eisenberg & J. Strayer (Eds.), *Empathy and its development* (pp. 47–80). Cambridge: Cambridge University Press.

Jones, E. E., & Sigall, H. (1971). The bogus pipeline: A new paradigm for measuring affect and attitude. *Psychological Bulletin*, **76**, 349–364.

Krebs, D., & Miller, D. T. (1985). Altruism and aggression. In G. Lindzey & E. Aronson (Eds.), *Handbook of social psychology* (3rd ed., pp. 1–72). New York: Random House.

Leary, M. R. (1983). A brief version of the fear of negative evaluation scale. *Personality and Social Psychology Bulletin*, **9**, 371–375.

Lennon, R., & Eisenberg, N. (1987). Gender and age differences in empathy and sympathy. In N. Eisenberg & J. Strayer (Eds.), *Empathy and its development* (pp. 195–217). Cambridge: Cambridge University Press.

Loehlin, J. (1987). *Latent variable models: An introduction to factor, path, and structural analyses*. Hillsdale, NJ: Lawrence Erlbaum.

Mehrabian, A., & Epstein, N. A. (1972). A measure of emotional empathy. *Journal of Personality*, **40**, 523–543.

Mussen, P., & Eisenberg-Berg, N. (1977). *Roots of caring, sharing, and helping: The development of prosocial behavior in children*. San Francisco: Freeman.

Paulhus, D. L. (1986). Self-deception and impression management in test responses. In A. Anglertner & J. S. Wiggins (Eds.), *Personality assessment via questionnaires* (pp. 143–165). Berlin: Springer-Verlag.

Pedhazur, E. J. (1982). *Multiple regression in behavioral research* (2nd ed.) New York: Holt, Rinehart, & Winston.

Pomazal, R. J., & Jaccard, J. J. (1976). An informational approach to altruistic behavior. *Journal of Personality and Social Psychology, 33*, 317–326.

Quigley-Fernandez, B., & Tedeschi, J. T. (1978). The bogus pipeline as lie detector: Two validity studies. *Journal of Personality and Social Psychology, 3*, 247–256.

Romer, D., Gruder, C. L., & Lizzadro, T. (1986). A person-situation approach to altruistic behavior. *Journal of Personality and Social Psychology, 51*, 1001–1012.

Rushton, J. P. (1980). *Altruism, socialization, and society.* Englewood Cliffs, NJ: Prentice Hall.

Schwartz, S. H. (1968). Words, deeds, and the perception of consequences and responsibility in social situations. *Journal of Personality and Social Psychology, 10*, 232–242.

Shields, S. A. (1987). Women, men, and the dilemma of emotion. In P. Shaver & C. Hendrick (Eds.), *Sex and gender* (pp. 229–250). Newbury Park, CA: Sage.

Snyder, M. (1986). *Public appearances and private realities: The psychology of self monitoring.* New York: W. H. Freeman.

Snyder, M., & Ickes, W. (1985). Personality and social behavior. In G. Lindzey & E. Aronson (Eds.), *Handbook of social psychology* (3rd ed., pp. 883–948). New York: Random House.

SPSS, Inc. (1983). *SPSSx User's guide.* New York: McGraw-Hill.

Stanhope, L., Bell, R. Q., & Parker-Cohen, N. Y. (1987). Temperament and helping in preschool children. *Developmental Psychology, 23*, 347–353.

Staub, E. (1986). A conception of the determinants and development of altruism and aggression: Motives, the self, and the environment. In C. Zahn-Waxler, E. M. Cummings, & R. Iannoti (Eds.), *Altruism and aggression: Biological and social origins* (pp. 135–164). Cambridge: Cambridge University Press.

Toi, M., & Batson, C. D. (1982). More evidence that empathy is a source of altruistic motivation. *Journal of Personality and Social Psychology, 43*, 281–292.

Wispé, L. (1986). The distinction between sympathy and empathy: To call forth a concept, a word is needed. *Journal of Personality and Social Psychology, 50*, 314–321.

Manuscript received November 16, 1987; revised April 21, 1988.

Developmental Psychology
1976, Vol. 12, No. 2, 175–176

Empathic Distress in the Newborn

ABRAHAM SAGI AND MARTIN L. HOFFMAN

University of Michigan

Simner (1971) showed that 2-day-old infants cry to the sound of another newborn's cry and that the cry is a response to the vocal properties of the other's cry. The infant cries less to inanimate sounds of the same intensity, including a computer simulation of a newborn cry. Simner suggests this reflexive crying may illustrate a primitive capacity for initiating and responding to peer-generated social stimuli. Hoffman (1975) suggests more specifically that it may signify an innate precursor of empathic distress, and cites several converging lines of supportive evidence.

To test the hypothesis of an inborn mechanism may require observing infants immediately after birth. In the present study, it was possible to come closer than Simner to this ideal: The average age of the infants tested was 34 hours (Simner's average was 70 hours). Additionally, whereas Simner's subjects were exposed to one stimulus, the present study also included a small subsample in which repeated measures were used.

The entire population of clinically normal full-term infants born in the University of Michigan Hospital from July 1974 to March 1975, whose mothers granted permission and had a normal medical history, pregnancy, and delivery, comprised the initial pool of subjects.

Since the same stimulus can elicit a different response depending on the infant's state, all subjects had to meet the criteria of Prechtl and Beintema's (1964) "State 3" (awake, alert, quiet, not engaged in gross bodily activity), the period of greatest responsiveness to external stimuli. Seventeen infants were eliminated for crying, sucking, or having both eyes closed immediately prior to testing, or vomiting or sneezing during testing. The final sample consisted of 28 males and 30 females randomly assigned to the three experimental conditions.

A tape recorder was placed below and to the side of the crib, the speaker about 60 cm from the infant's ears. One auditory stimulus—the spontaneous cry of another infant or a synthetic cry, each 81 ± 3 db. (re .0002 dynes) at crib

surface—was presented for 6 minutes. These stimuli were those of M. L. Simner, who kindly supplied his tapes. The synthetic cry was computer generated with the physical properties (e.g., burst length and sudden onset) of the spontaneous cry of a newborn, but easily recognized by adults as a nonhuman sound. Lighting was constant. Room temperature ranged from 24.4°C to 27.8°C. Babies were tested between 8 and 9 a.m., about 1 to 1½ hours before feeding time, when they are most likely to meet the State 3 criteria. The baby was placed in a supine position (for greatest sensitivity to external stimulation), lightly covered with a blanket from the waist down.

Twenty babies were exposed to the natural cry of another infant; 18 to the synthetic cry; and 20 to silence. In addition, 8 infants, randomly selected from the larger sample, were exposed to both stimuli: 4 to the natural cry on the first day and the synthetic cry on the second, and 4 in reverse order. Upon exposure to the stimulus, the baby's behavior was recorded, using Simner's (1971) definition of a cry: "an audible, intermittent vocalization accompanied by facial grimaces and increased motor activity lasting a minimum of 1–2 seconds" (p. 138). One tester operated the equipment, another observed. Observer reliability was 94% for the infant's state prior to testing and 100% for presence or absence of a cry in response to test stimuli.

The infants cried less often in response to the stimuli than in Simner's (1971) study, possibly due to their younger age. The pattern of crying, however, clearly replicates Simner's major findings. Although only a day old, infants exposed to a newborn cry cried significantly more often than those exposed to silence (maximum likelihood ratio = 6.66, $p < .01$) and those exposed to a synthetic newborn cry of the same intensity (maximum likelihood ratio = 9.61, $p < .005$). In the subsample in which repeated measures were used, exposure to the newborn cry also produced more crying than exposure to the synthetic cry (Cochran's $Q = 7.14$, $p < .01$).

The fact that 1-day-old infants cry selectively in response to the vocal properties of another infant's cry provides the most direct evidence to date for an inborn empathic distress reaction. The possible influence of simple learning mechanisms must also be considered, however, because test-

Thanks are due Adel Ayoub, Robert Borer, Lee Davis, Greg Hand, and Charles Tait for their help.

Requests for reprints should be sent to Martin L. Hoffman, Department of Psychology, University of Michigan, 529 Thompson, Ann Arbor, Michigan 48104.

159

ing was not done immediately after birth. Vocal imitation can probably be ruled out, since the newborn's response when exposed to another infant's cry appears to be a full-blown, spontaneous cry indicative of a distressed state. Simner too (personal communication) recalls the cry as lusty, fretful, and resembling a spontaneous cry. Thus, the infants seemed not merely to be making a vocal response to a vocal stimulus.

The tenability of conditioning as an explanation depends on whether it is possible in 1-day-old infants. It apparently is in the early weeks of life (Kessen, Haith, & Salapatek, 1970), but Sameroff (1971) concludes from his review of the research that the evidence for conditioning in 1-day-olds is weak. Crying behavior was not examined in any of these studies, however, and it is possible that a response so natural and frequent in newborns is more readily conditioned than other responses. Should crying be conditionable in 1-day-olds, credence is lent to Simner's (1971) hypothesis that the infant's cry in response to another's cry may be a conditioned vocal response to cues resembling the auditory cues associated with the infant's own past cries. Simner's formulation is limited, however, since, like the "vocal imitation" hypothesis, it ignores the evidence that a distressed state is part of the response. A more complete statement of the conditioning hypothesis would be that the infant's cry to another's cry may be a conditioned vocal-and-distress response to cues resembling the auditory cues associated with the infant's own past cries. This fits the classical conditioning paradigm, long the most parsimonious explanation of empathic distress in older children and adults (e.g., Humphrey, 1922). Cues of distress from another person evoke associations with the observer's own past distress, resulting in a distressed state in the observer.

The findings in this and Simner's study may thus signify a rudimentary empathic distress reaction at birth. Whether it is innate or learned—hypotheses which both remain plausible—is a topic for further research. Definitive experimentation, preferably in the delivery room, might reveal the conditioning or nonconditioned mechanism underlying the response.

Sex differences. Cultural stereotype views females as more empathic than males. Recent research supports this view in 4-year-olds (Levine & Hoffman, 1975). Simner (1971) reported that females cried more in response to another infant's cry in four different experiments, significantly in one. In the present study, females cried more in response to an infant's cry ($p < .06$); there were no sex differences in the other conditions. Despite the lack of consistent significance, the evidence is that in all five independent tests made to date, females cried more in the presence of cries from another infant. The likelihood that this pattern of results would occur by chance is less than .03. Female newborns may therefore be somewhat more specifically responsive than males to the cry of another infant. The stimulus in all five tests was a female newborn cry, however. The test must be replicated using a male newborn cry.

REFERENCES

Hoffman, M. L. Developmental synthesis of affect and cognition and its implications for altruistic motivation. *Developmental Psychology*, 1975, *11*, 607–622.

Humphrey, G. The conditioned reflex and the elementary social reaction. *Journal of Abnormal and Social Psychology*, 1922, *17*, 113–119.

Kessen, W., Haith, M. M., & Salapatek, P. H. Infancy. In P. Mussen (Ed.), *Carmichael's manual of child psychology*. New York: Wiley, 1970.

Levine, L. E., & Hoffman, M. L. Empathy and cooperation in 4-year-olds. *Developmental Psychology*, 1975, *11*, 533–534.

Prechtl, H., & Beintema, D. The neurological examination of the full term newborn infant. *Clinics in Developmental Medicine*, 1964, *12*, 1–72.

Sameroff, A. J. Can conditioned responses be established in the newborn infant: 1971? *Developmental Psychology*, 1971, *5*, 1–12.

Simner, M. L. Newborn's response to the cry of another infant. *Developmental Psychology*, 1971, *5*, 136–150.

(Received October 7, 1975)

4   The contribution of empathy to justice and moral judgment

Martin L. Hoffman

Few psychologists or philosophers can agree as to whether any moral principles are universal. Three broadly held principles, however, are often viewed as universal:

1. the principle of justice or fairness, essentially distributive justice and written about extensively by Immanuel Kant and his followers, which states that society's resources (rewards, punishments) should be allocated according to a standard equally applicable to all;
2. the principle of impartial benevolence, associated mainly with writers in the Utilitarian tradition, especially David Hume and Adam Smith, which states a moral act is one that takes into account all people likely to be affected by it – at the face-to-face level this has become a principle of caring about the well-being of others, including their need for self-respect, dignity, and avoidance of pain; and
3. the principle of maintaining the social order, derived largely from Hobbes's view that, without society, the individual would be constantly embattled, hence nothing.

The advocates of one principle do not deny the importance of the other two, but view them as subordinate.[1]

I think of these principles not as mutually exclusive precepts, but as "ideal types," any or all of which may be relevant in a given situation. When more than one are applicable, they are usually compatible – caring and justice, for example, reinforce each other in the case of honest, hard-working farmers who lose their farms because of economic forces beyond their control. However, these principles may be incompatible in some situations, as in voting for tenure when a candidate's performance is not quite up to the expected standard. If one likes the candidate and knows that one of his/her children is chronically ill, caring may move one to vote in his/her favor. At the same time, justice, may argue for a negative vote, or one might vote negatively to affirm one's commitment to the tenure system. One might even see the relevance of all three principles and be confused about how to vote, the issue finally turning on the intensity of one's feeling for the candidate and one's commitment to caring as a principle, versus one's commitment to distributive justice and to the tenure system.

Many psychologists have been concerned with justice/fairness and caring/consideration. Notions of justice are at the heart of Kohlberg's moral theory, which has been criticized for being overly cognitive and ignoring affect. Caring has been the focus of people like me who are interested in affect, especially empathy. The notion of maintaining the social order has been virtually ignored by psychologists, and I will say nothing more about it.

I have long been working on a scheme for the development of empathy, which I define as an affective response more appropriate to someone else's situation than to one's own.[2] I have described the scheme in detail (Hoffman, 1984); summarized evidence for empathy's status as a moral motive, that is, in contributing to prosocial behavior (Hoffman, 1978); theorized about empathy's role in moral internalization (Hoffman, 1983); traced empathy's roots in Western philosophy (Hoffman, 1982c); and speculated on its biological evolutionary beginnings (Hoffman, 1981). I have also investigated sex differences and the contribution of female sex–role socialization to empathy and to an empathy-based, humanistic moral orientation (Hoffman, 1970, 1975b, 1977). I believe that empathy as elaborated in my developmental scheme may provide the basis for a comprehensive moral theory, although to formulate such a theory one would have to expand the scheme in several directions. This chapter is a beginning attempt at such an expansion.

First, I briefly describe the scheme to pave the way for my argument, ending with five empathy-based moral affects: empathic distress, sympathetic distress, guilt, empathic anger, and empathic injustice. I then discuss how these affects may contribute to caring and justice principles, the role they may play in moral judgment and decision making, and the problem of empathic bias and how to reduce it. Finally, I speculate about the stabilizing effect that moral principles, as "hot cognitions," may have on empathy. Although I have long suggested a link between empathy, moral principles, and judgment (Hoffman, 1970, 1980, 1982b, 1984b), this is my first attempt to argue systematically for such a link.

Development of empathic moral affect

The scheme for empathic distress, an empathic affective response to another person's distress, starts with a simple innocent-bystander model – in which one encounters someone in pain, danger, or deprivation – and generates five empathic affects that are mediated by social cognitive development and various causal attributions or inferences.

The scheme includes five hypothesized modes of empathic affect arousal (I.A–E in Table 4.1), which have been described in detail and documented elsewhere (Hoffman, 1984a). I make four points about them here. First, they do not form a strict sequence of stages in the sense of subsequent modes encompassing and replacing preceding modes. The first mode typically drops out after infancy, owing to controls against crying; however, adults may feel sad when they hear a cry and some adults may even feel like crying themselves, although they usually control it. The fifth mode, being deliberate, may be relatively infrequent – for example, it may be used by parents and therapists who believe they can be more effective if they experience some of their child's or patient's feelings. The intermediate three modes enter at various points in development and may continue to operate throughout life.

Second, the existence of five arousal modes suggests that empathy may be overdetermined and hence may be a reliable affective response to another's distress. Thus, if only expressive cues (facial, vocal, postural) from someone in distress are provided, mimicry is available to arouse empathic distress in observers. If only situational cues are provided, conditioning and association are available. Ordinarily, the victim is present and all modes may be brought into play, which mode is dominant depending on which cues are salient. Even if the victim is not present, information about his or her distress communicated by someone else can produce empathy in an observer (through arousal modes I.D–E in Table 4.1).

Third, empathy may be self-reinforcing. Every time we empathize with someone in distress, the resulting cooccurrence of our own distress and distress cues from the other may increase the strength of the connection between cues of another's distress and our own empathic response and thus increase the likelihood that future distress in others will be accompanied by empathic distress in ourselves.

Fourth, most arousal modes require rather shallow levels of cognitive processing (e.g., sensory registration, simple pattern matching, conditioning) and are largely involuntary. Thus it should not be surprising that empathy appears to be a universal, largely involuntary response – if one attends to the relevant cues one responds empathically – that may have had survival value in human evolution (Hoffman, 1981).

Although empathy may usually be aroused by these simple involuntary mechanisms, its subjective experience is rather complex. Mature empathizers know the affect aroused in them is due to stimulus events impinging on someone else, and they have an idea of what that person is feeling. Young children who lack the self–other distinction may be empathically aroused without this knowledge. This suggests that the development of empathic distress corresponds to the de-

Table 4.1. *Scheme for the development and transformation of empathic distress*

I.   Modes of empathic affect arousal; operate singly or in combinations

    (Automatic – nonvoluntary)
    A.   Primary circular reaction; neonate cries to sound of another's cry
    B.   Mimicry; automatic imitation plus afferent feedback
    C.   Conditioning and direct association

    (Higher-level cognitive)
    D.   Language-mediated association
    E.   Putting self in other's place; other-focused and self-focused

II.   Development of a cognitive sense of others

    A.   Self–other fusion
    B.   Object permanence; other is physical entity distinct from self
    C.   Perspective taking; other has independent internal states
    D.   Personal identity; other has experiences beyond the immediate situation, own history, and identity

III. Developmental levels of empathy (coalescence of I and II)

    A.   Global empathy
    B.   "Egocentric" empathy
    C.   Empathy for another's feelings
    D.   Empathy for another's experiences beyond the immediate situation, general condition, future prospects
        1.   Empathy for an entire group

IV.   Partial transformation of empathic into sympathetic distress

    Begins to occur in transition from III.A to III.B; subsequently, one's affective response to another's distress has a pure empathic component and a sympathetic component

V.   Causal attribution and shaping of empathy into related moral affects

    A.   If victim is cause of distress, he/she may no longer be seen as a victim, so basis for empathy is removed.
    B.   *Sympathetic distress:* Victim has no control over cause of victim's distress
    C.   *Guilt:* Observer is cause of victim's distress
        Guilt over inaction: Observer, though not the cause, does nothing and therefore views self as responsible for continuation of victim's distress
        Guilt by association: Observer's group is cause of victim's distress
        (observer's or group's relative advantage may increase guilt further)
    D.   *Empathic anger:* Someone else is cause of victim's distress
        1.   Empathic anger may be reduced and/or turned toward victim, depending on context (e.g., if culprit was previously harmed by victim)
        2.   If culprit represents society, empathic anger may lead to social criticism and moral/political ideology
    E.   *Empathic injustice:* Contrast between victim's plight and character

velopment of a cognitive sense of others, the four broad stages of which are indicated in II.A–D in Table 4.1 (see Hoffman, 1975a, for evidence for these stages):

1. fusion, or at least a lack of clear separation between the self and the other;
2. awareness that others are physical entities distinct from the self;
3. awareness that others have feelings and other internal states independent of one's own; and
4. awareness that others have experiences beyond the immediate situation and their own history and identity as individuals.

Empathic affect is presumably experienced differently as the child progresses through these stages.

The resulting coalescence of empathic affect and social–cognitive development yields four levels of empathic distress (III.A–D in Table 4.1), which I now describe briefly (see Hoffman, 1984a, for details).

1. *Global empathy.* Infants may experience empathic distress through the simplest arousal modes (I.A–C in Table 4.1) long before they acquire a sense of others as physical entities distinct from the self. For most of the first year, then, witnessing someone in distress may result in a global empathic distress response. Distress cues from the dimly perceived other are confounded with unpleasant feelings empathically aroused in the self. Consequently, infants may at times act as though what happened to the other happened to themselves. An 11-month-old girl, on seeing a child fall and cry, looked as though she was about to cry herself, then put her thumb in her mouth and buried her head in her mother's lap, as she does when she herself is hurt. (For other examples, see Hoffman, 1975a; Kaplan, 1977; and Zahn-Waxler, Radke-Yarrow, and King, 1979.)

2. *"Egocentric" empathy.* With object permanence and the gradual emergence of a sense of the other as physically distinct from the self, the affective portion of the child's global empathic distress may be transferred to the separate image-of-self and image-of-other that emerge. The child may now be aware that another person and not the self is in distress, but the other's internal states remain unknown and may be assumed to be the same as one's own. An 18-month-old boy fetched his own mother to comfort a crying friend although the friend's mother was also present – a behavior that, although confused, is not entirely egocentric because it indicates that the child is responding with appropriate empathic affect.

3. *Empathy for another's feelings.* With the onset of role taking, at about 2–3 years, one becomes aware that other people's feelings may differ from one's own and are based on their own needs and interpretations of events; consequently one becomes more responsive to cues about what the other is actually feeling.

Furthermore, as language is acquired, children become capable of empathizing with a wide range of increasingly complex emotions. Empathizing with a victim's distress, children may also eventually become capable of empathizing with the victim's anxiety about the loss of self-esteem, hence with the desire *not* to be helped. Finally, children can be empathically aroused by information about someone's distress even in that person's absence. This leads to the fourth, most advanced level.

4. *Empathy for another's life condition.* By late childhood, owing to the emerging conception of oneself and others as continuing people with separate histories and identities, one becomes aware that others feel pleasure and pain, not only in the immediate situation but also in their larger life experience. Consequently, although one still responds empathically to another's immediate distress, one's empathic response may be intensified when one realizes that the other's distress is not transitory but chronic. Thus, one's empathically aroused affect is combined with a mental representation of another's general level of distress or deprivation. As one acquires the ability to form social concepts, one's empathic distress may also be combined with a mental representation of the plight of an entire group or class of people (e.g., the poor, oppressed, outcast, or retarded). (This empathic level can provide a motive base, especially in adolescence, for the development of certain moral and political ideologies that are centered around alleviation of the plight of unfortunate groups; see Hoffman, 1980, in press.)

When one has advanced through these four levels and encounters someone in pain, danger, or distress, one is exposed to a network of information about the other's condition. The network may include verbal and nonverbal expressive cues from the victim, situational cues, and one's knowledge about the victim's life beyond the immediate situation. These sources of information are processed differently: Empathy aroused by nonverbal and situational cues can be mediated by largely involuntary, cognitively shallow processing modes (mimicry; conditioning). Empathy aroused by verbal messages from the victim or by one's knowledge about the victim requires more complex processing, such as language-mediated association or putting oneself in the other's place.

The various cues, arousal modes, and processing levels usually contribute to the same affect, but contradictions may occur – for example, between different expressive cues, such as facial expression and tone of voice, or between expressive and situational cues. If one's knowledge of the other's life condition conflicts with the other's immediate expressive cues, the expressive cues may lose much of their force for an observer who knows they reflect only a transitory state. Imagine someone who does not know that he or she has a terminal illness laughing and having a good time. A young child might respond with empathic joy, whereas a mature observer might experience empathic sadness or a mingling of sadness and joy. Similarly, a mature observer's empathic distress (but not a child's) might decrease if the other person is known to have a generally happy life and the immediate distress is a short-lived exception. Clearly, the most advanced empathic level involves some distancing – responding partly to one's mental image of the other rather than only to the others' immediate stimulus value. (See Hoffman, 1986, for a more general discussion of the interaction of sensory, perceptual, and higher-order cognitive processes in generating affect.) This fits my definition of empathy, not as an exact match of another's feelings, but as an affective response that is more appropriate to the other's situation than to one's own.

Partial transformation of empathic into sympathetic distress

The transition from global to "egocentric" empathy (IV in Table 4.1) may involve an important qualitative shift in feeling: Once children are aware that others are distinct from themselves, their own empathic distress, which is a parallel response – a more or less exact replication of the victim's presumed feeling of distress – may be transformed, at least in part, into reciprocal concern for the victim. That is, they may continue to respond in a purely empathic manner – feeling uncomfortable and highly distressed themselves – but they may also experience a feeling of compassion, or "sympathetic distress," for the victim, along with a conscious desire to help, because they feel sorry for the victim, not just to relieve their own empathic distress.

Evidence for this shift comes from observational research (Murphy, 1937; Zahn-Waxler et al., 1979) and from anecdotes such as those cited earlier, which show that: (1) children progress developmentally, first responding to someone's distress by seeking comfort for the self and later trying to help the victim rather than the self; and (2) a transitional stage, in which children feel sad and comfort both the victim and the self, seems to occur at about the same time that they first become aware that others are distinct from themselves.

What developmental processes account for this shift? I suggested earlier that the unpleasant, vicarious affect that is experienced as a part of the child's initial global, undifferentiated self is transferred to the separate image-of-self and image-of-other that emerge during the self–other differentiation process. It seems likely that the wish, which is not necessarily conscious, to terminate the unpleasant affect is also similarly transferred to the emerging image-of-other and image-of-self. (See Hoffman, 1984a, for a more detailed discussion.) Consequently, the child's empathic response now includes two components: a wish to terminate the other's distress – the sympathetic distress component – and a more purely empathic wish to terminate distress in the self. The last three empathy development levels (III.B–D) may therefore describe the development of an affective response that has both an empathic distress and a sympathetic distress component.

A question may arise as to whether the pure empathic component is egoistic rather than prosocial. I have argued that it is both and may therefore be an important bridge between these two personality dimensions (Hoffman, 1981). In any case, it functions prosocially, because the other's distress must be alleviated if one's own distress is to end; this component must therefore be distinguished from the usual, primarily self-serving egoistic motives. The sympathetic distress component is obviously prosocial.

Causal attribution, empathy, and related moral affects

People are always making causal attributions, and there is evidence that they do this spontaneously (Weiner, 1985). It therefore seems reasonable to suppose that, when one encounters someone in distress, one will often make attributions about the cause, and the particular attribution made may determine how empathic affect is experienced. Consider now some causal attributions and the resulting affects (V.A–D in Table 4.1).

Sympathetic distress. One may respond to another's distress without making a causal attribution when the other's plight is salient, there are no causal situational cues powerful enough to draw one's attention from the other's plight, and one has no prior information about the cause. These conditions often exist when young children witness someone in distress, and were therefore assumed in my discussion of early developmental levels of empathy and its transformation into sympathetic distress. One may also feel sympathetic distress when there are cues or one has information indicating that victims have no control over their plight, as in serious illness or accidental injury. Sympathetic distress in mature observers may also be part of a complex ambivalent response, as when one condemns a man in the electric chair for his crimes while sympathizing with him because of information indicating that early experiences over which he had no control played an important role in his life.

Empathic anger. If the cues indicate that someone else caused the victim's plight, one's attention may to some extent be diverted from the victims to the culprit. One may feel anger at the culprit, partly because one sympathizes with the victim and partly because one empathizes with the victim and feels oneself vicariously attacked.[3] One's feelings may also alternate between empathic and sympathetic distress and empathic anger; or empathic anger may crowd out one's empathic and sympathetic distress entirely. Note that John Stuart Mill (1861/1979) suggested that empathic anger, which he described as "the natural feeling of retaliation . . . rendered by intellect and sympathy applicable to . . . those hurts which wound us through wounding others [serves as the] guardian of justice.'' A simple example of empathic anger is that of the 17-month-old boy in the doctor's office who, on seeing another child receive an injection, responds by hitting the doctor in anger.[4]

Empathic anger may also occur in complex contexts in which it is shifted from one target to another, along with the accompanying empathic and sympathetic distress. For example, if one discovers the victim did harm to the culprit on an earlier occasion, one's empathy for the victim may decrease, and one may begin to feel empathic and sympathetic distress for the culprit because of the hurt that led to the culprit's aggression in the first place; one may even empathize with the culprit's anger. Alternatively, one might discover that the victim has a history of being mistreated in his or her relationship with the culprit. In this case, one may assume the victim had a choice (why else would he or she continue the relationship?) and is therefore responsible for his or her own plight and thus is not a victim. One's empathic and sympathetic distress for the victim and empathic anger at the culprit may then decrease sharply. The empathic anger of young children is apt to miss these nuances, and if children's perceptions are confined to the immediate situation, they may respond in all these situations with simple empathic anger directed at the visible culprit.

A particularly relevant case here is one in which the observer blames the victim's plight – say, extreme poverty – on someone who is absent, especially when that someone represents the larger society or a powerful group within it. For example, one may see the victim's basic material needs as not being met because of society's neglect or the lack of an adequate "safety net." One may then feel empathic and sympathetic distress for the victim and empathic anger toward the powerful group or society as a whole.

Guilt feeling. The observer thus far in our analysis is an innocent bystander. If one is not innocent but the cause of the other's distress, the conditions may be ripe for feeling guilty,[5] that is, for a combination of empathic and sympathetic distress and a self-blame attribution. I have suggested that this combination may originate in discipline encounters in which parents point up the harmful consequences of the child's actions for others (Hoffman, 1983). Blaming oneself for another's distress may often result in empathic anger that is directed toward the self and thus may intensify the guilt feeling. Even if one is an innocent bystander but for some reason does not help, one may feel guilty because one blames oneself, not for *causing* the other's plight, but for contributing to its continuation by not intervening to help – the guilt is over inaction.

When one reaches the most advanced level of empathy development, one can not only categorize victims into groups but one can also categorize oneself as a member of a group. One may than have a feeling of guilt by association if one's group is seen as causing the victim's distress or benefiting from the same social system that disadvantages the victim. And, finally, I have suggested elsewhere (Hoffman, 1980) that one may feel guilty if one simply sees oneself as being in a relatively advantaged position vis-à-vis the victim. I call this "existential guilt" because one has done nothing wrong but feels culpable owing to life circumstances beyond one's control.

Empathic injustice. Other information beside that pertaining to the cause of the victim's distress may shape one's empathic response. I just mentioned that the contrast between the victim's plight and one's own good fortune may produce guilt feelings. Other contrasts are possible, such as that between the victim's plight and other people's good fortune. If one observes highly disadvantaged people in a context in which the extravagant life-style of others is salient, one may feel empathic injustice. Perhaps more important for our present purposes is the contrast between the victim's plight and his or her own general conduct or character. Thus if the victim is viewed as bad, immoral, or lazy one may conclude that his or her fate was deserved, and one's empathic and sympathetic distress might decrease. If the victim is viewed as basically good, however, or at least not bad, immoral, or lazy, one might view his or her fate as undeserved or unfair. One's empathic distress (or sympathetic distress, guilt, or empathic anger – whichever is appropriate) might then be expected to increase. Furthermore, the empathic affect may be transformed in part into a feeling that has elements in common with guilt and empathic anger but appears subtly different enough to be given a new name: empathic injustice.

An example of empathic injustice is found in the case of the 14-year-old Southern male "redneck" described by Coles (1986). After several weeks of joining his friends in harassing black children trying to integrate his school, this boy, a popular athlete,

> . . . began to see a kid, not a nigger – a guy who knew how to smile when it was rough going, and who walked straight and tall, and was polite. I told my parents, "It's a real shame that someone like him has to pay for the trouble caused by all those federal judges."
> Then it happened. I saw a few people cuss at him. "The dirty nigger," they kept on calling him and soon they were pushing him in a corner, and it looked like trouble, bad trouble. I went over and broke it up. . . . They all looked at me as if I was crazy. . . . Before [everyone] left I spoke to the nigger . . . I didn't mean to. . . . It just came out of my mouth. I was surprised to hear the words myself: "I'm sorry." (pp. 27–28)

After this incident, he began talking to the black youth, championing him personally, while still decrying integration. Finally, he became the black youth's friend and began advocating "an end to the whole lousy business of segregation." When pressed by Coles to explain his shift, he attributed it to being in school that year and seeing "that kid behave himself, no matter what we called him, and seeing him insulted so bad, so real bad. Something in me just drew the line, and something in me began to change, I think" (pp. 28).

The boy clearly seemed to experience sympathetic distress, empathic anger, and guilt. But what really seemed to move him was the contrast between the black youth's admirable conduct and the way he was being treated – it was as if the boy felt that this was a fine person who deserved better. Empathic injustice may be important because it seems closer than other empathic affects to bridging the gap between simple empathic distress and moral principle.

Complex combinations. Here is an example of the complex combination of empathic affects possible in moral encounters: A shabbily dressed man is observed robbing an obviously affluent person on the street. A young child might feel empathic and sympathetic distress for the victim and anger at the immediate, visible culprit. Mature observers might have these same feelings, but a variety of other empathic affects as well. They might feel guilty over not helping the victim. If they are ideologically liberal, they might empathize and sympathize not only with the victim but also with the culprit because of his poverty. The observers might view the culprit as a victim of society and feel empathic anger toward society. Furthermore, if the observers are affluent as well as liberal, they might feel guilty over being relatively advantaged persons who benefit from the same society. Ideologically conservative observers might not sympathize with the culprit but might respond with unalloyed empathic anger instead. They might also feel empathic anger toward society, but in this case because they view the victim, not the culprit, as a victim of society (because of inadequate law enforcement and citizen protection).

To summarize, the empathic reaction to someone's distress produces two basic affects: empathic distress and sympathetic distress. In addition – depending on various causal and other attributions – empathic anger, several types of guilt, and a feeling of empathic injustice may be generated. There is considerable research evidence that empathic and sympathetic distress (the research does not separate them) and guilt feelings function as motives for moral action (Hoffman, 1978, 1982b). Empathic anger has not yet been researched, but it seems reasonable to suppose that such anger includes a disposition to intervene and protect the victim in some way (although egoistic motives like fear may result in inaction). Also, since anger has long been known to "mobilize one's energy and make one capable of defending oneself with great vigor and strength" (Izard,

1977, p. 333), it seems reasonable to expect empathic anger to be an energizer of moral action, as suggested in this quotation from a letter to the *New York Times:*

> The pictures of starving children in Ethiopia are heartwrenching but feeling sad isn't enough . . . we send a check, the pictures disappear from TV screens, and soon we forget that millions are dying. . . . Instead we should feel outraged that in a world of plenty hunger still exists. Outrage produces action . . . etc. (February, 1985)

Research is needed to see if the letter writer is correct, not only in stating that empathic anger leads to action but that empathic anger is more likely to lead to action than is sympathetic distress.

Thus far, I have presented a scheme for empathy and empathy-related moral affects that may be aroused when the instigating stimulus is someone in pain or an otherwise distressing situation. If this scheme is to provide the basis for a comprehensive moral theory, these empathic affects, though generated by a bystander model, must be arousable in other types of moral encounters as well. Furthermore, these empathic affects must be congruent with the major moral principles. That is, the feelings, thoughts, and action tendencies associated with the affects must fit in with a principle's meaning and intent. Under these conditions, it would be reasonable to suppose that in the course of a person's development empathic affects will become meaningfully associated with moral principles, so that when empathic affect is aroused in a moral encounter this will activate the moral principles. The principles, along with the empathic affect, might then help guide the individual's moral judgment, decision making, and action. In some instances, the sequence might be reversed – the principle might be activated first and then its associated empathic affect elicited. The remainder of this chapter is concerned with these issues.

Empathic arousal in moral encounters

Empathic affects may be aroused not only in bystander situations but also in most other types of moral encounters. The reasons are as follows:

1. Human beings have the capacity for representation, and represented events can evoke affect, as shown in the voluminous mood-induction research in which all manner of affects are generated by imagining oneself in a relevant situation that one experienced in the past or simply made up (e.g., Harris & Siebel, 1975).
2. Human beings are capable of transposing stimuli and of imagining that stimuli impinging on someone else are impinging on oneself, and transposed stimuli can evoke empathic affect (Stotland, 1969).

3. The semantic meanings of events can become conditioned stimuli for autonomic arousal and therefore, presumably, for affect (Razran, 1971; Zanna, Kiesler & Pilkonis, 1970).

Thus, empathic affects should be arousable through the mediation of language and role taking (I.D–E in Table 4.1). The victim need not be present; one need only be informed about the victim.

Consequently, the bystander model can be intended to include instances in which one hears about victims second- or thirdhand – from parents, teachers, newspapers, or television. The model's essential features may also obtain when one is talking, arguing, or merely thinking about contemporary moral issues such as racial segregation, abortion, whether doctors should tell people how seriously ill they are, whether doctors should terminate life-support systems for brain-dead people, or how society should distribute its resources. If, in the course of these activities, relevant victims come to mind or are pointed up by others, one is then in the bystander's position of observing or imagining someone in distress. These situations are often more complex than the simple bystander model. At times they include competing principles and conflicting motives as well as pragmatic concerns, and the complexity may limit the vividness and salience of the imagined event, hence the intensity of empathic affects aroused. Nonetheless, these affects may still influence the moral judgments made in the situation.

Potential victims may also come to mind or be suggested by others when one is not in the bystander position but is contemplating an action that may directly or indirectly affect the welfare of others, with or without one's knowledge. One may be thinking of ways to resolve a conflict, break bad news to someone, go back on a promise, or simply satisfy some material need that at first may seem to have no bearing on the concerns of others. Or, one may be engaged in a task that clearly and explicitly requires making a moral judgment and decision. Consider the task of writing a recommendation for tenure. The instigating stimulus for engaging in the task is not the distress of someone, but a request from a colleague in another university. One might simply write a letter indicating, as objectively as possible, one's judgment of the candidate's competence. On the other hand, one might think about the candidate, imagining how he or she would feel and what would happen if tenure were denied, or one might imagine how one would feel if one were in the candidate's place. The empathic and sympathetic distress (or, more strictly, the anticipatory empathic and sympathetic distress) that one might feel as a result of this role taking might then influence the tone and content of the letter.

Writing tenure letters is one of many moral encounters that may be readily transformed into situations involving victims or potential victims. Indeed, it is difficult to imagine moral encounters in everyday life that do *not* involve potential victims and therefore are not likely to be so transformed. The likelihood that one's actions will affect someone's welfare is another important reason – along with the human tendency to react empathically to victims, whether physically present or imagined – for expecting empathy to play a significant role in a comprehensive moral theory. I now discuss a third reason: the congruence between empathy and the principles of caring and of justice.

Congruence between empathy and moral principles

Moral principles are often presented as abstractions. When they are concretized in actual life events, however, the victims and potential victims often stand out, and empathic affects become relevant.

Empathy and caring

The link between empathic affects, especially sympathetic distress, and the caring principle appears rather direct and obvious: The empathic affects and caring operate in the same direction – that is, toward considering the welfare of others. This link appears to be reflected in the empathic moral reasoning that often accompanies people's behavior when they encounter someone in distress. Consider this example from the book *Uncle Tom's Cabin*, reported by Kaplan (in press), in which an affluent, politically uninvolved housewife whose empathy for slaves she knew, who "have been abused and oppressed all their lives," leads her to oppose a newly passed law against giving food, clothes, or shelter to escaping slaves. Arguing with her husband, who supports the law on pragmatic and legal grounds, she verbalizes what amounts to a general principle of caring – "the Bible says we should feed the hungry, clothe the naked, and comfort the desolate," adding that "people don't run away when they're happy, but out of suffering." She becomes so intensely opposed to that "shameful, wicked, abominable" law that she vows to break it at the earliest opportunity.

This episode is reminiscent of Huckleberry Finn's moral conflict between his empathic feeling for Miss Watson's slave Jim, whom he helped escape, and both Missouri law and church teaching at the time, which strongly opposed helping slaves escape. In a famous passage, Huck first writes a letter exposing Jim's hiding place, but then, after a great deal of agonizing soul-searching in which his moral thinking is driven by conflicting moral feelings – sympathetic distress and guilt over the consequences for Jim if he is exposed, and the feeling of how awful a "sin" it would be to keep Jim's whereabouts a secret – he tears the letter up and says to himself, "All right then, I'll *go* to hell." As powerful as that passage is, the episode from *Uncle Tom's Cabin* goes beyond it for our purposes because it indicates that empathy may lead to a response that transcends the immediate, individual victim. More specifically, the episode suggests that the combination of empathic and sympathetic distress and empathic anger in a particular situation may provide the motive for affirming a general caring principle, which may then serve as a premise for the moral judgment that laws violating it are morally wrong.

Empathy and distributive justice

Although the link between empathy and justice is less obvious and less direct than that between empathy and caring, it does exist, as I hope to show in this section. To begin, there are at least three distinct, and seemingly mutually exclusive, principles of distributive justice:

1. *Need* – Society's resources should be allocated according to what people need: Those who need more should receive more; those who need less should receive less.
2. *Equality* – Each person has the same intrinsic worth, in some larger religious or philosophical sense (e.g., in the sense of Bentham's principle, "Everyone to count for one and nobody for more than one"), and therefore society's resources should be divided equally.
3. *Equity* – People should be rewarded according to how much they produce (their output) or according to how much effort they expend.

It seems obvious that choosing one of these abstract principles of justice becomes transformed into an empathy-relevant task as soon as one imagines the consequences of various distribution systems for certain people. If one imagines the consequences and empathizes with poor people, one may conclude that any truly moral distribution system must guarantee everyone at least a minimal level of well-being and may end up affirming the principle of need or of equality. In other words, need and equality appear to have a caring component that may be activated when one empathizes with people whose welfare may be adversely affected by a distribution system, thus transforming the distributive justice issue, in part, into a caring issue.

Alternatively, one might empathize with the needs and expectations of people who work hard and save for their families, and as a result one might affirm the principle of distributing resources according to *effort*. Consider this response of a 13-year-old male research subject to the question, "Why is it wrong to steal from a store?" "Because the people who own the store work hard for their money and they deserve to be able to spend it for their family. It's not fair; they sacrifice a lot and they make plans and then they lost it all because somebody who didn't work for it goes in and takes it." In this response, the subject has transformed an abstract moral question into an empathy-relevant one by imagining a particular victim. The response has a clear empathic-identification component: One empathizes with the other's effort, sacrifice, plans, and expectations about enjoying the fruits of his or her labor and with the other's disappointment and loss. There also appears to be an empathic-anger component, as well as a feeling of empathic injustice. The response thus suggests that effort, like need and equality, has a caring component, which in this case may be activated when one empathizes with people who work hard. Empathic affect may thus contribute to one's receptivity to the principle of equity based on effort. The size of the contribution depends on the extent of one's tendency to empathize with hard-working people rather than to derogate or compete with them or to empathize with the poor instead. Only research can provide the answer.

The principle of equity based on *output* is a different matter. Distributing resources on the basis of output seems to imply that the individual's welfare and internal state are irrelevant considerations. This would seem to rule out a direct link between empathy and output. There are at least two possible indirect links, however:

1. If output is assumed to reflect effort, as it often is, then my argument about the contribution of empathy to effort may also apply to output.
2. If distribution systems based on output motivate people to produce more, as many people believe, then there is more to go around and everyone benefits, including the poor (this reflects the trickle-down idea).[6]

It may thus be possible for empathic identification with the poor to lead one to affirm equity of output as a moral principle, but the route is circuitous and it seems far more likely that empathic identification with the poor will incline one toward the need or equality principles. A recent study of adults by Montada, Schmitt, & Dalbert (1986) supports this expectation. They found a positive correlation between a questionnaire measure of empathy and a preference for need, and a negative correlation between empathy and equity based on output. I found the same thing in an unpublished study of college students. When the subjects were asked to explain their choices, the high-empathy subjects tended to give explanations that included a concern for those who might be disadvantaged under other systems.

Need, equality, and equity are not mutually exclusive and may occur in different combinations. One principle may be dominant, the others playing a constraining role, as exemplified by the moral philosopher Rashdall (1907), who insisted that "equality is the right rule for distributive justice in the absence of any special reason for inequality" (p. 225); among the "special reasons" are need, output, and effort. Alternatively, a distribution system may be based on equity of output but may be regulated so that no one suffers if low output is due to forces beyond one's control (effort); no one, regardless of output, is excessively deprived (need); and vast discrepancies in wealth are not permitted (equality).

As an example of complexity, consider the first two drafts of the "Bishops Pastoral Letter on Catholic Social Teaching and the U.S. Economy" (1984, 1985). The analysis of the American economy in these documents appears to have been transformed into a situation relevant to empathic distress by imagining the economy's consequences for poor people. Thus the documents proclaim the Church's "tradition of compassion for the poor." Included are numerous statements describing in eloquent detail and empathic tone the plight of the poor – their "homelessness," "feelings of despair," "vulnerability," "the daily assaults on their dignity." The statement concludes that "gross inequalities are morally unjustifiable, particularly when millions lack even the basic necessities of life," and it characterizes present levels of unemployment and poverty as "morally unacceptable." In other words, the bishops' statement is an argument that starts with the expression of empathy and the compassion for the suffering poor. It attributes that suffering to the country's system of distributing resources. It then affirms need as a principle of justice and argues that the system is morally wrong because it is insensitive to so many people's needs. However, the statement also notes that absolute equality in distribution of resources, or distribution strictly according to need, is not necessary. In the end, it supports the principle of equity, pleads that equity be tempered with need and equality. The statement thus illustrates an important point: Empathy is more likely to operate in combination with other factors (economic, political, pragmatic) in deriving the complex moral prin' ples pertaining to distributive justice in modern society.

To summarize, in contemplating how society's resources should be distributed, one might focus on the implications for oneself and on the implications for others. For highly egoistic people, their own welfare is paramount and they are apt to be most receptive to distributive justice principles that coincide with their own condition: equity based on output if one is a higher producer, need or equality if one produces little. For empathic people, the welfare of others may be important and they may opt for need or equality even if they are high producers. Or, as seems more likely, a person's egoistic and empathic proclivities may both operate, the result being a distributive-justice orientation that combines the two – output tempered by need and equality, for example.

I have used the term *link* and suggested that empathic people opt for certain principles, but what exactly is the nature of the relation between empathy and moral principles and when and how does it become established? I comment only briefly on these matters. First, it seems obvious that, developmentally, empathic affects become part of most people's affective and motivational structures long before moral principles are seriously considered. At some point in late childhood or adolescence the individual is exposed to various moral principles, usually in a loose, scattered fashion. The "cafeteria" model seems appropriate here: The more empathic one is, the more receptive one should be to caring, need, equality, and perhaps effort.

Apart from this *developmental receptivity* to moral principles there is also the *activation* of moral principles already in one's repertoire. I have suggested that empathic affect arousal may activate related moral principles. It also seems likely that because of the congruence between empathy and principle discussed earlier, the two may be elicited independently. Either way, the resulting cooccurrence of empathy and principle may be expected to strengthen the bond between them, increasing the likelihood that both will be operative and will affect moral judgment in future situations. The influence of principles on moral judgment has been taken for granted (e.g., Kohlberg, 1969). Consider now the impact of empathic affects.

Empathy and moral judgment

Empathy's potential contribution to moral judgment is more complex than its contribution to principles, because here the relationship is mediated by complex reasoning in particular moral encounters. This reasoning is presumably based on moral principles, and it would simplify matters if there were a universal moral principle from which to derive the logically correct moral judgment for each situation. But, as I noted earlier, there are no universally accepted moral principles. We must therefore ask not only how people derive judgments from principles, but what determines which principle, if any, one chooses in the first place, that is, which principle is activated in a situation; and, when two principles are in conflict, what determines which one wins out. My thesis is that empathy plays a key role in all these situations.

David Hume (1751/1957) suggested more than 200 years ago that moral judgment ultimately depends on empathy. That is, moral judgment is based on feelings of satisfaction, pain, uneasiness, or disgust that result from the observer's empathy with the feelings of the person whose action is being appraised and with the feelings of those who are affected by this action. Hume's argument is as follows: First, it is obvious that we all applaud acts that further our own well-being and condemn acts that may harm us. Therefore, if we empathize with others we should applaud or condemn acts that help or harm others; and, unless we are abnormally callous, we will feel indignant (empathic anger) when someone willfully inflicts suffering on others. Empathy may thus guide the moral judgments we make about others. Furthermore, since people may be presumed to respond empathically to similar events in similar ways, empathy may thus provide the common informational input that impartial observers need to reach a consensus on moral judgments. Finally, Hume points out, we talk to one another about these events and respond empathically to each other's descriptions of the relevant acts and their consequences; these empathic responses provide further help in our efforts to reach a consensus. Although Hume does not discuss justice, my notion of empathic injustice can be used to apply Hume's argument to justice: We obviously feel indignant when we do not receive what we deserve because of our efforts or our output; it follows that, if we empathize with others, we should feel indignant when someone else does not receive what he or she deserves because of their effort or output.

Hume's view that empathy provides a reliable basis for consensus in moral judgment has been criticized by Rawls (1971), who argues that empathy lacks the situational sensitivity necessary for achieving a rational consensus. My own empathy scheme, summarized earlier, may solve this problem in part by assuming that at the most advanced empathic level one processes a network of cues that includes a knowledge of the other's life condition beyond the immediate situation. Mature empathy thus reflects a sensitivity to subtle differences in the severity and quality of the consequences that different actions might have for different people. It thus seems clear that empathy can contribute to informed moral judgments. Hume's claim that empathy provides the ultimate basis for reaching *consensus* on moral judgments is another matter, one that requires empirical testing.

Empathy's contribution to moral judgment can be illustrated by anecdotes and hypothetical illustrations. The examples I cited earlier are cases in point. The woman in *Uncle Tom's Cabin* not only affirmed a general caring principle but also used it as the basis for making the moral judgment that a law that violates this principle is morally wrong. The Bishops' Pastoral Letter not only affirmed a justice principle that incorporated need and appears to have been a direct outcome of empathic reasoning based on identification with the poor, but it also used that principle as the basis for the moral judgment that the country's allocation system is morally wrong because it creates many victims. Furthermore, the white Southern schoolboy incident not only illustrates empathic injustice, but also shows how empathic identification with a particular victim can, over time, foster a change in attitude toward a previously accepted social institution – racial segregation – with the result that one now judges that the institution is wrong.

In the research on moral judgment and decision making, subjects are typically asked how someone facing a particular moral dilemma should act and why such action would be better or worse than other actions. Or they may be asked to identify the moral issue in the dilemma. The situation is different in real life. To be sure, some occupations may require people to make judgments of others and decide whether they should receive certain punishments or rewards (such as a promotion or pay increase). For the most part, however, people's moral encounters do not begin with such a cognitive task. More likely, one's moral precepts are apt to be activated when one encounters someone in danger or distress and feels a conflict between the desire to help that individual and the desire to continue to pursue one's own goals of the moment; when one feels outraged by someone's inhumane or unjust treatment of another; when one discovers that one's actions have harmed another or that one's contemplated action may harm someone; when one realizes that one's contemplated action on behalf of someone may operate to the detriment of someone else; when one is tempted, or under external pressure, to act in a way that violates another's reasonable expectations (e.g., by breaking a promise, violating a trust, telling a lie).[7] Culture plays a role in all this, as does history. Deciding whether to have an abortion has recently become a moral dilemma (in which personal needs are placed against the violent consequences to the fetus) for some people who in the past might have considered it a moral dilemma (in which personal needs are placed against the physical danger to oneself). Advances in medical technology have added an element of moral complexity to the medical practitioner's former, relatively simple goal of prolonging life: Organ transplants save lives, but cost–benefit analysis may show that more lives could be saved if the money were spent differently.

There are many variations on these themes. What impresses me is that most moral dilemmas seem to involve victims or potential victims (and beneficiaries) of one's own actions. This means that in the course of thinking about what to do in these situations one may often be confronted with the image, or idea, of someone being helped or harmed by one's own action. This appears to be true even when one is not the actor but is compelled to judge or evaluate the action of others. It follows that empathy may often be aroused in moral judgment and decision making in life; and the empathy aroused, if my previous argument for a link between empathy and moral principles is correct, may not only have a direct effect on moral judgment and reasoning, but may also serve to activate one's moral principles and bring them to bear in the moral reasoning process, more or less along the lines indicated in the examples cited throughout this chapter.

In sum, I am arguing that most moral dilemmas in life may arouse empathy because they involve victims – seen or unseen, present or future. Since empathy is closely related to most moral principles, the arousal of empathy should activate moral principles, and thus – directly, and indirectly through these principles – have an effect on moral judgment and reasoning. This may also be true of moral reasoning in abstract situations, such as Kohlberg's moral dilemmas, provided the person making the judgment empathically identifies with relevant characters in them. Here are some examples of subjects' responses to moral questions that seem to reflect empathic identification operating in the service of moral judgment (Hoffman, 1970). The moral dilemma is an adaptation of Kohlberg's story about two men – Al, who broke into a store and stole $500, and Joe, who lied to a known benefactor about needing $500 for an operation. The subjects were asked who did worse, and why. Most answers, as expected, pertained to the need for law and order, the Ten Commandments, and the possibilities of getting caught. Although the item did not highlight a victim, one quarter of the subjects, who ranged from 11 years to middle age, seemed to transform it into one involving empathic identification with a victim – either an immediate victim of one of the men's actions or potential future victims.

For example, Joe's action was said to be worse because he made the benefactor feel betrayed by someone he trusted, because he made the benefactor lose faith in people and become bitter, because he misused the benefactor's faith and pity, or because people who really needed help would no longer be able to get it. Al's action was said to be worse because the storeowner worked hard for the money, saved for his family, and needed the money – this is the kind of response I described in discussing equity of effort. Note that these empathic-identification responses more than doubled in frequency when the focus of the question changed from the actor ("Who did worse?") to the observer ("Which would make you feel worse, if you did it?"). The empathic-identification responses in which Joe's act was deemed worse might appear to reflect a simple liking for the kind benefactor – a personal bias or halo effect rather than a moral judgment – but this is not the case. When asked "what kind of person" the benefactor was, the subjects who gave these empathic-identification responses were as likely as the other subjects to criticize him for being foolish or naive. In other words, they empathized with him and felt it was wrong to deceive him, although they were critical of him. These responses are more convincing as *moral* judgments because they transcend personal feeling for the person harmed.

Empathic bias and how to reduce it

The case for empathy thus far looks rather strong. There are problems, however, that might appear to limit empathy's contribution to all but the simplest of situations. One is that empathy may be biased in several ways. First, there is research evidence that observers are more empathic to victims who are familiar and similar to themselves than to victims who are different, although, I hasten to add, they are usually empathic to victims who are different – just less so (Feshbach & Roe, 1968; Klein, 1971; Krebs, 1970). Second, it seems that people are more apt to be empathically aroused by someone's distress in the immediate situation than by distress that they know is being experienced by someone somewhere else or that is likely to be experienced in the future. There is no empirical evidence for such a here-and-now bias, but it seems likely in view of the fact that several of the arousal processes noted in Table 4.1, especially the involuntary processes (conditioning, association, mimicry) are dependent on immediate situational and personal cues. These cues are absent when someone's distress occurs somewhere else or when it is likely to occur in the future.

These biases constitute a flow in empathic morality and raise questions about its applicability in situations involving conflicting moral claims, that is, situations in which one must make a moral judgment and decision and the welfare of several people or groups depends on one's action, but only some of these people are familiar or present in the immediate situation. First, is it a fatal flaw? The answer depends on two things: whether there is an alternative morality that is bias-free, and whether the bias in empathic morality can be eliminated or minimized. Regarding the first point, the most likely alternative is cognitive morality in the Kohlberg tradition, which states that one can solve moral dilemmas by applying the universal principle of justice to the particular situation and by reasoning out the solution. There are problems with this formulation. As I noted, it is unlikely that justice can be considered universal; in any case, there are several other principles beside justice, and justice itself has several variants. The question that follows is what determines which of these principles is chosen, or activated, in a particular moral dilemma? One's socialization into a particular culture or subgroup would seem to be a reasonable answer, as would one's needs and predilections of the moment, contextual cues, and perhaps the empathic affect that may be aroused along the lines I suggested. The principle chosen may also serve as a rationalization, not necessarily conscious, for one's own interests, as long suggested by philosophers in the tradition of emotive theory (Ayer, 1936; Brandt, 1979; Edwards, 1955).

Aside from these biases in choosing a moral principle, decades of research on ethnic and racial prejudice suggest that one's principles may be applied differentially to members of one's own group and members of other groups. Within one's group, one's moral principles are likely to be applied differentially to people who are present or absent, as I suggested may also be true of empathy. Moreover, the reasoning process, too, is open to question. There is considerable evidence that reasoning based on factual knowledge about the physical world is often unreliable, partly because of the human tendency to employ "availability" and other error-producing heuristics (Tversky & Kahneman, 1973). Surely the same must be true of reasoning in the moral domain. Thus, although this notion may seem counterintuitive, there are no a priori grounds for assuming that cognitive morality is any freer of bias than empathic morality. Whether it is freer of bias is an empirical question that awaits research.

The second question about the applicability of empathic morality is whether empathic bias can be reduced to a manageable level. The answer here is more complex. First, a correction for bias toward the here and now is built into my empathy scheme, as I illustrated earlier with the terminally ill person who is happy in the immediate situation. However, in order to be able to empathize with the victim's plight beyond the immediate situation, the observer requires information about the victim's condition in other situations, and this information must enter the observer's consciousness at the appropriate time. If the observer lacks the necessary information, it must be given to him or her; if the observer has it stored in memory, something in the situation must prime it so that it will be recalled. Furthermore, the observer must be sufficiently advanced developmentally to be able to process the information and realize that it may be a more compelling index of the victim's welfare than the victim's contradictory current behavior.

This brings us to the question of the role of moral education in reducing empathic bias, which I can only comment on briefly here. One thing moral education can do is teach people a simple rule of thumb: Look beyond the immediate situation and ask questions such as "What kind of experiences does the other person have in various situations beyond the immediate one?" "How will my action affect him or her, not only now but in the future?" and "Are there other people, present or absent, who might be affected by my actions?" If children learn to ask these questions, they should be able to enhance their awareness of all those who may be affected by their actions, whether present or not. In addition, to compensate for the here-and-now bias in intensity of empathic affect, children might be encouraged to imagine how they would feel in the place of those others. And, finally, a positive value might be placed on spatial and temporal impartiality, and children might be encouraged, insofar as possible, to give equal consideration to all of those who may be affected by their actions. Children cannot be expected to engage in this laborious process all the time (nor can adults), but with such moral education their empathic responses should at least be less exclusively confined to the here and now and should more closely approach the ideal of spatial and temporal neutrality.

As for the familiarity–similarity bias, Hume (1751/1957) declared that it was perfectly natural for people to empathize more with their kin than with strangers and that doing this was not necessarily incompatible with being moral. He also said that efforts must be made to minimize this bias and suggested that society can be organized so as to minimize it: People, each having a particular bias and knowing about their own and the other's bias, can devise systems of social rules that minimize bias and encourage impartiality. To this I would add a moral education curriculum that stresses the common humanity of all people and includes efforts to raise people's levels of empathy for outgroup members. Such efforts might include direct face-to-face cultural contact and training in role-taking procedures that are vivid enough to generate empathic feeling for people in circumstances that are different from their own. The combination of rule systems and empathy-enhancing moral education should expand the range of people to whom individuals can respond empathically, thus reducing familiarity–similarity bias.

How empathic bias may be reduced in life can be illustrated in the task of writing a letter of recommendation for a former student. When composing such a letter, we may empathize with the student, to whom we feel close. Thus when negative things about the student come to mind, we may experience a moral conflict in trying to decide whether to include this negative information and hurt his chances or withhold it and violate both our standards of honesty and our commitment to the collegial system of evaluating job applications. Our empathy for the student may lead us to withhold the information and tolerate the resulting guilt feeling. Or, we may also empathize with our peer colleagues, who need the information and are counting on us to be objective and tell the truth. Obviously the moral conflict would be more complex if in addition one had to consider whether one might be betraying the trust of these unseen colleagues.[8] We may even go one step further and empathize with people whom we do not know at all and who will probably never see our letter but whose welfare may nevertheless be affected by it, namely, the other applicants for the job. This situation would further complicate the moral conflict. Regardless of our final decision, the multiple empathizing, which clearly contributes to the moral conflict, may also reduce the potency of our initial empathic bias in favor of the particular student.

Here is an even more complex example adapted from an illustration used by Noddings (1984). In considering whether to sponsor a favorite graduate student's research proposal that requires deception, a professor might empathize with the student's pride in a well-written proposal, the student's fear that months of work will be wasted if the professor rejects the proposal, and the student's eagerness to get on with the job. This empathy for the student may be strong enough to motivate the professor to sponsor the proposal. So far, there appears to be no moral conflict. But the situation may be transformed into a moral conflict if the professor's belief that deception is wrong is activated. Deception may be too abstract a concept to elicit enough affect to compete with the professor's empathy for the student. But if the professor is aware of this fact and also of his or her empathic bias, he or she may try to compensate for the bias and penetrate the abstractness by thinking about subjects being harmed by the research – by imagining how a hypothetical subject, perhaps a person he or she cares about very much, might respond to the experimental manipulation. If the danger perceived is great enough, the professor's anticipatory empathic distress may be so intense that despite his or her empathy for the graduate student (and the fact that the proposal is otherwise satisfactory), the professor might refuse to sponsor the student's research. The professor's empathic revulsion might even be so great as to compel him or her to propose guidelines for the control of all research requiring deception. This example illustrates how the combination of biases – for the familiar and the here and now, all favoring the student – may be overcome by a more or less deliberate effort to empathize with exemplars of other people whose welfare may be affected by one's action.

As in the letter-of-recommendation example, the professor might go a step further and empathize with people who are unseen and perhaps unknown but whose welfare may be indirectly at stake – namely, other researchers whose careers might be jeopardized by excessive constraints on research or other people who may ultimately benefit from the research. As a result of this multiple empathizing, the professor might refuse to sponsor the student's research but might refrain from making rules that will bind other investigators. The outcome may be entirely different, of course, but whatever it is, the process illustrates, first, how one's initial empathic response may be biased toward familiar individuals and toward the here and now, and second, how the effects of that bias may be counteracted by empathizing with people who are not present but whose welfare may nevertheless be affected by one's actions.

This all sounds like traditional utilitarian moral reasoning: Consider the future as well as immediate consequences of one's action for people who are absent as well as present. But we should not lose sight of the role of empathy in providing both substantive input and motivation at various points in the reasoning process. In any case, it seems reasonable to conclude that although empathic morality may be flawed because of certain biases, it may be no more flawed than the most apparent alternative, cognitive morality in the Kohlberg tradition. Furthermore, empathic bias appears to be controllable, although to control it one may have to add a cognitive perspective that attempts to give equal weight to all people whose welfare may be affected by one's actions. With this perspective, empathy may not only contribute to moral principles but may also play a constructive role in complex moral judgments and decision making.

Moral principles as "hot cognitions"

I have suggested that empathy contributes to caring and most principles of justice through empathic identification with victims and potential victims of society and its institutions. What are the circumstances in which this process occurs? One possibility is that it occurs in the normal course of development in children who have been socialized to be empathic. Empathic socialization begins in early childhood (Hoffman, 1982b), but it is not until late childhood or early adolescence that children are able to comprehend the meaning of moral principles. It follows from my previous argument, then, that, to the degree that children are empathic, they should be receptive to the principles of caring, need-based justice, equality, and perhaps effort-based justice. In this cafeteria model, people are disposed to select from the moral principles available in society, those that fit their empathic dispositions. One internalizes the principles with little external pressure, because they are in keeping with one's empathic leanings.

The moral encounters one has through life may also play a significant role, because of the empathic affects often aroused. These empathic affects are most likely to be aroused in bystander situations in which victims are salient from the start. But they may also be aroused, as I suggested, in other situations in which victims do not become apparently until later on (e.g., when writing a letter of recommendation). In either case, the empathic affects may dispose one to act on the victim's behalf; such a response would be in opposition to one's egoistic motives in the situation and thus would instigate one type of moral conflict.[9]

A moral conflict is essentially a conflict between alternative courses of action. Therefore it seems reasonable to assume that, when one experiences a moral conflict, one inevitably wonders what to do, considers alternative actions, and anticipates consequences for others. Such thoughts may not only bring to mind victims and potential victims, thus arousing empathic affects, but may also bring to mind the guidelines to action, including relevant moral principles (caring, need, etc.) and associated norms to which one has been previously exposed and that have been stored in memory. The empathic affect and moral principles may be evoked independently, or empathic affect may be aroused first and then may prime the moral principles. Either way, the cooccurrence of a principle and empathic affect should produce a bond between them (or strengthen any existing bond). The result may be that the principle, even if learned initially in a "cool," didactic context (e.g., abstract intellectual discourse in which victims are not salient), acquires an affective charge. An interesting reversed sequence may then become possible: In future cool contexts, for example, in answering moral judgment research questions, the abstract principle may be activated first and this may trigger empathic affect. Such a sequence may explain the emotionality in my subject's explanation of why it is wrong to steal (see the section Empathy and distributive justice). In other words, as a consequence of being coupled with empathic affect in moral encounters, a moral principle may be encoded and stored as an affectively charged representation – as a "hot" cognition or category.

What exactly is represented in such a "hot" category? Probably anything that has been associated with the principle and its accompanying empathic affects in life, including verbal descriptions of the principle's content, as well as events in which the principle is violated – events involving victims, culprits, and actions that conform or violate the principle. These representations are apt to be charged with the empathic affects associated with them in one's experiences; and when one subsequently encounters an instance fitting one of these representations, one may be expected to respond to it with the category's affect (as is assumed to occur in general when hot categories are activated; see Fiske, 1982; Hoffman,

1986). Empirical evidence that moral principles are encoded as hot categories is lacking, but a study by Arsenio and Ford (1985) suggests that single instances of the violation of a moral principle may be so encoded. The findings – young children experienced negative affect when told stories in which a child acts inconsiderately toward another, and their later recall of these stories was aided by the induction of negative affect – suggest that violations of particular principles may be encoded as hot cognitions. Perhaps the same is true of categories of violations.

A potentially important implication of all this is that a person's affective and cognitive responses in moral encounters are due not only to the immediate stimulus event (cues from the situation and from the victim), but also to the affectively charged moral principles that one's action and other aspects of the stimulus event may activate. The empathic affect elicited in moral encounters may thus have a stimulus-driven component and a component driven by the activated, affectively charged principle. This may have important implications for prosocial action. In some situations, for example, the empathic affect elicited by the stimulus event alone may be too weak, perhaps because of a paucity of relevant cues from victims, to override the egoistic motives that may also be operating. But if one's caring principle were activated, its associated empathic affect might be released. This category-driven component, alone or in combination with the stimulus-driven component, may be powerful enough to exceed the threshold needed to override the egoistic motives. Activating one's moral principles may thus provide an additional source of empathic affect, with a resulting increase in one's overall motivation for moral action. The obverse side to this should also be mentioned. In some situations, the empathic affect elicited by the stimulus event alone may be so intense that it produces the disruptive effects of "empathic overarousal" (Hoffman, 1978). In these cases, if one's caring principle were activated and the stimulus event assimilated to it, the category-driven component might *reduce* empathic affect intensity to a more manageable level. Thus, the activation of an affectively charged moral principle may have a heightening or leveling effect and in general might function to stabilize one's level of empathic affect arousal in different situations.

In sum, empathy may play a significant role in determining whether one becomes committed to a moral principle by giving the principle an affective base. But once the principle is in place, activating it in future moral encounters may increase or decrease the intensity of one's empathic affective response. Moral principles may thus make it more likely that moral conflict will lead to effective moral action.

The hot-cognition concept also has implications for memory, as there is reason to believe that both affect and cognition contribute to memory. Recent research suggests that affect in general is an extremely powerful retrieval cue (Bower,

1981). In addition, I have argued that empathic affect associated with moral concepts acquired in early discipline encounters contributes to remembering (and internalizing) these moral concepts (Hoffman, 1983). The Arsenio and Ford (1985) study supports this view. On the cognitive side, a moral principle is, in part, a semantically organized category of knowledge (or prototype). Like other categories, it encompasses many instances and is shaped and made more complex over time in the process of accommodating to new instances. The fact that categorical knowledge is highly enduring in memory, for reasons spelled out by Tulving (1972), should therefore apply to moral principles. Thus, both the affective and cognitive components of a moral principle should help maintain it in memory, keeping it available for activation in future moral encounters.

Concluding remarks

My aim in this chapter has been to demonstrate the possible role of empathy in a comprehensive moral theory. To this end I have argued as follows:

1. When one witnesses someone in distress, one may respond empathically, that is, with affect more appropriate to the other's situations than to one's own. The most likely response is empathic or sympathetic distress, but, depending on the available cues and one's prior knowledge about the victim, one may make certain causal and other attributions that may transform these feelings into empathic anger, guilt, and empathic injustice.

2. The essential features of this bystander model, including the five empathic affects it can generate, do not require a victim to be physically present because human beings have the capacity for representation and represented events have the power to evoke empathic as well as direct affect. What is required is that a victim or potential victim be imagined, as may occur when one is told or reads about someone's plight, is engaged in conversation or argument about moral issues, or even makes moral judgments about hypothetical situations in a research project. Occasions like these, though cognitively and motivationally more complex than most bystander situations, may arouse empathic affects in a similar way. In other situations, one's own actions are at issue, and when one acts or contemplates acting in a way that may affect other people's welfare, imagining the consequences for them may be expected to arouse empathic affect. Thus many, perhaps most, moral encounters appear to involve victims and potential victims (and beneficiaries, although I focus on victims) and can be counted on to evoke empathic affects.

3. Empathic affects are by and large congruent with caring and most forms of justice. These are the prevailing moral principles in Western society and may be assumed to be the part of people's knowledge structures that are most often brought to bear in moral encounters. The content of these principles also makes

them relevant, in varying degrees, to issues involving victims. The moral principles may therefore be activated either by the empathic affects aroused in a moral encounter or by the relevance of their content to the victim dimension of the moral encounter. Either way, the resulting cooccurrence of the empathic affect and moral principle creates a bond between them that is strengthened in subsequent cooccurrences. Moral principles, even when initially learned in "cool" didactic contexts, may in this way acquire an affective charge and take on the characteristics of a hot cognition.

4. An important implication of the hot-cognition concept is that when a moral principle is subsequently activated even in didactic or research contexts, empathic affect may be aroused. Another implication is that empathic affects aroused in moral encounters may have a stimulus-driven and a category-driven component. The category-driven component may have a heightening or leveling effect on the intensity of the stimulus-driven component in any given moral encounter. The overall result may be to help stabilize the individual's level of empathic affective reactions in different situations over time.

5. Empathic affect may also make important contributions to moral judgment and decision making. The contribution may be direct, or it may be mediated by the moral principles activated by the affects. In either case, the contribution may be limited by empathic bias toward the familiar or toward the here and now. However, these biases may be reduced by socialization that highlights the commonalities among human groups, places high value on impartiality, and trains people in the techniques of multiple empathizing, that is, empathizing not only with people in the vicinity who may be affected by one's actions, but also with people who are absent.

A neglected question in morality research is that of why a person applies one principle and not another in a moral encounter. Cognitive moral theories have difficulty answering this question because they lack affective and motivational concepts. My suggestion that empathic affect may shed some light on this question may seem counter intuitive. Why should affect influence the selection of a principle? This is not a simple, unadorned affect, however, as I hope I have made clear, but an empathic affect informed by one's cognitive sense of others, one's relevant causal attributions, and, in the ideal case, one's knowledge of the importance of being impartial. Furthermore, the affects may be subject to conscious efforts to correct their characteristic biases, efforts such as empathically identifying with people who are absent as well as present, which may provide a number of relevant empathic affective inputs that are then worked into the moral reasoning and judgment process. These inputs, when congruent with one another, may lead directly to the final moral judgment or decision. When the inputs are contradictory (e.g., empathic joy on contemplating an action that will make someone who is present happy versus empathic distress on recognizing that the same action may harm someone who is absent), one must somehow weigh the relative importance of each. This may be a cognitive weighing, or one may base one's moral judgment on the input that includes the most intense affect, as in my example of the professor whose empathic concern for future research subjects finally outweighed his empathic concern for his graduate student.

My theoretical argument does not extend to this final phase of the moral reasoning process in which the importance of various inputs is weighed – not only empathic inputs but also moral principles and pragmatic considerations. Rather, my objective is to make sure that all relevant inputs, including empathy-based inputs, are taken into account. In this sense, my approach, as noted earlier, fits squarely in the long Utilitarian tradition in Western philosophy, which states that what is good is what benefits most people. Utilitarians often say that in any moral encounter one should consider the potential harm or benefit an action might have for all people – present or absent. I suggest that empathic affect makes an important contribution toward this end.

Before concluding, I want to correct a statement I made at the beginning of the chapter. There *is* an overriding principle on which there may be close to universal agreement, at least in Western philosophy. However, it has no particular content, but simply states that, whatever one's moral principle it must be applied impartially – to strangers as well as kin, to people who are absent as well as present, and to the future as well as the present implications of action.[10] This principle has been implicit throughout my argument.

Finally, I am *not* saying that empathic affects are an adequate substitute for moral principles or that actions guided by empathic affects automatically qualify as moral actions, as Blum (1980) and Gilligan (1982) seem to imply. According to Gilligan, an empathy-based caring morality is equal, and in many ways superior, to an equal-rights-based justice morality – even though justice morality proceeds from the premise that everyone should be treated the same, whereas caring morality does not require such impartiality. Gilligan's examples of caring do not reflect the complexities of having to care for two or more people, when one can only care for one and must make a choice, nor does she deal with familiarity and here-and-now-biases. Consider a doctor who cares for and goes out of the way to give all of his or her consulting time to a particular patient, but neglects others who are equally in need of attention. This doctor is obviously empathic and cares a lot, to the point of setting aside personal needs, but I would have difficulty calling this moral behavior. On the other hand, I do not go as far as Kohlberg and others, who seem to consider acts moral only if they derive from moral principles. The issue is complex, and I do not have an answer except to suggest a development criterion. The doctor in question may not be acting morally, but a young child, who, out of sympathetic distress, goes out of his or her way to help someone, may be acting morally.

I *am* saying that empathic affect may contribute to acceptance of moral principles in relevant situations and to the motivation to act in accordance with moral principles. Empathic affects may also contribute inputs to moral reasoning based on principles, and thus to moral decision making and moral judgment. My argument is not foolproof, as it is based mainly on anecdotal and hypothetical examples showing that people's moral reasoning and judgment sometimes have a quality of personal concern for others that seems to reflect an underlying empathic identification with them. There is also the research mentioned earlier showing that empathy correlates positively with a preference for need-based equity and negatively with a preference for output-based equity as principles of distributive justice. This research is encouraging but limited in applicability because causal inferences cannot be made (although empathy obviously predates moral principles developmentally and may therefore be the more likely antecedent). Furthermore, the research says nothing about process. We need experimental studies of how empathic and sympathetic distress, guilt, and empathic anger affect one's receptivity to certain moral principles as well as the moral reasoning and judgment used in applying these principles. Longitudinal research is also needed to explain how these empathic affects contribute developmentally to an internalized commitment to moral principles and to the moral reasoning and judgments based on them.

Notes

1. Utilitarians, for example, may view both justice and the social order as subprinciples instrumental in attaining impartial benevolence.
2. This definition differs from others, which require a close match between the affective response of the target person and that of the observer. The advantages of my definition have been discussed elsewhere (Hoffman, 1982a).
3. Empathic anger should be distinguished from the type of self-righteous indignation that serves to tout one's own moral superiority.
4. I thank Inge Bretherton for this example.
5. This type of guilt feeling should be distinguished from Freudian guilt, which results not from awareness of harming someone in the present, but from activation of early repressed childhood anxieties about losing parental love; it is often unconscious and may be experienced when no one else is involved (masturbation guilt).
6. There is reason to question this assumption. Though output-oriented societies apparently produce more than other societies, such comparisons may ignore important uncontrolled variables. Experimental research by Deutsch (1985), in which relevant variables were controlled, raises serious questions about whether distribution of resources on the basis of output actually does produce greater overall output. If it does not, is there any other reason for considering output equity a justice principle?
7. We may feel guilty about violating the expectations of others intentionally, or unwittingly, owing to our normal habits. We are apt to feel far guiltier, however, about breaking an actual promise, because in this case we not only violate another's expectations but we are responsible for having created those expectations in the first place. (We may, of course, feel an obligation

to keep a promise even if no one will be injured if we don't; this type of moral feeling appears to fall outside the domain of empathic morality.)

8. I stress the role of empathy in all of these examples, but we may be concerned about honesty and fairness without empathizing.

9. Other types of moral conflict involve opposition between principles, in which one's egoistic needs may not be an issue.

10. A contemporary Western philosopher who plays down the importance of impartiality is Blum (1980), who argues that it is morally appropriate to favor one's friends.

References

Arsenio, W. F., & Ford, M. E. (1985). The role of affective information in social–cognitive development: Children's differentiation of moral and conventional events. *Merrill–Palmer Quarterly, 31,* 1–17.

Ayer, A. J. (1936). *Language, truth and logic.* London: Gollancz.

Bishops' pastoral letter on Catholic social teaching and the U.S. economy: First draft (1984). *Origins, 14,* Nos. 22, 23.

Bishops' pastoral letter on Catholic social teaching and the U.S. economy: Second draft (1985). *Origins, 15,* No. 17.

Blum, L. A. (1980). *Friendship, altruism and morality.* London: Routledge & Kegan Paul.

Bower, G. H. (1981). Mood and memory. *American Psychologist, 36,* 129–148.

Brandt, R. A. (1979). *A theory of the good and the right.* New York: Oxford University Press.

Coles, R. (1986). *The moral life of children.* Boston: Atlantic Monthly Press.

Deutsch, M. (1985). *Distributive justice: A social psychological perspective.* New Haven, CT: Yale University Press.

Edwards, P. (1955). *The logic of moral discourse.* New York: Free Press.

Feshbach, N. D., & Roe, K. (1968). Empathy in six- and seven-year olds. *Child Development, 39,* 133–145.

Fiske, S. T. (1982). Schema-triggered affect: Applications to social perception. In S. Fiske and M. Clark (Eds.), *Cognition and affect: The Carnegie-Mellon Symposium* (pp. 55–78). Hillsdale, NJ: Erlbaum.

Gilligan, C. (1982). *In a different voice.* Cambridge MA: Harvard University Press.

Harris, M. B., & Siebel, C. E. (1975). Affect, aggression, and altruism. *Developmental Psychology, 11,* 623–627.

Hoffman, M. L. (1970). Conscience, personality, and socialization techniques. *Human Development, 13,* 90–126.

Hoffman, M. L. (1975a). Developmental synthesis of affect and cognition and its implications for altruistic motivation. *Developmental Psychology, 11,* 607–622.

Hoffman, M. L. (1975b). Sex differences in moral internalization. *Journal of Personality and Social Psychology, 32,* 720–729.

Hoffman, M. L. (1977). Sex differences in empathy and related behaviors. *Psychological Bulletin, 84,* 712–722.

Hoffman, M. L. (1978). Empathy, its development and prosocial implications. In C. B. Keasey (Ed.), *Nebraska Symposium on Motivation* (Vol. 25, pp. 169–218). Lincoln: University of Nebraska Press.

Hoffman, M. L. (1980). Moral development in adolescence. In J. Adelson (Ed.), *Handbook of adolescent psychology,* (pp. 295–343). New York: John Wiley & Sons.

Hoffman, M. L. (1981). Is altruism part of human nature? *Journal of Personality and Social Psychology, 40,* 121–137.

Hoffman, M. L. (1982a). Measurement of empathy. In C. Izard (Ed.), *Measurement of emotions in infants and children* (pp. 279–296). New York: Cambridge University Press.

Hoffman, M. L. (1982b). Development of prosocial motivation: Empathy and guilt. In N. Eisenberg, (Ed.), *Development of prosocial behavior* (pp. 281–313). New York: Academic Press.

Hoffman, M. L. (1982c). Affect and moral development. In D. Cicchetti (Ed.), *New directions in child development* (pp. 83–103). San Francisco: Jossey-Bass.

Hoffman, M. L. (1983). Affective and cognitive processes in moral internalization: An information processing approach. In E. T. Higgins, D. Ruble, & W. Hartup (Eds.), *Social cognition and social development: A socio-cultural perspective* (pp. 236–274). New York: Cambridge University Press.

Hoffman, M. L. (1984a). Interaction of affect and cognition in empathy. In C. Izard, J. Kagan, & R. Zajonc (Eds.), *Emotions, cognition, and behavior* (pp. 103–131). New York: Cambridge University Press.

Hoffman, M. L. (1984b). Empathy, its limitations, and its role in a comprehensive moral theory. In J. Gewirtz & W. Kurtines (Eds.), *Morality, moral development, and moral behavior* (pp. 283–302). New York: John Wiley.

Hoffman, M. L. (1986). Affect, cognition, and motivation. In R. M. Sorrentino and E. T. Higgins (Eds.), *Handbook of motivation and cognition: Foundations of social behavior* (pp. 244–275). New York: Guilford.

Hoffman, M. L. (in press). Empathy and prosocial activism. In N. Eisenberg, J. Reykowski, & E. Staub (Eds.), *Social and moral values*. Hillsdale, NJ: Erlbaum.

Hume, D. (1957). *An inquiry concerning the principle of morals* (Vol. 4). New York: Liberal Arts Press. (Original work published 1751).

Izard, C. E. (1977). *Human emotions*. New York: Plenum Press.

Kaplan, E. A. (in press). Women, morality, and social change: A historical perspective. In N. Eisenberg, J. Reykowski, & E. Staub (Eds.) *Social and moral values*. Hillsdale, NJ: Erlbaum.

Kaplan, L. J. (1977). The basic dialogue and the capacity of empathy. In N. Freedman & S. Grand (Eds.), *Communicative structures and psychic structures*. New York: Plenum.

Klein, R. (1971). Some factors influencing empathy in six- and seven-year-old children varying in ethnic background (Doctoral dissertation, University of California, Los Angeles, 1970). *Dissertation Abstracts International, 31,* 3960A. (University Microfilms No. 71-3862)

Kohlberg, L. (1969). The cognitive developmental approach. In D. A. Goslin (Ed.), *Handbook of socialization theory and research*. Chicago: Rand McNally.

Krebs, D. L. (1970). Altruism: An examination of the concept and a review of the literature. *Psychological Bulletin, 73,* 258–303.

Mill, J. S. (1979). *Utilitarianism*. Cambridge, MA: Hackett (original work published 1861).

Montada, L., Schmitt, M., & Dalbert, C. (1986). Thinking about justice and dealing with one's privileges; A study on existential guilt. In H. W. Bierhoff, R. Cohen, & J. Greenberg (Eds.), *Justice in social relations*. New York: Plenum Press.

Murphy, L. B. (1937). *Social behavior and child personality*. New York: Columbia University Press.

Noddings, N. (1984). *Caring*. Berkeley: University of California Press.

Rashdall, H. (1907). *The theory of good and evil*. New York: Oxford University Press.

Rawls, J. A. (1971). *A theory of justice*. Cambridge, MA: Harvard University Press.

Razran, G. (1971). *Mind in evolution*. Boston: Houghton Mifflin.

Stotland, E. (1969). Exploratory investigations of empathy. In L. Berkowitz (Ed.), *Advances in experimental social psychology* (Vol. 4). New York: Academic Press.

Tulving, E. (1972). Episodic and semantic memory. In E. Tulving & W. Donaldson (Eds.), *Organization of memory*. New York: Academic Press.

Tversky, A. & Kahneman, D. (1973). Availability: A heuristic for judging frequency and probability. *Cognitive Psychology, 5,* 207–232.

Weiner, B. (1985). "Spontaneous" causal thinking. *Psychological Bulletin, 97,* 74–84.

Zahn-Waxler, C., Radke-Yarrow, M., & King, R. A. (1979). Childrearing and children's prosocial initiations towards victims of distress. *Child Development, 50,* 319–330.

Zanna, M. P., Kiesler, C. A., & Pilkonis, P. A. (1970). Positive and negative affect established by classical conditioning. *Journal of Personality and Social Psychology, 14,* 321–328.

CHAPTER 7

Empathy, Role Taking, Guilt, and Development of Altruistic Motives[1]

Martin L. Hoffman

Introduction: Evidence of Altruism in Animals and Humans

Western psychology has evolved along lines seemingly antithetical to giving consideration for others a central place in the overall view of personality. The doctrinaire view, present in both psychoanalysis and behaviorism, has been that altruistic behavior can always be explained ultimately in terms of instrumental self-serving motives in the actor. The assumption of this chapter, by contrast, is that man is innately capable of both egoistic and altruistic motivation, and our aim here is to propose a theory of how the latter may develop in the individual. First, we will take a brief look at the relevant research literature—animal and human—to see if it is at all supportive of the idea that altruistic behavior may be based on other than selfish motives.

The evidence for altruism in animals is scanty, anecdotal, and often subject to alternative interpretations (See the recent controversy between D. L. Krebs, 1970a, 1971; and Hebb, 1971). Several of the detailed descriptive reports in the literature,

however, do seem to provide reasonably good evidence for altruistic rescue behavior. In one study, the experimenter inflicted pain on a chimpanzee, which then screamed, whereupon her cagemate began alternatively to pull her to safety and to attack the experimenter (Nissen & Crawford, 1936). A week later when the experimenter reappeared and the previously harmed animal approached him, the cagemate tried strenuously to pull her away and continued to do so for the brief period that the experimenter remained. Similarly, porpoises aid wounded members by raising them to the surface of the water for air (Hebb & Thompson, 1954).

In the human research, *altruism* has been implicitly defined as any purposive action on behalf of someone else which involves a net cost to the actor. Two types of altruistic behavior have been studied: (1) rescue, or helping another in distress; and (2) sharing, or making an anonymous donation to someone in need. The research in general presents a less bleak picture than that depicted in the social commentary following reports of bystander unresponsiveness in emergencies. In the studies reported thus far, anywhere from a sizable minority to all of the subjects (observers) have been found to help the victim when the observer was the only bystander. Among the more dramatic findings are the following: Darley and Latané (1968) found that 85 percent of their subjects attempted to help someone whom they thought was having an epileptic fit, and 90 percent of those helping acted within sixty seconds; all of Clark and Word's subjects (1972) rushed to help a man they heard fall and cry out in pain (average reaction time was nine seconds); and Schwartz (1970b) found that 59 percent of his subjects were willing to donate blood marrow to a stranger described as desperately in need, though warned in advance that a general anesthetic and a day in the hospital would be required and that they would feel sore for several days afterwards.

The findings with children are less dramatic but consistent. Murphy (1937) reports that the nursery school children she observed who had the necessary coping skills typically offered help to other children in distress. Using more structured observations of normal and retarded children in two age groups (3- to 5-year-olds and 8- to 10-year-olds), Severy and Davis (1971) found that 35 to 57 percent of the opportunities to help others were taken by the children. These figures are consistent with those obtained by Staub (1970a, 1971a, 1971b; Rosenhan, Moore, & Underwood, Chap. 13) in a more controlled laboratory setting. This consistency is particularly interesting in view of the restraint often shown by young children in laboratory studies.

There is also evidence that helping others is not associated with deprived need states in the actor, an association that would be expected if helping were a primarily egoistic need-satisfying act. Thus Murphy (1937) reports that though some of the nursery school children's helpful acts seemed calculated to win adult approval, many obviously were not (for example, shoving an attacker away from the victim, showing intense concern for the victim and being oblivious to others about him). Murphy also reports that the children who seemed most concerned about others in distress were among the more popular and emotionally secure members of the group. Jeanne Block (personal communication, 1972) reports a similar positive relation between helping behavior and such personal attributes as emotional security and self-confidence. Similarly, Staub and Sherk (1970) obtained a negative correlation between making charitable donations and the need for social approval in children. Finally, several studies (reviewed by Rosenhan, Moore, & Underwood Chap. 13) report evidence that situationally induced feelings of well-being, rather than deprivation, contribute to helping behavior.

It thus appears that helping and sharing, though often viewed as effective means of gaining rewards such as social approval, do not characterize the very people who have the greatest need for these rewards; nor are these helping behaviors associated with the arousal of egoistic needs in the situation. This makes sense when we realize that egoistic need deprivation very likely leads to a state of preoccupation with the self—with one's own needs, hopes, and fears. Such concern for the self should be expected to interfere with the individual's inclination to help others, rather than contribute to it. A state of well-being and need fulfillment, on the other hand, may very well facilitate prosocial behavior because it reduces pressures toward egoistic self-concern, leaving the person more open and responsive to the needs of others.

That people will help others when their own needs are not salient, indeed when they are in a state of well-being rather than want, lends credence to the view that an altruistic motive system separate from the egoistic may exist within the individual. The remainder of this chapter will be taken up with a theoretical account of the development of the altruistic motive. The scheme which will be presented rests ultimately on the human capacity to experience the inner state of others who are not in the same situation. This analysis attempts to pull together what is known about the individual's affective response to another person's distress (empathy, sympathy, guilt), on the one hand, and cognitive development and role taking, on the other.

Affective Response
to Another's Distress

Empathy refers to the involuntary, at times forceful, experiencing of another person's emotional state. It is elicited either by expressive cues which directly reflect the other's feelings or by other cues which convey the affective impact of external events on him.

The tendency to respond empathically to another in distress has long been noted in children and adults. Murphy (1937, p. 295) in her classic study described numerous instances of empathic responses in nursery school children and concluded that "experiencing distress when another is in distress seems primitive, naive, reasonably universal"—as natural a response as anger is to threats to the self (and, as with anger, only the specific form of empathy is due to learning). N. D. Feshbach and Roe (1968) found that 4- to 7-year-old children typically gave empathic responses to a series of slide sequences depicting other children in different affective situations. College students respond affectively, as indicated by physiological measures, when observing another person being administered electric shock or heat, or failing in a task (Berger, 1962; Craig & Weinstein, 1965; Stotland, 1969; Tomes, 1964; R. F. Weiss, Boyer, Lombardo, & Stich, 1973). Clore and Jeffery (1972) found that watching someone in a wheel chair for an hour produced feelings of empathy and diminished potency in the observer.

The various explanations for empathic distress boil down to two basic classical conditioning paradigms. One paradigm views empathy as developing early in infancy with the bodily transfer of tension from the caretaker to the child. A second, more general, paradigm holds that the unpleasant affect accompanying one's own painful past experiences is evoked by another person's distress cues which resemble the stimuli associated with the observer's own experiences. A simple example is the child who cuts himself, feels the pain, and cries. Later on, he sees another child cut himself and cry. The sight of the blood, the sound of the cry, or any other distress cue from the other child associated with the observer's own prior experience of pain can now elicit the unpleasant affect that was initially a part of that experience.[2] Because the process involved in the second paradigm is neither confined to early infancy nor limited to distress originating in physically communicated tensions, it opens up the possibility of a multiplicity of distress experiences with which the child can empathize.

EMPATHY AND ALTRUISM

The possible contribution of empathy to altruism has long been noted in the literature. In the 1920s Stern (1924) suggested that empathy contributes to such acts as attempting to comfort, help, or avenge a distressed person. Isaacs (1933) similarly viewed empathy as one root of reciprocity, the ability to take turns, and to cooperate through active sharing. And Anna Freud (1937), in discussing altruistic "surrender," saw the individual as projecting his own needs to others and then gaining vicarious gratification from his efforts to satisfy these needs. More recently it has been suggested that the parent's use of induction (discipline techniques that point out the harmful consequences of the child's act for others) contributes to moral development partly because it arouses empathy for the victim of the child's actions (M. L. Hoffman, 1963b, 1970, in press; M. L. Hoffman & Saltzstein, 1960, 1967; Saltzstein, Chap. 14). Aronfreed and Paskal (1965, 1966) have proposed a two-stage theory of empathy and altruism: Empathic distress results from observing another's distress in close temporal association with one's own experience of distress; the altruistic act is then acquired by observing another person's altruistic act in conjunction with the reduction of one's own empathic distress.

Most of these writers have stressed the affective and reinforcing properties of empathy, to the relative neglect of the cognitive. Since cognitive processes help determine how even the simplest emotion is experienced, the same must be true for a complex emotional experience such as empathy. It seems likely, for example, that the actor experiences not only the feelings but also some of the perceptions, thoughts, and wishes of the other person, as well as images of his own past distress and the actions of others who helped relieve it (these images may serve as cues to what might be done to help the other in the immediate situation). These cognitions may have obvious ramifications for altruistic motivation and action. More fundamentally, since it is a response to cues about the affective state of others, empathy must depend to a great extent on the actor's cognitive development, especially his level of self–other differentiation. We now turn to an examination of self–other differentiation, after which we will attempt to combine this differentiation with empathy to account for the development of altruistic motives.

Development of a Sense of the Other

The literature bearing on development of a sense of the other can be organized around three topics: attainment of object permanence in infancy; role taking, espe-cially in early childhood; and identity in later childhood and adolescence. Since our aim is a developmental synthesis of empathy and the sense of the other, we must estimate, within the limits of available data, the age at which each of these capabilities exists.

OBJECT PERMANENCE

To have a sense of the other means at the very least to be aware of the other's existence as a separate entity from the self. That the young infant lacks such awareness is indicated by Piaget's studies (1954) of object displacement. If, for example, a desired object is hidden behind a screen before the infant's eyes, he will before 6 months of age lose interest in it, as though it no longer existed. After that age he will typically remove the screen to obtain the hidden object. Not until 18 months, however, will the infant go after an object that has been *invisibly* displaced (i.e., first hidden in front of the child in a container, which is then hidden behind a screen and brought out empty after the object has been removed from it in the hidden place). From this pattern of behavior, Piaget and others infer that it is not until about 1½ years of age that the child shows true "object permanence," that is, a stable sense of the separate existence of physical objects even when they are outside his immediate perceptual field.

"Permanence" with respect to persons, more important for our purposes, appears to develop before object permanence (Fraiberg, 1969). The existence of stranger anxiety (Spitz, 1950) as early as 7 months suggests that at this age the child can carry an internal image of a preferred person, such as his mother, although a similar stimulus (e.g., another human face) is probably necessary to evoke the anxiety. S. M. Bell (1970) tested the child's ability to retrieve (1) a toy and (2) his actual mother when both had been visibly and invisibly displaced; Bell concluded that person permanence preceded object permanence by several months in most subjects. Early in the second year of life, then, the child has a sense of his mother—and perhaps other persons whom he values and interacts with frequently—as separate physical entities.

ROLE TAKING

Having attained a sense of the separate existence of persons, the child still has a highly limited sense of the other. He is bound up in his own point of view, which he regards as absolute: The world exists as he perceives it. According to Piaget (1932), it is not until about 7 or 8 years of age that this egocentrism begins to give way to the recognition that others have their own perspective. The research by and large supports Piaget's view. Its emphasis, however, has been heavily cognitive, dealing with the other person's perceptions and thoughts rather than with the other's affections and emotions. Furthermore, the tasks used often require the subject to utilize cognitive skills that may facilitate role taking at times, but not be critical to it. The result, as we shall see, may be an overestimation of the age at which the child becomes capable of role taking.

Consider first the studies of "perceptual role taking" (Flavell, 1968; Lovell, 1959; Piaget & Inhelder, 1956; Selman, 1971b). The procedures used in these studies are variants of the classic one devised by Piaget in which the child is seated facing a scale model of three mountains and tested for his ability to predict how the model would look to another child seated at various positions around it. In this type of task, the presence of the other person is incidental; the child could just as well be alone and asked what he would see if he were located elsewhere in the room. In other words, the skill tested bears on the child's conception of space and his competence in spatial relations—more specifically, the ability to imagine how things would look from different vantage points.[3] This ability is not necessary for assessing another's inner state except when such an assessment is dependent on visual stimuli to which the other, but not the observer, is exposed. In short, the tasks in the studies of spatial perspective shifting involve a cognitive skill which may contribute to role taking under certain conditions, but is not an essential part of it.

In other role-taking studies the subject is asked to communicate a message to someone whose perspective is deficient in some respect; the receiver is, for example, much younger than the subject or handicapped by being blindfolded (Chandler & Greenspan, 1972; Flavell, 1968). In a representative study by Flavell (1968), the child is shown an ordered series of seven pictures which tell a story in comic-strip fashion. After the child has narrated the story, the experimenter removes three of the pictures, leaving a four-picture sequence that illustrates a very different story. A second experimenter then enters the room, and the subject is told that this person has never seen the pictures before. The subject's task is to predict the story he thinks the newcomer will tell on the basis of having seen only the set of four pictures. One could attribute the failure of younger children on this task to their inability to keep the details of both stories separately in mind rather than to their inability to shed their own previously formed perspective and adopt the other person's fresh and naive one. The picture-sequence task thus appears to be primarily a cognitive one; and, as with the spatial tasks described previously, the subject can give the correct response without actually attending to the other person and making inferences about his perspective.

There is a small body of research dealing directly with the ability to infer another person's emotions in different situations. Borke (1971), for example, told 3- to 8-year-old children stories in which the main character might be perceived as happy, sad, afraid, or angry. Based on her finding that even the youngest children could correctly differentiate between happy and unhappy responses in the story characters, Borke concluded that children as young as 3 years of age are able to adopt the point of view of another, and consequently cannot be described as egocentric. Borke's conclusion may be questioned in light of an earlier study by Burns and Cavey (1957) which found that 3- and 4-year-old children who were shown pictures in which a child's facial expression was incongruent with the situation tended to overlook the incongruity and to respond in terms of how they would feel in the situation. This finding suggests that young children cannot assess another's emotional state when it differs from their own, although the measure Burns and Cavey used may have been too cognitively demanding to provide a true test of this ability.

To summarize, the dominant focus of the role-taking research has been on the cognitive aspects of the other person's perspective, and the tasks used typically put a premium on cognitive and verbal skills. When cognitive or verbal operations beyond the child's capacity are required, his actual role-taking capability may be masked. It follows that to estimate how early in life the child can take another's role requires evidence from studies employing measures that are minimally complex cognitively; thus far only Selman's measure (1971b) comes even close to this ideal. Selman's subjects were given a simple concept-sorting task and asked to predict what choices would be made on a similar task by another child from whom one of the test items had been hidden. Nearly all 6-year-old subjects could perform the task, while younger subjects did poorly. The question may be asked, however, whether younger children would show evidence of role taking in tasks requiring even less cognitive processing—for example, where the child already has the information necessary for assessing the other person's thoughts and feelings in the situation and is maximally motivated. To

provide a tentative answer, we must draw on anecdotal evidence in natural settings familiar to the child.

Although Flavell concludes from his research that the budding awareness of perspective differences does not occur until about age 6, he gives several anecdotal examples of cognitive role taking in 4- and 5-year-olds. An incident which I observed involved a still younger child. Marcy, aged 20 months, was in the playroom of her home and wanted a toy that her sister Sara was playing with. She asked Sara for it, but Sara refused vehemently. Marcy then paused, as if reflecting on what to do, and then began rocking Sara's favorite rocking horse (which Sara never allowed anyone to touch), yelling "Nice horsey! Nice horsey!" and keeping her eyes on Sara all the time. Sara came running angrily, whereupon Marcy immediately ran around Sara directly to the toy and grabbed it. Without analyzing the full complexity of Marcy's behavior, one can infer from her actions that she had deliberately lured her sister away from the toy. Though not yet 2 years of age, Marcy was capable of being aware of another person's inner states that were different from her own. While her behavior was Machiavellian rather than altruistic, this child demonstrated that she could take another's role. Yet had she been a subject in the experiments discussed previously, it is doubtful that she could have understood the instructions, much less performed the designated role-taking response.

The final example is in some respects less dramatic and depicts a cognitively less demanding behavior, but the child was only 15 months old and the context is more germane to our altruistic concerns. The boy, Michael, was struggling with his friend, Paul, over a toy. Paul started to cry. Michael appeared concerned and let go of the toy so that Paul would have it, but Paul kept crying. Michael paused, then gave his teddy bear to Paul, but the crying continued. Michael paused again, then ran to the next room, returned with

Paul's security blanket, and offered it to Paul, who then stopped crying. Several aspects of this incident deserve comment. First, it does seem clear that Michael assumed that his own teddy, which often comforts him, would also comfort his friend. Second, its failure to do this served as corrective feedback, which led Michael to consider alternatives. Third, in considering the processes underlying Michael's final, successful act, three possibilities stand out: (1) he was simply imitating an effective instrumental act observed in the past; that is, he had observed Paul being comforted with the blanket. This can be tentatively ruled out, since Michael's parents could not recall his ever having such an opportunity. (2) In trying to think of what to do, he remembered seeing another child being soothed by a blanket, and this reminded him of Paul's blanket— a more complex response than might first appear, since Paul's blanket was out of Michael's perceptual field at the time. (3) Michael, as young as he was, could somehow reason by analogy that Paul could be comforted by something that he loved in the same way that Michael loved his own teddy.

I favor the last interpretation, although it does postulate a complex response for a young child. Regardless of which, if any, of the three explanations is correct, the incident suggests that a child not yet 1½ years of age may be able, with the help of a very general form of corrective feedback[4] (Paul's continuing to cry when offered Michael's teddy), to assess another's specific needs that differ from his own. The same conclusion may be drawn from a strikingly similar incident recently reported by Borke (1972). This age is a far cry from the 5 or 6 years suggested by the laboratory research—a discrepancy too large to be explained strictly in terms of Michael's precocity.

In conclusion, it appears that just as person permanence may precede object permanence by several months, certain forms of role taking in familiar and highly motivating natural settings may precede the more complex forms investigated in the laboratory by several years. The child who can take the role of a familiar person at home may behave egocentrically in complex role-taking tasks in the laboratory because he cannot utilize the available cues regarding the inner states of others and must therefore rely on his own perspective. In other words, the rudiments of role-taking competence may be present before the child is 2 years old (not long after he has attained person permanence), although role-taking performance varies with the cognitive and verbal complexity of the particular task.

AWARENESS OF IDENTITY

The sense of the other as having his own personal identity, that is, his own life circumstances and inner states beyond the immediate situation, has been largely ignored in the literature. The conception closest to it is Erikson's concept (1950) of ego identity, which pertains to the individual's own sense of sameness through time. Erikson's view is supported by the likelihood that at some point the child develops the cognitive capacity to integrate his own discrete inner experiences over time, and to form a conception of himself as having different feelings and thoughts in different situations, but still remaining the same continuous person with one past, present, and anticipated future.

Research by Kohlberg (1966) suggests when this awareness of identity develops. He asked 4- to 8-year-old children if a pictured girl who wanted to be a boy could be one if she played boys' games or if she wore boys' haircuts or clothes. Kohlberg (1966) found that "by age 6 to 7, most children were quite certain that a girl could not be a boy regardless of changes in appearance or behavior" (p. 95)—in contrast to younger children, who were often thrown off by physical appearances and thought that girls could become boys by altering their appearance. This finding suggests that the child has a sense of stabilization and continuity regarding gender by about 6 or 7 years of age.

The findings on racial identity are similar. Proshansky (1966), after reviewing the research literature, concluded that a firm sense of one's racial identity does not appear to be established until about 7 or 8 years of age. Finally, Guardo and Bohan (1971), in a developmental study of self-identity in middle-class white children, found that 6- and 7-year-olds recognize their identity as humans and as males or females mainly in terms of their names, physical appearance, and behaviors—a finding that is consistent with the results for gender and racial identity. These children's sense of self-continuity from the past and into the future was still hazy, however. It was not until 8 or 9 years of age that more covert and personalized differences in feelings and attitudes made a contribution to these subjects' sense of identity—although even then most felt that their names, physical characteristics, and behaviors were the essential anchorage points of identity.

Sometime between 6 and 9 years, then, the child's conception of his own continuing identity appears to begin. This emerging sense of identity may be presumed to result by early adolescence in a broadening of his view of others. Once he has the cognitive capacity to see that his own life has coherence and continuity despite the fact that he reacts differently in different situations, the individual should soon be able to do the same with regard to others. He can then not only take the role of others and assess their reactions in particular situations but also generalize from these interactions and construct a concept of others' general life experiences. In sum, his awareness that others are coordinate with himself expands to include the notion that they, like himself, have their own identity as persons, which goes beyond the immediate situation. His perspective on others and his interpretation of their response in the immediate situation are thereby dramatically altered.

Development of Altruistic Motives: A Theory of Synthesis

The foregoing analyses of empathy and a sense of the other provide needed background for the following theory of altruistic motivation, which is essentially a developmental account of the synthesis of these affective and cognitive capacities.

EMPATHIC DISTRESS

Developmentally first is empathic distress. As discussed previously, this kind of empathy is very likely a conditioned affective response based on the similarity between distress cues from someone else in the immediate situation and elements of one's own actual distress experiences in the past. The neural capacity necessary for such a response is minimal, since both classical and operant conditioning are known to be possible in the early weeks of life (e.g., Kessen, Haith, & Salapatek, 1970). It follows that the infant is capable of empathic distress long before he has developed a sense of self or a sense of the other.

As a result of this lack of self–other differentiation, the child for at least most of the first year is presumably unclear as to who is experiencing any distress that he witnesses, and he will often behave as though he were experiencing it. That is, he sees the other's distress cues, and they automatically evoke an upset state in him. This global empathic distress includes unpleasant feelings which he wishes would terminate, and perhaps also images of his own and others' acts that would relieve or comfort him because they have comforted him in the past. He may then seek comfort for his own distress. This was recently illustrated by an 11-month-old child of a student of mine. On seeing another child fall and cry, she first stared at the victim, appeared as though she were about to cry herself, and then put her thumb in her mouth and buried her head in her mother's lap—her typical response after *she* has hurt herself and needs comforting.

This is obviously a very primitive response. We use the word *empathy* to describe it, but the child does not really put himself in the other's place and try to imagine what he is feeling. The child's response is rather a conditioned, passive, involuntary one based on the pull of surface cues associated with elements of his own past. If there is action, its dominant motivation is hedonistic—to eliminate discomfort in the self. Nevertheless, empathic distress is basic in the early development of altruistic motivation precisely because its occurrence shows that we may involuntarily and forcefully experience others' emotional states rather than only the emotional states pertinent and appropriate to our own situation—that we are built in such a way that distress will often be contingent not on our own, but on someone else's painful experience.

SYMPATHETIC DISTRESS

A major change in the child's reaction to distress occurs when he becomes capable of distinguishing between himself and others. When confronted with another person in pain, he still experiences empathic distress, but because of this new cognitive capacity he will now know that the other person, not himself, is in actual pain. The recognition that the other is actually experiencing the distress transforms the empathy *with* the victim, a parallel affective response, into sympathetic concern *for* the victim, a more reciprocal response. This is not to deny that the response may continue to have a purely empathic component, or that the child may also fear that the undesired event will happen to him. The important thing, however, is that

the quasi-hedonistic motive to alleviate the child's own distress ("I want to get rid of my distress") gives way, at least in part, to the more prosocial motive to alleviate the other's distress ("I want to get rid of his distress"); and this prosocial motive is a new addition to the child's repertoire. The transformation of empathic into sympathetic distress occurs in three stages, which are tied to the three levels of cognitive apprehension of the other: permanence, role taking, and identity. The three stages of sympathetic distress—each stage defined in terms of the synthesis of empathic distress and a cognitive level—will now be descirbed. Following this an attempt will be made to probe more deeply into the transition between empathic and sympathetic distress.

Empathic distress and person permanence. At the level of person permanence the child has acquired a sense of the other only as a physical entity. He knows that the other is the victim, and his empathic reaction is transformed by this knowledge into a genuine concern for the other. But he cannot yet distinguish between his own and the other's inner states (thoughts, perceptions, needs). Without thinking about it, he automatically assumes that the other's states are identical to his own. Consequently, although he can sense the other's distress, he does not understand what caused it nor does he know what the other's needs are in the situation (except when they happen to coincide with his own). This lack of understanding is often evidenced in the child's efforts to help, which consist chiefly of giving the other what he himself finds most comforting. In the example cited earlier, Michael's initial attempt to placate his friend is a case in point. I have also heard a description of a 13-month-old child who brought his own mother to comfort a crying friend, even though the latter's mother was equally available, and of another child the same age who offered his beloved doll to comfort an adult who looked sad. (At this age the child's helping behavior may sometimes be quite transitory, and the next moment he may strike the person he was just comforting.)

This first level of sympathetic distress is in some ways as primitive as the empathic distress described earlier—a passive, involuntary, and sometimes grossly inaccurate and transitory response to cues perceptually similar to those associated with the child's own past distress. It is a significant advance, however, since for the first time the child experiences a desire to help the other, though his effort to do so may be misguided because of his cognitive limitations. This motive to help is aroused by the awareness of someone in distress, although its qualitative aspects—including the conception of the nature and intensity of the other's distress and the type of action needed to relieve it—will depend on the child's level of cognitive development.

Empathic distress and role taking. At the second developmental level of sympathetic distress, the child has begun to acquire a sense of others not only as physical entities but also as sources of feelings and thoughts in their own right. That is, he is no longer certain that the real world and his perception of it are the same thing. He has begun to realize that others may have inner states that differ from his own, as well as different perspectives based on their own needs and interpretations of events, although he may be uncertain what their perspectives actually are. This advance, as mentioned in the discussion of role taking, is very likely the result of the child's cognitive development combined with experiences in which his expectations that others have identical inner states are disconfirmed by corrective feedback from them.

The awareness that the other has inner states independent of his own has profound effects on the nature of the child's response to distress. Though the affective distress aroused in him remains essentially the same, and though he may continue to project his own feelings on the victim as in the past, these reactions are now only part of a more conscious orientation to the other's state. The child is, moreover, aware of the guesswork involved and therefore uses other inputs besides his own empathic distress in formulating an idea of the other's needs and feelings—inputs such as specific information about which acts will alleviate the other's distress and which will not. Initially he may engage in trial and error based on his own past experience and then, like Michael in the example discussed earlier, alter his behavior in response to corrective feedback in the situation. Eventually the trial and error and reality testing take place internally, and external feedback is no longer needed except perhaps in new and complex situations.

For the first time in our developmental account, then, the child begins to make an active effort to put himself in the other's place, although he remains aware of the tentative and hypothetical nature of the inference he makes. He has now achieved genuine role-taking. His motivation to relieve the other person's distress is far less egocentric than before and it is based to a far greater degree on a veridical assessment of the other's needs. As a result, his attempts to help are more sophisticated and appropriate.

Empathic distress and identity. Despite this obvious progress, the child's response at the second level of sympathetic distress is still confined to the other's distress in the immediate situation. This deficiency is overcome at the third level, owing to a significant new input: the child's emerging conception of others, as well as of himself, as continuous persons with their own histories and identities. By the time he has reached the preadolescent years, the child is presumably fully aware that others react with feelings of pleasure and pain, not only in immediate situations but also within the context of their larger pattern of life experiences. He continues to react to others' momentary distress, but feels worse when he knows it is chronic. He may also imagine their repeated experiences of distress, even when these are not reflected in the immediate situation. In sum, being aware that others have inner states and a separate existence beyond the immediate situation enables the individual to respond not only to their transitory, situation-specific, distress but also to what he imagines to be their general condition. (The transitory and the general are ordinarily consonant, but when they conflict the individual's response will be determined by the latter, since it is the more inclusive, and hence more compelling, index of the other's welfare. An exception to this rule is when the cues of the transitory are far more salient than those of the general.)

This third level of sympathetic distress, then, consists of the synthesis of empathic distress and a mental representation of the other's *general* plight—that is, his typical day-to-day level of distress or deprivation, the opportunities available or denied to him, his future prospects, and the like. If this representation of the other falls short of what the observer conceives to be a minimally acceptable standard of well-being (and if the observer's own life circumstances place himself above this standard), this third level of the sympathetic distress response will typically be evoked, regardless of the other's apparent momentary state.

To summarize thus far, the individual who progresses through these three stages may reach the point of being capable of a high level of sympathetic response to another person in distress. He can process all levels of information—including that gained through his own empathic reaction, immediate situational cues, and general knowledge about the other's life. He can act out in his own mind the emotions and experiences suggested by these sources of information, and introspect on all of this. He may thus gain an understanding of the

circumstances, feelings, and wishes of the other, have feelings of concern for him, and wish to help—while all the time maintaining the sense that the other is a separate person from himself.

With further cognitive development the person may acquire the capacity to comprehend the plight not only of an individual but also of an entire group or class of people to whom he is exposed, such as those who are economically impoverished, politically oppressed, socially outcast, victimized by war, or mentally retarded. Since the observer is part of a different group, his own distress experiences may not be quite like those of the less fortunate group. All distress experiences have much in common, however; and by this stage the individual has the capacity to generalize from one distress experience to another. It may therefore be assumed that most people have the cognitive and affective requisites for a generalized empathic distress (although the salience of others' misfortune may be necessary to activate this capacity). Possible exceptions are people whose socialization has rendered them incapable of empathy, or whose status in life has permitted only the most superficial contact with less fortunate people (consider Marie Antoinette's apocryphal "Let them eat cake" in response to the peasants' clamoring for bread). In any case, the synthesis of empathic distress and the perceived plight of an unfortunate group results in the developmentally most advanced form of sympathetic distress.[5]

TRANSFORMATION OF EMPATHIC DISTRESS INTO SYMPATHETIC DISTRESS

A key assumption in this theoretical account is that with the development of a sense of the other, the child's self-oriented empathic distress is transformed into a true sympathetic concern for the other. The question may be asked, Why doesn't the child, once he realizes that the other is not actually in distress, simply feel relieved and ignore the other's plight? The answer requires a closer look at the transition between empathic and sympathetic distress.

As discussed previously, the child at first does not differentiate himself from others, and when he observes someone in distress he feels it is his own distress. He has unpleasant feelings that he wishes would terminate, and he may also imagine acts by others that will relieve or comfort him, perhaps because these acts have done so in the past. Since the young child experiences a global empathic distress which fuses his own feelings with his impressions of another, it seems reasonable to assume that his undifferentiated unpleasant feelings, wishes, and images would be subsequently transferred to both the separate "self" and the "other" which emerge from the global self later in development. That is, the properties of the whole become the properties of its emerging parts. As a consequence, the child's initial concern to relieve his own empathic distress becomes in part a sympathetic concern to relieve the distress of the other.

Second, the process of self–other differentiation is gradual and very likely subject to occasional regression, for example, when the child is fatigued or under tension. This means that in the early stages of differentiation he is only vaguely and momentarily aware of the other as distinct from the self. He must therefore go through a period of responding to another's distress by feeling as though his dimly perceived self and the dimly perceived other are somehow simultaneously—or perhaps alternately—in distress. That is, the self and the other slip in and out of focus as the person whose distress the child wishes to have terminated. Consider a colleague's child whose typical response to his own distress beginning late in his first year was to suck his thumb with one hand and pull his ear with the other. At 12 months, on seeing a sad look on his father's face, the child proceeded to look sad himself and to suck his thumb while pulling

his father's ear! An early period of subjectively overlapping concern such as this, in which the self and the other are experienced as "sharing" the distress, would seem to provide a further basis for a positive orientation toward the emerging other. The gradual nature of self–other differentiation is therefore important, because it gives the child the experience of simultaneously wanting to terminate the emerging other's distress as well as his own—thus providing a link between the initially hedonistic empathic distress response and the earliest trace of sympathetic distress. If the sense of the other were attained suddenly, the child would lack this experience; when he discovers that the pain is someone else's, he might simply react with relief (or even blame the other for his own empathic distress).

Though the child now responds with sympathetic distress, he is still egocentric; and his concern for the other may be due partly to his assumption that the other's inner states are the same as his own. When the child develops role-taking capabilities, the question that introduced this section may be reformulated as follows: Why should the child continue to be positively oriented toward others once he discovers that they are the sources of their own inner states? The reason I would advance is that in the course of discovering that others have their own internal reactions to situations, the child finds that although their reactions at times may differ from his, the differences are typically outweighed by the similarities. The role-taking literature, to be sure, stresses development of the capacity to grasp another's perspective when it differs from one's own. This is done only to make clear the nature of the child's progress away from egocentrism, however. In real life, when the child takes the perspective of others, he is apt to find that it is usually like his own except for minor variations. In the case discussed earlier, though Michael found out that he and his friend would want different comforting objects in the same situation, the basic feeling that he initially projected to his friend was shown by the final outcome to be veridical. That is, his assumption that his friend's basic emotional needs would be the same as his own was confirmed. Thus while moving away from the automatic, egocentric, assumption that the other's inner states are identical to his own, the child discovers both that others react as persons in their own right, and that their responses are often very similar to his own. The realization that his feelings resemble those experienced independently by others in similar situations must inevitably contribute to a sense of "oneness," which preserves and may even enhance the child's developing motivation to alleviate others' distress.

To summarize, there are three significant aspects of the child's early response to another's distress. These may account for the seemingly paradoxical notion that self–other differentiation, which might be expected to create a barrier between persons, and empathic distress, which is partially hedonistic, combine to produce the developmental basis for a motive to help others. Two of these aspects are manifest in the earliest stages of self–other differentiation: (1) the transfer of the unpleasant affect associated with the initial global "self" to its emerging separate parts (self and other) and (2) the subjective experience of "sharing" distress, which is due to the gradual attainment of a sense of the other and gives the child the experience of wishing the other's distress to end. The third aspect of the child's early response to another's distress, a growing awareness of the similarity between his own and the other's independent affective response to situations, occurs during the shift away from egocentrism.[6] When we add the fact that all children have the same basic nervous system, an increasing capacity for stimulus generalization on the basis of both conceptual and perceptual similarities, and many experiences in common during the long period of socialization, it

would appear that the human potential for a sense of oneness, empathy, and sympathy may well be enormous. The developmental synthesis of empathic distress and the cognitive sense of the other, postulated here, may thus be a fundamental fact of life for most individuals.

It should be noted that by *synthesis* we do not mean an instantaneous occurrence, but a reciprocal process in which the empathic and the cognitive enhance one another. Thus the empathically produced cues within the observer serve as one source of cognitive information about the other's state. The cognitive understanding of the other's state, on the other hand, may trigger, intensify, or give broader meaning to the observer's empathic response. Which of the two, cognitive or empathic, initiates the process of synthesis is presumably a function of personal style and the nature of the situation. Where there is close contact between observer and victim, the empathic response may be aroused prior to full comprehension of the victim's plight. In other situations, such as seeing a stranger drowning, cognitive comprehension may precede empathic distress.

THE ROLE OF COGNITIVE MEDIATION

Besides the central role that cognitive development plays in the transformation of empathic distress into the different forms of sympathetic distress, it also has an obvious mediational function throughout. The child's response initially is dependent on the physical similarity between cues of the other's distress and those associated with his own past distress. That is, he can respond only to visible types of distress such as cries over falls, cuts, bruises, and lost possessions. Further cognitive development enables him to respond on the basis of inferred as well as perceptual similarities, and verbal as well as physical expressions of distress—thus opening the door to a host of psychologically more subtle types of empathic distress such as those resulting from another's feelings of rejection and disappointment or his state of being unfulfilled. A growing capacity for cognitive mediation also enables the child to make inferences about another's distress on the basis of information about the other's life conditions, even when these differ from his own and the other person is not physically present. That is, knowing only the other's life condition may be sufficient for grasping his perspective and responding sympathetically. Finally, cognitive growth may eventually help the individual attain a generalized concept of distress experience which enables him to respond sympathetically to types of distress that he has not experienced himself.

The Relation between
Motives and Altruistic Action

The focus of this chapter is on motives; a full treatment of the relation between motives and action is beyond its scope. This topic cannot be ignored, however, since the importance of motives ultimately lies in their influence on behavior. The assumption implicit in our formulation is that motives do relate to action—that both empathic and sympathetic distress predispose the individual to act, though only in the latter case does he feel himself to be acting on the other's behalf. Developmentally, this means that as the child acquires coping skills, he will tend to use them in the service of these motives. At first, he simply enacts behaviors that have alleviated his own distress in the past, as exemplified in our earlier illustrations of empathic distress and the lowest level of sympathetic distress. Eventually he experiences doubt about the appropriateness of these acts for the other person; role taking and higher levels of cognitive processing begin to intervene between the motives and the act; and the child's response becomes more veridical in terms of

the victim's needs. Presumably there is also some feedback or reinforcement process throughout, whereby acts that successfully alleviate the other's distress are retained and repeated in the future. The corrective feedback which often follows unsuccessful, inappropriate acts may lead to trial and error or the operation of higher-level cognitive processes which in turn result in appropriate acts.

To date, there is only modest empirical support for the key point in this formulation—that sympathetic distress predisposes the person to act altruistically. In the intensive nursery school observations by Bridges (1931) and Murphy (1937), the younger children usually reacted to another in distress with a worried, anxious look but did nothing, presumably because of fear or lack of necessary skills. Had they been in the familiar surroundings of the home, however, these subjects might have responded more actively, as the 20-month-old son of a colleague did when a visiting friend, about to leave, burst into tears complaining that her parents were not home (they were away for two weeks). His immediate reaction was to look sad, but then he offered her his beloved teddy bear to take home. His parents immediately reminded him that he would miss the teddy if he gave it away, but he insisted—as if his sympathetic distress were greater than the anticipated unpleasantness of not having the teddy. His insistence may be indicative of the strong motivational potential of sympathetic distress.

In any event, Murphy (1937) found that for older children sympathetic distress was usually accompanied by an overt helpful act. The laboratory studies by N. D. Feshbach and Roe (1968) and Staub (1970a) also suggest that preschool and older children typically react to another child's distress with both sympathy and attempts to help. Finally, several other studies cited earlier, when considered as a group, provide evidence for a similar association between altruistic motivation and behavior in adults. Witnessing another person being shocked or failing in a task typically results in both an affective reaction, as measured physiologically, and an overt attempt to help (Berger, 1962; Craig & Weinstein, 1965; D. L. Krebs, 1970b; Stotland, 1969; Tomes, 1964; R. F. Weiss et al., 1973). In a similar study, DiLollo and Berger (1965) found that exposure to the pain cues of a victim in a simulated shock experiment resulted in a decrease in reaction time for a button-pushing response. Though this was not a helping response, the finding supports the idea that the individual's affective response to another's distress is accompanied by an overt response tendency.

It would appear, then, that sympathetic distress is accompanied by tendencies toward helpful action. Whether it motivates or is merely associated with the action is uncertain, although there is some evidence in one of Murphy's empirical generalizations (1937) that it may motivate: "As verbal and physical techniques develop to the point where the child can cope with a large portion of the varied situations to which he is exposed, an active response (to help) occurs and there is less likelihood of prolonged affective response" (p. 300). Thus when the child overtly helps the other, the affective portion of his sympathetic distress diminishes; when he does not help, the affect is prolonged. This applies both developmentally (more action and less affect with age) and within the same child at a given age. Latané and Darley (1968) found something similar with adults: Subjects who helped a person who seemed to be having an epileptic fit showed less emotion afterwards than those who did not help. These findings are all consistent with the notion that sympathetic distress predisposes the person to act; acting reduces the sympathetic distress, whereas inaction does not."[7]

Though sympathetic distress may predispose the child to act altruistically, it does not guarantee that he will act. Whether the child acts depends on other things besides the strength and developmental level of the altruistic motive. Action is more likely when the appropriate thing to do is obvious and within the person's repertoire, and less likely when there is little that he can do. The costs to the observer and the strength of competing motives aroused in him by the situation must also be taken into account. In an individualistic society such as ours, for example, altruistic motives may often be overridden by more powerful egoistic motives. Our society, moreover, often sends out mixed messages about altruism. Though encouraged by our traditional religions, for example, altruism is often suspect, regarded as serving the actor's egoistic needs to feel superior to the other, or viewed as an invasion of the other's privacy or a sign of insensitivity to his need to help himself. Finally, as noted by M. L. Hoffman (1970a) and Staub (1970a), American children are often socialized to behave altruistically and to follow the rules; but in some situations following the rules will interfere with altruistic action. In such a society altruistic motives may well have a reliable effect on behavior only in situations in which one encounters someone in distress and is not preoccupied with himself or subject to conflicting social norms.

Pending clarification in future research, I would suggest the following formulation of the relationship between altruistic motives and action. Distress cues from another person trigger the altruistic motive-and-response system. That is, the observer experiences sympathetic distress and his initial tendency is to act. If he does not act—because of situational counterpressures, competing motives, lack of necessary skills, or whatever other reasons —he will typically either continue to experience sympathetic distress or to cognitively restructure the situation to justify his own inaction, for example, by derogating the victim or otherwise convincing himself that the victim wanted or deserved what he got.

Guilt and Reparative Altruism

Thus far nothing has been said about what happens when the observer sees himself as the cause of the other's distress. Blaming oneself becomes possible once one has acquired the cognitive capacity to recognize the consequences of his action for others and to be aware that he has choice and control over his own behavior.[8] The combination of sympathetic distress with an awareness of being the cause of another's distress may be called *guilt*, since it has both the affectively unpleasant and cognitive self-blaming components of the guilt experience.

Personal or true guilt may be experienced directly as the result of commission (things the person did) or omission (things the person did not do which might have helped the other). This type of guilt, which has been found to relate to parental discipline (M. L. Hoffman, 1970a; M. L. Hoffman & Saltzstein, 1960, 1967), differs from the psychoanalytic conception of guilt. The latter is based not so much on the actual harm done to others as on the transformation of anxiety over loss of parental love into self-blame, and the direction of unsuccessfully repressed hostile impulses toward the self (see J. Gilligan, Chap. 8). Actually, little is known about the development of the guilt response. Though Murphy (1937) reports numerous instances of sympathetic distress in preschool children, she found few examples of guilt or reparative behavior. Harming others usually occurred in the context of a fight or argument, and the victim was typically helped by a bystander rather than the aggressor. In the few instances of accidental harm, however, the responsible child was sympathetic or made some spontaneous attempt at reparation. A boy on a swing who knocked a girl down, for example, gave her a long ride on the swing afterwards, pushing her gently all the while. Such instances suggest that young children are capable of an im-

mediate awareness and reaction to the harmful effects of their own behavior. There is also indirect evidence that their reaction may extend beyond the immediate situation: Children exposed to parental discipline which pointed to the harmful effects of their behavior were generally considerate of their nursery school peers (M. L. Hoffman, 1963b).[9]

Most of the 10- to 12-year-old subjects in our moral development research (M. L. Hoffman, in press; M. L. Hoffman & Saltzstein, 1967), some of which is unpublished, gave guilt responses to projective story completion items in which the transgression committed by the central figure was an act of commission (cheating, accidentally harming another) or omission (not helping a small child who later suffered as a result). In most cases the guilt feelings described by our subjects were followed immediately by the attribution to the story character of some sort of reparative behavior, which functioned to reduce his guilt. When reparation was precluded by the story conditions (it was too late for anything to be done), the guilt response was typically prolonged. (This pattern is similar to Murphy's finding, 1937, that sympathetic distress typically leads to action that diminishes the actor's affect, but if there is no action the affect is prolonged.) The central figures in the story were also often portrayed by our subjects as resolving to become less selfish and more considerate of others in the future. This suggests that one mechanism by which guilt may contribute to altruistic behavior is to trigger a process of self-examination and restructuring of values which may help strengthen one's altruistic motives.

Experimental evidence that guilt contributes to altruism has been obtained in a number of studies in which adults who were led to believe they had harmed someone showed a heightened willingness to help others. They did this by engaging in various altruistic deeds such as volunteering to participate in a research project

(Freedman, Wallington, & Bless, 1967), contributing to a charitable fund (J. W. Regan, 1971), and spontaneously offering to help a passerby whose grocery bag had broken (D. T. Regan, Williams, & Sparling, 1972). These studies are limited, since they showed only short-run effects (the altruistic deed immediately followed the guilt induction), and the subjects were all college students. Together with the story completion data for children, however, these studies support the view that guilt may result in a generalized motive for altruistic action beyond immediate reparation to the victim.

The fact that 10-year-olds in the M. L. Hoffman study (in press) show evidence of guilt over inaction is worthy of note. The central figure in the story completion items has really done nothing wrong but just happened to be present when someone needed help, and children are not often taught to feel bad over such inaction. I would suggest that the guilt the subjects projected was due to their sympathetic distress response to the victim, in combination with an awareness of what the central figure (with whom they identified) might have done to help were it not for his selfishness. Guilt over inaction thus appears to have much in common with sympathetic distress—the difference being that the observer is aware of something he could have done. Guilt over inaction is also very likely more advanced developmentally than guilt over the actual commission of an act, since the former requires the capacity to visualize something that might have been done but was not.

EXISTENTIAL GUILT

The human capacity for experiencing guilt even when no wrong has been done is illustrated still more dramatically in other situations. The well-known phenomenon of survivor guilt in natural disasters and in war is a case in point. A recent example is the Navy pilot whose right arm had been partially crippled by shrapnel, who said on being released after two years as a Vietnam war prisoner, "Getting released, you feel a tremendous amount of guilt. You developed a relationship with the other prisoners . . . and they're still there and you're going away" (*Newsweek*, 1972, p. 27).

This remark suggests that despite a person's own plight, he may feel guilty if he feels he is far better off than others. This possibility contrasts interestingly with "social comparison processes" (e.g., Festinger, 1954; Masters, 1972b), which focus on self–other comparisons in a competitive context, for example, the enhancement of one's self-esteem that may result from outperforming others. Keniston (1968) very neatly captures the essence of guilt over being relatively advantaged when he describes his sample of affluent young social activists of the mid-1960s as stressing "their shock upon realizing that their own good fortune was not shared . . . and their indignation when they 'really' understood that the benefits they had experienced had not been extended to others" (pp. 131–132). One of Keniston's respondents, in discussing some poor Mexican children he had known years earlier, vividly described his realization of relative advantage in a way that suggests its possible role in altruistic action.

. . . I was the one that lived in a place where there were fans and no flies, and they lived with the flies. And I was clearly destined for something, and they were destined for nothing. . . . Well, I sort of made a pact with these people that when I got to be powerful I might change some things. And I think I pursued that pact pretty consistently for a long time (p. 50).

I call this reaction existential guilt to distinguish it from true guilt, since the person has done nothing wrong but feels culpable because of circumstances of life beyond his control.

Existential guilt may take on some of the qualities of true guilt, however. The activist youth in Keniston's sample, for example, appears to have concluded that his privileged position makes it possible for him to do something to alleviate the condition of the less fortunate, and that if he does nothing he becomes personally responsible for helping perpetuate the conditions he deplores. For some individuals existential guilt may shade still further into a sense of individual complicity or true personal guilt, should they come to view the other's plight as due to the action of people with whom they identify, for example, parents or members of their social class.

Another example of existential guilt shading into true guilt comes from the response given by a Congressional intern to the question, Why are so many middle-class youth turned off by the very system which gave them so many advantages and opportunities?

They feel guilty because while they are enjoying this highest standard of living, American Indians are starving and black ghettoes are overrun by rats. . . . This goes on while they eat steak every day. Their sense of moral indignation can't stand this; and they realize that the blame rests on the shoulders of their class (*New Republic*, Nov. 28, 1970, p. 11).

The statements and actions of some of the white radicals of the 1960s suggest that existential guilt may at times be a far more potent motivating force than the simpler type of true personal guilt discussed earlier. Existential guilt may require continued activity in the service of alleviating human suffering rather than merely a discrete act of restitution in order to afford one a continuing sense of self-worth.[10] It also seems likely, as with true guilt, that the person who does nothing will continue to feel guilty, or will cognitively restructure the situation so as to justify himself or to deny his own relative advantage ("The other has other pleasures and enjoys living the way he does"; "He is a bad person and brought his misfortune on himself"; "I worked hard for what I have").

Another alternative may be to reduce the relative advantage by renouncing one's privileges or in other ways "identifying with the lowly." This alternative may take on the character of pure self-punishment and cease to be altruism. Indeed, for some individuals existential guilt may be an obstacle to the development of personal competence, achievement, and success. A recent study of achievement and fear-of-success motives (L. W. Hoffman, 1974) provides a possible illustration of this phenomenon. Horner's projective story cue (1968), "John finds himself at the top of his medical school class," drew the following response from a male college student: "John is perplexed upon hearing the news. He's mad that everything is so assured. Resents the fact that he's hereditarily good and others are not." If this response really does reflect guilt over competence and is representative, it might mean that existential guilt is contributing to the erosion of the competitive, individualistic ethic in the affluent highly educated group in which this ethic has traditionally been foremost.[11]

GUILT AND SYMPATHETIC DISTRESS

Though guilt and sympathetic distress differ, the preceding analysis suggests that these affective states at times overlap and enhance one another. Developmentally, guilt probably also relates to the levels of sympathetic distress discussed earlier. Thus at the second level (synthesis of empathy and role taking), the child will experience sympathetic distress when he is not responsible for the other's plight. When he is responsible for the other's distress, however, his sympathetic distress will be transformed into guilt feelings. With further cognitive development, this transformation can result from the awareness of not helping when one might reasonably have been expected to help. Eventually, with the capability of foreseeing the consequences of action and inaction, anticipatory guilt also becomes a possibility. From then on sympathetic distress may always be accompanied by some guilt, except when the situation clearly rules out the possibility of helpful action. In line with this analysis,

83 percent of the subjects in the Schwartz· study (1970b) who volunteered to contribute blood marrow said afterwards that they would have felt guilty or self-critical if they had not volunteered.

Similarly, at the highest level of sympathetic distress, if the focus of concern shifts from the other's general plight to the discrepancy between it and the observer's relatively advantaged state (in the absence of moral justification), sympathetic distress may be transformed into existential guilt. Since this comparison requires "decentering," in Piaget's sense of cognitively processing two aspects of an event simultaneously, existential guilt may be developmentally more advanced than sympathetic distress. Furthermore, once the capacity for this dual self–other perspective is attained, there is no reason to believe it will be abandoned in subsequent observations of unfortunate people. Existential guilt may then become part of all future experiences of sympathetic distress.

To summarize, (1) sympathetic distress is both a necessary developmental prerequisite and a continuing part of the guilt response; (2) guilt is the synthesis of sympathetic distress and of the awareness of one's blame or relative advantage; (3) once the capacity for guilt over inaction and relative advantage is attained, guilt may be part of all subsequent responses to another's distress in situations where one thinks that he might have helped the other or that he is relatively advantaged without justification. Guilt may therefore be important in any theoretical account of altruism which stresses sympathetic distress.

Implications for Socialization: Several Hypotheses

The theory presented here, that altruistic motives develop out of the synthesis of empathic distress and the child's increasingly sophisticated cognitive sense of the other, is essentially a theory of a naturally evolving process. Under normal conditions of growing up everyone acquires the capacity for sympathetic distress, assuming he is sufficiently secure emotionally to be open to the needs of others. The child's socialization experiences may nevertheless play an important role by strengthening or weakening the child's natural empathic tendencies, shaping his developing attitudes toward others, and placing more or less stress on competing motives which may neutralize the altruistic. Though peripheral to this chapter, three hypotheses about socialization that derive directly from the theory will be briefly presented in the hope that they will stimulate needed research. They are:

1. Sensitivity to the needs and feelings of others may be fostered by allowing the child to have the normal run of distress experiences, rather than shielding him from them, so as to provide a broad base for empathic and sympathetic distress in the early years.

2. Providing the child with opportunities for role taking and for giving help and responsible care to others—these with corrective feedback when he is unable to interpret available cues—should foster both sympathetic distress and awareness of the other's perspective, as well as the integration of the two.

3. Encouraging the child to imagine himself in the other's place, and pointing out the similarities as well as differences between him and others, may also make a significant contribution to the development of altruism.

Another hypothesis is that development of altruistic motives is enhanced when the child is exposed for a long time to loved models (parents) who behave altruistically and communicate their own thoughts and feelings as well as the presumed inner states of the persons they are helping. A special case is the model of consideration displayed by the parent in relation to the child (for example, the willingness, within limits, to accept inconvenience for the sake of the child and in other ways show consideration for his needs).[12] To make altruism salient in the child's life, the model should also communicate a general and deep concern with the moral and ethical dimensions of life within the family and outside it (for example, in handling such issues as playing with unpopular children). Parents should make it clear that desired behavior in any situation can be deduced from broad principles concerning human kindness and consideration.

Since encounters with another in distress often involve conflict between the needs of the actor and the other, the child's prior experience in conflict situations, especially with peers, must play an important role in the development of altruistic motives. Does he emerge from these situations with little understanding of the other's point of view and the feeling that differences between him and the other are irreconcilable; or does he emerge with greater understanding of the other as an entity like himself having similar feelings and needs, and with the recognition that differences can be worked out mutually? The outcome of a child's conflict ex-

perience depends in part on how the conflicts are handled by parents and other socialization agents (Hoffman, 1975).

Socialization can also foster personality characteristics which may be important in certain situations in converting a disposition to help into action. Courage and autonomy, for example, may be crucial when altruism requires taking the initiative in the absence of group support (London, 1970). Children may also be trained in specific ways of aiding others in non–conflict situations by appeals to motives such as mastery and autonomy ("Big boys help others") or by pointing out positive consequences of the child's acts for the recipient ("Now he feels good"). Finally, direct reinforcement of altruistic behavior may make a positive contribution, although total reliance on this approach would presumably have the effect of making subsequent altruistic action dependent on the continuation of reinforcement.

Future research has the vital task of determining the combinations of experiences that will develop a person who both feels compassion for his fellow human beings and acts upon it.

Chapter 7. Empathy, Role Taking, Guilt, and Development of Altruistic Motives

[1] This paper was prepared in conjunction with grant HD-02258 from the National Institute of Child Health and Human Development. It is an expansion of a paper presented initially at the NICHHD Workshop "The Development of Motivation in Childhood" in Elkridge, Maryland, 1972 and, in revised form, at the meeting of the American Psychological Association Honolulu, 1972.

[2] Once a person has experienced it, empathic distress may be elicited subsequently as a secondary conditioned affective response to distress cues. This possibility contributes an additional component to future experiences of empathic distress.

[3] Furthermore, the complexity of the tasks varies, and this affects the results. Thus Selman (1971) found perceptual role taking in 5-year-olds whereas Piaget and Inhelder (1956) did not find it before age 8 or 9. This discrepancy is probably due to the fact that shortly before administering the task Selman showed the subjects the entire experimental setup, in the course of which they undoubtedly had the opportunity to view the stimulus materials from the same vantage point as the other child. As a result their estimate of the latter's perception may have been aided by short-term memory. Piaget and Inhelder's subjects lacked such an opportunity and thus had to rely entirely on their imagination in constructing what the other child would perceive.

[4] The amount of feedback needed varies with the child's developmental level. A less mature child than Michael would require more specific and direct feedback, which may contribute to his very first stirrings of awareness that people's perspectives and needs differ. A more mature child requires less feedback, and at some point can supply his own; though his first tendency might still be to attribute his needs to the other person, he may correct himself internally before acting. Eventually the entire feedback process is short-circuited, the person's initial response tendency being based on a more veridical interpretation of the other person's state. Even the fully mature person may project his own perspective, however, if he lacks the necessary information. But this projection will be done with the advance expectation of corrective feedback—an expectation lacking in a young child like Michael.

In a recent laboratory study of communicative role taking (Peterson, Danner, & Flavell, 1972), 4-year-olds readily reformulated their initial messages when explicitly requested to do so by the listener, but they failed to do so in response to nonverbal, facial expressions of listener incomprehension and implicit verbal requests for additional help, such as "I don't understand."

[5] The plight of the group and of the individual are often consonant. When they conflict, the group's plight will ordinarily be more compelling, since group well-being is the more inclusive indicator of human well-being. When the distress cues from the individual are more salient, however, they may be largely instrumental in determining the observer's response.

[6] Another possible contributing factor is that empathic distress is from the beginning and perhaps through life largely, if not entirely, an involuntary response. The resulting awareness that other people's distress is inevitably accompanied by unpleasant feelings in oneself, given the basic positive orientation discussed above, may add to the child's sense of oneness with others.

[7] A study by R. F. Weiss et al. (1973) suggests a direct way to test the assumption that sympathetic distress predisposes the individual to act. They found a positive correlation between intensity of distress cues and speed of the subject's helping response. The subjects also sweated a lot when exposed to the distress cues. It should be possible to find out, using systematic physiological measures of emotional arousal, if arousal precedes the overt helping response, if its intensity relates positively to the speed of the response, and if it diminishes right afterwards—all of which would be expected if sympathetic distress predisposes the person to act.

[8] We deal here with the general structural basis for guilt. There are obviously individual differences. Some people feel guilty even when they have no choice, and some avoid guilt even when they have a choice.

[9] This was true only when the parent was generally not power assertive in his discipline

pattern. When highly power-assertive parents pointed out harmful consequences from the child's behavior, the child showed little considerate behavior. This finding suggests a possible "reactance" effect.

[10] In relating existential guilt to social activism I do not mean to imply that it was the only, or even the primary, motive for activism, only that it may have been a contributing factor.

[11] In L. W. Hoffman's study over two-thirds of the male subjects responded to Horner's items with responses indicating a negative attitude toward success. In Horner's original work (1968), done seven years earlier, less than 10 percent of the males gave such responses. Two-thirds of the females gave such responses in both studies.

[12] There are limits to how far the parent should go in making sacrifices. If parental generosity is overdone and not balanced with appropriate demands, the child, instead of identifying with the parental model, may grow to expect others to continue to make sacrifices for him.

3

The Moral Development of Forgiveness

Robert D. Enright
and the Human Development Study Group*

ABSTRACT

Although philosophers have argued the differential merits of justice and mercy for centuries, psychological researchers have emphasized justice. Forgiveness as a specific application of mercy is described in this chapter. The focus is on the one who forgives, not on the one seeking forgiveness. Forgiveness is defined here as a forswearing of negative affect and judgment, by viewing the wrongdoer with compassion and love, in the face of a wrongdoer's considerable injustice.

The concept of forgiveness is traced from its theological origins to modern-day philosophies. Two psychological models of forgiveness are then described: a social cognitive developmental and a social processing model. It is claimed that forgiveness can be an effective problem-solving strategy in releasing one's own anger and joining again in community with the other person.

Randy betrayed Fred's most intimate secret.

Fred, deeply hurt, must now decide on his response. Were Fred to consult the published philosophies of conflict resolution, he would soon find himself immersed in a heated debate about the most appropriate response. Fred may seek justice, in which he attempts to objectively assess the fair solution. The quest for fairness could lead Fred into such issues as punishment, restitution, and even

---

*This group consists, in alphabetical order, of Radhi Al-Mabuk, Pamela Conroy, David Eastin, Suzanne Freedman, Sandra Golden, John Hebl, Tina Huang, Younghee Oh Park, Kim Pierce, and Issidoros Sarinopoulos

legal sanctions were they to exist in our case of betrayal. On the other hand, Fred may have pity on Randy or simply let it go, or perhaps even forgive him the offense.

The philosophical tension between justice and mercy is ancient. The *lex talionis* (eye for an eye) justice of earlier societies is contrasted with the self-sacrificial love of later, ancient societies. Hobbes (1651/1952) saw humanity's primary motive as rational self-interest, whereas Hume (1740/1952) saw it as benevolence. Gouldner (1973) described reciprocity (giving back in proportion to what is given) and beneficence (giving something for nothing) as conflicting societal norms. In the study of moral development, Kohlberg and Power (1981) acknowledged the tension between fairness as reversibility (justice) and super-erogation (going beyond duty).

Forgiveness as a moral concept exists on the side of self-sacrificial love, benevolence, beneficence, and supererogation. It is a specific application of these overarching principles. It is a concept that has been explored in theology, philosophy, psychiatry, and counseling, but rarely in human development. To date there is only one published empirical study on the moral development of forgiveness (Enright, Santos & Al-Mabuk, 1989). It is scarce in the empirical literature perhaps because it is traditionally associated with theology, not science (Fitzgibbons, 1986; North, 1987; Shontz & Rosenak, 1988). Yet it is forgiveness, not justice, that is frequently labeled divine, sublime (Morrow, 1984), humanizing (Calian, 1981), courageous (Cunningham, 1985; Kaufman, 1984), healthy (Droll, 1984), restorative (Murphy, 1982), and fulfilling (Beck, 1988). In our view, Fred's forgiving Randy is in the best interest of both.

In initiating a theory of forgiveness development we first define forgiveness, explaining what it is and is not. Our focus is on the offended party who will forgive, not on the offender who might ask for forgiveness. We then discuss the philosophical objections to interpersonal forgiveness. Next, we turn to a description of pseudo-forgiveness, or false forms of forgiveness. Our attention then turns to locating forgiveness within two psychological frameworks: a social cognitive-developmental model and a social processing model. Locating forgiveness within cognitive development will necessitate a discussion of how forgiveness development differs from Kohlbergian justice development. A synthesis of the social cognitive-developmental and social processing models is then attempted. We conclude with some thoughts on interventions in forgiveness.

FORGIVENESS DEFINED

We begin with the ancient evidence from both the Hebrew Bible and the New Testament. The modern ideas will follow.

Hebrew and Jewish Concepts

The Hebrew Bible and the subsequent Jewish tradition represent the first thorough expositions of divine and interpersonal forgiveness. The primary Hebrew word, occurring 46 times in the Hebrew Bible, that we translate as "to forgive" is *sălah* (Vine, 1985). In this context it refers to God removing sin from the people. Two other words include forgiveness in their range of meanings: *kăpar*, to cover or atone for wrongdoing, and *nāsā'*, meaning to lift up a sin and carry it away (Vine, 1985).

According to Landman (1941), *sălah* has both a spiritual and a moral connotation, representing a free act of God's removing sin or a person's removing misdeeds of another by hiding them from sight. One of God's attributes is forgiving sinful individuals (Exodus 34:6–7), provided there is repentance and a willingness to improve one's conduct (Landman, 1941). In ancient Hebrew culture, an elaborate system of animal sacrifices accompanied repentance in the covering of sin by the divine authority (see the book of Leviticus in the Hebrew Bible).

In the Mishnah (Danby, 1933), an injured person grants interpersonal forgiveness conditional upon the offender's repentance toward the offended party (Landman, 1941; Newman, 1987). The offended is "duty bound" to accept a sincere apology and must not harbor resentment (Leviticus 19:18, Landman, 1941; Newman, 1981). Such demands, however, according to one Talmudic sage (cited in Landman, 1941), are limited to three such encounters before the offended person can justifiably withhold forgiveness; Davies (1920) makes the same point. Forgiveness restores the offender to the relation formerly enjoyed with the other person and community. Such a relation in the Hebrew community involves reciprocal love (Leviticus 19:18). Love here includes all psychological systems of affect, cognition, and behavior (Deuteronomy 6:5). In theory, peace of mind is also restored (Landman, 1941). According to Walters (1984), examples of interpersonal forgiveness in the Hebrew Bible include Esau forgiving Jacob (Genesis 33:4), Joseph his brothers (Genesis 45:15), David in relation to Shimei (2 Samuel 19:16–24), and Solomon forgiving Abonijah (1 Kings 1). Forgiveness in Jewish tradition is a moral duty because of the doctrine of *imitatio dei*, the imitation of God as forgiver (Newman, 1987; Shapiro, 1978).

Christian Concepts

In the Christian Bible, or New Testament, the primary Greek word, occurring 22 times, that we translate as "to forgive" is *aphiemi* (Vine, 1985). It signifies that sins are sent away, divine punishment is remitted, and harmony between God and the formerly sinful person is restored. The means for such removal of sin are repentance, as in the Hebrew Bible, and the loving acceptance of Christ's propitiatory sacrifice and resurrection to new life.

Three other Greek words include forgiveness in their range of meanings: *charizomai*, to bestow a favor unconditionally; *apoluō*, to release as a quasi-judicial act or to give up negative judgments and/or behavior toward an offender; and *agape*, to unconditionally love in a charitable or benevolent fashion (Strong, 1984; Vine, 1985; see Nygren, 1932 for a thorough exposition on *agape*, especially p. 81). Forgiveness here, thus, has the dual qualities of God's casting away of sin (conditional on repentance and acceptance of Christ's sacrifice) and drawing the person in love (without condition).

Interpersonal forgiveness in Christianity is to be strictly analogous to the divine form, similar to the *imitatio dei* discussed earlier (Matthew 18:21–22; Vine, 1985, p. 251). As one is forgiven, he or she must practice forgiveness toward others. In contrast to the Mishnah directives, one is to forgive the offender whether or not he or she repents (Lewis, 1980, p. 243). In this sense, the forgiver is demonstrating *agape* by unconditionally drawing the other in love. As in the Hebrew community, love is an addition of elements to affect (positive feelings), cognition (positive thoughts), and behavior (giving back to or serving the community) (see Mark 12:30–31; 1 Corinthians 13). In contrast to the Talmudic directive, the Christian must not set a limit on the number of times he or she extends forgiveness (Matthew 18:21). As in Jewish teachings, the forgiven is restored to a sense of peace. The forgiver, too, eventually experiences peace (Galatians 5:22).[1]

Insights from Philosophy and Psychology

Interpersonal forgiveness refers to one person forgiving another, not to the deity-human relationship or to one group "forgiving" another. A brief definition, drawn principally but not exclusively from North (1987), is this: Forgiveness is the overcoming of negative affect and judgment toward the offender, not by denying ourselves the right to such affect and judgment, but by endeavoring to view the offender with compassion, benevolence, and love while recognizing that he or she has abandoned the right to them. The definition becomes more

---

[1]In Islam's Qu'ran, God, Allah forgives offenses when the person repents, has faith, and performs good works. People also are to forgive one another (The 'Imrans 3: 134). God's love is conditional on one's righteousness (The 'Imrans 3: 134). Person-to-person forgiveness is likewise conditional. For example, one does not forgive tyrants or those who will perpetuate wrongdoing (Counsel 42: 40). Forgiveness in Islam is to give up resentment, blame, and punishment (Sch-he-rie, 1984, abstract 12901, p. 370). This is analogous in our definition (to follow immediately) of particular elements being *subtracted* from the affective, cognitive, and behavioral systems.

Many other world religions do not have the concept of an offended, holy God. In such cases, there is little mention of person-to-person forgiveness (e.g., some Native American religions, Buddhism, Hinduism, Taoism, etc.). When the emphasis is on being one with the whole, individual offense is often interpreted as caused by ignorance not sin. If everyone has the essential nature of a supreme being, personal forgiveness becomes unnecessary.

complex when we realize that forgiveness involves the affective, cognitive, and behavioral systems. When one forgives certain elements are subtracted from each system. Negative emotions such as anger, hatred, resentment, sadness, and/or contempt are given up (Richards, 1988). This may occur slowly, but it is eventually accomplished, specifically toward the injuring person in the context of the given offense. In the cognitive system, one ceases condemning judgments and the planning of revenge, where this was occurring. In the behavioral system, one no longer acts out the revenge (if such were occurring, however subtle).

When one forgives certain elements are added to each system. In the affective system, the negative emotions are replaced by more neutral emotions and eventually by positive affect, such as *agape* (see Cunningham, 1985; Downie, 1965; North, 1987). The latter includes the willingness, through compassion and love, to help the other. In the cognitive system, the offender may realize he or she has a right to negative emotions, yet is willing to forego them (North, 1987). Positive thoughts emerge toward the other, such as wishing her well (Smedes, 1984) and viewing him respectfully as a moral equal (Cunningham, 1985). In the behavioral realm, there is a willingness to join in "loving community" with the other, perhaps making overtures in that direction (Augsburger, 1981). Such overtures will depend on true change in the other. There is the potential for the forgiver to experience both inner release and a healed relationship (Augsburger, 1981).

The foregoing definition can be deepened with the following 10 points:

1. Interpersonal forgiveness is between people, not between a person and an inanimate object (Kolnai, 1973–74; Lambert, 1985; Murphy, 1982; Smedes, 1984). One does not forgive tornadoes or floods. The willingness to join again in loving community with a tornado most certainly would be absent. Kolnai restricts forgiveness only to interpersonal equals. A worker, then, could not forgive the boss. This, in our view, is too restrictive.

2. Forgiveness follows a deep, personal, long-lasting injury or hurt from the other person. The injury might be psychological, emotional, physical, or moral (Kolnai, 1973–74; Murphy, 1982; Murphy & Hampton, 1988; Smedes, 1984). In real life a deep injury might involve all of these areas at once (Eastin, 1988). O'Shaughnessy (1967) claims that the *relationship* must be personal; this excludes too many sources of hurt. We claim that the injury, whether intended or not, must be directed personally at the forgiver. The forgiver, therefore, does not forgive the Nazis for the Holocaust unless he or she was personally involved (Gingell, 1974). We acknowledge personal, indirect involvement, for example, of children whose parents are Holocaust survivors.

3. In our view, the offense is an objective reality, not merely a perception by the one offended. Kahrhoff (1988), in contrast, claims, "Everything that

happens outside our minds is neutral'' (p. 3). In his view, an offense can be so only if we perceive it as such. We acknowledge, for example, individual differences in physical abuse victims' perception of the violence. All will not experience the same depth or duration of emotional distress. Yet all will experience a certain emotional pain because of the objective occurrence. If all outside our minds is neutral, we wonder if Mr. Kahrhoff's mind is the culprit when his hand, upon touching a hot stove, feels pain.

4. Forgiveness is possible only when a person first has a sense of justice. One cannot feel a deep sense of moral injury without a sense of fairness (Brandsma, 1982; Hunter, 1978; Kohlberg & Power, 1981). This implies that children as young as 4 or 5 might need to forgive (see Enright, Franklin, & Manheim [1980] for a discussion of early childhood forms of justice).

5. There is usually an initial reaction by the injured party toward the injurer. It is one of *experiencing* the hurt as profound, followed by shock or disbelief, and culminating in anger or even hatred (Eastin, 1988; Fitzgibbons, 1986; Linn & Linn, 1978; Smedes, 1984).

6. Over time the injured party no longer seeks retaliation (Hughes, 1975). This is an internal response by the one injured (Droll, 1984), and may involve the giving up of narcissistic tendencies of disavowing the hurt (Cunningham, 1985).

7. The offender need not apologize for the injured person to forgive (North, 1987; Twambley, 1976). Otherwise, as an example, were the offender to die before a change of heart, the other is trapped in unforgiveness (O'Shaughnessy, 1967). Further, a gift given need not await a prior response from the other person. In fact, many see as we do the unconditional character of forgiveness (Cunningham, 1985; Downie, 1965; Smedes, 1984; Torrance, 1986). Some disagree with this (Dobel, 1980; Domaris, 1986).

8. The offender need not have intended the wrong (Downie, 1965). O'Shaughnessy (1967) and Murphy (1982) claim the opposite, but in our experience many an offender does not realize how much damage was done by his or her act. The requirement of intent, therefore, is too restrictive.

9. The difficulty in arriving at a forgiveness solution will vary with such external variables as the severity of the offense and the quality of the relationship prior to the injury (Newman, 1987). It will also vary with such internal psychological qualities in the offended person as his or her ability to understand forgiveness and to choose a forgiveness, in contrast to a justice, problem-solving strategy.

10. It is not always the case that one party offends and the other is offended. As Beatty (1970) insists, forgiveness is relational. Thus, it is conceivable to have an offended offender. Consider an unjustly fired worker who writes a scathing letter to her former boss. He is both offender and, now, offended by the letter. Both may have to forgive the other.

What Forgiveness Is Not

A complication arises in understanding forgiveness when we realize that the following are popularly considered synonyms of it: pardon, reconciliation, condonation, and excusing (Mawson & Whiting, 1923; Webster, 1979). Forgiveness is none of these.

Pardon, Legal Mercy, and Leniency. There is a consensus in the philosophical literature that pardon involves the world of jurisprudence, not interpersonal relations (Downie, 1965; Hunter, 1978; Kolnai, 1973–74; Lauritzen, 1987; Murphy, 1982; Murphy & Hampton, 1988; Roberts, 1971; Smart, 1968; Twambley, 1976). Cases of pardon usually involve a just authority overseeing laws by which the degree of punishment is established for each violation. When a person who breaks the law has punishment suspended or reduced below what is normative, there is pardon. The authority who commutes the sentence is rarely the one personally hurt by the defendant. Fred's forgiving Randy is not an official reduction in a deserved sentence, but a change in Fred's response toward Randy, who personally hurt him.

Suppose Randy broke the club's rules. An authority of the club would pass the legal sentence, or perhaps pardon him. Only those club members directly hurt by Randy's action could actually forgive him (Downie, 1965). One also can imagine situations in which legal mercy is not forthcoming for Randy, yet the personally-injured club members forgive him. Finally, we can imagine situations involving forgiveness in which the spectre of punishment, and therefore pardon, is entirely absent. If Fred were to forgive the long-dead Randy 25 years from now, it is peculiar to say that as Fred forgives he is pardoning Randy or being lenient with him (O'Shaughnessy, 1967).

Reconciliation. Forgiveness and reconciliation are occasionally conflated in the published literature (e.g., Lauritzen, 1987). While forgiveness is an *internal* release, reconciliation is a behavioral coming together again. Forgiveness may be a necessary condition for reconciliation, but it requires more (Williams, 1968). To truly reconcile, Fred must trust Randy (Horsbrugh, 1974; Kolnai, 1973–74; Smedes, 1984). Fred's reconciling, then, presupposes that Randy has changed and that a more just relation will ensue. The key difference is that when Fred forgives he removes all barriers he may have had in blocking the relationship. Now Randy must remove his barriers for reconciliation to occur.

Condonation and Excusing. Were he to condone Randy's behavior, Fred would first realize Randy's injustice but deliberately refrain from retaliation (Kolnai, 1973–74). Mitigating circumstance such as the need for companionship obviates any punishment Fred might give. In condonation, Fred puts up with the injustice. In forgiveness, Fred, rather than putting up with injustice, actively seeks to release Randy, to accept him despite moral injury. Condonation leaves the residual of smoldering resentment, while forgiveness does not. Condonation denies resentment; forgiveness overcomes it with compassion and love (North, 1987).

To excuse, on the other hand, is to judge the supposedly hurtful event as not worth a quarrel (Kolnai, 1973–74). Fred would conclude in excusing Randy that his behavior was not so wrong as to require strong emotional reactions. Although Neblett (1974) calls this condonation, it is not. In condoning, Fred acknowledges a moral infraction. In excusing there is no such acknowledgment, but rather an affective neutrality or indifference. Others (Lapsley, 1966) erroneously equate excusing and forgiveness. In Lapsley's example, a child implicitly concludes that the parent must meet all the child's needs. The child who is now an adult forgives the parent by realizing no parent can meet all needs. The debt is excused because the debt is and was imaginary. Excusing, of course, is based on the assumption that the injury inflicted is no injury at all. Forgiveness occurs in the face of acknowledged hurt.

Justification.   Rather than see no moral infraction in Randy's behavior, Fred sees something just or fair in it. Rather than betray a secret, suppose Randy stole Fred's car to drive an injured child to the hospital. Fred may see the thievery as justified with no need to forgive (Murphy, 1982). Forgiveness, in contrast, occurs when there is a deep, unjust hurt.

Self-centering.   Forgiving another is not motivated exclusively by the desire to be rid of strong negative emotions (Richards, 1988). The forgiver also looks toward the other, with a willingness to join in community with him or her. Even when such community is no longer possible because the offender has died, the offended party endeavors to change judgment of the other. Even when an offender continues unchanged, one who forgives nonetheless waits in the hope of such community.

Other Misconceptions.   Forgiveness is not the passive act of allowing angry feelings to diminish across time (Kolnai, 1973–74). Instead, it is an active struggle. It is not forgetting, because such deep offense is rarely blotted from consciousness (Kolnai, 1973–74; Smedes, 1984). It is not simply offering the words, "I forgive you." If there is underlying anger and resentment, there is no true forgiveness yet. At the same time, Fred need not be required to recite such words to forgive the long-dead Randy. Finally, forgiveness is not synonymous with mourning. As Hunter (1978) points out, forgiveness occurs in the psychodynamic context of aggression, not grief.

PHILOSOPHICAL OBJECTIONS TO INTERPERSONAL FORGIVENESS

As there has been a long history of forgiveness literature, so too has there been a litany of criticism directed against it. We will consider 11 cogent arguments against forgiveness.

Forgiveness as Weakness

Nietzsche (1887) is the primary spokesperson for the view that those who forgive are weaklings, incapable of asserting their right to a just solution. He, too, criticizes human love with a similar argument. A modern, psychological study (Trainer, 1981) elucidates why, perhaps, this view is not uncommon. Trainer found various approaches to forgiveness, one labeled role-expected. In this approach, the "forgiver" senses a moral or religious imperative to forgive, even though he or she is unconvinced of its merits. Unable to retaliate against the superior who offended, the "forgiver" grudgingly forswears justice, harboring resentment and low self-esteem. Perhaps it is this approach that Nietzsche observed and recorded. On the other hand, Trainer also found an intrinsic approach to forgiveness, characterized by self-acceptance, psychological strength, and respect for the other, even in the face of anger. The intrinsic forgiver values forgiveness in and of itself. North (1987) was describing this same approach when she said, "The forgiving character is one which is achievable only after a hard-fought battle, and should not be confused with timidity or moral feebleness" (p. 507).

Forgiveness as a Power Play

In contrast to the Nietzschian position, others claim that "forgiveness" can put the forgiver in a one-up position, thus dominating the "forgiven" (Augsburger, 1981, Cunningham, 1985; Smedes, 1984). As an example, were he to forgive Randy's betrayal of the secret, Fred may now consistently remind his friend that he (Randy) is under obligation. "You owe me one, Randy." Such maneuverings are not forgiveness, because the latter is to wipe the slate clean and come together again as interpersonal equals. Although North (1987) acknowledges a *moral* superiority by the forgiver for this (and only this) hurtful instance, she instructs, "Indeed, if the wrongdoer is to be 'lifted up' and 'raised' to his original position it is made easier if the wronged party goes some way to meet him, by 'lowering' himself in modesty and humility" (p. 507).

Forgiveness as a Reversal of Societal Justice

An excessive forgiving attitude by society may lead to our paroling criminals who will perpetuate crime. Philosophers such as Lewis (1980) and Roberts (1971) have wrestled with this question. The main problem with the argument is that it confuses forgiveness with legal mercy or pardon. Further, it is possible for societal justice and forgiveness to exist simultaneously, as in the case of Pope John Paul II, who forgave him while the would-be assassin remained in prison (Morrow, 1984). One who characteristically practices forgiveness certainly could participate on a jury and bring justice to bear as required. Forgiveness opens the door for society's receiving back the criminal, but it does not oblige us to hastily open the cell door.

Forgiveness as a Block to Personal Justice

Even though societal justice and forgiveness may exist side-by-side, one's personal justice is often set aside upon forgiving the other. Fred, for the pain endured, does not require a pound of flesh from Randy. Because it thwarts personal justice, forgiveness is considered by some to be immoral (Lauritzen, 1987; Smart, 1968). However, as Roberts (1971) counters, when one deliberately sacrifices a personal entitlement, as in forgiveness, one is acting mercifully, not immorally. The giving of a gift, as forgiveness is, hardly warrants the label "immoral." To forgive is first to be aware of a wrong done, thus placing the forgiver within, not outside, the moral arena. Further, the intent of a genuine act of forgiveness is to heal and join in loving community, hardly an immoral goal.[2]

Forgiveness as Perpetuating Injustice

Were a wife to forgive an abusive husband, she is vulnerable, once again, to his psychological and physical blows. Were she to forgive, she acts immorally (Lauritzen, 1987). Such thinking, while showing compassion toward the wife, confuses forgiveness and reconciliation. Forgiveness is an internal release; reconciliation is a behavioral coming together. In our example, the wife could forgive the husband, but not reconcile until he shows a *genuine* change in attitude and evidence of behavioral change, which of course may never come. Were she not to forgive, she is trapped with inner hatred that may be as abusive as and perhaps more long lasting than the physical violence against her.

Forgiveness as a Logical Impossibility

For Kant, forgiveness is a logical impossibility. Were he to forgive Randy, Fred would be wiping out the wrong done. Because it is impossible to cancel the betrayal (because it did actually happen), it is impossible to forgive. Minas

---

[2]There are exceptions to the complete forswearing of personal justice when one forgives. One case in point is seeking monetary compensation from someone who has physically debilitated the person through injury. For the nuances on compensation and forgiveness, see Enright & Zell (1989).

(1975) makes a similar argument in her discussion of deity-to-human forgiveness. An omniscient God could not become morally blind. As North (1987) perceptively argues, however, what is cancelled in forgiveness "is not the crime itself but the distorting effect that this wrong has upon one's relations with the wrongdoer and perhaps with others. If this is correct then forgiveness is possible even with God" (p. 500).

Forgiveness as Inducing Inferiority in the Other

Even though Fred, in forgiving, may not seek superiority over him, Randy may nonetheless feel inferior (Droll, 1984; O'Shaughnessy, 1967). After all, Fred's forswearing retaliation makes him, in Randy's eyes, better than Randy. The problem with this argument is that it assumes Fred must *tell* Randy of the forgiveness. This is not a necessary condition. Even if Fred were to tell Randy, who may misinterpret Fred's motives, this is no reason why Fred should not forgive. A gift rejected does not detract from the fact that it is a gift given.

Forgiveness as Inducing Inferiority in Self

Murphy (1982) correctly asserts that a too-ready tendency to forgive implies a lack of self-respect. His argument, however, is not targeted to forgiveness, but to one's hastening the process so that the outcome is less than genuine forgiveness. Our definition of forgiveness includes a distinct period of anger. Individuals who ignore the anger are not forgiving those who hurt them.

Forgiveness as a Lack of Respect for Others

This, too, is Nietzsche's. As Fred fails to show resentment, he shows that Randy is not worth taking seriously. Yet, if forgiveness involves *agape*, or a reaching out in love, the one who forgives is certainly valuing the other. As Fred acknowledges the hurt and nevertheless is willing to cancel the debt on that hurt, he is valuing Randy.

Forgiveness as Alienation

Droll (1984), citing Berger (1969), makes the interesting argument that forgiveness might separate us from our true nature as aggressive beings. Retaliation is more natural. Without debating the scientifically opaque question of our basic nature, let us only say that many in the helping professions claim that deep and long-lasting anger, not forgiveness, can be alienating to self and others (Brandsma, 1982; Fitzgibbons, 1986; Hunter, 1978). Because forgiveness restores positive evaluation and affect toward the other, it has potential to restore relationships, the antithesis of alienation.

Forgiveness as Producing Hypersensitivity to Hurt

Downie (1965) and Droll (1984) make the provocative statement that as one forgives, he or she may become overly sensitive to interpersonal hurts. The forgiver begins to pay very close attention to interpersonal slights, making them larger than they are simply by focusing on them. Yet to truly forgive is to honestly scrutinize the pain, not to distort it so one can forgive. If anything, the sincere practice of forgiveness should reduce hypersensitivity in those currently prone to perceptual distortion of the pain.

THE MORAL JUSTIFICATION OF FORGIVENESS

It should be clear that forgiveness when properly understood is not an immoral action. On the contrary, we consider it superior to a strict and exclusive adherence to justice for two reasons. First, because a forgiver views the other as equal and worthy of respect (see our definition above), any subsequent justice response must, out of necessity, include respect for the individual. Were the offended party still to harbor hate or contempt, a response of respect and equality, although possible, may be less likely.

Second, a community united in forgiveness is not united only by the justice requirements of order and obligation. There is the added component, *agape,* in which individuals are united in the loving support of one another. As Kohlberg and Power (1981) note, such a community goes beyond justice. Of course, none of this requires a person to forgive, primarily because forgiveness goes beyond duty.

THE PROBLEM OF PSEUDO-FORGIVENESS

Even though it may be morally justified, forgiveness has its dangers. Some truly believe they have forgiven when, in fact, they have not. Clinicians label these observed false forms as pseudo-forgiveness (Cunningham, 1985; Enright & Zell, 1989; Hunter, 1978; Thompson, 1983). Pseudo-forgiveness usually manifests itself within the context of psychological defenses.

Reaction Formation

Hunter (1978) was the first to observe this distortion on the forgiveness theme in a 45-year-old female client. A pillar of her church, she claimed to have forgiven her husband for various behavioral imperfections, but underneath and unaware she harbored resentment, mistrust, and blame. The outward forgiveness, as contradiction to her inward reality, helped block anxiety that would have otherwise flooded the ego. If manifested, the anxiety would force her to confront the hate she felt. This defense is so subtle that she did not realize the contradiction between her forgiveness pronouncements and the true nature of her inner reality. "Forgiveness" here does not release, but instead masks and perpetuates despair. Pattison (1965, p. 112) describes a similar situation.

Denial

Cunningham (1985) discusses the case of people refusing to acknowledge their emotional pain through denial. Perhaps this is tied to the narcissistic tendency to deny that others can hurt us deeply. In denying hurt, some deny their need to forgive. There is a tendency to just let the offense go, resulting in the possibility of lowered self-esteem and reduced personal integrity.

Projection

In projection the "forgiver" transfers his or her own sense of imperfection onto another (Cunningham, 1985). In fact, the other is innocent. The one using projection spends much time condemning and then "forgiving" the innocent.

Hunter (1978) believes that people practicing any form of pseudo-forgiveness have a certain smug quality about them that is evident even to those without clinical training. Having explored the concept of forgiveness, we are now ready to describe the two psychological models.

THE COGNITIVE DEVELOPMENTAL MODEL OF FORGIVENESS

One hesitates to postulate a new social cognitive developmental stage sequence because most attempts in this direction are not new. They are actually iterations on the Kohlbergian justice theme. Consider two examples. Prosocial moral reasoning (Eisenberg-Berg, 1979) concerns self-sacrifice. It thus appears to be on the supererogative side of the justice–mercy debate. Yet the dilemmas used to assess such reasoning place the domain squarely on the justice side. As one dilemma example, a man must decide whether to help a woman being mugged or protect himself. The research subject must weigh competing claims, assess the moral adequacy of each, and decide in favor of the more justifiable claim. This is a classic justice, not mercy, strategy. The competing claims here are always between self-interest and other-interest.

The other example is the moral domain of care (Gilligan, 1982, 1985). Care is that form of morality that seeks a resolution to Kohlbergian justice dilemmas through compromise or the minimizing of hurt. A prototypical dilemma is whether Heinz should steal a drug to save his dying wife. If one is deciding on how best to care through compromise for Heinz, his wife, and the druggist, one is involved in a justice problem-solving strategy. This is so because it involves identifying each party's interest, seeking a balance among justice claims, and optimizing interests where possible. The one major difference between Kohlberg's and Gilligan's approaches is this: Kohlberg asks for a reaction to the initial question of whether Heinz should steal the drug, whereas Gilligan focuses on issues further into the dilemma, once Heinz takes action and how he and the druggist will compromise in that action.

Might our attempts here be similar? We think not. There are major conceptual differences between Kohlbergian justice and forgiveness strategies. Forgiveness is a forswearing of justice. As North (1987) instructs, a forgiver knows that the wrongdoer has no *right* to compassion, but it is given nonetheless. In the prosocial work, subjects decide in favor of the other's interests when the other has a right to the goods or services.

When we ask for the *fairest* solution to a problem, forgiveness never enters the picture. As an example, suppose Billy runs to Mom, telling her that Jill unfairly took all the marbles. Although Mom could ignore it, she probably would engage in some form of justice reasoning. Whether she uses distributive justice, punitive justice, care reasoning, or another form, she is reasoning with a justice strategy of some kind. The parent would not think of forgiving the child in this context. On the other hand, Mom may ask Billy to forgive Jill. If so, and this is the crux of the justice-forgiveness distinction, she is abandoning her quest for the *fair* solution. Instead, she is seeking the compassionate solution, or the one beneficial to Billy's emotional health, or even the one most beneficial to Billy's and Jill's relationship.

One might press the point, arguing that a forgiveness option is part of a justice strategy. For example, in the Heinz dilemma, we could focus on yet a different aspect from Kohlberg or Gilligan, asking subjects what Heinz should do if the druggist conceals the drug. The subject must use a justice strategy to decide whether to seek retribution on his own, sue through the courts, or perhaps forgive. This, in fact, involves a justice strategy because one is considering the fairest action to correct a wrong. Anyone choosing forgiveness in the above exercise in all likelihood is confusing forgiveness with condonation or excusing the wrongdoer. If Mom, in asking Billy to forgive Jill, thought this was the *fair* solution, she, too, would be confusing forgiveness with acquiescence or condonation.

When the researcher places the subject exclusively into a forgiveness strategy, a set of questions different from justice emerges. How can I release the injurer from obligation? What steps must I take to forgive him? What conditions might make it easier for me to forgive her? What benefits might I expect in forgiving? Justice and forgiveness thus require the person to ask different questions.

Enright, Santos, and Al-Mabuk (1989), in validating a social cognitive-developmental stage model of forgiveness, asked this question: What conditions make it easier for someone to forgive a wrongdoer? They presented two scenarios taken from Rest (1979) in which a justice dilemma ended with a story character being emotionally hurt. As an example, the druggist hid the drug, the wife died, and Heinz is left bitterly angry. In two studies, subjects (grades 4, 7, 10, college, and adult) were asked to evaluate whether revenge, restitution, peer and authority pressure, and/or restored social harmony influenced the decision to forgive. Unconditional forgiveness was also assessed. A strong age trend and moderate relation to the Kohlbergian sequence was noted in both studies. The forgiveness stages, as validated in the above studies, are presented in Table 3.1. The Kohlbergian justice stages are included for comparison.

Five points are noteworthy regarding the forgiveness stages. First, the initial two stages involve a distortion of forgiveness, conflating it with justice problem-solving strategies. Second, the middle two stages, in which justice and forgiveness are no longer confused, imply that forgiveness is forthcoming only when there is considerable social pressure to do so. One senses a reluctance in these subjects to offer forgiveness unless the pressures are present. Third, Stage 5 no longer requires a certain condition to be present *before* forgiveness occurs, as is the case in stage 1 through 4. The condition must occur *after* forgiveness is extended. In Stage 5, the person is willing to offer forgiveness if, and only if, social harmony is restored by the generosity. Fourth, only Stage 6 captures the breadth and subtlety of the forgiveness concept. It is the only stage in which no condition is sought, either before or after forgiveness is granted. Fifth, the stages do not show rigid stage-like properties of a unified whole. Instead, most subjects showed evidence of two or more stages in their thinking. Such a pattern, however, occurred across adjacent stages; bimodal patterns were rare. Rest's (1983) description of cognitive-developmental stages more accurately captures the nuances of the forgiveness stages than does Kohlberg's (1976) description.

In theory, there is a relation between justice and forgiveness stages because of the common, underlying social perceptive-taking skills required at each Stage. As Kohlberg (1976) claims that his justice Stages 1 and 2 are prejustice, so too are forgiveness Stages 1 and 2 preforgiveness conceptions. As we have seen, Stages 1 and 2 confuse forgiveness with retributive and restitutional justice, respectively. The social perspective-taking demands require the focus only on one other person in Stage 1 and a reciprocal perspective in Stage 2. Stage 3 requires the more complex group perspective, while Stage 4 requires the systems or legal perspective. Stage 5 requires the perspective of a person within the systems or societal perspective capable of altering the system. Stage 6 requires the more complex perspective that principles take precedence over societal functioning and "the fact that persons are ends in themselves and must be treated as such," as Kohlberg (1976, p. 35) argues in Stage 6 justice. The higher forgiveness stages, thus, are more developmentally advanced than the lower stages because of the increasing complexity of the social perspective required at each higher stage.

TABLE 3.1
Stages of Justice and Forgiveness Development

	Stages of Justice	Stages of Forgiveness
Stage 1.	Punishment and Obedience Orientation. I believe that justice should be decided by the authority, by the one who can punish.	Revengeful Forgiveness. I can forgive someone who wrongs me only if I can punish him or her to a similar degree to my own pain.
Stage 2	Relativist Justice. I have a sense of reciprocity that defines justice for me. If you help me, I must help you.	Restitutional or Compensational Forgiveness. If I get back what was taken away from me, then I can forgive. Or, if I feel guilty about withholding forgiveness, then I can forgive to relieve my guilt.
Stage 3	Good Boy/Girl Justice. Here, I reason that the group consensus should decide what is right and wrong. I go along so that others will like me.	Expectational Forgiveness. I can forgive if others put pressure on me to forgive. It is easier to forgive when other people expect it.
Stage 4	Law and Order Justice. Societal laws are my guides to justice. I uphold laws in order to have an orderly society.	Lawful Expectational Forgiveness. I forgive when my religion demands it. Notice that this is not Stage 2 in which I forgive to relieve my own guilt about withholding forgiveness.
Stage 5	Social Contract Orientation. I am still interested in that which maintains the social fabric but I also realize that unjust laws exist. Therefore, I see it as just, as fair, to work within the system for change.	Forgiveness as Social Harmony. I forgive when it restores harmony or good relations in society. Forgiveness decreases friction and outright conflict in society. Note that forgiveness is a way to control society; it is a way of maintaining peaceful relations.
Stage 6	Universal Ethical Prinicple Orientation. My sense of justice is based on maintaining the individual rights of all persons. Conscience rather than laws or norms determines what I will accept when there are competing claims.	Forgiveness As Love. I forgive unconditionally because it promotes a true sense of love. Because I must truly care for each person, a hurtful act on his or her part does not alter that sense of love. This kind of relationship keeps open the possibility of reconciliation and closes the door on revenge. Note that forgiveness is no longer dependent on a social context, as in Stage 5. The forgiver does not control the other by forgiving; he or she releases the other.

THE PROCESSES OF FORGIVING ANOTHER PERSON

Even though studies of morality focus predominantly on the stage model, there are recent attempts at developing process models (see Enright 1980; Flavell, 1974; and Rest, 1983 for examples). The basic assumption of these process models is that a moral response involves a series of strategies executed to resolve a dilemma. The strategies include not only cognitive components, but also affective and behavioral components. As Rest (1983) correctly elucidates, the artificial trichotomizing of the field into independent categories of cognition, affect, and behavior fails to capture the subtlety, complexity, and integration of these systems. Process models integrate the three.

An example of a process model of forgiveness is presented in Fig. 3.1. The *Injury* is something that happens to a forgiver, not a strategy in which he or she chooses to engage. Following injury, there is characteristically a set of negative emotional reactions such as rage, self-doubt, and obsession with the injury (see Fitzgibbons, 1986 and Hope, 1987 for two of many examples). *Awareness* (Component 1) of the emotional pain is essential if forgiveness is to be put into practice because the pain acts, in part, as a motivator for resolution. This implies a certain level of self-reflection perhaps absent in the very young. The injury and the self-reflection on the pain produce a *Need* to resolve the conflict (Component 2). This is an awareness that one must think through the problem.

Deciding Among Strategies (Component 3) implies that the injured party must choose in a general way between justice and mercy. Each has substantially different implications for how the problem will be ultimately resolved. One will choose forgiveness as the resolution strategy if the *Forgiveness Motive* (Component 4) is strong. The forgiveness motive maximizes the probability that a forgiveness strategy will be adopted.

Decision to Forgive (Component 5) is a *cognitive* commitment to forgive the injurer. The forgiver at this point decides to give up resentment and punishment, even if there is an opportunity to punish. There still may be anger and unresolved, psychologically negative consequences present, but these no longer direct behavior; the commitment to forgive directs it.

Execution of Internal Forgiveness Strategies (Component 6) involves the cognitive activities of understanding the other and self differently, within more subtle contexts. It also involves expanded affect such as compassion and empathy toward the other. The strategies comprise the injured person's attempt to change the way the injury is now viewed, without distorting the facts. A *Need for*

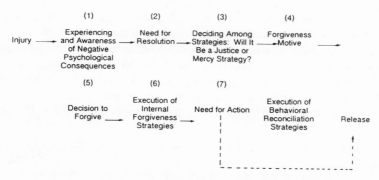

FIG. 3.1. Processes involved in forgiving someone.

Action (Component 7) is similar to Component 2. There must be an awareness that a behavioral response toward the other is necessary before forgiveness occurs. *Execution of Behavioral Reconciliation Strategies* is outside the scope of this chapter because it deals with interaction patterns rather than internal resolution in forgiveness. The dashed line between *Need for Action* and *Reconciliation Strategies* represents the possibility that reconciliation is either impossible (Randy is no longer among the living) or unwise (Randy remains unchanged). The forgiver can thus circumvent the *Reconciliation Strategy,* moving to *Release.* *Release,* like *Injury,* is not part of the person's active, psychological processes primarily because it *happens* to him or her; it is not directed by him or her. Release is the experiencing of diminished negative affect and increased positive affect toward the injurer.[3]

These processes are not considered rigidly inevitable or mechanical in that everyone who forgives necessarily passes through all. The sequence is logical, but not considered psychologically invariant. There will be both feedback and feedforward loops so that each component influences others. A more thorough description of Components 1–6 follows, gleaned from a review of the psychological, psychiatric, philosophical, theological, and case study literature.

A Detailed Look at the Processes

Experiencing and Awareness of Negative Psychological Consequences. There are seven predictable responses following deep injury. One is psychological defenses, such as denial, repression, projection, and reaction formation. The purpose of the defenses is to distance oneself from the pain. Case study examples can be found in Kiel (1986), Koerbel (1986), and Thompson (1983). While a positive development initially, the defenses work against healing if they prevent the confrontation of and active resolution of that pain. A second response, acknowledged in our definition of forgiveness, is anger or even hatred toward the other (Droll, 1984; Thompson, 1983; Trainer, 1981). The anger, like the defenses, is initially positive because of its cathartic effect (Cotroneo, 1982; Donnelley, 1982; Linn & Linn, 1978). Yet, if it continues, it can debilitate (Fitzgibbons, 1986). A third negative response is shame (Patton, 1985). The injury may lead to public embarrassment. Fourth, an obsessive emotional centering, or cathexis, on the injury may occur (Droll, 1984; Kiel, 1986). This, in all likelihood, emerges if the initial anger does not effectively resolve the problem. Fifth, cognitive rehearsal, in which the injured person continually rethinks the event, may be manifested (Droll, 1984; Eastin, 1988; Kiel, 1986). The person,

---

[3]We are not implying that the reduction in negative and the increase in positive affect is a passive process. The decision to forgive, reframing, and the nurturing of compassion (all described below) are only three examples of actively dealing with such emotions. Our point is that the work done toward release does not automatically or quickly lead to release. It usually takes time to unfold.

as an example, may be watching television or doing the dishes and finds oneself cognitively and unexpectedly reliving the painful event. Sixth, a comparison between one's own unhappy state and the perceived better state of the injurer is cognitively contrasted, perhaps intensifying anger, cathexis, and rehearsal (see Kiel, 1986 as one example). Seventh, as all this pain accumulates, the person may reevaluate his or her "just-world" hypothesis, concluding that the world is unfair (Flanigan, 1987). Depending on the extent of the person's previous just-world hypothesis, he or she may now feel out of control in this and other areas of life. The person's awareness of at least some of these responses leads to a need for resolution.

Need for Resolution.   This component is similar to Flavell's (1974) postulation of need before a social thought is generated, and to Rest's (1983) Component 1 in justice problem solving. The person must be sensitive to the injury and to his or her internal reactions if there is to be motivation to problem solve. The *Need,* in theory, develops with age (Flavell, 1974).

Deciding Among Strategies.   Forgiveness is not an inevitable response to injury. It must be chosen from a host of alternatives. The two broadest strategies are an interpersonal strategy (in which the injurer is involved) and a self-healing strategy (focusing on one's own affect, bibliotherapy, jogging, or other techniques that exclude the offender). Within an interpersonal strategy, involving the injurer, the two broadest categories are justice and mercy. Within justice, one might decide to pursue a legal sanction or personally seek fairness. An imbalanced justice-seeking strategy might include the injustice of revenge. Mercy could range from a forswearing of punishing the other to the more active forgiveness strategy which includes the positive affects of compassion and love. An imbalanced mercy-seeking strategy might include condonation that ignores the injustice.

Forgiveness Motive.   One is likely to choose forgiveness if there is a motivation encouraging it. This is both a subtle and complex development dependent on six (and perhaps seven) variables. First, one's social cognitive-developmental stage will influence a forgiveness motive. Stage of development as a process variable is similar to Rest's (1983) Component II in justice problem solving. As an example of stage influencing motivation, if the person predominantly reasons on Stage 1 (revenge-seeking) and there is no possibility of revenge, he or she is unlikely to be motivated to "forgive." On the other hand, a person predominantly reasoning on Stage 6 may possess a strong forgiveness motive because of the tendency to forgive unconditionally.

A second variable is cultural conditioning. Some cultures or subcultures do not consider forgiveness an acceptable conflict resolution strategy for certain injuries. One dramatic case in point is the Israeli Jewish community's response to the Holocaust. One study of 18 Holocaust survivors now living in Israel revealed that none considered forgiveness viable.[4] Consider one case study example that is typical of those interviews. These are excerpts, translated from Hebrew, of a now 60-year-old woman who was imprisoned at Auschwitz by the Nazis when she was 14 (in 1944). She lost all her family during the war. She says:

> I forgot a lot of things. But today, when I see a film or a memorial ceremony—now I can cry. In the past I did not cry. As I get older the memories become more painful because one understands the meaning of suffering. In the past I had feelings of anger and revenge. Nowadays I am angry because of the things that I lost during the war. Nowadays I am more angry in comparison with the period immediately after the war. There were times that I did not feel anything, but as time passes the anger is greater. I could not do what they [the Nazis] did. I am glad that the Holocaust did not change us to become more like the Germans. I would like the Nazis to be punished, but I'll not persecute them. I don't think that it is ever possible to forgive them. Life goes on, I did not explore the Holocaust all those years, I lost interest. The sting becomes blunted. The only way to help myself was by reading a lot of autobiographic books about that period. I looked for myself through the books. I have a friend who was with me in concentration camp. For many years we did not talk about it at all. Now we talk about the Holocaust, and then we feel that we have arrived home.

In the foregoing example, there is a conscious rejection of a forgiveness strategy in favor of justice's legal strategy. Bibliotherapy and catharsis are two psychological techniques she uses to promote self-healing.

A third variable influencing the forgiveness motive for some is immediate environmental encouragements/sanctions for forgiving, or its discouragement. Family, friends, and societal groups who encourage a forgiveness response may increase the motivation. In all likelihood, this variable interacts with one's social cognitive-developmental level. Those predominantly reasoning in Stages 3 or 4 who have such supports may develop a strengthened forgiveness motive.

A fourth variable is philosophical and/or religious education. Those who are taught about and who understand forgiveness may more readily consider it as the primary problem-solving strategy. The correlation between practice of a particular faith and forgiveness stage (Enright, Santos, & Al-Mabuk, 1989) is a related example here.

A fifth variable is time since the injury. The forgiveness motive, in theory, would be suppressed when there is still great anger present. As time reduces some of the powerful negative emotions, the forgiveness motive should appear more strongly, especially if the other variables that strengthen the motive are present.

---

[4]The discussion is based on the research of Mazor, Gampel, Enright, and Orenstein (1990). No forgiveness data are presented in this paper because all rejected it as a strategy.

Sixth, degree of suffering may influence the motive to forgive. In the case of the Israeli response to the Holocaust, the extreme horror may strengthen a justice motive, in contrast to a forgiveness motive. On the other hand, a lesser offense may make it easier to forswear resentment and feel more positively toward the injurer. One could also imagine, however, that debilitative emotional turmoil could be an incentive to forgive, because such emotions eventually may be released if forgiveness occurs.

A seventh variable, described in social psychology (Weber & Crocker, 1983), counseling psychology (Eastin, 1988), and theology (Mackintosh, 1927), is conversion. Conversion is a momentous "change of heart" (North, 1987, p. 503). To Weber and Crocker (1983), conversion involves cognitive interpretation of significant instances that dramatically alter one's view of the world. In our context, conversion is dramatic primarily because one's judgments of the other person and of forgiveness as a problem-solving strategy are now the opposite of previous conclusions. It is also dramatic because the time involved, while not necessarily sudden, is concentrated relative to the cognitive changes wrought. Support for conversion as an observed phenomenon can be found in Gurwitz and Dodge (1977). Within our context, conversion leads to the insight that revenge seeking destroys self and damages relationships; it leads to a deeper appreciation of mercy-seeking strategies. What was once seen as weak is now viewed as courageous (see Kaufman's [1984] insights here). What was seen as passive is viewed as active and affirming. What was once seen as ineffective and paradoxical is now viewed as efficacious and internally consistent. There are numerous case studies documenting people's turn to Christian faith because of intense emotional pain, and then choosing forgiveness strategies (see, as examples of conservative Christianity, Bristol & McGinnis, 1982; Kiel, 1986; Koerbel, 1986; and of liberal Christianity, the Amanecida Collective, 1987; Gentilone & Regidor, 1986). Conversion here is different from religious or philosophical education in that the former involves *insight*, whereas the latter may involve only knowledge and a sense of obligation. The majority of the case studies involving conversion show similar patterns: injury, intense negative emotions, despair, embracing new religious insights, forgiveness, and then release. One can imagine such insight into forgiveness developing without a concomitant religious experience, but to date all cases published involve the tandem of Christian insight and forgiveness when the "change of heart" occurs.

The forgiveness motive is analogous to the justice motive discussed by Rest (1983) under his Component III. It is also similar to the utilizer function in justice problem solving as described by Thoma, Rest, and Barnett (1986), in that a strong utilizer enhances the probability that the person will view a given problem as a justice issue.

Decision to Forgive.   For Neblett (1974), committing to forgiving the other is the crux of the entire process. The commitment may involve the language, "I forgive you'' to the offending party, but in our view, this is not necessary. Neblett correctly acknowledges various intentions by the forgiver: some may decide only to refrain from punishing the offender, others may also seek positive affect toward him or her, others may further seek a renewed relationship. Intention, not the language used, is central to discerning commitment. The commitment often includes fidelity to the internal forgiveness strategies until change in self is realized. Rest (1983) places the decision for action in justice under his Component III.

Execution of Internal Forgiveness Strategies.   The published literature describes six strategies commonly used in forgiving another. One involves cognitive reinterpretation of the injurer's qualities and the event. Various terms are used for this process, such as reattribution training (Al-Mabuk, 1987), positive cognitive attributions (Droll, 1984), reframing (Bandler & Grinder, 1982), rewriting past history (Guest, 1988), seeing with new eyes (Smedes, 1984), constructive alternativism (Smith, 1981), and reappraising the injury (Trainer, 1981).

Consider Smith's (1981) description of this process:

> It is possible to call to mind some past event, and to interpret it, perhaps with some memory of the constructs we formerly used to give it meaning, but now responding to it with *alternative* constructs, and, in meeting it with revised anticipations, we find it has different meaning and significance. (p. 304)

This first internal forgiveness strategy might be described as viewing the offender and the event *in context,* using appropriate social perspective-taking skills. Consider, as one example, a college student forgiving his father for love deprivation. The student may consider the father's own child-rearing history, the financial and familial pressures on the father at the time of the deprivation, and the lack of social supports within the community. Such perspectives would require Stage 3 and 4 abilities, as described by Selman (1980). In putting the father *in context,* the student focuses, not exclusively on the father's personality (as he may have done previously), but also on the environmental events surrounding personality formation. A more complex view of the father is likely to emerge. Alternative constructs are now cognitively considered. This is not done to condone or excuse the love deprivation, but to more deeply understand this injustice, still recognized as such.[5]

---

[5]Reframing is entirely different than the ''visualizing your parent'' exercise advocated by Bloomfield and Felder (1983). They ask the son or daughter (offended party) to imagine the parent (offending party) coming in love and respect even when this will not occur. We disagree with the approach because it is not grounded in reality, where genuine forgiveness must courageously center. They further advocate physical catharsis (punching a pillow) and writing a cathartic letter, which is not sent. This is not forgiveness in our view. It is getting even in imagination.

Such exercises as the above may foster empathy in the injured toward the injurer, our second internal strategy. Feeling how the injurer feels reduces aggression toward him or her (Cunningham, 1985; Droll, 1984; Kiel, 1986; Smedes, 1984).

Third, some have described the development and nurturance of compassion toward the injurer (Cunningham, 1985; Droll, 1984). In contrast to empathy, compassion is not simply feeling the other's pain, but also behaviorally *reacting* to that pain. It is to "suffer with" the other (McNeill, Morrison, & Nouwen, 1982). This is not masochism or a marked interest in pain, but a willingness and courage to cry with the miserable and be vulnerable with the emotionally troubled (McNeill et al., 1982). Perceived degree of threat from the injurer and time since injury will influence the emergence of this component.

Fourth, if one is to forgive, then he or she must "absorb the pain" (Bergin, 1988; Eastin, 1988). In some cases there is a cycle of revenge; Fred may respond revengefully to the injury, followed by Randy's retaliation, followed by Fred's aggressive response. Forgiveness stops this pattern when the forgiver absorbs the pain given. This is akin to accepting the injustice (Downie, 1965), and to accepting psychological scars. The pain absorbed may be physical, mental, emotional, or all three.

The point certainly is not to repress the pain until it boils over; it is to absorb and wait for release, not to absorb then harbor. Consider Bergin's (1988) insightful comments in the context of family dysfunction:

Is it important, then, for somebody, sometime in the history of a pathological family, to stop the process of transmitting pain from generation to generation? Instead of seeking retribution, one learns to absorb the pain, to be forgiving, to try to reconcile with forebears, and then become a generator of positive change in the next generation. The therapeutically changed individual thereby becomes intergenerationally transitional by resisting the disordered patterns of the past, exercising an interpersonally healing impact and then transmitting to the younger generation a healthier mode of functioning. (p. 29)

Two cognitive strategies (our fifth and sixth strategies for Component 6) involving self are also present in the literature. One is the exploration of the insight that the injured party needed forgiveness from others in the past (Cunningham, 1985). If the injured sees the self as imperfect, he or she may more easily explore reframing, empathy, compassion, and absorption of pain. The second strategy is a reframing regarding self, acknowledging a change in self as a result of the injury. As an example, Close (1970) describes a therapeutic case in which a sexually abused client would not forgive because she needed to see herself as sexually pure. Only after she cognitively acknowledged the permanent change in self because of the abuse could she forgive (see also Brink [1985] regarding the acceptance of changes in self and Pingleton [1989] regarding humility).

Developmental Features of the Process Model

The process model has five features that characterize it as a developmental model. First, certain aspects of the model cannot be taught, but must await a readiness for change. The psychological defenses are one case in point. Until a certain distancing from the emotional pain is realized, the person will not (nor should be expected to) relinquish the defenses. The "change of heart" and compassion are other examples. A second feature is the directional rather than arbitrary pattern of change. Each unit in the process brings one closer to a specific goal, that of forgiveness. Third, the end point is not psychologically equivalent to the initial point. The end point removes anger and perhaps revenge motives, and substitutes in their place *agape* and emotional release. *Agape* is developmentally superior to revenge, as seen in the social cognitive stage model. Fourth, in theory, as a person masters forgiveness he or she acquires expertise in it. This may involve initiating the process sooner, moving through quicker, skipping certain units, or releasing the other more completely. Fifth, also in theory, we would expect automatization eventually to occur (for those frequently practicing forgiveness) in which the person almost without thought chooses the forgiveness option over other options when deep injury occurs.

A SYNTHESIS OF THE STAGE AND PROCESSING MODELS

The processes described earlier are based on the assumption that the person is engaging in true forgiveness, not in pseudo-forgiveness or the other machinations described under the heading, "Philosophical Objections." A direct implication, therefore, is that those who forgive in this way have some understanding of Stage 6. This does not imply that a person must be consolidated on that stage, especially if we adhere to the new assumptions of cognitive-developmental stages discussed previously. Even young individuals, those consolidated on lower levels, may have some understanding of the Stage 6 concepts, and may be able to forgive to some degree.

Yet, not all will have such understanding or use it if they have. Thus the processes people go through in the name of forgiveness may differ widely. As a first step in elucidating the stage-process synthesis, let us consider examples taken from Trainer's (1981) research. She refers to three "types" of forgiveness: role-expedient (analogous to our Stages 1 and 2 in Table 3.1), role-expected (analogous to Stage 3 and 4), and intrinsic (Stages 5 and especially 6). The role-expedient forgiver, Trainer found, may *appear* to fulfill the *Decision to Forgive* component with the words, "I forgive you." Yet there is little evidence of *Internal Forgiveness Strategies,* as hostile, condescending judgments predominate. Rather than *Behavioral Reconciliation Strategies* being used, there are assertions of self-superiority. Rather than *Release* there is continued anger.

Trainer observed that role-expected forgivers also *appear* to fulfill the *Decision to Forgive* with spoken words. Yet because the *Negative Psychological Consequence* of reaction formation is still strongly present, there are no active *Internal Forgiveness Strategies* manifested. Instead, the injurer is viewed as superior. *Behavioral Reconciliation Strategies* are passive (Park, 1988) and not dependent on the other's changed behavior. Rather than *Release,* there is repressed anxiety.

People in Trainer's third forgiveness type, intrinsic, performed the forgiveness strategies as we already discussed in Fig. 3.1. Emotional release, in this case, was realized. The implication of this synthesis is that people on different stages may markedly differ in the processes engaged toward forgiveness.

SOME FINAL THOUGHTS ON INTERVENTION

In focusing first on the forgiveness stage model, we are not recommending the educational models typically used with the Kohlbergian justice paradigm. The plus-one exchange, as the most frequently employed strategy, may not be warranted for the forgiveness stage model because all other stages than Stage 6 distort the concept of forgiveness (see Enright, Lapsley, & Levy [1983] for descriptions of plus-one techniques). Thus, educating students with plus-one simply exchanges one distortion for a more complex one. Perhaps Rest's model of stages needs to be employed in education. All people are capable of using concepts higher than their consolidated level. Those with some knowledge of Stage 6 could thus benefit from an intervention on this stage. A focus on Stage 6 may not shift the person from the existing consolidated stage; perhaps such shift should not be the goal. Instead, drawing from Rest's notion of percentage of principled reasoning concept, our goal might be to increase the student's insight into Stage 6, no matter how small at first.

Educators might do well in assessing the forgiveness motive in each student by attending to the seven variables that may attenuate or strengthen the motive. Only those who are willing to engage in forgiveness should be so educated; forgiveness should never be forced upon anyone.

In this early phase of theory generation, we have focused intervention ideas more on the process than the stage model, especially with those suffering deep hurts. The active, psychological processes that could be exercised in such an intervention, extrapolated from the detailed discussion of Fig. 3.1, is in Table 3.2. The *Need* components are absent from this table because the interventionist does not engage the *Needs;* the student already does or does not possess them. In our view the process model should be used only by trained professionals or graduate students supervised by them. We question whether the model should be

TABLE 3.2.
Psychological Variables Engaged in a Process Intervention
on Forgiveness

1.	Examination of psychological defenses
2.	Confrontation of anger; the point is to release, not harbor, the anger
3.	Admittance of shame, when this is appropriate
4.	Awareness of cathexis
5.	Awareness of cognitive rehearsal of the offense
6.	Insight that the injured party may be comparing self with the injurer
7.	Insight into a possibly altered "just world" view
8.	A change of heart/conversion/new insights that old resolution strategies are not working
9.	Commitment to forgive the offender
10.	Reframing, through role taking, who the wrongdoes is by viewing him or her in context
11.	Empathy toward the offender
12.	Awareness of compassion, as it emerges, toward the offender
13.	Acceptance/absorption of the pain
14.	Realization that self has needed others' forgiveness in the past
15.	Realization that self has been, perhaps, permanently changed by the injury
16.	Awareness of decreased negative affect and, perhaps, increased positive affect, if this begins to emerge, toward the injurer
17.	Awareness of internal, emotional release

used within a typical intervention framework that sets time boundaries on the program. The professional who uses the model must be willing to invest in the participants' lives, for as long as it may take to forgive. We recommend, then, a criterion-referenced approach in which different ending points are possible for each participant. Research done in such a context would have to use the yolked-control group format in which each participant is carefully matched and yolked with another. Randomization would determine which in the yolked pair receives treatment first. Once criterion is reached (forgiveness is realized), the relevant dependent variables, such as degree of anger, anxiety, and self-esteem, could be readministered to that pair (from pretest) to assess the influence of forgiveness on emotional and psychological improvement. If forgiveness training/education/counseling proves effective, the control subjects could receive intervention. The major point in such a research design is that forgiveness takes time and is idiosyncratic for each of us. Intervention design should reflect this.

REFERENCES

Al-Mabuk, R. H. (1987). *The development of attributional processes with implications for forgiveness research.* Unpublished doctoral preliminary exam, University of Wisconsin—Madison.

Amanecida Collective (1987). *Revolutionary forgiveness: Feminist reflections on Nicaragua.* Maryknoll, NY: Orbis Books.

Augsburger, D. (1970). *The freedom of forgiveness: Seventy times seven.* Chicago: Moody Press.

Augsburger, D. (1981). *Caring enough to not forgive.* Scottsdale, PA: Herald.

Bandler, R., & Grinder, J. (1982). *Reframing: Neuro-linguistic programming and the transformation of meaning.* Moab, Utah: Real People Press.

Beatty, J. (1970). Forgiveness. *American Philosophical Quarterly, 7,* 246–252.

Beck, T. V. (1988). Forgiving. In J. Norris (Ed.), *Daughters of the elderly: Building partnerships in caregiving* (pp. 207–211). Bloomington: Indiana University Press.

Berger, P. (1969). *The sacred canopy.* Garden City, NJ: Anchor Books.

Bergin, A. E. (1988). Three contributions of a spiritual perspective to counseling, psychotherapy, and behavioral change. *Counseling and Values, 33,* 21–31.

Bloomfield, H. H., & Felder, L. (1983). *Making peace with your parents.* New York: Ballantine Books.

Brandsma, J. M. (1982). Forgiveness: A dynamic theological and therapeutic analysis. *Pastoral Psychology, 31,* 40–50.

Brink, T. L. (1985). The role of religion in latter life: A case of consolation & forgiveness. *Journal of Psychology and Christianity, 4,* 22–25.

Bristol, G., & McGinnis, C. (1982). *When it's hard to forgive.* Wheaton, IL: Victor Books.

Calian, C. S. (1981). Christian faith as forgiveness. *Theology Today, 37,* 439–443.

Close, H. T. (1970). Forgiveness and responsibility: A case study. *Pastoral Psychology, 21,* 19–25.

Cotroneo, M. (1982). The role of forgiveness in family therapy (pp. 241–244). In A. J. Gurman (Ed.), *Questions and answers in the practice of family therapy.* New York: Brunner/Mazel.

Cunningham, B. B. (1985). The will to forgive: A pastoral theological view of forgiving. *The Journal of Pastoral Care, 39,* 141–149.

Danby, H. (1933). *The Mishnah.* Oxford: Oxford University Press.

Davies, W. W. (1920). The law of forgiveness. *Methodist Review, 103,* 807–813.

Dobel, J. P. (1980). They and we have not paid dues. *Worldview,* January–February, 13–14.

Domaris, W. R. (1986). Biblical perspectives on forgiveness. *Journal of Theology for Southern Africa, 54,* 48–50.

Donnelley, D. (1982). *Putting forgiveness into practice.* Allen TX: Argus Communications.

Downie, R. S. (1965). Forgiveness. *Philosophical Quarterly, 15,* 128–134.

Droll, D. M. (1984). *Forgiveness: Theory and research.* Unpublished doctoral dissertation, University of Nevada-Reno.

Eastin, D. L. (1988). *The treatment of adult female incest survivors by psychological forgiveness.* Unpublished doctoral dissertation proposal, University of Wisconsin–Madison.

Eisenberg-Berg, N. (1979). Development of children's prosocial moral judgment. *Developmental Psychology, 15,* 128–137.

Enright, R. D. (1980). An integration of social cognitive development and cognitive processing: Educational applications. *American Educational Research Journal, 17,* 21–41.

Enright, R. D., Lapsley, D. K., & Levy, V. M. (1983). Moral education strategies. In M. J. Pressley & J. R. Levin (Eds.), *Cognitive strategy training: Educational, clinical, and social applications* (pp. 43–83). New York: Springer.

Enright, R. D., Franklin, C. C., & Manheim, L. A. (1980). Children's distributive justice reasoning: A standardized and objective scale. *Developmental Psychology, 16,* 193–202.

Enright, R. D., Santos, M., & Al-Mabuk, R. (1989). The adolescent as forgiver. *Journal of Adolescence, 12,* 95–110.

Enright, R. D., & Zell, R. (1989). Problems encountered when we forgive one another. *Journal of Psychology and Christianity, 8,* 52–60.

Fitzgibbons, R. P. (1986). The cognitive and emotive use of forgiveness in the treatment of anger. *Psychotherapy, 23,* 629–633.

Flanigan, B. (1987). *Forgiving.* Workshops at the Mendota Mental Health Institute, Madison, WI, September 25.

Flavell, J. H. (1974). The development of inferences about others. In T. Mischel (Ed.), *Understanding other persons* (pp. 66–116). Totowa, NJ: Rowman and Littlefield.

Gentilone, F., & Regidor, J. R. (1986). The political dimension of reconciliation: A recent Italian experience. In C. Floristan, & C. Duquoc (Eds.). Forgiveness [Special issue]. *Concilium,* April. Edinburgh: T. & T. Clark.

Gilligan, C. (1982). *In a different voice: Psychological theory and women's development.* Cambridge, MA: Harvard University Press.

Gilligan, C. (1985). *Response to critics.* Paper presented at the meeting of the Society for Research in Child Development, Detroit.

Gingell, J. (1974). Forgiveness and power. *Analysis, 34,* 180–183.

Gouldner, A. W. (1973). *For sociology: Renewal and critique in sociology today.* London: Allen Lane.

Guest, J. L. (1988). *Forgiving your parents.* Downers Grove, IL: InterVarsity Press.

Gurwitz, S. B., & Dodge, K. A. (1977). Effects of confirmations and disconfirmations on stereotype-based attributions. *Journal of Personality and Social Psychology, 35,* 495–500.

Hobbes, T. (1651/1952). *Leviathan.* In R. M. Hutchins (Ed.), *Great books of the Western world* (Vol. 23). Chicago: Encyclopaedia Britannica.

Hope, D. (1987). The healing paradox of forgiveness. *Psychotherapy, 24,* 240–244.

Horsbrugh, H. J. N. (1974). Forgiveness. *Canadian Journal of Philosophy, 4,* 269–282.

Hughes, M. (1975). Forgiveness. *Analysis, 35,* 113–117.

Hume, D. (1740/1952). *An inquiry concerning human understanding.* In R. M. Hutchins (Ed.), *Great books of the Western world* (Vol. 35). Chicago: Encyclopaedia Britannica.

Hunter, R. C. A. (1978). Forgiveness, retaliation, and paranoid reactions. *Canadian Psychiatric Association Journal, 23,* 167–173.

Kahrhoff, R. E. (1988). *Forgiveness: Formula for peace of mind.* St. Charles, MO: Capital Planning Corporation.

Kaufman, M. E. (1984). The courage to forgive. *Israeli Journal of Psychiatry and Related Sciences, 21,* 177–187.

Kiel, D. V. (1986). I'm learning how to forgive. *Decisions,* February, 12–13.

Koerbel, P. (1986). *Abortion's second victim.* Wheaton, IL: Victor Books.

Kohlberg, L., & Power, C. (1981). Moral development, religious thinking, and the question of a seventh stage. In L. Kohlberg, *The philosophy of moral development* (pp. 311–372). San Francisco: Harper & Row.

Kolnai, A. (1973–1974). Forgiveness. *Proceedings of the Aristotelian Society, 74,* 91–106.

Lambert, J. C. (1985). *The human action of forgiveness.* New York: University Press of America. Francisco: Harper & Row.

Kolnai, A. (1973–1974). Forgiveness. *Proceedings of the Aristotelian Society, 74,* 91–106.

Lamberg, J. C. (1985). *The human action of forgiveness.* New York: University Press of America.

Landman, I. (Ed.). (1941). Forgiveness. *The universal Jewish encyclopedia: In ten volumes* (Vol. 4). New York: The Universal Jewish Encyclopedia, Inc.

Lapsley, J. N. (1966). Reconciliation, forgiveness, lost contracts. *Theology Today, 22,* 45–59.

Lauritzen, P. (1987). Forgiveness: Moral prerogative or religious duty? *Journal of Religious Ethics, 15,* 141–150.

Lewis, M. (1980). On forgiveness. *Philosophical Quarterly, 30,* 236–245.

Linn, D., & Linn, M. (1978). *Healing life's hurts.* New York: Paulist Press.

Mackintosh, H. R. (1927). *The Christian experience of forgiveness.* New York: Harper & Brothers.

Mawson, C. O. S., & Whiting, K. A. (1923). *Roget's pocket thesaurus.* New York: Pocket Books.

Mazor, A., Gampel, Y., Enright, R. D., & Orenstein, R. (1990). Holocaust survivors: Coping with post-traumatic memories in childhood and forty years later. *Journal of Traumatic Stress, 3*(1), 1–14.

McNeill, D. P., Morrison, D. A., & Nouwen, H. J. M. (1982). *Compassion.* Garden City, NY: Doubleday.

Minas, A. C. (1975). God and forgiveness. *Philosophical Quarterly, 25,* 138–150.

Morrow, L. (1984). Why forgive? *Time,* January 9, 26–33.

Murphy, J. G. (1982). Forgiveness and resentment. *Midwest Studies in Philosophy, 7,* 503–516.

Murphy, J. G., & Hampton, J. (1988). *Forgiveness and mercy.* Cambridge: Cambridge University Press.

Neblett, W. R. (1974). Forgiveness and ideals. *Mind, 83,* 269–275.

Newman, L. E. (1987). The quality of mercy: On the duty to forgive in the Judaic tradition. *Journal of Religious Ethics, 15,* 141–150.

Nietzsche, F. W. (1887). *The genealogy of morals.* (trans. by P. Watson). London: S.P.C.K.

North, J. (1987)., Wrongdoing and forgiveness. *Philosophy, 62,* 499–508.

Nygren, A. (1932/1953). *Agape and eros.* (trans. by P. Watson). London: S.P.C.K.

O'Shaughnessy, R. J. (1967). Forgiveness. *Philosophy, 42,* 336–352.

Park, Y. O. (1988). *The development of forgiveness in the context of friendship conflict.* Unpublished doctoral dissertation proposal, University of Wisconsin—Madison.

Pattison, E. M. (1965). On the failure to forgive or to be forgiven. *American Journal of Psychotherapy, 19,* 106–115.

Patton, J. (1985). *Is human forgiveness possible?* Nashville, TN: Abingdon.

Pingleton, J. P. (1989). The role and function of forgiveness in the psychotherapeutic process. *Journal of Psychology and Theology, 17,* 27–35.

Rest, J. R. (1979). *Revised manual for the Defining Issues Test.* Minneapolis: Minnesota Moral Research Projects.

Rest, J. R. (1983). Morality. In J. Flavell & E. Markman (Eds.), *Handbook of child psychology* (Vol. 3, pp. 556–629) (P. Mussen, Gen. ed.). New York: Wiley.

Richards, N. (1988). Forgiveness. *Ethics, 99,* 77–97.

Roberts, H. R. (1971). Mercy. *Philosophy, 36,* 352–353.

Sch-he-rie, M. (1984). *The scale of wisdom, 6,* Qum, Iran: Propogation Center, first edition (Arabic).

Selman, R. L. (1980). *The growth of interpersonal understanding.* New York: Academic Press.

Shapiro, D. S. (1978). The doctrine of the image of God and imitatio Dei. In M. M. Kellner (Ed.), *Contemporary Jewish ethics* (pp. 127–151). New York: Sanhedrin Press.

Shontz, F. C., & Rosenak, C. (1988). Psychological theories and the need for forgiveness: Assessment and critique. *Journal of Psychology and Christianity, 7,* 23–31.

Smart, A. (1968). Mercy. *Philosophy, 43,* 345–359.

Smedes, L. B. (1984). *Forgive & forget: Healing the hurts we don't deserve.* San Francisco: Harper & Row.

Smith, M. (1981). The psychology of forgiveness. *The Month, 14,* 301–307.

Strong, J. (1984). *The new Strong's exhaustive concordance of the Bible.* Nashville, TN: Thomas Nelson.

Thoma, S. J., Rest, J., & Barnett, R. (1986). Moral judgment, behavior, decision making, and attitude. In J. R. Rest (Ed.), *Moral development: Advances in theory and research* (pp. 133–175). New York: Praeger.

Thompson, R. D. (1983). The Wesleyan and the struggle to forgive. *Western Theological Journal, 18,* 81–92.

Torrance, A. (1986). Forgiveness: The essential socio-political structure of personal being. *Journal of Theology for Southern Africa, 56,* 47–59.

Trainer, M. (1981). *Forgiveness: Intrinsic, role-expected, expedient, in the context of divorce.* Unpublished doctoral dissertation, Boston University.

Twambley, P. (1976). Mercy and forgiveness. *Analysis, 36,* 84–90.

Vine, W. E. (1985). *An expository dictionary of Biblical words.* Nashville, TN: Thomas Nelson.

Walters, R. P. (1984). Forgiving: An essential element in effective living. *Studies in Formative Spirituality, 5,* 365–374.

Weber, R., & Crocker, J. (1983). Cognitive processes in the revision of stereotypic beliefs. *Journal of Personality and Social Psychology, 45,* 961–977.

Webster's new collegiate dictionary (1979). Springfield, MA: G. & C. Merriam.

Williams, D. D. (1968). Paul Tillich's doctrine of forgiveness. *Pastoral Psychology, 19,* 17–23.

Developmental Psychology
1989, Vol. 25, No. 5, 820–826

Development of Friendship Reasoning:
A Study of Interindividual Differences in Intraindividual Change

Monika Keller
Max Planck Institute for Human Development and Education
Berlin, Federal Republic of Germany

Phillip Wood
Pennsylvania State University

Structure and content aspects of interpersonal understanding in friendship reasoning (based on Selman's, 1980, model) are investigated by examining microdevelopmental processes and individual differences. In a longitudinal study, 97 Icelandic subjects at 9, 12, and 15 years of age were interviewed about six issues concerning Ss' own close friendships. The sample was stratified according to gender, social class, and level of cognitive development. Results of the microdevelopmental analysis support the cumulative nature of the development of friendship reasoning. Statistically significant differences between issues obtain at each measurement. Furthermore, prerequisite relationships among issues are observed to emerge over time. Analysis of individual differences shows that social class and level of cognitive development exert a stable influence over time on friendship reasoning. The order of development of the issues is not affected by individual differences.

Several studies in recent years have investigated how children and adolescents interpret friendship and how this interpretation changes developmentally. In spite of differences in methodological approaches, there is convergence in the developmental changes described. Younger children tend to focus more on concrete aspects of interaction (e.g., sharing toys and material goods) whereas young adolescents, without necessarily rejecting the relevance of concrete aspects of interaction, emphasize the importance of more abstract dimensions, such as intimacy, trust, and faithfulness. They show greater awareness of the psychological aspects of friendship, of friends' personalities, and of the rules of reciprocity that govern interaction (Asher & Gottman, 1981; Berndt, 1986; Bigelow, 1977; Damon, 1977; Youniss, 1980).

In the cognitive–structural tradition, these developmental trends have been conceptualized as a sequence of hierarchically organized stages or levels (Selman, 1980; Selman & Jaquette, 1977). Selman defined a sequence of five levels of friendship reasoning that are assumed to form a hierarchy in which each lower level represents a necessary but not sufficient condition for the next higher level. Levels of friendship reasoning are assessed across various content aspects that represent unique fea-

tures of the friendship concept. These issues include the characteristics of an ideal friend, the meaning of closeness and trust as well as of conflict resolution, and the formation and termination of friendship.

The ability to differentiate and coordinate social perspectives hypothetically represents the cognitive "deep structure" of levels of reasoning about various issues of friendship (Selman, 1980). For example, the issue of trust has different meanings at each developmental level: At Level 1, trust is defined from the subjective perspective of one person as the predictability of the friend's concrete behavior. At Level 2, trust is understood in terms of a reciprocal relationship between friends in which aspects of the inner world (e.g., thoughts, intentions, secrets) can be shared. At Level 3, trust is understood as mutual and intimate sharing of personal experiences in an ongoing relationship. At Level 4, trust implies the awareness that intimacy and needs for independence must be balanced in order to maintain a satisfying relationship.

Selman (1976, 1980, 1981; Gurucharri, Phelps, & Selman, 1984; Gurucharri & Selman, 1982) studied friendship reasoning as one facet of general interpersonal understanding. He concluded that reasoning develops sequentially and is generally consistent across domains. Some content effects occur, but they are more pronounced in younger subjects (between 6 and 14 years of age) than in adolescents (Selman, 1980, p. 179). Thus, the data suggest that homogeneity across content areas may be a product of development.

Intraindividual Consistency in Friendship Reasoning

Contradictory results have been obtained regarding the consistency of friendship reasoning across issues. Oppenheimer and Thijssen (1983), using questionnaire items, supported Selman's interpretation of mutual dependency of friendship issues. Pellegrini (1986), in a study of children between 9 and 15 years

This research is part of Project Child Development and Social Structure, which is being carried out by the Center of Development and Socialization at the Max Planck Institute for Human Development and Education in West Berlin in cooperation with the Department of Social Science of the University of Iceland. Phillip Wood was supported by a grant from the National Institute of Aging (T32-AG00-110-02).

We thank Wolfgang Edelstein, Marvin Berkowitz, and Teresa Jacobsen for helpful comments. In addition, the helpful commentaries of the reviewers are gratefully acknowledged.

Correspondence concerning this article should be addressed to Monika Keller, Max Planck Institute for Human Development and Education, Lentzeallee 94, D-1000 Berlin 33, Federal Republic of Germany.

of age, using Selman's (1980) friendship interview, found a surprising amount of heterogeneity in reasoning about friendship concept issues. Pellegrini did not analyze age-specific differences, so whether reasoning becomes more homogeneous across content areas over time remains a question.

These findings raise more general questions about consistency and synchrony in development that have been extensively debated in cognitive developmental and social cognitive theory (Damon, 1983; Fischer, 1983; Flavell, 1972, 1977, 1982; Gelman & Baillargeon, 1983; Turiel, 1983). Friendship reasoning is a domain where this controversy can be fruitfully pursued. On one hand, friendship issues can be expected to have the close conceptual interdependencies that Flavell (1982) claimed are the basis for consistency and synchrony in development. On the other hand, the issues of the friendship concept measure distinct and theoretically meaningful aspects of the overall concept of friendship. The issues of trust and closeness may be seen as representing the central defining features of intimate friendship. On the other hand, the perception of the process of becoming friends follows from the basic meaning of friendship. Thus, conceptual changes in the meaning of trust and closeness will influence the evaluation of how friendship is established over time, whereas changes in the evaluation of how friendship is established are not expected to influence the basic meaning of trust and closeness in friendship. This assumption is congruent with Rest's (1983) functional model of moral problem solving, in which reflection of strategies is a later step than the definition of the problem elements themselves. Two types of relationship between the issues may obtain: First, trust and closeness may be "easier" with regard to the developmental level that subjects achieve. Second, certain precursor relations may obtain between issues. In this case, progression in the issues of trust and closeness may function as a necessary but not sufficient condition for further progression in the issue of friendship formation. Consequently, it is expected that the development of the issues of trust and closeness precedes the development of the issue of friendship formation.

Individual Differences in Reasoning About Friendship

Research in social cognitive development has generally given little attention to the role of social experience and individual differences in development. Because developmental sequences are often assumed to be universal, studies have concentrated more on differences in rates of development than on the organization of concepts within groups or the existence of multiple sequences in development (Fischer & Bullock, 1981).

Only two factors in the literature have been consistently considered as possible sources of individual differences in social cognitive performance (Shantz, 1983): general cognitive functioning and gender. Although research on gender-specific differences suggests that girls have a preference for dyadic relationships (Eder & Hallinan, 1978) and express more emotional concerns than boys (Berndt, 1986; Kon & Losenkov, 1978), corresponding differences have not been found in the level of interpersonal reasoning or friendship reasoning specifically (Pellegrini, 1985, 1986; Selman, 1980). General cognitive development has been found to be positively related to levels of both

interpersonal and friendship reasoning (Pellegrini, 1985, 1986; Selman, 1980). The relationship of general cognitive development to friendship reasoning across time has not been explored.

Social class is a construct rarely mentioned in social cognitive research. This construct is, however, a primary source of individual differences in social experience. Selman (1980) and Pellegrini (1985, 1986) found a moderately positive relationship between levels of interpersonal as well as friendship reasoning and social class. According to Selman, children from working-class origins lagged behind middle-class children between the ages of 7 and 10 years, but not in adolescence. Thus, early differences appeared to level off with age.

The present study explores the development and interrelationship of subcomponents of the friendship concept over time and examines microdevelopmental processes in light of individual differences.

Intraindividual Hypotheses

The development of the friendship issues is cumulative and sequential. Homogeneity in reasoning about the different issues of the friendship concept obtains so that, for each issue, a statistically significant difference *between* measurement occasions will obtain. Because the issues are distinct elements of the overall concept of friendship, however, we expect that systematic differences between issues *within* measurement occasions will obtain. More specifically, the overall level of development of the issues of trust and closeness will be higher than that for the issue of friendship formation. Finally, we expect processes of generalization or consolidation to lead to greater homogeneity between issues over time.

Individual Differences Hypotheses

Differences between individuals in friendship reasoning that are due to cognitive functioning and social class are expected to persist over time. Middle-class subjects and cognitively well-developed subjects should achieve higher levels of friendship reasoning. Gender should not be related to development of friendship reasoning, and differences between issues should not vary between groups.

Method

Subjects

Subjects came from a cohort of children who had entered the first grade of public schools in Reykjavik, Iceland. Of the 97 subjects included in this study, 23 girls and 28 boys are of lower- and lower-middle-class origin, and 22 girls and 24 boys are of upper-middle- and upper-class origin. Subjects were tested at 7 years of age on cognitive development and at 9, 12, and 15 years of age on their friendship reasoning.

Instruments and Scoring

Friendship conceptions. The friendship interview was a modification of Selman's (1980, 1981) procedure. Instead of eliciting reasoning about friendship within a hypothetical friendship dilemma, subjects were interviewed exclusively about their own friendships. The following six issues were explored in a semistructured interview using several open-ended questions: *motivation* (Why is friendship important? Why does one need a best friend?); *ideal friend* (What type of person makes a good friend? What are the special characteristics of a close friend? What is the difference between a good friend and a best friend? What makes friendship really close?); *trust* (What does it mean to trust one's friend? Why is trust in friendship important?); *conflict resolution* (What types of quarrels happen between friends? How are quarrels solved?); and *formation of friendship* (How does one go about making friends? What is needed to become good friends?).

All subjects were given standard questions, but interviews varied in the specific wording and order of some of the questions. Additional questions were asked when the child's comprehension seemed in doubt or when the answer was unclear.

Different interviewers interviewed subjects at different measurement occasions. The interviewers did not know the subjects' responses from the previous interviews and had no information about the social class of the subject. The same raters rated children from all three age groups (one of the raters was trained in Selman's "Harvard-Judge Baker Social Reasoning Project"). Because of the longitudinal design, the raters knew about the age of the subject but were blind to social class and sex as well as to the subject's interviews from the previous ages.

Two raters scored 30 interviews for each age group. Exact percentage of agreement in sublevel varied for the issues between 84% and 96%. Average agreement across the issues was 94%, 88%, and 90%, for the 9-, 12-, and 15-year-olds, respectively. Such agreement levels are comparable to those reported by Selman (1980) and Pellegrini (1986) for scoring full levels.

Interviews were scored according to a scoring manual by Selman and Jaquette (1977). On the basis of the present data, this manual was further elaborated in order to define transitional levels (Keller, Essen, & Mönnig, 1987). If the concepts expressed with regard to an issue were basically at a single stage, the issue was scored as *pure stage* (e.g., 0, 1, 2, 3, 4). If the concept represented stage mixture, it was scored as *transitional* with a predominant full stage and subordinate stage level, for example, Stage 1 (2), Stage 2 (1), and so on (where the number in parentheses represents the minor level).

Scoring examples are given for the transition between Level 1 and Level 2 in the issue of trust. At Level 1, trust means the unilateral predictability of concrete material acts (e.g., trusting that the friend takes care of things lent to her; that she goes to a store if she has said so). At Level 1 (2), in addition to this concrete behavior, the necessity of trust for the maintenance of a long-term relationship and the normative implications of a violation of concrete behavioral expectations are emphasized (e.g., they may become better friends if they trust each other; it makes a great difference if she betrays that). At Level 2, trust is interpreted as reciprocal access to each others' true feelings, thoughts, and intentions. Friends share their secrets and rely on each others' truthfulness (e.g., Friends will not blabber out secrets; you can trust that the friend tells the truth or keeps promises; friends don't betray each other). At Level 2 (1), these basic ideas are expressed but are either unelaborated or still interpreted in a Level 1 way (e.g., Trust means to keep promises and to trust that a friend won't hit you or tease you; a friend does everything you tell him provided he promised to do so; friends stand by what you have told them to do).

Given the theoretical five-stage model, scores can vary in sublevels of one-third of a full stage on a 13-point scale from Pure Stage 0 to Pure Stage 4. Scores actually varied between Transitional Level 1 (0) and Pure Stage 3 because of the age restrictions of the sample. The range of scores in each age group consisted of 5 to 6 sublevels.

Cognitive development. Two sets of standardized Piagetian tasks for concrete-operational reasoning were administered at age 7. The concept of conservation was assessed in eight content domains (number, substance, continuous and discontinuous quantities, area, two-dimensional

Table 1

Percentages of Sublevel Change in Global Stage Score of Friendship Reasoning From 9 to 12 and From 12 to 15 Years

Measurement occasions	Regression $-^1/_3$	Stability 0	Progression		
			$+^1/_3$	$+^2/_3$	$+^3/_3$
9–12 years	3	18	41	23	14
12–15 years	3	25	40	23	9

Note. Fractions represent portions, in thirds, of one full stage.

space, length, and weight), using a test developed by Goldschmid and Bentler (1968). The concepts of classification and class inclusion were measured using Smedslund's (1964) procedure. These tasks examine the ability to classify hierarchically and to compare classes and subordinate classes quantitatively.

The tasks were scored dichotomously as either preoperational or concrete operational (see Schröder, 1989, for a detailed description of the tasks and scoring criteria). A summary score of concrete-operational reasoning was derived by combining the scores for the Piagetian tasks. Groups representing either *high* or *low* cognitive development were defined by dividing the sample at the median. In essence, this procedure classified the two groups into preoperational and concrete operational 7-year-olds.

Social class. Björnsson and Edelstein's scale was used to assess the household heads' position in the social class system of Iceland. Research has shown that this scale is a valid indicator of family position in the emerging and complex system of social inequality in Iceland (see Björnsson, Edelstein, & Kreppner, 1977). Classes were dichotomized into lower (1–3) and higher (4–6) classes.

Results

Analysis of Microdevelopmental Aspects of Friendship Reasoning

Cumulativity and sequentiality. Patterns of progression, stability (no change between two measurement occasions), and regression in sublevel change between measurement occasions were calculated for the global stage score in friendship reasoning (computed as the mean of the six issues; see Table 1).

Regression between two measurement occasions occurred in only 3% of the cases, all within one third of a stage. Progression amounting to one third of a stage between two measurement occasions is the most frequent developmental pattern, whereas stability and progressions of two thirds of a stage are about equally frequent. Progressions of a full stage or more are rare.

Change patterns for the individual issues are somewhat different. In summary, between 9 and 12 years of age, the data evidence about 10% regressions for the issues of trust, ideal friend, and motivation and about 5% regressions for the three other issues. Between 12 and 15 years of age, conflict, trust, and motivation show about 10% regressions, and the other issues, considerably less. Most regressions were within one third of a stage. At the issue level, patterns of no change are observed in about 20% to 30% of the cases. Progression rates of one third, two third, or a full stage are distributed rather equally. Anything more than a full stage change occurs very rarely.

Table 2
Issue Specific Means at 9, 12, and 15 Years of Age

	Measurement occasions		
Issues	9 years	12 years	15 years
Trust	1.68[a]	2.02[a]	2.22[b]
Closeness	1.47[a,b]	1.97[a]	2.43[a]
Conflict	1.56[a,b]	2.00[a]	2.36[a,b]
Ideal friend	1.47[a,b]	1.84[a,b]	2.27[a,b]
Motivation	1.39[b]	1.86[a,b]	2.29[a,b]
Mechanism	1.42[b]	1.75[b]	2.22[b]

Note. For multiple effects, classes sharing a letter are not significantly different (Scheffé tests within age groups).

Homogeneity/heterogeneity. A five-way analysis of variance (ANOVA) with repeated measurements was computed to test the within-subject effects of Time of Testing (9, 12, 15 years) and Issues (motivation, mechanism, closeness, ideal friend, trust, and conflict resolution) and the between-group variables of Gender, Social Class (lower class and upper class), and Cognitive Development (high and low) on friendship reasoning. Because of unequal cell frequencies and occasional random missing scores, a General Linear Model (GLM) procedure within the SAS system (1986) was chosen, using the Individual × Time interaction as the basis for estimation of the mean square error.

For the variables relevant to the microdevelopmental analysis, time and issue, the results reveal statistically significant main effects for time, $F(2, 1,986) = 587.34, p < .001$, and issue, $F(5, 1,686) = 18.43, p < .001$, and a statistically significant disordinal Time × Issue interaction, $F(10, 1,668) = 3.78, p < .01$. Post hoc Scheffé tests revealed a strong developmental effect. All issues were significantly different from each other at each measurement occasion (see Table 2). Overall means of friendship reasoning for each time of testing were 1.50, 1.91, and 2.30, for the 9-, 12-, and 15-year-olds, respectively. Thus, across the 6 years, progression amounts to slightly less than a full stage on the average for all issues.

The effect of issue was tested for each measurement occasion (see Table 2, columnwise comparisons). Post hoc Scheffé tests showed that, for the 9-year-olds, trust was the highest scoring issue and significantly different from the issues of motivation and mechanism. For the 12-year-olds, trust, closeness, and conflict resolution were significantly higher than mechanism. For the 15-year-olds, the highest scoring issue of closeness was significantly different from trust and mechanism. Thus, the Time × Issue interaction was due to the fact that some issues changed their relative position over time. The most marked change was observed for the issue of trust, which was the highest scoring issue for both the 9- and the 12-year-olds but the lowest scoring issue for the 15-year-olds.

Consolidation. With regard to the assumption of increasing homogeneity or consolidation, results of the repeated measurement ANOVA revealed that the intraindividual differences between issues did not decrease over time (see Table 2).

Precursor relationships. Whether precursor relationships between issues obtain in intraindividual development was tested using the prediction analysis developed by Hildebrand, Laing, and Rosenthal (1977). Prediction analysis can be used to test for relationships of the following type: It holds for every person that development of a variable x precedes development of a variable y. The prediction coefficient indicates the amount of reduction in error in the prediction of a dependent variable if a specific pattern of distributions is hypothesized. The prediction coefficient can vary between 0 and 1. Tests compared the relationship of trust and closeness to friendship formation. The results yielded no prerequisite relationships between the issues for the 9-year-olds. For the 12-year-olds, the issue of closeness preceded the issue of mechanism with a prediction coefficient of .45 ($p < .05$). This prediction coefficient became stronger for the 15-year-olds (.94; $p < .001$).

Analysis of Individual Differences

An ANOVA with repeated measurements was computed for the variables relevant to hypotheses about individual differences—social class, gender, and level of cognitive development. The results revealed statistically significant main effects of social class, $F(1, 1,686) = 38.38, p < .001$, cognitive development, $F(1, 1,686) = 41.48, p < .001$, and gender, $F(1, 1,686) = 17.14, p < .001$. In addition, statistically significant Social Class × Sex, $F(1, 1,686) = 11.39; p < .001$, and Cognition × Sex × Social Class, $F(1, 1,686) = 13.27, p < .001$, interactions obtained. Post hoc Scheffé comparisons ($\alpha = .05$) of the Sex × Social Class interaction revealed that lower-class boys achieved the lowest level of friendship reasoning compared with the other three groups. Post hoc Scheffé tests ($\alpha = .05$) of the Sex × Social Class × Cognition interaction revealed that the interaction effects of cognition and class were more apparent in males than in females (see Figure 1).

More specifically, the effects of cognitive functioning were in the same direction for lower-class subjects: Lower-class/high-cognition males or females, respectively, achieved higher scores on friendship reasoning than lower-class/low-cognition males or females, respectively. Among the latter group, post hoc Scheffé comparisons evidenced that the lower-class/low-cognition males scored at the lowest level in friendship reasoning compared with all other groups ($\alpha = .05$). In the upper class, on the other hand, the effects of cognitive development were different for the sexes. For upper-class females, cognition was of no influence for level of friendship reasoning, whereas a marked effect of cognition on friendship reasoning was evidenced in the upper-class males: Post hoc Scheffé comparisons showed that upper-class/high-cognition males achieved the highest level of performance compared with all other groups ($\alpha = .05$).

Because no interaction was found between the issue variable and the between-group variables, we can conclude that the relationships between issues did not differ across subgroups. Prediction analyses within the subgroups supported this result. The precursor relationships found between issues within the subgroups were basically the same as for the entire sample.

Discussion

Microdevelopmental Analysis of Friendship Reasoning

The results of this study are in agreement with those reported by Selman (1980) for the longitudinal development of interper-

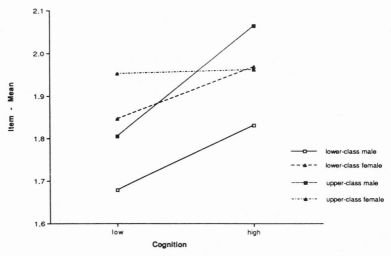

Figure 1. The triple interaction of Cognition, Socioeconomic Status and Sex.

sonal reasoning in subjects from the United States and, thus, support the cross-cultural validity of the theory. Results confirm the assertion that the developmental transformation of social reasoning structures proceeds in a slow and gradual manner as demonstrated by Selman and, for moral reasoning, by Colby, Kohlberg, Gibbs, and Lieberman (1983). In general, it takes about 6 years to advance one full stage from Stage 1(2) to Stage 2(3). On the average, we observe somewhat more regressions for the particular issues than is the case for the global stage score. Nevertheless, given measurement error, these results can be taken to support the claim that the development of friendship reasoning is a cumulative and sequential process.

The results further indicate that the development of friendship reasoning proceeds as a function of the interaction between the operative structure and the content. The main effect for time is relatively large compared with the issue main effect. This is taken to support the notion of a stage-like progression of the issues of friendship reasoning. However, the statistically significant issue effect implies that there is heterogeneity among the issues as well.

Some friendship issues are easier than others. This is true for the issue of trust at ages 9 and 12 and for the issue of closeness at ages 12 and 15 years, as was expected in view of the definitions of the core meaning of friendship. The issue of mechanism (strategies of friendship initiation) is the most "difficult" issue on all measurement occasions. It is difficult to say why trust undergoes such a marked change of position on the last measurement occasion in adolescence. The shift from a concrete conception of relationship in middle childhood to a conceptualization of relationship as intimacy, mutual caring, and loyalty

in adolescence appears to be more difficult to achieve for the issue of trust than is the case for other issues, especially the issue of closeness. One reason may be that, for the issue of trust, the transformation into Stage 3 reasoning involves prescriptive (moral) aspects such as loyalty and dependability, whereas the issue of closeness involves the descriptive aspect of intimacy. Prescriptive moral reasoning has been demonstrated to develop later than descriptive social cognition (Kurdek, 1978; Walker, 1980).

Differences in the difficulty levels of the issues do not inform the researcher about the structural relationships between the issues over time. In this study, the tests for precursor relationships between the issues show that such structural relationships emerge and become stronger over time. Thus, the data reveal that necessary but not sufficient relationships, as they have been assumed to exist between different tasks within a domain (Urberg & Docherty, 1976), occur between subconcepts within a conceptually rather homogeneous domain (see also Edelstein, Keller, & Wahlen, 1984). It is interesting that the strength of the hierarchical relationships shows a marked increase over time. This may be interpreted as a developmental increase in differentiation and coordination of subcomponents of social reasoning in the sense of Werner's (1948) orthogenetic principle. It must be kept in mind, however, that such integration refers only to the logical connection between issues and not to increasing homogeneity in reasoning over time. Neither does the task variance decrease nor do individuals get more homogeneous in their reasoning about the different friendship issues.

Individual Differences in Friendship Reasoning

The results support the hypothesis that individual differences affect the rate of individual development across the levels of friendship reasoning in a stable way over time. Even though these effects appear small compared with the overall developmental effect, it should be borne in mind that, on the average, differences of one third of a stage represent a difference of about 2 years in development. Differences in cognitive development at the age of 7 years exert a stable influence on the development of reasoning about friendship over the 6-year time span. Contrary to Selman's (1980) findings, gender and social class membership exert a stable influence on development over time. The interaction effects show that social class effects are most salient in the low-cognition group and in boys. The effects of gender and cognitive development are in evidence in the lower social class but are absent in the higher social class. Thus, lower-class subjects, and especially boys, appear to be deprived with regard to certain experiences that are relevant for the development of friendship reasoning. On the basis of previous findings that lower-class families in Iceland place less weight on affective and communicative processes in socialization (see Björnsson et al., 1977), we may speculate that role-taking opportunities (Kohlberg, 1969) differ between classes.

Finally, the results indicate that individual differences have no influence on the relationship among the issues. Both differences in issue difficulty and precursor relationships between issues remain stable across subgroups. Thus, the organization of the friendship issues and the developmental logic in the construction process as revealed by the developmental relationships among issues is universal in the culture assessed. This implies that the social experiences made in different "life worlds" of the culture under scrutiny are either irrelevant or sufficiently homogeneous so as not to affect the microdevelopmental processes assessed in this study.

References

Asher, S. R., & Gottman, J. M. (Eds.). (1981). *The development of children's friendships.* Cambridge, MA: Cambridge University Press.

Berndt, T. J. (1986). Children's comments about their friends. In M. Perlmutter (Ed.), *Minnesota Symposia on Child Psychology* (Vol. 18, pp. 189–212). Minneapolis: University of Minnesota Press.

Bigelow, B. J. (1977). Children's friendship expectations: A cognitive-developmental study. *Child Development, 48,* 246–253.

Björnsson, S., Edelstein, W., & Kreppner, K. (1977). *Explorations in social inequality: Stratification dynamics in social and individual development in Iceland.* (Studien und Berichte, Nr. 38). Berlin, Federal Republic of Germany. Max Planck Institute for Human Development and Education.

Colby, A., Kohlberg, L., Gibbs, J., & Lieberman, M. (1983). A longitudinal study of moral judgment. *Monographs of the Society for Research in Child Development, 48*(1–2, Serial No. 200).

Damon, W. (1977). *The social world of the child.* San Francisco: Jossey-Bass.

Damon, W. (1983). The nature of social–cognitive change in the developing child. In W. F. Overton (Ed.), *The relationship between social and cognitive development* (pp. 103–141). Hillsdale, NJ: Erlbaum.

Edelstein, W., Keller, M., & Wahlen, K. (1984). Structure and content in social cognition: Conceptual and empirical analyses. *Child Development, 55,* 1514–1526.

Eder, D., & Hallinan, M. (1978). Sex differences in children's friendships. *American Sociological Review, 43,* 237–250.

Fischer, K. W. (1983). Developmental levels as periods of discontinuity.

In K. W. Fischer (Ed.), Levels and transitions in children's development. *New Directions for Child Development* (Vol. 21, pp. 5–20). San Francisco: Jossey-Bass.

Fischer, K. W., & Bullock, D. (1981). Patterns of data: Sequence, synchrony, and constraint in cognitive development. In K. W. Fischer (Ed.), Cognitive development: *New directions for child development* (No. 12 pp. 1–20). San Francisco: Jossey-Bass.

Flavell, J. H. (1972). An analysis of cognitive developmental sequences. *Genetic Psychological Monographs, 86,* 279–350.

Flavell, J. H. (1977). *Cognitive development.* Englewood Cliffs, NJ: Prentice Hall.

Flavell, J. H. (1982). Structures, stages and sequences in cognitive development. In A. Collins (Ed.), *Minnesota Symposia on Child Psychology* (Vol. 15, pp. 1–28). Hillsdale, NJ: Erlbaum.

Gelman, R., & Baillargeon, R. (1983). A review of some Piagetian concepts. In P. H. Mussen (Series Ed.) & J. H. Flavell & E. Markman (Vol. Eds.), *Handbook of child psychology: Vol. 3. Cognitive development* (pp. 167–230). New York: Wiley.

Goldschmid, M. L., & Bentler, P. M. (1968). *Manual: Concept assessment kit—Conservation.* San Diego, CA: Educational and Industrial Testing Service.

Gurucharri, C., Phelps, E., & Selman, R. L. (1984). Development of interpersonal understanding: A longitudinal and comparative study of normal and disturbed youths. *Journal of Consulting and Clinical Psychology, 52,* 26–36.

Gurucharri, C., & Selman, R. L. (1982). The development of interpersonal understanding during childhood, preadolescence, and adolescence: A longitudinal follow-up study. *Child Development, 53,* 924–927.

Hildebrand, D. K., Laing, J. D., & Rosenthal, H. (1977). *Prediction analysis of cross classifications.* New York: Wiley.

Keller, M., Essen, C. von, & Mönnig, M. (1987). *Manual zur Entwicklung von Freundschaftsvorstellungen* (Manual for scoring friendship reasoning). Unpublished manuscript, Max Planck Institute for Human Development, Berlin, Federal Republic of Germany.

Kohlberg, L. (1969). Stage and sequence: The cognitive–developmental approach to socialization. In D. A. Goslin (Ed.), *Handbook of socialization theory and research* (pp. 374–480). Chicago: Rand McNally.

Kon, I., & Losenkov, V. (1978). Friendship in adolescence: Values and behavior. *Journal of Marriage and the Family, 40,* 142–155.

Kurdek, L. A. (1978). Perspective taking as the cognitive basis of children's moral development: A review of the literature. *Merrill-Palmer Quarterly, 24,* 2–28.

Oppenheimer, L., & Thijssen, F. (1983). Children's thinking about friendships and its relation to popularity. *Journal of Psychology, 114,* 69–78.

Pellegrini, D. S. (1985). Social cognition and competence in middle childhood. *Child Development, 56,* 253–264.

Pellegrini, D. S. (1986). Variability in children's level of reasoning about friendship. *Journal of Applied Developmental Psychology, 7,* 341–354.

Rest, J. R. (1983). Morality. In P. H. Mussen (Series Ed.) & J. H. Flavell & E. Markman (Vol. Eds.), *Handbook of child psychology: Vol. 3. Cognitive development* (pp. 556–629). New York: Wiley.

SAS programmer's guide for PL/I, Version 5. (1986). Cary, NC: SAS Institute.

Schröder, E. (1989). *Vom konkreten zum formalen Denken. Individuelle Entwicklungsverläufe im Alter von 7 bis 15 Jahren* [From concrete to formal reasoning: Individual developmental paths from childhood to adolescence]. Basel, Switzerland: Huber.

Selman, R. L. (1976). Toward a structural analysis of developing interpersonal relations. In A. D. Pick (Ed.), *Minnesota Symposia on Child*

Psychology (pp. 156–200). Minneapolis: University of Minnesota Press.

Selman, R. L. (1980). *The growth of interpersonal understanding.* New York: Academic Press.

Selman, R. L. (1981). The child as a friendship philosopher. In S. R. Asher & J. M. Gottman (Eds.), *The development of children's friendships* (pp. 242–272). Cambridge, MA: Cambridge University Press.

Selman, R. L., & Jaquette, D. (1977). Stability and oscillation in interpersonal awareness: A clinical–developmental analysis. In C. B. Keasey (Ed.), *Nebraska Symposium on Motivation* (Vol. 25, pp. 261–304). Lincoln: University of Nebraska Press.

Shantz, C. U. (1983). Social cognition. In P. H. Mussen (Series Ed.) & J. H. Flavell & E. Markman (Vol. Eds.), *Handbook of child psychology: Vol. 3. Cognitive development* (pp. 495–555). New York: Wiley.

Smedslund, J. (1964). Concrete reasoning: A study in intellectual development. *Monographs of the Society for the Research in Child Development, 29*(Serial No. 93).

Turiel, E. (1983). Domains and categories in social cognitive development. In W. Overton (Ed.), *The relationship between social and cognitive development* (pp. 53–90). Hillsdale, NJ: Erlbaum.

Urberg, K., & Docherty, E. M. (1976). The development of role-taking skills in young children. *Developmental Psychology, 12,* 198–203.

Walker, L. J. (1980). Cognitive and perspective-taking prerequisites for moral development. *Child Development, 51,* 131–139.

Werner, H. (1948). *The comparative psychology of mental development.* Chicago: Wilcox & Follett.

Youniss, J. (1980). *Parents and peers in social development.* Chicago: Chicago University Press.

Received September 21, 1987
Revision received February 16, 1989
Accepted February 23, 1989 ■

Children's Understanding of Moral Emotions

Gertrud Nunner-Winkler

Max Planck Institute for Psychological Research

Beate Sodian

University of Munich

NUNNER-WINKLER, GERTRUD, and SODIAN, BEATE. *Children's Understanding of Moral Emotions.* CHILD DEVELOPMENT, 1988, 59, 1323–1338. 4–8-year-old children's attributions of emotion to a story figure who violated a moral rule were studied in a series of experiments. Most 4-year-olds judged a wrongdoer to experience positive emotions, focusing their justifications on the successful outcome of his action, whereas almost all 8-year-olds attributed negative feelings, focusing on the moral value of the wrongdoer's action. A developmental trend from outcome-oriented toward morally oriented emotion attributions was also observed in children's judgments of the feelings of a story character who had resisted temptation. When morally evaluating a wrongdoer, only children above the age of 6 years took emotional reactions into account, judging a "happy" wrongdoer to be worse than a "sorry" one. 4- and 5-year-olds attributed positive emotions to a wrongdoer even if his transgression was severe and if he did not gain any material profit from it. However, they did not expect a person (even an ill-motivated one) to feel good if he or she unintentionally harmed another person or merely observed someone being hurt. These results are discussed in relation to recent research on children's developing conceptions of emotion and on the early development of moral understanding.

The nature of young children's morality is controversial: Kohlberg (1976) maintained that in the earliest stages (until 11 years) the child's morality is based on extrinsic features, moral obligation being both external and coercive. Similarly, Damon (1977) and Blasi (1982) described young children's moral reasoning as being based on purely instrumental factors. On the other hand, Turiel (1983) claims that even very young preschoolers possess a genuine understanding of morality (see also Keller & Edelstein, 1986; Döbert, 1987), being able to distinguish between moral and conventional transgressions and deriving their judgments from genuinely moral considerations such as welfare, fairness, and obligations. Furthermore, even the very young child's sensitivity to the needs of others and his willingness to forgo his own interests for altruistic motives has been amply documented in research on prosocial obligations and in observations of children's moral acts in real life (Eisenberg-Berg, 1982, 1986; Hoff-

man, 1982; see Radke-Yarrow, Zahn-Waxler, & Chapman, 1983, for a review).

The significance of morality for young children might be better understood if we knew more about the emotions children attach to morally relevant situations. In "functionalist" theories of emotion, "emotions are conceptualized as important internal monitoring and guidance systems, designed to appraise events and motivate human action" (Bretherton, Fritz, Zahn-Waxler, & Ridgeway, 1986, p. 530). Moral events are likely to provoke intensive and potentially conflicting feelings. A person who violates a moral rule may, for instance, experience joy at the success of his or her forbidden action, and/or shame, guilt, and remorse at his or her immoral behavior, and/or fear of its possible consequences. A person's behavior in situations of moral temptation may be influenced by the emotional consequences he or she expects a moral transgression to have. Thus the expec-

The research presented in this paper was conducted within the context of the *Munich Longitudinal Study on the Genesis of Individual Competencies* (see Weinert & Schneider, 1987). We would like to thank the members of the research group at the Max Planck Institute for critical discussions of the project, and Jens Asendorpf, Augusto Blasi, Merry Bullock, and Paul Harris for helpful comments and suggestions on earlier versions of this manuscript. We are grateful to Katrin Bandomer, Barbara Gollwitzer, and Martina Hascher for their assistance in data collection and the staff and children of various kindergartens in Munich for their friendly cooperation. The order of authorship is alphabetical. Requests for reprints should be addressed to G. Nunner-Winkler, Max Planck Institute for Psychological Research, Leopoldstr.24, D-8000 Munich 40, West Germany.

tation that committing a moral transgression will be followed by unpleasant feelings like shame and remorse may play an important role in motivating moral behavior.

Children's conceptions of the emotional consequences of moral transgressions are part of their larger conceptions of the situational determinants of emotion. Children's developing ability to infer emotions from situational cues has recently been investigated in a number of studies (see Bretherton et al., 1986, for a review). Even young preschoolers are quite proficient at attributing simple "general purpose" emotions such as happiness and sadness to other persons. They rarely, however, refer to more complex emotions such as pride, shame, remorse, or guilt in their spontaneous speech (Ridgeway, Waters, & Kuczaj, 1985). When presented with situations in which a character succeeded or failed in achievement or moral contexts for reasons of effort (lack of effort), good or bad luck, or intervention of others, only children above the age of 7 or 8 years appropriately infer complex emotions based on causal attributions such as pride, pity, anger, and shame (Thompson, 1987; Thompson & Paris, 1981; Weiner, Graham, Stern, & Lawson, 1982). Even if young children do not distinguish between shame, anger, and mere sadness or pride, gratitude, and mere happiness, they generally expect success to be followed by positive and failure by negative emotions (Barden, Zelko, Duncan, & Masters, 1980). This seems natural as long as a person's actions are in accordance with social or moral norms. If, however, an actor violates social or moral standards intentionally in order to attain a personal goal, his or her emotions may either be inferred from the success or failure of his or her goal-directed action or from the social or moral value of this action. That is, a successful wrongdoer may be expected to be happy at the success of his action or sad (sorry, ashamed) at having violated a moral rule.

In a study of children's knowledge about the experiential determinants of emotion, Barden et al. (1980) found that kindergartners differed from older children in their predictions of the emotions a person would experience who had committed a dishonesty that went undetected. When offered a choice between "happy," "sad," "mad," "scared," and "just OK," most 4- and 5-year-olds predicted that the person would feel happy, whereas 9–10-year-old children expected a scared or sad reaction. When asked about their own emotional reactions to hypothetical moral transgressions, these young children also predicted happiness. This finding is surprising from an adult's point of view since Zelko, Duncan, Barden, Garber, and Masters (1986) found that adults expected preschool children to feel sad or scared in response to having committed a dishonesty.

If the developmental trend observed by Barden et al. (1980) is a stable phenomenon, this may point to an important change in children's conceptions of the determinants of emotion between the preschool and the elementary school years. Young children may regard emotions as fully determined by the outcome of an action, whereas older children may expect the evaluation of this action with regard to moral or social standards to have an impact on a character's feelings. From the point of view of moral development, the finding that young children do not expect moral transgressions to have negative emotional consequences suggests that moral rules may not be understood as personally binding, and that anticipation of unpleasant emotional experiences may not intervene as a motivational force in guiding their behavior. The emotions children attribute to moral wrongdoers, however, may be highly dependent on situational variations affecting the salience of the moral transgression in comparison to the salience of the wrongdoer's profit. Thus, before far-reaching conclusions can be drawn, the generality of this developmental trend and the reasons for young children's assumed neglect of moral aspects in their attributions of emotion have to be investigated.

In the present series of experiments we studied children's developing conceptions of the emotional consequences of morally relevant actions. First, children's attributions of emotion to a story figure who had violated a moral rule as well as to a story figure who had resisted temptation to do so were investigated. We thereby attempted to replicate the developmental trend reported by Barden et al. (1980) and to explore whether young children's assumed tendency to neglect the moral evaluation of an action in their emotion attributions was a more general phenomenon. Second, we attempted to investigate whether children's patterns of emotion attributions in morally relevant situations were affected by situational variations, that is, by the severity of the moral transgression and the salience of the profit that a wrongdoer gained from his action. A third aim was to explore the criteria children use when attributing emotions to others in morally relevant contexts, that is, to identify the variables that they regard as determinants of a person's emotions.

Experiment 1

The first experiment was designed to replicate the findings reported by Barden et al. (1980), to make a first test of the generality of the expected pattern of emotion attributions, and to explore some possible reasons for these attributions. There are several possible explanations for the finding that young children attribute positive emotions to moral wrongdoers while older children attribute negative ones. First, a rather trivial reason for young children's pattern of emotion attribution might be that they do not know the moral rule in question. Given Turiel's (1983) findings that fundamental moral rules such as "you should not lie, steal, or break a promise" are clearly understood even by preschoolers, this explanation seems unlikely. However, children's rule understanding has to be controlled for. A second explanation might be that young children, being unable to conceptualize conflicting emotions (Harris, 1983; Harter, 1983), opt for the "good" feelings whenever a person is likely to be in emotional conflict. If this is true, their attributions of positive emotions would not reflect a neglect of morality but a generalized "good" bias.

This assumption can be tested by assessing children's emotion attributions to a person who resisted the temptation to commit a moral transgression. In this situation the protagonist could be conceived as being either sad at not having attained a desired goal (e.g., an attractive object that did not belong to him) or happy or proud at having behaved in accordance with moral standards. If young children's apparent neglect of moral aspects in their emotion attributions simply reflects a tendency to side for the "good" feelings in conflict situations, then there should be a high rate of positive emotion attributions both to a person who successfully committed a misdeed and to a person who resisted temptation. In contrast, attributions of happiness to a wrongdoer and of sadness to an actor who resisted temptation would point to a rather profound neglect of moral aspects in young children's conceptualizations of emotions.

Older children's attributions of negative emotions to moral wrongdoers may primarily reflect fear of sanctions; they may simply be better able than younger children to anticipate further consequences of one's actions. Yet older children may expect a wrongdoer primarily to be sad at having caused a victim's suffering or at having violated important standards of conduct. Barden et al. (1980) found expectations of both scared and sad reactions.

Children's justifications for their emotion attributions may provide insight into the kind of emotions children expect a wrongdoer to experience and the reasoning behind these emotion attributions. Second, emotion attributions in the case of resistance to temptation, where external consequences are most unlikely to occur, should reflect children's consideration (or neglect) of genuinely moral aspects such as conformity to moral standards or fairness toward others.

Older children may be more likely than younger ones to consider the moral evaluation of an action in their emotion attributions because they know about the conventional significance of a person's emotional reactions for the judgment of this person's moral worth. Adults understand that a person who shows remorse at a moral transgression is considered to be less evil than someone who displays indifference, or even joy. Thus, to display remorse is socially desirable. Research on the development of moral judgment in children has focused on the evaluation of intentions and outcomes (for a review, see Keasey, 1977). Whether emotional reactions enter into children's judgments of a person's moral worth at all and how different emotional reactions are evaluated has, to our knowledge, not been studied previously. One might speculate that once children begin to realize that it is socially unacceptable to display joy at a moral transgression, they will no longer openly attribute positive emotions to wrongdoers. An additional purpose of the first experiment was therefore to gather information on the development of children's judgments of emotional reactions to moral transgressions and their relation to developmental changes in emotion attribution.

In this experiment, we examined 4–8-year-old children's attributions of emotions to an actor who had committed an act of minor theft without being caught, and to an actor who had resisted the temptation to steal. Subsequent to this emotion-attribution task, children were asked to judge the moral worth of two actors who had both committed an identical act of stealing but who differed in their emotional reactions, that is, displayed joy versus sadness/remorse ("moral judgment task"). Stealing was chosen because this moral rule should be clearly understood even by 4-year-olds and because the temptation to commit a petty theft is likely to be a common experience in young children's everyday lives. Since Barden et al. (1980) did not find differences between the emotions children anticipated for themselves and for a story figure, we

TABLE 1

STORY A IN THE EMOTION-ATTRIBUTION TASK: EXPERIMENT 1

Episode 1
This is Florian and this is Thomas. They are in the cloakroom in their kindergarten/school, hanging up their coats. Thomas takes a bag with sweets out of his pocket and shows them to Florian. "Look, my aunt gave me these sweets." Florian likes this kind of sweets very much.

Episode 2
Later on, Florian is back in the cloakroom, where Thomas left his coat with the sweets. He is all by himself. He thinks about taking the sweets out of Thomas's coat.

Control Question
What do you think? Is Florian allowed to take the sweets? Why? (Why not?) You think that he is not allowed to take them. Florian also knows that this is not allowed.

Episode 3

Moral Version	*Immoral Version*
Now Florian goes to Thomas's coat hanger. He takes the bag with the sweets in his hand, but then immediately puts it back and goes back to the classroom. He has not taken any sweets from Thomas.	Now Florian goes to Thomas's coat, takes the bag with the sweets out of his coat, and puts it into his pocket. Then he goes back to the classroom. Nobody has seen him.

Test Question
How does Florian feel now? Why?

NOTE.—The girls received a version with girls as story figures.

restricted our investigation to the emotion attributions made to story figures.

Method

Subjects.—Sixty children, 27 boys and 33 girls, divided into three age groups, participated in this experiment. The mean ages of the three groups were 4-7 (range 4-1 to 5-0), 6-3 (range 6-0 to 6-11), and 8-4 (range 8-0 to 8-11). The 4- and 6-year-olds attended kindergartens and the 8-year-olds an after-school center.

Materials.—For the *emotion-attribution tasks,* two parallel stories were constructed that were illustrated by 19.5 × 13.5-cm colored drawings. For each story, a "moral" and an "immoral" version was constructed. Story A, concerning the theft of candies, is described in detail in Table 1. Story B is identical in structure to story A and takes place on a playground where children competed to collect chestnuts. In Episode 1, the protagonist was shown to have collected only a small number of chestnuts, whereas another child had collected a large heap. In Episode 2, this latter child climbed on the tree in order to collect more chestnuts, while the protagonist remained unobserved on the playground. In the "moral" version of Episode 3, the protagonist went over to the other child's chestnuts but then returned to his own small heap without taking a chestnut from the other child. In the "immoral" version, the protagonist took a large number of chestnuts from

the other child's collection and added them to his own.

For the *moral-judgment task,* two colored drawings, each showing a child with a toy car and two colored drawings of children's faces, one with a happy and the other with a sad expression, served as materials.

Procedure and design.—Each subject first received two emotion-attribution tasks. In one task, the subject had to judge the feelings of the protagonist who had behaved morally ("moral" story version) and in the other task those of the protagonist who had behaved immorally ("immoral" story version). Whether the children received the "moral" or "immoral" version first, or whether the "moral" ("immoral") version was story A or B, was counterbalanced. For each child, the protagonist in the stories was a same-sex child. The exact procedure is described in Table 1. The subjects attended to the experimenter, who told the stories and showed the pictures at the appropriate positions. The experimenter took care always to point to the story figure he was talking about when telling the story and asking the questions. The test question was, "How does [protagonist] feel now?" "Why?" Children's rule understanding was assessed by the control question: "Is [protagonist] allowed to take the [sweets/chestnuts]?" "Why?" ("Why not?") Those children who answered that the protagonist was not allowed to steal the other's possessions were told that the protagonist also knew that this was not allowed. This was done to ensure that children did not regard the story figure as ignorant of moral laws.

The emotion-attribution tasks were followed by the moral-judgment task. The experimenter announced that she wanted to tell the child a story about two boys (girls) who both had a friend. She showed the pictures of the children with the toy cars and said that both children had stolen a toy car from their friend. She then asked whether these children had been right to take the cars from their friends or not, and why. After the subject had answered, he or she was shown the picture of the child with the sad face and the picture of the child with the happy face. The experimenter explained, "This child [pointing to the happy face] is happy because she [he] now has the beautiful car. This child [pointing to the sad face] is sorry because she [he] took the car from his friend. Do you think that this child [happy] is worse or that this child [sorry] is worse, or do you think that they are both the same? Why?" The order of mentioning the happy and the sorry child in the test question was counterbalanced across subjects.

Results and Discussion

Emotion-attribution tasks.—Preliminary analyses showed that there were no significant effects of sex of subject or story content in either the "moral" or the "immoral" story versions on the number of children who attributed positive or negative emotions to the protagonist, nor were there any order effects. These variables will not be discussed further.

In the "immoral" story version, one 4-year-old answered "yes" to the question whether the protagonist was allowed to take the other child's possessions. This subject was dropped from further analysis. All other subjects answered "no" to the question testing their rule understanding in both the "moral" and the "immoral" story versions and were able to give a reason for this rule. Except for two children whose reason was that the other child wanted to keep the sweet for himself, all children gave norm-oriented justifications or pointed to morally relevant consequences (e.g., that one is not allowed to take another's possessions without permission, that taking them would be theft, that the other child would be sad if the protagonist took his sweet, or that stealing would be sanctioned). This indicates that even children of the youngest age group understood that the protagonist was forbidden to steal and could give adequate reasons for this rule.

Children's emotion attributions to the protagonist in the "moral" and the "immoral" story versions were classified as positive ("good," "happy"), negative ("sad," "bad," "not good," "not happy"), or ambivalent (e.g., "a little good and a little bad"). This classification was unproblematic, as most children used emotion terms that clearly were positive or negative. Interrater agreement was 90%. The few conflicting cases were resolved by discussion.

Ambivalent feelings were attributed only in the "moral" story version, by one 4-year-old, one 6-year-old, and three 8-year-olds. Two 4-year-olds in the "moral" and one 4-year-old in the "immoral" story replied with "I don't know."

In the "immoral" version, 14 (out of 18) 4-year-olds (74%) and eight (out of 20) 6-year-olds (40%) judged the protagonist to feel good after having stolen the other child's possessions, whereas 18 (out of 20) 8-year-olds (90%) judged him to experience negative emotions. The difference in negative emotion attributions to the wrongdoer was significant, $\chi^2(2, n = 58) = 17.97, p < .001$.

In the "moral" story version, 10 out of 17 4-year-olds (59%) and 14 out of 19 (74%) 6-year-olds, but only seven out of 17 (41%) 8-year-olds, judged the protagonist to experience negative emotions. Although the overall age difference in the attribution of negative versus positive emotions was not significant, $\chi^2(2, n = 53) = 3.91, p > .05$, the difference in emotion attributions between 6- and 8-year-olds was, $\chi^2(1, n = 36) = 3.90, p < .05$.

The majority of the 4-year-olds and almost all 6- and 8-year-olds gave justifications for their positive or negative emotion attributions. These justifications allowed us to distinguish emotion attributions that focused solely on the successful versus unsuccessful outcome of the protagonist's action from those that involved moral considerations. Children's answers were classified as outcome oriented if the reasons given for the protagonist's feelings were that he possessed (did not possess) the desired object or that he was successful (not successful) at taking (stealing) the desired object. Emotion attributions were classified as morally oriented if children reasoned that the protagonist felt bad (good) because he had stolen (not stolen) the object, because he had been "nasty" ("good"), or because he was afraid of inward (bad conscience) or outward sanctions. In the "moral" version, there were several cases where a child said that the protagonist felt bad be-

TABLE 2

NUMBER OF CHILDREN WHO GAVE OUTCOME-ORIENTED AND MORALLY ORIENTED
EMOTION ATTRIBUTIONS IN EXPERIMENT 1

| | STORY VERSION AND AGE | | | | | |
| | "Moral" | | | "Immoral" | | |
EMOTION	4	6	8	4	6	8
Outcome	6	12	3	12	8	2
Moral	5	7	17	3	12	18
Not classifiable	9	1	0	5	0	0

cause he had thought of stealing the object; this was classified as a morally oriented answer. Ambivalent emotion attributions were classified as morally oriented if at least one moral reason was given. A justification was considered unclassifiable if no reason was given, if the justification was tautological ("he feels good because he feels good"), or if the reason was uninterpretable with regard to the story ("he feels good because he likes to be in kindergarten"). Again, interrater agreement was high (89%). Table 2 shows the number of children of each age group whose emotion attributions were classified as outcome and as morally oriented or whose justifications were unclassifiable. Those children whose responses were unclassifiable are ignored for further analysis.

In both the "moral" and the "immoral" emotion-attribution tasks there was an age trend from an outcome orientation among the 4-year-olds to a moral orientation among the 8-year-olds. This age trend was significant for the "moral" version, $\chi^2(2, n = 50) = 10.19$, $p < .01$, as well as for the "immoral" version, $\chi^2(2, n = 55) = 17.50$, $p < .001$.

Table 2 shows two discrepancies. First, in the "moral" version the percentage of children whose answers were outcome oriented was higher among 6- than among 4-year-olds. As sample size was reduced considerably in 4-year-olds, the possibility of interpreting this "reverse" age trend is obviously limited. Some 4-year-olds may have had difficulties in understanding the "moral" story since it involved a protagonist giving up his original intentions without any external reason. Second, in the "immoral" story version most of the 6-year-olds' justifications were morally oriented, whereas in the "moral" version most were outcome oriented. Inspection of individual response patterns did not, however, yield significant differences.

A further analysis of children's justifications in the "immoral" story version revealed that none of the 4-year-olds, three 6-year-olds, and six 8-year-olds mentioned fear of external sanctions. However, in all age groups the majority of those children who gave a morally oriented answer focused on the fact that the wrongdoer had violated a moral norm ("he feels bad/sad, because he has stolen the sweet, because he is a thief, because one is not allowed to do this"). This suggests that the developmental change in emotion attributions is not primarily due to an increased awareness of possible external sanctions.

Moral-judgment task.—Among 4-year-olds, three children gave no answer or gave an uninterpretable answer to the question whether the "happy" or the "sorry" child was worse or whether they were both the same. Eighteen 8-year-olds, 14 6-year-olds, but only six (out of 17) 4-year-olds judged the "happy" child to be worse than the "sorry" child. Two 4-year-olds and two 6-year-olds judged the "sorry" child to be worse, and nine 4-year-olds, four 6-year-olds, and two 8-year-olds judged them to be both the same. Thus, the majority of the 6-year-olds and almost all 8-year-olds judged the child who was "happy" to be worse than the child who was "sorry," whereas the majority of the 4-year-olds judged them to be both the same. This age trend was significant (happy judgments vs. sad or same judgments), $\chi^2(2, n = 57) = 12.53, p < .01$.

All children who judged the happy child to be worse justified their answers by referring to the emotion this child displayed ("he is happy," "he is not even sorry for what he did"); those children who judged them to be both the same in their justifications referred to the fact that they had both committed the same deed. In the rare cases (four children) where the sad child was judged to be worse, no interpretable justifications were given.

The results of the emotion-attribution ("immoral version") and the moral-judgment tasks concur in suggesting that children begin to expect negative emotional consequences to follow a moral transgression at about 6 years, when they begin to understand the significance of emotional reactions for moral judgment. An analysis of individual response patterns showed that, in fact, 42 out of 59 children (71%) were consistent on the two tasks. That is, they either judged the happy child to be worse and gave morally oriented emotion attributions (28 children) or they judged them to be both the same (or the sorry child to be worse) and gave outcome-oriented emotion attributions (14 children). Of those children who were inconsistent, 11 judged the happy child to be worse while making outcome-oriented emotion attributions, whereas six showed the reverse pattern. Thus, a substantial proportion of those children who knew that a wrongdoer would be judged more leniently if he was sorry instead of happy still expected him to experience joy (29% in the total sample, 43% if only the 4- and 6-year-olds are considered).

In Experiment 1, Barden et al.'s (1980) results were replicated: young children tended to expect a wrongdoer to experience happiness, whereas older children expected him to experience sadness or fear. Children's justifications suggested that older children mostly focused on the moral transgression, whereas younger children focused on the outcome of the protagonist's action (i.e., the possession of a desired object). There was little evidence that the developmental change in emotion attributions was due only to older children's increasing awareness and fear of external sanctions that might follow a misdeed (even if it was not immediately detected). Rather, their emotion attributions mostly seemed to be based on genuinely moral considerations. Moreover, the developmental change from outcome-oriented toward morally oriented emotion attributions was a more general trend. A majority of the younger children expected a person who had resisted the temptation to commit a moral transgression to be sad at the negative outcome (i.e., at not having attained a desired object), whereas the older children expected this person either to be proud or relieved at having behaved morally or to be sad or ashamed at even having considered committing a moral transgression.

A parallel developmental trend was observed in children's moral judgments of wrongdoers who differed in their emotional reactions. Whereas most 4-year-olds based their judgments on the sameness of the two wrongdoers' actions, the majority of the 6-year-olds and almost all 8-year-olds judged the person who displayed joy to be worse than the one who displayed remorse. Thus, the older children's attributions of negative emotions to a wrongdoer may have been influenced by their knowledge about the conventional significance of these emotions in moral judgment. A sizable proportion of the younger children (4- and 6-year-olds), however, attributed positive emotions to a wrongdoer despite an understanding of the significance of these emotions in moral judgment. This suggests that an understanding that a joyful wrongdoer will be judged negatively does not suffice to alter young children's rather robust expectations about the emotions a wrongdoer will experience.

The findings of Experiment 1 suggest that 4-year-olds do not expect the moral value of an action to have an impact on an actor's emotions, whether the actor is a wrongdoer or a "moral hero." This finding cannot be explained by a failure to understand the moral rule in question. Although the wrongdoer's action was clearly understood as a moral transgression, and although it was emphasized that the wrongdoer himself knew about the validity of the moral rule, the moral evaluation of the protagonist's action did not enter into young children's attributions of emotion. Rather, 4-year-olds seemed to base their emotion attributions solely on outcome information.

In research on children's developing conceptions of emotion it has been shown repeatedly (e.g., Harris, 1983; Harter, 1983) that young children do not understand that a single situation can provoke both positive and negative emotions in the same person. Being unable to conceptualize emotional conflict, young children will attribute only one of two potentially conflicting feelings to a person at a given time. Children's responses to the "moral" story version in Experiment 1 indicate that they do not simply pick a "good" emotion whenever a conflict arises but rather are consistently oriented toward outcomes in their emotion attributions. This outcome dependency may be due to the salience of outcome information in the experiment. Young children's responses in a variety of tasks have been shown to be influenced heavily by physical, tangible aspects of a situation. In Experiment 1, the protagonist's action led or did not lead to the possession of a desired object, that is, to a tangible profit. Young children may have attributed joy to the wrongdoer (and sadness to the "moral hero") in this situation simply because this tangible profit was so much more salient than the action's moral value. Children's pattern of emotion attribution might be quite different if the salience of morality were increased. This assumption was tested in Experiment 2.

Experiment 2

In Experiment 2, we investigated whether young children's emotion attributions in morally relevant situations vary as a function of the salience of morality in a given context. Salience of morality was manipulated along two dimensions. First, a condition in which the protagonist's immoral action was motivated by his wish to possess an attractive object and, in fact, led to this possession (*tangible-profit condition*) was contrasted with a condition in which the protagonist's action was motivated by his wish to annoy another child and did not lead to a tangible profit for himself (*no-tangible-profit condition*). Note that in the tangible-profit condition the actor's primary motive is not immoral in itself: he breaks a moral rule in order to attain an attractive object, not in order to do harm to another. In contrast, in the no-tangible-profit condition the actor's motive to cause annoyance to another person is immoral in itself and furthermore does not even lead to any external gain. Moral aspects should, therefore, be more salient in the second condition than in the first one.

Second, we tested whether children's attributions of emotions were influenced by the severity of the moral transgression. Within the tangible-profit and the no-tangible-profit conditions, we contrasted a story in which the protagonist told another child a lie with a story in which he physically injured another child. Doing bodily harm to another person is regarded as a more severe moral transgression than lying or stealing—in fact, in lists of wrongdoings, physical harm is given the first place in rank orderings according to severity of transgressions by children and adolescents (see Elkind & Dabeck, 1977; Imamoglu, 1975; Stephenson, 1966, pp. 25 ff.). It also differs from lying or stealing in being an overtly hostile act that cannot be kept secret. Thus, the immorality of injuring another should be quite salient especially if this act is not motivated by the wish to attain some tangible profit. In order to control for young children's understanding that injuring a person is worse than lying, we asked them to judge which

protagonist had been worse subsequent to the emotion-attribution task.

Method

Subjects.—Twenty children, nine boys and 11 girls, participated in Experiment 2. Their mean age was 5-2 (range 4-1 to 5-11).

Materials.—Two dolls (about 8 cm high) and a 30 × 60-cm wide white cardboard "wall" were used to act out the story about telling a lie. The dolls were always of the same sex as the subject. In the tangible-profit condition, a paper model of an ice-cream cone was used to illustrate the actor's profit. This story is described in detail in Table 3.

The story about doing bodily harm, illustrated by 19.5 × 13.5-cm colored drawings, was situated on a playground where the protagonist met another child who was on the swing. He pushed the other child from the swing. This child was hurt and was described as being very sad and angry. In the tangible-profit condition, the protagonist's action was motivated by his desire to get onto the swing himself. In the no-tangible-profit condition, the protagonist did not want to get onto the swing because he used to get sick from swinging, but he wanted to annoy the other child, whom he disliked. The drawings clearly showed that the other child was crying and bleeding after falling from the swing.

Procedure and design.—Half the children were randomly assigned to the tangible-profit condition and the other half to the no-tangible-profit condition. Each child received two stories in counterbalanced order, one about telling a lie and one about injuring another child. After each story the test question and a control question were asked. The test question was, "What do you think? How does [protagonist] feel now?" "Why?" The control question was, "What do you think about what [protagonist] did: Was it right or was it not right?" "Why?" After the subjects had answered the test and control questions for both stories they were asked whether they thought that the story figure who sent the other child in the wrong direction was worse, or whether the story figure who pushed the other child from the swing was worse, or whether they were both the same. The order of asking about the two story figures was counterbalanced across subjects.

Results and Discussion

All children answered the control questions (rule understanding) correctly and could justify their answers with moral reasons. There was no significant difference between

TABLE 3

STORY VERSIONS IN EXPERIMENT 2 (Story Frame: Telling a Lie)

On his way home, John passes by the ice-cream van (situated behind the wall).

Tangible-Profit Condition	*No-Tangible-Profit Condition*
He wants to buy an ice cream, but he has no money in his pocket. He decides to run home quickly to fetch money.	He is not hungry and does not buy an ice cream.

On his way he meets Stephen. Stephen is looking for the ice-cream van. He asks John: "Do you know where the ice-cream van is today?"

Tangible-Profit Condition	*No-Tangible-Profit Condition*
John knows that there is only very little ice cream left today. He does not want Stephen to get there before him, as he might buy the last bit of chocolate ice cream which John likes so much.	John does not like Stephen. He wants to annoy Stephen.

John says, "The ice-cream van is there" (points to the wrong direction).

Control question (story understanding): Will Stephen find the ice-cream van? You are right, he will not find the ice-cream van. He will be annoyed.

Tangible-Profit Condition	*No-Tangible-Profit Condition*
John goes home, gets money, and buys a large portion of chocolate ice cream.	. . .

the emotion attributions in the tangible-profit and the no-tangible-profit conditions. Thus, the data were collapsed across these conditions. In the story about telling a lie, 15 out of 20 children attributed a positive emotion to the wrongdoer, four a negative emotion, and one gave no response. In the story about doing bodily harm, 13 out of 20 children attributed a positive emotion, five a negative one, and two gave no response. Subjects were largely consistent between stories: of the five inconsistencies, three attributed a negative emotion to the wrongdoer in the story about doing bodily harm and a positive one in the story about lying, while two children showed the reverse pattern.

In the tangible-profit condition, children who attributed positive emotions generally justified their answers by the profit the protagonist gained from his action ("because he now has an ice cream," "because he is now on the swing"). In the no-tangible-profit condition, the positive emotion attributions were justified by the protagonist's success in annoying the other child (e.g., "because he annoyed him very much").

Children's answers to the question concerning which of the two story characters was "worse" showed that they regarded injuring a person as a more severe transgression than lying: Eighteen out of 20 children replied that the child who had pushed another child from the swing was worse than the one who had told a lie. As in Experiment 1, however, the majority of the children expected the child who had injured another child to be happy.

The results indicate that neither the severity of the moral transgression nor the tangibility of the profit gained through an immoral action affect young children's emotion attributions. They do not seem to consider the moral value of a person's action when judging his or her feelings, even if moral aspects are made quite salient. The finding that young children expect a wrongdoer to experience joy even if he caused severe distress in another person is counterintuitive from the point of view of everyday experience and of research on young children's spontaneous concern for others' well-being as displayed in their prosocial acts.

One explanation for this discrepancy might be that young children react with empathic, prosocial emotions to other persons' distress, but that they do not yet *conceptualize* these emotional reactions. They might lack an understanding of empathic, other-oriented, basic moral emotions even though they react empathically in response to others' distress. Thus, they may generally expect a person to feel happy if he or she is not negatively affected herself, regardless of what happened to others.

Another possibility is that young children are not profoundly unaware of moral emotions but that they neglect morality in their emotion attributions whenever an actor's personal motives are in conflict with moral standards. The present findings suggest that young children expect people to be happy whenever they get what they want, regardless of whether this wish is in accordance with moral standards. This would suggest that young children's criteria for judging a person's feelings rest on whether there is a match between a person's motive and the outcome of his or her action. However, one might argue that there is not sufficient evidence from Experiments 1 and 2 to support this interpretation since we did not investigate children's attributions of emotion to a neutrally or well-motivated actor who harmed another person unintentionally. Children might have based their emotion attributions solely on outcome, regardless of motive; that is, they might attribute joy whenever an actor successfully produces some conspicuous effect regardless of its moral evaluation and regardless of whether or not it was intentional. In order to test these explanations, we studied emotion attributions in situations where another person was harmed unintentionally by the protagonist and where the protagonist merely witnessed another person's distress.

Experiment 3

Experiment 3 was designed to investigate whether young children's attributions of positive emotions to wrongdoers are restricted to cases where harm is done to another person intentionally, that is, where an action outcome matches the actor's bad motive. We tested three alternatives to this possibility.

First, young children's emotion attributions may be due to a lack of reflexive awareness of prosocial, empathic emotions. They may expect someone to feel good whenever he or she is not negatively affected by an event, regardless of other persons' feelings. If this were the case, then positive emotions should be attributed even to a bystander who witnesses another person's distress without having caused it.

Second, we tested whether young children attribute positive emotions whenever a person has been a causally effective agent, that is, produced some visible effect in the real world, regardless of whether this effect is intended or not. Evidence relevant to this question was presented by Yuill (1984), who tested 3–7-year-olds' comprehension of the relation between motives and outcomes of action by presenting them with matching and mismatching outcomes. When asked to judge an actor's satisfaction, even 3-year-olds ex-

pected a person who had a *neutral* motive toward another character but did harm to him by mistake to be sad. This suggests that young children consider intentionality when judging an actor's emotions. We attempted to replicate this finding by creating a condition in which a neutrally motivated actor unintentionally harmed another person.

In contrast to the judgments of neutrally motivated actors' emotions, Yuill found that when children were asked to judge the feelings of a person who had a bad motive toward another character, 3- and 5-year-olds did not distinguish between cases of motive-outcome match (i.e., the actor wanted to hurt someone and succeeded in doing so) and cases of mismatch—either in recipient (i.e., the actor intended to hurt person A but by mistake hurt person B) or in value (i.e, the actor wanted to hit another person with a ball, but this person caught the ball). This suggests that children's emotion attributions in value-laden contexts may differ from those in neutral contexts.

A third possibility might thus be that young children form a stereotype of a "bad character," who is assumed to experience joy whenever he succeeds in doing harm to others, regardless of whether this effect corresponds to his intentions or not. If this were the case, positive emotions should be attributed to an ill-motivated actor even if he did harm to a person whom he did not intend to hurt, that is, if there was a mismatch in recipient between his motive and the outcome of his action.

In order to test whether any of these possibilities can account for young children's emotion attributions, we contrasted a condition in which a protagonist intentionally harmed another person (*intentional harm done by ill-motivated actor*), with a condition in which an actor wanted to do harm to person A but inadvertently harmed person B (*unintentional harm done by ill-motivated actor*), with a condition in which the protagonist, who had no bad motive toward another person, harmed this person unintentionally (*unintentional harm done by neutrally motivated actor*), and with a condition in which the protagonist witnessed as a bystander an accident in which another person was hurt (*bystander*). Table 4 shows the response patterns that are expected under each of the four hypotheses outlined above.

In order to replicate the findings of Experiment 2, we chose a situation in which the victim was physically injured. In addition to judging each actor's feelings, children were

TABLE 4

HYPOTHETICAL RESPONSE PATTERNS IN EXPERIMENT 3

	EXPERIMENTAL CONDITION			
RESPONSE PATTERN	Intentional Harm Done by Ill-motivated Actor	Unintentional Harm Done by Ill-motivated Actor	Unintentional Harm Done by Neutral Actor	Bystander
1	+	+	+	+
2	+	+	+	−
3	+	+	−	−
4	+	−	−	−

NOTE.—Response patterns: 1, protagonist feels good if not negatively affected himself; 2, protagonist feels good if causally effective; 3, ill-motivated protagonist feels good whenever he does harm; 4, protagonist feels good only if he does harm intentionally; +/−, positive/negative emotion.

asked to judge the four protagonists morally. Experiments 1 and 2 showed that young children clearly understood the moral rules in question. Therefore, it is likely that they will judge an ill-motivated actor who does harm to another person to be "bad." However, we cannot rule out the possibility that they might also judge an actor who has no bad motive but does damage unintentionally to be "bad," basing their judgments solely on outcome, regardless of motive.

Method

Subjects.—Twenty-four children, 13 boys and 11 girls, participated in this experiment. Their ages ranged between 4-6 to 5-11 (mean age 5-3).

Materials.—Four story frames were constructed. Each of these was used to generate four different stories. An example of the four

stories derived from the story frame "bicycle" is given in Table 5. The other three story frames were analogous in structure. Their topics were playing with toy building blocks in the kindergarten, playing catch on the playground, and playing in the sandbox. The victims were hit by a toy building block, fell (by accident or by being pushed) on the playground, and got hurt from a load of sand in the eyes, respectively. The stories were illustrated by movable colored figures that were shifted around appropriately on the table while each story was told.

Design and procedure.—Each child received four stories, one for each of the four experimental conditions (intentional harm done by ill-motivated actor, unintentional harm done by ill-motivated actor, unintentional harm done by neutral actor, bystander).

TABLE 5

STORY VERSIONS IN EXPERIMENT 3 (Story Frame: "Bicycle")

Intentional Harm Done by Ill-motivated Actor
Tom (protagonist), Peter, and John are cycling on the playground. Tom does not like Peter. He wants to annoy Peter. Tom drives his bicycle into Peter's way so that Peter falls off his bike and hurts his leg. Peter is sad and cries.

Unintentional Harm Done by Ill-motivated Actor
Tom, Peter, and John are cycling on the playground. Tom does not like Peter. He wants to annoy Peter. Tom drives his bike into Peter's way to make Peter fall off his bike. However, Peter gets out of Tom's way in the last moment. Right there John comes by. John cannot stop anymore. He falls off his bike and hurts his leg. Tom did not want to hurt John. John is sad and cries.

Unintentional Harm Done by Neutral Actor
Tom, Peter, and John are cycling on the playground. Suddenly, Tom drives his bike by mistake into John's way so that John falls off his bike and hurts his leg. Tom did not want to hurt John. John is sad and cries.

Bystander
Tom comes to the playground. John and Peter are there already, cycling around. Suddenly, John makes a sharp bend with his bike. He loses balance and falls off his bike. His leg is hurt. John is sad and cries.

NOTE.—The girls received story versions with girls as story figures.

The assignment of story frames to experimental conditions was counterbalanced across subjects. The experimental conditions were presented in four different random orders.

The experimenter introduced the task by saying that she wanted to tell the child some stories about children of his or her own age. She then told the first story, while manipulating the figures on the table. Care was taken to ensure that it was always perfectly clear which story figure the experimenter was talking about. In order to avoid a confusion of story contents, the experimenter produced an attractive toy after each story and played with the child for about 5 min before proceeding with the next story. After each story, the subject was asked the following questions: *emotion-attribution question:* "What do you think? How does [protagonist] feel now?" If the child did not reply spontaneously to this question, the experimenter proceeded: "Do you think [protagonist] is happy or do you think [protagonist] is sad?" "Why?" The order of mentioning "happy" and "sad" was varied from story to story. *Moral-judgment question:* "Was [protagonist] bad or was she [he] not bad?" "Why?" *Control question:* "Did [protagonist] hurt [victim] intentionally or did he [she] hurt him [her] not intentionally?" In the bystander condition this question was replaced by: "Did [protagonist] hurt [victim] or did he [she] watch [victim] being hurt?"

Results and Discussion

Preliminary analyses revealed no effects of sex of subject or order of presentation of experimental conditions on children's emotion attributions and moral judgments. All children answered the control questions about the protagonist's intention correctly. Table 6 shows the number of children who attributed positive or negative emotions to the protagonist and who gave positive or negative moral judgments in each of the four experimental conditions.

The majority of the children (79%) expected the protagonist in the intentional harm–ill-motivated actor condition to experience positive emotions. In contrast, only one child attributed positive emotions to the protagonist in the cases of motive-outcome mismatch (unintentional harm–ill-motivated or neutral actor). In the bystander condition, five children (21%) judged the protagonist to feel "good" (or "just normal," one subject). One of these children said that the bystander felt good because he could help the other child, whereas two children expected him to feel good because he was not injured himself. Table 6 shows that in all conditions except for the intentional harm condition the majority of the children judged the protagonist to feel sad or bad. This suggests that the majority of the subjects distinguished in their emotion attributions between a case where the outcome of an action matches the actor's bad motive and cases of motive-outcome mismatch. An analysis of individual response patterns confirmed this impression: 17 out of 24 children attributed positive feelings in the intentional harm condition and negative feelings in all three other conditions, that is, conformed to response pattern 4 (see Table 4). Of the remaining subjects, four children attributed negative emotions to the protagonist in all four conditions, one child judged all four protagonists to feel good, and two children showed other patterns.

Moral judgments did not follow the same pattern as emotion attributions. The majority of the children judged the protagonist who had a bad motive to be "bad." This was the case in both the intentional harm and the unintentional harm–ill-motivated actor conditions, although in the latter case one-third of the subjects (eight children) gave a positive

TABLE 6

NUMBER OF CHILDREN MAKING EMOTION ATTRIBUTIONS AND MORAL JUDGMENTS IN EXPERIMENT 3

	EMOTION ATTRIBUTION		MORAL JUDGMENT	
EXPERIMENTAL CONDITION	Positive	Negative	Positive	Negative
Intentional harm done by ill-motivated actor	19	5	2	22
Unintentional harm done by ill-motivated actor	1	23	8	16
Unintentional harm done by neutral actor	1	23	20	4
Harmful event witnessed by bystander	5	19	23	1

judgment. Six of these children, however, justified their answer by saying that the protagonist was bad with regard to the target person but not bad with regard to the victim. This suggests that they considered value of motive in their moral judgments. Almost all children judged the protagonist who had no bad motive not to be bad: 83% of the children did so even if the protagonist had unintentionally done harm to another person. In the intentional harm condition, 17 children judged the ill-motivated actor to be bad but expected him to feel good; the reverse pattern did not occur, McNemar's test, $\chi^2(1) = 15.05$, $p < .001$. In the unintentional harm condition, 20 children judged the neutrally motivated actor positively morally and expected him to experience negative emotions; one child showed the reverse pattern, McNemar's test, $\chi^2(1) = 15.4$, $p < .001$.

The results of Experiment 3 support the assumption that children around the age of 5 years attribute positive emotions to a person who harmed another one only if he or she did so intentionally, that is, that they base their emotion attributions on the criterion of a match between an actor's motive and the outcome of his action. This suggests that the ability to coordinate motive and outcome information may develop even earlier than observed by Yuill (1984). Yuill found that 3- and 5-year-old children based their emotion attributions on a match between motive and outcome when neutral motives but not when bad ones were involved. Our results indicate that 5-year-olds distinguish between the feelings of an ill-motivated actor who hurt the target person and those of an ill-motivated actor who missed the target person but hurt another person instead. This was observed by Yuill only in 7-year-olds. We also found that, in their moral judgments, children judged an actor who had no bad motives not to be bad, although he had unintentionally caused damage. In Yuill's study, this age group's moral evaluations were in between "good" and "bad" in a similar condition.

Our study differs from Yuill's in story content and in response mode. Story content may be a relevant issue, since Yuill's story frame (intending to hurt someone with a ball) may be less plausible than the straightforward aggressive acts chosen in our story. Response mode may have increased task demands in Yuill's study because children had to indicate the *degree* of positive or negative feelings (of "goodness" or "badness") on a four-point-scale, whereas in our study they only had to make a binary choice.

Rating scales have been shown to be cognitively more demanding for young children than paired comparisons (e.g., Lohaus, 1986).

The present results indicate that 5-year-olds do not generally expect a person to be happy at another person's distress (or at the fact that she herself is not in distress), nor do they expect an actor to be satisfied with anything he did, regardless of whether he produced an effect intentionally or not. As in Experiments 1 and 2, the majority of the 5-year-olds expected the successful wrongdoer to experience positive feelings even though their moral judgments showed that they were clearly able to assess the moral value of the action correctly. In contrast, when there was no conflict between the protagonist's motives and moral values, the protagonist was judged to be sad at having hurt another person. In the unintentional harm—neutral actor and the unintentional harm—ill-motivated actor conditions, about half of those children who attributed sadness or regret justified this response by referring to the actor's intentions ("because he did not want to hurt him"), while the other half focused on the damage done to the victim ("because he hurt the other child," "because the other is sad," etc.). In the bystander condition, negative emotion attributions were justified with concern for the victim by almost all children ("because he sees that the other child is hurt," "because he is afraid that the other's leg might be broken"). This indicates that young children are not profoundly "egocentric" in their emotion attributions, and that they can conceptualize empathy or concern for others. Thus, children as young as 5 seem generally aware of the existence of "moral emotions." When personal motives and objective moral values conflict, however, they seem to focus on personal motives, ignoring moral values when attributing emotions.

General Discussion

The present study showed a clear change between the ages of 4 and 8 years from outcome-oriented toward morally oriented attributions of emotions to a moral wrongdoer. Most 4-year-olds, though clearly aware of the validity of moral rules, expect a wrongdoer to experience positive emotions even if the transgression is severe and no material profit is gained through it. They do so, however, only if the transgression is intentional. A person who harms another unintentionally or who witnesses another's distress is expected to feel sadness, regret, or pity. In cases of conflict between personal motives and moral standards, young children thus seem to focus solely on the relation between personal motives and action outcome when judging the actor's feelings. In contrast, older children tend to judge emotional states in relation to moral standards.

Preschoolers' emotion attributions seem to be based on a quite consistent and reasonable "theory of emotions": An actor is judged to be happy if he gets what he wants, and sad if the outcome of his action does not match his motive. This "theory" is useful in everyday life because it allows one to distinguish between the feelings that differently motivated persons will experience in response to the same event. Results by Gove and Keating (1979) indicate that young children find it difficult to spontaneously provide explanations for differing feelings at the same outcome (e.g., being happy vs. sad in response to receiving a gift). The present results suggest, however, that when given information about two persons' motives (e.g., neutral vs. bad motives) they are able to infer different feelings at the same outcome (e.g., happiness vs. sadness at having hurt another). Four- and 5-year-olds do not seem to confound the objective evaluation of a person's action with his or her feelings about this action. They clearly distinguish between "being bad" and "feeling bad." In contrast, their rigorous application of the rule that a person's feelings are determined by the relation between a person's motives and the outcome of his or her actions leads to a complete dissociation between objective evaluations and subjective feelings in the case of moral transgressions.

This account of young children's theory of emotions is obviously limited to cases where a person is described as having some specific intentions or goals. It cannot explain children's emotion attributions in cases where, as in Experiment 3, a person merely witnesses or unintentionally causes harm. The fact that, in Experiment 3, young children attributed sadness or pity to the bystander, and sadness or regret to the unintentional harmdoer, indicates that they recognize that emotional states are not exclusively determined by the attainment of subjective goals; they may also be affected by moral considerations involving empathic concern with a victim's suffering or concern with the actor's moral integrity that has been endangered by unintentional rule violation. Thus, it appears that empathic considerations enter into young children's conceptions of the determinants of emotion but that they are set aside when they

are in conflict with the emotions expected to arise from personal goal attainment.

One might argue that this neglect of moral considerations in conflict situations is part of young children's more general failure to conceptualize ambivalent and conflicting emotions (Harris, 1983). This would explain why moral emotions (which are recognized as long as they do not conflict with emotions arising from goal attainment) are set aside in conflict situations. However, if the failure to conceptualize ambivalence were the only reason for young children's neglect of morality in their emotion attributions, one would expect that, when moral aspects are made salient (as in Experiments 2 and 3) they would neglect the pleasure derived from goal attainment and base their emotion attributions on moral considerations. This was, however, not the case. Furthermore, one would expect a high frequency of ambivalent emotion attributions among older children, who, according to previous findings, are able to conceptualize ambivalence. Most 8-year-olds, however, did not focus on emotional conflict but clearly expected the wrongdoer's emotions to be determined by moral rule violation (Experiment 1). These findings suggest that the developmental trend observed in children's emotion attributions may be due to an age-related change in children's understanding of morality.

In accordance with findings by Turiel (1983), preschoolers showed an elaborate moral knowledge, being able to give perfectly adequate reasons why rules should be binding and distinguishing between transgressions of different severity in accordance with adult standards. Yet young children do not seem to be aware of the significance of conformity to moral rules for a person's self-evaluative and empathic emotions. Thus, children may first come to know moral rules in a purely *informational* sense, that is, they know that norms exist and understand why they should exist. Not until several years later, however, do they seem to treat them as personally binding obligations the intentional violation of which will be followed by negatively charged self-evaluative emotions or genuinely empathic concerns.

This interpretation of early moral learning processes throws a new light on the controversial findings about young children's morality: The young child may simultaneously display a genuine understanding of the validity of moral rules and a purely instrumentalist orientation in questions of behavior in moral conflict situations. The contradictory findings in research on early moral development may thus be partially explained by differences in the kind of moral understanding that was investigated. Turiel (1983) asked children whether a protagonist's behavior was "right or wrong," "why it was considered right or wrong," and "whether it would still be considered wrong if there were no rule," that is, he studied the knowledge and justification of moral and social rules. In contrast, Kohlberg (1976), as well as Blasi (1982) and Damon (1977), presented children with moral dilemmas, asking them what the protagonist should do. That is, they did not question children about the validity of moral rules but about the principles which, according to the child's understanding, should guide behavior in conflict situations. If young children consider a person's satisfaction to be fully determined by the fulfillment of personal intentions, they will regard prudential, not moral, rules as the principles that should guide behavior.

This interpretation rests on the assumptions of functionalist theories that emotions signal the differential significance of various aspects of reality. Young children's "amoral" emotion attributions may thus signal a morality that has not yet gained motivational force in guiding their behavior. This seems to contradict observations of very young children's prosocial acts and empathic emotions in real-life situations. Yet, in spontaneous altruistic behavior, a child acts on his or her (prosocial) intentions. Though this may well be considered part of morality, it is not directly relevant to the present issue: we have been dealing with situations in which spontaneous needs and interests collide with moral norms and therefore ought to be suppressed.

Real-life situations in which personal goals collide with moral norms would be more directly relevant to our assumptions. Little is known about young children's emotional reactions in such situations. Is there a developmental change from joy at goal attainment to guilt and remorse at rule violation in children's emotional reactions that is similar to the change observed in their emotion attributions? As Harris (1987) has pointed out for other domains of emotional development, children may show an emotional reaction long before they become reflexively aware of such emotions and their causes, attributing them to actors in hypothetical situations. One might speculate that only at the level of conscious awareness do emotional consequences attain a motivating function in guiding behavior. Further research is needed to explore the relation between children's behavior and emotional reactions in moral conflicts and the emotions they attribute to other persons acting in them.

References

Barden, R. C., Zelko, F. A., Duncan, S. W., & Masters, J. C. (1980). Children's consensual knowledge about the experiential determinants of emotion. *Journal of Personality and Social Psychology, 39,* 968–976.

Blasi, A. (1982). Kognition, Erkenntnis und das Selbst. In W. Edelstein & M. Keller (Eds.), *Perspektivität und Interpretation: Beiträge zur Entwicklung des sozialen Verstehens* (pp. 289–319). Frankfurt: Suhrkamp.

Bretherton, I., Fritz, J., Zahn-Waxler, C., & Ridgeway, D. (1986). Learning to talk about emotions: A functionalist perspective. *Child Development, 57,* 529–548.

Döbert, R. (1987). Horizonte der an Kohlberg orientierten Moralforschung. *Zeitschrift für Pädagogik, 33,* 491–511.

Damon, W. (1977). *The social world of the child.* San Francisco: Jossey-Bass.

Eisenberg-Berg, N. (1982). The development of reasoning regarding prosocial behavior. In N. Eisenberg-Berg (Ed.), *The development of prosocial behavior* (pp. 219–249). New York: Academic Press.

Eisenberg-Berg, N. (1986). *Altruistic emotion, cognition, and behavior.* Hillsdale, NJ: Erlbaum.

Elkind, D., & Dabeck, R. F. (1977). Personal injury and property damage in moral judgments of children. *Child Development, 48,* 518–522.

Gove, F. L., & Keating, D. P. (1979). Empathic role-taking precursors. *Developmental Psychology, 15,* 594–600.

Harris, P. L. (1983). Children's understanding of the link between situation and emotion. *Journal of Experimental Child Psychology, 36,* 490–509.

Harris, P. L. (1987). *Transition mechanisms in emotional development and in the young child's concept of emotion.* Paper presented at the ESF Workshop on Transition Mechanisms in Cognitive-Emotional Child Development, Grächen, Switzerland.

Harter, S. (1983). Children's understanding of multiple emotions: A cognitive-developmental approach. In W. F. Overton (Ed.), *The relationship between social and cognitive development* (pp. 147–194). Hillsdale, NJ: Erlbaum.

Hoffman, M. (1982). Affect and moral development. In D. Cicchetti & P. Hesse (Eds.), *Emotional development* (pp. 83–103). San Francisco: Jossey-Bass.

Imamoglu, E. O. (1975). Children's awareness and usage of intention cues. *Child Development, 46,* 39–75.

Keasey, C. B. (1977). Children's developing awareness and usage of intentionality and motives. In C. B. Keasey (Ed.), *Nebraska Symposium on Motivation* (Vol. 25, pp. 219–260). Lincoln: University of Nebraska Press.

Keller, M., & Edelstein, W. (1986). Beziehungsverständnis und moralische Reflexion. Eine entwicklungspsychologische Untersuchung. In W. Edelstein & G. Nunner-Winkler (Eds.), *Zur Bestimmung der Moral* (pp. 321–346). Frankfurt: Suhrkamp.

Kohlberg, L. (1976). Moral stages and moralization: The cognitive-developmental approach. In T. Lickona (Ed.), *Moral development and behavior: Theory, research and social issues* (pp. 31–53). New York: Holt, Rinehart & Winston.

Lohaus, A. (1986). Zum Einsatz von Antwortskalen in der Datenerhebung bei Kindern und Jugendlichen. *Zeitschrift für Entwicklungspsychologie und Pädagogische Psychologie, 18,* 214–224.

Radke-Yarrow, M., Zahn-Waxler, C., & Chapman, M. (1983). Children's prosocial dispositions and behavior. In E. M. Hetherington (Ed.), P. H. Mussen (Series Ed.), *Handbook of child psychology: Vol. 4. Socialization, personality, and social development* (pp. 469–545). New York: Wiley.

Ridgeway, D., Waters, E., & Kuczaj, S. A. (1985). The acquisition of emotion descriptive language; Receptive and productive vocabulary norms for ages 18 months to 6 years. *Developmental Psychology, 21,* 901–908.

Stephenson, G. M. (1966). *The development of conscience.* London: Routledge.

Thompson, R. A. (1987). Development of children's inferences of the emotions of others. *Developmental Psychology, 23,* 124–131.

Thompson, R. A., & Paris, S. G. (1981). *Children's inferences about the emotions of others.* Paper presented at the biennial meeting of the Society for Research in Child Development, Boston.

Turiel, E. (1983). *The development of social knowledge: Morality and convention.* Cambridge: Cambridge University Press.

Weiner, B., Graham, S., Stern, P., & Lawson, M. E. (1982). Using affective cues to infer causal thoughts. *Developmental Psychology, 18,* 278–286.

Weinert, F. E., & Schneider, W. (Eds.). (1987). *The Munich Longitudinal Study on the Genesis of Individual Competencies: second report.* Munich: Max Planck Institute for Psychological Research.

Yuill, N. (1984). Young children's coordination of motive and outcome in judgments of satisfaction and morality. *British Journal of Developmental Psychology, 2,* 73–81.

Zelko, F. A., Duncan, S. W., Barden, R. C., Garber, J., & Masters, J. C. (1986). Adults' expectancies about children's emotional responsiveness: Implications for the development of implicit theories of affect. *Developmental Psychology, 22,* 109–114.

Journal of Personality and Social Psychology
1990, Vol. 58, No. 4, 709–717

The Family Origins of Empathic Concern:
A 26-Year Longitudinal Study

Richard Koestner
McGill University

Carol Franz
Harvard University

Joel Weinberger
Derner Institute, Adelphi University

This study examined whether adult empathic concern was associated with parent behavior in early childhood. Subjects were drawn from a longitudinal sample first investigated by Sears, Maccoby, and Levin (1957). At age 31, 75 subjects completed the Adjective Checklist (Gough & Heilbrun, 1965, 1983), from which an index of empathic concern was derived. Scores on this index were regressed on 11 parenting dimensions derived from maternal interviews when the subjects were 5 years old. The results revealed a significant multiple R indicating that, taken together, the parenting dimensions predicted the level of empathic concern at age 31. Adult levels of empathic concern were most strongly related to the following parenting dimensions: paternal involvement in child care, maternal tolerance of dependent behavior, maternal inhibition of child's aggression, and maternal satisfaction with the role of mother.

A wide variety of meanings have been associated with the concept of empathy within the psychological literature. A consensus seems to have emerged, however, that empathy can most usefully be viewed as a multidimensional construct with significant cognitive and affective components (Goldstein & Michaels, 1985). The abilities to discriminate other people's emotions and to assume their perspectives are the central cognitive capacities associated with empathy (Feschbach, 1975). The affective component of empathy, often referred to as "empathic concern," can be defined as "the tendency to experience feelings of sympathy and compassion for others" (Davis & Oathout, 1987). Questionnaire inventories of empathy differ in the extent to which they assess the affective or cognitive component; for example, the Mehrabian–Epstein Scale (1972) can be viewed as relatively affectively oriented, whereas the Hogan Scale (1969) is more cognitive in its focus (Davis, 1983a). The emotional component of empathy, which is the focus of the present investigation, has demonstrated considerable predictive power in the realm of prosocial moral reasoning and prosocial behavior (Batson, Bolen, Cross, & Neuringer-Benefiel, 1986; Davis, 1983b; Eisenberg-Berg & Mussen, 1978). For example, among college students, empathic concern was positively related to viewing and contributing to the annual muscular dystrophy telethon; more cognitive aspects of empathy, such as role

taking and fantasizing ability, were unrelated to either viewing or contributing (Davis, 1983b).

Social philosophers have long been interested in the developmental origins of an empathic disposition. Not surprisingly, a number of psychological researchers have suggested that parenting practices may influence the development of empathy and related responses in children (cf. Eisenberg-Berg & Mussen, 1978; Hoffman & Saltztein, 1967). In a recent review of this literature, Barnett (1987) proposed that the development of empathy is most likely to occur in a family environment that (a) satisfies the child's own emotional needs and discourages excessive self-concern, (b) encourages the child to experience and express a broad range of emotions, and (c) provides opportunities for the child to observe and interact with others who encourage emotional sensitivity and responsiveness. Because these conditions focus on emotional responsiveness, it can be hypothesized that they are particularly likely to foster the emotional component of empathy (empathic concern).

There is evidence that stable individual differences in empathic responsiveness appear in children as early as age 2 (Radke-Yarrow, Zahn-Waxler, & Chapman, 1983); thus, one might conclude that early parenting experiences are of primary importance in the development of empathic concern. The present investigation offered a unique opportunity to use a prospective longitudinal research design to examine whether parent behavior in early childhood is related to the long-term development of empathic concern. Subjects were drawn from a sample first investigated by Sears, Maccoby, and Levin (1957) and most recently followed up by McClelland and Pilon (1983). When subjects were 5 years old their mothers were interviewed about their parenting behaviors as well as the parenting behaviors of their spouses. These interviews were then rated for a variety of specific maternal and paternal behaviors. Factor analyses of these ratings revealed (a) eight *maternal dimensions*—warmth, strictness, restricts sexuality, inhibits aggression, tolerates dependency, satisfaction with role as mother, use of physical pun-

This research used the *Patterns of Child Rearing, 1951–1952* data set (made accessible in 1979, raw and machine-readable data files). These data were collected by R. Sears, E. Maccoby, and H. Levin, and are available through the archives of the Henry A. Murray Research Center of Radcliffe College, Cambridge, Massachusetts. This study was funded by fellowships granted from the Seaver Institute and by a grant from the Fonds Pour La Formation De Chercheurs Et L'Aide A La Recherche (FCAR-Quebec).

Correspondence concerning this article should be addressed to Richard Koestner, Psychology Department, McGill University, 1205 Dr. Penfield Avenue, Montreal, Quebec, Canada H3A 1B1.

ishment, and use of praise; and (b) three *paternal dimensions*—involvement in child care, firmness in discipline, and warmth. At age 31, 75 of the original subjects were administered the Adjective Checklist (ACL; Gough & Heilbrun, 1965, 1983), from which an index of empathic concern can be derived (see Matthews, Batson, Horn, & Rosenman, 1981). The central purpose of the present study was to examine the relation between empathic concern at age 31 and the 11 parenting dimensions that were coded when subjects were 5 years old.

Relatively little attention has been given to the question of whether early parenting practices relate to later *adult* levels of empathic concern. One study employed a retrospective design to examine the relation between college students' memory of parenting experiences in middle childhood and their current level of empathic concern, as measured by the Mehrabian–Epstein Scale (Barnett, Howard, King, & Dino, 1980). Compared with students with low empathic concern, those who scored high reported that their parents had (a) spent more time with them, (b) been more affectionate with them, and (c) discussed feelings more with them. However, Barnett (1987) noted that these findings must be interpreted with caution because "individual differences in empathic disposition may tend to lead people to differentially distort or recall their parents' characteristics" (p. 151). More generally, Halverson (1988) has recently concluded that studies on the constructive nature of memory cast strong doubts regarding the accuracy of retrospective reports about the type of parenting one has received. It would seem that a prospective longitudinal research design, such as that offered by the present investigation, is necessary to convincingly demonstrate a relation between parenting practices and adult empathic concern.

The parenting dimensions available in this study do not match exactly those identified by Barnett et al. (1980) as related to empathic concern. However, there is enough conceptual overlap to offer three hypotheses. Because time spent with parents was a strong predictor of empathic concern in the Barnett et al. (1980) retrospective study, we hypothesized that father involvement in child care would facilitate the long-term development of empathic concern. Indirect support of such a hypothesis is provided by studies showing that fathers who were involved in the care of their children foster altruism and generosity, prosocial behaviors that have been associated with empathic concern (Rutherford & Mussen, 1968). Because none of the mothers in this study were employed outside the home, it is more difficult to calibrate the amount of time they spent with their children. However, a crude index of the amount of time spent together is perhaps reflected by the degree to which the mother tolerated dependency (e.g., allowing the child to remain nearby while preparing dinner). It might also be proposed that tolerating dependency in a 5-year-old reflects nurturance, responsiveness, and acceptance of feelings on the part of the mother, all of which have been positively associated with the development of prosocial behavior in children (Sigel, Dreyer, & McGillicuddy-De-Lisi, 1984). Thus, our second hypothesis was that maternal tolerance of dependent behavior would be positively associated with the development of empathic concern. Finally, we expected that parental affection, as reflected in ratings of maternal and paternal warmth, would be positively associated with later empathic concern. This prediction received support in the Bar-

nett et al. (1980) study and was also confirmed for adolescent boys in a study by Eisenberg-Berg and Mussen (1978).

It can be argued that even if the present investigation were to find a strong relation between early parenting experiences and adult levels of empathic concern, it would not be possible to infer causality. As Maccoby and Martin (1983) have noted, such a correlation might reflect the perseveration of the child's behavior from age 5 to age 31, with the parents' behavior at age 5 having merely been an *effect* of the child's behavior at that time. The possibility that empathic concern is a stable dispositional trait is highlighted by Matthews et al.'s study (1981), which employed a twin design to show that there is a strong genetic component to empathic concern.

In hopes of untangling the independent contributions of parenting practices and children's disposition, we will also examine the relation of adult levels of empathic concern to ratings of children's behavior in school made by their teachers when they were 5 years old. Specifically, adult empathic concern will be examined in relation to six dimensions of children's behavior reported by teachers: activity level, gets along with others, quarrels and fights with others, shows evidence of a conscience, emulates the teacher, and seeks help and attention from the teacher. Another source of information about children's dispositions is provided by interview ratings based on mother's descriptions of the child's behavior at home. Of particular relevance to the present question are ratings of the extent to which mothers described their children as sociable, dependent, aggressive, and disobedient at home. Because empathic concern has been associated with prosocial behavior, children with this disposition should be more likely to get along with others and inhibit aggressive behavior both at home and in school. To the extent that adult empathic concern is unrelated to descriptions of children's behavior, we can be less concerned that the relation between parenting experiences and adult empathic concern can be discounted as merely reflecting the continuity of children's disposition.

Because the ACL-derived measure of empathic concern has not been widely used, we will examine its relation to other personality constructs. Specifically, in this study it was possible to examine the correlation between empathic concern and social motives such as the need for affiliation, power, and achievement (McClelland, 1985) as well as with values as assessed on the Rokeach (1973) Values Inventory. Empathic concern should correlate positively with the need for affiliation (defined as "a concern with establishing and maintaining warm relationships") and with prosocial values (e.g., loving and equality). On the other hand, empathic concern should correlate negatively with the need for power and achievement (defined respectively as "a concern with having an impact on others" and "a concern with standards of excellence") as well as with values that emphasize self-direction (e.g., independent and a sense of accomplishment). Finally, it can be predicted that women will score higher on empathic concern than men. Eisenberg and Lennon's (1983) review of gender differences showed that in 16 of 16 studies, females scored higher than males on self-report measures of empathy, including measures of empathic concern.

Method

Procedure

Subjects were drawn from a longitudinal sample first investigated by Sears et al. (1957) and followed up by McClelland and Pilon (1983).

When subjects in this sample were 5 years old, their mothers were interviewed about their parenting behaviors as well as the parenting behaviors of their spouses. These interviews were transcribed and then rated for a variety of specific maternal and paternal behaviors (see Sears et al., 1957, for a description of rating procedures and interrater reliability figures).

Factor analyses of parenting ratings. Separate factor analyses were performed on (a) 42 maternal style ratings, (b) 7 ratings of the mother's management techniques, and (c) 9 paternal ratings. In all cases we used principal-component factor analysis followed by varimax rotation. Data from the entire original sample of 379 subjects were used, and all ratings were standardized prior to the analyses. The analysis of maternal style ratings yielded six dimensions: warmth (eigenvalue = 3.25), strictness (eigenvalue = 4.23), restricts sexuality (eigenvalue = 4.83), inhibits aggression (eigenvalue = 2.57), tolerates dependency (eigenvalue = 2.72), and role satisfaction (eigenvalue = 2.84). Analysis of the mother's management techniques revealed two dimensions: use of physical punishment (eigenvalue = 2.05) and use of praise (eigenvalue = 2.68). The analysis of paternal ratings yielded three dimensions: involvement in child care (eigenvalue = 1.63), firmness in discipline (eigenvalue = 2.77), and warmth (eigenvalue = 2.13). Subscale scores for each dimension were created by calculating the means of all ratings that loaded at least .30 on a particular factor. (See Appendixes A and B for listings of the dimensions and factor loadings of all items; see Appendix C for correlations among parenting dimensions.)

Teacher ratings of children's behavior in kindergarten. Each of the children in the original Sears et al. study (1957) was rated on six dimensions by his or her kindergarten teacher: (a) level of activity, (b) the degree to which the child gets along with peers, (c) the degree to which the child quarrels and fights with peers, (d) the extent to which the child emulates the teacher, (e) the extent to which the child shows evidence of having a conscience, and (f) the extent to which the child seeks help and attention from the teacher. All ratings were made on 7-point Likert scales.

Mother's ratings of children's behavior. Four ratings based on the interviews with mothers measured the extent to which children displayed the following behaviors at home: sociability, dependency, disobedience, and aggression.

31-year-old follow-up. At age 31, 75 of the original 379 subjects (38 women and 37 men) were followed up and administered a variety of personality measures, including the ACL (Gough & Heilbrun, 1965, 1983), Thematic Apperception Test (TAT-)derived measures of social motives (McClelland & Pilon, 1983), and the Rokeach (1973) Values Inventory. McClelland and Pilon (1983) reported that this 31-year-old sample was representative of the original sample on a host of demographic indices. To ensure that our sample was also comparable with the original one in terms of parenting experiences, we performed *t* tests between the 75 subjects and the remaining 304 from the original sample on all 11 parenting dimensions. No differences approaching significance emerged (*p*s > .15), suggesting that the 31-year-old sample was representative of the original sample on both demographic and parenting variables. McClelland, Constantian, Regalado, and Stone (1982) have provided a full description of the follow-up procedures.

Empathic concern. The ACL (Gough & Heilbrun, 1965, 1983) requires a person to circle any of 300 self-descriptive adjectives. Matthews et al. (1981) identified 13 adjectives that reflected empathic concern for others. Of those identified, 8 were scored positively (scored "+1" if circled and "0" if not circled) and 5 were scored negatively (scored "+1" if not circled and "0" if circled). Positive adjectives were emotional, generous, helpful, kind, sensitive, softhearted, sympathetic, and warm; negative adjectives were cold, hardhearted, self-centered, selfish, and unemotional. An individual's score on the index of empathic concern was derived by summing the number of +1s scored for these 13 adjectives. Index scores ranged from 5 to 13 in our sample.

Matthews et al. (1981) reported that the ACL-derived index of empathic concern was unidimensional and showed an acceptable level of internal reliability—the alpha coefficient was .70. These authors demonstrated the concurrent validity of their new empathic concern index by showing that it correlated highly with the widely used Mehrabian–Epstein Feelings Inventory (1972), *r*(86) = .47, *p* < .001.

Social motives. Motive measures were obtained from content-coding imaginative stories told in response to each of six TAT-like picture cues. The pictures were drawn from a standard set used in previous research to elicit stories to assess motive dispositions (cf. McClelland & Jemmott, 1980). All stories were coded, according to standard systems, for the need for affiliation (Heyns, Veroff, & Atkinson, 1957), need for achievement (Atkinson, 1958), and need for power (Winter, 1973). Coding was done by professional coders who had demonstrated their ability to score at least at the level of 85% agreement with expert coding. All scores were corrected for their regression on the total number of words in the six-story protocol. The reliability and validity of TAT-derived motive measures were described at length by Koestner and McClelland (in press).

Values. All subjects completed the Rokeach (1973) Values Inventory, which requires the rank ordering of each of 16 terminal values (e.g., "a world of beauty") and 16 instrumental values (e.g., "independent"). Schwartz and Bilsky (1987) recently showed that these 32 values are organized into seven motivational domains: enjoyment, maturity, achievement, self-direction, restrictive conformity, prosocial, and security. Because we were particularly interested in the relation of empathic concern to the prosocial and self-direction value domains, we created domain scores by summing responses to the values identified by Schwartz and Bilsky (1987) as belonging to the following two domains: *prosocial*—honest, loving, forgiving, helpful, equality, and belief in God; or *self-direction*—broad-minded, logical, independent, intellectual, imaginative, sense of accomplishment, and self-respect.

Results

Parenting Origins of Empathic Concern

Subjects' scores on the 13-item empathic concern index (alpha coefficient = .69) were regressed on 12 variables. Sex was entered first into the regression equation, and the 11 parenting dimensions were entered in a stepwise fashion thereafter. The questions of interest were (a) Would the multiple *R* indicate that the parenting dimensions are significantly associated with later empathic concern? and (b) Which of the 11 parenting dimensions would be the best individual predictors? A significant multiple *R* of .60, *F*(8, 67) = 4.63, *p* < .001, indicated that, taken together, the parenting dimensions predicted the level of empathic concern at age 31. The results for each of the individual predictors are shown in Table 1. The standardized regression coefficient (*β*) indicates the degree of relation between each dimension and empathic concern, whereas the significance of each effect was estimated by a *t* test. The betas and significance tests that are reported were those obtained after all of the independent variables had entered into the regression equation.[1] Pearson correlations between empathic concern and the parenting factors are also provided. It can be seen that two of the parenting dimensions significantly predicted empathic concern: paternal involvement in child care (*β* = .37) and maternal tolerance for dependent behavior (*β* = .26). Two marginally significant effects (.05 < *p* < .10) were also found: maternal inhibition of the child's aggression (*β* = .19) and maternal role satisfaction

---

[1] The results are similar if the standardized regression coefficients are taken at the step at which each independent variable entered the regression equation. These betas were as follows: sex, .21; father involvement, .38; mother tolerates dependency, .25; mother inhibits aggression, .20;

Table 1

Standardized Regression Coefficients (Betas), Pearson Correlations, and Significance Tests of the Relation Between Parenting Dimensions and Empathic Concern at Age 31

Predictor	Standardized regression coefficient (β)	Pearson correlation	t test
Sex			
(M = 1, F = 2)	.17	.21	1.70*
Parenting dimensions			
Paternal involvement in child care	.37	.38	3.67***
Maternal tolerance of dependency	.26	.23	2.61**
Maternal inhibition of aggression	.19	.25	1.89*
Maternal satisfaction with role	.18	.22	1.81*
Use of praise	−.11	−.01	−1.06
Paternal firmness in discipline	.10	−.06	1.01
Maternal strictness	.10	.25	0.96

Note. Four parenting dimensions failed to enter into the regression equation because they increased the R^2 by less than 0.01. These dimensions were paternal warmth, maternal warmth, maternal restriction of the child's sexuality, and use of physical punishment.
* $p < .10$. ** $p < .01$. *** $p < .001$.

($\beta = .18$). A marginally significant effect for sex of child was also found ($\beta = .17$), indicating that females scored higher on the index of empathic concern than males. Contrary to predictions, maternal and paternal warmth were unrelated to empathic concern.

Moderating Role of Sex on the Relation Between Parenting and Empathic Concern

To examine whether the relation between parenting and empathic concern is conditional on the sex of the child (as suggested by Abraham, Kuehl, & Christopherson, 1983), a second analysis regressed empathic concern on sex, the 11 parenting dimensions, and the 11 Sex × Parenting interactions. Essentially, the Sex × Parenting product is analogous to the two-way interaction term in an analysis of variance, accounting for the joint effects of each parenting dimension and sex on level of empathic concern (see Cohen & Cohen, 1983). This regression revealed marginally significant ($ps < .10$) interactions for Sex × Maternal Strictness and Sex × Maternal Inhibition of Aggression. To interpret these effects, the correlations between parenting dimensions and empathic concern scores were calculated separately for men and women. These correlations showed that maternal strictness led to greater empathic concern for women ($r = .44$) but not for men ($r = −.14$). Similarly, maternal inhibition of aggression was associated with greater empathic concern for women ($r = .46$) but not for men ($r = −.14$). Because these interactions were not expected and only approached significance, they will not be considered in the Discussion section.

Teacher Ratings at Age 5 and Empathic Concern at 31

Adult empathic concern scores were unrelated to the six teacher ratings: activity, $r = −.05$; gets along with peers, $r = .08$;

father firm in discipline, .13; maternal role satisfaction, .19; mother restricts sexuality, −.04; maternal strictness, .12; and maternal warmth, −.03.

fights with peers, $r = .00$; emulates the teacher, $r = .07$; shows evidence of a conscience, $r = .04$; and seeks help from the teacher, $r = .00$.

Maternal Ratings of Child at Age 5 and Empathic Concern at 31

Adult empathic concern scores were unrelated to three of the ratings derived from mothers' descriptions of their children's behavior: sociability, $r = .02$; dependency, $r = −.06$; and aggression, $r = .11$. However, a significant negative relationship was found between children's disobedience at home and later empathic concern, $r = −.30$.

Correlates of Empathic Concern at Age 31

We predicted that empathic concern would correlate positively with the need for affiliation and with prosocial values and that it would correlate negatively with the need for power and achievement as well as with values that emphasize self-direction. These predictions were largely confirmed: Empathic concern correlated positively with need for affiliation, $r(75) = .30$, $p < .05$, and with prosocial values derived from the Rokeach survey, $r(75) = .21$, $p < .10$. On the other hand, empathic concern was negatively related to values emphasizing self-direction, $r(75) = −.26$, $p < .05$, and to need for achievement and need for power ($rs = −.12$ and $−.10$, respectively).[2]

Discussion

The results indicate that there is a relatively strong association between early parenting experiences and adult empathic concern. Parenting behaviors accounted for 36% of the variance in adult empathic concern scores, a percentage that compares favorably with effects typically found for child-rearing practices (Maccoby & Martin, 1983). Parenting behaviors reflecting the

[2] In this study it was also possible to examine whether self-reported empathic concern related to nonverbal sensitivity as measured by the

amount of time spent with the child were most predictive of later levels of empathic concern. Thus, children whose fathers were very involved in their care and whose mothers were tolerant of dependency were most likely to report high levels of empathic concern at age 31. Contrary to predictions, adult levels of empathic concern were unrelated to parental affection toward the child.

The influence of paternal involvement in child care on later empathic concern was quite astonishing. This single dimension accounted for a greater percentage of the unique variance in empathic concern scores (13%) than the three strongest maternal predictors combined. These results appear to fit with previous findings indicating that prosocial behaviors such as altruism and generosity in children were related to active involvement in child care by fathers (Rutherford & Mussen, 1968). It can be speculated that these results have implications for research on the long-term developmental outcomes of children who experience divorce prior to age 5, because diminished paternal involvement in child care is a concomitant of the vast majority of divorces (Biller, 1981). At a minimum, the strength of these results supports the recent emphasis on the importance of considering fathers' contributions to child development (cf. Lamb, 1981).

The positive relation between maternal tolerance of dependency and later empathic concern can be interpreted in different ways. First, if it is assumed that tolerance of dependency is likely to lead to greater levels of mother–child interaction, then the results support Barnett et al.'s (1980) findings. It can also be proposed that tolerance of dependency reflects nurturance, responsiveness, and acceptance of feelings on the part of the mother, all of which have been positively associated with the development of prosocial behavior in children (Sigel et al., 1984). The fact that maternal inhibition of aggression also was related to empathic concern provides an interesting counterpoint to the apparent empathy-enhancing effect of tolerance of dependency. Taken together, these two findings suggest that differential responsiveness to children's affiliative and aggressive impulses may promote the long-term development of empathic concern. This conclusion contrasts with Barnett's (1987) contention that empathy is most likely to develop in a family environment that encourages the child to experience and express a broad range of emotions. It should be noted that both teacher and maternal descriptions of children's dependent and aggressive behavior did not relate to later empathic concern.

The finding that mothers who are satisfied with their role are likely to raise children who are high in empathic concern can be more easily understood when one considers the specific ratings that went into this factor. Mothers scoring high on this di-

mension have positive attitudes about themselves, about their roles as mothers, and about their family situations. They are also confident about their child-rearing skills and make sure they behave in an authoritative rather than submissive manner toward their children. It can be speculated that mothers who are secure and confident in their roles may facilitate the development of empathy in two ways: (a) Confident, nonanxious mothering will likely foster a secure mother–child attachment, which has been identified as important to the development of concern for others' feelings (Barnett, 1987); and (b) happy mothers who feel good about themselves are probably more likely to be able to attend to children's feelings and concerns and thereby serve as a model of empathic concern.

The present study failed to confirm a relationship between parental affection and empathic concern. This failure to replicate Barnett et al.'s (1980) results may well be due to the fact that we employed prospective rather than retrospective methods. It may be that retrospective accounts of parental warmth are especially vulnerable to selective memory biases. It should be noted that a review of the developmental literature on prosocial behavior concluded that a relationship with parental warmth and acceptance had not been firmly established (Radke-Yarrow et al., 1983).

In contrast to the association found between parenting dimensions and adult levels of empathic concern, children's behavior as reflected in teacher and maternal ratings generally failed to predict later empathic concern. Thus, children who were described as getting along with their peers and emulating the teacher in kindergarten were no more likely to develop high levels of empathic concern than were children who were described as active and quarrelsome. Similarly, children who were described by their mothers as sociable and nonaggressive at home were no more likely to develop empathic concern than were those who were described as unsociable and aggressive. However, mother's report of obedience problems was significantly negatively associated with later empathic concern. Interpreting this finding is complicated because obedience problems may reflect any of the following causes: (a) The child has a difficult temperament, (b) the parents set high standards for obedience, (c) the parents lack the limit-setting skills necessary to ensure appropriate behavior on the part of their child, and (d) the family context is unstructured and disorganized, therefore promoting disobedient behavior.

Because our measure of empathic concern has not been widely used, we also examined its relation to other personality constructs. The results showed that empathic concern correlated positively with need for affiliation and with prosocial values derived from the Rokeach survey, whereas it was negatively related to values emphasizing self-direction and to need for achievement and need for power scores. Consistent with previous research (Eisenberg & Lennon, 1983), women in our sample scored somewhat higher on empathic concern than men. On the basis of these results, we conclude that the index derived from the Adjective Checklist can serve as an acceptable replacement for other empathic concern scales. However, its use seems most appropriate with archival samples when there is no opportunity to introduce a more standard index of empathic concern such as the Mehrabian–Epstein (1972) or Davis (1983a) measure.

It is important to note the limitations of the present investiga-

---

audio version of the Profile of Nonverbal Sensitivity (PONS; Rosenthal, Hall, DiMatteo, Rogers, & Archer, 1979). We found a nonsignificant correlation of $-.07$ between these two measures. The lack of correlation between self-reported empathic concern and nonverbal decoding skill is not surprising. Rosenthal et al. (1979) reported an r of only .08 between self-ratings of interpersonal sensitivity and performance on the PONS. Furthermore, reviews of the construct validity of empathy measures have failed to note any consistent relation between questionnaire measures of empathy and performance measures of nonverbal sensitivity.

tion. First, all parenting ratings (including those of the father's behavior) were derived from mothers' self-reports—it would no doubt have been preferable to have buttressed these reports with observational data. Second, all ratings were made concerning parenting behavior toward the child until he or she was 5 years old—it cannot be assumed that the same pattern of behavior (e.g., tolerating dependency) would yield the same effect if the child were older than 5. Finally, the cultural frame of our sample—early 1950s baby-boom era—must be remembered when generalizing from these results.

To review, our results suggest that children are most likely to grow up to be empathically concerned adults when both of their parents enjoyed being involved with them and when their affiliative and aggressive needs were differentially responded to, with the former being permitted and encouraged and the latter inhibited. The results also indicate that children who present minimal problems with regard to disobedience in the home are especially likely to develop high levels of empathic concern as adults. The composite picture that emerges regarding parenting behaviors likely to promote the long-term development of empathic concern resembles the authoritative pattern of parenting described by Baumrind (1967, 1971a). Authoritative parenting is "reflected in a pattern of family functioning in which children are required to be responsive to parental demands, and parents accept the reciprocal responsibility to be as responsive as possible to their children's reasonable demands" (Maccoby & Martin, 1983, p. 46).[3]

The strength of the relation between early parenting experiences and an adult personality measure is startling given the wealth of recent evidence that genetic factors play a far more central role in the development of personality than do environmental factors (Plomin & Daniels, 1987). Consider the conclusion recently offered by McCrae and Costa (1988): "The growing body of evidence suggests that the way in which parents raise their children has limited formative impact on their children's future personality" (p. 432). Although we cannot rule out temperamental and genetic explanations, our results suggest that parenting behaviors in early childhood can have a lasting impact on the course of personality development.

---

[3] It might also be argued that the family context in which empathic concern is most likely to flourish parallels Baumrind's (1971b) description of "harmonious" families in which interaction between parents and between parents and children proceed with little conflict or need for exercising firm control. The potential role of family harmony as a contextual feature likely to foster the development of empathic concern is supported by ratings made concerning the degree to which the mother and father appeared to possess similar personalities, attitudes, and habits. These ratings of parental similarity were significantly positively associated with adult empathic concern, $r = .25$, $p < .05$. This variable was not included in the factor analyses reported earlier because it did not relate to parental behavior toward the child.

References

Abraham, K. G., Kuehl, R. O., & Christopherson, V. A. (1983). Age-specific influence of parental behaviors on the development of empathy in preschool children. *Child Study Journal, 13*, 175–185.

Atkinson, J. W. (1958). Towards experimental analysis of human motivation in terms of motives, expectancies and incentives. In J. W. Atkinson (Ed.), *Motives in fantasy, action, and society* (pp. 288–305). Princeton, NJ: Van Nostrand.

Barnett, M. A. (1987). Empathy and related responses in children. In N. Eisenberg & J. Strayer (Eds.), *Empathy and its development* (pp. 146–162). New York: Cambridge University Press.

Barnett, M. A., Howard, J. A., King, L. M., & Dino, G. A. (1980). Antecedents of empathy: Retrospective accounts of early socialization. *Personality and Social Psychology Bulletin, 6*, 361–365.

Batson, C., Bolen, M. H., Cross, J. A., & Neuringer-Benefiel, H. E. (1986). Where is the altruism in the altruistic personality? *Journal of Personality and Social Psychology, 50*, 212–220.

Baumrind, D. (1967). Child care practices anteceding three patterns of preschool behavior. *Genetic Psychology Monographs, 75*, 43–88.

Baumrind, D. (1971a). Current patterns of parental authority. *Developmental Psychology Monographs, 4*, 1–103.

Baumrind, D. (1971b). Harmonious parents and their preschool children. *Developmental Psychology, 4*, 99–102.

Biller, H. B. (1981). Father absence, divorce and personality development. In M. Lamb (Ed.), *The role of the father in child development* (pp. 489–552). New York: Wiley.

Cohen, J., & Cohen, P. (1983). *Applied multiple regression/correlation analysis for the behavioral sciences*. Hillsdale, NJ: Erlbaum.

Davis, M. H. (1983a). Measuring individual differences in empathy: Evidence for a multidimensional approach. *Journal of Personality and Social Psychology, 44*, 113–126.

Davis, M. H. (1983b). Empathic concern and the muscular dystrophy telethon: Empathy as a multidimensional construct. *Personality and Social Psychology Bulletin, 9*, 223–229.

Davis, M. H., & Oathout, H. A. (1987). Maintenance of satisfaction in romantic relationships: Empathy and relational competence. *Journal of Personality and Social Psychology, 53*, 397–410.

Eisenberg, N., & Lennon, R. (1983). Sex differences in empathy and related capacities. *Psychological Bulletin, 94*, 100–131.

Eisenberg-Berg, N., & Mussen, P. (1978). Empathy and moral development in adolescence. *Developmental Psychology, 2*, 185–186.

Feschbach, N. D. (1975). Empathy in children: Some theoretical and empirical considerations. *Counseling Psychologist, 5*, 25–30.

Goldstein, A. P., & Michaels, G. Y. (1985). *Empathy: Development, training and consequences*. Hillsdale, NJ: Erlbaum.

Gough, H., & Heilbrun, A. L. (1965). *The Adjective Checklist manual*. Palo Alto, CA: Consulting Psychologists Press.

Gough, H., & Heilbrun, A. L. (1983). *The Revised Adjective Checklist manual*. Palo Alto, CA: Consulting Psychologists Press.

Halverson, C. F. (1988). Remembering your parents: Reflections on the retrospective method. *Journal of Personality, 56*, 434–443.

Heyns, R. W., Veroff, J., & Atkinson, J. (1957). A scoring manual for the affiliative motive. In J. W. Atkinson (Ed.), *Motives in fantasy, action, and society* (pp. 205–218). Princeton, NJ: Van Nostrand.

Hoffman, M. L., & Saltzstein, H. D. (1967). Parent discipline and the child's moral development. *Journal of Personality and Social Psychology, 5*, 45–57.

Hogan, R. (1969). Development of an empathy scale. *Journal of Consulting and Clinical Psychology, 33*, 307–316.

Koestner, R., & McClelland, D. C. (in press). Social motives. In L. Pervin (Ed.), *Handbook of personality theory and research*. New York: Guilford Press.

Lamb, M. E. (1981). *The role of the father in child development* (2nd ed.). New York: Wiley.

Maccoby, E., & Martin, J. A. (1983). Socialization in the context of the family: Parent-child interaction. In E. M. Hetherington (Ed.), *Handbook of child psychology* (Vol. 4, pp. 1–102). New York: Wiley.

Matthews, K. A., Batson, C. D., Horn, J., & Rosenman, R. H. (1981). The heritability of empathic concern for others. *Journal of Personality, 49*, 237–247.

McClelland, D. C. (1985). *Human motivation*. New York: Cambridge University Press.

McClelland, D. C., Constantian, C. A., Regalado, D., & Stone, C.

(1982). Effects of child-rearing practices on adult maturity. In D. C. McClelland (Ed.), *Development of social maturity* (pp. 209–248). New York: Irvington Publishers.

McClelland, D. C., & Jemmott, J. B. (1980). Power motivation, stress and physical illness. *Journal of Human Stress, 6,* 6–15.

McClelland, D. C., & Pilon, D. A. (1983). Sources of adult motives in parent behavior in early childhood. *Journal of Personality and Social Psychology, 44,* 564–574.

McCrae, R. R., & Costa, P. T., Jr. (1988). Recalled parent-child relations and adult personality. *Journal of Personality, 56,* 417–434.

Mehrabian, P. A., & Epstein, N. (1972). A measure of emotional empathy. *Journal of Personality, 40,* 525–543.

Plomin, R., & Daniels, D. (1987). Why are children in the same family so different from one another? *Behavioral and Brain Sciences, 10,* 1–16.

Radke-Yarrow, M., Zahn-Waxler, C., & Chapman, M. (1983). Children's prosocial dispositions and behavior. In P. H. Mussen (Ed.), *Handbook of child psychology* (pp. 469–546). New York: Wiley.

Rokeach, M. (1973). *The nature of human values.* New York: Free Press.

Rosenthal, R., Hall, J. A., DiMatteo, M. R., Rogers, P. L., & Archer, D. (1979). *Sensitivity to nonverbal communication: The PONS test.* Baltimore, MD: Johns Hopkins University Press.

Rutherford, E., & Mussen, P. H. (1968). Generosity in nursery school boys. *Child Development, 39,* 755–765.

Schwartz, S. H., & Bilsky, W. (1987). Toward a universal psychological structure of human values. *Journal of Personality and Social Psychology, 53,* 550–562.

Sears, R. R., Maccoby, E. E., & Levin, H. (1957). *Patterns of childrearing.* Evanston, IL: Row Peterson.

Sigel, I. E., Dreyer, A. S., & McGillicuddy-DeLisi, A. V. (1984). Psychological perspectives of the family. In R. Parke (Ed.), *Review of child development research* (Vol. 7, pp. 42–79). Chicago: University of Chicago Press.

Winter, D. G. (1973). *The power motive.* New York: Free Press.

Appendix A

Items and Factor Loadings for Maternal Dimensions

Factor loading	Dimension label
	Maternal warmth
.48	Mother's responsiveness to infant's crying.
.72	Amount of mother's affectionate interaction with baby, beyond routine care taking.
.57	Amount of fun taking care of small babies.
.82	Warmth of affectional bond: mother to infant.
.53	Amount of affectional demonstrativeness: mother to child.
.43	Does mother find time to play with child just for her own pleasure?
.47	Nature of affectional relationship: mother to child.
	Maternal restrictiveness regarding sexuality
.76	Permissiveness for going without clothes indoors. (reversal)
.67	Amount of pressure that mother has applied for modesty indoors.
.78	Permissiveness for masturbation. (reversal)
.49	Severity of pressure that has been applied against masturbation.
.80	Permissiveness of sex play among children. (reversal)
.53	Severity of pressure that has been applied against sex play.
.80	Mother's level of sex anxiety.
	Maternal strictness
.35	Severity of mother's handling of feeding problems.
.39	Amount of restriction of physical mobility during meals.
.55	Amount of restriction in the use of fingers for eating.
.54	Amount of restriction of interruption of adult conversation.
.75	Level of demands, table manners.
.59	Amount of pressure for conformity with table manners and restrictions.
.57	Level of standards, neatness and orderliness and cleanliness.
.48	Pressure for conformity to restrictions and standards: neatness and orderliness.
.45	Strictness about bedtime behavior.
.37	Strictness about noise.
.41	Restrictions on radio and TV.
.37	Giving child regular jobs and encouraging child to accept these.
.45	Mother's realistic standards for obedience.
.42	Does mother carry through on obedience demands?
.38	Mother's permissiveness for aggression toward parents. (reversal)

(Appendix continues)

Appendix A (*continued*)

Factor loading	Dimension label
	Maternal tolerance of dependency
.66	Mother's response to dependency.
.74	Permissiveness for dependency.
.73	Extent to which mother rewards dependent acts, complies with demands.
.50	Amount of punishment for child's dependent responses, and amount of irritation mother feels. (reversal)
	Maternal inhibition of aggression
.76	Level of mother's demands for child to be aggressive toward other children. (reversal)
.72	Extent to which parent has encouraged child to fight back. (reversal)
.63	Permissiveness for inappropriate aggression toward other children. (reversal)
.40	Keeping track of child.
	Maternal role satisfaction
.32	Mother's attitude toward the mother role.
.55	Mother's acceptance of current situation.
.64	Mother's self-esteem.
.78	Mother's child-rearing anxiety. (reversal)
.51	Mother submissiveness to child. (reversal)

Appendix B

Table B1
Items and Factor Loadings for Maternal Management Techniques

Factor loadings	Dimension label
	Use of praise
.75	Praise for table manners.
.61	Praise for obedience.
.64	Praise for nice play.
.83	Extent of praise.
	Use of physical punishment
.84	Extent the mother spanks.
.88	Use of physical punishment.
.53	Use of reasoning. (reversal)

Table B2
Items and Factor Loadings for Paternal Dimensions

Factor loadings	Dimension label
	Paternal firmness in discipline
.75	Father's standards for obedience: how strict is he?
.56	Percentage of father to mother discipline.
.83	How lenient is father with child. (reversal)
.78	Does mother think father is too strict?
	Paternal involvement in child care
.85	Does father ever stay with child when mother is out?
.79	How much does father do these days in connection with taking care of child?
	Paternal warmth
.78	Amount of coldness and lack of affection between child and father. (reversal)
.76	Nature of affectional bond, father to child (index of father's hostility). (reversal)
.66	Extent of father's positive feeling when he discovered wife was pregnant.

Appendix C

Correlations Among Parenting Scales

Variable	1	2	3	4	5	6	7	8	9	10
1. Father's involvement in child care	1.00									
2. Mother's tolerance of dependency	.05	1.00								
3. Mother inhibits aggression	.02	−.02	1.00							
4. Father's firmness in discipline	−.11	.01	−.10	1.00						
5. Mother's satisfaction with her role	.12	.15	.09	−.01	1.00					
6. Mother's restriction of sexuality	.04	−.17	.24	.07	−.06	1.00				
7. Mother's strictness	.16	−.10	.09	.22	.10	.33	1.00			
8. Mother's warmth	.11	.28	.06	−.10	.26	−.19	−.08	1.00		
9. Father's warmth	.31	.19	.11	−.26	.26	−.03	.09	.27	1.00	
10. Use of praise	.08	−.01	.07	.03	.08	.01	−.08	.28	.09	1.0
11. Use of physical punishment	.07	−.21	−.06	.04	−.14	.25	.15	−.16	−.10	−.03

Note. All correlations are based on data from the 379 subjects available from the Sears, Maccoby, and Levin (1957) study. $r > .10$ reflects $p < .05$. $r > .17$ reflects $p < .01$. $r > .21$ reflects $p < .001$.

Received August 30, 1988
Revision received July 1, 1989
Accepted July 26, 1989 ■

281

Education and the moral emotions

BEN SPIECKER

1 Introduction

Moral philosophers and psychologists such as R.M. Hare and L. Kohlberg have often been reproached for giving insufficient attention to the question of which moral emotions may be found in a 'decent' or moral human being (Williams, 1973: 207).[1] It seems to me that this reproach is justified and the neglect is particularly felt in the field of moral education. The capacity for experiencing moral emotions – e.g. guilt – is a necessary condition for being a moral person. We feel entitled to blame someone for not feeling repentance after wilfully harming someone else.

But can we educate moral emotions? Nowadays it is often said that our emotions can be distinguished from each other, and justified, on the basis of their cognitive–evaluative component.[2] And because these evaluations can be influenced, the phrase 'education of emotions' is not a contradiction in terms. Moral emotions are taught; if a child breaks the rules it learns not only *that* (or *why*) it should feel guilty, but also (as its parents make clear) *what* feeling guilty means. The child learns a whole range of what is considered *proper* behaviour – from 'don't look so insolent' and 'go and apologize' to correct

43

attitudes toward an offence: 'You should feel terrible about what you've done' (cf. Arman-Jones, 1985: 9).

The rational tradition (Kant, Piaget, Kohlberg) has made its influence strongly felt in the field of moral education and development; in this tradition moral learning is not considered to be a matter of supplying missing emotions and motives, but of developing our innate intellectual capacities. According to this conception, education initiates the child into the forms of knowledge. Matters such as attachments, tendencies and character receive less attention (White, 1984). However, in order to maintain a well-ordered and just society, it is precisely these ties, moral sentiments and motives that are of decisive importance.

In this article, I want to explore further the question of what we understand by moral emotions and sentiments and in what way these can be influenced or educated. I shall distinguish two subclasses of moral emotions, and subsequently examine in more detail their *logical* and *developmental-psychological* relations to one another. In conclusion, I will make a number of observations about the discussion between L. Kohlberg and G. Gilligan, because I think that their controversy can be illuminated by means of the subclasses of moral emotions that have been distinguished.

There are no clear classification-criteria which distinguish (moral) emotions from attitudes, motives or traits of character. Most emotions and motives are also regarded as virtues and vices – e.g. envy, benevolence and lust (Peters, 1974: 182; see also Rorty, 1980). Some emotions are by nature motivational – feelings of obligation, regard or respect for a moral principle in the case of conscientiousness – and form an integral part of certain virtues. Virtues, and thus vices as well, include both specific wants and feelings. If we say of someone that his character is friendly or sympathetic, then we also imply that this person is capable of having certain feelings and emotions (e.g. tenderness). The same applies to the term 'attitude'; a moral attitude (e.g. respect for persons) logically implies certain emotions and feelings (Dent, 1984: 16). Thus, two types of virtues, called by D. Hume the 'natural' and the

44

'artificial', correspond to the two subclasses of moral emotions which I will distinguish.

2 Two subclasses of moral emotions

What do we consider to belong to the category of moral emotions? We could ask whether moral emotions are distinguished from other emotions by specific manifestations of behaviour or characteristic sensations (cf. Richards, 1971: 250). Neither case is satisfactory; one's face can turn red as a result of either shame or anger, warmth or exertion. Nor do physical sensations form a necessary condition for moral emotions to occur or be distinguished. The physical sensation of anger, for example, will differ from case to case: a dry mouth, shaking hands, a pounding heart. On the other hand, the explanation a person gives for experiencing a moral emotion *is* characteristic of one subclass of moral emotions. Among other things, this explanation implies that the person thinks he has broken a moral rule or principle, or is intending to do so, and is, moreover, of the opinion that there are no excusing conditions. For instance, I can feel guilty when I wilfully treat someone else unkindly or deliberately break a promise. In turn, I feel indignant when someone else fails to keep a promise. Moral emotions which result from consciously transgressing a moral principle should disappear after the relationship with the other(s) has been re-established. Reconciliation can be effected by confessing guilt, by showing regret, by asking for forgiveness, and so on. That some moral emotions are logically dependent on the conviction that moral rules or principles are applicable to us can be explained by comparing the emotions 'shame' and 'embarrassment' (Bedford, 1967: 85). The behaviour of a person who feels embarrassed will often not differ greatly from that of someone who feels ashamed; nevertheless, both find themselves in different situations. Moral shame occurs when someone breaks a moral standard; a necessary condition for the correctness of a statement such as 'she is ashamed of herself' is that the person in question feels

45

that she has acted wrongly. This person can be blamed because she can be held responsible. On the other hand, a person can be embarrassed both without his knowledge and without his responsibility. For the behaviour of small children who have been put under our responsibility, we can probably feel both shame and embarrassment.

One can, on the basis of the above, draw the conclusion that there is a subclass of *moral* emotions, of which a necessary condition is formed by the awareness that moral rules apply to oneself and to others and that in some cases these rules are broken. But breaking a moral rule in one's actions or experiencing immoral emotions – immoral emotions (malice) can also call up moral emotions (indignation) – does not in itself form a sufficient condition, as it is possible that a person deliberately goes against moral principles without experiencing moral emotions. I will call this subclass of moral emotions (moral) *rule*-emotions. With this type of moral emotions the cognitive evaluation consists of considering a moral rule or principle to be applicable to oneself and to others.

Moral rule-emotions are thus connected with moral rules, and only a person who has mastered these rules can have these emotions. These *rule*-emotions are rational: for, in principle, a person can explain and justify why he experiences these emotions.

I have already touched on the relationship between moral emotions and virtues. Rule-emotions correspond to, or are a part of, what are called the 'artificial' or non-teleological virtues or traits of character (reasonableness, justice). The non-teleologically virtuous person experiences and acts on the basis of these motivating rule-emotions; he shows respect for the moral law, he feels obligated to keep his promise, or, formulated more generally, he has a predilection for justice (Steutel, 1986). The bearer of artificial virtues cares about moral rules, he has acquired the disposition of a positive commitment to moral rules and is inclined to evaluate certain conflicts and situations with the help of these rules.

I come now to the second type of moral emotions, the *altruistic* emotions, sometimes called 'natural attitudes'. The

46

moral character of these altruistic emotions is not always sufficiently recognized – this may be the result of a 'genetic fallacy'. Owing to the fact that the instinctive wants and urges of young children have to be socialized, the attitudes and moral emotions of adults are wrongly taken to be a mere masking of these natural urges (cf. MacIntyre, 1967).

In developmental psychology, actions motivated by altruism are often taken as a form of 'pro-social behaviour', as actions that are intended to aid or benefit another person or group without the actor's anticipation of external rewards (Mussen and Eisenberg-Berg, 1977: 3). The operationalization of this concept frequently comes down to 'helping behaviour' or 'compliance' (see Wispé, 1978; Bridgeman, 1983). But from a conceptual point of view, not all helping behaviour is altruistic; if an attractive student stopped me on the campus and asked for my name, I would probably give it to her, but not because I felt altruistic (Krebs, 1978: 143–4).

Altruistic emotions, such as feelings of compassion, concern, generosity and sympathy, are directed at other people (or animals) specifically in the light of their weal and woe (cf. Schopenhauer, 1840; Blum, 1980). In particular, parents and educators stress the importance of these altruistic emotions explicitly when speaking of the aims of education and the future of their children. Parents hope and strive to have their children grow up to have a good character and to become pleasant, trustworthy and compassionate persons, who know how to love and who have enough friends (cf. Peters, 1974: 331; White, 1984). The so-called 'natural' (or teleological) virtues are also formed by helping the child to acquire altruistic emotions.

The central altruistic emotions are directed at those fellow human beings who find themselves in misery, who are in distress, or who suffer; they are 'moral' in that they involve a regard for the good of other persons (feelings of pity) (cf. Schopenhauer).[3] These emotions have a cognitive component as well: it does make some difference whether the other feels embarrassed or is suffering. The content of the cognition, however, does not in itself form a sufficient condition for

47

speaking of an altruistic emotion. An element of feeling should also be involved: one should be '(painfully) struck' or 'touched' by the distress of the other. Nevertheless, there is no question of one 'typical' feeling; concern for another person (or animal) can involve feelings of shock, hope and (afterwards) relief, in which the component of physical sensations can also make itself felt.

Altruistic emotions are to be distinguished from moods (excitement, elation, depression) and from personal feelings (admiration, respect); neither being in a good mood nor being fond of a person forms a necessary condition for having altruistic emotions. When I am in a bad mood I can still feel pity for a neighbour who is in trouble, even though I dislike the neighbour.

On what grounds now can the distinction between rule-emotions and altruistic emotions be justified? Up to this point I have not got beyond making the distinction between observing the *condition* of other persons in the light of their weal and woe on the one hand and judging a person's *actions* (or one's own) by a moral principle on the other hand. Rule-emotions presuppose that an action is judged with the aid of a moral rule. Because the judgement is based on a rule, one may expect to find that persons involved in identical situations in which rules are broken have the same rule-emotion(s); if X and Y are both witnesses to Z's theft, one can reasonably expect both X and Y to be indignant about the offence.

In altruistic emotions, a judgement based on a moral rule does not form a necessary condition for experiencing these emotions. Nowadays, as the psychologist R.B. Zajonc observes, emotions are all too often considered as exclusively *post*-cognitive, i.e. occurring only after considerable cognitive operations have been completed. Against this view, Zajonc argues that we cannot be introduced to a person without experiencing an immediate feeling of attraction or repulsion, though we may completely fail to notice the other person's hair colour: 'But seldom do we escape the reaction that the other person impressed us as pleasant or unpleasant, as nice or irritating' (1980: 153, 156).[4]

48

Compassion, friendliness and helpfulness presuppose only that one reacts to certain characteristics of a situation or to the condition of the other, i.e. that one recognizes or understands that someone else needs help, and that this perception leads one to undertake charitable actions. Forming a judgement is no necessary condition, as is being sensitive, being receptive to the weal and woe of the other. The friendly or caring person does not as a rule act in order to be virtuous; he is rarely aware that he acts morally (Blum, 1980). In order to justify his altruistic emotion, it is not necessary for a person to call upon a moral rule. If X, filled with care, hurries to help Y, X does not necessarily need to be convinced that he is acting in accordance with a general reason or principle. An altruistic emotion and the corresponding wish to watch over or promote the other's well-being, or to lighten his suffering, can be justified by referring to the weal and woe of the other, to his situation or condition which 'strikes' us. Depending on the result of the intervention, acting out of compassion is characterized by, among other things, feelings of pleasure, relief, joy ('a load off our minds'), sadness or frustration. If altruistic emotions are to occur, a necessary condition is also formed by the perception and understanding that all is 'not well' with the other(s). This does not of course rule out the possibility that perception and understanding can *also* be influenced by a moral rule; X is worried about Y because Y is, in his actions, less and less concerned with moral principles.

In my opinion, the distinction between both subclasses can also be further elucidated with the help of two types of duties, called *perfect* and *imperfect* duties by Kant and 'Rechts-' and 'Tugend-' or 'Liebespflichten' by Schopenhauer (Kant, 1978: 87; Schopenhauer, 1979: 57, 110, 125). Perfect or 'Rechts-' duties are those duties which do not allow an exception in favour of an impulse; these duties not only state what we may not or may never do – do not steal, kill, lie – they also, when the rules are transgressed, compel us to undergo those emotions which I have earlier called rule-emotions. The altruistic emotions, on the other hand, are connected with the imperfect duties or 'Liebespflichten', in which there are no rules which

49

concretely dictate when we should do what or which altruistic emotions we should experience. We will show
differential reactions to transgressions of the two types of
duties. Unjustly not showing rule-emotions will be considered
a *'vice'* ('Laster'); failing in the altruistic emotions will be
understood as a 'lack of virtue' ('Untugend') (cf. Nunner-
Winkler, 1984: 349).

The altruistic emotions form part of the 'natural' (or
teleological) virtues. The bearer of these 'natural' virtues is
characterized by the disposition of a positive commitment to
the fate of his fellow man (Steutel, 1986). The motivating
emotions of this person are interwoven with the perception of,
and sometimes with the judgement of, the weal and woe of the
other. In his actions, he strives after a certain aim (*telos*) – to
abolish the sufferings of fellow man.

To distinguish both subclasses from a logical point of view
may sound plausible, but the question of how children acquire
these emotions is of completely different order. I will attempt
to prove that in the development of a child both types of moral
emotions influence each other in such a way that, on the one
hand, the altruistic emotions form, from a *developmental–
psychological* point of view a condition for acquiring the rule-
emotions, while on the other hand (the development of) the
justification of the altruistic emotions, the degree to which
they are *proper*, is influenced by rule-emotions. Finally, I will
explore the issue of (the development of) the *justification* of the
moral rule-emotions.

3 The development of moral emotions

In the development of a child, the elementary altruistic
emotions appear first; this type of moral emotions have
primacy from an *ontogenetic* point of view.[5] Small children are
quickly touched by the cries of pain and sorrow of other living
beings. Their empathic capacities are not yet 'corrected' by
cognitive evaluations. The infant is not yet capable of making a
subject–object distinction; it does not yet have a (complete)

50

concept of 'person'. Given the limited cognitive abilities, a number of emotion-terms cannot as yet be applied to the infant; we do call these children 'friendly' but not (yet) 'charitable', they are 'teasing', but not 'malicious' (cf. Arman-Jones, 1985).

I assume that learning either type of moral emotions will be made possible to a large degree by *identical* pedagogical conditions. For a child the learning process consists of acquiring moral rules and concepts about acts such as promising and comforting, traits such as honesty and faithfulness, and emotions such as indignation and sorrow. Adults stimulate these learning processes by encouraging children to imagine themselves in the position of another (role-taking opportunities) and by pointing out to children, in their pedagogical procedures, what the results of their actions are ('inductive discipline'). Because the altruistic emotions are primary in ontogenetic perspective, I will examine the development of these moral emotions. In doing so I will pay particular attention to the works of the developmental psychologist M.L. Hoffman.

Learning altruistic emotions presupposes that infants have a 'cognitive sense of others'. At the end of the first year of life they attain person permanence and become aware of others as physical entities distinct from themselves; a year later they have become vaguely aware that others have their own feelings and thoughts. In as much as a young child does not yet have a sense of others as separate entities, it experiences the distress of others as its own unpleasant feelings. According to Hoffman, we can, in this case, speak of a precursor of empathy or of an involuntary 'global empathy'. As the acquisition of language progresses, the child will be more capable of identifying the emotions of others, and its role-taking capability will increase.

How does the developmental shift take place from one's personal empathic distress to a concern for the victim, to a feeling of compassion or sympathetic distress? According to Hoffman it is reasonable to assume that the experience of an unpleasant effect includes the wish or motive that it be

51

terminated. Such a motive is then transferred to other persons (Hoffman, 1984a: 116, 1984a). Hoffman does not explain exactly how this transference takes place; he characterizes the infant too much as a solitary explorer of the social environment, and thus takes too little account of the *pedagogical* context. Is it not much more plausible that a child's acquisition of elementary feeling of sympathy can be understood because of the specific relationship (a relationship *sui generis*) which these children often have with their caretakers? Is it not this early parent–child relationship in particular that is often characterized specifically by a wealth of altruistic emotions flowing from the caretakers? Where else do we often see the whole range of altruistic emotions but in those cases in which the adults who feel responsible for them act as loving and caring 'double-agents' (J. Shotter) of the needs and interests of babies and infants. The adult voices the child's needs and interests, and interprets its actions as expressions of feelings and emotions (hunger, pain, happiness), and subsequently reacts to these in a caring manner. The shift from empathic distress to sympathetic distress described takes place, one could say, only if a young child has been taken up in a network of actions motivated by altruistic emotions.

As a result of its empathic capacity the child learns what the consequences of its actions are for others and also that it feels sad or guilty if it hurts others. According to Hoffman, it is of great importance to point out to a child the inner condition of others in forming the empathic capacities and the altruistic emotions.

> The experiences are exemplified by the parent's use of inductive discipline, which calls attention to the pain or injury caused by the child's action or encourages the child to imagine how it would feel to be in the victim's place. Third, we expect role-taking opportunities in positive contexts to help sharpen the child's cognitive sense of others and increase the likelihood that they will pay attention to others, thus extending their empathic capability (Hoffman, 1984b: 290).

By using this inductive discipline technique, however, the child

52

is at the same time also informed about the moral rule or norm 'considering others'. Besides indicating harmful consequences of the child's action for the other, inductive discipline often also communicates the moral rules the parents adhere to. In these inductions parents also show and motivate their rule-emotions, which supports the conjecture that the development of rule-emotions becomes possible by virtue of altruistic emotions.

That a child only acquires the rule-emotions if it does not have a disturbed bond or relationship with adults is an assertion which is often heard. A child only has 'authority guilt' when it trusts a caretaker, when it is attached to, and scared of losing the care and love of, the 'significant other'. The absence of certain moral feeling or emotions sometimes is evidence of the absence of certain 'natural attachments' (Rawls, 1972: 486). For the sake of its relationship with its parents or caretakers the child will be inclined to confess its faults and to seek reconciliation. All this presupposes, however, that a young child has an (elementary) capacity for empathy; it must be able to feel or perceive the feelings (happiness, anger) of the parents. Moral *rule-emotions seem to be able to come into being only on the basis of the elementary altruistic emotions*, such as fellow-feelings or sympathy.

Educators also call upon the altruistic emotions in forming the 'artificial' virtues corresponding to the rule-emotions. As has been said before, the moral agent is characterized by a positive attitude towards moral rules, and this means that she is dedicated to these rules in a benevolent, upright and loyal manner. Educators not only try to teach children to act according to moral rules and conventions, they also want them to do so with 'heart and soul' and 'in the right spirit'. They teach children the rule 'stealing is wrong' by pointing out to them that they also do not enjoy losing things they are attached to, and that they would also be angry or sad in such cases. In short, educators call upon feelings of sympathy and upon fellow-feelings in forming 'artificial' virtues as well. A moral person seldom acts only from feelings of 'pure' duty to rules. If a person says she feels obliged to do something, then in

53

many cases she also indicates that this feeling of duty involves altruistic emotions. If I worry about a sick friend, feelings of care and compassion make me feel obligated to go and see that person (cf. Neblett, 1981: 17).

4 The justification of moral emotions

After having touched on the influence of altruistic emotions in forming rule-emotions, in the form of a *condition of genesis*, I will now examine the influence the opposite way around. Altruistic emotions can be *justified*, and *corrected*, with the help of rule-emotions; rule-emotions also determine whether the altruistic emotions displayed are *proper* or *improper*, especially in relation to the scope, duration and intensity of these emotions. Rule-emotions such as feelings of guilt, justice and duty form, one could say, a *condition of justification* for the altruistic emotions.

It can be said that a person who has the disposition of a positive commitment to the well-being of his fellow man also has a positive attitude towards his *own* altruistic emotions. He identifies himself with these emotions and may even count it his duty to have these emotions; he can reproach himself – and worry – that he failed to have feelings of compassion or care for the other.

When a firm believer in Apartheid forgets his nationalistic, perfect duties for a moment and supports a black man who has been shot and takes him to safety, we will not call him a caring or friendly person if he later despises himself for his helpfulness. The person who is only now and then prepared to help, or who only helps one certain category of fellow human beings, is not the bearer of 'natural' virtues either; his actions are strongly determined by moods and prejudices. Unreliability, prejudice and strict partiality are vices, while feelings of lovelessness, indifference, distrust and contempt are immoral emotions. Although altruistic emotions are in any case, and even in the first instance, directed at the weal and woe of the fellow human beings one is closest to (one's family and

54

friends), they are also, if they are corrected by the rule-emotions, always concerned with the well-being and distress of other human beings (and animals). It is not coincidental that in the parable the Good Samaritan's compassion is directed towards an unknown man, probably from Judea, who is in trouble (Luke, 10: 25–37).

Rule-emotions, in particular the sense of justice, can counter (the danger of) the limited scope of the altruistic emotions. When this *limited* sympathy (Warnock) is not forced open, the danger threatens that people will only love passionately, and be loyal to, their own country, their own race or family and will, with great fanaticism, cold-bloodedness and indifference, humiliate and kill strangers and outsiders. Caring fathers and loving husbands have had their share in the massacres and genocides of this century. And when the love of one's own country and people leads to fanaticism, it becomes possible for the four hijackers of the ship *Achille Lauro* to execute 69-year-old Leon Klinghoffer, who had been confined to a wheelchair for years (*Time*, 21 October 1985). The distinction that B. Williams draws between the psychopath and the amoralist is of importance in this context. The crimes of the psychopath appal us because this human being is not capable of showing any feeling of sympathy or compassion whatsoever. The amoralist, however, does show some affection and does occasionally care for others. The mafia hitman, as we know him from the movies, does care for his dog, his mother, his child and his mistress. This gangster is still recognizably amoral, because he is extremely short on fairness and other general considerations:

> ... this man is capable of thinking in terms of others' interests, and his failure to be a moral agent lies (partly) in the fact that he is only intermittently and capriciously disposed to do so. But there is no bottomless gulf between his state and the basic dispositions of morality (Williams, 1972:25).

To have altruistic emotions with respect to special persons is a necessary, but certainly not a sufficient condition for being a moral agent. The tentative conclusion can be drawn that the

55

moral person has in any case acquired both types of moral emotions and their corresponding 'natural' and 'artificial' virtues.[6]

In concluding this part I will briefly explore the development of the capacity to *justify* moral rule-emotions. In order to have rule-emotions a person must have acquired a disposition of positive concern for moral rules and principles. A child will first acquire the moral rules, conventions and codes, and then – if the right pedagogical conditions are realized and the child has the necessary cognitive capacities – it will acquire the moral principles. With the help of these more abstract principles a moral person can justify or criticize the operative moral rules (Peters, 1974). This means that, in the development of the child, the motives and reasons for having rule-emotions will change. The manner in which a child perceives moral rules is to a high degree dependent on its cognitive development; Kohlberg's theory of the stages of moral development can offer us insight into this point. The justification which a child gives for its rule-emotions will vary according to the level of moral judgements which the child has attained – pre-conventional, conventional, or post-conventional. In any case, three forms of guilt can be distinguished: authority guilt, association guilt and principle guilt (Rawls, 1972 : 467). 'Association guilt', for example, presupposes that the person is acquainted with the standards or rules which are fitting for the roles and duties of the individual in different social contexts such as family and school, and that she has thus acquired the cognitive capabilities needed to look at matters from different perspectives. Not only does the nature or justification of a certain rule-emotion change, the 'same' emotions – for example, 'guilt' from fear of losing a parent's love – can at a later stage no longer be called 'moral' (but 'neurotic').

5 The controversy between Kohlberg and Gilligan

Because of the fact that both types of moral emotions

56

presuppose and influence each other, important light can be shed on the controversy between Kohlberg and Gilligan.[7] Gilligan, as we know, criticizes Kohlberg's theory of moral development, because the experiences and concerns of women are insufficiently reflected in this theory. Kohlberg's conception of adulthood is out of balance, favouring the separateness of the individual self over its connection to others. On the basis of the responses of pregnant women to structured interview questions regarding the moral dilemma of whether to continue or abort a pregnancy, Gilligan concludes that the sequence of a woman's moral development follows a three-level progression from an initial focus on the self through a societal perspective, the discovery of the concept of responsibility as the basis for a new equilibrium between self and other, to a universal perspective. At this third level, both individual needs and conventions are subsumed under the moral principle of non-violence (Gilligan, 1977 : 483, 492). Gilligan stresses the centrality of the concepts of responsibility and care in a woman's construction of the moral domain, and she indicates that there is a close connection in women's thinking between concepts of the self and conceptions of morality (1977 : 516). According to Gilligan (1977), there are two distinct moral domains and moral languages, the domain of care and responsibility and the domain of justice and rights. The morality of responsibility which women describe stands apart from the morality of rights which underlies Kohlberg's theory (1977 : 509). The first domain is more typical for women and corresponds to the experience of the self as part of relationships, as 'connected self'; moral judgements, on the other hand, follow impartial rules defining rights and duties (cf. Lyons, 1983).

In his reply, Kohlberg admits that the 'principle' of altruism, care and responsible love has not been adequately represented in his works (Kohlberg et al., 1983 : 20). But he denies – and I think rightly so – that there are two different moral orientations. A morality of care and a morality of justice is a distinction made in the minds of all human beings, be they male or female (a belief also held by Gilligan in 1983). The growth of

57

justice and the ethics of care do not represent two distinct tracks in the stages of moral development (Kohlberg *et al.*, 1983 : 139). According to Kohlberg, many moral dilemmas do not pose a choice between one orientation or another, but almost always call out a response which integrates the two orientations; in the Heinz dilemma the concerns for justice and care are often very hard to distinguish.

At first glance Kohlberg's conclusions seem to correspond to what I have asserted in relation to the two types of moral emotions. It is important, however, to stress the fact that Kohlberg is still interested only in the development of moral *judgements*:

> ...we partially accept Gilligan's differentiation of two orientations in moral *judgment* which may vary in stress from person to person and from situation to situation (Kohlberg *et al.*, 1983 : 138; my italics).

Gilligan's emphasis on the orientation of care and responsibility has (only), according to Kohlberg, broadened the moral domain beyond his initial focus on justice reasoning (Kohlberg *et al.*, 1983: 139). Care and responsibility, and also altruistic emotions such as compassion and concern, are thus subsumed under the category of moral judgement or reasoning. Gilligan, however, can be reproached for the same thing, though to a lesser degree. She repeatedly speaks, in connection with care, love and responsibility, in terms of a different 'mode of moral *judgment*', of a different 'way of thinking about conflict and choice' (1983: 49, 55, 58; my italics). Gilligan does not sufficiently recognize the specific nature of altruistic emotions, and it could be said that, in her research, she understands implicitly and describes this subclass of moral emotions as rule-emotions. But it is quite possible, as I have argued, that an explicit cognitive evaluation is omitted precisely in those cases where our altruistic emotions directly motivate us to act morally.

In Kohlberg's view, special obligations and relationships of care presuppose but go beyond the general duties of justice, which are necessary but not sufficient for them. Considera-

58

tions of a special relationship – to one's own family and friends – are supererogatory, go *beyond* the duties owed to another on the basis of a person's rights (Kohlberg *et al.*, 1983 : 20–21). Many parents who take care of and protect their children do not however – always – feel themselves placed in a moral dilemma. They – often – act directly from feelings of love and care and not – constantly – from considerations of the rights of their child. Parents and caretakers do not – always – do more than they know they are obliged to, and are thus neither moral heroes nor saints. Most of the time they are motivated 'simply' by moral altruistic emotions.

Notes

1 R.S. Peters criticizes Kohlberg's theory of moral development for the fact that his system does not deal with the *affective* aspects of development (Peters, 1981 : 171). And G. Warnock states in his reply to R.M. Hare that

> ignorance is not a linguistic failing, nor is crass insensitivity, nor callous indifference. It is not through the study of language that these things are to be – as far as they ever will be – cured (Warnock, 1979 : 14).

2 I refer to the publications of W.P. Alston (1967), E. Bedford (1967), A.I. Melden (1969), G. Pitcher (1975) and J. Wilson (1971).
3 In his criticism of the ethics of Kant, Schopenhauer stressed the point that only those actions which are motivated by the weal and woe of others can be called truly 'moral'. Only in one case are actions not *egoistic* in nature:

> ... nämlich wenn der letzte Beweggrund zu einer Handlung, oder Unterlassung, geradezu und ausschliesslich im *Wohl und Wehe* irgend einer dabei passive betheiligten *Andern* leigt, also der aktive Theil bei seinem Handeln, oder Unterlassen, ganz allein das Wohl und Wehe eines *Andern* im Auge hat und durchaus nichts bezweckt, als dass jener Andere unverletzt bliebe, oder gar Hülfe, Beistand und Erleichterung erhalte. *Dieser Zweck allein* drückt einer Handlung, oder Unterlassung, den Stämpel des *moralischen Werthes* auf; ... (...) (...) es ist das alltägliche Phänomen des

59

Mitleids, d.h. der ganz unmittelbaren, von allen ander-
weitigen Rücksichten unabhängigen *Theilnahme* zunächst
am Leiden eines Andern und dadurch an der Verhinderung
oder Aufhebung dieses Leidens,...Dieses Mitleid ganz
allein ist die wirkliche Basis aller *freien* Gerechtigkeit und
aller *ächten* Menschenliebe (1840: 105, 106).

4 According to Zajonc preferences, or what he also calls 'affective
reactions' or 'affective judgments' [sic], need not depend on
cognition; we are therefore often unable to verbalize the reasons
for our attitudes or preferences. In my opinion, however, these
preferences do depend on *concepts* ('nice', 'attractive'), and also on
cognition, but not necessarily on a deliberate cognitive *evaluation*.

5 According to R.S. Peters the concern for others develops much
earlier in a child's life and does not require the same level of
conceptual development to be operative as does justice or even
honesty. It can be learned and encouraged by the example of
others. Of course, this concern for others can be exhibited at
different levels which vary according to a person's imagination
and sophistication about what constitutes human welfare.

But it certainly can get a foothold in a person's moral life
earlier than justice, because it is not necessarily connected
with rules and social arrangements, as is justice. This was one
of the reasons which led Hume to distinguish the artificial
from the natural virtues (Peters, 1974: 313).

6 J.L. Mackie states that, though *self-referential* altruism is a natural
virtue, it remains true that what we morally approve of and regard
as virtues in this area involve a wider concern for others than
either instinctive affection or immediate social intercourse would
produce. Humanity, generosity, compassion, clemency and
fairness must therefore be counted as *partly* artificial virtues with
respect to their approved range of application (Mackie, 1980: 127).

7 See also the publications of L. Kohlberg *et al.* (1983), N. Plessner
Lyons (1983), B. Puka (1983), *Ethics, 92*, April 1982 (special issue
on 'Virtue, Sex and Gender: Some Philosophical Reflections on
the Moral Philosophy Debate'; contributions of O.J. Flanagan,
B. Puka, L. Kohlberg and others), G. Nunner-Winkler (1984).

60

References

Alston, W.P. (1967). Emotion and feeling. *In* P. Edwards (ed.), *The Encyclopedia of Philosophy*, Vol. 2, pp. 479–86. New York/London.

Arman-Jones, C. (1985). Prescription, Explication and the Social Construction of Emotion. *Journal for the Theory of Social Behavior*, 15, 1–21.

Bedford, E. (1967). Emotions. *In* D.F. Gustafson (ed.), *Essays in Philosophical Psychology*, pp. 77–98. London/Melbourne.

Blum, L.A. (1980). *Friendship, Altruism and Morality*. London.

Boyd, D. (1983). Careful Justice or Just Caring: A Response to Gilligan. *Philosophy of Education: 1982. Proceedings PES*, 63–70. Normal, Ill.

Bridgeman, D.L. (ed.) (1983). *The Nature of Prosocial Development. Interdisciplinary Theories and Strategies*. New York.

Cochrane, D.B., Hamm C.M. and Kazepides, A.C. (eds) (1979). *The Domain of Moral Education*. New York.

Dent, N.J.H. (1984). *The Moral Psychology of the Virtues*. Cambridge.

Ethics (1982). Special issue on moral development, 92.

Gilligan, C. (1977). In a Different Voice: Woman's Conceptions of Self and of Morality. *Harvard Educational Review, 7*, 481–517.

Gilligan, C. (1983). New Maps of Development: New Visions of Education. *Philosophy of Education: 1982. Proceedings PES*, 47–63. Normal, Ill.

Hare, R.M. (1979). Language and Moral Education. *In* D.B. Cochrane, C.M. Hamm and A.C. Kazepides (eds), *The Domain of Moral Education*. New York.

Hoffman, M.L. (1983). Affective and Cognitive Processes in Moral Internalization. *In* E.T. Higgens, D.W. Ruble and W.W. Hartup (eds) *Social Cognition and Social Development*, Cambridge.

Hoffman, M.L. (1984a). Interaction of Affect and Cognition in Empathy. *In* C. Izard, J. Kagan and R.B. Zajonc (eds), *Emotions, Cognition and Behavior*. Cambridge.

Hoffman, M.L. (1984b). Empathy, its Limitations, and its Role in a Comprehensive Moral Theory. *In* W.M. Kurtiness and J.L. Gewirtz (eds), *Mortality, Moral Behavior, and Moral Development*. New York.

Izard, C., Kagan, J. and Zajonc, R.B. (eds) (1984). *Emotions, Cognition and Behavior*. Cambridge.

61

Kant, I. (1978). *Grondslagen van de ethiek. Grondslag voor de metafysica van de zeden.* Meppel.

Kohlberg, L., Levine, Ch. and Hewer, A. (1983). *Moral Stages: A Current Formulation and a Response to Critics.* Basel, London and New York.

Krebs, D. (1978). A Cognitive-developmental Approach to Altruism. *In* L. Wispé (ed.), *Altruism, Sympathy, and Helping. Psychological and Sociological Concepts.* New York.

Kurtiness, W.M. and Gewirtz, J.L. (eds) (1984). *Morality, Moral Behavior, and Moral Development.* New York.

Lyons, N.P. (1983). Two Perspectives: On Self, Relationships, and Morality. *Harvard Education Review,* 53, 125–45.

MacIntyre, A. (1967). Egoism and Altruism. *In* P. Edwards (ed.), *The Encyclopedia of Philosophy,* 463–6, New York.

Mackie, J.L. (1980). *Hume's Moral Theory.* London, Boston and Henly.

Melden, A.I. (1969). The Conceptual Dimension of Emotions. *In* Th. Mischel (ed.), *Human Action, Conceptual and Empirical Issues,* pp. 199–221. London.

Mussen, P. and Eisenberg-Berg, N. (1977). *The Roots of Caring, Sharing and Helping.* San Francisco.

Neblett, W. (1981). *The Role of Feelings in Morals.* University Press of America, Inc.

Nunner-Winkler, G. (1984). Two Moralities? A Critical Discussion of an Ethic of Care and Responsibility Versus an Ethic of Rights and Justice. *In* W.M. Kurtiness and J.L. Gewirtz (eds), *Morality, Moral Behavior, and Moral Development.* New York.

Peters, R.S. (1974). *Psychology and Ethical Development.* London.

Peters, R.S. (1981). *Moral Development and Moral Education.* London.

Pitcher, G. (1975). Emotion. *In* R.F. Dearden, P.H. Hirst and R.S. Peters (eds), *Reason. Part 2 of Education and the Development of Reason,* pp. 218–39. London and Boston.

Puka, B. (1983). Altruism and Moral Development. *In* D.L. Bridgeman (ed.), *The Nature of Prosocial Development. Interdisciplinary Theories and Strategies.* New York.

Rawls, J. (1972). *A Theory of Justice.* Oxford.

Richards, D.A.J. (1971). *A Theory of Reasons for Action.* Oxford.

Rorty, A.O. (ed.) (1980). *Explaining Emotions.* Berkeley.

Schopenhauer, A. (1840). *Preisschrift über das Fundament der Moral.* (Reprinted 1979, Hrsg. von H. Ebeling, Hamburg.)

62

Sichel, B.A. (1985). Woman's Moral Development in Search of Philosophical Assumptions. *Journal of Moral Education*, 14, 149–61.

Spiecker, B. (1984). The Pedagogical Relationship. *Oxford Review of Education*, 10 (2).

Steutel, J.W. (1986). Education, Motives and Virtues. *Journal of Moral Education*, 15, 179–88.

Warnock, G.J. (1979). Morality and Language: A Reply to R.M. Hare. *In* D.B. Cochrane, C.M. Hamm and A.C. Kazepides (eds), *The Domain of Moral Education*. New York.

White, J. (1984). The Education of the Emotions. *Journal of Philosophy of Education*, 18, 233–44.

Williams, B. (1972). *Morality*. London.

Williams, B. (1973). Morality and the Emotions. *In* B. Williams (ed.), *Problems of the Self*, pp. 207–99, Cambridge.

Wilson, J. (1971). *Education in Religion and the Emotions*. London.

Wispé, L. (ed.) (1978). *Altruism, Sympathy, and Helping. Psychological and Sociological Concepts*. New York.

Zajonc, R.B. (1980). Feeling and Thinking. Preferences need no Interferences. *American Psychologist*, 35, 151–75.

63

Education, Motives and Virtues[1]
Jan W. Steutel

Abstract
Most parents value highly their children growing up to be just, sincere, reliable, kind and helpful people. This string of adjectives refers to certain qualities of character which are also called virtues. In this paper, I shall subject the typical motives (wants and aversions) of the virtuous human being to a conceptual investigation. Based on the results of this analysis, it will be possible to draw up an inventory of a number of important tasks educators face if they wish to cultivate virtuousness in children.

1 Formulation of the problem

As we know, J. B. Wilson has, in various articles, undertaken an interesting attempt to inventory the qualities of the morally educated person. In this paper I shall make a start with a similar attempt by subjecting our concept of *virtuousness* to a partial analysis. Stimulating the development of children into virtuous persons is an important aim of moral education. By clarifying which components or subdispostions constitute this comprehensive educational aim, I hope to make visible the contours of the tasks the educator faces if he or she wishes to cultivate virtuousness in a child. However, before I proceed with this analysis, I shall first state the problem more precisely by way of three separate points.

In the first place, I shall leave what are called the instrumental virtues completely out of consideration and confine myself to an analysis of the *intrinsic* virtues. This latter group of character traits, among which we can for example count honesty, fidelity, impartiality and kindness, is constitutive of the morally good life, since the practising of these virtues consists, *ceteris paribus*, in carrying out morally right or commendable actions. On the other hand, instrumental virtues are not constitutive of the good life but are a part of the means necessary for practising the intrinsic virtues successfully. If, for example, we count helpfulness as an intrinsic virtue, then we shall in all probability see diligence as an instrumental virtue; someone who is lazy will now and again not succeed in offering necessary or commendable assistance. In a similar manner, steadfastness, self–control, temperance and daring can be considered instrumental virtues.[2]

In the second place, my analysis of intrinsic virtuousness will be limited to one aspect only: what are the typical *motives* of the bearer of intrinsic virtues? Or, more accurately, if a person shows his intrinsic virtuousness in his actions, what are the wants and aversions which cause him to act?[3]

Jan W. Steutel is Lecturer in Education at the Free University, Subfaculteit Pedagogische Wetenschappen, De Lairessestraat 142, 1075 HL Amsterdam, The Netherlands.

In answering this question I am interested both in the *dispositional* and *occurrent* wants and aversions of the human being with intrinsic virtues. The difference between these two types of wants and aversions can be illustrated by the statement 'Person X is *angry*'. The adjective 'angry' can, depending on the context, refer either to a disposition of X (for example, if, within the framework of a character description, we mean that X is an angry sort of person) or to an occurrent emotion of X (if we make the statement at a moment when X is growing purple with anger). Because anger is normally attended by the desire 'to inflict an injury or harm upon the person who provokes one's anger' (Dent, 1984, p. 54), we can in the first instance speak of a dispositional want and in the second instance of an occurrent want. In general I would put it as follows: an occurrent want or aversion is a concrete-individual event; it is a mental process or a 'happening' in consciousness. Dispositional wants and aversions, however, are not concrete-individual events. It is nevertheless possible partially to clarify the meaning of terms referring to dispositional wants and aversions by formulating a series of subjunctive conditionals. Such statements refer to lawful connections between classes of concrete-individual events, among which are occurrent wants and aversions. [4]

In the third place, I immediately want to make a distinction between two sub-classes of intrinsic virtues. The practising of some virtues, such as kindness, generosity, friendliness and charity, involves 'a direct concern for the happiness and well-being of others' (Wallace, 1978, p. 128). Because the bearer of this sub-class of intrinsic virtues carries out the corresponding actions with the *telos* of looking after the well-being of the one(s) he acts for, I shall from now on call these traits of character *teleological* virtues. The practical realization of other intrinsic virtues such as justice, honesty, sincerity and fairness is, however, by no means necessarily linked to such intentions. I can inflict on X a just punishment which will seriously damage his well-being; or, if I tell X the truth, it is not impossible that he will be seriously shocked, or his happiness be permanently disturbed; and at times it is fair that I act solely for my own well-being. Looking after the well-being of others is thus not the typical motivating background for the practising of these dispositions. The bearer of these virtues will rather do the corresponding actions because of their moral rightness. For this reason I shall from now on call these traits of character *non-teleological* virtues.[5]

On the basis of these three qualifications we can formulate the central question of this paper as follows: *what are the characteristic dispositional and occurrent wants and aversions of the bearer of non-teleological and teleological virtues?* In answering this question we will be able to make an inventory of a number of the tasks facing the educator who wishes to stimulate virtuousness in a child.

2   Motives and non-teleological virtues

In the field of moral philosophy, the literature deals with a variety of motives which are considered typical of the bearer of non-teleological virtues. I allude here, for example, to respect for the moral law, to a sense of duty or obligation, to love for truth and to a sense of justice. It is true that these motivating emotions are not all identical; moreover, one can argue about whether or not these motives are characteristic of the bearer of non-teleological virtues. Nevertheless, I believe that we can reduce this series of activating emotions to the same denominator because these emotions all belong to one class of wants and aversions; and the characteristic motives of the person with non-teleological traits form, in my view, part of this class.

In order to determine the nature of this class of wants and aversions it is important to draw attention to a certain measure of *parallelism* between non-teleological virtues on the one hand and moral rules or principles on the other. For example, the moral principles of justice correspond to the virtue of justice; and the moral rules which are constitutive of making promises and agreements go with the virtue of fidelity. This insight makes it possible to point out an important quality that the bearer of non-teleological virtues possesses: such a person is characterized by a certain disposition, namely by a *positive concern for the corresponding moral rules.* Or, formulated differently, a human being with non-teleological traits is someone who cares about the corresponding moral rules. This positive concern can be looked upon as the interweaving of dispositional wants and aversions, for someone who is positively affected by the demands of moral rules *wants* these rules to be followed by everyone (the dispositional want) and *does not want* human action to be in conflict with these rules (the dispositional aversion).

Take for example the virtue of justice. To this virtue correspond the principles of justice, including the formal principle of distributive justice. In his *Ethica Nicomachea* (1934 edn, pp. 266-73) Aristotle has already given an explication of this rule. In my opinion we do not do this Greek philosopher an injustice if we formulate the formal rule of distributive justice (RDJ) as follows:

> (RDJ) When goods are distributed, persons who are relevantly different should receive unequal amounts and persons who are not relevantly different should receive equal amounts.

And what now typifies the just human being? That he is, among other things, positively concerned with the RDJ, that is to say, that he possesses a dispositional want with regard to the general following of the RDJ and a dispositional aversion to the general transgressing of the RDJ. The same applies, *mutatis mutandis,* for the other non-teleological virtues.

In section 1 I wrote that statements about dispositional wants and aversions are interwoven with subjunctive conditionals in which classes of concrete-individual occurrences are connected with each other. This also applies to the disposition of a positive concern for moral rules. Besides other subjunctive conditionals, the statement 'X is positively concerned with moral rules' is also analytically interwoven with conditional statements referring to connections between classes of certain *occurrent cognitions* on the one hand, and specific *occurrent wants and aversions* on the other. If X possesses a non-teleological trait, then X will, if he is of the opinion that the corresponding moral rules are relevant to his actual situation (occurrent cognition), experience, in a normal frame of mind, either an occurrent aversion to performing actions which, according to him, are in conflict with these rules, or cherish an occurrent want to perform actions which, according to him, are in accordance with these rules.[6] These occurrent wants and aversions constitute the characteristic motivation factors of actors with non-teleological virtues. They are the causal result of certain occurrent cognitions, namely *the realization of the actor that the relevant moral rules apply to his situation.* For this reason every bearer of non-teleological virtues is, under normal circumstances, motivated to perform virtuous deeds as soon as he is of the opinion that the corresponding moral rules are relevant to his actual situation, that is to say, when he realizes that the relevant moral rules require him to act in a certain way.

Suppose X is a just human being who wants to divide a few goods among his children (Y and Z). In this case we should not think only of material goods such as food, clothing, toys, pocket-money and enough room in the house, but especially of non-material goods, among which are all kinds of help, attention, guidance and instruction. In principle, everything Y and Z want and of which there is a certain shortage (the demand is larger than the supply) qualifies for a just or an unjust division. In this case the RDJ offers only a *formal* guideline to X. The rule says only *that* an unequal division between Y and Z must be based upon relevant differences, without indicating *what* the possible relevant differences could be. The principle merely requires an unequal division to be well-founded so that arbitrariness and partiality are ruled out; but on which *material* criteria X should base the division (for example: sex differences, age, level of development or personality features), the RDJ gives no answer.

Now if X, on the basis of his material criteria, discerns relevant differences between Y and Z, and is thus of the opinion that he should divide the goods unequally (the occurrent cognition), then X will experience an equal division as negative (the occurrent aversion) as well as feel attracted to an unequal division (the occurrent want); and if X, on the basis of his material standards, does not accept relevant differences between Y and Z, and is therefore of the opinion that he should divide the goods equally (the occurrent cognition), then X will experience an unequal division as repugnant (the occurrent aversion) and feel a positive inclination towards equal distribution (the occurrent want). The *then*-clauses of these subjunctive conditionals refer to the complex motive of X to display acts of distributive justice; and the *if*-clauses refer to the causal conditions under which these wants and aversions occur: X's realization that the RDJ is relevant to his situation or, formulated another way, X's particular moral judgements concerning the demands of the RDJ in his own situation.

But suppose that X fulfils an important political position and has to divide goods which are in great demand among the people. In doing so he adheres strictly to the RDJ: no one can catch him out in arbitrariness of partially. On closer investigation however, it appears that X follows the RDJ solely with the intention of building up a good reputation in order to obtain the same position or a higher one in the next elections. According to the analysis I have given, X acts from motives characteristic of the bearer of non-teleological virtues. For he will, if he is of the opinion that the RDJ is relevant to his situation, also possess the described wants and aversions. Nevertheless, there is something clearly amiss with his motives. They are motives which are obviously *not* characteristic of the just human being.

This counter-example brings to light the incompleteness of my analysis. In order to perfect this analyses, and in concurrence with R. B. Brandt (1970, p. 30,34), I shall call the characteristic motives of the bearer of non-teleological virtues *intrinsic* wants and aversions. I suggest the following definition: X has an intrinsic positive concern for a moral rule if, and only if, X's realization that this rule is applicable to his situation, is, in a normal frame of mind, a *sufficient* causal condition for the occurrent want or aversion to act either in accordance or in conflict with this rule respectively. X's particular moral judgement concerning the demands of the moral rule in his situation is thus sufficient for the complex motive to act virtuously to occur. Other cognitions concerning the actions in question are not required.

Using this definition we can rule out the counter-example described above. The politician's mere awareness that the RDJ is relevant to his situation is not a sufficient condition for the wants and aversions to occur. For that to happen, his conviction that the following of the RDJ contributes to building up his reputation is a requirement. This man is thus not intrinsically but *extrinsically* motivated.

What are the most important consequences of this argument for the practice of education? If I see it correctly the foregoing analysis makes it clear that the educator is faced with two central tasks if he wishes to stimulate the virtuousness of a child. These two tasks correspond respectively to the occurrent cognitions described above on the one hand, and to the occurrent wants and aversions on the other.

In the first place, the educator will have to cultivate the child's *ability for moral judgement*. When a child has acquired this ability he is generally capable of determining when the moral rules are applicable to his own situation. When an ability for moral judgement is effectively put into practice this results in the occurrence of the right cognitions with respect to the demands of moral rules in specific situations. Because these cognitions underlie the putting into practice of the non-teleological virtues, the ability to make particular moral judgements is a necessary component of the complex disposition of virtuousness.

Having at one's command this ability for moral judgement implies that one has *knowledge* of moral rules. This knowledge is not necessarily built up of propositions regarding the general requirements of moral rules ('knowing *that*'), but is concerned more with the competence to apply moral rules in concrete situations ('knowing *how*'). In the same way as a human being with an ability for linguistic judgement can distinguish between correct or incorrect speech utterances, the bearer of an ability for moral judgement can generally determine whether or not his behaviour is in conflict with moral rules; and as little as linguistic ability need involve explicit knowledge of the rules of linguistic usage, does judging according to moral standards imply the ability to formulate these rules. The educator wanting to impart to his children the capacity to judge morally thus need not convey explicit knowledge of moral rules: 'principles . . . are normally not inculcated by their verbal repetition, but by example, demonstration, and other practical means.' (Hare, 1952, p.63).

In the second place, the educator must promote a *positive attitude towards moral rules.* Like an ability, an attitude is also a disposition; in contrast to an ability, however, an attitude does say something about the wants and aversions of a person. It is only when a child has gained this positive attitude that the cognitions described above will result in the occurrence of the appropriate wants and aversions. Someone who makes use of his ability for moral judgement and thus, for example, realizes what he should or should not do under certain circumstances according to the RDJ, will not be motivated to act in a just manner if he lacks a positive attitude to the RDJ. That is why the educator should not only stimulate the development of an ability for moral judgement but should also see to it that the child gains a positive attitude to moral rules. This attitude is by nature intrinsic, in the meaning of this word as defined above. This point especially is important in education. According to a great many pedagogues and developmental psychologists, children, during a certain phase, follow moral rules due to extrinsic reasons. They carry out the right actions and do not do the wrong things in order to obtain approval, avoid punishment, keep the love of their parents, or to fulfil other needs. However, in order to become a bearer of non-teleological virtues a fundamental turnabout is required: the change from extrinsic to intrinsic motivation. This transition does not take place only in the area of moral development (although not nearly with all children) but also in other areas of life. R.S. Peters, notably, has pointed out this phenomenon. As we know, he defines 'education' as 'initiation in worth-while activities', which include, for him, not only the area of morality but also the areas of science, aesthetics, religion, etc. And what applies to the initiation in forms of life generally, applies to the development in the specific area of morality as well: 'Somehow or other the individual must come to care sufficiently about what is intrinsic to these worth-while activities so that he no longer has any need of extrinsic motivation' (1966, p.62).

3 Motives and teleological virtues

Feelings of duty and obligation, respect for the moral law, a sense of justice, etc. — these are generally considered to be the typical motives of the human being with a good character. In the preceding section I interpreted these motivating emotions as wants and aversions testifying to a positive concern for moral rules. Together, these wants and aversions form the incentives characteristic of the bearer of non-teleological virtues.

In the field of moral philosophy, the literature deals not only with feelings of duty and obligation, a love for truth, etc., but also compassion, affection and care for one's fellow-man, and respect for the needs, wants and concerns of others. This class of motives, which I will call the *benevolent* emotions, is also deemed typical of the virtuous human being. Benevolent emotions are the opposite of malevolent emotions, among which we can count hate, resentment, envy and revenge. Malevolent emotions incite us to frustrate the needs, wishes and concerns of the other, to undermine his well-being or to interfere with his happiness; benevolent emotions motivate us to carry out actions which promote the welfare of the other, relieve his needs or come to the good of his interests. This group of motivating emotions is, in my opinion, characteristic of the bearer of teleological virtues. These activating emotions also form part of a genus of wants and aversions. In this section I shall attempt to determine the generic nature of these wants and aversions as well as indicate how these motivating factors distinguish themselves from the wants and aversions of the person with non-teleological character traits.

We can also regard the person with teleological virtues as having a certain disposition. For example, someone who is philanthropic, benevolent, helpful, charitable, compassionate, generous, or friendly, is characterized by a *positive concern for the welfare of his fellow-man*. And this disposition too is a collection of dispositional wants and aversions. Someone who is concerned about the welfare of others *wants* things to go well for his fellow-man (the dispositional want) and *does not want* things to go ill for his neighbour (the dispositional aversion). This characterization immediately makes an important difference between teleological and non-teleological virtues perceptible. The object, or content, of the characteristic wants and aversions is not the same. In the case of non-teleological virtues, the concern for moral rules matters, while in the case of teleological virtues, a concern for the weal and woe of the other is essential (cf. Table 1).

Table 1

	Non-teleological virtues	Teleological virtues
Disposition	Positive concern for moral rules	Positive concern for the welfare of one's fellow-man
Dispositional want	Want regarding the general following of the rules	Want regarding the well-being of one's fellow-man
Dispositional aversion	Aversion regarding the general transgression of the rules	Aversion regarding the misfortune of one's fellow-man

The statement 'X is positively concerned for the welfare of others' can also be clarified in part with the help of subjunctive conditionals in which classes of concrete-individual occurrences are interrelated. And here too conditional statements are at stake which refer to connections between classes of certain *occurrent cognitions* on the one hand and specific *occurrent wants and aversions* on the other. If X has a positive concern for the welfare of his fellow-man, and if he realizes that the actions he contemplates undertaking will seriously damage the interests of Y, or will make Y unhappy, or will thoroughly undermine Y's well-being (the occurrent cognition), then X will, in a normal frame of mind, experience a disinclination to carry out these actions (the occurrent aversion); and if X is of the opinion that his actions will lighten Y's grief, or will provide a substantial contribution in lifting Y out of his miserable condition, or will relieve the distress Y feels (the occurrent cognition), then X will, under normal psychic circumstances, feel attracted to carrying out these actions (the occurrent want). The characteristic motives, which enable us to explain the morally right or commendable behaviour of a human being with teleological virtues, are thus composed of occurrent wants and aversions which in turn are the causal results of specific cognitions, namely *the actor's judgement as to the effects of his actions on the welfare of others*. These wants and aversions stimulate the bearer of teleological character traits to conduct himself in a helpful, charitable, friendly or generous manner, and withhold him from conducting himself in an unfriendly, rude, indifferent or cruel manner.

The cognitions described particularly clarify the differences between the motives of the teleologically virtuous human being and the motives of the bearer of non-teleological qualities. The wants and aversions of the latter are connected with judgements concerning the demands of moral rules in specific situations; the wants and aversions of the former, however, are interwoven with judgements on the effect actions have on the welfare of one's fellow-man[7] (cf. Table 2).

Table 2

	Non-teleological virtues	Teleological virtues
Occurrent cognition	The judgement that action A ought to be carried out	The judgement that action A promotes the well-being of others
Occurrent want	Want regarding A	Want regarding A
Occurrent cognition	The judgement that action A ought not be carried out	The judgement that action A damages the well-being of others
Occurrent aversion	Aversion regarding A	Aversion regarding A

Now let us assume that a politician wishes to promote the welfare of others with the intention of winning votes in the next elections. To achieve this goal he gives money to different charities, organizes a great many charity bazars, and puts special charity stamps on all his letters. It is true that such a person behaves, in a certain sense, charitably, but he lacks the virtue of charity. Nevertheless, he conforms to the analysis given; he too acts because of wants and aversions which are connected with his conviction that these actions are for the good of others.

In order to rule out this counter-example, I shall once again refine my analysis, regarding the motives of the bearer of teleological virtues as *intrinsic* wants and aversions, which I shall define as follows: X has an intrinsic positive concern for the welfare of others if, and only if, X's realization that his actions will in actual fact either promote or damage the well-being of others, forms a *sufficient* causal condition, if he is in a normal frame of mind, for the occurrences of either wants or aversions with respect to the carrying out of these actions.

The politician's judgement of the effect his actions have on the welfare of his fellow-man is *not* sufficient for the occurrence of the want to carry out these actions. It is only because he is of the opinion that his conduct will result in vote gain that he has the desire to act charitably. Because of this extrinsic motivation, he lacks the teleological virtue of charity.

Having presented the specific motives of the possessor of teleological virtues, I shall now once more touch upon the most prominent consequences of this analysis for educational practice. The educator wanting to impart to a child the teleological virtues is also faced with two central tasks. Once again, these tasks are related to the cognitive and motivational aspects of virtues, in this case the teleological virtues.

In the first place, the educator will have to stimulate the *empathy* or *imagination* of a child. I have explained earlier that the wants and aversions of the bearer of teleological virtues are connected with cognitions concerning the effects of one's actions on the welfare of others. These cognitions encompass a certain insight into the frame of mind of one's fellow-man, and particularly into his actual or possible misfortunes. The occurrent want to carry out actions which will relieve the needs of the other is dependent on an insight into his *actual* misfortunes, while the occurrent aversion regarding actions which will cause one's fellow-man grief is bound up with a certain realization of his *possible* misfortunes. For an effective understanding of the real or eventual need of a fellow human being, a well-developed imagination is a necessary condition. I refer here to an ability to understand the inner world of the other, to gain insight into the quality and intensity of the other's experiences by imagining what it is like to be the other or to be in the other's situation (cf. Hare, 1981, pp.90–99). This does not mean placing oneself in the other's situation while maintaining one's *own* attitude of mind. (What would I experience and want, if I were in his shoes, with *my* psyche?) It means imagining oneself in the position of one's fellow human being with *his* state of mind. (What would my experiences and preferences be if I imagine myself to be in his place, with *his* experiences, wants and aversions?) It is only by following this last course that it is possible to understand the inner world of the other by approximation. For this reason the educator who wishes to promote a child's teleological virtuousness must stimulate his imagination; for the effective putting into practice of this ability results in an adequate understanding of the other's sphere of experience, including the occurrent cognitions concerning his actual or possible misfortunes.

In the second place, the educator must promote a *positive attitude towards the welfare of one's fellow-man.* Just as an ability for moral judgement is not necessarily attended by a positive attitude towards moral rules, an ability for empathy is not always attended by a positive attitude towards the well-being of others. 'I might know exactly how others feel and how my actions affect them', writes Warnock (1979, p.113), 'and yet simply not care, or I might even take pleasure in causing them annoyance and distress'. For example, a malicious human being is all too often capable of placing himself in the position of the other without in any way being motivated to lift him out of his miserable condition. On the contrary, he will take pleasure in the misery and distress of the other (cf. Scheler, 1923, pp.19–24; Hare, 1981, p.99). The second task of the educator is thus primarily concerned with fostering *fellow-feeling* or *sympathy* in a child. It is only when this task is completed that the putting into practice of one's empathy will be followed by a *sharing* in someone else's misfortunes, attended by the occurrence of the appropriate wants and aversions.

Fellow-feelings can be divided into two groups: sympathetic *joy* and sympathetic *suffering,* or compassion (cf. Scheler, 1923, pp.143–44). Sympathetic joy occurs when the sympathetic human being realizes that the other feels happy, is glad, is in an exuberant mood or is experiencing a sense of well-being; compassion is a reaction to the insight that the other is depressed, feels unhappy, experiences fear, suffers pain or feels despairing. The modes of compassion (such as mourning, pity, commiseration) particularly stimulate us to promote the well-being of our fellow-man, or withhold us from undermining his welfare. That is why the educator, if he wishes to promote the teleological virtuousness of a child, must not only stimulate the empathy of the child but must also favour his inclination towards sympathy. Only then will the occurrent cognitions concerning the actual or possible misfortunes of the other result in feelings of compassion, that is to say, in occurrent wants to act with charity, mercy and helpfulness, and in occurrent aversions with regard to unfriendly, rude or undermining conduct.[8]

Notes
1. This article is a revised version of some parts of previously published essays (Steutel, 1984; Steutel (Ed), 1984, pp.39–67).
2. The terms 'instrumental' and 'intrinsic' are taken from Hare (1981, pp.192–93). The distinction between these two sub-classes of virtues is also made by other moral philosophers (cf. Warnock, 1971, pp.78–79).
3. Brandt in particular has designed an intriguing motivational theory of virtues and vices (1970, pp.27–30; 1976, p.430–33). However, his central claim 'that trait-names designate desires and aversions' (1970, p.27), should be watered down somewhat. In the first place, it seems much more natural to take the instrumental virtues as capacities (cf. Wallace, 1978, pp.60–89) or perhaps even as skills (cf. Roberts, 1984, pp.237–46). In the second place, Brandt has too little eye for the fact that a person can stand back from his wants and aversions, that is to say that he can reflect on and evaluate them, can identify himself with them or not, and can intervene if necessary (cf. Dent, 1984, pp.152–84). My analysis of our concept of virtuousness in terms of wants and aversions is confined to the intrinsic virtues, and is, moreover, a partial one.
4. At the moment it is not popular to interpret occurrent wants and aversions as phenomena of consciousness. Goldman (1970, pp.86, 91–99; 1976, pp.67–84) is one of the few representatives of this phenomenological conception within the field of analytical philosophy. I think, however, on the strength of reasons which I cannot bring forward within the scope of this essay, that this interpretation is the least untenable.
5. This distinction between these two types of intrinsic virtues is in no way a new one. Related distinctions can be found, for example, in Hume (1739–40, pp.477–84, 574–91) (between natural and artificial virtues), in Schopenhauer (1840, pp.110–28) (between 'Menschenliebe' and 'Gerechtigkeit'), in Jackson (1978, p.234–37) (between charity and justice), and in Wallace (1978, pp.90–158) (between benevolence and conscientiousness).
6. The clause 'in a normal frame of mind' means that X is not drunk, or under hypnosis, or undergoing the psychic (by-)effects of medicines, or upset, etc. (cf. Brandt, 1970, pp.35–36). It cannot be expected of the intrinsically virtuous human being that the relevant cognitions will lead to the appropriate wants and aversions if he is in an abnormal frame of mind.
7. The distinction between teleological and non-teleological wants and aversions corresponds to Spiecker's (1984, pp.243–244) division of moral emotions into altruistic emotions and emotions of principle.
8. At a later stage I hope to go into the differences and similarities of this analysis of intrinsic virtuousness on the one hand, and Peters' (1981, pp.24–44, 92–110) discussion of the virtues, and Wilson's (1973, pp.41–68) rendering of the qualities of a morally well-educated person on the other hand.

References
ARISTOTLE (1934 edn). *The Nicomachean Ethics:* Loeb Classical Library. G. P. Goold (Ed). London: Harvard University Press.
BRANDT, R. B. (1970). 'Traits of character: a conceptual analysis', *Amer. Phil. Quart.,* **7**, 1, 23–37.
BRANDT, R. B. (1976). 'The psychology of benevolence and its implications for philosophy', *The J. of Phil.* **73**, 14, 429–53.
DENT, N. J. H. (1984). *The Moral Psychology of the Virtues.* Cambridge: Cambridge University Press.
GOLDMAN, A. I. (1970). *A Theory of Human Action*: Princeton, New Jersey: Princeton University Press.
GOLDMAN, A. I. (1976). 'The volitional theory revisited'. In BRAND, M. and WALTON D. (Eds) *Action Theory. Proceedings of the Winnepeg Conference on Human Action.* Dordrecht/Boston: D. Reidel Publishing Company.
HARE, R. M. (1952). *The Language of Morals.* Oxford: Oxford University Press.

HARE, R. M. (1981). *Moral Thinking. Its Levels, Method, and Point.* Oxford: Clarendon Press.
HUME, D. (1739–40). *A Treatise of Human Nature.* Selby-Bigge, L.A. and Nidditch, P.H. (Eds) (1978). Oxford: Clarendon Press.
JACKSON, J. (1978). 'Virtues with reason', *Philosophy,* **53,** 229–46.
PETERS, R.S. (1966). *Ethics and Education.* London: Allen and Unwin.
PETERS, R.S. (1981). *Moral Development and Moral Education:* London: Allen and Unwin.
ROBERTS, R.C. (1984). 'Will power and the virtues', *The Phil. Rev.,* **93,** 2, 227–47.
SCHELER, M. (1923). *Wesen und Formen der Sympathie.* Hrsg. von M.S. Frings (1974). Bern/München: Francke Verlag.
SCHOPENHAUER, A. (1840). *Preisschrift über das Fundament der Moral.* Hrsg. von H. Ebeling (1979). Hamburg: Felix Meiner Verlag.
SPIECKER, B. (1984). 'Opvoeding van (morele) emoties', *Pedagogische Studiën,* **61,** 6, 236–46.
STEUTEL, J.W. (1984). 'Opvoeding, deugden en motieven', *Pedagogische Studiën,* **61,** 6, 247–60.
STEUTEL, J.W. (Ed) (1984). *Morele Opvoeding. Theoretisch- en Historisch-Pedagogische Opstellen.* Meppel/Amsterdam: Boom.
WALLACE, J.D. (1978). *Virtues and Vices.* Ithaca, NY: Cornell University Press.
WARNOCK, G.J. (1971). *The Object of Morality.* London: Methuen.
WARNOCK, G.J. (1979). 'Morality and language: a reply to R.M. Hare'. In COCHRANE, D.B., HAMM, C.M. and KAZEPIDES A.C. (Eds) *The Domain of Moral Education.* NY/Ramsey: Paulist Press.
WILSON, J. (1973). *The Assessment of Morality.* Windsor: NFER Publishing Co.

Altruism and Moral Development

BILL PUKA

What is so great about altruism? Much behavior, perhaps most behavior going under that name, seems designed to win friends and gain approval, or to boost sagging self-esteem, or even to play out maternal fantasies. The most dramatic cases of altruism seem to border on masochism. Is any of this especially noble?

Worse yet, altruism seems discriminatory from the moral point of view. Justice bids us to render each her or his due. Certainly we must count ourselves equal to anyone else, equally worthy of our due. Why then is it better to fulfill someone else's interest or enhance someone else's welfare rather than our own? In fact, why is it not worse to be altruistic than to be just or even to be self-interested? After all, altruism involves a significant loss to someone, a sacrificing of one's interest for another, whereas self-interest does not, justice need not. More interests would be served, it would seem, if we each catered to our own, for the most part.

Still, there seems to be something more praiseworthy about going out of your way for others than merely doing your part. Our moral exemplars are not drawn primarily from among the merely fair or just and certainly not from among the selfish or prudent. We admire those who have conscientiously dedicated themselves to their community or to humankind in general and at some personal cost. Are our feelings misplaced here, or do we admire merely the unselfishness of these rare people?

The extraordinary virtues of altruism derive from four main sources. One is altruism's tendency to increase overall welfare or the ratio of benefit over burden. The other three involve desirable traits expressed in altruistic acts or embodied in altruistic character, that is, preference for the good; insight and sensitivity; and self-mastery. Altruism typically occurs where others are in dire need or are liable to experience great benefits that they cannot partake of unassisted. Increased good accrues from altruistic acts largely because there are many others and only one self.

The personal sacrifice involved is not desirable in itself but necessary as a means that is outweighed by the benefit to others. From the perspective of consequences, altruism should not be considered preferable to justice, or even to prudence, except where this ratio of benefits between self and other holds. The example just offered of a dyadic relationship in which one person merely sacrifices her or his interest to satisfy the like interest of another is not especially worthy (at best). It also is not especially frequent. Even in close love relationships where such altruism might occur most, the altruist presumably reaps great satisfaction from what is more an expression of love than an act of sacrifice, a means of communicating devotion, enhancing bonds of affection, and bettering the relationship generally.

Altruists are admirable both because they make the right choice of values and because they make that choice at some sacrifice to their self-interest. Either in a particular decision to act or in the many choices which contribute to developing altruistic motivations, the altruist puts good-enhancing values generally above self-enhancing ones. For this effort in behalf of the good, she or he merits our appreciation.

We typically associate the character trait of altruism with personal wisdom and maturity. Altruists are often valued because they seem to have an especially high level of understanding regarding their own nature and value and that of others. We are tempted to think that being altruistic requires a high degree of self-mastery and personality integration, bringing feelings and attitudes into line with moral principles and freeing oneself from fears, anxieties, and insecurities regarding the dangers that others and life in general present. Altruists must have a well-developed self-concept and high self-esteem, we think. How else could they afford to risk and give away so much? Must they not be inwardly expansive to be outwardly so?

Though it is difficult to demonstrate precisely which character traits are valuable, from the moral point of view, traits of deep understanding, personality integration, empathy, and high self-esteem will surely fall on the list. When we add in the additional qualities of sensitivity and compassion that normally accompany true altruism, its worth seems assured. In the truly altruistic act we see these traits and the character they compose in action. We value such acts largely because of the personal qualities they express.

Psychological research has verified some of our common-sense beliefs regarding the motivations and traits of altruists, especially as concerns locus of control and role-taking ability. (See, for example, Staub, 1978.) Due to the focus of this research, however—its emphasis on childhood and the relation of situational variables to behavior—little has been discovered about the comparative level of personality integration or cognitive "maturity" of altruists. Limited research by cognitive developmentalists suggests that level of cognitive–moral structure significantly affects choice and behavior, with greater conceptual sophistication leading to more principled and morally valid judgment. (See, for example, Haan, Smith, & Block,

1968; Krebs & Rosenwald, 1977.) If, in fact, our level of understanding is related to altruism as our commonsense beliefs suggest, we should expect more adults than children to be characteristically altruistic, where factors other than cognitive structure are equal. We should also expect to find more instances of true altruism, altruism motivated by altruistic motives, among adults. Moreover, we should expect to find an inordinate number of altruists at the highest levels of cognitive–moral development. The highest levels of moral–cognitive structure should embody the moral logic of altruism.

Surprisingly, the most widely discussed and empirically supported conception of moral-cognitive development, Kohlberg's moral stage theory, portrays *justice* as the highest level of moral cognition and moral logic. His research suggests that altruistic motivations do not demonstrate superior levels of moral understanding, but merely particular desires to go beyond the call of duty, perhaps even beyond the call of morality. (See the appendix for a brief account of Kohlberg's view.)

ALTRUISM AND JUSTICE STRUCTURE

Among the many psychologists and philosophers who have objected to the justice emphasis in Kohlberg's theory, some have been motivated by a preference for altruism. They find it hard to believe that someone whose rationales for acting are merely fair and righteous can be more morally sophisticated than someone who is kind and compassionate. They see much of what they like (i.e., caring, concern, love, and community) at Kohlberg's Stage 3, and they wonder if his ordering of stages and interpretation of data is not skewed to his ideological tastes or even gender identity.

There is much that can be said in reply to these reactions. For one thing, they often fail to take seriously Kohlberg's crucial distinction between structure and content. Critics such as Gilligan (1977) simply will not let Kohlberg confine his scope to cognitive-moral structure, as he defines it. Instead we find Kohlbergian stages portrayed as levels of personality development, as ego stages, perhaps, in which *styles* of thought and behavior, attitudes toward personal liberation and love, are figured into "stage" transitions. There is no reason to think that a person reasoning at the highest stage of justice could not use some lessons in caring and warmth, in taking on and feeling the power of responsibilities. There are certainly more and less humane world views that are open to someone at a certain cognitive stage, not to mention different moral beliefs and skills. Some of these nonstructural aspects may be crucial to moral judgment (more crucial than structure), especially where reasoning relates to behavior. Still, this is not the stuff of Kohlberg's stages. It is the *structure* or logic of caring, compassion, and altruism that must be contrasted with his stage of justice.

Critics often make unfair comparisons between the least desirable motivations that can underlie justice (judgmentalism, self-serving prudentialism, begrudging egalitarianism) and the ideal motivations for altruism (e.g., love and compassion).

At the moral root of justice, however, is a respectfulness for the value, autonomy, and uniqueness of each individual. Kant described this motivation as a kind of nondiscriminating reverence and love. Critics should reformulate their argument by comparing the best motivations of both perspectives and showing how love and compassion surpass reverence and respect. The altruist must be portrayed as feeling that she or he should do what the just person considers nonobligatory but admittedly better. Here the superiority of altruism would be based on the assumptions of justice; altruism is justice and something more.

The rationale one finds for altruism at Stage 3, however, is clearly something less. It is a conventional altruism of "in-group conformity" for the most part. Those who support this stage against principled stages fall into the sort of trap Kohlberg has set even for himself in caricaturing altruism as a set of adolescent "feelings". To merit a hearing, critics must offer rationales of altruism that are as sophisticated philosophically and as integrated and differentiated conceptually as Kohlberg's highest stages. They must portray altruism as an overall theory of morality rather than a special emotion or particular set of obligations and virtues.

This is not an easy matter. Conceptions of altruism as a general moral "stance" on life are more spirit than refinement. The lack of clarity in even traditional philosophical theories of benevolence or love, (agape) make them less adequate than theories of justice in performing crucial moral functions such as resolving conflicts of interest. Moreover, utilitarian views, which embody an altruism of sorts, are flawed in ways that make altruism seem inappropriate for morality altogether. Let us consider this point briefly.

Put very simply, the rationale of utilitarian obligation is that we should act so as to foster the maximum welfare of all. This is an altruistic principle in that each individual often will be required to sacrifice her or his own interest, even surrender her or his rights, where this will increase the well-being of others. Such a view does not account for our recognition that some less than ideal activities are not wrong, but merely less than best. It makes every ideal thing we could do obligatory on pain of immorality.

It might be possible to reconstruct utilitarianism so that it offers an additional set of weak or imperfect obligations to do best or better. Such a view would then have to provide a way to order or balance these two sorts of obligations and in a way that somehow renders justice inviolate while giving altruism "punch." This would be difficult and would detract from the traditional virtue of utilitarian theory, which is simplicity. Moreover, even if the altruistic obligations of utility could be worked out, there would still be the problem of ordering goods or utilities by their moral importance and of protecting individuals from majority tyranny.

Consider the first point. If we defined altruism merely in terms of maximizing good or social welfare or of enhancing the happiness or satisfactions of others, then our moral exemplars would come from among the ranks of famous comedians and rock'n'roll stars rather than, for example, civil rights leaders or servants of the poor. This is so, at least, where the former celebrities were devoted to their audiences and where the latter devotees ruffled feathers or worked obscurely in small locales.

Sacrificing oneself for interests of any sort—to increase soap opera watching opportunities in America, for example—hardly qualifies for moral commendation. Sacrificing one's desires for social justice to help sadists or Nazis derive their most treasured pleasures in the suffering of others is despicable altruism.

Utilitarianism mistakenly has been viewed as a moral principle, when in fact it is a principle of social interest and prudent choice in a conventional or positivistic sense. It has a "pro social" orientation in much the way psychological research in this area has. Moral psychology, moral development research, by contrast, is concerned with what society or the individual *should* want, from the *moral* point of view. Altruism in the moral sense involves enhancing the well-being of others in certain ways and, ideally, for certain reasons. It serves the best interests of others and fosters morally permissible (merely permissible) ones, primarily as a way of respecting or caring for their possessors.

On utilitarian principles we may be obliged to infringe the free choice of others where they are unwilling to cooperate in social progress, to foster the greater good of the many. This is the majority tyranny problem. The legacy of human nature theory, especially before behaviorism got hold of it, is that our psychology is organized by its cognitive, active, willful side. At least this is how it should be seen where we are considering how to relate to others, to cooperate or contend. To respect and value persons, which is what morality is all about, we must view their aims through their perspectives, as they choose to set priorities and pursue them. Any moral view that sees people primarily as experiencers or welfare-holders misses the point. Coerced or coercive altruism, paternalistic or otherwise, is morally unacceptable, regardless of its good effects overall.

JUSTICE AND MORALITY

Despite these problems in defining a structure of altruism, there seems good reason to be dissatisfied with justice alone as the defining concept of moral development. Even those who view justice as the centerpiece of moral thought and development speak of going beyond the call of duty, of acting in supererogatory fashion. As mentioned previously, we associate our moral exemplars with kindness and love rather than mere fairness. Kohlberg and the schools of moral theory with which he identifies concentrate on moral obligations, on rights and duties that, at the highest (Stage 6) level, will apply to all persons equally. Yet when we speak of going beyond the call of duty we do not mean going beyond morality. Those who exemplify love and kindness in their stance toward others are exemplary and admirable within the moral realm, whether they act out of obligation or not. A most adequate form of moral thought should accommodate this moral logic. A highest stage of moral reasoning should incorporate supererogatory rationales and correctly.

A careful look at Kohlberg's Stage 6 indicates that a great deal of behavior we would intuitively consider altruistic is required by justice. This follows primarily from his interpretation of the Kantian principle of nondiscrimination which bids us to weigh the value of our interests equally with those of others in rendering each her or his due. Kohlberg portrays this principle best through the logic of his ideal role-taking or "moral musical chairs." Two examples might suffice:

1. If someone needed a ride to get to an appointment and you are the only person willing (or able) to drive her or him, you are obligated to do so as long as the cost to you is not greater than the loss would be to the person missing the appointment.
2. If you are walking over a bridge and see someone drowning whom only you could feasibly help, you are obligated to rescue that person so long as this would not increase the likelihood of your drowning beyond that of his or her drowning or make it likely that both of you will drown.

According to Kohlberg, these are the only conclusions you could come to if you really had to occupy all the relevant positions in each dilemma. You would consider it legitimate to expect the person to drive or rescue you and you would be willing, in good faith, to inconvenience yourself or even seriously risk your life "in return."

As we normally understand duty, both of these cases would go beyond it. It might be a bit callous of you not to drive someone in need to an appointment. It might even be wrong or unfair of you not to do so when that person really needs it and it would be "no big thing" for you to help out. However, you need not take on his or her situation, take on his or her utility prospects, feeling obliged to bear almost as much inconvenience in helping as he or she would if not helped. This would ignore that person's responsibility for having made the appointment, for conducting her or his life in a way that leads to such foreseeable needs and dilemmas.

Likewise in the drowning person case, no one owes another a 45–50% risk to one's life on grounds of mere fairness. We are not being unfair to someone when we have insufficient courage to "play hero." It is true that it might be better to set up our interrelations so that people could depend on this much aid from each other, as much as we now expect from a close family member, but this would not represent the merely just society. It would be the humane society in a true sense. The potential savior is not obliged to right the tragedies of nature or accident, even if her or his conceptions of just desert should not rest upon them. (We should not fault or reward people morally for what they cannot help.) When asked, "Why won't you bear the risk I am bearing? Why do you choose to stay safe and dry while I am the one to drown?" The potential saviour can answer, "Because you are the one who fell in the water, not me." This may sound too heartless to bear if we do not add to his reaction, "But, my God, how I wish it had never happened to you, how I wish I could save you without putting my life in dire peril, without knowing that, if I jumped in, there's as much chance I'll never come out as not." The person who respects the high and equal value of human life should feel this way but need not jump in the water.

We may even feel that the potential saviour *should* attempt a rescue and that we are morally obliged to be heroic to some extent, if not to this great extent. I would agree. This obligation, however, if it exists, is an obligation to go beyond the call of justice or fairness. It is an obligation of benevolence or kindness in some moderated form. In these ways, Kohlbergian justice at the highest stage can be said to accommodate altruism but not in the right way. Stage 6 is structurally inadequate in assimilating the moral logic of moral altruism.

In ancient ethical texts, justice was seen as the moral virtue that organized all other virtues and balanced them in proper, relative proportions. No doubt this approach influenced Kohlberg, as an avowed Platonist, in choosing justice to define moral thought. However, these ancient conceptions lacked content. They directed us to be properly courageous or generous or honest without indicating how and where to draw the line of propriety. Moreover, many virtues they placed under justice's wing would fall outside the realm of universal rights and duties that justice commands in Kohlberg's stages. It is mistaken to think that only justice, rather than one of these other virtues, can provide the general structure for organizing the moral domain. Benevolence and prudence have also been tried in that position; utilitarianism is the evidence.

Modern justice is a particular moral concept that performs certain limited roles in morality. It falls in the moral category of right, as does rights, rather than in that of good or ideals. In his early writings such as "From Is to Ought," Kohlberg (1981) defines the role of morality as ordering competing claims and resolving conflicts of interest among persons. Kohlberg's moral judgment interview presents moral dilemmas to get at moral reasoning in this way. According to Kohlberg, morality does its job best when it resolves such dilemmas by showing impartial respect for the equal value and autonomy (rights) of those involved, regarding their occurrent, nonwrongful interests.

Actually, resolving such conflicts, and in this impartial way, is the special function of justice. When considering what we should do morally, we might also wonder how to assess the relative quality of interests, values, or intentions and how to advance them. We might consider how to set ideals for character development, life-style, and career choice, or for social progress. When considering how to treat people, we may accord respect to their potential for development, their best and ideal interests (seen as possible future interests) rather than to their actual interests alone. Moral reasoning must be concerned with all these moral issues.

Importantly, however, justice is commitedly neutral regarding the relative quality of interests, values, and ideals. The impartial respect it renders people as equals requires that their different conceptions of the good life and worthy character be ignored. In this way, justice can never be expected to tell the whole story; it must rely on other moral concepts to complement its role. In the particular school of justice with which Kohlberg aligns, that is, deontological justice, this concept functions as a filter device on values and a side constraint on their pursuit. It does not guide our behavior, development, or forms of interaction toward ideals. It does not exhort or oblige us to be better. Rather it sets minimal standards of acceptable behavior and takes a neutral stance toward all values, interests, or pursuits that are permissible or nonwrong. The very definition of deontology implies this for justice. It defines any concept in the moral category of right as logically independent from the concept of good and as not forwarding or maximizing good.

Seen from the category of right, deontological justice is normally concerned with according respect to individual autonomy. It ranks equal individual liberty absolutely (or near absolutely) above all considerations of value and above all interests. In this way, it takes freedom out of the realm of values, making equal respect for persons as autonomous beings a prior-to-value consideration. This is a far cry from any teleological conception that defines right (and justice) solely as promoting values. Moreover, because respect for persons normally accords persons equal *maximum* freedom (as much freedom as each can exercise without infringing on each other's freedom), deontological justice normally includes no teleological component at all. It cannot obligate people to advance the good once it has said that anything an individual may want to do is morally acceptable, so long as it does not coerce others. Being unwilling to develop kindly motivations or to make a social institution more humanistic does not involve coercing someone. It does not violate anyone's rights.

A moral concept that excludes so many moral concerns on principle cannot represent the logic or structure of morality as a whole. However, it could be argued that once we see what justice implies, once we recognize the deontological truth that equal respect for the autonomy of persons is primary, the primacy of justice in morality must be accepted also. It is not that justice excludes all other moral considerations, it is that other moral considerations become dubious or unruly beside it or that they must be subsumed within it. On the first view it is recognized that teleological (good-enhancing) obligations to advance overall good oblige us to infringe personal liberty if necessary. This places supposedly moral principles in the uncomfortable position of requiring immorality. Thus there is no place for them within the realm of obligation. Such principles might represent "hypothetical imperatives" for supererogation, however—"if you want to be saintly, loving or admirable, do such and such."

On the second view, teleological principles could be used to support justice and respect for liberty. Thus we should develop certain virtues of courage, honesty, sympathy, and generosity regarding the needs and burdens of others; we should promote a willingness to compromise our interests and cooperate in joint projects insofar as this fosters commitment to the principles of justice and compliance with them.

Neither view is likely to satisfy the altruist. It is not merely a question of *if* you happen to want to be loving. You *should* want to be! Altruism should not merely foster justice and stop short of going beyond it. It should strive to go beyond justice and strive mightily, and it should inspire others to do the same. Altruists and nonaltruists alike may sense that the trouble with justice, its tendency to dominate morality, comes from its obsession with coercion. Put another way, the modern conception of justice, and of deontological justice in particular, is tailored to providing a moral foundation for the coercive nature of political and legal systems. The conception of justice provided by John Rawls (1971) and which Kohlberg often cites to explicate Stage 6, is explicitly designed for that purpose. Like other deontological conceptions, it arises from the social contract tradition that asks how a government can have the authority to order its citizens around, to set rules for them, to threaten them with fines and imprisonment, and to make good on these threats through direct coercion. The answer this tradition offers is that citizens reasonably can be expected to accord government these powers voluntarily, to legislate these powers on themselves by unanimous, if tacit, consent. Citizens would do this to provide assurance that interpersonal conflicts of interest or over fairness will be resolved peaceably and in a regular, nonarbitrary fashion, and that shared expectations for fair cooperation will be set publicly and followed. (Such publicized expectations will avert unresolvable conflict and resentment down the road.)

How does government assure that people will abide by its rules? By force! The government is a coercive power monopoly (among other things) that backs its procedures with threats. The rights we surrender it to create this power, legitimately, are rights to *enforce* our rights. We do not surrender the rights themselves. Consider—we not only have the right to life, but, most likely, the right to enforce that right. This is the right to infringe the liberty of someone threatening our life, perhaps even to violate her or his right to life, in defense of our (right to) life. The logic of enforcing rights, of rights to enforcement, is different from that of morality generally or even of rights, that is, *moral* rights, in particular. Enforcement, after all, is coercion. Coercion is a prima facie moral wrong. The moral question of coercion is one of when it is legitimate to do what would otherwise be wrong. This would be a question of justifiability or excusability rather than a question of right, per se. Normally enforcement deals with how to deal with people who have committed injustices, not merely with people as autonomous beings worthy of equal respect. Moreover, when enforcing rights we must worry about the evils of making a mistake or of abusing power much more than in normal cases of respecting life or liberty.

Given these special and atypical considerations of enforcing morality and the special social contractarian need to rally unanimous consent among divergent individuals, it is no wonder that the principles of justice derived emphasize individual freedom above all, maximum toleration of diverse interests. No one would be willing to risk having the values of some enforced by government on others, even if these values seemed best, and, indeed, why should anyone be so willing? Whether or not deontological principles or rights should be enforced (over the noncoercive opposition of pacifists and anarchists), teleological principles or duties should not, in general. This does not make them supererogatory or hypothetical. It merely leaves them matters of morality per se.

Consider the issue of enforcement in the context of utilitarianism. What is the problem of majority tyranny? It is that some are allowed or obliged to coerce others, to make them suffer burdens they would not choose to bear, to advance the good of others. The few, here, have done nothing wrong. They do not deserve to be discriminated against at the expense of their liberty and welfare. Suppose, however, that we confined morality to its proper realm, the realm of noncoerce advice-giving, or guidance; inspiration and the setting of legitimate expectations, and so forth. Here utilitarian principles would direct us to initiate good actions, develop good traits in ourselves and foster them in others, and seek cooperation in socially progressive ventures. These principles would form the basis for *exhorting* others to do likewise, for *praising* them when they did, or *criticizing* them when they did not. Such principles would not advise that we coerce others but offer strong advice or apply strong pressure. Coercion or the threat of coercion is precisely what morality is designed to avoid.

Of course such a pragmatic basis for morality may seem insufficient. It may be most practical for some individual in some particular instances to bend others to her or his will if she or he can get away with it. No good-enhancing principle, including utilitarianism, has come up with a totally acceptable way to guarantee each individual, or moral practice generally, against coercion. At the same time, so-called *ideal utilitarian principles* have been advanced which argue for the high quality of freedom and equality as values and direct us to maximize them. These may be combined with rule–utilitarian principles, which direct us to adhere strictly and foremost to a rule of equal individual liberty as the best means of advancing overall good. Here we approach the deontological good quite closely. We could go even farther in transcending the crude categories of deontology and teleology altogether by adopting a narrower conception of morally acceptable liberty to make room for direction on how to use some liberties better. These two types of principles would then combine in what is termed a *mixed conception,* protecting right and fostering good in a more balanced way.

The point is that deontological justice, as embodied in Kohlberg's Stage 6, does not represent, should not dominate, and cannot subsume morality adequately. Somehow it must be complemented, conceptually, with significant rationales for promoting values. Put another way, if people naturally develop to Stage 6 and if Stage 6 truly represents the structure of their moral reasoning on the whole, then Stage 6 structure is not morally adequate. It is not the highest level of moral reasoning. Of course, it may be the highest level of *natural* development in moral reasoning, since the moral competence people develop spontaneously through social interaction may not be very high.

A more reasonable assessment of Stage 6, and one with which Kohlberg recently has come to agree, is that it represents reasoning about matters of justice in particular, not morality in general. After all, it was generated empirically (insofar as it has been supported empirically) by a research technique that pulled for fair resolutions to conflicts of interest. This instrument also focused on questions of law—should someone be punished for doing wrong, what is the relation of law to society—which is the special province of deontological justice. Since stage descriptions account for responses to such questions, we can expect a justice bias, a political or legal bias as well, in Kohlberg's theory. We can expect, also, that teleological rationales of utility and perfection will be represented as nonstructural or orienta-

tional components of moral judgment, where they arise empirically. This has occurred in Kohlberg's work on substages.

To fill out the empirical basis for defining stages of moral development, we must
pose different sorts of moral questions that concern ideals of character and community development or ordering of values. We may then discover that moral reasoning
on the whole does not develop naturally and in Piagetian stages or that the structure
of moral development does not correlate neatly with justice development; Stage 6
justice may not occur in Stage 6 morality. More likely we will discover that the
structure of reasoning about nonjustice issues is compatible with the structure of
justice but alters importantly the precise nature and extent of obligations.

IF NOT JUSTICE, THEN WHAT?

Objections to Love as an Alternative to Justice

As noted, various conceptions of altruism, benevolence, or love (agape) have
been advanced as alternatives to justice theory. Although they are inspiring and
imaginative, they are too vague to be of much practical use to the moralist. Love has
been defined, for example, as an intuitive union with the essence of another person
or all persons. (Consider the modern conceptions of love offered by humanistic
psychologists such as Fromm, Maslow, and May.) If such conceptions are not
practical, we must doubt that they could ever define a natural structure of cognitive–moral thought. Such structures arise, after all, as solutions to conceptual
problems that occur as people interact with others. Utilitarianism as a form of
benevolence theory is much more detailed and practicable than love theories, but it
is seriously flawed, as we have seen.

In Kohlberg's offhand rejection of love conceptions, love has appeared either as a
particular (moral) emotion or virtue that cannot organize the structure of moral
reasoning or as a rationale of supererogation that cannot place obligations on all
people. Recently, in his book *The Philosophy Of Moral Development,* Kohlberg
(1981) placed certain conceptions of universal love in a metaphorical "Stage 7."
Here they function as a kind of religious or spiritual metaphysic that lends meaning
and worth to being moral in general. In answering the question "why be moral,"
they have great value for moral thought, yet they are not really part of that thought.

Perhaps the most pointed criticism Kohlberg has offered of a sophisticated principle of love concerns its inadequacies in resolving moral dilemmas. Love cannot
resolve some dilemmas at all because it is totally on the side of each conflicting
party. Kohlberg often raises the hypothetical case of two altruists slowly dying of
thirst on a desert despite a canteen containing enough water to save one of them. On
one interpretation of altruism, they may each feel obliged to empty the canteen into
each other and thus they may end up passing the canteen back and forth, without
either drinking, until they both die. (Of course, if one dies first. . . .)

On a second interpretation of love or altruism, or regarding other sorts of dilemmas, total concern for each person may lead to equal sharing. Here altruism or love will reduce to justice. Yet since justice is a more clarified concept with a more explicit rationale, we should prefer it to love where their effects are the same. Last, if loving concern does not lead to equal justice when it resolves a conflict of interests, it is objectionable because it is discriminatory or unjust. On all these grounds justice is to be preferred.

Responses to Objections to Love

A plausible response can be offered to each of the previous objections against love or altruism. The vagueness and impracticability problem can be handled by merely specifying a clear conception of these concepts, a conception of love or altruism that is as explicit as that of Stage 6 justice. How this can be done will be considered in a moment. Insofar as such an account can portray love or altruism as a general moral principle, criticisms of love as a particular (moral) emotion or virtue or pantheistic metaphysic will be beside the point.

Transforming supererogatory conceptions of love or altruism to morally obligatory ones is primarily a matter of building in moderation. To require that all people be altruistic is inappropriate only because it asks more than we can reasonably expect of people. In effect, it discriminates against the vast majority who do not have the extraordinary degree of compassion, self-esteem, etc., to fulfill duties of love in stride. Note that being just, especially in Kohlberg's sense, often requires sacrificing strong self-interests. Duties of justice will be easier to fulfill for those who are especially empathetic or moralistic. However, we feel that justice does not ask so much of anyone that she or he could not reasonably expect the same of others in return. The problem with good-enhancing or teleological priniciples is that they direct us to *maximize* the good across all persons. This is not an accident. Given the nature of value and the virtue of rational prudence, which all moral principles should embody, it would make no sense to prefer less good to more or most. By contrast, the teleological tradition needs a principle of right that will be rational for each person and will give equal consideration to the moral burdens each bears. Such a principle would direct each of us to promote the welfare of all to a sizable (but not overly burdensome) extent.

Two substantial problems would have to be faced in formulating such a principle. The first is one of precision—where to draw the line of moderation. Do we require people to advance 75% of the welfare that utilitarian altruists would predictably generate, or to exert 65% of the effort they would exert in maximizing good? The second is how to guarantee equality. It is possible that the approximate equality needed in bearing altruistic obligations could be established by a rule–utilitarian principle, as suggested previously, but this is unclear.

An alternative approach might be to construct an altruistic logic through a complex of different principles that limit, balance, or moderate each other. In a sense, deontological justice is designed to do this, to place side-constraints of right on the pursuit of good. Unfortunately justice does not pose sufficient obligations to foster good that might then be limited by an arena of permissible slacking off. I will take the balancing approach in posing an altruistic stage of moral cognition, a stage of moderate altruism. Its great advantage is that it can build in rival principles, a circumscribed principle of justice, for example, thereby borrowing the virtues of these alternatives. Where justice is guaranteed as a component of altruism, we can meet the criticism that loving resolutions of conflicts of interest will not only be nonjust, but *un*just. We can also fend off the criticism that such conflicts cannot be resolved. If justice can resolve them, our justice-and-more can resolve them also. This is true at least where the revisions of and additions made to a justice rationale do not decrease its validity or hamper its effectiveness. The component principles of a complex love rationale have to be combined or ordered in a clear-cut and regularized manner. Only in this way can we avoid uncertainty in deciding what weight each will have relative to each other in deciding a case.

It is important that we assess the merits and demerits of a love or altruism rationale against those of justice structure. Just as altruism may have difficulty resolving conflicts of interest, justice may have difficulty (if it has anything to say at all) prescribing ideals of character and community. (A mixed or complex conception of love or altruism could deal with both issues.) Where love may sometimes be nondiscriminating regarding who gets what or whether anyone gets the goods, justice may be unacceptably indifferent as to what goods people should pursue.

The justice advocate can hardly fault love or altruism for reducing to justice in some instances. Yet it is a mistake to think that because love may resolve conflicts of interest fairly, it is limited to fairness in handling all moral problems. The structure of altruism that I will suggest, however, usually would add additional considerations to fairness even in resolving conflicts of interest. However, many of the standard Kohlberg dilemmas happen to be structured so that the additional obligations of altruism cannot take hold. I see this as a methodological problem in Kohlberg's research that we will consider shortly.

ALTRUISM AS JUSTICE AND MORE

Defining the precise structure of a Stage 6 level altruism would be equivalent to defining the logical foundations of an ultimately valid moral philosophical theory. This is too long (and too technical) a story to tell here. Moreover such a story may have limited relevance to moral development, since *natural* development may not extend this far. The structure of a cognitive–moral stage in the Kohlbergian sense, must be derived meticulously from data.

It may be useful to consider, however, how such data might be generated and what structure it would show. We might also speculate on how moral rationales that have shown up in the data, which define various Kohlbergian stages, might be integrated and differentiated to form a principled altruism. Since stage progression shows moral logical progress through integration and differentiation of this sort, our speculative account might represent a plausible hypothesis of how more than just development would proceed.

As I read Kohlberg, the main rationales that arise and recur in moral stages are an individual rights rationale, prominent at Stages 2, 4, and 5A; a liberal egalitarian justice rationale, prominent at Stages 3B and 6 (if there is a Stage 6); a utilitarian rationale, most prominent in Stages 4B and 5B; and a value hierarchy that ranks life over liberty over property, with greater clarity as development progresses. Subsidiary or less frequent rationales also arise along the course of development: a just deserts rationale, at Stages 2A and 4A in particular; a catering-to-needs rationale, most prominent in Stage 3; and a perfectionist rationale, which occurs at various B substages and especially at Stages 3B and 5B. (Perfectionist rationales direct us to develop our natural gifts and virtues on the individual level and to foster excellence or exemplary individuals in our society.) All the foregoing rationales of natural development are prominent within moral philosophical theory in more refined form. They provide the building blocks for a principled stage of altruism.

The main conceptual problem to be solved at the highest level of moral cognition is how to accommodate the conflicting demands of deontological right and teleological good. Within Stage 5, for example, Kohlberg describes an opposition between an individual rights rationale, respects the equal autonomy of each individual, and a rule–utilitarian rationale, which tries to tailor this respect to practices that advance the overall good of society. According to Kohlberg, until these rationales are universalized and ordered so that all persons as persons are respected equally (not merely as members of particular societies) and equal respect is made prior to advancing the good (advancing the good becomes a form of rendering equal respect), the greatest level of structural adequacy cannot be achieved. Ideally we might wish to show how this problem can be solved by combining the primary rationales of Stage 5 in a way that embodies the logic of altruism and meets the Kohlbergian criteria of integration, differentiation, reflective equilibrium, reversibility, correlativity, universality, prescriptivity, abstractness, etc. This would build the case for a structure of altruism on the structural and philosophical foundations Kohlberg accepts—a formalist, deontological altruism. Of course, these criteria are challengeable, and we may wish to challenge Kohlberg's philosophical assumptions, especially, in making our case. We do not have to tailor altruism to the peculiar structural difficulties of Stage 5 insofar as this stage is defined with a bias toward justice.

For now let me suggest that a promising way around the deontological–teleological problem, the problem of infringing individual liberty for the greater welfare, is through a principle of perfectionism. People will be altruistic voluntarily, finding the self-sacrifice quite bearable, where they have developed and strengthened other-oriented motivations such as empathy and caring. Through such development, also, we can foster true altruism or love, altruism rendered out of altruism, loving acts expressing loving. This development can be stimulated and reinforced during childhood years, primarily, thereby mitigating problems of indoctrination and authoritarianism. Before a child has a developed sense of autonomy and an elaborated self to determine, the fostering of certain character traits will not be an imposition, nor need it feel like one. Early training of this sort can also help motivate compliance in later life with obligations to make oneself, and others, more spontaneously giving.

By itself, a principle or rationale of perfectionism is not strong enough to support altruism. People who develop kindly feelings slowly, who are at present underdeveloped, or who hearken most to nonaltruistic motivations (and obligations) will exhibit precious little altruism in their daily behavior. Therefore, we might add a rule–utilitarian principle that ranks the value of altruistic motivations and their predictable aims highly. This would be termed an *ideal* utilitarian principle because it would place certain values (ideals) above others and would rank morally worthy or desirable ones highest.

Let us assume, for the sake of prudence and clarity, that both of the above principles define right or obligation in terms of *maximizing* altruism. Now we will need some way to moderate these obligations without sapping away their strength. For this purpose I would suggest circumscribed individual rights, accompanied by a limited principle of egalitarian justice. In designing these rationales we want to limit the permissible use of liberty so that our perfectionist and ideal utilitarian obligations can hold sway; it is not OK, morally, to act in ways that neglect or impede the development and expression of altruism. At the same time we want to respect the equal autonomy of persons. Positing equal rights, as opposed to a general liberty principle, allows us to pick the sorts of liberties we will sanction morally. Duties will not be placed on others to refrain from interference in any nonwrong thing a person wants to do. Rather, people will be given specific rights to do specific things, or types of things, and we will be duty-bound to give them right of way. (Consider the Bill of Rights as an example of this rationale, although such rights are political.) By defining these rights so that less than a maximum amount of general liberty is sanctioned—even within particular rights, perhaps—altruistic obligations are given room to operate. At the same time, the essential moral personality, that core of each person we respect as an equal, is guaranteed room to function autonomously. In an ideal account of moral rights, we might wish to sanction only those liberties that express the traits of the morally essential personality.

An egalitarian justice rationale would be added to the structure of altruism to distribute moral obligations and unearned welfare equally among persons. Obligations to help others at personal sacrifice would be distributed equally thereby, avoiding the majority tyranny and unequal burden problems of utilitarianism. (Ideally, subrationales of just desert and need should form parts of this principle, weighted or ranked relative to each other.)

It is an important defect of Kohlbergian (and Rawlsian) justice that the particular needs and meritorious efforts of individuals are all but ignored in deference to respect for the equality of essential personhood. Kohlberg talks at Stage 6 of the equal value of life and, only indirectly, of respect for equal liberty. Yet respondents to Kohlberg interviews talk of just deserts, rewards and punishments for accomplishments and faults, and of the value of property. Why is Stage 6 justice silent on these aspects of human personality and activity? Is it not more cognitively sophisticated to differentiate both the moral core and the moral fringe of human personality, as well as the interests and deserving "claims" of each, and then to integrate these in one's rationale of respect?

It is important to ask how the sorts of moral rationales I have just identified have been differentiated and integrated in Stage 6 structure. It seems to me that the liberal justice bias in Kohlberg's view has suppressed strong natural rights and just deserts aspects of justice as well as teleological rationales. By contrast, the structure of altruism I propose distinguishes many aspects and roles of justice and respect. It relegates that portion of Stage 6 justice that invokes altruism (e.g., risking one's life to save a drowning person) to appropriately good-enhancing rationales.

Yet how are these rationales to be integrated? There are several possibilities. To accomplish our goals of moderating altruism and equalizing its moral demands, we might rank-order rationales as follows: rights over equal liberty over perfectionism over ideal rule–utilitarianism. This retains the primacy of right over good as the deontologist demands. It relieves the few of extraordinary sacrifices to enhance the many. Yet above all it protects basic liberties even from the tyranny of betterment, while giving betterment a fighting chance.

Working out the details of this structure would be extremely difficult. The particular rights to be granted and their scope would have to be specified and justified, as would the relative weight of just deserts to claims of need. The precise implications of ranking perfectionism absolutely over ideal utilitarianism would have to be explicated. Would people be able to hide behind their own self-development—leave me alone, I am working on my empathy—to avoid being generous or boosting ideals of community? Are the combined rationales of altruism reversible and universalizable? Do they match the criteria of adequacy as well as justice alone does at the Stage 6 level?

Perhaps the most complex problems arise in ranking the ideals to be advanced by the rationale of ideal utility and in justifying the overall superiority of altruistic ideals and motivations. With regard to the perfectionist principle as well, we might ask, "Why should we develop our propensities for love; why not courage, honesty or integrity? Why not appreciation of beauty?" My reliance on the perfectionist principle as the key to generating structural altruism is highly problematic. Of all rationales appearing in Kohlberg's data, this is one of the most infrequent. If my speculation regarding moral structure is to have any empirical relevance, how can it rest so heavily on such an undistinguished feature of observed natural development?

In my view, the sorts of stimuli that would elicit statements about duties to (altruistic) development have not been presented in Kohlberg's research. On the contrary, the sorts of questions Kohlberg's moral interview asks make perfectionist responses inappropriate. Consider the Heinz dilemma, for example, in which a man is so desperate to save his wife's life that he is contemplating robbery to acquire needed medicine. In such a last minute and desperate situation, with life hanging in the balance, can we contemplate Heinz's possible obligation to feel empathy for the greedy druggist who will not sell the lifesaving drug at less than an outrageously high price? Should Heinz use this occasion to practice stoic acceptance or instruct the druggist on virtue? Might he return to his wife empty handed and consider with her what she might learn from this disappointment in her waning moments of suffering and consciousness? (I am caricaturing the perfectionist stance, but hopefully one gets the drift.) Lifeboat dilemmas that ask whom to throw overboard to save a sinking ship are similarly inhospitable to developmental suggestions.

Consider next the story of a father who heartlessly reneges on a promise to his son. The question asked on Kohlberg's interview is whether the son should respect the father's unjust request. A respondent is very unlikely to say that the son should go to his father and try a little developmental stimulation. Nor would we expect the son to take it upon himself to act so as to develop his own character. This would be nice, but hardly to be expected of children under the (psychological) gun or of those considering what children in that situation should do. The situation wreaks of injustice and pulls for a just resolution.

Developing one's moral virtues or those of others takes time and perhaps some informal planning. It usually occurs within stable but expanding social contexts, not bizarre and terminal ones. The moral aims approached by perfectionist duties involve what sorts of persons to become, what sorts of relationships to establish and how to steer their growth, what kinds of community to aim for. To get at reasoning about these issues, we might pose situations in which people are asked to give moral advice or instruction on developmental issues. "Should I stay with my boyfriend (or husband) and try to work out our problems even now that the feeling has faded and a romantic alternative stands temptingly in the wings?" "Should I bring my child up in a religion? If not, how should I deal with my religious mother-in-law as the time for each religious rite of passage arises and is missed?"

We also might pose alternative career choices. The first places one in joint enterprise with high energy materialists pursuing economic gains. The second weds one to burned-out social activists struggling haltingly toward lofty but unlikely ideals. "Subjects" might be asked which option one should choose and why. Such choices might be posed in terms of competing duties: Should one devote oneself to one's own moral development when there are people in need of aid or where there are gross injustices to be opposed? Should one forego the developmental environment of a social change organization to pursue a high salary that could be used to bankroll this organization? The same sorts of questions could be generated regarding our choice of friends or mates.

Questions of these sorts will not only produce evidence, pro or con, for a naturally developing perfectionist rationale, but will also show how people rank values and ideals, and whether or not they can justify these rankings. There is a values clarification exercise that presents succinct paragraphs posing various approaches to life; the approach of hedonism, striving for individual accomplishment and success, devotion to spiritual enlightenment or cultural pursuits. "Subjects" could be asked to assess the relative merits of these styles as conceptions of the morally worthy or good life: "Do you feel that it is wrong to pursue life-style X in preference to life-style Y? Do you feel we are obliged to pursue one life-style more than the other, or would it merely be better to do so, or is morality indifferent to such choices? Are these choices irrelevant to morality?''

Based on the evaluations of ideals people offer and their reasons for them, we may be able to define an expanded, naturally developing value hierarchy that is a logical extension of stage structure. The relativity we normally associate with value judgments may then be explained away, at least in part, as a function of inadequate stage development. Some rankings will reflect the structural inadequacies of lower stages. Hopefully the motivations and ideals of altruism and love would tend to be ranked highest by people at principled stages. This would provide some basis for arguing that there are ideals that all people tend to recognize as superior and toward which all people might be expected to strive.

APPENDIX

Kohlberg has outlined the assumptions of cognitive developmental theory as follows:[1]

> 1. Basic development involves basic transformations of cognitive structure which cannot be defined or explained by the parameters of associationistic learning and which must be explained by parameters of organizational wholes or systems of internal relations.
> 2. Development of cognitive structure is the result of processes of interaction between the structure of the organism and the structure of the environment, rather than being the direct result of maturation or the direct result of learning (in the sense of a direct shaping of the organism's responses to accord with environmental structures).
> 3. Cognitive structures are always structures (schemata) of action. While cognitive activities move from the sensorimotor to the symbolic to verbal-propositional modes, the organization of these modes is always an organization of actions upon objects.
> 4. The direction of development of cognitive structure is toward greater equilibrium in this organism-environment interaction i.e., of greater balance or reciprocity between the action of the organism upon the (perceived) object (or situation) and the action of the (perceived) object upon the organism.
> Social development is, in essence, the restructuring of the (1) concept of self; (2) in its relationship to concepts of other people; (3) conceived as being in a common social world with social standards: Social cognition always involves role-taking, i.e., awareness that the other is in some way like the self, and that the other knows or is responsive to the self in a system of complementary expectations. Accordingly developmental changes in the social self reflect parallel changes in conceptions of the social world.
> The core of the cognitive–developmental position, then, is the doctrine of cognitive stages. Cognitive stages have the following general characteristics:
> 1. Stages imply distinct or qualitative differences in children's modes of thinking or of solving the same problem at different ages.
> 2. These different modes of thought form an invariant sequence, order, or succession in individual development While cultural factors may speed up, slow down, or stop development, they do not change its sequence.

[1]Source: From L. Kohlberg, ''Stage and sequence: The cognitive–developmental approach to socialization. In D. A. Goslin (Ed.), *Handbook of socialization theory and research*. Chicago: Rand McNally, 1969. Pp. 348–353.

3. Each of these different and sequential modes of thought forms a "structured whole." A given stage-response on a task does not just represent a specific response determined by knowledge and familiarity with the task or tasks similar to it.

4. Cognitive stages are hierarchical integrations. Stages form an order of increasingly differentiated and integrated structures to fulfill a common function.

Kohlberg's Levels and Stages of Moral Judgment[2]

Level I—Preconventional

Stage 1. It is right to avoid breaking rules backed by punishment, to obey for its own sake, to avoid physical damage to persons and property, to avoid the superior power of authorities.

Egocentric point of view: Doesn't consider the interests of others or recognize that they differ from one's own; doesn't relate two points of view. Actions are considered physically rather than in terms of psychological interests of others. Authority's perspective is confused with one's own.

Stage 2. One should follow rules only when it is to someone's immediate interest; acting to meet one's own interests and needs and letting others do the same. Right is also what's fair, what's an equal exchange, a deal, an agreement. You should serve your own needs or interests in a world where you have to recognize that other people have their interests, too.

Concrete individualistic perspective: Aware that everybody has his own interest to pursue and these conflict, so that right is relative (in the concrete individualistic sense).

Level II—Conventional

Stage 3. One should live up to what is expected by people close to you or what people generally expect of people in your role as son, brother, friend, etc. "Being good" is important and means having good motives, showing concern about others. It also means keeping mutual relationships, such as trust, loyalty, respect and gratitude. You must be a good person in your own eyes and those of others. You must care for others and believe in the Golden Rule. You desire to maintain rules and authority which support (stereotypically) good behavior.

Perspective of the individual in relationships with other individuals: Aware of shared feelings, agreements, and expectations which take primacy over individual interests. Relates points of view through the concrete Golden Rule, putting yourself in the other guy's shoes. Does not yet consider generalized system perspective.

Stage 4. You must fulfill the actual duties to which you have agreed. Laws are to be upheld except in extreme cases where they conflict with other fixed social duties. Right is also contributing to society, the group, or institution. You must keep the institution going as a whole, to avoid the breakdown in the system "if everyone did it," or the imperative of conscience to meet one's defined obligations.

Differentiates societal point of view from interpersonal agreement or motives: Takes the point of view of the system that defines roles and rules. Considers individual relations in terms of place in the system.

Level III—Postconventional

Stage 5. You should be aware that people hold a variety of values and opinions, that most values and rules are relative to your group. These relative rules should usually be upheld, however, in the interest of

(continued)

[2]Source: Adapted from L. Kohlberg, "Moral stages and moralization: The cognitive developmental approach." In T. Lickona (Ed.), *Moral development and behavior.* New York: Holt, Rinehart, and Winston, 1976. Pp. 34–35.

Level III—(Continued)

---

impartiality and because they are the social contract. Some nonrelative values and rights like life and liberty, however, must be upheld in any society and regardless of majority opinion. You must have a sense of obligation to law because of your social contract to make and abide by laws for the welfare of all people's rights. A feeling of contractual commitment, freely entered upon, to family, friendship, trust, and work obligations. Concern that laws and duties be based on rational calculation of overall utility—"The greatest good for the greatest number."

Prior-to-society perspective: Perspective of a rational individual aware of values and rights prior to social attachments and contracts. Integrates perspectives by formal mechanisms of agreement, contract, objective impartiality, and due process. Considers moral and legal points of view; recognizes that they sometimes conflict and finds it difficult to integrate them.

Stage 6. One must follow self-chosen ethical principles. Particular laws or social agreements are usually valid because they rest on such principles. When laws violate these principles, one acts in accordance with the principle. Principles are universal principles of justice, the equality of human rights and respect for the dignity of human beings as individuals. As a rational person one must believe in the validity of universal moral principles and a sense of personal commitment to them.

Perspective of a moral point of view from which social arrangements derive: Perspective is that of any rational individual recognizing the nature of morality or the fact that persons are ends in themselves and must be treated as such.

REFERENCES

Gilligan, C. In a different voice: Women's concepts of self and morality. *Harvard Educational Review.* 1977, *47*,(4), 481–517.

Haan, N., Smith, M. B., & Block, J. The moral reasoning of young adults: Political–social behavior, family background and personality correlates. *Journal of Personality and Social Psychology,* 1968, *10,* 183–201.

Kohlberg, L. *The philosophy of moral development* (Vol. 1). New York: Harper & Row, 1981.

Krebs, D., & Rosenwald, A. Moral reasoning and moral behavior in conventional adults. *Merrill–Palmer Quarterly,* 1977, *23,* 79–84.

Rawls, J. *A theory of justice.* Cambridge, Mass.: Harvard University Press, 1971.

Staub, E. *Positive social behavior* (Vol. 1). New York: Academic Press, 1978.

Commentary to Feature Review

THE FUTURE OF MORAL PSYCHOLOGY:
Truth, Intuition, and the Pluralist Way

Richard A. Shweder and Jonathan Haidt
Committee on Human Development, University of Chicago

What are the recent theoretical developments in the study of moral psychology? The publication of the *Handbook of Moral Behavior and Development* (Kurtines & Gewirtz, 1991) provides us with an excuse to assess the state of the art. It also provides us with a chance to engage in some augury (and perhaps influence the future) by making an educated guess about where the discipline is heading. We assess the current state of moral psychology in the light of a history of conflicts along three theoretical fronts: cognitivism versus emotivism, pluralism versus monism, and intuitionism versus rationalism. We foresee the consolidation of a cognitive-pluralist-intuitionist theory of moral psychology whose main tenet is that moral appraisals (this is good, that is right) are grounded in self-evident truths (intuitions), saturated with local cultural meanings, and activated by means of the emotions.

SOME PRINCIPALS OF MORAL PSYCHOLOGY: THE CURRENT STATE OF THE ART

The 40 chapters contained in the *Handbook* make it clear that the voice of Lawrence Kohlberg still dominates the current scene. The reference lists contain 143 references to Kohlberg's work, more than twice the number for any other author. A survey of all entries in the PsycLit data base under the descriptor "moral develop-

ment" confirms this picture: Sixty percent of the entries for 1991 either employ or criticize Kohlberg's theory and methods.

Kohlberg's preeminence derives from the fact that in the wake of the "cognitive revolution" of the 1960s, he temporarily gained the upper hand over psychoanalysts, radical relativists, and social learning theorists in the battle between cognitivism and emotivism. Moral cognitivism is the position that qualities such as goodness, rightness, justice, or beneficence are real and knowable and that moral statements can therefore be either true or false (see Gewirth, 1984). A cognitivist approach to moral development tries to identify the particular mix of intellectual skills (e.g., perspective taking) and interpersonal experiences (e.g., caretaking) that makes it possible to apprehend or figure out moral truth. The basic point of cognitivist theories of moral psychology is that everyday moral appraisals (e.g., that the police officers in the Rodney King video behaved in a morally repulsive way) can be right or wrong; they are not subjective or inculcated tastes, opinions, or attitudes, as emotivism would have it. Kohlberg succeeded at driving home the cognitivist's point about the objective reality of justice, which he viewed as the supreme moral truth.

The most influential and widely cited critic of Kohlberg's theory is Carol Gilligan. Gilligan's importance derives from the fact that in the wake of the feminist revolution of the 1970s, she temporarily gained the upper hand over Kohlberg in the battle between pluralism and monism. She can be credited with the claim that the realm of moral truth is diverse, not homogeneous, and consists of an ethics of care as well as an ethics of justice.

Address correspondence to Richard A. Shweder, University of Chicago, Committee on Human Development, 5730 South Woodlawn Ave., Chicago, IL 60637.

336

Finally, research on the importance of moral emotions flourished during the 1980s, as the cognitive revolution branched out into multiple skirmishes, including the battle of intuitionism versus rationalism. Cognitive intuitionists (e.g., Kagan,1984; Lazarus, 1991) assume that moral appraisals are generated rapidly and automatically, without deliberate reflection or deductive or inductive reasoning. They assume that verbal judgments about actions and goals (this is right, that is good) and morally relevant emotional appraisals (pride, disgust, empathy, shame, guilt, anger, dread) are grounded in a base set of nondeducible and noninducible self-evident truths, for example, that it is wrong to inflict pain arbitrarily, that it is right to treat like cases alike, that it is right that wrongs should be repaired.

Ironically, if the cognitive intuitionists win the day, the emotions (reinterpreted as a rapid system of cognitive appraisal) may well be restored to their rightful place in the study of moral development. It is not just emotivists who believe that "emotions may be the gatekeeper to the moral world." Cognitive intuitionists believe it as well (see Lucas, 1971; Moore, 1903/1966; Ross, 1930; Seung, 1993; Shweder & Sullivan, 1993; also Strawson, 1949, p. 24, from whom the "gatekeeper" quote is drawn).

SOME PRINCIPLES OF MORAL PSYCHOLOGY: THE EMOTIVIST LEGACY OF DAVID HUME

Hume described the state of the art in moral philosophy in 1777 (1777/1960). His description is astonishingly accurate for moral psychology in 1993: "There has been a controversy started of late . . . concerning the general foundation of Morals; whether they be derived from Reason, or from Sentiment; whether we attain the knowledge of them by a chain of argument and induction, or by an immediate feeling and finer internal sense; whether like all sound judgments of truth and falsehood, they should be the same to every rational intelligent being; or whether like the perception of beauty and deformity, they be found entirely on the particular fabric and constitution of the human species" (p. 2). Hume believed there were only two possible resolutions to this controversy concerning the foundation of morals.

The first possible resolution is the cognitivist resolution, that moral qualities are objective and universal qualities of events in the world and can be apprehended by means of reason through a "chain of argument and induction," and that moral appraisals can reasonably be judged to be true or false.

The second possible resolution is the emotivist resolution, that the moral qualities of events in the world do not exist aside from people's sentimental reactions to those events, including their feelings of approval and disapproval. For emotivists, morality (like beauty) is in the mind of the arbiter. Moral appraisals are not subject to determinations of truth and falsehood, and cannot be judged against rational standards. They are simply declarations of preferences and values.

Given those two choices, Hume opted for emotivism. Having ceded to reason nothing more than the instrumental capacity to calculate the most efficient means for achieving a given end, he argued that appraisals about which ends in life are bad and which ones are good must be rooted entirely in people's passions, interests, and will. This led Hume to a series of breathtaking emotivist conclusions, from which he had the intellectual courage not to shrink: "Reason is and ought to only be the slave of the passions, and can never pretend to any other office than to serve and obey." "Reason alone can never be a motive to any action of the will." "Tis not contrary to reason to prefer the destruction of the whole world to the scratching of my finger." (See Hume, 1739–1740/1969, pp. 460–463.) In Hume's emotivism, ends may provide the rational justification of means, but nothing can provide a rational justification of ends.

One can develop a cognitivist theory or an emotivist theory about any kind of mental state. The distinction between cognitivism and emotivism is not peculiar to the study of moral appraisals. There are cognitivist theories of the emotions and emotivist theories of inductive reasoning. The mark of a cognitivist theory is the assumption that mental states serve primarily a representational function. The mark of an emotivist theory is the assumption that mental states serve primarily nonrepresentational functions. Cognitivist theories explain a mental state by reference to facts or truths about the objects and events which that mental state "re-presents" (sometimes inaccurately), on the assumption that such objects and events exist and can be invoked as external standards for explaining and judging (as rational or irrational) mental states. Emotivist theories explain the occurrence and character of a mental state without assessing the veracity of the mental state vis-à-vis the objects or events it represents, on the assumption that no such objects and events exist aside from the mental representation of them.

Prior to the cognitive revolution of the 1960s, emotivist theories of moral psychology flourished and were used to explain the apparent diversity of moral appraisals across history and culture (e.g., why eating beef is judged a sin in Delhi but not in Dallas). It was widely recognized that moral disagreements are interminable. Emotivist theories offered a simple explanation for why moral disputes go on forever: There are no moral facts. Morality is nothing more than a system of inculcated, reinforced, or introjected values, evolved to serve some pragmatic (nonrepresentational) function such as influencing people to do what you want, coordinating social activities, or balancing intrapsychic conflict anxiety.

THE COGNITIVIST LEGACY OF LAWRENCE KOHLBERG

It is a striking fact of intellectual history that emotivist theories have nearly disappeared from the intellectual landscape of moral psychology. This disappearance is due largely to the bold formulations and fortunate timing of Kohlberg (1969). Kohlberg argued that judgments about the moral world could be true or false, better or worse, just like judgments about the physical world. When children learn to conserve mass in Piagetian tasks, we do not hesitate to say they are developing a more correct, adequate, and true understanding of the physical world. Kohlberg's cognitivism employed the same logic for moral judgments. Kohlberg drew on Rawls (1971) to make philosophical claims about the superiority of justice reasoning. He backed up these claims with longitudinal and cross-cultural evidence that justice reasoning was in fact the endpoint of moral development. Kohlberg made the world safe for cognitivism.

Hume (and Kohlberg) saw only two possible resolutions to the "controversy started of late . . . concerning the general foundation of Morals." The cognitivist resolution implied that morals "should be the same to every rational intelligent being," at least upon sufficient reflection, and "we attain the knowledge of [morals] by a chain of argument and induction." Kohlberg endorsed both of these propositions. But cognitivist theories come in many varieties. Much of the recent work in moral psychology can be seen as a challenge to one or the other of the two propositions, from within the framework of a cognitivist theory. Pluralists like Gilligan disagree with monists like Kohlberg about the first proposition, and intuitionists like Kagan disagree with rationalists like Kohlberg about the second.

PLURALISM VERSUS MONISM

Moral appraisals seem to differ widely across people, cultures, and historical periods. They differ at the level of actions deemed morally obnoxious; in India, for example, among Brahmans, it is highly immoral for a son to eat meat or cut his hair during the 10 days that follow the death of his father (see Shweder, Mahapatra, & Miller, 1987/1990). Moral appraisals also differ in terms of the moral qualities (e.g., rights, duty, care, sanctity) that are salient in judging the rightness or goodness of an action or goal.

Shweder (1984) described three strategies for dealing with this apparent diversity across time and space. The *universalist* strategy (exemplified by Elliot Turiel) is to interpret apparent difference as superficial, and to seek commonality in a more universal deep structure. The *developmentalist* strategy (exemplified by Kohlberg) is to acknowledge the existence of differences and to rank them as stages, from primitive to advanced. Both of these strategies are forms of moral monism, asserting that there is only one correct or mature morality. In contrast, the third strategy, *moderate relativism*, is a form of moral pluralism, accepting that there can be more than one correct and mature morality. Gilligan (1982) argued against the prevailing monism of morality research in the 1970s, which seemed to rank women as deficient in the one true morality of justice.

Kohlberg and others have pointed out that the mere existence of difference between groups is not evidence that a measuring instrument is biased. We do not throw out our measuring tapes when they tell us that women are, on average, shorter than men. But Gilligan's (1982) now-famous critique of her ex-advisor said more than this. Gilligan asserted that people have two moral "voices," or ways of talking and thinking about moral issues. Kohlberg measured only the development of the justice voice, ignoring (or missing the sophistication of) the care voice. Gilligan found in narrative analyses that American women use the care voice more than the justice voice, while American men do the reverse, yet she noted that both genders use both voices. However, studies of moral reasoning in hypothetical dilemmas have generally failed to find gender differences (Walker, 1991). Some scholars think Gilligan misread the difference between justice and care as a gender issue.

Whether the two moral voices are associated with the two sexes or not, Gilligan has, by common consensus, won the argument for pluralism. Kohlberg, Levine, and Hewer (1983) acknowledged that there is more to the moral domain than justice reasoning, and they specifically cited an additional cluster of virtues including "charity, love, caring, brotherhood, or community" (p. 19). This cluster is not homogeneous, however, and there is ambiguity about how the ethics of care is to be conceptualized: as a sensitivity to other people's needs? as the particularistic side of justice in its guise as mercy? as the role obligation of guardianship?

More recently, cultural psychologists have been exploring forms of limited pluralism. The moral value of justice may be recognized in some form in all cultures, yet there are additional moral goods that are often used in sophisticated (or "postconventional") ways to resolve moral dilemmas. Japanese see a moral value in preserving group harmony, even in some cases when justice might be compromised (see Markus & Kitayama, 1991). Indians see a moral value in meeting one's social role obligations, even when these may conflict with the demands of justice (Miller & Bersoff, 1992; Shweder & Much, 1991; Snarey & Keljo, 1991; for a powerful theory of limited pluralism, see Fiske, 1991, 1992).

Shweder, Much, Mahapatra, and Park (in press; see also Shweder, 1990) find that moral discourse tends,

Richard A. Shweder and Jonathan Haidt

cross-culturally, to make use of three distinct but coherent clusters of moral concerns. These three ways of talking about morality are labeled the ethics of *autonomy* (concerns about freedom, rights, harm, and justice), *community* (concerns about duty and the collective enterprise), and *divinity* (concerns about purity, sanctity, and the realization of one's spiritual nature). Haidt, Koller, and Dias (in press) found that people of high and low social class in Brazil and North America made differential use of these three ethics when judging acts that were harmless yet offensive (such as eating one's dead pet dog or cleaning one's toilet with the national flag). And Balle-Jensen (1993) has confirmed that North American college students are unusual in their almost exclusive reliance on the ethics of autonomy. Older Americans of the same social class are more willing to talk about the moral issues of community and divinity.

INTUITIONISM VERSUS RATIONALISM (AND NATURALISM)

How exactly does one discover or figure out moral truths? Hume described cognitivists as relying on a "chain of argument and induction." But in fact one can be a cognitivist yet hold any of three views on how people acquire moral knowledge. One can be a cognitive rationalist, a cognitive naturalist, or a cognitive intuitionist.

Theories of cognitive rationalism argue that knowledge of moral truth comes from a process of argumentation and deductive reasoning. Kant, for example, was a cognitive rationalist. So was Kohlberg, who was a Kantian as well. Both Kant and Kohlberg tried to counter Hume's emotivism by grounding a cognitivist theory of morals not in the instrumental means-ends reasoning that Hume parodied so effectively, but rather in the principle of consistency inherent in deductive reasoning. They proposed a method for deducing right conduct from the logic of noncontradiction, as in Kant's categorical imperative. (The critiques of this famous and failed attempt to derive substantive moral conclusions from a purely formal logical principle are voluminous; see Seung, 1993).

Theories of cognitive naturalism, in contrast, argue that the methods for acquiring knowledge of the moral world are similar to the methods for acquiring knowledge about the natural world: observation and inductive reasoning. The idea is that actions that are right and outcomes that are good exhibit certain defining properties, which can be observed directly with the senses, much the way one can observe the defining properties of a tiger. Turiel is an eminent contemporary cognitive naturalist. He argues that moral violations, such as murder, contain intrinsic features, such as harm, which are directly observable (Turiel, 1983; Turiel, Killen, & Helwig, 1987).

Most philosophers, however, are uncomfortable with the idea that goodness or rightness or even harm is a natural property (like redness) that anyone with a normal sensory apparatus can see. Yet almost everyone allows that appraisals of rightness and goodness are unavoidably made about almost all of the actions that one does see. How is this done? Cognitive intuitionists offer a third kind of account.

Theories of cognitive intuitionism assume that moral properties (e.g., rightness, goodness, beneficence, justice, sanctity, fraternity) are objective and knowable but apprehended as self-evident truths. Such theories assume that moral knowledge is distinct from other forms of knowledge (knowledge of geometry, knowledge of minerals, knowledge of how to build a house) in that it cannot be derived solely from deductive reason (e.g., a principle of consistency or universalizability) or instrumental reason (e.g., knowledge of the most efficient use of means to accomplish a given end) or inductive reason (e.g., systematic observation of the natural properties of objects and events in the world).

Theories of cognitive intuitionism assume that the project of grounding moral appraisals in deductive, inductive, or instrumental reason has failed. Such theories assume that what this failure implies is not that emotivism is right and objective moral qualities do not exist, but rather that objective moral qualities are neither logical properties nor observable properties. Theories of cognitive intuitionism assume that moral qualities are objective properties of a different kind, properties that are open to the rational intuitive capacities of the human mind or nervous system. They can be activated without reflection. They are not dependent on deliberative reason or argumentation to bring them on-line.

One attractive feature of cognitive intuitionism is that it makes it possible to tell the following kind of story about moral pluralism. Following Ross (1930), imagine that the human mind has intuitive access to a plethora of self-evident, abstract moral truths (e.g., fidelity, gratitude, reciprocity, justice, beneficence, self-improvement). These truths are so self-evident that if someone were to deny that, for example, it is right to treat like cases alike and different cases differently, you would suspect either that they did not understand the meaning of those words or that they were not sincere in their denial. Yet there are too many such truths. They cannot all be activated at once. They cannot be institutionalized simultaneously in social practices. Some cultures specialize in the truths of justice and fidelity, others in the truths of duty and care, others in the truths of purity and pollution, and so on.

Moreover, the various objective moral qualities open to apprehension by the intuitive mind are only the abstract "frames" or the "gross architecture" within which

363

societies historically implement and develop their local and quite divergent moral practices. Thus, for example, although moral appraisals are grounded in an original multiplicity of self-evident moral truths, it is not, on first glance, immediately obvious to an Anglo-American observer precisely why it is morally obnoxious for a Brahman male in India to eat chicken or have a haircut in the days immediately following the death of his father. The case does become self-evident, however, once one recognizes it for what it is: a powerful combination of reciprocity, care, duty, nonmalfeasance, and other intuitively available moral qualities.

To recognize the case for what it is, however, one must know the kinds of things orthodox Hindus in India know about death pollution. One must know about the difficulties faced by a reincarnating soul in its attempt to escape from the bondage of the corpse. One must know about the ascetic techniques employed by living relatives (abstaining from sex; fasting from all "hot" foods, such as chicken) to facilitate the absorption of death pollution into their own bodies as a form of assistance to the spirit of the dead. One must know about the migration of pollutions to the extremities of the body. One must know how to remove the pollution by cutting off all head hair, which is done only after the soul is on its way, typically 12 days after the death. In other words, historical and cultural understanding is essential for moral appraisal, yet there is always more to a moral appraisal (the intuition of an abstract moral truth) than only historical and cultural understanding can provide. Taken together, however, moral intuitions and cultural-historical understanding work hand in hand to turn the reality of a cognitive moral pluralism into a credible theoretical possibility.

According to this cognitive-pluralist-intuitionist view, there is such a thing as moral truth, and it is a heterogeneous collection of goods, known through culturally assisted intuition. The base set of abstract, self-evident moral truths is universal but accessed differentially and with particularizing substance.

A second attractive feature of cognitive intuitionism is that it makes it possible to acknowledge the difference between fast and slow cognitive processes, without assimilating this difference to the distinction between "affect" and "cognition." Moral reasoning, like any other kind of explicit and conscious problem solving, is slow. Yet moral intuition, like all intuitive knowledge, is rapid and introspectively opaque. Margolis (1987) argued that most of cognition consists of rapid, intuitive pattern matching, followed (when people are called upon to explain themselves) by slow, ex post facto propositional reasoning. Applying this view to the study of moral development suggests that cognitive rationalists such as Kohlberg focused their attention on the slow, ex post

facto processes. These processes depend on verbal, deductive, and inductive abilities, which improve throughout childhood, accounting for Kohlberg's age trends. Yet studies of moral intuition find few age trends. Turiel's (1983) method can be reinterpreted as a way to probe children about their moral intuitions (using a series of yes/no questions), and studies that have used this method typically find that 5-year-old children have intuitions similar to those of adults within their own communities.

According to cognitive intuitionism, emotions are the "gatekeeper to the moral world." Emotions "tell us how the world is in a very vivid way" (D'Andrade, 1981, p. 191; also see Shweder, 1993). Emotional responses, it is now generally thought, involve rapid, automatic, and unconscious cognitive appraisals of the significance of events for personal well-being. Lazarus (1991), for example, has proposed a cognitive theory of the emotions in which emotions serve a representational function. In Lazarus's view, the emotions are mental maps of certain kinds of truths. The experience of anger is a representation of a certain kind of interpersonal event (e.g., a demeaning personal insult) that exists both inside and outside the anger, in the mental state and in the state of the world that is represented emotionally.

Crucially, many of the cognitive appraisals that have been postulated as causal conditions for an emotional experience are quite similar to the self-evident truths of morality. Anger is about injustice and the perception of a demeaning personal insult. Sympathy is about harm and suffering. Shame and guilt are about the right and the good. Disgust is about degradation and human dignity. (For more on the emotional basis of morality, see Haidt, Koller, & Dias, in press; Hoffman, 1991; Kagan, 1984; Solomon, 1976).

Kagan (1984) has long argued that moral psychology should pay more attention to the emotions: "Beneath the extraordinary variety of surface behavior and consciously articulated ideals, there is a set of emotional states that form the bases for a limited number of universal moral categories that transcend time and locality" (p. 119). In other words, if cognitive intuitionism gains the upper hand over cognitive rationalism, we will soon recognize what many peoples of the world have been telling anthropologists for a long time: The mind of the moralist is located in the heart, which is, paradoxically, a cognitive organ, and it is through the heart that we come to know moral truth(s). That is our augury.

Acknowledgments—This essay was developed with support from the John D. and Catherine T. MacArthur Foundation Health Program Research Network for Successful Midlife Development (MIDMAC).

Richard A. Shweder and Jonathan Haidt

REFERENCES

Balle-Jensen, L. (1993). *Shweder et al.'s ethics of autonomy, community, and divinity: A theory and an exploratory study*. Manuscript submitted for publication.

D'Andrade, R.G. (1981). The cultural part of cognition. *Cognitive Science, 5,* 179–195.

Fiske, A.P. (1991). *Structures of social life.* New York: Free Press.

Fiske, A.P. (1992). Four elementary forms of sociality: Framework for a unified theory of social relations. *Psychological Review, 99,* 689–723.

Gewirth, A. (1984). Ethics. *Encyclopaedia Britannica* (Vol. 6, pp. 976–998). Chicago: Encyclopaedia Britannica.

Gilligan, C. (1982). *In a different voice: Psychological theory and women's development.* Cambridge, MA: Harvard University Press.

Haidt, J., Koller, S.H., & Dias, M.G. (in press). Affect, culture, and morality, or, is it wrong to eat your dog? *Journal of Personality and Social Psychology.*

Hoffman, M.L. (1991). Empathy, social cognition, and moral action. In W.M. Kurtines & J.L. Gewirtz (Eds.), *Handbook of moral behavior and development: Vol. 1. Theory* (pp. 275–302). Hillsdale, NJ: Erlbaum.

Hume, D. (1960). *An enquiry concerning the principles of morals.* LaSalle, IL: Open Court. (Original work published 1777)

Hume, D. (1969). *A treatise of human nature.* London: Penguin. (Original work published 1739–1740)

Kagan, J. (1984). *The nature of the child.* New York: Basic Books.

Kohlberg, L. (1969). Stage and sequence: The cognitive-developmental approach to socialization. In D.A. Goslin (Ed.), *Handbook of socialization theory and research.* Chicago: Rand McNally.

Kohlberg, L., Levine, C., & Hewer, A. (1983). Moral stages: A current formulation and a response to critics. In J.A. Meacham (Ed.), *Contributions to human development, Vol. 10.* New York: Karger.

Kurtines, W.M., & Gewirtz, J.L. (Eds.). (1991). *Handbook of moral behavior and development* (Vols. 1–3). Hillsdale, NJ: Erlbaum.

Lazarus, R.S. (1991). *Emotion and adaptation.* New York: Oxford University Press.

Lucas, J.R. (1971). Ethical intuitionism II. *Philosophy, 46,* 1–11.

Margolis, H. (1987). *Patterns, thinking, and cognition.* Chicago: University of Chicago Press.

Markus, H.R., & Kitayama, S. (1991). Culture and the self: Implications for cognition, emotion, and motivation. *Psychological Review, 98,* 224–253.

Miller, J.G., & Bersoff, D.M. (1992). Culture and moral judgment: How are conflicts between justice and interpersonal responsibilities resolved? *Journal of Personality and Social Psychology, 62,* 541–554.

Moore, G.E. (1966). *Principia ethica.* Cambridge, England: Cambridge University Press. (Original work published 1903)

Rawls, J. (1971). *A theory of justice.* Cambridge, MA: Harvard University Press.

Ross, W.D. (1930). *The right and the good.* Oxford: Oxford University Press.

Seung, T.K. (1993). *Intuition and construction.* New Haven, CT: Yale University Press.

Shweder, R. (1984). Anthropology's romantic rebellion against the enlightenment, or there's more to thinking than reason and evidence. In R. Shweder & R. LeVine (Eds.), *Culture theory.* Cambridge, England: Cambridge University Press.

Shweder, R. (1990). In defense of moral realism: Reply to Gabennesch. *Child Development, 61,* 2060–2067.

Shweder, R.A. (1993). The cultural psychology of the emotions. In M. Lewis & J. Haviland (Eds.), *The handbook of emotions.* New York: Guilford.

Shweder, R.A., Mahapatra, M., & Miller, J. (1990). Culture and moral development. In J. Stigler, R. Shweder, & G. Herdt (Eds.), *Cultural psychology.* New York: Cambridge University Press. (Original work published 1987)

Shweder, R.A., & Much, N. (1991). Determinations of meaning: Discourse and moral socialization. In R. Shweder, *Thinking through cultures: Expeditions in cultural psychology.* Cambridge, MA: Harvard University Press.

Shweder, R.A., Much, N.C., Mahapatra, M., & Park, L. (in press). The "big three" of morality (autonomy, community, and divinity), and the "big three" explanations of suffering, as well. In A. Brandt & P. Rozin (Eds.), *Morality and health.* Stanford, CA: Stanford University Press.

Shweder, R.A., & Sullivan, M.A. (1993). Cultural psychology: Who needs it? *Annual Review of Psychology, 44,* 497–523.

Snarey, J., & Keljo, K. (1991). In a *Gemeinschaft* voice: The cross-cultural expansion of moral development theory. In W.M. Kurtines & J.L. Gewirtz (Eds.), *Handbook of moral behavior and development: Vol. 1. Theory* (pp. 395–424). Hillsdale, NJ: Erlbaum.

Solomon, R. (1976). *The passions.* Austin: University of Texas Press.

Strawson, P.F. (1949). Ethical intuitionism. *Philosophy, 24,* 23–33.

Turiel, E. (1983). *The development of social knowledge: Morality and convention.* Cambridge, England: Cambridge University Press.

Turiel, E., Killen, M., & Helwig, C.C. (1987). Morality: Its structure, function, and vagaries. In J. Kagan & S. Lamb (Eds.), *The emergence of morality in young children.* Chicago: University of Chicago Press.

Walker, L.J. (1991). Sex differences in moral reasoning. In W.M. Kurtines & J.L. Gewirtz (Eds.), *Handbook of moral behavior and development: Vol. 2. Research* (pp. 333–364). Hillsdale, NJ: Erlbaum.

341

ACKNOWLEDGMENTS

Eisenberg, Nancy, Paul A. Miller, Rita Shell, Sandra McNalley, and Cindy Shea. "Prosocial Development in Adolescence: A Longitudinal Study." *Developmental Psychology* 27 (1991): 849–57. Copyright 1991 by the American Psychological Association. Reprinted by permission. Courtesy of Yale University Sterling Memorial Library.

Staub, Ervin. "A Conception of the Determinants and Development of Altruism and Aggression: Motives, the Self, and the Environment." In Carolyn Zahn-Waxler, E. Mark Cummings, and Ronald Iannotti, eds., *Altruism and Aggression: Biological and Social Origins* (New York, NY: Cambridge University Press, 1986): 135–64. Reprinted with the permission of Cambridge University Press. Courtesy of Yale University Sterling Memorial Library.

Bickman, Leonard. "Social Influence and Diffusion of Responsibility in an Emergency." *Journal of Experimental Social Psychology* 8 (1972): 438–45. Reprinted with the permission of Academic Press, Inc. Courtesy of Yale University Sterling Memorial Library.

Borofsky, Gerald L., Gary E. Stollak, and Lawrence A. Messé. "Sex Differences in Bystander Reactions to Physical Assault." *Journal of Experimental Social Psychology* 7 (1971): 313–18. Reprinted with the permission of Academic Press, Inc. Courtesy of Yale University Sterling Memorial Library.

Batson, C. Daniel, Jim Fultz, and Patricia A. Schoenrade. "Distress and Empathy: Two Qualitatively Distinct Vicarious Emotions with Different Motivational Consequences." *Journal of Personality* 55 (1987): 21–39. Copyright Duke University Press 1987. Reprinted with the permission of the publisher. Courtesy of Yale University Sterling Memorial Library.

Batson, C. Daniel, Janine L. Dyck, J. Randall Brandt, Judy G. Batson, Anne L. Powell, M. Rosalie McMaster, and Cari Griffitt. "Five Studies Testing Two New Egoistic Alternatives to the Empathy-Altruism Hypothesis." *Journal of Personality and*

Social Psychology 55 (1988): 52–77. Copyright 1988 by the American Psychological Association, Inc. Reprinted by permission. Courtesy of Yale University Sterling Memorial Library.

Blasi, Augusto. "The Psychological Definitions of Morality." In Jerome Kagan and Sharon Lamb, eds., *The Emergence of Morality in Young Children* (Chicago, IL: Chicago University Press, 1987): 83–90. Reprinted with the permission of the University of Chicago Press. Courtesy of Yale University Divinity Library.

Carlson, Michael, Ventura Charlin, and Norman Miller. "Positive Mood and Helping Behavior: A Test of Six Hypotheses." *Journal of Personality and Social Psychology* 55 (1988): 211–29. Copyright 1988 by the American Psychological Association, Inc. Reprinted by permission. Courtesy of Yale University Sterling Memorial Library.

Eisenberg, Nancy, Paul A. Miller, Mark Schaller, Richard A. Fabes, Jim Fultz, Rita Shell, and Cindy L. Shea. "The Role of Sympathy and Altruistic Personality Traits in Helping: A Reexamination." *Journal of Personality* 55 (1987): 41–67. Copyright Duke University Press 1987. Reprinted with the permission of the publisher. Courtesy of Yale University Sterling Memorial Library.

Sagi, Abraham and Martin L. Hoffman. "Empathic Distress in the Newborn." *Developmental Psychology* 12 (1976): 175–6. Copyright 1976 by the American Psychological Association. Reprinted by permission. Courtesy of Yale University Sterling Memorial Library.

Hoffman, Martin L. "The Contribution of Empathy to Justice and Moral Judgment." In Nancy Eisenberg and Janet Strayer, eds., *Empathy and Its Development* (New York, NY: Cambridge University Press, 1987): 47–80. Reprinted with the permission of Cambridge University Press. Courtesy of Yale University Sterling Memorial Library.

Hoffman, Martin L. "Empathy, Role Taking, Guilt, and Development of Altruistic Motives." In Thomas Lickona, ed., *Moral Development and Behavior: Theory, Research, and Social Issues* (New York: Holt, Rinehart and Winston, 1976): 124–43. Reprinted with the permission of Thomas Lickona, copyright holder. Courtesy of Yale University Cross Campus Library.

Enright, Robert D. and the Human Development Study Group. "The Moral Development of Forgiveness." In William M.

Kurtines and Jacob L. Gewirtz, eds., *Handbook of Moral Behavior and Development* (Hillsdale, NJ: Lawrence Erlbaum Associates, Publishers, 1991): 123–52. Reprinted with the permission of Lawrence Erlbaum Associates, Inc. Courtesy of Yale University Sterling Memorial Library.

Keller, Monika and Phillip Wood. "Development of Friendship Reasoning: A Study of Interindividual Differences in Intraindividual Change." *Developmental Psychology* 25 (1989): 820–26. Copyright 1989 by the American Psychological Association. Reprinted by permission. Courtesy of Yale University Sterling Memorial Library.

Nunner-Winkler, Gertrud and Beate Sodian. "Children's Understanding of Moral Emotions." *Child Development* 59 (1988): 1323–38. Reprinted with the permission of the Society for Research in Child Development. Courtesy of Yale University Sterling Memorial Library.

Koestner, Richard, Carol Franz, and Joel Weinberger. "The Family Origins of Empathic Concern: A 26-Year Longitudinal Study." *Journal of Personality and Social Psychology* 58 (1990): 709–17. Copyright 1990 by the American Psychological Association, Inc. Reprinted by permission. Courtesy of Yale University Sterling Memorial Library.

Spiecker, Ben. "Education and the Moral Emotions." In Ben Spiecker and Roger Straughan, eds., *Philosophical Issues in Moral Education and Development* (Philadelphia, PA: Open University Press, 1988): 43–63. Reprinted with the permission of Open University Press. Courtesy of Open University Press.

Steutel, Jan W. "Education, Motives, and Virtues." *Journal of Moral Education* 15 (1986): 179–88. Reprinted with the permission of Carfax Publishing Co. Courtesy of Yale University Sterling Memorial Library.

Puka, Bill. "Altruism and Moral Development." In Diane L. Bridgeman, ed., *The Nature of Prosocial Development* (New York, NY: Academic Press, 1983): 185–204. Reprinted with the permission of Academic Press. Courtesy of Yale University Sterling Memorial Library.

Shweder, Richard A. and Jonathan Haidt. "The Future of Moral Psychology: Truth, Intuition, and the Pluralist Way." *Psychological Science* 4 (1993): 360–5. Reprinted with the permission of *Psychological Science*. Courtesy of Yale University Sterling Memorial Library.